Earle Birney, 1979.

EARLE BIRNEY

A Life

Elspeth Cameron

VIKING

Viking
Published by the Penguin Group
Penguin Books Canada Ltd, 10 Alcorn Avenue, Toronto, Ontario, Canada
M4V 3B2
Penguin Books Ltd, 27 Wrights Lane, London W8 5TZ, England
Viking Penguin, a division of Penguin Books USA Inc., 375 Hudson
Street, New York, New York 10014, U.S.A.
Penguin Books Australia Ltd, Ringwood, Victoria, Australia
Penguin Books (NZ) Ltd, 182-190 Wairau Road, Auckland 10, New
Zealand

Penguin Books Ltd, Registered Offices: Harmondsworth, Middlesex,
England

First published 1994

10 9 8 7 6 5 4 3 2 1

Printed and bound in Canada on acid free paper ∞

Canadian Cataloguing in Publication Data

Cameron, Elspeth, 1943-
Earle Birney: a life

Includes bibliographical references.
ISBN 0-670-82874-2

1. Birney, Earle, 1904–   - Biography.
2. Poets, Canadian (English) - 20th century -
Biography.*   I. Title.

PS8503.I72Z6 1994   C811'.54   C94-931853-1
PR9199.3.B5Z6 1994

See page 685 for copyright acknowledgments.

*For Janice Dickin McGinnis
from whom
I learned to appreciate the West*

Introduction

Earle Birney expected a biography. In 1927, when he was only twenty-three, his mentor, Professor G.G. Sedgewick, wrote: "If, in your exact scholarly way, you wish to affix an accurate date to this letter (which no doubt you will preserve for future publication), I hereby state for the benefit of yourself and posterity (whether your own or of others) that this is being written at 2 p.m. of the afternoon of God's Holy Day on, or in nearest contiguity to, 15 October—"[1] The remark was a ponderous jest, but was serious too. The eccentric and illustrious Sedgewick had marked Birney out as an exceptional person destined for greatness, if not as a scholar, then as a creative writer. In doing so, Sedgewick confirmed the ambition Birney's mother had harboured for him. She, too, saved his letters; the diary she insisted he write on a trip with her when he was twelve; and his childish literary efforts, such as an English essay he wrote at age nine called "The Saskatchewan Rebillion" [sic]. By 1944, the biography that would someday appear had become a joke with his friends. His Toronto neighbour, Corinne Hagon, playfully speculated on the role she might play in such a work in a letter she sent him during the war. "Perhaps some biographer will one day come searching for me in my Villa on the Riviera begging me to let him see the letters which the famous Canadian poet, Earle Birney, wrote during World War II!"[2] The first request for his manuscripts arrived from the University of Buffalo Library in January 1945 (he sent them drafts of six of his poems).[3] And, although he cleanly excised his private life from *Spreading Time*, the partial autobiography he published in 1980, Birney keenly hoped that a future biographer would include it. "Keep my letters, darling," he wrote poet Elizabeth K. Campbell after an ecstatic summer holiday he spent with her in 1948. "If ever I do anything to make my life worth recording, I want you to be part of that record. I am proud that you love me and wish that my world could know it right now. Perhaps, some day, chance will make that possible."[4] For years, Birney was preparing to write a full autobiography. But aside from four somewhat reticent articles on his adolescence in Erikson which appeared in the unlikely magazine *B.C. Outdoors* in 1980, he was unable to write comfortably about his own life. Perhaps that was because, as he flippantly commented on submitting a report of his activities as writer-in-residence at the University of Toronto in 1965–66, "Hope somebody can untangle my life story from the attached. I've never been able to myself."[5]

"Untangle" is the word. The materials Earle Birney hoarded and sold to various public repositories must be one of the most complete records of a person's life ever compiled. The main collection of his papers at the University of Toronto's Thomas Fisher Rare Book Library contains more than 20,000 files; and some of those files contain hundreds of letters. Massive numbers of photographs and various recordings—audio and visual tapes alike—are also stored publicly. It is possible to see the four-inch long, beaded moccasins that were his first shoes; his appointment books (filled to the brim with engagements); his extensive correspondence (he wrote to fifteen different "Browns," including poet Audrey Alexandra Brown and critic E.K. Brown); periodic stock-takings of his physique, like one in 1948 that notes his car (a 1946 Dodge Super de Luxe coach), his height (6'½"), his weight (150 lbs.), his hat size (6¾) and his collar size (14½–15); his books, which are filled with annotations he used in teaching or in public readings; drafts of his much-revised poems; lists, which he endlessly compiled, of the furnishings of each of his residences (including handkerchiefs, ashtrays, light bulbs, suspenders, cook books, laundry bags and sewing oddments), of the mailing addresses of his friends (one is twenty-one pages with about fifty names to a page); of periodicals all over the world that might publish his poems; of his academic notes, both as a student and as a professor (tiny notebooks in precise, cramped writing of the vocabulary for *Beowulf*, for example); even a four-page list called "Marine Shore Fauna" he started on holiday in the summer of 1950. The collection includes such recherché items as: his father's schedule and fees for painting, plastering and wallpapering in the summer of 1926; a piece of embossed wallpaper from the hall of the Château de Montmorency near Ghent, Belgium, where he was billeted during the war in October 1944; a receipt for a money order of $40.00 sent to his friend Herman Singer on 11 January 1961 (with the added note: "he never acknowledged"); the yellow library slips from the books he used in preparing his Ph.D. thesis; a cancelled cheque of Stephen Leacock's for $243.15—a donation to Upper Canada College on 7 May 1934; a traffic violation ticket for parking in the wrong lot at the University of Waterloo, 5 February 1968; the postcards his father collected during the Great War; his Bank of Montreal Savings Book for 1946–48, with a notation by Birney "the first thousand"; his mother's membership card for the Vancouver Horticultural Society; and a letter cancelling his credit cards with the Vancouver Home Oil Company on 30 January 1969.

Birney knew the value of his materials. "i'm very busy cataloguing my old poems & nail-clippings i sold to the u of t library," he wrote one friend (oddly, considering that one thing he could not stand was to be in the same room with someone clipping toenails). That sale of papers, which took place in more than one deal during the mid-sixties (the first and largest batch was sold in 1966), garnered for Birney the equivalent of a year's salary—approximately $20,000[6] all told.

Birney sorted carefully through all his materials before allowing them to be catalogued anywhere. "[I'm] trying to decide what I should preserve for a dubious and hypothetical and probably indifferent Posterity," he wrote a friend.[7] The resulting materials must be regarded with some skepticism, despite the apparent integrity of the collections and despite the fact that they contain much material that Birney must have known would not reflect well on him. It is a warts-and-all collection.

But Birney was uncommonly shrewd and habitually secretive. Some of his letters appear in more than one library. As one friend recalls, "Esther used to say, 'Oh my God, he's selling his *toenails* to the university, his laundry list, his you-name-it!' She said that he used to write two of everything so that he could sell [them]. He always used to have an extra of everything so that he could put it into the University of Alberta, Toronto, Vancouver—I know, I *have* some of them."[8]

Certainly, as I researched this biography, I came across several duplicates of items in various Birney collections. I have also come across occasional letters in which Birney has clearly concealed certain passages—usually just a sentence or phrase—by typing over them. And in a few letters, whole sections have been cut out and the partial letter photocopied.[9]

Who was Earle Birney? What was he like? These are the questions I have most often been asked during the six years I have worked on this book. Immersion in his materials, in the reminiscences of many who knew him, familiarity with the places that shaped him (including Shetland, Calgary and the ranch land nearby, London, Banff, Vancouver and Toronto), and experience of the emotional timbre of his life have gradually taken shape for me in two images of Birney: one from Scandinavian mythology, the other from literature.

In many ways, Birney resembles Loki, the Old Norse god, who represents the principle of change. Dynamic and unpredictable, exciting and mischievous, the red-haired Loki is the Scandinavian version of the trickster figure who appears in many cultures. "The trickster is greedy, selfish, and treacherous," writes one expert on Norse myths, "he appears in comic…situations, and yet he may be regarded as a kind of culture hero, who provides mankind with benefits like sunlight and fire. At times he even appears as a creator… He is…a kind of semi-comic shaman, half way between god and hero, yet with a strong dash of the jester element, foreign to both, thrown in."[10] The parallel with Prometheus, a figure who gripped Birney's imagination in his poem "Vancouver Lights," is striking. The darker side of the playful, inventive Loki is the cruel predator; "even when fettered, he remains an agent of destruction, causer of earthquakes."[11]

Like other trickster figures, Loki takes various shapes, often those of animals. But the creature he is associated with most often is the spider, who is a trickster in some other cultures as well. Not only was Loki supposed to have invented the net, but his name closely resembles the Scandinavian word for spider (or spiderlike insects): "locke."[12]

Birney's ingenious craftsmanship, his penchant for playful satire, his Nordic appearance (like the early Vikings he was "tall as date-palms, and reddish in colour"[13]), and his restless, predatory temperament, all call to mind Loki. He loved poetry, but loved much else, and lacked the single-mindedness to dedicate himself to it, or to anything else. He enjoyed seeing sparks fly in literature as in life. Irony, he wrote in his first essay on Chaucer, the literary subject he pursued for years, "is concerned with a clash of forces." He could not resist revision. There are at least five "David"s and four "El Greco"s. And like Loki, he took many shapes. Oliver Yorke, David Brownstone, Richard Miles, Vanlo (short for Vancouver L[eft] O[pposition]), Earle Robertson, Rufus, Abe (a rearrangement of his initials), Henry Scott Beattie (a real person, under whose name he ghost-wrote a letter for *The Canadian Forum*),[14] Mr. Cottingham-Ross, B.C. Birney and Earle Binning—these, and no doubt others that eluded my research—were his pseudonyms. He even eluded self-definition: "I am pretty well Celt in blood and instincts, when I'm not mixed up with feeling Norse or Canadian or just International," he wrote. He may have appreciated Chaucer most of all because he considered him "a slyboots."[15]

As he grew older, Birney more and more resembled Don Quixote, a literary figure who had long intrigued him and to whom he occasionally compared himself. The spindly old white-bearded knight tilting at windmills, inspired by visions so idealistic they eclipse reality, suggests almost exactly the fervent dedication to causes that pricked Birney to action. For Leon Trotsky, for various journals, for the rights of poets and other beleaguered members of society, for Canada, for the cause of Creative Writing, for numerous organizations, such as the Canada Council or the League of Canadian Poets, he was ready to give his all. He remained a naïve visionary until the end: easily

galvanized into action for goals he idealized and just as easily disenchanted by mankind's inefficiencies and fallibilities in realizing
them. As with Don Quixote, the fervour with which Birney
threw himself into causes (while Esther—his stolid Sancho
Panza—attended to practical details) had its ridiculous side. His
zeal for the "happenings" and "Love Ins" of the late sixties made
him a curiously grotesque figure among groups of young hippies.
And the sudden collapse of more than one of the love affairs he
initiated made him a figure of fun among his friends. In a typically layered allusion in "Vancouver Lights," he referred to
Aldebaran, the star that is the eye of Taurus, his astrological sign.
"The Old Baron" (Aldebaran) was himself. Noble, old in the
ways of the world—no matter what his age—a determined,
argumentative, bullish man.

Aldebaran is red—the colour Birney most associated with himself. "Matchstick," "Rufus," his Utah group "The Sparks," his
"red" politics, his red sports car, even "Birney" (which puns on
"burn"): all suggest the fiery zeal, inflammatory temper, burning
lust, and intellectual fire that were his nature. Red and yellow and
orange—the colours of flickering flames—were his favourite hues.

Both Loki and Don Quixote are restless spirits, in quest of
something (the joys of disruption or the conquering of evil) or,
perhaps, in flight from something. "restlessness is the ness one
goes by," he wrote poet George Johnston in 1979, "a motto of
my own life (& i appreciate the ambiguity or irony of 'ness' since
in my skull these days are shetland places-to-see-soon one must
go to Lunna Ness to get to the Out Skerries & around Helli
Ness or No Ness to reach Monsa)."[16]

Was his restlessness a movement towards or from? Mainly
from, I think. In flight from all constriction, in flight from certain realities such as the conventions of society which require
some sacrifice of self-interest, in flight from the person who most
tried to impose those conventions: his mother. And after her, any
woman who expected him to stay in sight long enough to control him. Birney exhibits what some theorists consider an archetypal male drive to elude commitment: what David Malcolmson
calls "escape from the devouring mother,"[17] and which Camille
Paglia describes in her discussion of the poet Byron—"[he] keeps

moving, reclaiming space from mother nature… 'Run, run, run,' say a dozen classic rock songs. To grow a plant must put down roots. So keep young…"[18] So vivid was this impulse to flee confinement—the enclosing walls of the house, and the woman whose presence dominates there—that he frequently went to great trouble to make love outside.

Long ago, Dr. Samuel Johnson confessed to his biographer, James Boswell: "if I had no duties, and no reference to futurity, I would spend my life in driving briskly in a post-chaise with a pretty woman; but she should be one who could understand me, and would add something to the conversation."[19] Substitute airplanes and a red Volvo for Johnson's post-chaise, and this fantasy was realized in the life of Earle Birney two centuries later, with a series of women for the most part so beautiful, so exceptional in character and talents, and so accepting of Birney's flaws (including his relationships with other women), it is astonishing. These women were so numerous I have had to exclude all but the most significant among them. Remarkably, most of them remained his friends and Esther's when others supplanted them.

My grasp of Earle Birney—as distinct from the way others might view him—crystallized in a dream I had the night of 11–12 February 1991, when I was mid-research. In this dream, I was climbing mountains somewhere on the west coast with Birney and some other people. It was sunny and pleasant. Suddenly a line from "David" came thundering out of the sky, as if God were speaking: "MOUNTAINS FOR DAVID WERE MADE TO SEE OVER." The implication of this dramatic pronouncement lay in the idea of "conquest." Earle Birney, I reflected in my dream, was a "conquistador" who somehow was Don Quixote. The "quixotic" aspect of the dream hinged on a Birneyesque linguistic pun: "*con*" (French slang for woman's genitals, also "deceive" and "against") and "quest." From this—and from a reversal of "see over" to "oversee" (and, for that matter, "oversea")—I concluded, still in my dream, that Birney had transferred his conquest of nature to a literal "con" "quest" of women, that these women "adored" the "conquest" ("conquistador"), and that his essential aim in life was to "see over," to "oversee" or control, and to do so by moving "over seas."[20]

As my dream indicates, I have had the sense of climbing enjoyably with Birney up the mountain of material I faced. Despite the fact that when Penguin Books Canada invited me to write this book in the fall of 1987, it was not possible to interview Birney, I had interviewed him about Irving Layton in 1982, and therefore had a good sense of his physical presence and mannerisms. But my feeling of working with him resulted most of all from coming across a letter from Gabrielle Baldwin, in which she described for him the doings of a judge and his wife with whom she briefly lived during the war, and of a girls' private school nearby where she knew a number of school mistresses.[21] The place was Barrie, Ontario; the judge was Judge James G. Harvie; the school was Ovenden College. At the time this letter was written, I was a two-year-old child in the nearest house just up Dundonald Street. The Harvies were friends of my parents; the judge's wife, Bettina, would later be my art teacher; and I would come to know several of the school mistresses. I was intrigued with Ovenden because the uniformed girls used to ride their horses past our house, a sight that seemed romantic and remote to me. It was with a frisson of recognition that I read this letter which brought Birney's life so close to mine.

My research for this book has been helped by many others. First, I thank Wailan Low for her encouragement. She has efficiently given me letters of permission, addresses of people to interview, access to information, photographs, tapes, and read the manuscript to correct errors without trying to interfere with my views. Esther Birney, the person who knew Earle most intimately and over the longest period of time, has warmly and generously shared her reminiscences. Rosemary Baxter, Earle's cousin in Aberdeen, who is an avid family historian, made available far more material about the Robertson side of his family than I could ever use. In Aberdeen she showed me the lock of Earle's red-gold baby hair kept in a family locket. John Archer, who knew Birney well in the 1930s, has read and offered suggestions for that section of my manuscript. Numerous friends and family members have told me what they remember of Birney's life: by telephone, FAX, electronic mail, audio tape, letter and interview. Some of them will be disappointed not to find themselves quoted. Most will realize that to quote even one sentence from each of Earle Birney's friends would be a two-volume work in itself. And, since almost every day of Birney's life after about age twenty is documented (and re-documented) in the letters he saved, the information I gleaned otherwise sometimes served mainly to confirm or lend a sense of the personalities involved to what was already clear. To all those who helped me in this way, I am deeply grateful.

There have been librarians, too, who have assisted in ways that exceed a strict definition of their responsibilities. I am grateful to Anne Yandle, Librarian Emerita, and Christopher Hives, University Archivist, Special Collections Library, UBC, for many thoughtful and time-saving acts on my behalf. Jon Whyte, Curator of the Heritage Collection, made time to assist me at the Whyte Museum of the Canadian Rockies in Banff and to reminisce about Birney. I thank Anne Goddard, Archivist of the Manuscript Division at the National Archives of Canada, particularly for drawing my attention to a recent acquisition of Miriam Waddington Papers, which contained important letters, and Lorna Knight at the National Library of Canada, for looking through numerous files other than Birney's on my behalf. I also appreciate the help I received from Apollonia Steele at the University of Calgary Special Collections Division, especially in duplicating photographs. Above all, it was a pleasure to work in the Thomas Fisher Rare Book Library at my own university. During those months I came to know many of the staff there: Richard Landon, Director, and a former UBC student, kindly shared his views of Birney with me. He and Katharine Martyn, Assistant Director, were pleasant and helpful. I appreciate the interest in my project shown by Debra Barr, who generously steered me through the Birney materials she was familiar with from preparing her *Guide to the Papers of Earle Birney in Canadian Repositories* (1987), and shared her journal entries and recollections concerning Birney. Tom Reid, Library Technician, told me of his interviews with Birney on the subject of Trotskyism and helped me understand Birney's politics in the thirties. Librarian Margery Pearson arranged for my carrel and assisted me in many ways; Manuscripts Librarian Edna Hajnal and Librarian Luba Hussel answered endless questions cheerfully; and Library Technicians Albert Masters, Cynthia King and Jennifer Ramlochan and Bibliographical Assistant Sarah Sung were helpful on many matters. I also appreciate the assistance I received from Kirk Baddley, Archivist at the University of Utah Archives, in tracking down information about Birney's time there. Geoff Ott, Manuscript Division, National Archives of Canada; Linda Oliver of the E.J. Pratt Library, University of Victoria, Toronto; Michael Moosberger, Records Manager and Archivist in the Department of Archives and Special Collections, University of Manitoba Libraries; the staff of the Queen's University Archives; Gene Bridwell, Special Collections Librarian at the W.A.C. Bennett Library, Simon Fraser University; and Charlotte White, William Ready Division of Archives and Research Collections, McMaster University Library, Hamilton, Ontario also assisted me. Working with such experts is a privilege.

I was more than fortunate to have research assistance from a number of quarters. Susan Lamb, a Toronto doctoral candidate in English who became a friend during this project, took on a number of delegated tasks with good humour, carefully read my manuscript unasked, and unexpectedly helped me with numerous insights and challenges. My friend Professor Janice Dickin McGinnis, University of Calgary, obtained materials from the Glenbow Institute in Calgary on my behalf. My colleague Professor David M. Hayne, University of Toronto, brought me an important article on Birney's work with Margerie Lowry. Professor Sherrill Grace at UBC assisted with the Lowry sections of the book, and Professor John Lennox at York University helped locate information. Sheryl Salloum generously shared her interview with Birney. York doctoral candidate Charles M. Levi shared his research on student organizations in the 1930s and checked a number of political references for me. And Levi's thesis adviser, Professor Michael Horn, York University, read two chapters of my manuscript and made useful suggestions. My friend Jennifer Gough, who formerly worked in the Office of Protocol for the Ontario government, generously volunteered to help me track down photographs and permissions. Christina Tasikas, Kelly Cook and Christopher Cheatle helped at different times with clerical and other tasks. Working with these colleagues and young people has been a happy experience, and I thank them for all they did.

It saved much time to have Jack David and Robert Lecker's extensive bibliography of works by and about Earle Birney from *The Annotated Bibliography of Canada's Major Authors*,[22] a luxury I did not have with my biographies of Hugh MacLennan and Irving Layton. Readers interested in the frequently complex publishing history of specific works by Birney, or in the wide range of critical studies of his writing, should consult this book.

It has been a pleasure, too, to have the cheerful assistance of the staff at University College. Jean Smith was especially helpful transcribing my interviews. And Carol Robb efficiently dispatched many of the administrative responsibilities relating to my research grant. I am also grateful to Eleanor Dennison and Audrey Dennie for their help.

To my editor, Meg Masters, who was involved in life issues herself during the time I was writing, I am grateful for the warm encouragment she was able to give not only before and after but also during her maternity leave. Mary Adachi, my entertaining and energetic copy editor, was a pleasure to work with.

Without the support of the Social Sciences and Research Council of Canada, who generously funded my project, this book could not have been written.

For special reasons, I want to thank Bill Stauble, Gale Bildfell, Greg Johnstone, and David, Leopold and Anatol McGinnis. I am grateful, as always, to my parents, Bertah and Donald Cameron, my sisters, Christina and Alexandra Cameron, and especially my children—Beatrix, Hugo and Henry—for their love and support.

Elspeth Cameron
University of Toronto
Friday the 13th of May, 1994

Contents

EARLE BIRNEY

❧ *1* ☙

THE GREAT DIVIDE

The boy whom Private William George Birney left behind him when he went off to the Great War in 1916 was not the same boy he found on his return ten months later. Will Birney loved his "Sonny Boy" and his wife, Martha, almost as much as he loved adventure. He had promised on marrying Martha in Revelstoke, British Columbia, in 1898 that he would not abandon her to serve "the old Traditions of True Britishness"[1] in the Boer War,[2] as so many other Canadian men had done, on one condition: that she let him go to the next one. So now that Britain had declared war on the Hun, there was no holding back the forty-nine-year-old sign-painter and paper-hanger, who was eager to join the other three hundred or so men from the mountain resort town of Banff, Alberta, who had already enlisted. Moreover, he was grateful to boost his meagre income with an army wage.[3] Suffused with the romantic illusions typical of the time, he became one of the "hardy young sons of the mountains," who were, according to the Banff *Crag and Canyon,* "clear-eyed, clean-living, strong-muscled, virile—like the Vikings of old."[4]

The Birneys' only son, Alfred Earle, thrilled with pride in his father, who was elevated in his eyes on the 19th of October 1915

1

to the gallant role of soldier from among the lower ranks of the town's labourers. For a boy teetering on the brink of adolescence, the experience was dazzling: "It was great striding beside him up Banff Avenue, for everyone to see how good he looked in uniform with a Red Cross badge on his arm and, on his second leave, an Acting Lance-Corporal's stripe as well."[5] Young Earle's own self-important speech a month later on behalf of the Cadet Corps to their leader, who was joining up, was excruciatingly formal and clichéd: "You have been very patient with us during your period of instruction," he enunciated clearly, as his mother—who had reason to encourage his public speaking—had coached him to do, "and we hope that we may show by our conduct and example, as you have by yours, the advantages of such a training."[6]

For the eleven-year-old boy, the war was the most exciting thing that could have happened. Never mind that one of his chums who had added two years onto his age to enlist had been shot in the head at the Battle of St. Julien within the first month of going overseas.[7] Never mind his young schoolteacher's stricken reaction to the loss of that bright sixteen-year-old student, nor his mother's "tragic-like" sighs when she read news reports of other Canadians lost, wounded or killed. War was fun. Especially for a boy like Earle who had been peddling the *Canadian Pictorial Review* and the *Calgary Herald* to augment the slim profit his father made crafting signs and papering walls—a pittance his mother supplemented by taking in tourist boarders during the summers and assisting as a self-taught midwife at some of the town's births. War was a bonanza. Because the war sold papers ("there was an archduke murdered in Serbia in June and headlines of mobilizations and ultimata in July... Germany declares war on Russia, [then] on France"),[8] he had been able to buy his first bike—a second-hand Bluebird—in the summer of 1914. Long would he remember the bright red headline BRITAIN DECLARES WAR ON GERMANY on the August 4 edition of the *Herald*:

I remember racing Joe up the Station Road with our papers sagging down our wire carriers almost onto the

front tire, and the cool air rushing at us, and the sunshine lighting up a snow speck way up on top of
[Mount] Rundle. Even with all the load, I felt like I
was soaring and it seemed kind of surprising that my
bike was sticking on the road and not leaping right
into the air and staying there, the way I felt.... I was
sold out in an hour and made nearly three bucks
because there were a lot of tips. People were shouting
across the street to each other and some of them were
laughing and gosh you felt important—almost like the
guys in the poem in the reader about how they
brought the good news from Ghent to somewhere,
only we didn't have horses.[9]

When the time came as 1915 drew to a close for Private
William G. Birney to leave for Calgary, where he was temporarily posted before going overseas at the end of March 1916, it was
an occasion to be marked by a professional photograph of the
close-knit family of three. Standing like protective brackets on
either side of their cherished child were the handsome rangy soldier whose strong bones and wide waxed moustache seemed at
odds with his dark, sensitive eyes and the unsmiling woman
who, though smartly elegant in her jaunty hat, looked grimly
forlorn. Between them, in natty tailored tweed knickers and
jacket stood Earle, a bookish, sweet-faced, freckled boy whose
skinny frame, carroty hair and sudden bursts of temper had
earned from the classmates who delighted in provoking him the
nick-name "Matchie," for "Matchstick."

Will Birney's affection for his son and wife was exceptional,
even given the situation which spurred its written expression.
Letters criss-crossed every few days: first from Calgary, where
Private Birney was stationed in Victoria Barracks with C Section
of the Canadian Army Medical Corps; then from "Somewhere-
in-Belgium" (probably Hooge near Sanctuary Wood, since he
was not on the Verdun front, but somewhere else where bom-
bardments were taking place on 6 June 1916) where he served
during the Ypres Salient as an ambulance driver and stretcher
bearer with the 8th Field Ambulance, C.E.F. ("Oh but the sights

one sees here is enough to put you batty if you were not blessed with good nerves");[10] and later, having been promoted to Corporal and put in charge of the Dressing Room, from France during the Battle of the Somme (known as The Bloody Somme, in which 24,029 Canadian soldiers died). These letters, filled with endearments and concern, suggest that it was chiefly Will Birney whose tenderness nurtured the little family. "My, my, your faces come up before me all the time my Darlings. God bless you," he typically wrote Earle from Calgary before leaving for overseas. "Send me a *Crag and Canyon* Son if you have one and kiss mother for me and mother kiss you for me."[11]

Always solicitous of the health of his "Sonny Boy," who had already succumbed as a child to serious bouts of whooping cough and pneumonia, he wrote to Martha on another occasion, "I do hope Earle is getting better for we must have some fun together when I come home [on weekend leave], so you must tell him to do as he is told and get well. I'll bring him up some medicine when I come."[12] He advised Martha to keep Earle home when the temperature dropped below 30 degrees lest he get pneumonia, and told Earle himself: "Dont work too hard sawing wood Son for you can overdo it."[13] Even from far-off Belgium he advised dosing Earle when his stomach was bad with "1 or 1 1/2 grams Calomel at night and before breakfast a good dose of salts...the Calomel cleans the bowels [and] the salts take it away."[14] After his final visit in late March before leaving Canada, he wrote to his "Two Heroes,"

> Ah me, it takes all I can do to keep a stiff upper lip sometimes my Dear, but the knowledge that God is watching over us and will help us to bear the sacrifice we are making gives me heart.[15]

In response to a letter enclosing a verse written by Earle, he closed his reply: "Now Dearies good night and God bless us all & keep us safe. That was a fine verse of Earls [sic]. Now good night my Dears. Write Soon and give my regards to all friends. Night, night, Daddie."[16] And when Earle sent overseas the essay that won the IODE Empire Day Prize at school (an occasion marked by patriotic songs and a dramatic version of Longfellow's "Hiawatha")—a jingoistic effort called "The British Navy,"[17] which traced the navy back to Alfred the Great (his namesake)— Will's pride was unbounded:

> I read that Essay to my Tent-mates before they knew who wrote it and when they found out the verdict was that Dad's Son was sure some Boy to be proud of. Don't get *Swell-head*, old Chap.[18]

These affectionate feelings were fully reciprocated by Earle, who at Martha's insistence had begun a diary in awkwardly pencilled handwriting after his father left. In entries punctuated with expressions such as "awful funny," "dandy," "something fierce," which he had gleaned from *Boys' Own Papers*, *Puck* and the Ralph Connor novels he and his father admired, he described frequent crying sessions shared with his mother, notably the "last dinner" with his father after attending the Banff Union Church service:

> The parting was the worst thing that I've ever experienced. Daddy switched on the light in the sitting room and took a last look. We stood and saw him go down to the station and the thought crossed our minds "Would he ever return to us." We had an awful crying spell after he left and then we heard the toot of the train. To me it was the worst sound I had ever heard.[19]

The absence of his father left Earle in the hands of his mother, a situation that was not entirely to his liking. Not only did he deeply miss his warm, feckless, fun-loving father, but relations with his mother had never been easy. His statement, much later, that he had been born "with enough violence to make it impossible for my mother to have further children,"[20] suggests the sense of guilt Martha unwittingly induced in her son. A grey miasma of guilt also surrounded his knowledge that he had lost an older brother—William—who had died in the first week of life a year before he himself was born.

Martha had endured brutal treatment as a child from her sometimes drunken father, Robert Robertson, a subsistence Shetland crofter and fisherman who, when angered, lashed his children with fish-hooks. Martha, understandably, was a strict teetotaller. And, though Will was clearly religious, his was a gentle, benign Christianity, while hers was the stern stuff of rigid Presbyterianism. At the centre of her life were the services, Sunday Schools (which she frequently taught), prayer meetings, women's groups and choirs of the Banff Union Church, and she expected her son to attend morning and evening services, as well as Sunday School, every Sunday. She aspired not only to stainless morality, but to the stable respectability her own childhood lacked. Though she was usually cheerful and sociable, and her assistance at confinements was kindly, many noticed an underlying bitterness in her and, not surprisingly in one who had endured much pain in powerless anguish, the tendency to supervise and control the doings of others. Banff's public school principal, an affable bachelor named Charles W. Brown, for example, writing to Earle when he was away from Banff at a summer job in 1919, refers almost comically to Martha's aggressive morality:

> I am afraid if I were to say what other forbidden things I do on Sunday, your good Presbyterian mother would taboo me, or possibly consign me to the bottomless pit. Were we living in the days of the Inquisition, and your mother an orthodox Catholic, I would be fuel for an auto-da-fe. But what can a would-be Christian do, who has no wife nor family when he sees household duties to be done with which school duties interfere.... I suppose that mother of yours would suggest a Mrs. Brown be installed in the kitchen, civilized enough to adorn a parlor chair and receive callers occasionally...[21]

The socially ambitious Martha dressed her son fastidiously, fretted about his health and his skinny body, insisted that he take piano lessons (so he could in time play the organ), and made sure his attendance at Sunday School was impeccable and productive (he had been awarded a certificate for exceptional memorization of Scripture from the Toronto office of the Presbyterian Church in Canada at age six). She made it clear that the career she had in mind for her exceptionally bright young gentleman was that of Presbyterian minister.[22]

To the pressure Martha had exerted all along on her only child was now added the irritability that directly arose from her anxieties for Will—a situation she most assuredly could not control. It appears, too, that Earle—whose red hair and amber eyes resembled hers and her mother's—had either inherited her tendency to become suddenly irascible, or had copied such behaviour in self-defence. That he and his mother occasionally blew up at each other is implicit in such admonitions as the following in Will's letters home: "just quit your scrapping now and be mother's man till Dad comes back."[23] Martha, faced with the possibility she might never again see her husband alive, clearly regretted some of her earlier behaviour towards Will. This is implicit in his response to a letter[24] from her: "Yes, darlings, it is as you say I don't think we appreciated one another as we should but my Dear Girl you never did anything to beg my forgiveness for."[25] That the tender-hearted Will had a knack for handling both Martha and Earle is clear in his son's later recollection of an incident in which he dealt with his son after he had lost his temper in school and sworn at a teacher:

> the contretemps had stirred up something bitter and reckless in my make-up. Luckily, it was a gene my father understood. He took me out on the porch and quietly pointed out that I had a choice. Either I could apologize, make my mother happy and prevent this obstacle to a higher career, or I could quit school.... His attitude amazed, flabbergasted me. My father obviously didn't think more schooling was...as important as *my freedom*, my freedom of choice. I think he handled me with much wisdom. Quietly he let me see the gulf of mediocrity I could be trapped into for life if I let my temper and pride and souped-up sense of justice prevent me from even finishing high school.[26]

In Will's absence both Martha's and Earle's fiery irritability flared unbridled. Earle's diary (which reported Martha's frequent headaches and bouts of "rhumitizim") at times reads like the work of a testy old man full of impatient resignation. ("It is pretty lonely without dad but we'll have *to stand it*.") As a man, he would recall, "my loving and cheerful mother became gloomier and shorter tempered as the months wore on."[27]

Somehow, in the process of adapting to the stark reality of his father's absence and his mother's omnipresence, Earle became a man. He took to heart his father's frequent admonition that he become the head of the family and noted Will's advice to Martha that in his absence—and perhaps forever—she must lean on her son ("'my little substitute.' I hope he will not have to be but if so you will know you have a Son who is the making of a real man and a better one than his Dad"[28]). Earle comforted his mother when she cried; he took her up breakfast or helped her cook and dust; he squired her on such outings as a train trip to Calgary to visit some family friends (typically listing all the train stations along the way); he even heeded his father's instructions to see that he and his mother celebrated her eighteenth wedding anniversary on the 18th of August ("Be good to her for she is good to you").[29]

And, at the same time as he adopted his father's tender nurturing attitude towards his mother, he also appropriated his father's right to arbitrary absences from Martha's watchful eye. His diary records an occasion when he refused to accompany her to a church function and attended a Charlie Chaplin movie instead—a bid for independence she would not have approved of. Though the childish pursuits of stamp-collecting, skating, tobogganing and swimming at Banff's sulphurous hot-springs pool continued, and the scholastic achievements of the school "bookworm" developed apace, a third dimension to Earle Birney—neither his father's sweet solicitude nor his mother's ardent zeal—gained strength and validity. With a shrewd secretiveness, he asserted his passionate need for success on his own terms and for the indulgence of what had that year become intense sexual curiosity. In imitation of the wartime newspapers whose power to stir interest he well understood, he began with a school chum to write and circulate an underground paper. When it was apprehended by a teacher outraged at the crude sketch of a soldier engaged in sex with a woman standing under a tree, he was whipped with the cat-o'-nine-tails—a crisis bravely endured that put an end to the teasing of his peers and ensured his status. He helped organize a boys' club[30] which had a secret meeting place up in a treehouse and eluded Martha on delicious hikes in the mountains far from the oppressive house where he increasingly felt trapped. Dropping his boyish newspaper sales job in favour of the more manly work of delivering meat for the town's sometimes drunken butcher, he used the entrepreneurial skills he had gained as a newsboy to augment his income by renting out to the senior boys packets of flagrant pornography prepared by a Banff photographer. And, with what can only be described as prodigious energy, he also sold copies of the *Calgary Eye-Opener*, a satirical, anti-religious, sly and gossipy publication of which he later observed, "my mother would have burned at once any [copy] that came into her hand."[31]

At the end of the few months' diary he had undertaken at his mother's urging, he charted his progress over the year since his father's departure in spidery handwriting as if trying to measure his transformation:

January 1st, 1916

1916	Identifacation [sic]	(1917)
name	Earle Birney	
age	11 years	(12 yrs)
height	4 ft. 11 inches	(5 ft. 2½)
weight	74 pounds	(78 lbs.)
hair	"rusty"	(auburn)
shoe size	3½	(4)
moccasin size	5	(5½)
P.O. Box	142	
Residence	Squirrel St.	
Town	Banff	
Province	Alberta	
Size of Collar	12	(12½)
Size of Hat	6⅝	(6⅞)[32]

The family photo taken to mark the return to Banff of Corporal William G. Birney, who was eventually discharged on 7 March 1918 as unfit for further service on account of sickness, shows Earle no longer a gentlemanly little dandy, but a lanky and outdoorsy young man standing head and shoulders above his father and mother. Casually dressed in an open-necked shirt and workman's cloth cap, his outspread arms bracket his seated parents: on one side his father, now grey-haired, with arms akimbo, and on the other his mother comfortably dressed and hatless, her tanned face aglow, her hands almost relaxed.

⚜ *2* ⚜

LOWLANDS AND HIGHLANDS

Earle Birney's earliest recollections are of marching in the Calgary Orangemen's Parade "as a sort of child mascot" at about age five and of being taught to dance the minuet.[1] These memories of a cherubic boy with red-gold curls and immaculate little suits suggest a childhood more elevated than might have been predicted for a child born to virtually destitute parents in a shack[2] on the south bank of the Bow River in the shadow of Calgary's Old Langevin Bridge on a day of the month that was ominous for Shetlanders: Friday, 13 May 1904. As Martha well knew, anything begun on a Friday the 13th was bound to fail.

The name "Earle" was among those titles of nobility like "Prince" and "Duke" which were appropriated for first names in Britain in the seventeenth century, perhaps as a revolt against Puritan naming practices. Birney later made much of the fact that the name was a mistake, due to his mother's florid Scottish accent when pronouncing "Errol" to the registrar. Since she could read, and might readily have altered "Earle" to "Errol," even informally, her acceptance of this error suggests that she was not particularly displeased with the name's aristocratic overtones. After all, she had chosen "Alfred" (which means "elf counsel") after Alfred the Great as a first name for this special child. The

11

result was an impressive name that mimicked nobility, for formal address follows the same pattern: as in Alfred, Lord Tennyson or Charles, Prince of Wales. Alfred Earle Birney, who was crowned with the downy hair like burnished gold that proclaimed him a descendant of the strikingly handsome Martha and her auburn-haired mother, was clearly a child of whom much was expected. He would not only compensate for his older brother, William, whose death had left an aching void in his mother's heart, but—if his health and education were carefully tended to—he could surely rank above the lowly fortunes of his working-class parents. But somewhere just back of the regal "Earle" lurked "Errol"—an old Scottish place name and surname possibly linked to the Latin word for "wanderer."[3]

Though the Birney family came from England (and the family claimed to be Anglo-Irish), their roots—like Martha Robertson's—must have stemmed from Scotland, for the name Birney (or Birnie) is a Scottish place name from the northernmost highlands in the romantic Moray district that can be traced as a surname back to the mid-thirteenth century.[4] Alfred Earle Birney was the first of his father's family to be born in Canada. His grandfather William Birney was born in London, England, in 1835 and left his apprenticeship to a butcher in Leighton Buzzard in Bedfordshire to serve in the Crimean War at age twenty-one, then was off to the Indian mutiny two years later. He was said to have farmed in Bedfordshire for a time before emigrating with his wife and eldest son, Will, to Guelph, Upper Canada, where he worked as a butcher. After the death of his wife in childbirth with her second child, the elder William remarried and fathered six more children.

William Birney intended to have his eldest son, William George, join his Guelph meat business, but at age fifteen, young Will ran away. Judging from the career that followed—if the rapid succession of jobs he took can be called a career—he rebelled at any thought of foregoing the "barefoot boyhood existence, fishing and swimming-holes in summer, sugar-tapping and school fights in winter...mainly between the sons of the Knights of Columbus [and] the sons—like himself—of the Loyal Orangemen."[5]

With feckless panache, the eternally restless and boyish Will hitchhiked on hay wagons to Chicago that summer of 1880; then rode west to Calgary herding some of the horses from the U.S. south which were essential for pulling the wagons essential in pre-railroad times, in exchange for a rifle, a saddlebag of grub and a horse. On arriving in Calgary he cashed in on the excitement of the first Alberta railroad, riding between Lethbridge and Medicine Hat as a brakeman. Will soon caught the fever of the California gold rush (a fever from which he was never entirely cured), sniffed the challenge of battle and joined Coxey's Army in the great eastward march of the western unemployed on Washington in the 1890s, then quit soon after, when he realized it didn't tally with his Conservative politics.

Ironically, Will's impulsive bid for freedom from his father's business eventually converted his father to the west. At the lowest point in his peripatetic career, Will turned to his father for money to pay off his gambling debts. When his father came west to bail him out and insisted in exchange that his errant son take up a trade (an apprenticeship in paper-hanging and sign-painting which conveniently presented itself), he too felt the magnetism of the west, put a down payment on a ranch at Priddis in the Bow River Valley near Calgary, returned to Guelph to sell his butcher business, and promptly came back with his third wife. There the couple raised six more children, and made a success of Deer Spring Ranch, where William finally died at age seventy-five.[6]

After deserting Coxey's Army, young Will tried his luck at prospecting in the Selkirks and the Kootenay Mountains of British Columbia. Having failed there, he moved on to Rossland nestled high in the Rocky Mountains, grubstaked a claim, and worked his trade in town until such time as he made it rich, an eventuality he seems always to have felt was near at hand. It was in the dining room of Rossland's Halcyon Hotel that he looked down from his ladder and glimpsed what he thought was the most heavenly red-haired waitress he'd ever seen, briskly carrying her tray past. It was the twenty-two-year-old Martha Robertson.

For a Christmas engagement present, Will gave Mattie, as he sometimes called her, a copy of Robert Burns's poetry. For their wedding—a modest affair in Kootenay on 17 August 1898—he gave her a hunter watch with their initials and the date of their wedding intertwined on the silver cover.[7]

Martha Stout Robertson had also fled home at age fifteen in 1890 with what was probably more justification than Will had. She was the seventh of twelve children born to the handsome, black-haired Robert Robertson and his wife, Barbara Laurenson, both from old Shetland families of sailors, fishermen and crofters, who eked out a subsistence on the treeless barren northern moors where "five acres and a cow" constituted a farm and the bitter cold was kept at bay in the tiny thatched crofts by burning peat sods and bundling up in sweaters knit from thick local wool.[8] Martha recalls, above all, her father's drunken rages. In one of these her little finger was bent permanently crooked when he violently grabbed a fishnet she was mending. Another left her with permanent scars after a whipping with fish-hooks. Old Robbie Robertson seems to have been a force as uncontrollable as the seas that swirled treacherously around the bleak Shetland croft in which he and his family hunkered down on the Island of Bressay off the west coast. To him and to his father, the family attributes their vigour. Family legend has it that the elder Robert Robertson—Martha's grandfather—was descended from "a Highland Irish woman with very black hair and a good profile who settled in Bressay and lived to be very old." With pawky humour, the Robertson descendants speak in their vivid dialect of Scandinavian and Scottish phrases about his ingenuity in settling for free by transporting stones in his boat stealthily under cover of mist across from Bressay to Lingness on the mainland and building a new croft below the high-tide line where taxes could not be levied. So sly was this building enterprise that no one noticed the croft, let alone smoke from its chimney, until one day the mist cleared and "the lum was reeking."[9]

His son Robert—Martha's father—was noted for his charm and his inability to resist women. He was only nineteen when he married the twenty-two-year-old Barbara Laurenson in 1862 at Nesting, and it wasn't long before his penchant for affairs was common knowledge. As the result of one of these in 1877, when he was thirty-five, he and his family (which by then numbered eight children) were evicted from the croft at Bressay. The father of a local girl, who was under sixteen, took Old Robbie to court for the lying-in expenses of his daughter, whose newborn daughter Robbie had fathered. Family history has it that Barbara, his gentle, long-suffering wife, who had given birth to her eighth child only a week before her husband's illegitimate daughter was born, rowed a boat to the court to plead on her own behalf, "Who's going to give milk [i.e., support] to *my* baby?" At the time of this crisis, Martha—until then the youngest child—was not yet two. And though she would later speak of her father's violence, she never mentioned this scandal.[10] A few years later, Robert left his family to live in a croft nearby where he took in a sixteen-year-old housekeeper, who immediately became pregnant, giving birth eventually to a child so handsome there was no mistaking his father.

If the Robertsons were vigorous, the Laurensons were intelligent and enterprising. Portraits of two of them hang in the Town Hall in Shetland's capital, Lerwick: Arthur Laurenson (b. 1829), who travelled to Norway, Sweden and America for literary and linguistic study; and George Reid Morrison, Arthur's first cousin (b. 1819), who was master of the *Bulldog* in the Crimean War and later a staff-commander known for his supression of slavery and piracy on the south and west coasts of Africa and China. One of Morrison's grandsons, G.T. Manley (who was later an evangelical missionary), was Senior Wrangler in Mathematics at Cambridge in 1893 while his classmate Bertrand Russell took fifth place.[11]

At fifteen, Martha—like many Shetland girls who sought work as nurses or servants away from Shetland where there was nothing but croft work for them to do—left home for a job in Edinburgh where she became a servant to a doctor.[12] Eventually Magnus, one of her older brothers who had jumped ship at Nanaimo on the east coast of Vancouver Island and was working in a coal mine there, sent her passage money to join him in the mid-1890s. Martha thus took her part in the dispersal of the Robertson family which was characteristic of Shetlanders in that generation. Of her eight siblings that survived into adulthood, four emigrated to western Canada (all sponsored by Magnus) and two moved south to Glasgow. Only two remained in Shetland.

The main image of her energetic father which Martha passed on to her son in stories embellished with Shetland phrases (such as "a sudden tide lump at heaved up and flang her clean ower"; or "he would even go awat tae the lochs in Delting tae shoot dukes you know idda winter time")[13] was that of the drunken fisherman of the North Sea from whom she had fled.

"Wicked Old Robbie," as his descendants refer to him, seems to have had unusual skills as a storyteller himself. That, at least, is the main tribute paid the "kindly" and "cheery" adventurer, "skilled [at] seamanship," in his 1936 obituary:

> His more intimate associates will remember always his reminiscences which he could tell so graphically, inter-mingled with rich humour when the occasion demanded that the hearer had no dull moment in his company—in fact so vividly told that one felt, at the end of his stories that the scenes in his experiences had been enacted over again in person with him.[14]

A talent for tales was a quality Martha herself either inherited or acquired from the oral culture of Shetland. Certainly her son was to begin his literary memoirs with his recollections of her stories told with a broad Shetland accent—an accent deriving from Scottish and Norse pasts so deeply intermingled that the unique dialect even today is largely incomprehensible to an English-speaker from elsewhere. "I absorbed 'poetry' before I could read," he would later write,

> without knowing what it was. My mother's musical voice brought me lovings and lamentings from her Scottish childhood. "Noo I lay me doun to sleep" and "Humpty-Dumpty" and other intercontinental chants for an Anglophone baby echoed down from a Shetland croft to my corner of the single bedroom on the Albertan ranch. At three I was prattling "Jesus wants me for a sunbeam"; at four reciting the Lord's

Prayer and the Twenty-Third Psalm in the Morningside Sunday School.[15]

Years later the slightest mention of such songs could trigger an instant response: "there was a special moment," he wrote Olaf Ruhen, whose *Harpoon in My Hand* (a book about whaling in the Tonga Islands) he was reading, "when I suddenly felt very kindred to you, for my Shetland mother also sang me 'Robin Grey' and many another old Scottish song, from the first times I can remember."[16]

Such early experiences and impressions may have been more deeply imprinted on Earle than on most young children, for he saw almost no human beings other than his parents for the first six years of his life. "My father moved around my consciousness as the definition of a man," he would recall later. "He was something accepted and uncompared, a being enormously high, scarcely ever still, but with the trick of making anything he did seem, at the moment, as important as a ritual, whether it was planning a barn or sugaring his porridge. This is not to say that he could not be merry or playful, but even building a snowman was a challenge to his craftsmanship."[17] Martha must have seemed the very definition of woman, her traits also "accepted and uncompared." Though there was the odd guest and he was taken occasionally on visits to relatives and friends in Calgary, which dazzled him with its hustle and bustle, its "mansions," its street-lights, and he later was taken to the Sunday School taught by his mother, he spent the vast majority of his early life alone with Will and Martha on the ten-acre bush farm eighty miles from Calgary and two miles east of Morningside—a little flag station near the Edmonton line—which Will, with his unflagging optimism, referred to as a "ranch" and named "The Bonnie Doon." "I was a solitary child," Earle would later recall with more than a hint of regret. "I knew chunks of [Robinson] Crusoe by heart, he was Me, & I can still go back to him."[18] It was Martha who read to her son, and soon began teaching him with alphabet blocks and Will's celluloid stencils for painting letters on signs.[19] By four, their alert and responsive "Sonny Boy" could read.

If Will had had his way, the family would have been even more remote. He favoured striking out much further north to Peace River, five hundred miles north of Calgary. Martha favoured settling in Calgary, a booming town she thought would surely have customers for signs, paint and wallpaper, a business she anticipated could provide enough profit to invest shrewdly in real estate. The Bonnie Doon was a compromise. Martha held him to his wedding promise of no further prospecting and now insisted on a location near a railway (which ruled out Peace River) while Will convinced her that he'd feel "fettered" in Calgary, which had become too civilized for his adventuresome tastes, and that the future of the shining new province of Alberta lay in farming.

For six long and difficult years, Martha and Will—and Earle, as soon as he could help with chores—cleared scrub from around the three-room shack of one-ply board and planted vegetables and ploughed uneven ground and chopped wood and shot deer. And even though Morningside was safe compared to the territory further north, one of Birney's lasting memories when he was about five was one of stark terror: "my mother once stood in a farmhouse door warding off a crazed half-breed with a shotgun while I peered around behind her apron."[20] Despite the family's efforts, on their weekly visits to the market in Lacombe, there were scarcely five cents to spare for a bit of chocolate for Earle. And during the hard valley winters, Will had no choice but to leave Martha to run The Bonnie Doon so he could find painting or wallpapering jobs in Calgary or Lethbridge in order to buy seed and the family's Easter renewals of clothes, a last-ditch measure which suggests that Martha's vision for the family's future had been more sound financially than her husband's.

Yet photos of Earle at The Bonnie Doon hardly depict a ragged ruffian. Quite the contrary, a bonnier child, his shining well-fed face surrounded by masses of golden curls, could hardly be imagined. Somehow there was money enough to dress him at age three in a Buster Brown middy outfit, knee stockings and high-buttoned boots. Despite the drab facts of his life, he looked like the child of a prosperous family.

Accustomed as he was to long stretches of time alone and adult company when there was any, it is not surprising that Earle was terrified by school. In his lonely fantasies at Bonnie Doon, he had imagined himself as the fast-talking auctioneer he once observed in fascination on a trip to Lacombe,[21] or as "a missionary to China, the nearest place I thought of as having heathens."[22] He appears to have begun school in Calgary mid-year, sometime in early 1911. Even though he had been too lonely on the farm, the rough-and-tumble of a room full of children was devastating. And the fact that he could already read and write made him a freakish figure of fun. He recalls that coming down with whooping cough that spring triggered a "merciful" release from school. On the doctor's advice that the child's health required a move from the farm in the valley to the fresh air high in the mountains, Will and Martha moved to Banff, a town named after the resort town in the Moray district of northern Scotland from which the name Birney had come. Will—no doubt eager to move on again and relieved to find a good excuse to extricate himself from yet another failed enterprise—sold up the farm. As for Martha, life centred on the health of her alarmingly thin little boy and the move to Banff promised at least some of the amenities of civilization.

Banff in the summer of 1911 was one of the most spectacular resorts in the world. It was advertised in folders of the Canadian Pacific Railway as "Fifty Switzerlands in One." Nestled high in the Rockies 130 miles west of Calgary, the little town founded in 1883 and frequented by wealthy American and European climbers and naturalists, was surrounded by a 1.6 million-acre national park along the eastern slope of the Continental Divide. To the east, the majestic Banff Springs Hotel overlooked the muddy main street with its apothecary shop, Chinese laundry, railway station, stables, curio stores boasting furs and the stuffed heads of bears, moose, mountain goats and wolves, as well as crafts by the Stoney Indians, and the supply shops run by myriad outfitters; to the west, the sulphur hot springs that were the resort's original *raison d'être* and were enshrined in The Sanitarium—a spa hotel—bubbled their hot brimstone vapours into the lower and upper public baths: one an indoor "Cave," the other an outdoor "Basin." Adventurers from around the world tested their climbing skills—sometimes with tragic results—on the snow-capped peaks that surrounded the town like a ring of awe-inspiring giants. In their crevices and lofty sills lay the surprise of flowery meadows, pungent thickets of pine, spruce and fir, thundering waterfalls, clear green lakes and expansive glaciers. Down below in the town, the icy Bow River slid past on its way east towards Calgary.[23]

The farm Will had believed would make the family rich—even with the sale of their horse Comet thrown in—yielded only enough to buy a little property 15 feet by 30 feet on Squirrel Street in Banff facing Mount Norquay, Stoney Squaw and the Cascade Mountains, and some lumber towards building a house.[24] Meanwhile, they camped in a tent on the Bow River where Echo Creek flows in and spent what for Earle was an idyllic summer, eating fresh-caught fish and long corrugated loaves of fresh bread from the local bakery. "It was the edge of the great mountain-woods; the junction of the two streams was a cold deep mystery haunted by great trout and clever grayling," he would write later.[25] By fall, Will had a rudimentary shell of a little house in place, complete with a sign that may have been a gentle reprimand aimed obliquely at the spats of Martha and Earle: "KWITCHERKIKIN."

In October, Earle—no doubt apprehensively—entered the Banff Public School, one of ten seven-year-olds among forty-one children aged five to thirteen. By his own account later, he was unpopular: "introverted, quarrelsome, timid."[26] But though he was still being teased and picked on, this was not Calgary. The most gorgeous natural haunts in Canada lay just outside the door; the school was small; and home was a short walk, not twenty miles away. By January, he was among those few promoted to the *Second Reader*, assuming an unenviable role in which he would be cast until adolescence as academically precocious. What remains of his school-work conveys an impression of a boy who was sensitive—perhaps to a fault—artistic and observant. A series of three poems interspersed with carefully detailed and whimsical sketches about the chickadee, the loon and the woodpecker, for example, are delightful and fresh:

Woodpeckers are surprising birds
With hooks on all their toes,
By which they hang straight up and down
On any tree that grows.

Some folk think 'peckers peck for fun
And like to whack & thump,
But they must carve their beds and board
From some old log or stump.

And though they hammer hard all day
They're always dressed up neat,
With orange hats or polka vests,
Or laundered shirts with pleats.

. . . .

And if a worm can duck his beak
(A worm that's smart and small),
He sticks him with a long hooked tongue
As sharp as any awl.[27]

A mysterious sickness in the fall of his second year—thought to
be Rocky Mountain fever resulting from a tick bite—added to
the fact that by summer's end Will had still not finished their
house, induced Martha to take Earle out of school to accompany
her back to Shetland for her first return visit. From the end of
the first week of November to the middle of March 1912,
mother and son travelled by colonist car to Montreal, saving
money by cooking their own meals on a stove at the end of the
coach, and travelling steerage on the Donaldson Line aboard the
old *Athenia* (Cunard)[28] to Glasgow.

Earle would later recall with pleasure that winter in Shetland.
At first, he and his mother lived on a remote peatbog called
Hellister, in Weisdale, where the seven-year-old boy had a
beloved one-eyed sheepdog. Then they moved in with his grandmother in Lerwick—the woman from whom he had inherited
his tall, thin frame, warm brown eyes and red hair. Her kindness
to her grandson contrasted with Martha's strictness. "She was
always on at him to be up and doing," one family member

recalls. "'Play?' she would say, "What's this word 'play'?"[29] Earle
would later recall seeing "Up-Helly-Aa," the impressive Viking
celebration in which a longboat is set aflame at sea. "My uncle
was a Guyser Jarl and rode in the great ship for the procession,
and my cousins and I made a small wooden galley in great
secrecy, for some reason, in the toolshed."[30] Earle hated Glasgow,
where he and his mother visited her older brother William
Robertson, a sea captain, because "the bully boys were out, saw
he was a foreigner, and were terrible and rough."[31] But he liked
Edinburgh. Ironically, considering that concern for his health
had in part prompted the trip, he came down with pneumonia
after a visit to Edinburgh Castle—where he was thrilled to sit
astride a cannon. "My childhood memories of those treeless isles
are mainly connected with having double pneumonia and having
to wait for a doctor, *the* doctor, to be rowed over from another
island."[32] He returned home thinner and paler than when he
had left.

This disruption of his second year at school in Banff, which
confirmed rather than dissipated his sense of his physical vulner-
ability, his closeness to his mother, the almost pompous bookish-
ness that had resulted from a childhood among adults—mostly
Martha who recognized his quick intelligence and pressured him
to excel—and his spindly awkward frame combined to ensure an
unhappy time among his hardier peers. Though it is an extreme
example, one occasion he bitterly recalled later indicates the
anguish he frequently felt at the time:

> I remember the first attempts to teach skiing to kids in
> Banff. I remember seeing [Alpine mountaineer]
> Conrad Kain's street being pointed out, but I don't
> remember having any direct connection with him
> except that he was one of the people that stimulated
> the...parents to buy skis. [The] schools wouldn't put
> up the money and those Austrian-Swiss people who
> came in...didn't have any money particularly them-
> selves, [but] they did want to start skiing.... We were
> practically forced onto skis, and our parents were
> forced to find the money to buy the skis. They built a

slide, a small ski jump, and then we were taught...to jump.... Of course, we were trying to learn on our own to manouevre on the level, but it was such a primitive undertaking.... And at the same time, they started to build a big slide.

I was still very very thin and light in weight, and on my first jump, there was some kind of cross draft and I was blown around in the air and landed upside down. One of my skis broke—it was a cheap ski anyway—and a splinter of it went into the top of my left knee. I was out of circulation—as far as sports went—for nearly a year. This was very annoying to me because I had started skating. I had learned to skate just before I came to Banff, and I was trying very much...because I had been a lonely child and because I was thin, and so on. I had perhaps more than the usual desire to identify with the crowd and the herd and all that, and I was constantly being rejected by the group because I was no bloody good in team sports. I was always getting cracked up and hurled sideways and everything, especially in hockey. I was always boarded, and I learned to skate faster because I was always trying to get away from the other guys. These were the old days—seven man hockey—and I was made the rover. I really began to develop a speed in skating [which] Lou Crosby (Canadian speed skater) noticed. I felt very bucked that a guy like [him] had noticed me, and [thought] that I might be a great speed skater myself. I was beginning to work at this and then this damned skiing accident bunged me up for a long time. It gave me this kind of childish hostility against skiing, so I never skiied [again] in my life. [I] never went back to a pair of skis from then on, one of the great deprivations of my life.[33]

The physical disadvantages Earle experienced as a boy were not all that caused others to reject him. His achievements at school—he was skipped ahead a grade twice—and his artificially "adult" learning, encouraged by his ambitious parents, and a certain "mother's boy" aura resulting from Martha's insistent protectiveness made him paradoxically a condescending know-it-all and something of a sissy. He desperately wanted to be a part of school athletics, but could not hold his own, except in skating where he "learned to skate fast just to escape being killed... I felt superior in some ways, in others inferior. But never equal," he said later. "I always wanted integration with other people—on my own terms."[34]

In a 1913 issue of the *Canadian Pictorial* one Alfred E. Birney is singled out for the feature "Our Agents' Corner." Under a photo of the owlish bespectacled nine-year-old in a natty straw hat and impeccable knickers, jacket and tie, hands carefully grasped behind his back, reads a caption:

> Alfred E. Birney
> Banff, Alberta
> Alfred has been doing splendid work since he started business with us, more than a year ago, and he certainly has earned his place in the "Pictorial" as one of our best boy agents. Good luck to him![35]

⋙ 3 ⋘

DOWN IN THE VALLEY

On the 26th of March 1922, the seventeen-year-old Earle Birney wrote in some distress, enclosing fifty cents, to a graphologist he had seen advertised in a paper his father received from Ottawa called *The Veteran*:

Dear Graphologist:

This is a specimen of my handwriting. I want you to tell me what particular line of work I should make my life-work. I am only turned 18 years, and at present am trying to make enough money, via pick & shovel, to put me through college. I have not yet made up my mind what to take up, and am worried that I may choose something in which I will not succeed.

When at, High School, my favorite study was Chemistry, and so I have often thought of training for a position as Analytical Chemist. My mind wavers between that and studying law, for many of my friends, also my parents, think I would make a good lawyer. I'm afraid the only claim for talent in that direction is my argumentative disposition!

Perhaps my writing is not matured enough for you
to tell, but I am sure that you can help me better than
anyone else;

yours hopefully,
A.E. Birney[1]

Birney had good reason to be distressed. He had already
embarked on one career which had gone awry. He had hoped to
win the one-hundred-dollar scholarship for top marks in the
Kootenay District in his last year of high school, a scholarship
that might have enabled him to go on to university. But the
never-ending chores and odd jobs for cash that were by now
chronic in his family cheated him of the time he needed to study,
and he stood second. Disappointed, frustrated and angry, he had
taken his parents' advice to take up a job for which his high-
school principal had referred him as a junior clerk in the Creston
Bank of Commerce. Although the salary was abysmal (forty-five
dollars a month, less than he had been making in his summer
job as a fruit-picker and packer), his parents persuaded him that
it was an opportunity for a commercial education. Who could
tell? He might become a rich bank manager in the end.

Even if his parents had not harboured high aspirations for his
future, he knew he did not want to throw himself into daily
drudgery, as they did, simply to make ends meet. For some time
now he had been torn: like his father he loved the excitement of
the new, but he could also see his father's wild schemes for what
they really were—the naïve belief that somewhere, somehow, in
the pioneering enterprise of the great north-west, something
would pan out. Sometime he'd get lucky.

Now that Birney was a teenager, and an observant and shrewd
teenager, he could see that the end result of his father's restless
enthusiasms was nothing more or less than backbreaking physical labour, fraught with let-downs and for little material gain.
His father's last venture had proved that beyond any doubt.
When Will was finally discharged from the Armed Forces on 7
March 1918, three months after his return from the front, he
was assessed as eligible for only a 10 per cent pension instead of
the full pension he had counted on. Birney would later recall

that his father had returned home "a pale skeleton of the man I knew as my father"; that he was "shell-shocked"; and that his hands trembled from some sort of neuralgia that made it impossible to paint or wall-paper. This seems an exaggeration, given that Will's letters do not indicate much distress during his service overseas and clearly indicate that he was never closer than three miles to the front; and also given the fact that Will eventually returned to his trade. Certainly, although he had turned grey during the war years, as a fifty-year-old man probably would have anyway, his photos after returning do not give an impression of a man either pale or skeletal.

The Birney family, however, were convinced that Will needed a change from painting and papering. First he worked as a towel attendant at the Cave and Basin public baths. Then, when interest-free loans for veterans were announced, it was back to farming—this time a fruit farm on the other side of the Rockies in British Columbia's Creston Valley, near the little town of Erickson, about two hundred miles west of Banff. In June 1918, having chosen a ten-acre farm on which he put a down payment of one hundred dollars borrowed from the government's new Soldiers' Civil Re-establishment Fund, he rented the Squirrel Street house and mortgaged the rest. Full of hope, Will descended with his little family into the fruitful valley he was sure would make his fortune.

As far as Earle was concerned, it was a reversion to life near Morningside—a reversion he didn't relish. Not only was he leaving his Banff chums—with whom he had finally managed to fit in—but the move promised to be a regression to the arduous, isolated life of loneliness he recalled from his early years. Worse, now that he was fourteen, he would be expected to do a man's share of the work. Looking back much later, Birney described his days on the Creston farm almost in awe of how hard he and his parents worked. Not surprisingly, given Will's judgement and his finances, the place was run-down, largely impossible to cultivate, populated by indifferent livestock—including a shack full of sick hens—and irrigated by a stream with the disarming tendency to dry up when most needed. The Birneys picked strawberries and raspberries from dawn to dusk, sorted and packaged them, drew water when there was any, cared for livestock, drove produce daily to the Erickson railway station, weeded, fended off predators and garden pests with guns, traps and poison, mended and repaired an endless series of items and devised irrigation systems to survive the dry spells.

And yet, there was a side to this life that enthralled Earle. Among his age-group, he was accorded instant status as a swimmer and outdoorsman—a kid, after all, from a larger, more cosmopolitan world than their own. Unhappy as he had been to leave the rugged heights of Banff, the softer landscapes of the Creston Valley afforded pleasures of their own. Behind the Birney's tiny, almost windowless house sloped Goat Mountain, a mere hill compared to the pinnacles looming over Banff, but one that was lush with a more delicate undergrowth and populated with songbirds. "I had only to walk a few yards out of sight of the grey box of our house," he would later recall, "and be into jade firs and hemlock alive with chattering squirrels and chipmunks, blackbirds trilling in the clean blue sky overhead, robin red-breasts on the fence-posts."[2] And though the creek had nothing of the majesty of the Bow River that swept past Banff, "the little willow-shaded creek with its two comical kingfishers, chattering and noisy as they dove for smallfry and bugs afforded glistening pools fringed by purple tangles of wild pea-vine and swordferns and violets" in which he could fish and—on hot summer days—dive naked into the mysterious chill green depths. And along the bank, hidden by "corpses of old logs interspersed with new growth slim as bamboo,"[3] was a special secret spot where he could lie far from the tiny cramped house and make love in his imagination to the ladies' underwear ads torn from the Eaton's catalogue. Later he would theorize that masturbation—"the first seed-casting"—is "the real break-through from male virginity." And for him, that breakthrough was inextricably linked to being outdoors, surrounded by the intense sensual impact of the natural world. "For me, [that first seed-casting] is entangled with the rank smell of crushed wild-parsnip-leaves and the cool damp of a ditch I lay in at 13, the almost-dried July creekbed running through the berry orchard, the wild blackberry canes roofing me from the pickers over in the raspberry canes, but peering I could just see the mountainous bare legs of Dumb Annie, the halfbreed picker from the end of the hillroad. The smell of semen was also the wild parsnip smell, & I'd cracked the universe, leapt armed from my own head, all the girls of the world were waiting, and god struck dead."[4]

More than ever now, the young Birney was obsessed with the one subject his parents never broached: sex. He developed one crush after another—several simultaneously—on the local girls he gradually met his first summer, then went to school with at Creston. Dora, Frances, Vivienne, Urva, Eunice: his whole being was dazed with lust, an adolescent lust perhaps all the sweeter for being so completely taboo and separate from the rest of his existence. One of these girls—Frances Lyne—would later recall how Earle appeared to her. "When a new boy comes to town there is excitement at school, especially when that boy is tall, with red hair and brown eyes! Earle's parents were very proud of him and ambitious for him. Some way or other he must have the very best education possible. The school was a one-room affair, with a tiny lab added on. There was just one teacher to teach all subjects. He was a graduate of London University and a clever man, but *not* a disciplinarian. Consequently much fun was had by all! Earle was an only child who had a very long walk each day back and forth to school and he enjoyed the companionship of his school mates. Our fun was simple—tennis, hiking, camping, climbing Goat Mountain, going to parties and picnics."[5]

The social events in which Earle awkwardly took part—learning to waltz to the strains of "Beautiful Dreamer" from Eunice, a younger girl who had unexpectedly kissed him one day at the fountain, or the Christmas party where all, including the "tuneless" Earle, joined in with the piano to songs like "I Love You Truly"—were merely tantalizing. He wanted a partner who burned as he did, afire with desire.

The lanky, carrot-headed teenager—now over six feet tall—was an awkward bundle of contradictions. He fully shared the boyish rambles and fishing expeditions his father loved. The week that "lives fresher in my mind than all the others of my boyhood," he would later write, was a school fishing trip spent feasting on yellow plums and black cherries fresh from the orchards, climbing the hills of the Border Country, sitting just out of sight near the evening campfire holding hands with Frances. At last he could play the role of hero, not the skinny bumbler. After catching a large fish while precariously perched on a ledge, he recalls his triumphant return:

> Cheers went up from the supper table when I stumbled in with my 3½ kilos of trout, cheers partly of relief that there wouldn't need to be a search party for my own drowned body, but I think some of it was for me, for rescuing my own male image. I could never have met those faces at supper on the last night without a real char dangling from my hand.[6]

But despite his delight in play, he applied himself almost mercilessly to work at school and on the farm; he indulged to excess in his erotic daydreams and made clumsy forays to find any girl he could to share his sensuality; yet he was still in some ways unusually infantile. That, at least, is his own decription of his behaviour on an occasion in which he recklessly tried to imitate his father driving the democrat wagon standing up. He was thrown off and sprained his wrist:

> What really made me loathe myself was that I had let out a shriek...as if the hand had broken clean off. I had to be given mother's patent painkiller, and when the laudanum, or whatever lurked in it wore off, I started weeping from the pain and was put to bed and comforted by my mother, like a baby, while my father looked on silently. I felt he was once more disappointed in me.... I'd failed to take the consequences like a man, not even like a little man.[7]

With these strong and contradictory impulses waging a tug-of-war inside him, the sixteen-year-old Birney set off by bike in his first suit with long pants, a snap-on bow tie and celluloid collar for his first real job. Perhaps it would prove to be his career.

"I never knew a job could be so boring," he later wrote. In the two-storey white bank on Creston's main street, the new clerk learned to use an adding machine, and dispensed ink, nibs and forms to the tellers. In slack times, he was allowed to peck at the typewriters, his first encounter with such machines. Lunches were lonely, since the other staff went home for lunch. Birney dreamed away these hours reading the few fishing books someone had left there—visions of a paradise lost. By New Year's, he was transferred two hundred miles west by paddle-steamer to the bank branch at Vernon, another orchard town. Though his salary was increased to fifty-five dollars his expenses increased to forty-five dollars, even though he took the most rudimentary unheated bare room above the bank and ate meals in the cheapest restaurant. Now he had really left home, an occasion marked by his father's gift of the family bible with the inscription "Good luck son."

His dutiful letters home from Vernon (one of which is his first typed letter)[8] indicate clearly that, despite an underlying current of homesickness, the young Birney was trying his utmost to do what his parents wanted. He reiterated how much he is learning about business, dazzled by the machines that can perform every mathematical function ("Pretty soon they won't need any human beings at all but will have machines to take out the drafts!!!").[9] He wrote with resolve about the practical aspects of his newly independent life, and firmly declined his parents' offer to take him back home—an offer that suggests they were having difficulty letting go of him:

> ...it is doing me good to get away amongst strange people & have to depend on myself. It sure is a great experience, & will come in handy when I will have to go away someday for much longer periods. Besides it seems so silly to quit after having only been here a couple of weeks. People will think that I didn't have enough in me to be able to go on by myself...[10]

Martha, in particular, pressured him about his meals, sent him packages of cake, shortbread, ginger snaps, jam and butter, reminded him to be prudent with money, inquired about whether he was meeting the right kind of people and if he was going to church. To all of this, Earle responded patiently and responsibly ("I have a glass of *milk* at dinner. The rate is 50c a meal; but that is as cheap as can be got anywhere"[11]). His greatest expense was having four teeth filled for twelve dollars, an expense for which he'd regrettably had to dip into his savings. "Don't worry about my finances," he staunchly wrote. "I have it all figured out & will just break even, at the most. And, if I want more money I will write home for some, before I will draw on my savings." He reported in detail about the church services he'd attended—sometimes twice on Sunday. (He heard sermons on "Missions in China," "The Life and Work of St. Patrick," "Spiritualism" and "Amusements.")

As for his own amusements, here too he tried his best to conform to the standards set at home. He borrowed a bicycle from another clerk to take a spin round the town, describing the sights (especially the Court House) in a letter home. He borrowed skates and went skating. He declined his parents' offer to send Sunday School papers and books. ("There are about a dozen books in the sitting room here—such as [W.M. Thackeray's] "Vanity Fair," [Ralph Connor's] "The Sky Pilot in No-Man's Land"[12] & other good books.")[13] He attended a basketball match, and proudly reported that he got in free because there was no attendant at the door. He went to concerts—"an organ recital in the English Church" and a "simply lovely" organ and violin performance of Beethoven's "Minuet in G." He went to a series of lectures by the Horticultural Society on fruit farmer problems.[14]

He made it clear that he was socializing with the kind of people his parents would approve of:

> I went to a meeting of the Young People's Guild, to which I was invited at church Sunday night. They have a dandy club composed of young people who, for the most part, work as clerks in the different stores, banks, offices, etc. around here. They are the nicer bunch, who go to church, & are very sociable… I am going next Monday night to their social. Their meetings are held in a special little room in the back of the Presby[terian] Church.[15]

The social highlight of the year was a dance in aid of the Children's Gymnasium Fund, with music by the Banff Orchestra:

> Just got in from the dance. Had a good time. Mr. Field [the clerk who had lent him the bicycle] was very good to introduce me to a great number of ladies. I danced pretty near all the dances. Very swell affair—beautiful ball dresses, etc. The Banff Orchestra sure is good— just like trained musicians. I went over and talked to Hutchins, who plays the piano. He remembered me...[16]

When Martha complained that she had danced very little at a dance in Banff, he gallantly replied, "Sorry you didn't have more dances, Mother. You sure would have had if I'd been there. Never mind, I'll take you up for every circle one-step the next dance I'm at in Creston. Eh? How's that?"[17]

But young Birney could not conform to the life his parents hoped for. Try as he might, the more he knew about banking, the less he liked it. To be caged in a bank serving customers and computing figures—machines or no machines—for years before there could be any hope of rising to managerial status was a deathly existence. Somewhere, a flicker of life in Birney flamed into an impulsive and fiery rebellion. Finally in April he succumbed to a temptation set in his path by a young salesman in the music store where he had passed his time listening to classical records after hours.

He angrily resigned his job, and with what was left after buying a one-way ticket to Banff from the ten-dollar bonus the manager gave him the passionate young man who, though starved for sex for almost three years, had been fed nothing but a few kisses, a few fumbling embraces, and countless polite socials, headed for the brothel he knew was somewhere just beyond the town's limits. "My girl, young but motherly, seemed unaffectedly pleased to be priestess at my deflowering," he would later recall.

> Her name, she said, was June, June Nightingale. There was a fresh medical certification tacked on her bedroom

wallpaper, testifying—rightly, as it turned out—to her good health. We danced before and after. I cannot remember getting so much pleasure and benefit from such an expenditure on any other night of my youth. It was the only really exciting and fulfilling evening in all my Vernon days.[18]

Rising up from the valleys back into Banff, where his parents had returned after giving up on the Creston Valley farm, was like an ascent back into life itself for Birney. His job on a survey crew that summer at fifteen dollars a month more than his bank salary, plus living expenses, promised fairly substantial savings towards a vague dream future. But much more important, the thrill of returning to the outdoors life among the mountains made this a memorable and happy summer for him.

The work involved surveying a scenic road and assessing the potential for hydro-electric power and water for a resort high in the undeveloped Waterton Lakes Park, a national park of more than two hundred square miles of wilderness in the south-west corner of Alberta on the Great Divide near the U.S. border. The four-man crew, headed by Murdoch, a crusty Scots engineer whose drunken recitals of the poetry and Greek drama he had learned at a British public school may have encouraged Birney to aspire to a university education,[19] tented at first in the Townsite at Waterton Lake, sharing meals and man-talk in the bunkhouse where some thirty construction workers at work on the resort site were stationed. Then they backpacked up through the craggy panoramic mountain scenery, hacking a swath, surveying the road-site and weighing the pros and cons of Cameron Falls as a dam site, to the very top of the Continental Divide. Birney's later account of breaking through in early August to the highest point of their survey registers something akin to religious awe—not the religiosity of the Presbyterian Church, but a sense of powerful and mysterious forces at work in nature:

The stream filtered away then and disappeared under the needle-carpeted roots of immense Douglas firs, larger even than those back by Cameron Falls. They had been growing there for perhaps two thousand years in the rich alluvium left by the Cameron before it found a fault in the bedrock and funneled the present canyon a mile away over the valley. Pillar after pillar the dark creatures stood in a dreamy silence broken only by the fitful chatter of chipmunks. A vegetable species in almost sole possession they climbed to join a sky-bright canopy so high and continuous that only an occasional sunshaft quivered down to the moss and pale wood flowers and huckleberries that alone had learned to survive in the living space of these mammoths. "The Cathedral" [we] got the habit of calling [it].[20]

The summer marked many achievements for the seventeen-year-old Birney. He overcame an unpleasant bout of food poisoning without succumbing to the childish urge to return to his parents in Banff. He acquired a different sort of education by listening to the men: "the contests in dirty jokes, the tough verbal quarrels...the competitive tales of logging accidents, maimings, deaths, the endless chewing over of their experiences of strikes and firings and sweating sadist bosses, the boasts of wanderings and gargantuan benders and whorings across Canada and into wartime Europe." And, in relation to one of his fellow-workers Bob Snaid, a nineteen-year-old Queen's University student who treated him like "a novel type of yokel," but who knew nothing of camping or mountaineering skills, he learned how to assert himself and succeed. "Between those strangely educational, companionable evenings and the sunny workdays... I was happy, putting on muscle, eating hugely, doing my job well now."

During the next winter, as his savings slowly grew, Birney lived at home, working on the road crew in Banff and at other odd jobs. The next summer he was off to the mountains again, as part of a five-man crew assigned to exterminate mosquitoes in the interests of better tourist trade. The RCMP (Royal Canadian Mosquito Patrol), as they called themselves, shared a tent, and in a spirit of fun tackled their task with ingenuity. Leo Tefler, a University of Alberta engineering student who was among the crew, records that he and Birney used to make up alternative lines of doggerel verse as they worked together cutting a trail around the margin of the Vermillion Lakes. On weekends, as if their work weren't exercise enough, the two would climb the mountains around Banff—Mount Inglismaldie and Mount Norquay (where they came across a dead mountain goat)—with Tefler, a more experienced mountaineer than Birney, leading the way.[21]

But summers on park jobs—no matter how exhilarating—and outdoor labour while living with his parents during the winter left some things to be desired for the young man who had taken his copy of *David Copperfield* along on his first survey job, and now found himself engrossed in pulp magazines and popular science journals in the little time he had to read at all. He liked spending time with the winter relief gang ("this kind of man I'd never known before"); he thought some of them were very fine men. But he recognized that they were "doomed."[22] What *was* he to do with his life?

The graphologist to whom he appealed that March, just before he turned eighteen in May 1922, thought he should become a chemist or a mechanical engineer.

CHARACTER DELINEATION

You are a game sort of chap and one who would succeed at whatever line you took up. When you have talents that fit in well for two or three jobs, as you have, it is always difficult I know to decide in which direction to make the plunge. Listing your assets one sees the language gift, continuity, close exact reasoning that holds like a chain, a love for facts, system, positivism, a talent for mathematics, a tenacious memory, thoroughness, ideality, clear judgement, painstaking and plenty of executive, and the observation that sees everything at a glance.

You will never want for friends and the optimism and buoyancy you have shows the best of health. If you have weaknesses, they are that you do not study causes enough and do not blow your clever horn as much as you might. Both will improve as you grow older.

If it was left to me to pick out your job, I should be inclined to say the chemistry, or some line of mechanics like motor engineering. You have the exactness and hand talents for either. Then there is an undercurrent of love towards the chemistry which will mean something. I am sure you argue well, but do you like talking until the other side is talked out? Are you not a little weak in your ability to read human nature?

Perhaps this will help you to decide better. I would go a lot by what is called "feeling it in your bones." Write whenever you feel like it, and next time do not trouble to send the fee. I would like to hear what a really clever chap like you has decided to do.[23]

❦ *4* ❧

SOCIAL CLIMBING AND
INTELLECTUAL HEIGHTS

Tucked away in the "Local News Notes" of the 23 September 1922 issue of Banff's *Crag and Canyon* among birth announcements, notices of overnight motor jaunts to Calgary, a report that one Dr. Fowler from New York had bagged five Rocky Mountain sheep and two goats from a month's big-game outing and a declaration that the Banff Springs Hotel had the most successful year in its history were three announcements concerning the Birney family. A tribute, no doubt, to the social ambitions of Martha Birney who liked to see their names in print. Her son Earl (the local paper still could not be relied on to spell his name with an "e") and his friend from the mosquito patrol, Leo Tefler, "made the ascents of Inglismaldie and Girouard mountains last Sunday." This was no mean feat. Though the two mountains stood nearby, just north-east of the town, they were both almost 10,000 feet.[1] A second notice alerted Banff's citizenry that, though young Earl may have been "connected" with the lowly Mosquito Control branch of the Parks department that summer, he had left last Wednesday for Vancouver to test his intellectual mettle at new heights "in Arts and Chemistry at the University of British Columbia." The third notice was more important, signalling as it did a recognition that a new phase in their only child's life was reason enough to uproot the whole family from the life they had known for eleven years.

> Mr. and Mrs. W. G. Birney are planning to remove to Vancouver for the winter months, leaving here about the first of October.

Birney, it seemed, had taken to heart the advice of the Ottawa graphologist and had in mind a degree in chemical engineering from UBC. Later he would explain: "I took first year arts, with all the science I could pack in, intending engineering the next year (they required first year arts as preliminary)."[2]

The University of British Columbia Birney entered in the fall of 1922 was a far cry from today's complex establishment on the wooded western-most tip of the peninsula that juts out insolently into the Pacific Ocean. Though this idyllic location had been set aside under the University Endowment Act of 1907 and architectural plans had been devised for a few essential buildings, fledgling construction of the first of these—a Science building—had been abandoned at the outbreak of the Great War in August 1914. Like a gaunt skeleton in the wilderness, the ribbed girders stood as if they were a testimony to an educational era past instead of the harbingers of one to come. Meanwhile, the few hundred students of the university that had begun in 1906 as McGill University College of British Columbia (an extension-affiliate of Montreal's McGill University) attended classes at Fairview. Fairview (or the "Fairview Shacks" as they came to be called) was a temporary campus completed in 1912, which consisted of two frame, shingled buildings (Physics and Chemistry) and a rough shack (Applied Science) on the site of the present Vancouver General Hospital whose stone walls were then being constructed at the south-east corner of Laurel Street and 10th Avenue. Postwar disarray necessitated industrial and economic restructuring and development everywhere on a scale that meant massive provincial debts. Meanwhile, growing university enrolments and concomitant operating costs at Fairview meant high-pressure demands for increased provincial funding. The result of this financial impasse was that, for the first time, UBC was forced by the government's refusal to cover all its costs to relinquish its unique position as the only provincial university in Canada offering free education, and levied annual tuition fees of forty dollars. Earle Birney was in the second Freshman class to pay such fees, which had risen in a year to fifty dollars.[3]

Other budget cuts—slashed salaries, shelved gymnasium plans, a relinquished Home Economics Department and the abandonment of a faculty insurance plan—increased pressure from those involved with UBC on the government to complete the West Point Grey campus buildings so they could move from Fairview. The Board had agreed to such cuts with the expectation that the University would open at West Point Grey in the fall of 1921. As time passed, the cramped conditions at Fairview had become intolerable.

When the student ranks swelled from 724 the year before Earle Birney arrived to 1,200 in 1922–23—his first year—some labs and classes had to be repeated to accommodate increased numbers of students; the famous "Chemistry Tent" was set up on the "Campus"; and nearby church space and even distant Sunday School facilities were commandeered as classrooms. The government's delay in developing the West Point Grey campus combined with the deterioration of the Fairview site to create an explosive situation.

That explosion was gathering force all through the summer of 1922 while Birney was exterminating mosquitoes and mastering mountains near Banff. At about the same time he was seeking the graphologist's advice in March which was to propel him into a chemical engineering program at the west coast university, UBC's Students' Council had launched a fierce campaign to "Build the University." By the time Birney enrolled that fall, persistent student petitioners had collected 17,000 signatures. The campaign gained momentum, fuelled by newsletters to sixty daily and weekly B.C. newspapers, free advertising donated by business firms and window displays of photographs showing the crowded conditions at Fairview. The campaign burst into its zenith during "Varsity Week, October 22–28": numerous speeches were mounted in theatres, church halls and auditoriums and a complete canvass was made of Vancouver, swelling the petitioner poll count to 56,000. It culminated in The Pilgrimage or Great Trek, a foot-parade of students with floats and decorated cars chanting a song which began "We're through with tents and hovels" through downtown Vancouver, by streetcar to the western terminal at 10th Avenue and Sasamat, then on again by foot to the Point Grey campus. There they swarmed over the empty frame structure of the Science Building, hanging banners from its four unwalled floors. Finally, into the hollow centre of the Cairn—a rectangle of masonry on the site of the Main Mall—each student cast a stone. An account of the campaign was placed inside and the top was sealed. The inscription on the Cairn said, "To the Glory of our Alma Mater Student Campaign 1922–23." Among the 1,178 students in The Great Trek was Earle Birney who, knowing nothing of university life and having roughed it in tents and shacks for much of his life, might not have understood what all the fuss was about. What must have been clear, however, was an exhilarating enthusiasm for education and the power of a united student body to legislate against their legislators.

Though it would be two years before the West Point Grey campus was ready for classes, the campaign succeeded. A few days after The Great Trek, the petition endorsed by 77,000 signatures was presented to the government. A week later, B.C.'s premier, the Honourable John Oliver, announced that his Government would float a loan of a million and a half dollars for the immediate construction of University buildings at West Point Grey. As a jubilant headline in the student newspaper *The Ubyssey* trumpeted, GOVERNMENT SEES THE POINT!

Meanwhile, the Birneys settled into a small house in the working-class district of South Vancouver at 163 East 39th Avenue where Will soon established himself as a painter and decorator. The couple—guided as usual by Martha's wishes—joined the South Vancouver United Church and the local horticultural society. Their social life at first consisted largely of visits with John Robertson, Martha's nephew, and his wife, Cissie (known as Uncle John and Aunt Cissie to Earle), who had left their small store in Three Hills, Alberta, to join the Birneys in Vancouver.

Earle that first year was an outsider, diligently applying himself
to his courses in English, Physics, Geometry, Trigonometry,
Algebra, Economics and Latin in order to justify his parents'
inordinate investment in his future. In all but Economics and
Latin (in which he got seconds), he had first-class marks, and his
overall average was Class I.[4] But not only had he entered UBC at
a critical and dramatic point in its history as a institution, his
class—Arts '26—was itself exceptional. His was the class responsible for ending initiation. They were the last freshmen to endure
the humiliation of being led by pairs of sophomores from
department to department where they were decorated with various colouring materials and scared by unseen sources; then to be
marched downtown where they were forced to walk on their
hands and knees to the middle of the huge circle formed by older
students and write compliments to the sophomores in whitewash; next made by seniors to polish streetcar tracks; then to a
bonfire of boxes at Union Station where they had to do a snake
dance; and finally submit to a procession through a "spanking
machine."[5] Arts '26 was also the first class to organize a freshman
rugby team, a precedent that was followed thereafter. And their
parties soon became legendary: the Freshette Tea, the Freshman
Reception, the hike of two hundred freshies to Capilano Canyon
north of the city, the class party at Valentine's with orchestra and
home-made cake, the theatre outing to the Capitol, High Jinks
night and the Arts Men's Smoker.[6]

Birney gingerly sampled these social delights among young
people more sophisticated than himself. Later he would describe
himself then as "a backwoods loner" with "hillbilly taste." His
summer after his first year at UBC was spent once again "in
happy illiteracy" (except for the biology and palaeontology texts
for his second-year courses, and his father's gift of the 1913
Oxford Canadian Verse which he read for its "satisfying descriptions of wilderness things approximating what I knew") as boss
of a four-man crew on mosquito patrol again around the
Vermillion Lakes. It convinced him that he "would always be,
like my father, an 'outdoors man.'"[7]

And yet, despite Birney's sense that summer that he "would
never grow different,"[8] the winds of change had been set in

motion. He had abandoned his aspiration to become a chemical engineer because his lab marks in Physics convinced him that he was deficient in the mechanical talents. Still interested in theoretical science,[9] he had decided to stay in Arts and become a research geologist.

But another decision decidedly at odds with this modification of his science career choice at the end of his first year was to have far-reaching effects. He had tried out for the next year's reporter staff on *The Ubyssey*, and had been accepted.

Birney's own account of how and why he went after the job of cub reporter is unconvincing. In his literary memoir *Spreading Time*, he attributes his interest to a campus uproar that resulted from the visit to UBC of Sir Henry Newbolt, an Australian poet whose patriotic poem "Drake's Drum" triggered anti-British "boos" from the many First World War veteran-students then at the university. The staff of *The Ubyssey* backed this anti-imperialist response and produced a clever, insulting parody, "Henry's Horn," which spurred Sir Henry—by then in Edmonton—to demand an apology, which the president gave, but not the students. The president then fired *The Ubyssey*'s editor-in-chief, and the rest of the paper's staff resigned in the throes of a campus civil war over freedom of the press. According to Birney, this incident was "an immense stimulus" to him, made him realize that poetry "had powers to provoke battles," and induced him to keep reading the student newspaper and reflect on its role as a training ground for fledgling journalists. This, in turn, "awakened…forgotten desires, formed in my *Calgary Herald* and *Eye-Opener* newsboy time, to be 'some day' a real newsman."[10]

The framework of Birney's memoir—which emphasizes Canadian writing and writers and casts his life in terms of what prepared him to be a literary figure—focuses on the *Canadian* aspect of this incident. He interprets the veteran-student and *Ubyssey* staff alliance against Sir Henry with hindsight as "an assertion of cultural independence" and, by implication, suggests that it reinforced his own nascent nationalism. But at the time, Birney was not bound for a literary career; nor was he a nationalist.

It is more likely that—aside from observing that journalism offered opportunities to indulge in angry diatribes—he was repeating a pattern that had already become well established in his behaviour. His conformation to "expected" or "conventional" behaviour—which was undoubtedly more rigidly enforced because he was an only child—made him feel stifled and impotent and unhappy; these feelings provoked him to initiate a secretive "other" life which usually ran counter to his apparent behaviour. That is what he had done when his mother's watchful eye and strict regulations oppressed him while his father was overseas. Then he had become a purveyor of pornography behind the scenes, while on the surface he had worked hard to flog the respectable *Calgary Herald*. Later, while conforming to the polite social codes of the young people at Creston, he had developed a full-blown fantasy life apart from his parents and society. Now, as he struggled in lonesome misery, feeling like a hayseed amongst his intelligent cultured peers in order to fulfil his parents' hopes for a life better than theirs as some kind of scientist with a good income while they literally watched his every move, something in him rebelled again. The blow-up over Sir Henry *was* an immense stimulus. It brought to the surface feelings of anger about "freedom" that had surely been simmering during a year in which chemical engineering had failed to exact his dedication. Unable to confront the parents who were perhaps too eager to sacrifice anything for what they believed was best for their "dear Son boy," he regained a feeling of power and control over his own fate by diverting those aspects of his unruly personality into another self-contained compartment. His tender-hearted father would not make him feel guilty by being mildly disappointed, and his sharp-tongued moralistic mother would not hurt him by haranguing him if he let them think he was following their sensible plan. Meanwhile, his own life-blood could flow freely into a wider, deeper channel than anything either of his parents could have imagined. Those were the "forgotten desires" awakened by recollecting his newsboy days.

Ironically, Earle Birney's bid for another more exciting, more powerful life did not remain the hobby or extra-curricular interest it might have become in a steadier nature. It soon overtook and overturned his aim to become a research geologist. The catalyst in this transformation, which was at least as astonishing as the chemical experiments Birney had been studying, was a remarkable English professor who almost literally cast a spell on the young man who had casually decided to sit in on one of his courses.

Though Garnett Sedgewick (or "Doc" as he was familiarly known) was a short man of rather ordinary features, his presence in the classroom and outside it was nothing short of stupendous. This dapper little Nova Scotian with a Harvard Ph.D. had studied under the great Shakespeare scholar George Lyman Kittredge. His talent for witty remarks and his dramatic flair, especially before large classes, made him—despite his height—a larger-than-life campus character. He used to approach the boys in the front-row seats as he lectured, for example, remove the tie from one of them and, without skipping a beat of his lecture, put it on himself—a gesture that signalled his approval.[11] He wore white, buttoned spats which he called "spatterdashes" and a flowing scarf, and he carried a walking stick. His hair was always impeccably close-cut. "He was absolutely superb," recalls Sadie Boyles, a fellow-student of Earle's who worked on the *The Ubyssey* with him. "The way he read poetry was really memorable. His recitations of Shakespeare were magnificent. The way he read illuminated whole poems. He was an actor *manqué*: his voice was resonant and he could ring all the changes an actor would ring in a voice. He loved performing."[12]

Sedgewick's approach to learning—aside from exposing students to the glories of dramatized literature—was to mock and rant at anything that failed to meet the highest literary standards. This inevitably included student essays. One of the many humorous depictions of Sedgewick in the student yearbook is a cartoon called "'Doc.' Sedgewick and His Reaction to a Freshman Theme." In it, Sedgewick strolls nonchalantly up to his desk, puffing on a cigar; begins to read the essay; puffs heavily on the cigar; wipes either tears or sweat from his eyes; begins jumping up and down shouting "Bilge, Bilge"; knocks over the desk and scatters the essay; and finally passes out on his back on the floor, hand clasped over his head, still uttering the word "Bilge." According to Birney, "From even Victorian literature as Sedgewick taught it I was getting wit, sophistication, artistic standards and value judgements.... [He] shocked parishpumpery and intellectual laziness out of me, and replaced it with Arnoldian love for the 'best that has been thought in the world.'... [He was] the most brilliant and inspiring teacher I ever encountered, and one of the finest human beings."[13]

According to Roy Daniells, who studied at UBC and later became Head of English there, it was common for students to refer to Sedgewick's Shakespeare course (English 409) as "the course in Sedgewick:"

> He would discourse upon himself; upon one or the other of his many godsons [he excluded women from his classes]; upon his Mother and the harsh and unfeeling way she treated him (he said); he would speak of Harvard, Berkeley, Chicago and other centres of learning he knew; but most [often] and most eloquently he discoursed, of *Musquodoboit*, where he was born and brought up; Musquodoboit, the Athens of Nova Scotia...that fountain-head of ministers, statesmen and professors; it lay somewhere in the woods near *Halifax*, but was vastly larger, more venerable and more important. This discourse he would vary by long sessions of bullying some innocent football-player, some chosen victim who would be verbally pilloried for his shortcomings (real or imagined) and whose deficiencies were slowly canvassed with sadistic joy.
>
> Why did two hundred or more people, including the honours students sit through all this with close attention? Because, between the personalities and the horseplay, scenes of Shakespeare were read and interpreted with unmatched clarity and precision. Because the whole warmth and tragic value of the Elizabethan drama would suddenly seem to flower....
>
> It was not for nothing that his doctoral thesis, later published as a book and recently re-printed, was on *irony*—on that device in drama and elsewhere in which the *actual meaning* of the speaker is the opposite of his apparent one, in which the end aimed at is not the *apparent end....*

He made us see that learning is difficult, and litera-
ture, to which it gives access, a ravishing delight.[14]

The eccentric "Doc" Sedgewick encouraged his favourites—all male—to call him by his first name and visit him at home in the evening. He lived alone with his mother, who had raised him unaided, doted on him, and now looked out for his every comfort, acting more or less as his cook and hostess while he entertained his young men. Almost every evening he held court, and his guests were expected to bring good cheer in both senses. Drinking and chatting wittily until late into the night, Sedgewick exercised the formative influence of friend and mentor over his adoring protégés.

Under Sedgewick's spell, Birney blossomed. By the end of his second year, having achieved only a second-class average in his science program overall, he shone in English. "I first became aware of him," recalls his classmate Sadie, "in 1923 when we were in the same group for English 200 (composition)...when [Professor] Freddy Wood read out Earle's superb essay on a Heifetz recital, which inspired from that motley sophomore class a moment of stunned silence and wonder that any one of us could write so magnificently well."[15] Two of his other essays—"The Bunkhouse" and "My Boarding House," which were both descriptive essays romanticizing poverty in situations he had known first-hand—drew kudos. The former: "Observation is quite effective"; the latter "This essay shows promise: there is feeling for words that is good."

As a cub reporter for *The Ubyssey* Birney published his first two poems: "Dormit Flumen" (the river sleeps) and "'Shun!" Together they represent two of the main aspects Birney was later to develop as a poet. "Dormit Flumen," a descriptive poem based, according to another of his classmates, Ted Morrison, on a river scene Birney saw as the train he had taken westward slowed to cross a trestle bridge,[16] strikes a romantic nature theme with a dark undercurrent:

"The river seems to doze." So broad and deep
That one would think it never could be changed,

But always flow in undisturbed sleep
And to the end of time its quiet keep.

. . . .

But now, see how each drop from sleep awakes;
Black rocks disrupt the calm with jagged crests;
True danger, not vague fear; the river shakes
Into resistant turmoil. Silence breaks

And gives its place unto the awesome roar
Of thundering falls...[17]

"'Shun!" on the other hand, is a short, adept exercise in witty wordplay based on social observation:

Light deceptions,
Sweet acceptions,
Interceptions,
With few exceptions,
Frosh Receptions.[18]

During that year, Birney met Lionel Haweis, a sensitive gnomelike, middle-aged poet who was an assistant librarian in the university library and entertained literary-minded students informally at his cottage in Cypress Park (which had to be reached by the North Vancouver ferry). There his plump, untidy wife and exquisite daughter served wonderful snacks. Haweis's little teas and picnics focused on creative writing—readings and discussion—and he encouraged his dozen or so followers to call themselves "Ganeshers" after the Indic god Ganesh ("He of the Elephant Head, Remover of Obstacles") as if their meetings constituted a secret society.[19] He made a gift to Birney of his own book of poems, *Little Lanterns.*

The Ganeshers also had picnics and swims on the log-strewn beaches part of the way around the tip of Point Grey. There, as the wine bottle was passed around, the discussion would be of literature. Sometimes they would all be off to the Lannings' (parents of one of Birney's classmates) at Grey Rocks for the weekend. "I remember one famous time," recalls Sadie Boyles, "watching Earle swimming the breast-stroke with his long legs looking like a spider."[20]

Not surprisingly, given his literary awakening, Birney was promoted at the end of the year from cub reporter to an associate editorship at *The Ubyssey*. By the time he returned from a lucrative summer spent peddling subscriptions to *Maclean's*,[21] (a job he quit because his devious methods as a salesman led to self-contempt), then house-painting on contract, he had abandoned science for the program he would pursue with excitement and brilliance for his last two years: the Honours course in English Language and Literature.

Even Birney's appearance changed. Gone was the lean, muscled outdoorsy chap in his peaked workman's cloth cap who had been photographed atop any number of mountains. In his place appeared a softer, more sensitive young man, almost languid, whose longish sand-red hair waved gently back from a high, clear brow. He thoroughly looked an Arts man, an English honours student and a poet. Looking back on himself at nineteen, he would say: "I was as romantic as hell."[22] The *Province's* scathing rejection of a descriptive poem about Vancouver at night as viewed from Grouse Mountain (the literary editor thought it "awkward," lacking in spontaneity and "a little beyond you"[23]) hurt Birney deeply.[24] But on campus, he was invited to join the Letters Club, an honour extended to a select few English students, where he gave the club's first paper under the aegis of Anglophile "Doc" Sedgewick, who steered him away from an interest in Canadian poet Marjorie Pickthall to report on the sublime in Rupert Brooke. In his third year he was also president of the Pianists' Club (despite the fact that, by all accounts, he was not a good piano player),[25] a group who exchanged ideas on international modes of music and gave instrumental and vocal concerts. There he presented another paper written for Sedgewick on Elizabethan music.

Birney's bond with Sedgewick deepened, and was complicated by the arrival of a new young professor of American literature whom Sedgewick had hired from Berkeley to make the sixth full-time teacher of impressive academic stature (two, other than Sedgewick, Harvard Ph.D.'s; a *Docteur des Lettres* from Brussels;

an Oxford M.A. with a London doctorate almost completed; and a Harvard M.A.). Some of Sedgewick's students realize with hindsight that his emotional orientation was homosexual, though there is no evidence that he was involved in anything more than close friendships with his protégés. But Frank Wilcox—an elegant, tall, slim man who dressed like a "fop"[26]—was a practising homosexual. And Birney, for a brief time, became one of his lovers.[27] The story "Night," which he published in the 13 October 1925 *Ubyssey*, suggests something of this situation. It is a sinister, descriptive piece about two men alone in the midnight street who approach, pass and look back at each other, which concludes: "And after I had reached my bed, I lay in restless thought for long, black hours. For, somehow, I could think of little but you, and our great friendship of last year."

In an era of chaperones and deans of women who kept a close watch on coeds, an era where "vamps" were regarded as fallen women, Birney—like many young men of his era—suffered intense sexual frustration. His emotional and physical orientation was strongly heterosexual. But he had found it difficult to attract young women. Not only was he convinced he was "a Banff hillbilly," he was too poor to be able to afford to court the coeds. And his pale, gangly looks were far from fashionable in an era that favoured stockier men who were dark and sporty, not in the way Birney (who liked hiking and swimming) was, but team athletes on rugby, hockey and basketball teams. He was not at all the suave hail-fellow-well-met girls seemed to prefer. His was a complicated, difficult, intense personality which was not easy to warm to.

One of the girls who attracted him, Florence Kerr, wrote a long "autopsy" of his character in the summer of 1924. She found his character filled with "contradictions and characteristics…in the most extraordinary combinations." Because of his "intellectual brilliance," she wrote, "You have the ability to become…a *truly great* writer…and, of course, a deep thinker." In her opinion, he had hardly begun to tap his "creative genius." He had "a very keen aesthetic sense—a natural and highly developed love for the beautiful in Art & Nature." But he was also "strongly materialistic" and oddly "cynical"—"I suppose," she speculated rather romantically, "because of shattered ideals and bitter disillusion-ments over love-affairs in your youth." She thought he showed a "*dangerous* tendency toward self-depreciation." His artistic tem-perament made him prey to "inexplicable depths of moodiness," "unaccountable heights of serenity," "vitality" and "nervous energy." As a person, he was "open-minded," "persevering," "humorous," "witty," "courteous" and "sympathetic (very rare among boys)." On the other hand, she found him "inclined to be dogmatic," "selfish" and "self-indulgent." Though he was "very impractical, especially where ideals are involved" ("you would have fitted beautifully into the court of King Arthur," she chided), he was also "practical in little things" ("especially in comparison with other boys"), such as drying dishes and butter-ing toast. And, despite these profound contradictions, she found that his "aimiable, easy calm naturalness when you are in 'Company' makes you a welcome visitor."[28]

Florence Kerr half expected Birney himself to laugh off this character analysis. ("I can almost hear you laughing and saying 'Har har!' like the villain in the play," she concluded.) But she added, "I may have missed by a mile, but I don't think so."

The Earle Birney who entered his final year at UBC—as a member of the first class to graduate from the West Point Grey campus—was hardly the lonely ineffectual outsider who had begun four years before. His "Uncle" John Robertson was earn-ing his living driving a student bus around the UBC campus. But Earle had risen in life to become a powerful and important presence. The October 15 *Vancouver Province* displayed his photo as editor-in-chief of *The Ubyssey* "boosting" the university publication with the caption "Mr. Birney has shown himself a youth of considerable talent, and has been a prominent student of the University of Vancouver." His editorials and other writings for *The Ubyssey* were by turns intelligently observant ("the spe-cialist is generally the most successful but not thereby the happi-est of men"),[29] idealistic ("By no means should we cringe and fawn before a stagnant form of public opinion [British patrio-tism]")[30] and playful ("Phoenix-like, the birth of the grill on the altar of the cafeteria has not been accomplished without burning pains").[31] Because he was now editor-in-chief, Birney was invited

to join the prestigious Sigma Epsilon Chapter of Zeta Psi fraternity as one of its charter members by a group of men whose
backgrounds from wealthy families could not have been less like
his own. As one of the "drunken Zates," as they were known, he
began "to come into the 'Pub' [for Student Publications Board]
and cock a tipsy eye at the other editors in the morning."[32] As a
Zate, he not only acquired the mandatory ritual scar inside his
right forearm, he acquired social clout. It was a coup that finally
made courting girls easy.

Once he had been selected to head *The Ubyssey* in the spring of
1925, he was targeted by downtown journalists for a summer
job. He eagerly seized the most lucrative, as managing editor for
the *Point Grey Gazette*. There he wrote editorials, published some
of his own undergraduate fiction written in the short-story class
Birney and others had pressured Sedgewick to give (Sedgewick
had mercilessly criticized them all and begged them never to
publish) under the pseudonym "Abe"—a rearrangement of his
initials, filled the paper with jokes, puzzles, statistics and the like
with a hand well-practised from *The Ubyssey*. He even wrote the
ads.

Ironically, it was because of an incident on this job that he gave
up any thought of becoming a "real newsman." The sex slaying
of a local housemaid named Janet Smith, and the alleged police
kidnapping and torture of an innocent Chinese houseboy
intended as a scapegoat for the socially prominent murderer,
introduced Birney to corruption in high places and demonstrated the impotence of the press.[33] Caught in a web that eventually made the case notorious, his idealistic view of journalism
was crushed. Birney concluded that newswork was a dirty business in which he wanted no part.[34]

But the job provided him with an ancient model-T Ford. For
years he had been practising the Charleston in *The Ubyssey* office
known as the "Pub." "I can still see him," recalls Ted Morrison,
who was also on the Pub Board, "this thin, red-haired fellow in
long flannels with a pipe sticking out of his mouth, flipping his
feet back and forth. It was comical, really. He did it so he could
take his part at the class parties and get invited around. He was
shrewd in his way."[35] Now that Birney was not only editor-in-

chief of *The Ubyssey* but also a Zate with a car, he had, to some extent, his pick of the girls.

Some were not willing. Like Kathleen Baird, an associate editor that year on *The Ubyssey*. "He used to lure girls to ride with him," says Ted Morrison. "He was supposed to be driving Kathleen home at night. One time, she told me, he leaned across and attempted a little fondling. She was very strait-laced. She grabbed the steering wheel and told Earle, 'If you don't leave me alone, I'll turn this car into the ditch!'"[36]

Others were readily wooed. Most important among these, was a beautiful dark-haired freshie called Jessie MacPhail, who lived at the boarding house her mother had kept to support herself after Jessie's father left them. The affair was doomed from the start. Jessie already had her eye on Kenneth Noble, the man she would eventually marry. "I fell in love with Kenny at first sight," she recalls. "But he had gone away to study in Berkeley. I thought he'd marry a California girl, and I didn't believe in sitting on the shelf, so I kept several beaux that year. Earle used to take me to the Caf' for tea or orange squash. And we went to parties at people's houses where we'd dance to the piano. He used to pick me up in his old Ford with the top down. That looked sophisticated, even if it did have to be started with a crank. We used to stick the hood on from inside (women then didn't want their hair ruined). I'd be late as usual (girls liked to be late for their beaux). We'd go to The White Spot at 70th and Granville for hamburgers and coffee at forty cents. There were clubs, too, with a four-piece band, where you had to pay a dollar to get in. We danced the fox trot, the one-two step or the waltz. Earle was good-looking: straight and very slender. He had a very thin face and reddish-white-pinkish skin. He had really bony hands with red hair all over his wrists and hands. He was flat-footed. He should have had special shoes. He used to dance with his hand around my waist and wave his other hand just a little. I'd hold it to stop him. But he was a good enough dancer."[37]

Mrs. MacPhail insisted on meeting her daughter's beaux, and was not too impressed with Earle. She did, however, take to Martha, who was not only as strict as she was in parental surveillance, but, since she herself had a mother whose family were from Inverness and Skye in Scotland, she warmed to the woman from Shetland.

Earle's romance with the grey-eyed beauty whose main preoccupation was gorgeous clothes and parties ended with the return of Ken Noble. (Eventually, they would marry and Noble's appointment to the Canadian Trade Commission took them both off to Singapore.) It was a blow to an already frail ego. "He had many unhappy love affairs [at UBC]," Ted Morrison recalls, "and he felt them quite intensely."[38]

When the frustrations—and more important, the expenses—of courting were more than he could bear, Birney turned to prostitutes. "Only Nadine's house understood," muses his autobiographical character, Gordon Saunders, in *Down the Long Table*, whose behaviour corresponds to Birney's later confessions about his undergraduate years,[39] "three dollars once a month, cheaper than taking nice girls to supper dances, less frustrating. Only the poor understand."[40]

What Birney's classmates saw was an ambitious, socially conscious, somewhat lecherous, campus character. It was taken for granted that he was a top student who had gained a Class I average in both his last two years. That is clear from the write-up that appeared for the class of '26 in the *Totem:*

ALFRED EARLE BIRNEY
The "flaming youth" of the Publications Board. Has worked his way from reporter to editor-in-chief by sheer ability and plenty of nerve. Socialistic tendencies tempered with idealism. Besides being a Charleston expert, he acquires honors in English. Hobbies: Editorials, Chaucer, badminton—not forgetting the Letters Club and scholarships. Assets: A very old Ford. Liabilities: Very young Freshettes. To him, "a thing of beauty is a joy forever."[41]

But much more than this summary by his peers had gone on under that colourful surface. The mountaineering romantic and lonely outsider from a working class family was transformed by the end of his UBC days to a sophisticated ironist who mixed easily among men from the campus's most prestigious fraternity and aspired to marriage into a class far above his own. Even his graduating essay on Chaucer's irony signalled this rise in status and expectations. Though it bears the unmistakable imprint of Sedgewick, who as an expert on the subject was Birney's somewhat overbearing adviser (towards the end, Birney rebelled by handing in a carelessly prepared version of his essay), it contains a number of observations that betray Birney's own frame of mind—one far more wide-ranging than the romantic naïveté with which he entered university. Irony, as he defined it, echoed something of Florence Kerr's keen analysis of his own character: "a form of speech in which the real meaning is ostensibly concealed in order to emphasize the presence of conflicting elements." And as for Chaucer as an ironist: according to Birney, he was "making game of romantic youth, of the short but earnest passions of the stripling." His essay was intelligent, well researched (once Sedgewick goaded him on) and impressively written. Like Chaucer, he was interested in a wide range of human experience—from extreme poverty to wealth, from religious to secular, from courtly to corrupt. And he was as comfortable with the coarse language of the survey camp as with effete discussions of sublime poetry. Again and again, he notes Chaucer's "detachment" as if to disengage himself from experiences (like his many unhappy love affairs) which had pained him. In a remark that may have been an early attempt at defining his own position, he wrote that "the best artists would be men not only careful to remain aloof from the material they shaped, but aloof even from their own shaping of it." With a touch of Sedgewickian pomposity, he also observed, "I have always thought it one of the distinguishing marks of even the most stirring ironists...that they were still plagued because life, especially human life, had not measured up to their youthful expectations."[42]

~❧ 5 ❧~

A DYING FALL

On 20 June 1926 Birney wrote excitedly to his Banff mountaineering chum, Leonard Leacock, who was studying music at
Mount Royal College in Calgary, "I just heard a couple of days
ago that I've been given a Toronto fellowship—$500 & free
tuition for one year (and no teaching work). I leave towards the
end of September."[1] Birney was one of two British Columbia
graduates who had snagged two of the seven Toronto grants.

Earle was spending the summer working with his father house-
painting, plastering and paper-hanging at seven dollars a day,
while Martha earned what she could by taking in a student
boarder. Though Birney had also applied to the University of
California graduate school at Berkeley, where several UBC students he knew had already gone, the family's financial fragility
was such that Toronto's bid could not be refused. In his spare
time that summer, Birney read and read in preparation. "I have
plunged into an orgy of "modern productions," he wrote
Leacock. "Edw[ard] Carpenter, Bertrand Russell, [Petr
Alekseevich] Kropotkin & [Mikhail Aleksandrovich] Bakunin,[2]
[H.G.] Wells and [Bernard] Shaw have ministered to my anar-
chical or communistic prejudices, while Rose Macaulay (have
you read 'Told by an Idiot'?[3]), George Moore (Heloise &

Abelard, publ'd this year, a remarkable piece of work), Aldous Huxley, etc. etc. have ministered to my less worldly moments." "If you can get it," he added in a quick P.S., "you ought to read a book by a young German, Otto Weininger, called in the Eng. translation 'Sex & Character.'[4] Sex is treated philosophically in the most amazing manner. Different from any sex book I've ever read. Really a work of genius—though of an insane genius. Most astounding & unheard-of conclusions reached through the most relentless logic."[5]

By the end of September, Birney was installed in the Toronto chapter of his fraternity Zeta Psi at 118 St. George Street near the university campus. Immediately, he realized that living at the Zate house was far from being the cheapest student accommodation. "You had better stay where you are if you are comfortable, rather than running around," his mother wrote when he offered to save money by moving, "unless something unforeseen turns up, for you would not save more than $5.00 per and you will perhaps have more comforts & companions, and that's worth more than money sometimes."[6]

Birney felt heavily the responsibility of proving himself to others. He knew his parents were sacrificing so that he could have the best and—more important to Martha at least—*meet* the best. He also knew that Sedgewick was banking on him: "It will be a very happy & profitable experience if you just keep to business—& I am sure you will. A good many of my hopes are set on you, my Earle: I am expecting that your record at Toronto will be the best yet: it *can* be, it should be with a clear road ahead of you, it must be, it will be."[7]

Sedgewick knew a number of the Toronto English professors with whom Birney would study: W.H. Clawson, the "meticulous, diffident, benign"[8] Anglo-Saxon and Chaucer expert, who like Sedgewick had studied under Kittredge at Harvard; Malcolm W. Wallace, Renaissance scholar and moralist, and Pelham Edgar, who taught modern fiction and poetry, Henry James in particular. He urged Birney to take full advantage of his new situation at the university and in Toronto generally. "You will find Wallace all that you anticipate, I am sure: he will meet you more than half-way always, & at the same time he will let you alone. I am sure, too, that Clawson will be interested genuinely in your Chaucer work, that he will have an ear for its values & that he will point out some further roads. Besides, there are interesting pictures to see & above all, music to hear—really noble music to hear. And you will save a dollar or two (even to the detriment of the college & fraternity boot-legger) to hear a little of it."[9]

But Birney at first felt too anxious and homesick to do much of anything. And Sedgewick's fatherly advice overlooked the stark fact that Birney had to count every penny and already felt guilty about wasting money on room and board at the fraternity. He was told to buy a new suit in Toronto while his mother was having her old winter coat "turned" so it would last a bit longer. Even with his parents' scrimping and saving, there were to be many concerts and college events he would have to forego for lack of money.

The attitude his parents took encouraged this anxiety and loneliness. Completely oblivious to the manifold ways in which their son had grown and changed during his four years at UBC, probably incapable of grasping it, they continued to treat him as if he were a little boy, instead of the remarkably intelligent, capable and shrewd twenty-two-year-old young man he had become. Their letters to him that fall differ not at all from those they sent to the Creston bank more than six years earlier. "Well *Son Boy*," his mother wrote in her first letter, before he'd even reached Toronto or sent her an address, "we sure are lonely without you coming in at night. We don't seem to mind it so much during the day, but it seems so lonely at night. Daddy has had such a dreadful cold since you left. he cough [sic] just dreadfully all night."[10] After receiving his first letter (sent immediately on his arrival), she wrote, "I will send your quilt tomorrow, and I do hope your cold will be all gone by now. Have you bought your winter underwear yet?"[11] In another letter to "Dear Son Boy" (her enduring nickname for him, one that may have punned on "sun" in reference to the reddish gold hair he shared with her),[12] she wrote: "I thought of you this morning when I was making the pancakes and wondered to my self if you would ever get pancakes for breakfast where you are, and what time you have to be down.... Have you bought your new suit yet? if you have send me a bit cut from that large seam on the back of the pants so I can see what its like."[13] Later she wrote, "'Yes' we are glad you can get to see all the plays for that price, and also I am glad you will have some exercise at the gym. be careful & don't get colds. hope you didn't take cold seeing the football game."[14] Her letters end with such endearments as: "so night, night, son," "God bless you and keep you," and "Now Darling with heaps of love I will close."

The Birneys wrote to their Dear Son Boy about their dinners with John and Cissie Robertson, their evenings of whist, their attendance at church, Will's outings to the Orangemen's Lodge, Martha's Horticultural Society teas, the antics of their boarder, Jack, and "Daddy's work" (he was working on Lionel Haweis's house that fall). They sent him flowers from their garden, violets and primroses pressed between the pages of their cramped writing, misspelled and often unpunctuated; they fussed about his physical well-being and were incurious about his intellectual life except to ask vaguely about his "work"—unidentified essays to be written and exams to be sat. They prodded him to write more often, and became anxious if they did not hear every few days. On one occasion, the steely side of Martha shows clearly through her almost relentless sentimentality. "Well young man I know one thing you did last week, that I have not done for *22 years.* and that is "*forgot my Birthday.*" Poor Dad was so sure you would not forget that he bet me a box of *chocklates* [sic] that you wouldnt and he of course lost & had to *pay up.* now old Dear put it down in your *brain somewhere* that poor Mother has a birthday two days before "Hawelleen" [sic] and and [sic] does not like to think she is forgotten."[15] When Birney apologized, she played the martyr: "'Yes' Dear I know that you just forgot and it came just at the time when you were busy with your Essays, but it kind of hurt at the time because you are all I have and I was lonely. I wish you would not bother to send anything now, as it is so near Xmas."[16]

Given this cloying and guilt-inducing atmosphere from home—well-intentioned as it was—it was not surprising that Birney needed outlets elsewhere. Though it took him a little

time to break free from the homesickness he felt at first, he eventually established a life for himself that his parents would never
have guessed. He knew what college life was supposed to be like.
As one of the "drunken Zates" at UBC, he had more than sampled a type of fun his parents would not approve. Through the
summer, and now into the fall, he was receiving letters from his
fraternity brothers filled with descriptions of the high times they
were having. Dal Grauer, for example, who had gone to Berkeley
to do post-graduate work in economics, had bought a Dodge
coupe which, he said, "heightened my poverty but lessened my
chances of chastity." On one weekend jaunt with a friend, they
hit the road aimlessly, ended up at the house of his friend's parents and found the parents away "but they didn't take their pre-
war stock [of liquor] along. Accordingly," Grauer went on, "we
sipped rare wine & discussed deeply philosophical subjects till 1
a.m., at which hour we felt so damn good we hit the road again.
Arrived in Sacramento the next morning, where Hugh knew
some very 'cheek' young ladies (as the French say). One of them
owned a Lincoln in which we disported ourselves for the rest of
the day. The young lady I had is heiress to $1,500,000, but she
felt just the same as one of these $5. gals."[17]

And he was corresponding with Frank Wilcox, who was spending a summer at Duncan on Vancouver Island with Bruce
Macdonald, one of the Zates. His letters were coy, playfully erudite and affectionate. "You probably doubted my earnest assurance that I was going to write you from my retirement," Wilcox
wrote. "Under ordinary circumstances such skepticism would
have been very just, but my overpowering affection for you will
not let me sleep o'nights until I have given this expression to
it.... If you are ever over here on the island, you will find our
latchstring hanging out. It is simple fare that we offer you, but
you know the words of Scripture about the handful of herbs
where love is. In the meantime, rejoice, and be happy, O my
Earle; do nothing unworthy of you, but if you do, be sure to tell
me, so that I can have at least a vicarious delight in your sin."[18]
And his friend Ted Morrison, who had replaced him as editor-
in-chief of *The Ubyssey*, boldly queried him, "Are the girls in
Toronto quite as pretty as the U.B.C. variety?" So candid were

Birney's confidences that Ted wrote: "I don't object to Huxley, my dear Earle, but your Chaucerian bluntness is, at times, more than should echo down the tiny labyrinthine whorls of a maiden's ears."[19] He only showed "bits" of Earle's letters to his curious girlfriend (and later wife) Mary.

Birney was pleased to be invited to the homes of his professors—especially Pelham Edgar's, where he lunched from time to time and on one occasion met the excruciatingly shy poet Raymond Knister.[20] Edgar, he would later recall, "was the great guy for me that year. He...treated me as if I were really an adult, and not a graduate student. He had the same worldly courtliness Sedgewick had. He stimulated me to vast readings in the novel, and he made me feel I had a gift for writing, though at that time I was trying nothing but criticism, seminar papers."[21] But these occasions had nothing of the panache of Sedgewick's soirées, of which he continued to hear enviable reports. "I called upon Sedgewick," wrote Morrison, "taking the usual refreshments with me and spent an enjoyable evening discussing 'harlotryes' and Balzac as a Catharsis of eroticism."[22] And Sedgewick himself reported other occasions: "Ted & Don Calvert were there last evening, warmed, likewise, by drinks (their own drinks too) but not permitted to be nearly as warm as the Ambrosial-Haired desired. The drinks were such as Ted might be expected to produce: bizarre in combination & expensive of purchase & deadly in effect. To wit: Catto's best and, of all potables, Yellow Chartreuse! The last was a tribute to me, for it is my favourite liqueur. (How in hell *do* you spell that word?) But Ted was desirous, in fact he valde desiderated, inducing (or to induce according as you choose your verbal) me to drink one Chartreuse & then one Catto & to repeat the process until the Cataclysm."[23]

By about the middle of November, Birney had his course work (Edgar's "Recent English Fiction and Poetry," M.W. Wallace's "Wordsworth" and "Milton and Seventeenth Century Literature" and W.H. Clawson's "Chaucer and his School") well under control, and under Clawson, he began his thesis on "Drummond of Hawthornden," an obscure seventeenth-century Scottish poet. He had established rapport with his professors intellectually and—in a sedate way—socially, and was attending the music concerts and plays which his parents and Sedgewick encouraged him to take in. But he had also managed to get underway a personal life that was the best he could do to duplicate the college life he knew went on elsewhere. His letter of 21 November to Leonard Leacock tells of myriad new delights. "Spiritous liquors are being consummed as regularly as when I last wrote you. Each weekend has seen a 'big' intercollegiate game, followed by celebrations either for victory or defeat (they are the same when celebrated). McGill, Queen's & Varsity have tied for the championship as you probably have noticed.... There remains... one game—Queen's–Varsity, next Saturday, which certainly should be a WOW with high heels. I'm actually casting aside centuries of Caledonian safety appliances [gifts from his mother], to bet for Varsity the coming game.... I'm beginning to win at bridge and billiards now too, and have ordered a case of ale for Xmas on the strength of it. One of the 'brothers' has a drag with O'Keefe's brewery and he got the House a reduction on beer and ale.... (There are 24 qts to a case, by the way).... I've been to 3 debutante dances, on general invitations to the fraternity: at Hunt Club, Jenkins Art Gallery, King Edw[ard] Crystal Ball Room. Wonderful times! Know some of the cream & much of the milk in Toronto society (only to dance with). Heard Lawrence Binyon lecture on Tung Art—very erudite & well-spoken. Saw 'Gent[lemen] Prefer Blondes' (in play) by N.Y. Stock Co. Funny as hell—wisecracks too clever to be vulgar. And, oh, such back-chat! Read the book? I stayed away from Hart House Masquerade, but seems to have been great as ever. Have learned to shoot crap—but find it more comfortable to watch—Thank God I do."

In a brief P.S., he is exuberant about coming events: "Hooray! The 'Varsity' staff invited me to their dance next Tuesday, and entered my name in their 'draw' for partners. I drew one of the two good-looking females in the forty. Hooray again! I've just had a bid to a birthday party Saturday!"[24] But the Monday after the Queen's–Varsity championship game and the Saturday birthday party, Birney learned that his father was dead.

In a shaky hand he wrote at once, "My dearest Mother: Tike

broke the news to me to-night after supper, and I hardly knew what I have been doing since, but I want to try and write a few lines tonight. I have just come back from telegraphing. Dear mother I do want to come home: I am sure it will be good for us both. I have figured it out and I will have enough money to go and come on, and still return again in May. I phoned Dr. Wallace and he told me it would be perfectly all right for me to leave and return as long after New Year's as I wanted, and that I would not have to worry about my standing. The only thing that holds me back until I hear from you is, would the extra $150 be better saved for next summer, not for myself—for I am sure of a job somewhere in Vancouver as soon as I get back—but for you. Have you enough cash in the bank to carry on? If you have, I think it would not be a waste of money for me to spend the next four weeks with you. Its not that I can't face the Christmas here, but that I am so afraid you will make yourself ill all by your-self.... I am leaving it to you to decide, but if you would rather not decide, just say so by letter."[25]

Martha, who was well buttressed by Cissie and John, her minister Dr. A.D. Archibald, and her friends, decided that $150 was too extravagant an expense for the luxury of having her son come to Vancouver. Will had actually fallen sick a week earlier, had lapsed into a fever thought to be the grippe, then into a coma for two days before dying on Friday the 26th of a brain haemorrhage. His funeral at South Hill United Church and his burial in a flag-covered coffin at the Soldiers' Plot of Vancouver's Mountain View Cemetery had taken place the day Earle learned of his death. Though Martha had written him at each stage of the illness, its seriousness had not been apparent until it was too late even for her to have last words with her husband.

For Earle, especially after the summer close to his gentle, affectionate father, it was a terrible loss, and he grieved openly. His fraternity generously moved him away from the rambunctious doings of the house on St. George Street and into a quiet hotel nearby. He was unable to attend classes or concentrate on his assignments. All he could think of in a jumble of confusion was his mother and his increased responsibility to her and the keen regret he felt at not having told his father how much he loved him. He wrote Martha every day for the next few days, and frequently after that. "Your letter telling of the end came today and it made me feel very bad," he wrote. "But I am glad that he passed so quietly. It was an end such as he would have desired I am sure, clean and quiet, but oh, why did he ever hear of that cursed job! I am sure that was the immediate cause, for every time he added a note in your letters it was always to say he was tired but 'just must carry on'. That is a great & good memory of him to keep with me, along with the other memories of his love & his sacrifices for me, but oh, I would rather have my living Dad. For I am just struck with remorse, Mother, at the thought of all the thoughtful acts towards him I left undone. It was very good of you to tell me how he blamed himself, but I think I knew all along that he loved me; it isn't that, its that I loved him all along but was so undemonstrative and reserved about it that now I am not even sure that he knew how much I loved him."[26] The coincidence of his father's death seemed almost punitive to Birney. "It is awful to think that I spent all last Saturday and Sunday enjoying myself, with father dead and not knowing it."[27] Elsewhere he wrote, "its an awful thing to feel one may have helped foreshorten one's father's life."[28]

Just as had been the case when his father went away to war in 1914, he was thrown closer to his mother; she would become the main focus of his life and his full responsibility. "You are all I have in this world now, Mother, and we must try and not brood over the past, but just look ahead together," he wrote on 15 December, by which time he had regained his equilibrium somewhat and had resumed his classes and assignments. "We will never forget our Daddie's gentle and loving heart, though, nor his patience and sincerity."[29]

He took comfort from the fact that Sedgewick had taken the time to attend the funeral, escorted there by two Zates from UBC. He was also grateful for the company of Tike, his Vancouver friend in Toronto, who studied quietly at the hotel with him, got him out for long walks in Toronto's bitter zero weather, and exercised with him at the Hart House gym. He was soothed by the letters that came from friends and relations—especially Sedgewick's which reassured him about his mother's well-being (he had earlier sent a telegram reinforcing her decision that he stay in Toronto) and described the funeral with dignity and sensitivity.[30]

But the facts were grim. Martha's finances were meagre, and she faced the effort of trying to obtain a soldier's widow's pension she was not at all certain of having. Earle might have to quit his studies and find a job to support them both. Pelham Edgar wanted to get him a fellowship to go on in England, but if he were to continue his studies anywhere, it would have to be closer to his mother. As he would recall later, "I could see my mother had to have me closer around—I was the only child."[31]

After Christmas, greatly sobered, Birney moved from the Zate house into a room at Knox College, which he bitterly described as "the breeding ground for Continuing Presbyterianism."[32] It was a fall from sartorial splendour into a miserable, soul-cramping hell. Even his incisive observations were tainted with cynicism. He drafted a short Chaucer-style sketch based on a dinner conversation between an "Aggressive Religionist," "The Humble Petitioner" and a "Repressed Youth," who is described as an "Arts student boarding in Knox because it costs him less and his parents want him to have a religious environment. [He] looks like a moulting woodpecker."[33] The final bawdy pun in this self-deprecating remark may well have been intended.

∼§ *6* §∼

A GREAT DEPRESSION

The invitation was addressed to Mr. A.E. Birney at 2519 Ridge Road, Berkeley, California, where he was a boarder at Farnsworth Inn. In careful, florid script it read:

Mr. & Mrs. George Reuben Potter
1544 Le Loma

At Home

Sun. March 17th
4–6 p.m.[1]

It was at this 1929 gathering, hosted by an assistant professor of English who specialized in the Bible and Elizabethan literature and typical of its time and place, where young people and their elders sipped tea and nibbled on cakes and cookies while they chatted, that Earle Birney, a Ph.D. student in his second year at the University of California, met Barbara Barrett, a twenty-one-year-old undergraduate from the Phi Beta sorority who was just about to complete her B.A. in English.

A second invitation followed from the vivacious young woman with whom Birney had fallen immediately in love. Would he

66

come to dinner at her mother's at 2236 Summer Street? And, she chided playfully, somewhat in the manner of Shakespeare's Rosalind, her favourite character, "Is it because Canadians don't like to receive phone calls that Mrs. Farnsworth's phone is out of joint?"[2]

The dinner at the Barretts' rambling old house, where they summered away from the heat and bustle of San Francisco, was entrancing. The early California spring had brought the large garden with its cool brook and apple tree to a flowery green magnificence of bright marigolds and poppies, and intense blue delphiniums and bachelor buttons. Brud, Barbara's younger brother, entertained as usual on the piano. It was an oasis of beauty, liveliness and culture. A fit setting for the uncommon spritely beauty of the blue-eyed, dark-haired Barbara herself.

At once, despite the fact that they were both students in the same university who saw each other frequently, a correspondence sprang up between them that was to be intense and lengthy. "Good morning, Scarecrow darling," Barbara—or Bobbie, as she was known—wrote to "the tall young Canadian" whose pronunciation of the word "house" ("hou-oose") so intrigued her, within a week of that family dinner.

> Are you flapping in the wind? I'm doing toil and trouble. I've decided I want to be a witch—"thrice the brinded cat hath mewed—thrice and once the Hedge Pigge whined, Harper cries 'tis time, 'tis time." Ummmm. I would make you an incantation and cast a shadow on your life.
>
> We would be a good pair—you in a barren field at twilight with a gray wind creaking through [your] clothes—and me a weird sister incanting you.[3]

The imaginative and literary cast of Bobbie's letter was to be typical. To her, Earle was not the desperately diligent student, building up a formidable set of notes on file cards in shoeboxes, he was her "Erol-Elf," her "elf-mortal," her "nice-oaf," her "Diggory Venn," a "Clym Yeobright" to her "Eustacia Vye,"[4] her "nice funny grandfather," her "funny little boy" and her "romantic child." Bobbie—in a word—was fey. Her world was peopled with airy-fairy creatures of which her "elf" Earle immediately became a part. Lying next to the little stream in her garden, he read the poetry of Rupert Brooke to her and compared her to the virgin goddess of the hunt, Diana. She in turn rhapsodised about him, of her "gay elf-mortal with little dancing gold lights—reflections of his hair, perhaps—in his brown, brown eyes and in between times there is a pouting little boy that makes me want to laugh at him and kiss his ear tips."[5] The young woman whose favourite colours were orchid and lavender described what for her had been an ideal day spent with him: "Idle and sunshiney—we swam a lot and toasted in the sun a lot and in the afternoon read and talked by the brook and watched the butterflies drifting over the garden and a blue dragon fly rested on one of the gold wisps of your hair."[6]

Almost at once, Bobbie noticed a difference between Earle's letters and his actual presence. The "letter-you," as she called him, was more sure of himself and less frightening than Earle in the flesh, much as she clearly adored his tanned and freckled skin, his fine straight nose, "the little apostrophe crease" in his forehead, his gold-red hair and his lean angularity. The "letter-you," she wrote,

> seems so entirely invulnerable and sophisticated—and—well mentally "engineering." Something in you sits back comfortably and says "well, it's only a question of time till he will win entirely" and I feel quite satisfied there's a feeling of rightness about it, "the will of god" etc.
>
> But there's a 'little boy' quality in the "real-you," a wistfulness and in some ways a naivete that frightens me. It makes me realize I'm a responsible adult who may hurt the little boy. With the "letter-you," you see, I'm relieved of all responsibility—I may light-heartedly leave everything to you and Providence.[7]

What the somewhat vain and immature Bobbie longed for was someone to seize her life and direct it. Earle, an experienced and intellectually brilliant twenty-five-year-old with a distinct edge over the other graduate students in terms of his knowledge and training in literature, seemed ideal to answer this need. Describing herself as "plastic" and referring to "my clay-like character," she invited her "Efficient Pedagogue" to guide her. "I shall be a model wife in one way," she wrote in the summer of 1929 to Birney who had had to return to Vancouver to earn money teaching in UBC's summer session and was living with his mother. "[M]y character will be 'moulded' by my husband.... Perhaps women *are* passive—I know I anticipate the day when I will let myself be 'moulded'—definitely by the person in whom I have implict trust. That's why I think, Grave-Elf—I have the feeling of 'rightness' in the thought of being yours for always—I feel quite sure I'd become as lovely a person as I ever could be, if I were in your hands."[8] Rather like the little fairy-tale character Thumbelina, Bobbie yearned to be enfolded and protected in a world far from reality. "If my mind could curl up comfortably in yours," she wrote Earle, "and say 'Well here I am—come to stay' I should be perfectly happy."[9]

Birney, no doubt flooded with certain new authority from teaching his first classes as a Berkeley teaching fellow—a formidable course that surveyed English literature from Old English to the moderns—took charge. His performance in most of his courses had been excellent. In his first year, 1927–28, he had taken a philosophy course on Plato (A), Old French (B and C), a seminar on the background to Chaucer, taught by associate professor Merritt Y. Hughes (A) and a reading course gauged to his thesis topic: an expansion of his earlier work on irony in Chaucer (A). At the time he met Barbara in his second year, he was taking a course on the Anglo-Saxon epic *Beowulf* from associate professor Arthur G. Brodeur (A), Germanic philology (A), Gothic German (B) and Old Norse (B). He would go on to complete a course in Bibliography with Professor Benjamin P. Kurtz (B) and another reading course the following year.[10] These studies were quickly broadening his knowledge and giving him a sense of power.[11] He advised Bobbie especially on what to read. He warned her that James Joyce's *Ulysses* was "too worldly" for her, but recommended Aldous Huxley's *Chrome Yellow* and Noel Coward's *Antic Hay*. From the lists he instructed her to make, she read most of George Bernard Shaw, May Sinclair's *A Cure of Souls* (lectures on preaching by John Watson), Roger Fry's *The Arts of Painting and Sculpture*, Huxley's *Two or Three Graces, and Other Stories* and *Point Counter Point.* They discussed Chaucer's *The Romance of the Rose*, Edna St. Vincent Millay, Katherine Mansfield, and the poetry of Sir Charles G.D. Roberts. Turning what may have been a deliberately blind eye on Birney's strong political and social opinions (issues she was blithely unconcerned about) and rejecting outright the wistful boyishness that frightened her, Bobbie developed a lopsided view of her elf-mortal as a creature of almost superhuman strength. Her word for the quality she most admired (or rather needed) in him was the opposite to her own "plastic" nature: he had "tempered-ness," as if he were girded in armour like a courtly knight. "I hold to the thought of your—what does one call it—I can only say the 'tempered-ness' that makes your identity genuinely significant. To form and keep beliefs, aims, to be able to follow them—that seems to me the ideal of life. And to know that you are doing that comforts me. If I were yours forever and ever, I'd be sharing in your aims and beliefs, wouldn't I?"[12]

In fact, some of Bobbie's values ran directly contrary to Earle's. She saw herself as "a retarded Blue Stocking of the 1900s"; he was ardently left-wing, and urged her to read about "the Labour Party and all the women in the House of Commons."[13] But she had no sympathy for his "interest in people, in society rather than material self-advancement."

> ...your saying that riches—highly developed material property—was always built up by some form of slave labour—...I realized when I read it that the idea simply didn't touch me—that if I were a New York millionaire the idea of the tenement district would simply not phase [sic] me—I would label it a "social problem" and go serenely on spending my millions on fox furs![14]

Despite this philosophical abyss, Earle began pressing her to marry him long before she was ready. Perhaps because he admittedly felt an "ugliness"[15] inside him and knew that poverty prevented him from dressing well (he wore "old brown shoes that hurt his arches"[16]), he was flattered that this sylphlike beauty could look up to him and adore even his "wide inane grin."[17] "Dear talker-about-marrying," she flirtatiously addressed him, "There's such an air of assurance in the way you talk of 'the house you could give me'—Earle, dear—I really don't plan to belong to anyone for years and years.... And dear-Elf—please—let's don't talk about us-in-the-future—yet—let's just be happy about this summer and next year."[18] Though he pressed his fraternity pin on her when their courses ended in the spring of 1929, she returned it a few days later, explaining she wanted to be free during the summer while he taught again at UBC. He unwisely insisted that she visit him in Vancouver to meet his mother who had sent Bobbie a "very proper little note" informing her she must not smoke in her presence. The two women—each passionately needing Earle for her own purposes—did not get along.

The problem, as always, for Birney, was money. His skills as a painter and decorator might well come in handy if he were to build or repair a house, but he had no income aside from his meagre teaching fellowship and the pittance he earned as a sessional lecturer during the summers at UBC. Nor had the materialistic Bobbie any money, despite the fact that her family had clearly been recently well-to-do. Her father's job as director of the Schmidt Lithograph Company in San Francisco was not enough to keep the family in the languid cultured leisure the Barretts had come to expect. Bobbie herself had had to take a job she loathed in the personnel department of the Emporium, a downtown department store, during the summers—a job that loomed across her future like a life sentence—and she complained frequently in her letters about how poor her family had become, a situation that continuously threatened her attendance at university and made even the buying of the fashionable clothes she adored a rare and special event. Earle was so desperate financially that he resorted to what he called "Canned Cheat." "What I did," he later confessed,

> was find a girl who took almost verbatim notes—she knew shorthand, was a patient fearful plodder, wanted

to pass. I paid her, with love and chocolates (since she had money enough) for a loan of a beautifully turned-out re-Englishing of her notes; I used the notes to give a 4-hr. cram course, the night before the exam.... [It] attracted 100 students...at $10 a head, of which I got 50 cents...to avoid the soul-destroying process of attending...lectures & personally taking notes.[19]

The romance between Bobbie and Earle burgeoned during the next year. Birney, anticipating intimacies, moved out from under the watchful eye of his landlady, Mrs. Farnsworth, and into a shack on the side of San Francisco's Telegraph Hill with his fraternity brother and close friend from Vancouver, Hendrie Gartshore (known to his friends as Hank). Hendrie was an elegant fellow from a wealthy family with whom Earle had frequently knocked about during his summers at home. Together they would ride about in Hank's old yellow jalopy. Hank loved "making whoopee," and playfully described himself as being "as shrewd as a Tudor King." He delighted in teasing Birney, especially about money, perhaps out of jealousy, since Birney was "the most brilliant [student] that I know": the previous spring when he had made $195 on his oil stocks in one day, he wrote to his friend, "You're only a poor starving student, and I'm to be a millionaire."[20]

Earle and Bobbie—now a graduate student with a fellowship—saw each other daily. Marriage became increasingly likely, as Bobbie, who was also an exceptional student, absorbed the material of her formal and informal studies under Earle's tutelage.

When a teaching position in English opened up in the fall of 1929, Earle applied. There was every reason for him to expect to be given the assistantship: he was an outstanding student, "the ablest of this year's graduates," one of his UBC professors had written;[21] he was deeply committed to teaching as a social responsibility; he had proven himself a capable teacher in his courses the two previous years; and his extra teaching experience in UBC's summer sessions gave him an advantage over his peers at Berkeley. Certainly he wanted the position desperately. It is not too much to claim that he pinned all his hopes on obtaining it. If he were to be successful, his salary would be sufficient to marry Bobbie. And the job would serve as a stepping-stone to a future career as an academic. As the Depression closed in on the eve of 1930 and jobs everywhere were becoming scarce, Birney saw this position as his only hope.

When that hope was dashed and the job was awarded to his exact contemporary and UBC friend Ted Morrison, who had replaced him when he left Vancouver as editor-in-chief of *The Ubyssey*, Birney was distraught. Already worried deeply about his eyesight, which was deteriorating terribly under the strain of so much study, and about the "incipient balding"[22] he had fretted about to Leonard Leacock, the blow to his vanity, his self-esteem and his future was intolerable. The knowledge that another fraternity brother, Harry Cassidy, who after obtaining his Ph.D. from Berkeley in 1926 had taught at the University of North Carolina and Rutgers University, had recently joined the department of Social Science at the University of Toronto as an assistant professor[23] was salt in the wound. The letters he dispatched must have been alarming, judging from the responses he received. His friend Hendrie noticed "a nervous speed" as if he were "hopping around on your toes" and told him not to "be reckless of this or that (say, your time or yourself) from mere impatience."[24] Professor Dewart Lewis, to whom Birney applied for a position outside the English department, wrote to placate him after reading his anguished letter. He explained that decreases in enrolment had resulted in fewer appointments and went on to say:

> We were all very much surprised when the catalog for next year appeared showing Ted as an assistant. Obviously there is something personal that has affected that appointment; and I suppose it is solely due to Ted's standing in the eyes of the great God Ben[jamin Lehman, Professor of 19th century literature]. You, however, look at the business in a personal way, as if it reflects the attitude of the department to you. I don't feel that way about it exactly. I think it reflects only Lehman's attitude to Ted. You will say

that Lehman isn't chairman of the department; true, but he might as well be for the influence that he has over the chairman [Prof. R.P. Utter]. The whole thing is that Ted made a hit with Benny while you have had little or nothing to do with him....

I think the event that has taken place contains no reflection on you whatever. You were just not Lehman's favourite, but certainly no disgrace attaches itself to one for failing to have become anyone's favourite. You have your teaching fellowship, which is a means of subsistence, and you can come back here on exactly the same basis as that of last year. Your own committee and the other men with whom you have to work have not changed their attitude to you, and you can finish up your work for your degree next year thumbing your nose most cordially at Lehman and his crew. You would be making a serious mistake to take any other attitude to the affair....either you or Ted would have been good for the job—and Ted had the influence on his side.[25]

As if she were alternately chiding and soothing a small child, Bobbie wrote to her "Dear old Silly":

Stuff and nonsense! What a funny little dum [sic] bunny you are to get all excited and miserable over that associate professorship [sic]. And this talk of "failing"—why, my dear one would think that extra title (and the $25!) were a doctor's degree and a start in life and a verdict all rolled into one to hear you talk.

I admit I felt a little sting in its being Ted...tho' I realize it must mean quite a lot to him (more than to you, dear, really—because your goal is nearer and because you have wider interests and are cleverer (Aren't you?). But just because I know you did want it, I can't be happy about Ted's getting it.... And of course I wanted to bash all their noses for being so unfair—since you *did* want it. But as for its "meaning"

anything—about "success" or "failure"—I think its all
nonsense.... and now you'll have time to work on
your thesis won't you—and as soon as the exam is
over, it'll be pretty straight sailing to a point where little "associate professorships" at Cal. are paltry noth-
ings...

As for that English department, at first I wanted to
blow it all up and then I wanted to dash down and
demand an explanation in a very high-handed manner. I think one *must* be high-handed with it don't
you—maybe that's how Ted got the silly appointment—he's pretty much that way in all his attitudes,
isn't he? Anyway, they're old meanies to give the job to
Ted when you've given them more of your time—and
I could tweak their noses.

...But pooh—as for its cramping your style in your
oral [exam], I don't believe a word of it. They can't
take your knowledge or your intelligence away from
you, whatever "attitude" some of the old sillies may
have.... I can't help but tweak your ears a little and
call you a great donkey for pulling such a long face
about it and persuading yourself that your whole
Future depended upon it.[26]

Bobby was wrong to dismiss Earle's worries about his oral
exam. As he completed his second—and final—year, Birney was
even more seriously crushed when Professor John S.P. Tatlock—
"one of the big three [in North America] in Chaucer scholarship"[27]—who was crucial to his academic career because he was
to be his thesis adviser—gave him an "E" on his final exam.
Birney was convinced that Tatlock had it in for him personally
and felt he wouldn't have a degree "for years and years."[28] Again,
Bobbie, who commented on his "recurring sense of failure" and
observed that there was obviously "an internal wound [that] may
cause more trouble than we realize," tried to calm him:

The only really unfortunate results that silly old exam
could have is to embitter your thoughts and your living

permanently. Don't you know, darling, that it doesn't matter what you do or what you are as long as you keep your personal integrity, your "tempered-ness"—from being eaten into by bitterness?

...I love you, first you—not what you are going to "do in the future..." no one can realize more than I the handicaps that you have right now—and I know that because of those handicaps—this Cal business, your eyes, money—that the odds are...against our doing anything significant according to outside standards.... I'm willing to take the chance.[29]

And, in a masterly letter of paternal affection, G.G. Sedgewick offered analysis and advice that suggested that Birney may have been handicapped by his lower-class background in that he lacked the personal skills that were second nature to students raised in middle-class homes:

I remember a certain first draft of an Honours Essay chapter [Birney's on "Irony in Chaucer"] that was manhandled bloodily, with most depressing effects upon the Soul: but somehow Good was the net result of Ill, to improve on our Victorian friend. I know what sort of work you can do, & I do not believe that even the icicle Tatlock will refuse to melt when such work is presented to him: consequently, I shall not worry—except about the Eyes. Don't get impatient with me if I modify that just a little, and say two things that do cause me a bit of worry about yourself: it won't take me too long to say them, & the utterance comes out of what knowledge & affection you know.

First, you have always been a bit casual about observance of rules & regulations & observances: I have suffered a little at times—let me say that because you can't expect many people to see enough of you to be able to put that fact in its proper place. It is irritating to find a stranger casual about such things.

Second (to be pedantic about points) you do give

people who don't see much of you the impression of boredom & indifference with respect to important matters about which you *don't* feel bored & indifferent: it looks like the "side" & airiness & superiority of, say, Arnold at his snottiest—without the Arnoldian corrective. I know how infuriating gratuitous omniscience can be, but I will try my hand at it! I can understand bigger men than T. [Tatlock] & F. [Willard E. Farnham] stiffening their necks in the presence of such a combination of qualities & remaining adamant in refusal of an arrangement that someone else would wangle in five minutes. Very probably that combination was never exhibited; but if there was any hint of it, the mischief would be done: I have seen it done in the presence of wiser & more worldly people than professors: to be specific, I have wrought such mischief myself.

Apparently, Tatlock has not remained quite adamant: I beg of you, as one of my dearest friends, to meet him half-way & in a placable spirit. Even if you have to swallow misunderstanding & injustice, there is no reason in getting thwarted & perhaps embittered for the sake of an important "principle"—or, what is worse, being diverted from your track.

...The point is this: you have done good work, you have unusual ability as a scholar & a critic:—this is not apple-butter—I have staked my little reputation (not anything except to me) on it. It hurts me to have you misjudged. But it would hurt me far more to see you off the track: and it has hurt me—this the last time—to see you thwart yourself for failure to soften some surface mannerisms that don't matter a damn, really, but that do matter, somehow in society.

There—I have pulled your ears—& they are *not* nice long silky ones—they are burry & spiky, & they stick out stubbornly: I love the ass under them even when he acts obscenely & courageously. You won't be irritated, will you?[30]

But Birney *was* irritated by Sedgewick's lecture, though not nearly so much as he was hurt and angered by what seemed to him Bobbie's uncomprehending (she thought him "too parsimonious")[31] and frivolous response.

His failure to obtain the assistantship at Berkeley and his perhaps greater failure (or inability) to heed Sedgewick's advice and set things right between himself and the Engish department induced Birney to begin at once making other plans. He had never liked Berkeley anyway: "you have probably read something of American colleges," he had written early in 1929 to Leonard Leacock, "and when I tell you that this is the second-largest on the continent you will realize that rolling-mill education, hollow standards, big business methods, pedantry and piddling formalities are in their finest florescence here. I'm sticking it because it would waste too much of my precious youth to go anywhere else and because, God pity me, the degree is quite marketable. (The standard for the doctorate is really high, because they are attempting to build up a Harvard-of-the-West reputation for the place; they already have Harvard faculty, by virtue of the climate's appeal)."[32] By the end of the year he had found a position as a lecturer at the University of Utah in Salt Lake City. He would abandon his Ph.D. studies at the University of California (where he had fulfilled the rigorous English requirements and a Minor in Germanic Philology) with only the thesis to complete, and establish himself at Utah for a year. Once this plan was firm, he persuaded Bobbie to become engaged. This time—a year after the date she had returned his fraternity pin—she accepted the pin as a pledge and agreed to wait out the summer working in her old Emporium job and taking the six-week program of M.A. courses, while Birney lived with his mother in her reduced circumstances at 365 East 38th Ave. in Vancouver, and painted houses or exterminated caterpillars to bring in whatever money he could. Extravagant though it must have been, he gave her a delicate scarab brooch as a parting gift. They were to be married the following spring in a "pagan" ceremony "with rites at a brook or with flower petals," which Bobbie was already feverishly imagining.[33]

But the summer of 1930 dealt Birney a personal crisis as debilitating as the professional one he had just weathered.

At first, his correspondence with Bobbie was all an engaged couple could want. Bobbie sent him news of her continuing readings, thanked him for the books and notes he had left to help her study, lovingly enclosed *The New York Times* book reviews he'd requested and reported that she was dutifully reading two San Francisco newspapers a day. She daydreamed of the red-haired little boy they would have, and announced her wish to choose a dog they could dote on together in the meantime. He sent her equally loving reports of his doings, pleased that Hendrie was fulfilling his duty by playing tennis with her, visiting for dinners and walks, and squiring her platonically to concerts and movies, as he had asked him to do. Earle's "vivid, sensuous and revealing" descriptions of the cool mountain glades and swimming haunts of British Columbia and his recollections of his childhood prompted her to urge him to write short stories and poetry again, as he once had at UBC, but not at all since then. "You are a part of what you write. I don't think you would ever describe anything Californian in that way. Write me some short stories, darling—one about your aunt [in Shetland] and one about your father."[34]

Birney began writing creatively again. And Bobbie, whose literary sophistication was increasing by leaps and bounds (she now liked Virginia Woolf and had plans to have a career after marriage), sent him sensitive and gentle criticism in return. "I was so happy about the poems," she wrote to her "dear fiery spirit," her "gold-head," her "Sticking-Out-Ears," her "dear brown Elf." "Especially the first poem, tho' I think the sonnet is better. It really is fine, Erol. The only line I don't like is the last one of the octet (is that the right word?)—doesn't it break the figure? The imagery before that is so 'fluid.'"[35] On another occasion, after detailed analysis, she wrote: "The dance and quiver of the rhythm in 'its antique, gay quicksilver oath' is wonderful, darling—its so exactly moon on water. Were you conscious of doing that or was it planned—did you say 'I want words that dance and quiver' and then pick those out or did you use the words and then realize that they were quite perfect? In other words 'Are you a conscious artist?'"[36]

But into this meeting of minds crept a more serious discussion.

Bobbie noted, as she had from the outset of their relationship, that the "letter-Earle" was not the same as the "real-Earle." When she could see him daily, that made little difference. But now that they were engaged and separated by thousands of miles, it took on a more sinister aspect. In a letter that greatly irritated Earle, she wrote, "Your letters are more arrogant and decisive in some ways than you are.... I like that side of you very much, but I have the feeling, too, that I'm not seeing all of you in your letters."[37]

Indeed she was not seeing all of Earle. Still smarting from the sense of failure he would always feel about losing out to Ted Morrison (even in his autobiography he would omit his Berkeley experience), suffering from his eyesight problems and severely lonely for Bobbie, he sought comfort in affairs: first with a young woman he met, then—more seriously—with a married woman called Mary. In what was probably an attempt to be honest with his future wife and bring together the two extremes in his relationships with women—a courtly tenderness with "nice" girls like Jessie and Bobbie and an uninhibited sexuality with prostitutes and easy women—which was characteristic of the young men of his generation, Birney confided in Bobbie.

At first she encouraged him—thinking herself 'modern' in contrast to her puritanical mother. The current literary controversy that swirled around D.H. Lawrence's *Lady Chatterly's Lover* that summer seemed to mark off a new, freer generation. Birney had been quick to seize on this novel, writing out sections of it in his letters. And Bobbie, for whom *Ulysses* had been "too worldly" only two years before, loved it, possibly because she cast herself as Lady Chatterly to the working-class Earle as the "gamekeeper" Mellors. She found the sexual descriptions "beautiful," especially the part about "threading flowers in her maiden hair."[38] She was enthralled, too, by the last afternoon spent with Earle before he left for Vancouver, when the two had come very close to consummating their passion: "the feel of your cream-smooth skin and the unexpected rough fuzziness of your satyr-thighs was in my fingers—the touch of your hand on my breast."[39] "I didn't mind your taking that girl," she wrote when she first heard of Irene. "...I laughed aloud...at your giving *me* carte-blanche—darling—with all your little card boxes [of thesis notes] full of irony, I don't think you realised how funny that was."[40] Three weeks later, when Earle had taken up with Mary, she wrote "don't dramatize yourself as an adulterer—what's in a name? I don't understand my curious indifference to your sex activities. I have so little emotional reaction to an incident—which most women seem to tear their hair about—that I wondered again if I did love you."[41] Soon, Bobbie began wondering whether Earle might feel "so lecherous" once they were married, a speculation that increased when Earle went further to confide that he had for some time vented his sexual frustrations with "chippies." "The idea of your picking up chippies with desire of copulation with them," she wrote, "seemed repulsive and somehow degrading to myself. I don't see why if you can satisfy yourself with girls like that, you care about taking me. The idea of your coming from such girls to me seems loathesome. Surely you can't ask me to do that—ever. I didn't mind about Mary so much—I felt that she was a beautiful and fine sort of woman—I only was disappointed to see that your love for me was less complete than I thought."[42]

Bobbie predictably discussed the issue with their mutual friend, Hendrie, who—despite the fact that he had proposed visiting whore-houses with Birney and had recently caused a small scandal in Bobbie's family by spending the night with one of her girlfriends—took Bobbie's side. The issue for both of them was Earle's cool detachment, his separation of sex from love. It was a matter Hendrie had already chided Earle about. "You must have a well of cruelty in you," he had written more than a year earlier when Earle had been involved with another married woman in Berkeley just before meeting Bobbie. "You wouldn't speak the obvious, and so you wouldn't say you're sorry for Viola. But that detached coldness, analysing her pompous weaknesses? She was courageous, and she was in a horrible position, with no advantage, none whatsoever, and trying, probably, not to coerce. You've never been like that."[43] Now he was chided for the same thing by Bobbie: "your intellectualizing process is much more complete than mine, more than anyone's I know. Perhaps it *is* possible for you to separate the sexual act from all forms of love or affection. It wouldn't be for me—that isn't just 'feminine' either, because Hendrie said it wasn't for him."[44]

By September, the stage was set for the complete disintegration of his dreams of the previous spring. His mother was incensed at a couple of telegrams she had received for Earle by phone. Bobbie's father, who visited Vancouver that summer, blew up at Earle about his friend Hendrie's indiscretions. Ted Morrison's oral exam had been, unlike Birney's, "a cinch," and Barbara had been assigned to him as an assistant reader. Fumes from the paint and the poison used for extermination had taken a further toll on his eyesight, and on the 15th of September he had a painful operation to straighten his septum, which had largely caused his eye pain. The week-long visit en route to Utah in late September, which he had been banking on to consolidate his engagement to Bobbie, was a dismal affair, partly because he brought his mother with him. Instead of waiting for him to help her choose a dog, Bobbie invited Hendrie to help her. They named their woebe-gone hound dog, which was given to "grinning so absurdly,"[45] "Earle" or "Erol-dog" and joked openly, "Look out for Earle." Bobbie lost in a train station washroom the lovely scarab pin Earle had given her.

But the final blow came in a letter of 26 October 1930 from Bobbie to Earle in Utah, where he had taken up residence with his mother. In an earlier letter, his fiancée had chafed at Hendrie's "lax and loose-fibred" sexual escapades: "Heaven help the woman he marries!" she had exclaimed at the end of May. Now, she wrote, "I've fallen twenty fathoms deep in love with Hendrie," as if expecting him to share her elation. "It was sudden and a little bewildering.… Hendrie called up at supper time and said that he didn't know how it had occurred—whether Aladdin had rubbed his lamp—but anyway we were going to be married right away.… I was perfectly well aware of all the things I disapprove of in him—his conservatism and emotional Puritanism, his romanti-cism. And I don't like blue eyes in men and Hendrie's nose is impossible; a fine well-shaped nose has always been so important to me in a husband; and he isn't a bit tan. Nevertheless—" Instead of assuming the role of romantic hero, a Clym Yeobright to Bobbie's Eustacia Vye, Birney was consigned to the unlovely and painful role of Diggory Venn, the odd-looking reddleman covered with red dust, who is fated to be the rejected suitor.

Two weeks later he also heard from the friend he had entrusted with his fiancée: "Of all the thousands of girls that there are, it is too bad that I should fall in love with your girl. I'm devilishly sorry for that. But I do love her, with everything I own; and I can't withdraw from that, even for you. I haven't written to you before, not because of lack of guts, I think—as you say—but because of confusion.... It's possible that I may have influenced Bob's feeling about you.... I had no such intention. I had been fond of her for so long that, although the change in magnitude was great, the change in position was really quite slight...like taking one step from a tiny room to a huge room in the same house, a house that I was already in."[46]

✂ 7 ✂

DESERTED

The first assignment that Mr. A. Earle Birney (as he formally introduced himself) gave to the medical students at the University of Utah, where he replaced an English instructor on a year's leave in the fall of 1930, was to write a character description of himself. The assignment was somewhat puckish. In the mirror of these descriptions, Birney could not only assess his students' literary level, but could also size up their views of him, a one-way communication that put them at a disadvantage. He kept two of these surprisingly candid first impressions, which suggest that Birney in his late twenties appeared a strange cross between Peter Pan and Ichabod Crane. "Eagerly, I waited in my seat to get a first glimpse of my new teacher, hoping audible sounds would replace that soft hushed voice of the former instructor," began one by what may have been the only woman in the class.

> One by one, young men marched in the class room and were seated. At last, came a tall slender man, who chose to place his books on the front desk. He removed his over-coat and leisurely took a seat on the desk beside the books. Surely, this must be the gentleman, for no Fresh-man could acquire such privileges.

84

He was dressed in a brown tweed suit; raised his eyes with an upward frown, which, *we all know*, means, mercy for others and spoke in clear distinct tones.

As he swung his feet to and fro like a child, one might, by close observation, discover more childish phases. Even his blue plaid socks were slightly wrinkled down over the wee tan oxfords.[1]

The other essay designated Birney a Canadian, and ended with the bracketed supplication: "Mr. Birney, please do not take this too seriously." "The most noticeable thing about him are his long, dangling arms and legs," it went.

He has a peculiar loose-jointed walk. His step is light and springy and his arms swing wildly about like those of a scarecrow in a hurricane.

His rather long neck has one of the most protruding Adam's Apples I have ever seen. When he is talking it wiggles in and out of a collar which is too large for his skinny neck in an amazing manner, reminding me of an ostrich swallowing oranges at a terrific speed.

His face, which has a sallow complexion, is topped with a rather sparse growth of reddish-brown hair. His eyes, peering from behind his horn-rimmed spectacles, are of a pale blue color. [Here Birney, correcting, has written: Look again.] An enormous blood vein, running perpendicular to his nose, swells noticeably when he is angry or talking forcibly. His mustache is the same color as his hair, and unless you look closely you will not see it.

His hands are long and skinny with clearly visible veins weaving around them. They are very delicate in appearance. The huge yellow gold ring on the third finger of his left hand seems to weigh it down.

His rather loose fitting suit is unkempt and disheveled. The trousers are short and baggy in the knees. This gives his feet a large appearance. The sleeves of his coat are wrinkled which shortens them, showing his bony wrists. A white handkerchief is usually tucked into the end of the left sleeve.

Although his outward appearance is nothing to boast about, there is a great amount of intelligence hidden behind his wrinkled forehead.[2]

After the usual remarks justifying the A-minus Birney gave this description, he added whimsically: "You may have a moral effect on me—I am thinking of having my suit pressed."

This playful approach to teaching must have lightened the course. English 21—a survey—was heavy going, especially for students like Birney's who were not specialists. Even such esoteric works as Sir Thomas Malory's *Morte Darthur*, Sir Philip Sidney's *Astrophel and Stella* and Sir Thomas Browne's *Religio Medici* were included. But Birney threw himself into the enlightenment of students who—this being a Mormon institution—were unusually conservative. With aplomb he offered on one test, for example, a list of statements to be marked as right or wrong that included such assertions as: "The Elizabethans were fond of puns, but Shakespeare never descended to them" and "Machiavelli was an Italian Renaissance painter."[3] His marking methods show a commitment that is striking. He analysed the results of each test in almost excruciating detail—presumably to improve both future performance and the tests themselves. He listed highest and lowest scores; calculated the average; laid out the grade distribution overall; listed common misconceptions; and singled out special data, such as the most difficult question. For Birney, as a brief interchange in his continuing correspondence with Bobbie Barrett makes clear, the aim of academic teaching was noble and worthwhile. In it he glimpsed a chance to "change a few minds, or make them grow, the best that come my way."[4] Whereas Bobbie (who after marrying Hendrie would teach for a time herself) thought academe was "too cloistered" and teaching "a silly business," Birney liked the *purpose* of his work at Utah, and was happy, despite the fact that a temporary post at the University of Utah, in the heart of Mormon country, was a far cry from his original ambitions.

After his crushing disappointments—academic and personal—
at Berkeley at a time when the Depression was circumscribing
opportunities everywhere, Birney had turned to his UBC mentor, Sedgewick, for advice. Sedgewick, who clearly missed young
Birney and the vociferous circle of friends he used to entertain
("I am not able any longer, either in energy or desire, to replace
them")[5] as much as Birney missed the man he looked to as his
father after his father's death (he had written affectionately that
he had not "grow[n] off" from Sedgewick),[6] carefully considered
the options. He "demurred" at any thought Birney might have of
teaching in boys' schools. He discouraged him from applying to
UBC (where there were no jobs anyway) until he had spent "a
year or so in some really big place." Of the graduate schools with
good mediaevalists where Birney might complete a Ph.D. in
Chaucer, he recommended Wisconsin, New York University,
Whitman, Chicago—but especially, Harvard. Above all, he
urged Birney to get a Ph.D. "I don't care a rap for the mere possession of a Ph.D. degree," he wrote:

> But you know well that it (or its equivalent, i.e. publi-
> cation) is a necessity in the market, as things now are.
> That damned degree… gives you kinetic energy:
> bluntly, the power to pull up stakes & go. And you
> will never be secure, paradoxically enough, unless &
> until you have just that power. And when you have it,
> or have it within near grasp, then is the time to return
> here.[7]

As for Utah, where Birney finally had to go, since it was the
only place to offer him the instructorship he needed to earn a living, Sedgewick simply wrote, "As for the Mormons, you
wouldn't mind them a bit—for a year at least: you could save
money."[8] So it was off to Utah that Birney went, at a salary of
$2,200 with no expectation that his instructorship would last
any longer than the year.

Birney seems to have intended to imitate Sedgewick in his first
real academic job. Like Sedgewick, he honoured teaching as a
profession; and like Sedgewick, he set up house with his mother,

who left Vancouver with him in his old Studebaker as soon as UBC's summer school was over.

But Mrs. Birney was not like Mrs. Sedgewick, content to play the submissive hostess to her son's friends and students. Nor was Birney cut out to play the genial, ironic celibate, like Sedgewick. Much as mother and son loved each other, their quick tempers flared at close quarters, and Martha's judgemental presence oppressed, rather than complemented, her son's. It can't have helped that Birney's Studebaker (his means of escape from Martha's watchful eye) collapsed in November and that he broke his arm tobogganing over the Christmas vacation. To make matters worse, Martha took a keen and persistent dislike to Utah, or so Birney wrote to Barbara Barrett. "I think your mother would never by temperament be 'happy' anywhere, do you?" Bobbie wrote in reply.[9] Sometime after February, Martha returned to Vancouver, where she would remain, to the simple pleasures of her garden and church socials. And Birney moved into a flat with the other new English instructor, Herman Singer, and began what in retrospect he would describe as "good days, though I didn't particularly realize it at the time."[10]

Singer, who was to be the model for the fictional character Van Bome in Birney's 1955 novel *Down the Long Table*,[11] was an affable, gleaming-haired, burly Dutchman, whose stocky handsome frame and powerful bass voice inspired envy in the lanky Birney who—like his fictional counterpart Gordon Saunders—saw himself as "a failure born of failure…a leper,"[12] and who often thought of himself as too scrawny and thin-haired to be attractive. But envy was subsumed in delight at Singer's playful disposition. Like Birney, Singer aspired to be a writer, and the two intrepid bachelors—aside from the typical youthful indulgences of beer, cards, tennis and casual dating, along with visits to the town's blind pig for bootleg whiskey and gin—shared a keen and whimsical observation of those they encountered around the University of Utah, and playfully competed in mock debates and wordplay. At the bottom of each month's accounts—meticulously kept in parallel columns listing everything from telegrams to kindling for their coal—they tried, for example, to outdo each other in bawdy comparisons indicating they were "square" for the month. "Square as the ass of Ed Wynn's parrot" concludes the February account; for March it was "Square as the bubs of Greta Garbo"; for May—one signed by Birney—it's "Square as my morning section."[13] And they collected gaffs from various student essays and exams to amuse each other, one notably cited in *Down the Long Table* when Van Bome, humped over the desk in the narrow cell they share as an office, his shirt slung over the chair back in the desert heat, holds up a "Morm-moronic [exam] bluebook" and asks his flatmate: "what do you suppose Miss Young means...when she tells me the friars of the Middle Ages were led by Asses? ...St. Francis? Or do I have to credit her with a thought?"[14] It was observations like these that led Birney in his novel to describe the student body at Utah as "a flock of desert hillbillies."[15]

In December of his second year at Utah, Birney reviewed *Pen*, the student literary magazine, in the *University Chronicle*. There his style is ponderously professorial, though there is no doubt his judgement is sound and his insights penetrating. "One sympathizes with the editors who fly from sophomore sex-thrillers and freshman true-confessions—even if the latter are seared with the Scarlet Letter of the English department," he writes, with more than a touch of Sedgewick's irony, "but one doubts if the flight may not be occasionally to greater evils."[16] And in the May issue of *Pen*, he published a poem based on his childhood visit with his mother to his Scottish relatives, "At My Shetland Grandaunt's."[17]

But Birney was not simply a devil-may-care bachelor dedicated in his serious moments to making his mark as a budding academic and transforming the lives of his students. There was another, secret side to his life in Utah—a side which, judging both from his correspondence at the time and from *Down the Long Table*, was far from trivial. He was deeply in love with Catherine Fisk, the wife of Vernon Fisk, an assistant professor of Botany. When their affair began is unclear. But from a postcard written by Birney to his mother in September 1931, he mentions that the very evening that he and Herman arrived back for their second year at Utah from their separate summers—Birney from teaching in UBC's summer session—they had dinner at the

Fisks. This suggests that they were already good friends; and the card implies that Martha, who had left Salt Lake City seven months earlier, knew Vernon and Catherine Fisk too. From her photo, Catherine, on whom the character of Anne in Birney's novel is based, was a very pretty, rather serious, dark woman with a perfect oval face. At some point, probably in the spring or summer of 1931,[18] they became lovers. Without spare money or a car, and oppressed by the necessity of meeting where neither her husband and young son nor Herman could find out about their liaison, Birney had Catherine pick him up in her car and drive in the opposite direction from the dense waters of Great Salt Lake through the sage-spiced desert to the green canyon that lay hidden in the elephant-grey Wasatch Mountains to the east of the city. There, high above the city among the sweet-scented pines, rustling aspens and sheltering sumac, he made tender love to the woman he found breathtakingly beautiful, the woman who soothed his hurts and fulsomely, without the coyness of virginal unmarried women like Jessie or Bobbie, restored to him the conviction that he was desirable. "I remember Catherine," he wrote Herman Singer much later, "when we were up Emigration Canyon [a hot May afternoon] playing the two-backed game while Vernon sweated in his lab."[19] To her, he seemed "one man in a thousand."[20] Unequivocally, he wanted her for his wife, and said so.

Though *Down the Long Table* has the advantage of hindsight, it offers an introspective analysis by Birney of himself as compartmentalized. Gordon Saunders, the largely autobiographical central character, discusses his sense that there are several Gordons. He clearly identifies "little Gordon," "a nice boy who did all his lessons and tried to keep his academic nose clean in the hope to be a Great Harvard Professor someday."[21] He can also single out "Gordy," "that slick go-getting twerp." "He's the one who wants to own a house, a car about the same size, a streamlined wife, four kids and a yacht.… He's a man of business who can bully half-bankrupt store-keepers, clap them on their crooked backs and flatter them, feed their stinking prejudices, and sign them up for quarter-page ads they don't need. He corralled all the pavement and sewer contractors and stampeded them into thinking, if they didn't advertise in his cheesy little rag, its owner, who was also Chairman of Works on the Municipal Council, would chuck their next bids in the public ashcan."[22] And he readily adopts also the insulting sobriquet "Man of Sin" that is hurled at him during a contretemps with his chairman, who has heard that he reads "sexy" poems by Robert Herrick to his English class and now accuses him of having added the coarse jest: "what this country needs is more gin and less virginity."[23] This "Man of Sin" Gordon is quick-tempered, passionate, sensual and uncontrolled. Chafing against the repressed climate of a Mormon institution; indignant at the strictures of poverty, hard work—both physical and mental—that have plagued his twenty-seven years; filled with self-loathing at his own longing for material success; haunted by the fear of failure and convinced of his ugliness; this Gordon rebels as if for life itself. And in that rebellion he glimpses something both noble and ridiculous. As his gorge rises against the sadistic fatuousness of his chairman, the image of himself as a spindly Don Quixote comes to mind: "Whoa, whoa," he admonishes himself, "riding at windmills again."

It was Birney's ability to compartmentalize himself that dissuaded Catherine from leaving her husband and, more especially, her son for him. Though, as his novel makes clear, Birney could not ever have limited himself to a placid life as "little Gordon," steadily and politely working his way upward towards becoming a professor, because he is addicted to the con games that enhance his pocketbook and the tempers and passions of the "Man of Sin" in him surge too strongly and disruptively from his core to be resisted. Neither could he abandon himself entirely to his love for Catherine. Her highly emotional letters detail his "realism" and "ruthlessness" and decline his requests for marriage not, as Anne says to Gordon in *Down the Long Table* because he is a "mamma's boy" who doesn't want to have to raise her children, but because, unlike her, Earle is only partly committed:

> I can see now that your work comes first and that all
> the finest in you is concentrated on *that*. Seems to me
> you are learning to live entirely from the outside and

to be lacking of something within.... At one time you were so tender and it was so becoming to you and oh how I should love to make you that way always... Just thinking of you these days has made me a less responsive mother, an irritable daughter-in-law and a cruel wife... For Vernon I feel only great pity and for you a hungry longing that's eating my heart away and to see you again—oh I'd pay so dearly....

We can't marry. You wouldn't marry me if you could. And it wouldn't be right to go on this way. Perhaps for you because you look on love in a very different way. But for me it would be nothing but misery. Your work will supplement home life, love and all of it. But I've nothing. You are free to do as you wish and choose without compromising. I'm not. Can't you see your love would be everything to me, but you have learned not to put it first in your life.... Make your plans without me, dear.[24]

Those plans proved more difficult to make than Birney could have foreseen. Though he readily obtained a fellowship of $750 (in his novel, Birney reduces this amount to $500 to make Gordon's case more pathetic) to attend the University of Toronto's graduate school, the University of Utah—which did not offer the Ph.D. he needed to complete—was in such financial straits because of the Depression that it could make no commitment whatever to hold open a position for his return. Nor, for the same reason, could Toronto offer any hope of renewal of his fellowship beyond one year. Bleak though these career prospects were, it was even more painful to leave without Catherine, for she—like Anne in *Down the Long Table*—had become pregnant with his child and, without telling him, had had an abortion.

❧ *8* ❧

SYLVAN DREAMS

On Wednesday 14 July 1933, a sylphlike nineteen-year-old sprang lightly onto the train coach at Toronto's Union Station. Her heart-shaped face framed by glossy auburn waves was animated. Sticking her return ticket cheekily between her teeth, she waved winsomely at the two people who saw her off—a dapper, puckish young graduate student named Roy Daniells, who had brought her two oranges and a bar of chocolate for the trip, and her mother, "Mrs. J.," a large mother hen of a woman who clucked to an indifferent porter that this was the first time her daughter had left home. And so far away! Vancouver![1]

By her own account later, the trip was no exception to the stream of dramatic incidents that usually overflowed Sylvia Johnstone's young life. "A fanatical old missionary woman set upon me to make a convert to the faith," she wrote en route in her helter-skelter scrawl to her brother Ken,

> at night she prayed God would bring me to the light
> & sorrowed after my lost soul then as a parting gift
> she pressed into my unwilling hands the enclosed
> pamphlet. Keep it for me as a curio of the train trip.[2]

Sylvia was immune to conversion. She was already as dedicated to Trotsky's cause as any nun to her Saviour. "All the people on the train knew I was a Communist," she went on, relishing her adventures.

> & the old woman found it a pleasant morsel for gossip. I had lots of arguements [sic] & was in several ticklish spots with the conductors who seemed to like me face, for they would chat to me on every occasion—asking me such questions as—Haven't you ever seen the Rockies before?—to which I would reply—"Oh—uh—uh well you see this is the first time I've had a *real good* look at them heh heh"—"Well where do you live in Vancouver?"—"Oh around 48th St." "Over near the _____ district"—"Yes, yes how many children did you say you had I bet they [sic] cute, do you raise chickens? gasp, gasp—" And that's the way it went.[3]

Sylvia was travelling fast and furious to join Earle Birney, the comrade with whom she was determined to set up a Trotskyist nucleus in the west-coast city wracked by unemployment in this the most wretched summer of the Great Depression.

Vancouver had been one of the first Canadian cities to suffer in the wake of the stock-market crash of October 1929 because the lumber trade came to a halt, orders for canned salmon dropped and the glut of wheat on international markets bit into water-front exports (prairie grain export fell from a high of $238 million in 1929 to just over $100 million by 1934).[4] Within months, breadlines were forming outside the City Relief Office. Communists began at once to arrange demonstrations: in December 1929, unemployed men raided the City Relief Office and hundreds paraded in the streets. In the autumn of 1930, R.B. Bennett's federal government responded to the national economic calamity with relief projects and direct financial assistance to the provinces. By the end of 1930, there were 7,000 Vancouver men on relief, and a month later there were hundreds more as men from other provinces, in flight from harsher climates, rode the rods west. In the autumn of 1931, when unemployment in

B.C. had reached 28 per cent, the highest in Canada, Premier Tolmie (a Conservative) had to take action. Relief camps to harbour such transients were set up in far-flung areas of the province with the intention of using the cheap labour of unemployed single males to build roads and airports in exchange for room, board and cash payments of just over one dollar a day, which dropped to seven-fifty a month and then to twenty cents a day.[5] Eventually there were 237 such camps and 18,340 men—about one-third of the total number in Canada on this type of relief. Before long the financial strain on Vancouver and B.C. led to the deportation of immigrants, and the disqualification of married men. The spring of 1933 witnessed the appearance of the provincial Co-operative Commonwealth Federation Party (CCF) some months after the national party under the leadership of "the bearded ethereal idealist"[6] and social activist J.S. Woodsworth was established at Calgary in July 1932. The "visionary socialism" resulting from the coalition of such reformist groups in Canada as radical socialists, female activists and followers of the social gospel was aimed at remedying Depression ills. (By the 1933 provincial election, the CCF were able to nominate candidates in forty-eight of the forty-nine ridings.)[7] At about the same time as Sylvia arrived in Vancouver, the "Regina Manifesto," which declared the CCF's election platform, was being formulated by 150 delegates at the Regina Conference (19–21 July). On 1 June, a few weeks before she had boarded her train west, the relief camps passed from provincial control to the federal Department of National Defence—a national move in the direction of "militarization" which made the Communist appeal of revolution decidedly more attractive. From all parts of the province, stirred to action by militant activists, the lonely ill-fed men in the camps ignored the physical danger of the police attacks they correctly expected and began to march by the thousands on Vancouver where more than one-tenth of the population were also on relief. Splinter groups of every shade of red—many of them with international connections and ambitions—had sprung up around the city, each certain it had the right degree of revolutionary fervour, the best means of righting the ills of a capitalist society gone awry.[8]

Sylvia Johnstone had been named after the British suffragette Sylvia Pankhurst and schooled by her ardently political mother for a life committed to a better world—a just world in which women would finally assume their rightful roles. Her first words as a toddler—quite literally—had been "Down With Men." Oddly, considering these views, "Mrs. J." (as even her three children called her) had plotted a ballet career for her youngest child and only daughter, who passionately studied from age eight to fourteen, taught for a year, but then abandoned dance for more serious studies at the University of Toronto. Almost at once, tuberculosis interrupted those studies, and Sylvia languished for more than two years at a rural sanitorium before resuming her courses in Toronto.[9] She'd had to finish her exams—some of them junior matriculation subjects which she had failed to complete in high school—in early July before she could leave for Vancouver. Somehow she had fit in a Spartacus meeting (the Trotskyist youth organization) on the 10th, marched in the Anti-Fascist parade on the 11th and had her hair cut and permed before leaving.[10]

Birney had had no option but to leave Toronto in May. His meagre fellowship had run out, and he returned to Vancouver to spend yet another summer teaching at UBC while living with his mother.

The twenty-nine-year-old whom Martha Birney welcomed back into her cramped quarters in South Vancouver bore almost no resemblance to the twenty-eight-year-old she had last seen the summer before. Then he had been her "dear Son Boy," solicitous of her health and her garden; dutifully reporting later from Toronto that he was "holding strongly" to his diet, "Breakfast: bowl of bran, scrambled eggs, hot & cold water. Lunch: fresh fruit. Dinner: small chop (not fried) or boiled fish, raw vegetable salad, whole wheat brown toast, postum or water"; and assuring her that he had stopped smoking.[11] He had taken a room in the men's residence of University College at 73 St. George Street, the elm-lined street he had no reason to love, where even the collegial nights of bridge-playing did little to alleviate the stifling atmosphere of respectable gentility. The high point of his few months there proved newsworthy: in a bridge game he dealt, he got all thirteen hearts, bid a grand slam, but lost to an opponent who overbid him in the only more powerful suit, spades. The paper quoted "Burney's" [sic] response as "What do you know about that?" to which Birney himself later added, "I said a lot more than that."[12]

The incident so enraged him he gave up bridge. And with it the role of the chummy, respectable graduate student he had presented to his mother. Nostalgic for the rakish bachelor life he had thrived on with Herman Singer in Utah, he moved in with Roy Daniells, a graduate student in English he had been lunching with weekly during the fall along with Alf Bailey, another English grad student, and Robert Finch, a Fellow in the French Department who had just returned from the Sorbonne. All four would one day be poets. But in the absence of Canadian journals interested in poetry (though Bailey had already published two chapbooks), they were students weaned on the Metaphysicals, W.B. Yeats and T.S. Eliot who dabbled in poetry—Birney in nothing more than satiric verses that gave vent to his spleen at what he considered the slavish subservience of the other three to traditional forms.[13]

Daniells and Birney found the ideal digs: Tom Thomson's tawdry tar-paper shack in the Rosedale ravine. For the three years before his death in 1917, Thomson had painted his greatest northern canvases in this cramped, primitive building—originally a cabinet-maker's shop—that he loved because it reminded him of the quarters in which he had been billeted as a guide in Algonquin Park.[14] It was bliss to Birney. He returned not only to batching it with another west-coast fellow (Daniells was from Victoria) whose ingenious literature examinations (one written in rhyming couplets) he had marked at UBC summer sessions when Daniells had been a second-year student, but to roughing it in a sylvan ravine that echoed his happier outdoor times out west.

Before Christmas that year his Chaucer thesis and seminars in linguistics commanded all his energy.[15] Groping to locate his own ideological position among his lunch friends (according to Birney, Finch looked to French models like poet Paul Valéry; Daniells was engaged with German poets like Rilke and was reading Adolf Hitler's *Mein Kampf*, Bailey was a follower of Carl Jung and deep into post-Frazer studies of "primitive" religion and anthropology), Birney recalls his own interest focused on James Joyce, André Breton and Dadaism as he "[wavered] between 'philosophical' anarchism and social democracy."[16]

Excellent though he was as a scholar, Birney was not gripped by academe. His aching eyes constantly reminded him that he was not made for marathons of stultifying library work. He knew well that some of his curiosities could never be satisfied by books alone. He had not found anyone to stir his passion like Catherine Fisk, whose absence he felt deeply. Nor had he found his voice as a poet. When he was younger, such limbos of loneliness were simple homesickness. Now that he was approaching thirty, his sense of an ideological vacuum took on far greater meaning. What did he really believe in? To what, or to whom, could he dedicate his formidable mind, his unusual energy, his physical and imaginative passion?

Politics was in the air, and Birney suddenly began breathing it in in huge draughts. Possibly because Daniells was spouting *Mein Kampf*, though more likely because, like Gordon Saunders in his novel *Down the Long Table*, he stumbled upon some radical left-wing rallies in Toronto, Birney had "launched on a crash program of 'leftwing' reading, starting with the *Communist Manifesto*...and Marx, Engels, Kautsky, Plekhanov, Lenin, Stalin, with side glances into the literature of the new (Canadian) League for Social Reconstruction" [LSR] and the incipient CCF party.[17]

One of those "side glances" must have fallen on *The Spark*,[18] the journal of the University of Toronto Student League for Social Reconstruction, for Birney refers to it in *Down the Long Table*.[19] Certainly, once the LSR and the CCF were organized, student study groups sprang up to discuss their ideologies. Such issues as the plight of the poor, freedom of speech, opposition to fascism and the flaws in a capitalist system of economy and education provoked feisty debate. Though Canadian university students involved in left-wing political groups in the thirties were a decided minority (according to one expert, "perhaps 5 per cent of students joined or participated regularly in reform-oriented organizations, [and] the last half of the decade involved more students than the first"[20]), the University of Toronto was one of the centres for such activity. The Student Christian Movement (SCM), a member group of the Canadian Youth Congress, of which U of T graduate Kenneth Woodsworth, the son of J.S. Woodsworth, became national secretary, campaigned for peace and social justice. Some SCM advocates, like Victoria College student Northrop Frye, promoted religion over politics; others promoted "radical ideology and mass action."[21] The Young Communist League (YCL), whose activities mainly took place off-campus, held some on-campus activities as part of their united-front and popular-front efforts. Since Toronto police routinely broke up Communist meetings or infiltrated them and filed reports on all suspects and because university officials were unpredictably repressive in their dealings with student debates and editorials in the late twenties and early thirties, such activities were surreptitious and were frequently co-operative endeavours with the SCM. Though at its peak, the YCL had seventeen hundred Canadian members, notably in Toronto, Montreal, Winnipeg and Vancouver, only a fraction were university students. Birney found himself cheek by jowl not only with SCM debaters like Norrie Frye, but with far more radical students like Stanley Ryerson (great-grandson of Egerton Ryerson) who, according to one classmate, was "the number-one Communist around"[22] and Dorothy Livesay, a Toronto M.A. and poet (though only twenty-four, she had published two books of poems—*Green Pitcher* and *Signposts*) who had just returned from the Sorbonne, found herself a job as a social worker and become an avid Communist.[23]

According to Birney in his memoirs, it was at a gathering at the home of his fellow Zate from Berkeley days, economist Harry Cassidy, now a professor in the university's department of Social Science,[24] that he met Dee Livesay along with Ken Johnstone, a roguish young man who worked at Canada Packers meat factory and was leader of the Trotskyist youth of Toronto, and his younger sister, Sylvia, whom Ken called "The Brat."

Livesay—a Stalinist—would later clearly recall meeting Birney: "The long-limbed, sandy-haired young man—obviously with much of the Scot in him—was guest at a tea party in Harry Cassidy's house when I first met him, in 1933. That was in Toronto, in the deep of the Depression. Earle Birney hailed from the University of B.C., they said; he was finishing his M.A. at the University of Toronto.... His concern was English literature; but neither he nor anyone else present seemed to be interested in talking about literature. The talk was of how to get a job; of economics and Marxism; of a possible world war."[25]

Together Ken and Earle took on Stalinist Dorothy Livesay over the role of the German Communist Party, which—stupidly, they thought—had refused to join forces with German socialists against Hitler because its members thought them "social-fascists." Suddenly something deep inside Birney clicked into place. Here, at last, was something into which he could throw himself, a purpose worthy of his mind, his heart, his soul. His delight in Ken, his attraction to the coquettish Sylvia, his temperamental incompatibility with the fierce Dorothy, his delight in the intellectual stimulation of the debate in which he, Ken and Sylvia found themselves in passionate accord was a heady mix. "I...was delighted to find at last, in Johnstone and his beautiful sister," he would later recall,

> two informed and clear-thinking minds able to expose Stalin's policies as not only tactically disastrous, as I thought, but basically unMarxist, Bonapartist not Leninist. That night began my conscious involvement in "the class struggle," and a seven-year loyalty to the cause of reforming the Third International or building a new one.[26]

It was not surprising that Birney found his cause in the Trotskyist movement. That spring of 1933 was a crucial one: it ushered in the darkest year of the Great Depression; it marked the recently elected F.D. Roosevelt's "New Deal," which favoured the trade union movement in the United States; and, in Germany, Adolf Hitler came to power. The victory of the Nazis was a devastating blow to German Jews, workers and leftists. It appeared to be a sinister portent of things to come in the rest of

Western Europe. Many tens of thousands of people, particularly young people, were galvanized into political life as a result.

Leon Trotsky, the organizer of the Soviet Red Army, and second only to V.I. Lenin as the leader of the Russian Revolution of 1917, had warned that the German Communist Party (KPD) must form a united front with the Social Democratic Party (SPD) to crush the Hitlerites or else they would both be destroyed, along with the unions, and every other democratic institution. Trotsky had been one of the founders of the Communist, or Third, International (known as the "Comintern") and remained one of its most influential leaders until his expulsion from it in 1928 by Joseph Stalin. Despite losing the factional struggle in Moscow, his words still commanded an international following of millions of leftist workers.

Trotsky pointed out that an amalgamation of the KPD and SPD would constitute a far greater force than the Nazis. But the Comintern, following the instructions of the Stalin leadership in Moscow, pursued a different strategy. They considered that the main danger was not the Nazis (who were dismissed as an insignificant and transitory phenomenon) but rather the continuing influence of the social-democrats over a large section of the German working class. If this obstacle could be overcome, reasoned the theoreticians of the "Third Period," then the KPD would become hegemonic within the German proletariat and would soon come to power. One of the KPD catch-phrases which encapsulated this idea was "After Hitler, us!" A tactical corollary was that instead of proposing a fighting alliance with the social-democrats against the Nazis, the KPD concentrated its energies on doing battle with the social-democrats, whom it dubbed "social-fascists."

Birney was, at the time, oblivious to these polemics underway within the communist left internationally. But he was soon to be swept into them, as a partisan of Leon Trotsky whose analysis of events in Germany was so powerfully vindicated with Hitler's victory, the rapid destruction of the KPD, the SPD and the unions, and the descent into fascist barbarism.

The bankruptcy of the Kremlin's sectarian attitude, and the failure of any component of the Stalinized Comintern to criticize

the policy even after the results were clear, led Trotsky to con-
clude that the attempt to return the Third International to its
revolutionary origins was hopeless and that it was necessary to
form a new, Fourth, International.

The German experience was an important political factor in the
division between the Trotskyists and Stalinists, but there had
been many others. Trotsky and Stalin represented the two major
political poles within the international communist movement
after Lenin died in January 1924. The Russian Revolution of
1917 had been made by the working class led by its own revolutionary party, but in one important regard it deviated from the
classical model of socialist revolution developed by Karl Marx in
the nineteenth century. Russia was not an advanced capitalist
society, but rather a backward semi-feudal one in which the
working class was a tiny minority—more than 80 per cent of the
population were peasants. According to Marxist theory, a socialist
revolution was not possible in such circumstances "unless, as both
he [Lenin] and Trotsky expected, revolution in Russia kindled
the flame of revolution in the advanced countries of the west."[27]

This internationalist perspective lay at the heart of the Russian
Revolution which was undertaken as a gamble on the prospect
of the European Revolution as a whole. Trotsky continued to
adhere to this political program throughout his life, but Stalin,
who was more skilful at machine politics, gradually came to view
this as hopeless and chimerical. By December 1924, he devised
what he considered to be a shrewder and more practical perspective than that of World Revolution—"Socialism in One
Country." While there was no support in the Marxist canon for
such a theory it did fulfil the immediate requirements of the
regime:

> ...psychologically its impact was enormous. It supplied
> a positive and definable goal. It dispensed with vain
> expectations of help from abroad. It flattered national
> pride by presenting the revolution as a specifically
> Russian achievement, and the building of socialism a
> lofty task in the fulfilment of which the Russian pro-
> letariat would set an example to the world. Hitherto

the dependence of the prospect of socialism in Russia
on socialist revolution in other countries had occupied
a central place in party doctrine. Now the order of priority was reversed. Stalin boasted that the victory of
the revolution in Russia was "the beginning and the
premise of world revolution."[28]

The entire axis of Trotsky's struggle against Stalin, which was to
play such an important part in the life of Earle Birney, took place
over this counterposition between "Socialism in One Country"
and "World Revolution"—that is, Russian nationalism vs.
Marxist internationalism.

Birney was not only drawn to Trotsky's internationalist, revolutionary perspective, he also sympathized with his views on education and culture. Stalinist "culture" was little more than a
crude tool to indoctrinate the masses, and virtually all forms of
artistic expression were suppressed, save that of "Socialist
Realism," which was dedicated to celebrating the regime and its
leader. Trotsky, on the other hand, upheld the artistic policy of
the early years of the revolution and insisted that the state had no
right to attempt to regulate culture. The Bolsheviks had sought
to create a society in which the educational and cultural capaci-
ties of all the citizens would be free to develop. For Stalin, the
artist was a servant of the state, incorporating communist doctrines into his work. But for Trotsky, the artist needed freedom
from rules and regulations in order to create the finest work possible. To Birney, who was temperamentally rebellious when faced
with constrictions of any kind, Trotsky's conception of the artist
as free spirit seemed grandly ideal.[29]

It was after the tea at Harry Cassidy's that Birney began avidly
reading the works of Marx, Lenin and Trotsky in the university
library. Unlike most of his fellow university students, who were
made more cautious by the sharp downturn in the economy
because they were primarily intent on using the university as "a
stepping stone to a more secure professional career,"[30] Birney
seized on the idea of revolution as if heeding voices from long
ago. The Depression had brought to the fore the very social and
economic issues with which he and his parents had struggled all

their lives. Poverty? He had tasted those humiliations many times over. He'd heard his mother bitterly decry her fate as an uneducated immigrant. The plight of the working class? He'd seen it all. Homeless and camping, subsistence farming, boarders, road gangs, that endless struggle, and never, ever, enough money. The blithe indifference of bourgeois capitalists? He'd seen that, too. His fraternity brothers, the "drunken Zates," had not understood why he couldn't keep up with their carefree social antics, and his comfortable professors at Berkeley had had no idea how crucial it had been for him to have fellowships. Long before the Depression polarized politics, Birney was acutely sensitive to social injustice. "I am housepainting, paperhanging, etc.," he had written to his friend Leonard Leacock in 1926, the summer he spent working with his father for seven dollars a day.

> I see… that Fred Ethridge has been appointed super-intendent of some mines (Cottontail?) in central B.C.; apparently a very good position.… It is rather tempting to speculate on the fact that Leo [Telfer]—who was twice as capable in applied engineering—is probably toiling away (at Toronto, I believe) as geology asst. at about $50 a month. And Leo will probably get his Ph.D. and acquire great knowledge and still continue to get not more than a third of the wages of a mine manager. "'Scurious-like, said the tree-toad.'"[31]

And four months after this letter, his overworked, underpaid father had died.

Intrigued now by the vivid spectrum of newly articulated political positions, Birney sampled Toronto's left-wing fare like a seasoned gourmet. It had not taken long for him to size up the Young Communist Leaguers, or, rather, for them to size him up. Though drawn to their energy and keen to assert the rights of the working class, he could not throw in his lot with what seemed to him the unthinking emotionality of the Stalinist position. Branded a Trotskyist before he had any idea what the term meant, he was bounced from their social problems club as the result of a speech cribbed from Trotsky he would later use in

Down the Long Table.[32] His interest in Cassidy's LSR position—a position shared by professors Frank Underhill, the liberal-nationalist historian[33] who with Montreal lawyer and poet F.R. Scott was the League's guiding light, and Eric Havelock, the classicist at Victoria College who was a Christian socialist, as well—drew him in the direction of social reform, especially since he found himself at the hub of the LSR's inception [it had begun in the winter of 1931–32 when sixty-eight U of T professors signed an open letter on behalf of Communists who were persecuted in Toronto].[34] But though these professors were intelligent and probing, something about the gentle piety of the party position left him cold. Still, even after the mesmerizing meeting at which he met Ken and Sylvia Johnstone and began to articulate what was to become a firm and lengthy commitment to Trotskyism, he wavered. By his own account, the "cherubic and very intelligent" Norrie Frye, with his "bright straw-coloured curls"[35] "almost diverted [me] back to my earlier skepticism about human affairs," at a Victoria College student debate.[36] Birney attributes his ultimate commitment to Trotsky to the fact that he was not essentially skeptical, but "by nature an optimistic sort of revolutionary.... [I] decided to cast my dice with the creator of the Red Army, and his brilliant Canadian supporter, the Toronto lawyer Maurice Spector,"[37] a man whom Frye thought a fraud.[38]

Birney met Spector, the only Canadian ever to be a member of the Executive Committee of the Communist International, who had been ruthlessly expelled from the Communist Party of Canada (CPC) in 1929 for his Trotskyist views, at the Johnstones' house at 34 Brownville Avenue in the working-class town of Weston beside the Humber River, just west of Toronto. Spector boarded at the house of one of Ken's friends on Medland Crescent on the south side of the nearby stockyards. "Mrs. J." and her children held Trotskyist discussions as informal as they were rambunctious. Birney's fictional depiction of these Sunday meetings in *Down the Long Table* suggests that they were a wildly idiosyncratic mix of articulate and well-informed political views from the likes of Spector and Jack MacDonald, a trade union leader and the CPC's founding chairman who had also been expelled from the CPC in 1929 for his independent views; less articulate but well-informed discussions with the Johnstones' working-class neighbours and student chums; stridently expressed opinions on such matters as the rights of women from the warm and welcoming "Mrs. J."; and cocky sibling banter between Ken and Sylvia, whose many suitors competed for her approval by their skill in political debate.

A description of an afternoon at the Johnstones by Roy Daniells—whom Birney eagerly tried to recruit to the Trotskyist cause—suggests that Birney's rollicking fictional descriptions were not greatly embellished.

> The Johnstones were visited today by an old uncle of Mrs. J.'s aged eighty-five and suitably "sans eyes, sans ears, etc." In the overflowing goodness of her heart she took him (he is an ardent Bible student) to a picnic of the L.O. [Left Opposition]. She told him what a great leader they had (Trotsky) and the old boy seemed to desire confirmation as to his Biblical soundness of doctrine. However, everything seems to have gone off very happily, and he appears to have thought he was at Bible Students' or similar picnic. At the end she told him to stand up for the hymns, so he took off his hat and bowed his head for the Doxology…and joined in spirit with the strains of the Internationale. After which Mrs. J. said she would introduce him to two of the preachers, or speakers, …Maurice and Jack Macdonald [sic]!!! The former, unperturbed as usual, said he had just been meditating on a certain scripture. (Which seems to have been a fact: he saw one on a roadside noticeboard.)[39]

Not only were high jinks like this the order of the day. For some of the young male visitors at the Johnstones, political fervour was indistinguishable from adoration of Sylvia, a situation Birney comments on obliquely in his novel when the character based on Ken describes them as "the Sunday night suitors, faithful and unrewarded. It's like the *Odyssey*—without Ulysses."[40]

Among these "Sunday night suitors" were both Birney and

Daniells, a situation which soon began to strain their friendship. As Sylvia put it to Earle, "Roy is splendid company when he's feeling witty Isn't he? he's really at his best; now you're at *your* peak when you are mercilessly knocking down point by point some unfortunate's brilliant exposition. And I'm at my best," she added with mock humility, "writing Latin Composition examinations. We all have our moments."[41]

By the time Birney left for Vancouver in the spring, their rivalry for Sylvia had become a classic love triangle. This time, Birney had no intention of being cheated of his girl, as he had been cheated of Barbara Barrett by Hank Gartshore when he had had to leave her to teach summer school in Vancouver. Like a knight from one of the mediaeval texts he had been studying, he heroically undertook to organize a Trotskyist nucleus in Vancouver on the side while he taught summer school, partly in order to prove his worth to the woman ten years his junior who openly spoke of herself as the Canadian Rosa Luxemburg (the romantic martyr to the revolutionary cause in Germany).[42] Indeed, Birney thought of himself and Sylvia as the legendary lovers Troilus and Criseyde; Daniells he cast as the worldly Greek who successfully seduces the fickle Criseyde and thereby causes Troilus to die of a broken heart.[43] Daniells, meanwhile, had written some Hiawatha poems, and was playfully casting Earle and Sylvia as Hiawatha and his beautiful wife noted for her merry laugh, Minnehaha. And out of this a game developed in which Daniells—possibly because of his twinkling impish smile—was identified with Pau-Puk-Keewis, the "merry mischief maker" known as the "Storm-Fool" in Longfellow's poem, who dances so superbly at the wedding of Hiawatha and Minnehaha.[44] All three referred to Roy as Puck, the mischievous sprite of English folklore. But beneath this arch literary banter, a real contest raged. "I wish I had definitely obtained from you before you left the exact attitude you wished me to take toward her, during the interim before she leaves," a badly smitten Daniells wrote Birney in Vancouver after an evening at the Johnstones. "As Sylvia and I have become extremely good friends, it is probably a good scheme to take the most extreme view for the sake of avoiding all danger and treat the problem as though there were some chance of my doing you damage." He told Sylvia that he was "[not] one of the suitors" and urged her to marry Earle.[45]

Birney's prickly reply was instantaneous:

> Hah! as Maurice [Spector] would say. Hah! You expect me to weep over your plight, and you, YOU, Sssssnake-a-de-grassssS, you "hope to see a fair amount of Sylvia" during a time which I had flattered myself was to be devoted, every hour, every minute, to getting [her] teeth fixed, packing and speeding across the continent to spend what remnant of the summer is left, with me. How can you reconcile that? I, who must in two months be plunged into all the rural idiocy of Utah for another long, lonely, friendless and stupid winter—no B.M.s [British Museum, where Daniells would be studying], no London, no England, no Europe, no wisdom, no sea, no life, no Sylvia—I am to be kept chafing in Vancouver for what is almost certainly the only visit to be deigned me ever, I am to be turning on a spit of expectation roasted with the fires of time and unavailing passion, in order that you, who have by now seen as much of the girl as I, may snitch hours, days, WEEKS, from the pittance Time and Space allot me. Ah, subtle Diomedes, I see thee…. I don't make friends easily and, too, my fate has sent me from pillar to post almost yearly. The result is I'm continually on the verge of making friends, lovers, comrades, and losing them to find others.[46]

Once alert to the risk of losing Sylvia, Birney wrote often and at length to forestall the possibility. "When I first met Sylvia," he explained in relief as Sylvia finally sped towards him by train,

> I was almost impatient that she meet you—selfish desire to show off my brilliant friends to her, to show her off to you, plus scientific impulse to educate you into what seemed to me higher standards of feminine

companionship... the experiment was almost alarmingly successful.... you are a very charming and intelligent fellow, with a great many virtues I don't possess, and I am a lover. Not an average jealous one, perhaps, but one who was so deeply burned by a parallel episode... that he is now prepared to kill off any number of men friends, however dear, to keep the girl he loves.[47]

Tensions in this triangular relationship ran like a leitmotif through their correspondence the rest of the summer. On the surface, Birney and Sylvia threw themselves into their great cause. Following his instructions from the executive of Toronto's Left Opposition via Ken, Birney fired off regular reports of his progress. Letters flew back and forth between Birney and Ken, Maurice Spector, and Babe Pearlstone, a Trotskyist editor circulating the periodical of the Communist Party of America, the *Militant*. These suggest that the Toronto branch was, as Ken put it, "far from being any smooth-running machine."[48] Birney was often frustrated: Spector took a long time writing and ignored Birney's plea for a Vancouver visit to help consolidate his efforts; Pearlstone was inefficient in sending copies of *Militant*. The prospect of establishing a Vancouver branch was daunting.

But undaunted, Comrade Birney—as he began calling himself—threw his heart and soul into the task like a gangly latter-day Don Quixote, sustained by the conviction that a new and better world would one day be ushered in by the Fourth International. He drew on his old newspaper experience to set up distribution of the *Militant*; the Canadian Trotskyist paper, *The Workers' Vanguard*; the *Modern Monthly* and various other pamphlets and bulletins. Circulation was almost ridiculously small; the first "newsie" he dealt with—E. Rolston, whose stand at 138 East Hastings Street was just west of the Royal Theatre—sold only six copies of *Militant*. Well, it was a start. He contacted all the professors he hoped he could convert, and began proselytizing: "An English professor here, Dr. W.L. MacDonald,[49] is working on a history of eighteenth century... lit., and I am going to feed him what I can of Marxian aesthetics," he wrote Ken. "He

is reading Trotsky's History of the Rev. now, and we left him
and his wife some Militants.... We were up at a weekend camp
with an old friend of mine [Helen M. Hughes] & her husband
[Everett C. Hughes], both are teachers of sociology at McGill.
We worked on 'em."[50] He even had a go at the irascible
Sedgewick. "Garnett has taken up a position of uninformed and
incurious amusement regarding the whole subject, but I undermine him day by day without his really being aware of it," he
confided to Daniells.[51]

Swinging into his undercover activities with all the relish he
had once accorded his earlier secret lives—which he had devised
mainly to elude his ever-watchful mother—he assumed a pseudonym which was, ironically, his mother's surname "Robertson."
Thus could he simultaneously vindicate her unjust youth and
thumb his nose at her disapproval of Communism. In this guise,
he checked out Vancouver's left-wing groups: the YCL, the SPC
(Socialist Party of Canada), the CLDC (Canadian Labour
Defence League), the WIR and the WUL (Workers' Unity
League). Birney thus played his role in the impact which the
post-revolutionary politics of Russia, which focused on the fundamental conflict between Stalin and Trotsky, was having on
Canadian trade union affairs. "Workers were [being] exorted to
separate from 'reformist' organizations like the All-Canadian
Congress of Labour and to join truly 'revolutionary' unions in
order to prepare for the coming revolution, which, Tim Buck
[leader of the Communist Party of Canada, which until 1936
was an 'unlawful association' under Section 98 of the Criminal
Code] predicted in 1929, 'will make the late War look like a
chicken fight.' No trade unions corresponding to this revolutionary ideal existed in Canada. There were, however, three national
unions of miners, loggers and garment workers that were sufficiently communist in complexion to be persuaded to join the
Workers' Unity League to give the red union central its first
skeletal form in 1930–31."[52] Birney's role was a tiny—one might
say inescapably futile—one. It was, in fact, a role within a role
within a role. As a Trotskyist he was opposed to Stalinist
Communism, which, in turn, opposed the social democracy
movement in Canada represented by the CCF. Though Birney

could not espouse the CCF cause, he was equally wary of the
revolutionary fervour of the Workers' Unity League, which was
the central core of the movement of "Red" trade unionists in
B.C. in the 1930s. His ideological position was tougher than
that of the CCF, but more complex, international and idealistic
than Stalinist doctrines. And, quite apart from the ideological
position to which he was deeply committed, the challenge of
operating as a sort of "double agent" spying on both Communist
and socialist activities under a pseudonym to build up a new
brotherhood of comrades challenged his managerial talents and
his imaginative intellect to the hilt. He found ways to recruit
from his UBC classes to start up a YCL study class two nights a
week: twenty to twenty-five students that were "the supposed
'pick' of the 200 YCLers in the town," and used his position to
attract new members, including even that most unlikely candidate for Communism, his old flame Jessie MacPhail. "We're
starting with the *Manifesto*," he reported to Ken. "Later I think
they want me to take up [Alexander] Losovky's *Problems of Strike
Strategy* etc. which ought to force me to show my hateful Trotsky
horns. By that time, perhaps I can exert a little influence on the
tender minds. If I don't work hard, however, those same minds
may grow to realize how abysmal is my own ignorance."[53] His
own reading included John Strachey's *Coming Struggle for Power*
and Sidney Hook's *Towards the Understanding of Karl Marx.*[54]

That Birney had time to read these political tracts or anything
at all other than the works he was teaching at UBC was astonish-
ing. Not only was his eyesight continuing to plague him, but he
was also teaching for the first time Jane Austen's *Pride and
Prejudice*, Sir Walter Scott's *Old Mortality*, Oliver Goldsmith's
The Vicar of Wakefield, Richard Sheridan's *The School for Scandal*,
Euripides' *The Bacchae*, Henrik Ibsen's *A Doll's House* and
William Shakespeare's *Julius Caesar.*[55]

Even here he found ways of disseminating left-wing ideas.
"Very glad you've been sliding some of the class struggle into
Eng. II," he wrote Daniells, who was doing his best to convince
the Johnstones to change their opinion of him as *not* a Marxist
nor a revolutionary.[56] "*Robinson Crusoe* is excellent evidence. So
is *The Vicar of Wakefield*."[57]

And once Sylvia arrived, he somehow found time to court her, showing her the Vancouver sights. "Since the very day I came I haven't been home one single evening," she wrote Roy on 25 July in a letter composed during a Socialist meeting.

> The very day I arrived Earle had a full timetable planned. We've gone out every afternoon too. To-day we went to the Suspension bridges & climbed down to the bottom of the canyon—the river was teeming with salmon about 2 feet long—they jumped right out of the water every few seconds. Went to Stanley Park & walked all through it, saw Seven Sisters, Siwash Rock—totem poles, gathered sea-shells, saw a big long snake. Have been bathing twice.[58]

Sylvia attended Earle's lectures (including one in which he gave a Marxist interpretation of 1760–1830 literature) and—at his urging—Doc Sedgewick's. (He called her in jest an "Impudent Young Hussy"; she thought him "the finest bourgeois specimen Birney [has] yet produced.") She visited his friends; she "piloted" Mrs. Birney around the public gardens.

But Birney's strenuous schedule wore her out. "Both Earle and Mrs. Birney direct my time," Minnehaha lamented to her Puck. "I have hardly any time to myself & you know how that is something unusual for me—sometimes I ache for home.... We're always tearing around like mad here and everything is punctual you know how blighting to my soul that would be."[59] Even when she was sick and wanted to go to bed, the Birneys were relentless: "both Earle and Mrs. Birney wanted to drag me off this evening," she wrote her brother,

> Earle to a YCL study group & Mrs. Birney to her sister Cissie's. I refused tho' I think Mrs. Birney's peeved about it—no fooling that woman is a Tartar—Earle says I get along with her better than anyone else— Well, I'd hate to get along with her badly then. She goes on about Communism something terrible & told me last night that I'd darn soon be a capitalist if I had

the chance it was just envy that was biting me & a lot
of other nice things like that—she and Earle fight like
the dickins [sic] too, I'd love to get away from here. I'd
come home like a shot only for the work here.[60]

On another occasion, she confessed her relief at having an
evening alone; "but it won't be for long. Mrs. Birney soon gets
bored with her sister & then back she'll come. You see Mrs.
Birney thinks that if you take a book up to read your [sic] just
wasting time or else your sulking & she'll find something for you
to do.... Earle says she was always like that with him & he
always hated his home & got away from it when he was sixteen.
I can fully understand why."[61]

Though there was one troubling incident when Earle exploded
at Sylvia because she refused to write a long outline on the early
nineteenth century European statesman François Guizot and
Prince von Metternich for a speech he was to give, a "fearful battle" that made her long for Daniells's "calm serenity,"[62] the two
revolutionaries worked hard and happy for the Trotsky cause.
They persuaded a second "newsie" to sell their journals: Bruno
Censie of 163 West Hastings at the corner of Cambie.[63] "We
have been taking turns hanging around the newsstand trying to
get contacts with workers interested in the *Militant*," she
reported to Daniells in a letter signed Minnehaha. "We made
quite a few contacts.... I met a woman about 30 years of age
Comrade [Lizzie] Campbell. Through her I joined the Women's
& Girls' Club & was made Secretary...there's twenty dollars in
the treasury too! They've elected me as the club's representative
to a Worker's Training School to study economics & oratory
to...train promising workers to be leaders! What do you think of
that?"[64] Only Sylvia's voice disappointed Birney: it faded whenever she was nervous. Otherwise she really was like Rosa
Luxemburg, and he gloried in her.

By the end of the summer at Ken's request, Birney submitted a
formal report to the Toronto branch of the International Left
Opposition that recommended Sylvia's acceptance as a member.
Comrade Sylvia Johnstone and Comrade Earle Robertson had
established a tiny Trotskyist nucleus. "On [September 13th] we

took formally into the organization two comrades: Dave Olsen [a forty-year-old revolutionary worker within the local lumbermen's unions, strike organizer & former CP member in charge of literature] and Jim Sheridan [a twenty-one-year-old YCL study group leader who had excelled in Birney's group] and constituted about them a group which has pledged itself to work for the breakup of the local bureaucracy and for the application of correct Marxist-Leninist tactics to the work in British Columbia and internationally, and are prepared to study the platform and literature of the Left Opposition with a view to becoming actual members."[65] These four were Fred Grange, a forty-year-old organizer of the Deroche [Relief] Camp strike the previous June; A.M. Stephen, a fifty-year-old history and English teacher with twenty-five years' experience in the old SPC; Comrade Peever, a fifty-year-old organizer of B.C. relief camp strikes; Comrade "Tom," a thirty-year-old trade unionist; Tom Bissett, an Irish worker in South Vancouver who circulated left-wing pamphlets, but steered clear of any party; and Comrade A. Zen, a new female recruit whom Birney had met only once, but who was said to have several Ukrainian comrades. The later cast of characters and events in *Down the Long Table* bore an uncanny resemblance to this report.

By the end of summer, too, despite the fact that Sylvia had kept up a flirtatious correspondence with Daniells, Sylvia agreed to marry Earle and move with him to "the rural idiocy of Utah" to set up another nucleus. Early in the summer she had confided to Ken that she was "not romantically in love [with Earle], but [was]...very fond of him," possibly because, as she also wrote, "in this 'Get your woman business' he could show the Mounted Police force *plenty*. The idea is utilize every weak moment & then hold them to their word." She would be back "without the ring": "I can't say I'm dying to get my feet in the glue."[66] But by late August, she had succumbed.

In a testy letter to Daniells whose oblique courting of Sylvia had reached what Birney thought were absurd proportions (three letters from Daniells had just arrived, one of which was black-edged to indicate Daniells's "mourning" for his lost love), Birney asserted his victory.

I think your sending such an envelope was a piece of damfoolery quite unworthy of you. It seems to have sprung out of a *reductio ad absurdum* of your pose of being the Courtly Lover.... why don't you love the girl honestly, and be honest with me too.... We are going to be married.... I am very anxious that neither Sylvia nor I should lose any of our friends simply because we decided to live and work together under a bourgeois dispensation. Gain or loss of friends will be decided by their acceptance or rejection of us as revolutionaries.... Are you willing to read and to work for communism when you are utterly remote from the Toronto circle, and have no hope of marrying Sylvia? ...For God's sake, take a genuine *intellectual* interest in communism. Read the *Manifesto*, read *Wage Labour & Capitalism*, read Engels' *Comm[unist] Utopia & Scientific*, read books on Russia, read Trotsky, read and subscribe to Marxist publications, join the comm[unist] party in England, or the L.O. if you can find it and can't get along in the Party. But *do* something... I don't want to quarrell [sic] with you Roy, ...It's rotten luck you should have fallen in love with S. too, and I feel like a cad talking so severely to you when I have all the happiness.... If I really didn't care, you see, I wouldn't write you at all.[67]

The plan was that Sylvia would return to Toronto and persuade her mother to allow her to marry Earle. But first, he wanted to show her Salt Lake City. With the ever-vigilant Mrs. Birney in the back seat, they drove through "a desert dust storm in Idaho which choked our carburetor for awhile and gave us the sensation of being choked too."[68] According to a much later account, the nearer they got to Salt Lake City, the more Earle tried to persuade her to marry him—not later, but at once.

One of the ways Earle tried to persuade Sylvia was by telling her that if it was found out by the principal of his university that he had travelled with such a young

woman, he would lose his job. It was such a scandalous thing to do. And it's not difficult to believe that
in that Mormon city it would be outrageous. And
finally, just before they reached Salt Lake City in the
late afternoon, Sylvia decided to agree, if the licence
office was still open. She would marry him, but she
would have to go home that same day and tell her
mother. After putting his mother on a train back to
Vancouver, he dashed off to the licence office, came
back with the licence, and they proceeded to find a
minister and set up the marriage.

Though Sylvia was only nineteen, he must have lied at the
licence office, for the newspaper announcement of their wedding
gave her age as twenty-one[69]—the legal minimum age for marriage without parental consent. Sylvia much later recalled her
distress at the speed with which Earle had precipitated events.
"As soon as the car pulled up to the office, I started to cry and
Earle dashed out and got me an ice-cream cone. And so all
through the wedding I licked this ice-cream cone and that's how
we got married. After the marriage, Earle took me to the station
and I was put on the train for Toronto. It was the most miserable
trip because he forgot to give me any money." The marriage was
never consummated. Sylvia would later refer to this episode as
"the fours hours of marriage."[70]

~§ 9 §~

A BURNING ISSUE

Taking advantage of a four-day college recess for American Thanksgiving at the beginning of December 1933, a small but determined cohort comprised of two University of Utah faculty and six students[1] set off by car to check out Carbon County, about one hundred miles south-east of Salt Lake City. The faculty member at the wheel was Earle Birney. The group was called "The Sparks," a name Birney had pirated from the radical student newspaper *The Spark* at the University of Toronto. Their mission was to investigate firsthand the scandalous aftermath of the coal-miners' strike which had made local headlines.[2]

The strike was one of many plaguing such U.S. states as Kentucky, Pennsylvania, Illinois and New Mexico. It had begun as a peaceful march to present petitions to county commissioners about such grievances as irregular pay, virtually mandatory use of company scrip at stores where food prices were inflated by 50 per cent, intolerable working conditions in the mines and equally intolerable living conditions in the Carbon County Camp. Trouble had resulted when differences arose between two unions. "Civilian Marshall Law" had been declared, and somewhere between one hundred and three hundred (reports differed) deputies—some as young as fifteen—had been appointed and

117

armed with tear gas, rifles and hoses. Picketers had been assaulted; the strike leaders had been charged with "criminal syndicalism" (the equivalent of Canada's Section 98 at the time) and jailed, along with a dozen or so other strikers. There were allegations of homes roughly entered at night, rifle-butt assaults on women and men alike, threats of shooting, seizures without warrants. In late September, a committee of Salt Lake City's more liberal citizens had sent a number of resolutions in protest to President Roosevelt, the state's Governor Blood and Sheriff Bliss, among others, as well as to the press.[3]

Now, on 1 December, the little delegation of Sparks "crashed the headlines" of Salt Lake City's papers.[4] The university's president, George Thomas, who held stock in some of the mines involved, was not amused. He had done all he could to crush the enterprise, cancelling outright The Sparks' charter as a student organization and ordering them bluntly to cancel the trip. But Birney had ignored his fulminations, claiming he and his group were acting as "private citizens." And he shrewdly refused to accept an offer from the National Miners' Union to pay their expenses.

Birney and his Sparks returned after two days, jubilant. Not only had they discovered that the allegations were largely true, but in their absence, the Sparks whose parents had forbidden them to go had succeeded in circulating a petition among faculty and city liberals protesting the president's suspension of their club. Thomas reinstated The Sparks on one condition: that they restrict future activities to campus. Their response? An open report of their findings in Carbon County—including Birney's criticism of the "ultra-leftist and ill-timed policies of the National Miners' Union in Carbon"[5]—at their next club meeting. "The result has been not only a good deal of publicity for the miners' plight," he wrote to Arne Swabeck,[6] an editor at the *Militant* in New York, "but also a great strengthening of my reputation in the C[ommunist] P[arty] locally and in general working class circles in Salt Lake. I intend to cash in on this...by pressing our point of view at party meetings. The *Student Review* is presumably accepting a 7000 word story of mine on the trip."[7]

Birney had prepared the inflammatory expedition of The

Sparks cagily. Immediately on returning to Utah with Sylvia, he had assembled half a dozen former students for a weekly study group, soon adding to this core any student worker or even any young capitalist between age fifteen and thirty he could enlist. His texts were Karl Marx's *The Communist Manifesto*, Friedrich Engels's *Socialism, Utopian and Scientific*, and pamphlets on contemporary problems—especially the increasingly alarming situation in Germany. Within a month, an average of fifteen students attended each meeting, some of them tempted, perhaps, by Birney's social lures such as wiener roasts and plays. He next persuaded them to draw up a constitution and apply for official status as a college club to host speakers interested in social problems from faculty and downtown. He himself addressed the first meeting of The Sparks on "Russia's Challenge to Students." "Our immediate practical aim," he wrote J.P. Cannon, another *Militant* editor in New York and secretary of the Communist League of America, "is to arouse interest in Carbon County conditions. Next week we build up 'respectability' by presenting a socialist preacher and prominent reformist in the state to explain fascism. (I'm going to coach him a bit beforehand to make sure there's no hitch.) The next week we're having Crouch, NMU organizer of the Carbon strike."[8] The preacher's talk attracted a record audience of fifty; at the end of Crouch's talk, by prearrangement, Birney proposed the Carbon County delegation.

The day before he defiantly led his Sparks to Carbon County, Birney and three of his most dedicated comrades sent off their applications to New York for the cards that would make them official members of the Communist Party.[9] While he made this major political decision and readied himself for the Carbon trip, on his desk lay a letter from Harry Cassidy, the Toronto economics professor (and former Berkeley graduate student) at whose home he had first felt drawn to the Trotsky cause, asking for money to support Canada's League for Social Reconstruction and gently chiding him: "What luck have you had as a lone Communist among your Mormon friends?"[10] At the end of December, in a letter that exaggerated somewhat his success as a Left Opposition (LO) organizer ("I've now got a political discussion club with about fifty members, including several from the faculty"),[11] he stated that he would probably be fired as a result of his trip to Carbon County, and, though he well knew that the CCF were rapidly gaining ground in B.C., politely declined to contribute to the LSR, the organization which had given rise to the CCF.

Birney's openness in the Carbon County venture and his new status as a card-carrying member of the Communist Party—under the pseudonym of Paul Robertson—in early 1934 marked his definite commitment to the Trotskyist vision of a new world order. That vision—at least as it specifically applied to him—issued from Toronto and New York. From Toronto, Jack MacDonald had written: "A decision seems to have been made internationally to lay the foundations for the organization of a new international. This will make our own work of even greater importance and at the same time sharpen the fight between the Stalinists and ourselves, so no stone can be left unturned."[12] And in New York, J.P. Cannon, who had heard all about Birney's activities in Utah from Maurice Spector and the Johnstones on a recent visit to Toronto, had written: "It will be of the greatest importance for our movement to get a stable nucleus established in Salt Lake City as that will be another connecting link on the coast. Recently we have formed several new branches in California and if we get good connections in Denver and Salt Lake, it will make a tour [for LO speakers] to the coast feasible."[13] In setting up a Trotskyist nucleus in Salt Lake City, just as he had in Vancouver, Birney was forging an important link in the chain of cities in which the potential for a North American workers' revolution could gradually be realized and—through educating uninformed students, disconsolate workers and even the odd disillusioned bourgeoisie—was laying a small part of the organizational groundwork through which a Fourth International might one day come to be.

His energy and ingenuity was prodigious. He contacted everyone he could think of, not only his old Toronto and Vancouver comrades, with whom he continued to debate Marxist theory and local practice by mail, but also those who were spearheading the U.S. movement: B.J. Field at Pioneer Publishers, the New York disseminator of LO books, pamphlets and other materials;

S.L. Solon, university editor, and Gilbert Frank at *Modern Monthly*; James P. Cannon, T. Stamm and Arne Swabeck, editors of the *Militant*; Joe Carter, secretary of the National Youth Committee of the Communist League of America and editor of their publication *The Young Spartacus*; Fred Zelman of the National Student League (NSL); and Theodore Draper, associate editor of the *Student Review*. All responded to Birney's overtures. Who else in Salt Lake City subscribed to *Modern Monthly*? No one. How should he link his Sparks with a national organization, and which one? "Let us say you plan an anti-war conference," replied Draper, who advised joining the NSL. "'Sparks' takes the lead. 'Sparks' is not NSL. But there will be members of NSL in 'Sparks.' The NSL meeting will be devoted to thrashing out problems of the conference before they reach the floor of 'Sparks,' being the leading and most energetic workers in 'Sparks' etc. In this way, 'Sparks' will be won piece-meal. It must be emphasized that the NSL must, on no account, be hidden."[14] "Of course," Birney responded, "if I hadn't been so Don Quixotish I would have arrived at it for myself long ago."[15] S.L. Solon, on the other hand, urged Birney to groom The Sparks so that they could eventually join the Spartacus Youth Clubs under the LO.

What Birney wanted most of all was to obtain LO publications: both for what he called "the baby branch" in Vancouver, which he ran by remote control through Dave Olsen, and for his new nucleus in Utah. Despite the fact that he was teaching English courses and supposedly preparing his Ph.D. thesis on Chaucer, and despite the fact that he still had "a pair of violently protesting eyes,"[16] he dedicated most of his time and energy and money to the LO cause. The booklist he ordered in September from Pioneer Publishers (and which cost him the hefty sum of $14.55) was typical: *The Permanent Revolution, The Real Situation in Russia, The Draft Program of the Communist International, The Strategy of the World Revolution, World Unemployment and the Five-Year Plan, Communism and Syndicalism, The Revolution in Spain, The Spanish Revolution in Danger, Problems of the Chinese Revolution, History of the Russian Revolution* (3 vols), *Whither England?, In Defense of the Russian*

Revolution, Schachman: *The Left-Opposition,* and Swabeck: *Unemployment and the American Working Class.*[17]

Nor was Birney content simply to have such publications himself. He drew on his friendships in Toronto, Vancouver and Berkeley—some almost amusingly bourgeois, like Garnett Sedgewick or Hendrie Gartshore and Barbara Barrett—to provide mailing lists for left-wing publishers to disseminate their information. He listed six English professors, a chemist, a psychologist and an electrical engineer from the University of Utah's faculty—"at least liberal elements with sufficient means to subscribe"; two Salt Lake City comrades—Emerson Sturdevant and Joel Nibley; three UBC English faculty—W.L. Macdonald and Stella Lewis, in addition to Sedgewick—and their colleagues, historians A.C. Cooke and F. Soward, and economist Henry Angus; at Toronto he targeted Harry Cassidy, economists Lorne T. Morgan and J. Parkinson, and the Chairman of English at University College, R.S. Knox, an Aberdonian with an Oxford veneer; at McGill he sought the support of sociologist Everett Hughes and his wife, his old UBC friend Helen McGill Hughes; economist Allen Buchanan at Berkeley was listed; and "some scattered addresses"—not only Barbara Barrett's, but also his former roommate Herman Singer's, now at Berkeley; Sallee Creighton in Toronto; H.R. Offord, a Vancouver friend now working in a lab at Berkeley; and former UBC friends—Mary Duncan Carter, now in Montreal; Geoffrey Bruun, a historian at New York State University; also Hilton Moore in Washington; and Carman Sing in New York. It was an impressive and rapidly expanding network.

Birney's New York contacts were dazzled by his meteoric drive. "It is quite remarkable," Solon wrote in October, "that in such a short time you have managed to gather about you a number of students and young workers interested in Marxism." A month later he added, "You are certainly carrying on your work at an amazing pace!"[18] "I admire very much your true fire and activities," wrote Viktoria Lorenz, a German Doctor of Law in flight from fascism, for whom Birney had gone to endless trouble in arranging a lecture tour for her talks on behalf of the National Committee in Aid of Victims of Fascism. "It would be only good," she went on in her broken English, "if we had not only in Salt Lake City but everywhere and especially in each university people like you.... I only fear...that you might be too careless and lose your position which gives you just this great power and influence."[19] It was a thought that had already occurred to Birney.

But compared to the real work of igniting young minds, desperate workers and liberal-minded bourgeoisie to the Marxist-Leninist ideas that would defeat Stalinism and transform the world from the destructive economic grip of capitalism and the devastating impact of fascism to an equitable, classless society, the English courses that had challenged Birney when he began at Utah now seemed pallid and remote. "I...am chiefly occupied this winter with sub-normal freshmen," he wrote disconsolately to Sedgewick in one of the few letters of his that year that were not specifically Trotskyist, "...and disgruntled pre-medics whose dean has gone cultural and demanded from his fledglings a knowledge of English literary masterpieces."[20] Despite the fact that he was trapped by an English syllabus he had no hand in designing, he began to find ways—such as exposing the social and political biases of an author or letting a class debate on fascism supplant the day's lesson—to "slide in" (as he put it) his LO beliefs. This meant a recasting of his courses that involved extra preparation.

No wonder he griped to Ken Johnstone by November, "I find myself wishing I were three people. There's this campus group, our L.O. faction, the CP, the Marxian class, my looming duties as agit-prop head, work with Belle Taub [an organizer] in the I.L.D., my classes, my themes [to mark], a tough course in modern poetry coming up (I have to read literally hundreds of modern poets before March), my thesis, and all my background reading.... I've read [Isaac Don] Levine's *Stalin*, and am practically finished with [Leon] Trotsky's *My Life*. I'm also reading [Vladimir Lenin's] 'What is to be Done,' 'Left-Wing Communism,' [*Left-Wing Communism, an Infantile Disorder*], [Leon Trotsky's] 'Whither England,' some Marxian study courses, 'Humanity Uprooted,' [Alexander Dunlop] Lindsay's introduction to 'Capital' [*Karl Marx's Capital; an Introductory Essay*] and some others."[21]

Birney was not only pondering that winter what was to be done with the world's economic and political system. He was also wondering what was to be done about his wife, Sylvia. She had not returned from Toronto, where she had fled in dismay after their ignominious "four hours of marriage." Her mother was firmly opposed to the marriage and had refused to allow Sylvia to rejoin him.[22] At first, Birney had hoped that she still loved him. But now she was pleading that physical problems prevented her from travelling. Perhaps something was seriously wrong—an appendix? Or a cyst? Perhaps she had been too immature emotionally at nineteen to leave her mother? He suggested that she and Mrs. J. come out at Christmas and that Mrs. J. stay on for a few months. But as the weeks passed and his distress that his marital victory over Roy Daniells may have been pyrrhic, he began to doubt that she had ever really loved him: "Believe it or not," he wrote Ken, who had been feeding him bulletins about his sister, "the worm is turning. Sylvia, and you, and I, have all been periodically concerned about whether she loved me or not. Lately, I've begun to give myself a break. You say, 'cement the real love, *which is growing.*' Growing where? To be quite frank, my little plant of affection seems to be drooping. Somehow, the actual facts obtrude more and more between the assurances; e.g., Sylvia's boundless and growing love urged her to put a major portion of the continent between us; her letters grow thinner and fewer; as Christmas approaches, talk of seeing me here fades beyond even a perceptible whisper. Personally, I'm interested in life in this world."[23] To his mother, to whom he had turned in distress, he wrote: "I have done nothing about an annullment [sic] yet.... I intend to write Ken soon and explain the whole thing...as he is capable of dealing intelligently with the matter, and has always tried to make Sylvia see things properly. There is no use writing Sylvia because she would not even answer, nor present my case fairly to her family.... There is little use in writing Mrs. Johnstone. She has no control over Sylvia, nor has anyone else.[24] On 20 November, he made one last effort—"a 4,500-word invitation to the dance"—to persuade her to return, but added in a separate letter a request and an angry warning to Ken that suggested that Birney found Sylvia's revolutionary ideas limited in one respect at least: "I agree with your remarks about the inconvenience of testicles. I've never known any eunuchs that I recognized.... Perhaps they don't lose fire after all. The trouble is not with our balls, dear Brutus, but with the ubiquitous bourgeois and his hypocritical sex training. If Sylvia had never been infected with the racial heritage of sex superstition and misinformation and unhealthy psychophysical reactions, things would be a good deal different. Can't you dig out one good sex book from somewhere and make her understand it? Havelock Ellis, say.... Well, she may be the new Rosa Luxemburg, but if she doesn't value me, it won't be long before I'll stop valuing her.... In the meantime, look after that gal. If she needs her appendix examined take her to a doc—and not an osteopath either. Send me the bill. Make her exercise if you have to throw her downstairs."[25]

Sylvia and Mrs. J. did not come for Christmas. Instead, Birney took refuge with "the only woman who has never lied to me, my mother."[26] He spent what he called "the bourgeois vacation" "rejuvenating" the "baby branch" of the LO there, which in his absence had diminished to a mere flicker.

Back at Utah for the spring, he singed more feathers. Taking a Marxist approach to his second review of the student literary magazine *Pen*, he "told the students to stop writing coy verses to the moon or empty stories about their adolescent sex life and realize that the great literary material today was the great struggle against capitalism and for collectivism."[27] The editor, a banker's son backed by a wealthy college fraternity, refused publication. "I have protested to the Faculty Publication Council and am forcing him to print it," Birney wrote Viktoria Lorenz with impish glee, despite a bout of hay fever. "It must all sound very childish to you, and of course it is, but it's fun for me. I may even split the fraternity here. The downtown papers are playing it up."[28] In the end, President Thomas intervened to back the editor against the Publications Council and Birney. "My only revenge," Birney wrote Lorenz, "was to expose it in a public lecture[29] I gave downtown shortly afterwards. The *Student Outlook*—a left-socialist college monthly in New York is printing a story...on it. But locally I am defeated."[30] The Sparks, however, triumphantly circulated a petition that engaged 60 per cent of the student body—approximately 1,800 signatures—to transform the college bookstore (Birney had accused the bookstore of "graft and corruption") into a co-operative, profit-sharing enterprise.[31] And Birney arranged visits that spring from the "hard-boiled"[32] Max Shachtman, a *Militant* editor who had been refused entry into Canada; Monroe Sweetland, from the American Socialist Party who represented the Student League for Industrial Democracy; and Walter Relis, a student activist from Cuba. In the end, mainly because he was impressed with Sweetland, but not at all with Relis, he opted to align The Sparks with the Student League for Industrial Democracy. As many of his correspondents acknowledged, Birney left the Salt Lake City branch in good shape.[33] Even years later, he was still remembered as the one responsible for "an assortment of redhots off the iridium tip of the [LO] vanguard." As one correspondent put it to Birney, "As far as I could make out, your footprints on the sands of whatchacallem *are* intellectual Salt Lake. I wonder what it would have been hadn't you ever been there."[34]

By the time Birney left Salt Lake City, the question of whether he would be rehired by the university was a moot point.[35] So was any question of accepting the appointment he had been offered in New York to work on the Trotskyist party newspaper, the *New International.*[36] Thanks to Pelham Edgar at Toronto, he had won a Royal Society of Canada Fellowship of $1,500 to complete his thesis at the University of London, England. While he waited in Vancouver that summer, he worked on the one hand—his right, as he jested[37]—to advance his Ph.D. thesis, and gave on the other hand—his left—LO speeches. Dodging both the RCMP[38] and the Stalinites who were keeping an eye on him, and rekindling his Vancouver nucleus from four to twelve, Birney was impatient for the freighter that would take him via the Panama Canal to London on the 19th of August, not so much to complete his thesis on Chaucer in England, but mainly so that he could continue his LO work in Europe.

He sensed that it was a momentous turning point. Before leaving, having just turned thirty that May, he made out his first will: all his property in Salt Lake City was to go to his brightest Spark, Reinhold Smith, in trust for the Communist League of

America; the rest of his property, including his car and his bank accounts, was to go to his mother; should his mother die before him, it was to go to Jack MacDonald in trust for the Workers' Party of Canada. "Ken...has talked to you about the possibilities of my being of service in France," he wrote Maurice Spector before he left, "and perhaps I realize the multiple handicaps, especially in regard to the language and to greenness in the movement, which will keep me from doing much; but what I can do I want to. Naturally, too," he added, picturing himself in Europe at last and within striking distance of Trotsky himself, "I'd like nothing better than to meet the Old Man."[39]

~§ *10* §~

RIPE FOR ENGLAND

On the 27th of September 1934, Earle Birney arrived in England feeling all life laid out before him. His excitement as he stood peering with his weak eyes through the dark at 2:30 a.m. on the deck of the freighter *S.S. Filleigh*, which had chugged down from Vancouver Island on the 19th of August, past Washington, California and Mexico, through the sweltering muggy heat of the Panama Canal, then across the Atlantic and up into the cool North Sea, was palpable. "Yesterday morning early (2:30 a.m.) we sighted the Bishop Rock Light, on the Scilly Isles—the farthest west of England," he wrote later that day to his mother, who had taken him there when he was six. "I woke to find we were opposite the cliffs of Hastings. By noon I was taking pictures of the white cliffs of Dover, and watching innumerable trawlers of all countries...dipping their sharp prows into the heavy swell."[1] So great was Birney's sense of importance and so diligent the wide-ranging journals he sent home that he admonished his mother to save them for future publication.

The vote of confidence in Birney's scholarship represented by the Royal Society Fellowship—especially during those lean years of the Great Depression—was enormous. In his letter of congratulations, Pelham Edgar, the Toronto professor whose recommendation was

128

instrumental in Birney's success, spelled out his expectations. Birney was to find "responsible supervision" for his thesis on Chaucer's irony at Queen Mary College of the University of London; if he could do so without paying the seventeen-pound fee (Birney's idea), so much the better; he was to report on his progress to Edgar every couple of months. With restrained, almost fatherly affection, Pelham added: "You are ripe for England and I shall be interested to hear of your adventures. So please sometimes on a separate sheet the personal touch."[2]

Birney seized what London had to offer as if it were but another mountain range to be conquered and he a lanky colossus striding from one pinnacle to the next. Despite his "first English cold" and a keen determination to hoard his money, within less than two weeks he had managed to see Regent's Park, Admiralty Arch, Buckingham Palace, the Parliament Buildings, Big Ben, the BBC, All Souls' Church, Canada House (where he glimpsed R.B. Bennett and High Commissioner Ferguson and ran into old Toronto fellow-student Alfred Bailey, who also had a Royal Society Fellowship), Westminster Abbey, the International Exhibition of Inventions at Central Hall, the models and children's toys in the Science Museum, and the Old Curiosity Shop immortalized by Charles Dickens. He had walked by day through Piccadilly Circus, Leicester Square, Oxford and Regent streets (where he bought his mother a Liberty scarf for her birthday), High Holborn, Tottenham Court Road, Pall Mall, Chancery Lane, Seven Dials, Soho, the Strand, Marble Arch and across Westminster Bridge. And he had strolled by night through Fleet Street, along the Victoria Embankment (where he saw Waterloo Bridge, Cleopatra's Needle and the statue of Boadicea). He had stood under Nelson's column, where his father had stood during the war, and mused on the Landseer lions cast from guns recovered from the wreck of the *Royal George*, and watched the sheep graze in Green Park before taking a bus along Park Lane and another over the Holborn Viaduct.

Despite the fact that he was thirty, Birney's letters to his mother give a singularly boyish impression. He is elaborately solicitous of her birthday; he reports every detail of the English flower gardens, promising to send her seeds; he tells her his most minute physical complaints and eating habits; he enumerates every detail of his expenses, even "an eight-penny haircut (plus tupenny tip)";[3] he reports he has located an adviser, Dr. B. Ifor Evans, and focuses dutifully on the work he immediately undertook in the British Museum. Just as he had in the Creston Bank at age seventeen, he seemed in his letters home to have become every bit what his parents had hoped for: an upstanding middle-class citizen with a profession and experiences far above either of theirs.

But there were rumblings that suggested his volcanic nature could not be contained in this role. The breadth and detail of his observations on ranging all over London indicated that he fostered interests more vast and curiosities more probing than any thesis topic—no matter how fascinating—could satisfy. His delight in sheer physical activity, now a habit from years of camping, farming, mountain-climbing, hiking and jobs involving tough physical labour, guaranteed he would feel restless and imprisoned at a desk. His horror of loneliness—recalled all too well from a childhood spent too much by himself—can be felt in his long letters to his mother, the only woman, for the moment, to whom he felt close. He had urged Catherine Fisk to leave her husband and come with him, but she had sensibly refused.[4] He had soon found a casual woman, a pretty theatre usher named Thelma Spackman, but this affair did little to alleviate his sense of an inner abyss. His eyes suffered from long and concentrated reading. Above all, to withdraw from the exciting swirl of contemporary politics into the serene calm of the Reading Room of the British Museum with its Wedgewood blue dome was no heavenly zenith for his brilliant mind; it was like being entombed. "I rest my eyes," he wrote his mother, "by leaving the Reading Room and wandering among the countless exhibits in this greatest museum in the world."[5] His letters home recount endless temptations that draw him from his thesis (a visit to the Tower, the Lord Mayor's parade, plays) and record virtually no enthusiasm for the thesis itself. "There seems no end to the work I must do," he wrote petulantly, "every time I open a book I find a reference to two other books I haven't seen. The worst of this museum is that it contains everything you want—you can't excuse yourself on the grounds that they haven't got the book anyway, the way I could in other places."[6]

Earle Birney was ripe for England, but—much as he tried—not quite in the way Pelham Edgar and his mother expected. Politics, not scholastics, engaged his heart and soul. Comrade Earle Robertson, not Earle Birney aspiring Ph.D., was in the ascendant. As he had intended all along, the ardent radical quickly sought out Trotskyist comrades because of his commitment to the Fourth International and his keen desire to render service to the great cause. Within two weeks of his arrival in London, on 12 October, he had made contact with a small group of Trotskyists and headed off to the Plenum of the International Communist League in Paris with two of them, Denzil Harber and Stuart Kirby, a recent graduate of the London School of Economics. Harber and Kirby were leading members of a small group called "the minority" which was in the process of forming the "Marxist group in the Independent Labour Party" as a means of organizing their supporters in that party. Harber and Kirby, who spoke French and assured Robertson that they could find cheap accommodations in Paris, provided an ideal entrée at an opportune moment into the international political theatre. One of the central issues at the Plenum was whether or not to accept Trotsky's advice to the French Trotskyists to join the French Socialist Party as a tactic—the so-called "French turn"—by which they might extend their influence in a milieu which could be expected at that time to be favourable to their ideas.[7] According to John Archer, a comrade of Harber and Kirby's who decades later wrote a Ph.D. thesis on British Trotskyism in the 1930s, "It may be that [Robertson] found the meeting so stimulating partly because he had an important contribution of his own to make to it, not merely with his political experience in Utah and in Canada behind him, but as a voice from the New World supporting the 'French turn.'"[8]

The political group known as "the minority" into which Birney stumbled that fall of 1934 was at a key stage in its own evolution. It had emerged as a "minority" in the first Trotskyist group in Britain, which had itself come into existence in the fall of 1932 after its founders were expelled from the Communist Party. That first group had begun to call itself "The Communist

League" in the summer of 1933. At about the same time, Trotsky had suggested to its members that they should join the Independent Labour Party (ILP) which had broken away from the control of the Labour Party at the end of July 1932. Since then, sentiments were being expressed in the League in favour of Stalinism and pacifism, an influence Trotsky feared would be disastrous, as indeed it was. However, the older members of the Communist League did not want to abandon their independent existence to enter the ILP. To the disappointment of Trotsky, who hoped the Communist League would be politically mature enough to accommodate members both within and without the ILP, a split occurred in December 1933 between those who wanted to apply the idea of the "French turn" to join the ILP and those who did not. It was "the minority" who abandoned the Communist League and joined the ILP.[9] Now, just as Robertson appeared in their midst, "the minority" had drawn around themselves those members of the ILP who had showed varying degrees of sympathy for Trotsky's ideas to form the "Marxist Group in the ILP."

On his return to London and Paris, Robertson moved into Kirby's flat at 18 Harpur Street and eagerly took part at meetings of the Holborn and Finsbury branch of the ILP to which Kirby and Harber belonged, one of four local branches in London.[10] There, among the sixty or so comrades comprising these four groups (they occasionally met jointly), he quickly aligned himself with those few (fifteen or so) who in early October, just days before he had joined them, had formed the Marxist Group at a meeting of the Clapham branch of the ILP, at which Bert Matlow—soon to become a friend of Robertson's—and other supporters of Trotsky, had presided. "To join," according to John Archer, "you had to agree to work to persuade the members of the ILP to agree to break off the relations of the ILP with Stalinism and pacifism—or, in a certain sense, to go through the experience of trying [to see] whether this was possible—because [we] thought, not inaccurately, that these relations were leading the ILP to self-destruction." The Marxist Group also wanted to put an end to running independent candidates in elections in which an ILP candidate could split the working-class vote and thereby enable a candidate from a bourgeois party to win. And long-range, the Group hoped to present the revolutionary aims of the Trotskyists in terms of the immediate concerns of the working people—such as pay, job security, housing and peace— and thereby mobilize workers apart from the "official" leaders and, ultimately, test by experience how far the "official" Labour leaders would go in meeting their demands. It was not, however, necessary for new members of the Marxist Group to accept the call for a Fourth International because it was expected that that would be the predictable outcome of experience in the group: "to accept the other two points—a break with Stalinism and a 'turn' to the rank and file of the Labour Party—[and to take part in the] common struggle for these, soon convinced earlier doubters that the call for the Fourth International was a necessary one and consistent with their general views," observes Archer.[11]

Almost immediately after Robertson, Harber and Kirby returned from Paris, it became necessary for the British Trotskyists to formalize their relations with the International Secretariat of the International Communist League in Paris. According to Archer, "Documents coming from [the secretariat] were arriving by post, and decisions had to be reached about how, to whom and by whom these documents were to be distributed. At this stage the question of a central direction of the work of the ILP had not yet presented itself, as it would in the spring of 1935, when the preparations had to be planned to intervene in the ILP's annual conference at Easter, by which time everyone was agreed about the [desirability of the] Fourth International."[12]

It was at a meeting held at 18 Harpur Street two months later, in December 1934, that twelve members of the Marxist Group (informally called the "inner group"), including Earle Robertson, Denzil Harber, Stuart Kirby, John Archer, Bert Matlow, Margaret Johns, Esther Heiger, Ted Grant and Hans Vojda [or Vadja], formally declared themselves to be heading the fight for the Fourth International in Britain. "We could all pretty easily keep in touch with each other," John Archer recalls, "and were soon to produce a mimeographed pamphlet containing our translation from the French text of Trotsky's article, 'Behind the

Kirov Assassination,' the main aim of which was to refute the allegations in the Stalinist press linking the killers to Trotsky. Kirby did most of the translation and the design."[13]

To this group of unemployed former students and factory workers from London's East End, Robertson appeared like a beacon of inspiration. Indeed, his arrival in their midst coincided with the peak period of Trotskyist influence in the ILP.[14] After a slow start, momentum in the Marxist Group began to build. According to John Archer, it was Earle Robertson who galvanized them:

> A sense of urgency had been injected into their work by the Plenum of the International Communist League in October 1934, where the delegates from Britain met for the first time a Canadian Trotskyist who was to spend somewhat over a year in London and who had had experience, as a member of the Communist League of America, of working "underground" in the Communist Party of U.S.A. This man contributed an optimism and dynamism to the Trotskyists in the I.L.P., helped to raise their theoretical level and, especially during his early months in Britain, encouraged the development of their contacts in the provinces.[15]

Archer remembers Comrade Robertson as "a lean, slightly irritable man with red hair and a red moustache, a man who would learn anything, a man who was furnishing his mind richly."[16] "Earle never talked of his career," he recalls, "though I had a definite impression he wanted to be a university teacher."[17] Margaret Johns, another comrade in whom Robertson briefly became romantically interested around Christmas, remembers him as "long and lean and fierce—one of those very tough-looking wiry people—intense and *very* intelligent. He was quite ginger, red-haired. You couldn't call him handsome, but he had a sort of personal magnetism. He was not the kind of person you could ignore. He could be quite irritable. I felt that life continually scratched him, that it impinged on him."[18]

The Marxist Group was led by Bert Matlow, whose wife, May, was its secretary. C.L.R. James, a black intellectual from Trinidad, was also a member. Margaret Johns makes it clear that Robertson was more sophisticated politically than her London comrades:

> Although he was not from England, Earle was very useful because of his inside work. A lot of us were pretty new. He had been close enough to know what was happening. He got a lot of books and papers from the States.[19] He had a very good grasp of what he was doing politically. He could get quite heated politically and come up with all the arguments. He was full of ideas about what we should do next. He was more idealistic than practical. He was an academic. He was preoccupied with theories rather than practicalities. He was an *ideologue*.[20]

Certainly, Birney's knowledge of Marxism and his commitment to Trotskyism had deepened as a result of his experiences in Toronto, Vancouver and Salt Lake City, and specifically as a result of his extensive and continuous readings. He had come a long way since admitting to Don Calvert, a former graduate student acquaintance in English at Toronto, in 1933, when discussing Granville Hicks's new book on American literary history (*The Great Tradition*): "I'm by no means a competent Marxist yet. That takes time, application and experience. It's difficult, of course, for you to give the [Marxist literary critical] method credit when its work seems so defective... My own emotionalities, both in my thesis and in my talks with you...may have misled you into thinking the Marxian approach is 'merely the sociological distorted by a revolutionary bias.'"[21]

By the fall of 1934, "time, application and experience" had made Birney sufficiently sophisticated politically to stand out among his new British colleagues. Trotsky's teachings had been absorbed so thoroughly into his every fibre that Marxism typified many of his simplest observations. Even crossing the Atlantic on board the *S.S. Filleigh* (where his shipboard reading was Gustave Myers's *History of Canadian Wealth*, a study of capitalist exploitation), he had written to his mother of grinning slyly to one of the crew while the captain offered his reactionary opinions about strikers and the way labour was ruining industry. Later, he told her he took on the captain at cribbage games in an attempt to modify his views. Elsewhere he professed disgust that the only British radio news "is snob news—all about Prince George and his engagement ring, and the rest of the nincompoop royalist parasites."[22] Throughout the trip, he analysed many aspects of life at sea (where "the caste system has neatly petrified"), and shipping generally, from a Marxist perspective. "Here we are," he wrote, "carrying eight thousand tons of lumber nine thousand miles to England in order that we may prevent Russia or Sweden from sending it five hundred miles to England. In this mad world of decadent capitalism, any absurdity is possible."[23] Similarly, in London, he followed news of the Spanish Civil War, checked out the mansions of the capitalists on Park Lane, contrasting them to the slum streets of Seven Dials, and soon began reporting on his own political activities from his new base at 18 Harpur Street.[24] "I gave a lecture, under another name, on the Canadian Working Class, at an Independent Labor Party hall," he wrote in November to his mother, who had no idea her son was using her maiden name as an alias. "And last night I went with some comrades to another similar Hall to see some working-class films, and hear songs and see a play in celebration of the anniversary of the Russian Revolution."[25] Two weeks later—after deploring the public money spent on the wedding of "that useless, stupid sot" the Duke of Kent, which was attended by "all the bums of European royalty and ex-royalty"—he reported:

> I went to hear a debate between a fascist and a socialist. It made you realize how close the inevitable fight is. There were four fascists there in full uniform— black shirts, etc. They pretend to be "socialists" themselves, you see, but of course they admit they are going to keep the present capitalist system and just rule without parliament. They praise Hitler and Mussolini

up to the skies, of course, and circulate all manner of lies against everybody else. They are ruthless, determined adventurers, who, unfortunately, are growing daily in numbers. Last week some of them raided a restaurant where socialists and communists go to eat after meetings. They picked on the Jewish-looking ones and started a fight. There were enough honest workers there however to give them an honest licking.[26]

And he commented that the defeat of the CCF candidate A. Sinclair (by the Liberal candidate H.G.T. Perry in the Fort George riding) in the November 1933 B.C. election "shows you that the capitalists won't let you reform things peacefully. They use all the power of money to defeat you."

Despite his commitment to Trotskyism and his fierce declarations against the capitalist system, Birney kept one foot in the capitalist camp himself. Birney's working-class background made him indignant at a system which exploited and subjugated the poor. But the imprecations of his self-sacrificing parents to better himself in the world, their insistence on propelling him up the social ladder, had also resulted in honing his social skills as a young gentleman to near-perfection. Birney may have worked on survey crews and road-gangs—as he was fond of asserting in left-wing circles—but he had also belonged to the most exclusive fraternity at UBC and Toronto and taken part fully in their social life, consorted extensively with elegant sophisticated people like Doc Sedgewick, and was now thoroughly hooked into a far-flung old boy network of family friends, fraternity brothers and an educated élite of fellow-students from four universities. Though he "kicked myself for doing it," Birney waited two hours in the rain to catch a glimpse of "the Old Man [King George V] and Buxom Mary...driving in a closed Rolls-Royce from the Palace to the opening of the House of Lords."[27] And at the same time as he was attending meetings as an impassioned comrade, he was using various letters of introduction (and would later send polite "bread-and-butter" notes) from family and friends to make quite different contacts. "I've dined twice with

Sir George May and family," he wrote his socially ambitious mother, in a letter that also described his Trotskyist activities, with no apparent sense of incongruity:

> You remember Bruce Macdonald [a Zate from UBC] gave me a letter to his daughter? I got in touch with her, and since then we've gone to several places in her carriage, such as the Zoo. I made it quite clear I was poor, so we split expenses and only go to cheap things.... I am going again [to dine] next Friday. Very amusing, particularly as Sir George is a well-known Conservative. He knows I'm a "bolshevik" and so we both know where we're at, and no harm done. We discuss political theory a good deal—neither really giving an inch, of course, but quite polite. He's rather better than most in his position in that he admits there's a change coming soon and that the workers will bring it about. But of course he's hanging on to his own position as long as he can. Had an excellent dinner last time: pheasant with burgundy, no less.[28]

The train trip Birney made north through England into Scotland on a three-guinea "month pass" in late February 1935 was typical of the way he successfully savoured Britain without sacrificing any of the sides of his complex personality. Ostensibly, he was visiting the Manchester Library to meet several noted professors in his field. As far as his Trotskyist comrades were concerned, he was looking at labour conditions firsthand. Armed with letters of introduction from them to fellow-travellers in the north, Birney frequently stopped off as he passed through Stoke-on-Trent, Manchester, Liverpool, Southport, Blackpool, Carlisle, Edinburgh and back down through York to talk with comrades and investigate the appalling poverty and working conditions of the working class. From Stoke-on-Trent, for example, he took a bus into a little mining town on the edge of the "Potteries" and stayed with an ILP miner and his wife. But he was also taking advantage of the introductions provided by his mother and Bruce Macdonald to friends of middle-class or higher standing who entertained him with dinners, plays and excursions to museums. Aside from York, whose mediaeval ruins intrigued him, and Edinburgh, which he found beautiful, Birney disliked most of the places he saw. He especially detested Glasgow, which he referred to as "the world's ass-hole" on his return.[29] Raw, rainy weather and bug-infested beds did not help. But his appetite for firsthand experience was clear; not simply academic experience, or political experience, or sophisticated experience, or cultural experience, but *all* experience. It is difficult to imagine a three-guinea rail pass (which Birney with characteristic financial acumen worked out to be less than one cent a mile) being more fully used.[30]

By spring, Birney had made grudging but significant progress on his thesis. His research work in the British Museum was almost complete, and he began planning how and where he would write up his findings. And he had established himself as an important figure in the ILP. He and his flatmate, Stuart Kirby, and a comrade from Clapham had been temporarily suspended from the ILP in January 1934 for disrupting a meeting of the Friends of the Soviet Union in Conway Hall. The three ILPers attended the meeting to sell copies of the *New Leader* and to hear what explanation would be given for the "Kirov affair," which they had followed closely as a result of Kirby's translating Trotsky's "Behind the Kirov Assassination" in December. S.M. Kirov, a leading Soviet functionary who had replaced Zinoviev as head of the Leningrad organization of the Soviet Communist Party, had been murdered. Zinoviev had been arrested and more than one hundred others had been executed. According to John Archer, "These reports had disturbing effects on many liberal-minded people in the West who entertained the hope that the stress and strain of the years of the First Five Year Plan and of forced collectivisation were giving way to greater harmony in Soviet life."[31] At first there had been speculation that the assassin represented lingering White Guard sympathies or terrorist factions within the Communist Party, then Trotsky's name was dragged in.[32] Robertson and his Trotskyist comrades, infuriated, rushed to his defence. When the platform speakers (confident of their predominantly Stalinist audience) made vague statements implicating

Trotsky in the Kirov affair, the three comrades called out repeatedly for evidence or proof.[33]

By 20 April, the date of the annual conference of the ILP in Derby, Robertson was reinstated, had been chosen to attend as the Holborn and Finsbury delegate and had also been made a member of the executive of the ILP's North London Federation.[34] According to John Archer, "the Marxist Group (which now numbered about one hundred members) reached the peak of its influence in the ILP at the Derby conference at Easter 1935, though the leadership did not recognize [it] at the time."[35] The Marxist Group—who through Robertson contributed more to the ILP debates than ever before—was divided over several issues, such as whether or not to withdraw from the ILP and seek some form of association with the Labour Party, and were overwhelmed, in any case, by "intense conflict in the ILP about the Party's attitude to the Italo-Abyssinian conflict."[36] Robertson, who was well prepared with documents worked out beforehand with John Archer, Ted Grant and Stuart Kirby, opposed the Labour Party's support for the League of Nations plan for economic sanctions to check Italian aggression against Abyssinia because he viewed the League as an imperialist agent. (The Stalinists also backed the League of Nations plan for sanctions while at the same time the Soviet Union was selling oil to Italy.)[37] He also questioned the idealization of the USSR as a "workers' state." And he supported the strategy of a General Strike as an effective means of preventing war. But a European war seemed inevitable, and Birney—unlike his father in the Great War—had no intention of serving: "You can bet the capitalists won't get *me* to shoot other men and get shot just to help them increase their riches, while they stay safely behind the battle."[38] After the Derby Conference, the whole ILP, and therefore the Marxist Group also, became more and more isolated from the working class and the realities of political life. Though Comrade Robertson had taken a striking role alongside his "young, voluble, self-confident and inexperienced"[39] comrades in their bid for a better world order, he had been unable to have much impact on the major developments of the time. He had been tilting at windmills.

On May Day 1935, Birney set off by train, far from the madding crowd and the imprisoning walls of the British Museum, to the lush Dorset coast Thomas Hardy described so sensually. There in a tiny caravan poised "in the shelter of a pine-copse"[40] atop a hill overlooking the village of Lulworth, he re-created as best he could the outdoorsy, camping conditions he had so loved as a boy. As always, he responded to nature from the depths of his being: "I've tried to draw you a picture of the site," he wrote his mother,

> but I assure you it's much more beautiful... I'm on top of a long gorse-covered hill, and my little door opens on a view leading right down to the village below.... Below the village is the cove—a perfect little horseshoe, with a beach of tiny pebbles, all shiny flint, polished by the waves... Along the beach from the cove are some green-watered sea caves, once actually used by smugglers... Farther along the beach, which runs for miles, are other bays, huge weathered rocks, some with holes bored through by wave action to form an arch. It is only five minutes walk down the other side of my hill to one of the wildest & finest parts of this coast—the most beautiful along the Channel. All the cliffs are shining white chalk, except where a cranny has allowed earth to gather and flowers to bloom.[41]

There, where he could stride the beaches and hike among the sheep through the daisied fields—probing ancient inscrutable barrows, or musing on the history implicit in Roman ruins, or chatting with the farmer who supplied his milk and eggs—he would settle in to write his thesis.

Much as Birney loved his little caravan and routine there—working mornings and evenings, and resting his eyes and his soul outdoors during the afternoons—the isolation did not suit him. At first he counteracted his profound loneliness by inviting Hans Vojda from the Marxist Group who had been sharing Esther Heiger's flat at 1 Hampton Street, to stay with him. But more specifically, he needed a woman. Before long, Esther, one of the comrades he had met in the Holborn group and with whom he had become involved after Margaret Johns, had agreed to join him. Not only did Esther cook and manage the caravan for Birney, she was also a trained stenographer well able and willing to type his thesis professionally.

Esther Heiger was an earthy, jolly woman four years younger than Earle, who, by the time she met Birney, had left the scientist she had married on 4 November 1929, Israel Heiger, a dark-haired, pale-complexioned, remote man absorbed in his research on the cancer-producing factor of cigarettes, who expected Esther to be "the little housewife in a tiny little house in the suburbs."[42] This was not the role for Esther, who in the early 1930s had met the charming Hans Vojda, a Hungarian exile in flight from political oppression, on a trip to Austria and had invited him to come and live with Israel and herself. Hans, who was as committed to being in the world as Israel was to ignoring it, became her lover and moved with her into the Hampton flat where their relationship eventually became amicably platonic.[43]

The feisty, vibrant Esther, born in 1908, whose Russian-Jewish parents had imbued her with socialist ideas and whose older brother David had included her in a radical group of his friends since 1927, had experienced the capitalist system firsthand as a secretary in her father's fur factory. "Dad was a socialist; not a revolutionary," she would later write:

> but certainly an enthusiastic supporter of the Russian Revolution. This event (when I was about nine) was the most momentous happening of my life. It brought with it the conviction that Utopia could arrive in our time. It meant that I would probably see the International Working Class triumphant before I died. Human nature would become non-predatory; everyone would have a piano and sufficient food, they would enjoy art galleries and love their neighbour. Who needed a Messiah? We would have a do-it-yourself Kingdom of God on Earth. All this would come about quite simply by the withering away of the competitive system.[44]

Esther was now deeply committed to Trotskyism. "I felt that there was no time for academics like Israel in a world that was going to blow up any minute. And that we had to do what we could to get the Fourth International landed and get the workers of the world to unite against the capitalists. And so we would talk and argue about such things [at our meetings], and pass resolutions and write briefs. And it was at one of these meetings that someone said to me: 'You haven't met our new comrade. So when the meeting broke for coffee he took me down to meet Earle. And here was this neat-looking fellow, small-featured, wearing rimless glasses, who spoke with a twang, and I said, 'Oh no, you must be a Yankee.' 'I'm not a Yankee,' he said indignantly. 'I'm from Vancouver.' And I said, 'Isn't that in South America?' And he had to look at me twice, I seemed so stupid. Then he said, 'No, Vancouver's on the west coast of Canada.' And I said, 'Has Canada *got* a west coast?'" "I often wondered," she later wrote, "if he married me to improve my geography."[45]

Esther believes that she owed her affair with Earle to the toss of a coin. By March 1935, Stuart Kirby had been replaced by John Archer in the Harpur Street flat. "Earle told me that he and Archer evidently discussed me," Esther recalls, though Archer claims the story is apocryphal.[46] "And Archer said, 'I'd like to take her out,' and Earle (whom I had taken around London: 'It was very much the Canadian colonial glad to be shown around by a true Londoner'[47]) said, 'Well I'm going to ask her to come out.' And they said: 'Well, let's toss.' And Archer lost the toss and Earle won it. So I can't say it was a great love attraction. He was terribly, terribly thin and blonde, and I liked short, thick-set dark men. And I remember thinking as he stood in front of the mantelpiece in my house talking about his trip to Paris, 'This is strange. This man has been to one of the greatest cities in the world and he's being very boring about it.' But he looked nice and, you know, good men are hard to find. And Earle had the prestige of being the head of the whole British Trotskyist group—he and Bert Matlow. He was a wonderful speaker on behalf of Trotskyism.[48] And he said appreciative things like: 'I've never known anyone to know more about Marxism than you do.' And I felt glowing. And we really believed that the workers were *not* going to shoot at each other this time; they were going to shoot their officers." Esther would later write of the first time she and Earle "had intercourse." "After it was over, I said something about wishing we could be within sound of the sea. Earle said rather scathingly, 'Oh, you're one of the poetic kind.' Had I followed my intuition I would have said, 'You're damn right I am' and left him. But I recalled that good communists are not mushy and romantic, so I changed the subject—probably talked of the minutes for the next meeting!"[49]

According to Esther, it was she who suggested a summer place and found the caravan in the first place. "He loved that place. I don't know where I found the van," she recalls. "It was quite small; just two people could sleep in it. He stayed down there reading and getting on with his thesis and I would come back and forth [from London]. I typed his Chaucer thesis and became very admiring of Chaucer. I caught Earle's enthusiasm and have had it ever since. I typed these endless pages of exposition and footnotes—Oh, those *footnotes!* I, who had turned down an orthodox education and dropped out of high school, somehow felt this was very worthwhile."

It was also a job during a time of massive unemployment. And Earle and Esther, in the unromantic style of fellow-travellers, worked out an equitable arrangement, sharing expenses. As Esther remembers it, "There was never anything sentimental, or 'you come and be my dear, dear little companion.' I remember very distinctly that when we decided to go to the country, I thought, 'Ah! We've taken the next step to being a pair.' And not too long after that, when we had been living together for a month or two, he said something like, 'I can't offer you honourable marriage.' So in a way he was an honourable man. He never lied about that."

Earle didn't lie to Esther, but he certainly concealed her existence in his life. His letters to his mother never mention her, except for references to a "typist." Quite the contrary, he spoke often of his loneliness (presumably during Esther's absences in London), a strategy that both spared him his mother's disapproval and engaged her pity: "I have lived a very solitary existence—sleeping, cooking, eating, writing. My eyes stand up pretty well; though having to rest them is the very devil, for I've nothing else to do. I see no one most days, but the farm-wife when I go for milk and to see if any mail has come for me. But I have sunshine and flowers and birds at last, and how pleasant they are after a winter in London. But if only you were here to share them with me."[50]

It wasn't long before Esther encountered Earle's temper. "It was spring," she recalled, after living with him only a couple of months, "and he said, 'Soon the tulips will be out!' And I laughed and said, 'Oh, is *that* how Canadians say "tulips"?' And he was so angry he just walked away from me. I suddenly felt, 'Good Lord, this man's really very short-tempered, isn't he!'"[51]

Within two weeks of moving to setting up camp in Dorset, Birney and Esther had produced 30,000 more words for the thesis.[52] Prof. W.H. Clawson, the Chaucer expert in Toronto, was pleased, writing of these chapters that the work was "excellent" and probably "publishable in entirety."[53] Not content to restrict himself to his scholarly work, Birney also began work on a novel.[54]

Birney's main preoccupation was his future employment. The Depression was at its worst, and unemployment in England, as elsewhere, had reached terrifying proportions: "well over two million on the dole," he wrote, "not to speak of the millions more who work for a pound a week, on half-time, etc."[55] Now that his Royal Society Fellowship had almost run out, and he was buckling down to complete his thesis, Birney tried to secure his career. In mid-April, he heard back from Utah that his contract would not be renewed. "[Sherman B.] Neff [the department's Chairman] has refused to recommend me, solely on political grounds," he explained to his mother."[56] Toronto also had nothing to offer him, explaining that "they had been cut $250,000, and must fire even some they have now."[57] The fact that his old rival for Sylvia, Roy Daniells, whose career had been just one step ahead of his own and whom he saw briefly that summer when Daniells vacationed in England, had just acquired a position at Toronto was aggravating in the extreme. His old Zate friend Hilton M. Moore at the University of New York backed his application there, but to no avail: no vacancies. To his mother he wrote, "I would like nothing more than to get a job

in Vancouver, so I could be company for you, and be with you…
But nothing so far."[58] As a last resort, he had listed his name for
night classes under the London County Council. No wonder
Birney wrote to Pelham Edgar that life was looking "bleak and
barren ahead."[59]

Birney did not complete his 860-page thesis by September as
he had hoped. In his official five-page report to the Royal Society
(which he sent very deliberately from Canterbury, the city associated with Chaucer's famous *Tales*, where he had moved with
Esther in the caravan at the beginning of July) he made a highly
emotional and personal plea for extension of his fellowship. After
outlining the six chapters he had finished, describing his research
methods and detailing his plans for completion of the one hundred to two hundred pages still to be written, Birney portrayed
himself—partly with justification—as a "victim." He took the
Society representatives to task for not responding to any of his
interim reports and reminded them that he had given up the
renewal of his Utah job at a salary higher than $1,500 to accept
the fellowship, implying that this cost him his Utah job. He
vented his frustration both at "a stupid economic system" and at
the futility of his academic achievments and extensive teaching
experience.

> The plain fact is that, despite repeated attempts to get
> work in England, in Canada, in the United States, in
> the profession for which I had fitted myself, I am still
> completely without prospects…. There is no work for
> me, here, there, or anywhere, either in university,
> school, or kindergarten. Even if I were to go once
> more out of my chosen profession into unskilled labor,
> where I began my working life and through which I
> saved my cents to go to college, there is still no work. I
> am faced with returning, on what remains of my fel-
> lowship money, to my home in Vancouver, there to sit
> and wait until I can establish residence "privileges."
> Then I may have the "privilege" of working in a relief
> camp at twenty cents a day…. if you consider my win-
> ter's work of any value you will be interested surely.

Whether you can do anything to help depends entirely upon whether there is any vacancy of which you have knowledge, or whether you can grant me any extension of my fellowship. There is still much that I can do in Chaucer research. I am having to hurry my thesis far too much and to leave untouched certain important aspects....[60]

He did not mention the time he had invested in the Marxist Group. The Royal Society neither found him a position, nor renewed his fellowship. Edgar wrote, urging him to expand his contacts, but to little avail. In a letter from Roy Daniells that must have piqued Birney, partly because Daniells had become more pretentious and "haute-bourgeois" while he had become more radically left-wing, he learned that there was a glimmer of hope for a position at Toronto; since E.K. Brown had just left to become Chair at the University of Manitoba, there was no mediaevalist.[61] For some reason—possibly because his political activities were so time-consuming—Birney had not yet contacted two of the English Chaucer scholars who might have helped him: C.S. Lewis at Magdalen College, Oxford and G.R. Owst at Cambridge. The former replied in a somewhat dismissive letter to Birney's request for a meeting in October: "My own belief is that modern criticism reads into Chaucer rather more irony than is actually there, but that, at this distance of time, no disputed case can be decided with any certainty. This reflection might have given my criticism some value at the *beginning* of your work: but at your present stage you can, I suspect, be helped only by those who are in some agreement with you."[62] The latter was more encouraging. Though he made it clear he would have no time for months to read Birney's work, he did have tea with him at the Hotel Vanderbilt on 3 November, and later wrote: "You certainly seem to me to bring together a vast collection of useful references, your extended analysis of mediaeval satire should be very interesting.... I hope to enjoy your published work, if & when it appears. Yes: I think you could use my name as reference, altho', on our present slender acquaintance, I do not think it will be of much use to you."[63]

So great was Birney's talent for living cheaply, however, that he pinched pennies for another six months. His political convictions were now fuelled by anger at his personal situation and, in the absence of any foreseeable job, he threw himself into politics with new vengeance. But his absorption in his thesis over the summer had coincided with—and possibly had some influence upon—the "period of stagnation"[64] for the Trotskyists in the ILP which occurred around the time Italy invaded Abyssinia in August 1935. It was a slump from which they would never recover, for by the following summer—after the hopeless defeat of all the ILP candidates in the November 1935 election which clearly showed that no faction of the ILP was reaching the masses—the Marxist Group disintegrated and several of its members—including Earle Robertson[65]—immediately joined the Labour Party.

Now Comrade Robertson began planning for a visit to see the Old Man, Leon Trotsky himself. As he completed the thesis back in London with Esther, he prepared the trip with Ken Johnstone, who was technically still his brother-in-law and who had come to England with hopes of becoming an international journalist. As Esther remembers it, the trip was part of an ambitious scheme to integrate the ILP Trotskyists with other groups moving towards the Fourth International. "Trotskyists were being disseminated and assassinated left and right, and Earle—along with C.L.R. James, Bert Matlow and Ken Johnstone—was negotiating with other European Trotskyists. They kept it very secret."[66]

Birney's contributions to the discussion within the Marxist Group on the characterization of the ILP leadership's policies on the question of "sanctions" against fascist Italy for the invasion of Abyssinia had first caught Trotsky's attention. A major article which Trotsky wrote on the ILP in September 1935 (which appeared in the *New International* in December of that year) entitled "The ILP and the Fourth International" had credited the ILP leadership with taking a correct position on the sanctions question. A month later, in an October 20 addendum to the article, entitled "A Necessary Addition," Trotsky learned of criticisms raised by Birney and corrected himself on this question:

In my article I approved of the attitude of this party on the question of sanctions. Later, friends sent me a copy of an important letter from Comrade Robertson to the members of the ILP. Comrade Robertson accuses the leadership of the party of maintaining pacifist illusions, particularly in the matter of 'refusal' of military service. I can only associate myself wholly with what is said in Comrade Robertson's letter.[67]

Evidently the great Russian revolutionary was impressed with the acumen of his young Canadian disciple. No doubt this predisposed him to the idea of a visit from Birney and his friend Ken Johnstone.

On Sunday, 15 November, Comrades Robertson and Alexander (Johnstone's pseudonym) landed in Bergen, Norway, en route to Hönefoss where Trotsky and his wife Natalia Ivanovna were secluded at the home of Konrad Knudsen, a Socialist member of the Norwegian Parliament. There Trotsky worked in comparative peace and freedom until, in the course of August 1936, the Norwegian government interned and isolated him under pressure from the Kremlin following the trial of the "Sixteen" and the executions that ensued.[68]

The trip was truly a pilgrimage. Like mediaeval knights from the era Birney had been immersed in through his thesis, the two Canadians proceeded in awe and reverence to pay homage to the great man whose ideas had inspired their loyalty and commitment for five years. "Yesterday crossed mountains by marvellous scenic railway to this place where we will be for several days," an exhilarated Birney wrote on a postcard to his mother. "Food marvellous & cheap. Hotel clean & cheap. Weather still fairly warm. Lovely air."[69]

The two apprehensive acolytes met with Trotsky on the 19th, 20th, 21st and 22nd of November (Birney would later exaggerate this to five days).[70] "Those five days, during each of which we talked and ate and walked with Trotsky," he would later write in awe,

are almost a dream world... I shall never forget the

impact of his personality. Genius is a word one should use only a few times in a lifetime; one meets only a few if any... Trotsky was a man who instantly impressed one with the authenticity of his genius. It wasn't his fine soldier's carriage, his powerful square shoulders and great chest and head, nor even his flashing deepset eyes. All that one may find in lesser men. It was the feeling of a mind that was equipped with twice the cylinders a man's mind possesses, and the engine of the mind running silently and smoothly and with perfect efficiency. Whatever the subject—and Trotsky never dodged a subject—he would speak about it with information, judgment and humour. And he would, without ever harping on Marxism, manage often to make one see that whatever the human phenomenon discussed, embedded in it were problems for the present and the future, problems for which a socialist society alone offered answers.[71]

Comrade Robertson presented the great man with a five-page outline of the Canadian situation in order to brief him.[72] Even here, Trotsky outdid the Canadian comrades who had worked hard and long to prepare their outline. "I remember how he enjoyed, and how he made us enjoy, correcting us as to the exact population of Canada.... Somehow he had got the latest Canada Year Book and had been checking on us quietly."[73] Trotsky's secretary had warned them that politics was off-limits as a subject at dinner, "When, unhappily, I forgot the rule," Birney recalls, "and made some feeble crack about the British Labour Party, Trotsky instantly shifted the conversation to English literature."[74] Robertson and Alexander raised subjects they knew were relatively trivial: "what to him must have been childish points of strategy...personalities obtruding in the tiny British section...squabbles inside the American party [and] lethargy on the Canadian partylot."[75] But the two awestruck Canadians had the privilege of accompanying the Old Man to a small, crowded local movie house where they watched an old set of newsreels from the Great War, including some brief views of Lenin orating in the Red Square, and some of Trotsky himself. "[He] seemed quite oblivious of possible dangers, quite happy to have the change of a movie, elated when Lenin flashed on the screen, and richly amused by seeing himself. We said goodbye to him in the market square after the show. He put his arms around both of us, in a familiar and heartwarming gesture, and sped us on our way. We never saw him again."[76]

During their visit to him, Trotsky reported in a letter as follows: "We now have here two Canadian comrades, Rob(ertson) and John(stone) working in England in the Marxist Group of the ILP. We discussed for four days the Br(itish) and Cdn. questions and I had the opportunity of becoming more clearly acquainted with the situation in their movements and our links with them. And now we are proceeding to discuss American questions."[77] Trotsky's answers to their questions were recorded in a pamphlet Robertson published on their return, called "Conversations With Trotsky."[78] The cover suggested a news scoop of the utmost importance:

FOR PARTY CIRCULATION ONLY
SHOULD THE ILP ENTER
THE LABOR PARTY?
SHOULD THE ILP FORBID GROUPS?
SHOULD THE ILP CONTINUE UNITED
FRONTS WITH CPGB [COMMUNIST PARTY
OF GREAT BRITAIN]?
SHOULD THE ILP HAVE OPPOSED
THE LP IN THE LAST ELECTIONS?
A literal report of answers to these and many other
pertinent questions, as given by the greatest living
Marxist, Leon Trotsky,
Norway, November 1935.
Price One Penny
PUBLISHED BY E. ROBERTSON
OF THE HOLBORN & FINSBURY ILP.
London, England
LEON TROTSKY ON THE ILP
(Conversations with E. Robertson.)

Clearly for Birney the most important issue that was discussed during the visit was the rather complicated situation of the British Trotskyists, and especially their relationship to the ILP. There were several small Trotskyist groupings. But the one which Birney was attached to, the Marxist Group within the ILP, was the main group. The entry into the ILP, which took place in mid-1934, had originally been Trotsky's idea, after the ILP had split from the Labour Party in 1932. At that time Trotsky had imagined that perhaps the "left centrist" ILP could be won to revolutionary politics and enrolled as the British section of the Fourth International. By 1935 this prospect was receding, but Trotsky still held out hope that a substantial section of the ILP (which at its high point after leaving the Labour Party claimed 25,000 members) could be won over.

Though the blurb for "Conversations with Trotsky" emphasized the aspects of his interview that bore most directly on these ILP issues, Birney questioned Trotsky about a much wider range of issues while he was in Norway, including the role of the League of Nations; the probable line-ups in what they both saw as a looming inter-imperialist conflict; and the proper attitude for communists who wished to defend the Soviet Union in time of war. Another, more immediate, topic on which Birney queried Trotsky was how to manage the sometimes subjective quarrels that erupted within the tiny Trotskyist nuclei. Trotsky suggested that disputes among petty-bourgeois intellectuals divorced from the larger workers' movement often had a tendency to become excessively "sharp and bitter" and commented that in general the leaderships of such groups had to win the political confidence of the membership rather than attempt to impose their will with rigid sets of rules, expulsions and other measures.

There are several questions raised in the version of the conversations with Trotsky that Birney produced which George Breitman, the late editor of Trotsky's works in English, suggested are mistaken. One is an assertion attributed to Trotsky that Britain and America was "the most fundamental" contradiction between the imperialists. This contradicts other contemporary observations by Trotsky. As Breitman points out, it is perhaps significant that "Birney sent Trotsky a copy, but Trotsky did not initial it, as he often did with summaries of discussions made by visitors to indicate that he found them generally accurate."[79]

The pilgrimage to Hönefoss could not forestall the inevitable difficulties of the ILP. Birney and Johnstone had worked out a proposal for bringing the entry to a conclusion and moving towards affiliation with the Labour Party which, although formally to the right of the ILP, was a genuine mass party in which the Trotskysists could potentially win much greater influence. And, in a letter written in July 1936, Trotsky summarized the results of their conversation:

> Since the last visit of R. [Robertson] and A. [Johnstone], I formulated my observations in this sense: that there isn't much to be done with the ILP. The three of us worked out a definite proposal for our British comrades (a manifesto to the party, collection of signatures, etc.). Comrade Schmidt [a senior leader of the Dutch section] went to England and judged the plan to be incorrect. Naturally this was not without its influence on the comrades, as well as on me. I immediately said to myself: Schmidt knows the ILP better than I do; perhaps he sees in the ILP such aspects as escape me; therefore the decision [to break politically] should perhaps be postponed.[80]

At the time of Schmidt's visit in January 1936 Trotsky had written Birney to advise him that Schmidt would be making "his investigations in England" in his capacity as a comrade who "should be playing the role of Secretary for the Fourth International." He continued:

> You also certainly know about the excellent struggle that he has waged in his own party against the SAPists. At the same time I would like to underline the fact that Schmidt is tied by long friendship to the head of the ILP and that he has perhaps a certain uneasiness, not to say mistrust, toward our friends as "sectarians." He would perhaps rather be inclined to insist on the

necessity of our comrades continuing their work in the
ILP. I am bringing up all these circumstances in order
to make mutual understanding easier.[81]

While Trotsky had agreed with Birney and Johnstone that the
ILP was in all probability lost for the Fourth International and
that it was time to move on, he was apparently indicating in this
letter that he was prepared to defer, at least temporarily, to the
conclusions he anticipated would be drawn by Schmidt. The fact
that he wrote to Birney in advance of the visit was an indication
that the young Canadian revolutionist had impressed his teacher
considerably on his visit a few months earlier. By April, Trotsky
concluded that the ILP's further movement to the right had confirmed the original orientation that he, Johnstone and Birney
had proposed and demonstrated that further time spent in this
group was time wasted. The ILP was shrinking (Trotsky estimated its size in April 1936 as 3,000 members) and concluded
that it was not qualitatively closer to revolutionary politics than
the hardened reformist leadership of the Labour Party. For every
militant the Trotskyists "might win in the ILP, there are hundreds in the Labour Party."[82] Schmidt continued as an ILP
patriot in the movement for the Fourth International for another
few months before he decamped for social-democracy.

It is clear from Birney's pamphlet, as well as from the reverence
with which he later alluded to his visit with Trotsky, that the
episode was a high point of his life. Comrades Robertson and
Alexander returned from Hönefoss fired with political fervour
and more deeply committed to the Fourth International.

Almost at once, they used the remarkable opportunity of a visit
to the continent to see what was going on in Germany firsthand.
Within a week they were off to Berlin on a special deal that
offered a 40 per cent reduction on the train fare. Literally surviv-
ing on beer and bread and cheese (Limburger for Birney;
Gorgonzola for Johnstone) and staying in hotels that were open
brothels, the two set out to size up Nazi Germany. According to
Johnstone, who hoped to "break into print" with the *Toronto
Evening Star*, while Birney attended a party rally to hear Hitler,
he went to a cellar café to savour wine, women and song, and got

himself into such trouble he left his raincoat behind with most of their money in it. On 2 December, their last day, the two set off to walk through the famous working-class Wedding district, where Karl Liebknecht and Rosa Luxemburg had been murdered in 1919. As Johnstone describes it:

> It was a drizzly Sunday morning and I was not surprised that the streets were deserted. But I was mystified when I heard the music of an approaching band and the blinds on the windows stayed down. It was the black-uniformed Schutzstaffel, Hitler's elite....
>
> Suddenly we were in the middle of a sea of flailing fists. I got one crack on the nose that brought the blood gushing, and another that rapidly closed my left eye before I could start cursing and fighting back. As soon as our attackers heard our non-German voices they vanished as suddenly as they had appeared. We were left in the company of a sympathetic Red Cross nurse (she accompanied such parades customarily to take care of similar mistakes) and two embarrassed policemen, who took us to the nearest police station, where we heatedly demanded apologies. The police generously offered to produce the culprits (they were known, since it was their job to beat up non-saluters) and let us each take a free punch.[83]

An incensed Birney, who only had his hat knocked off, demanded "that a public apology appear in the German press, accompanied by an order prohibiting the assault of anyone, German or foreigner, who failed to salute. This was, of course, refused. But fear of what we could tell the outside world drove the police to promise that they would insert a similar notice in Nazi internal party organs."[84] The two fellow travellers also contacted the British Consul in Berlin, made sure an article appeared in the Canadian press,[85] and Birney wrote a long piece about the episode for the ILP's *New Leader* about his "week's experiences as an ordinary tourist in Berlin."[86] As usual, he had packed an enormous number of excursions into one short trip.

He could report on the endless troop parades, the huge air ministry building being erected in Berlin, the worsening economic condition, the high price of meat, the unavailablity of vegetables and butter, the empty churches. Though he tried to visit a concentration camp, he was told they were off-limits for tourists. He did visit a model "Work-Service" camp where all youths were obliged to spend six months. Even these were distressing, "simply an arrangement for the forced exploitation of the youthful labour power under military conditions." As for Jewish youth and workers, these were "in a worse plight, for they cannot come even to these camps. And now the 'cold pogrom' is in full swing. If a German happens to be friends with a Jew, he is liable to be visited by hooded S.S. men, wearing the skull and crossbones, and warned that punishment will be visited upon both if the slightest social intercourse is continued. This, on top of the economic boycotting of Jews, is driving many to suicide. For Jews, there is now only exchange of good[s] with each other, and, for social life, the synagogues—which are consequently crowded."

"The Berlin Incident," as he called it, strengthened Birney's already strong commitment to his political ideals and, incidentally, bound him closer to the Jewish woman who had proven herself over the summer to be of indefatigable practical help and a loyal comrade. "The real hope...is in the power of the class-conscious workers to direct the democratic struggle into the overthrow of the Capitalism upon which German Fascism is obviously based." But, despite his firsthand experience, his political acumen and his indignation, Birney could not imagine the holocaust to come. "There is no doubt," he predicted, "that the mass-basis which Hitler acquired, especially in the middle class, is rapidly falling away, and with that must disappear the personnel by which an elaborate police spy-system is maintained....a workers' victory in France, or the overthrow of Mussolini in Italy, will be the beginning of the end for Hitler, and the breaking of the shackles which bind German workers to the savage dictatorship of finance capital."

11

LEVELLING OUT

In March 1936, two fellow travellers crossed the Atlantic engaged in a mission which bonded them: to do all they could to further Trotsky's Fourth International. But Earle Birney and Esther, who had now reassumed her maiden name, Bull, could not have been otherwise less alike. The intense, tall and spindly scholar and his jolly, heavy-set and round-faced comrade were not only physical opposites, they were temperamentally at odds. Birney was a romantic, an energetic Don Quixote of lofty ideas and aspirations, who imagined himself in heroic terms; Esther was a pragmatist, an earth-bound Sancho Panza whose self-deprecating humour and sarcastic barbs grounded her comrade by pricking his ballooning ego and reminding him of the vanity of human wishes.

But for the moment, their common purpose blinded them to the obvious. They arrived in New York and visited Birney's old political chum Maurice Spector, who was as deeply engaged as they were in the great Trotskyist cause. Then to Toronto where they stayed with the Johnstones, their common political purpose neutralizing any feelings that might have lingered after the fiasco of Earle's marriage to Sylvia. Esther, who reacted to life strongly and vocally, soon complained bitterly of the Canadian climate:

"It was a dreadful winter," she recalls. "The weather was awful. And the suburban area [of Toronto] way, way out west looked like the Russian salt mines to me. I was very depressed. I got a bad cold, then bronchitis, and I asked my father to send me some money to come home. But father said, 'Listen, you've made your bed. Make the best of it.' Father was fond of Earle and felt it would be better for me to stay with him. So there I was, not feeling well and just hating this grey, snowy, cold, miserable Toronto. Sometime in April I said I'd better go out to Vancouver. So I got on a train and came out to Vancouver while Earle remained in Toronto and finished up his Ph.D."[1]

According to Esther, arriving in Vancouver to stay with Mrs. Birney was no panacea either. Though she loved the English greenness of B.C. and thought Mrs. Birney "a fantastic gardener," life with the Presbyterian Martha Birney—who was nothing short of appalled at a situation in which her son was living with a woman before he was legally free of Sylvia—was difficult. "Here I was age twenty-eight, arriving in Vancouver. I got off the train and stood on the platform looking around, and this tall woman dressed in black with grim features and a white face and her lips set, looks me up and down and says: 'Well, you've got a better chin than the other one.' It was like the rabbit and the boa constrictor!"

Sharing a house with Mrs. Birney, as Esther remembers it, was a daily battle to see who was top dog. "That woman didn't smile or say a pleasant thing to me. I would light a cigarette, and she would disapprove. She was heavily 'the parent'; and I was heavily 'the child.'"[2] Later Esther would write with considerable bitterness,

> I was alone in a strange country, I had no belief in myself, and I had little that had been satisfying or sustaining in my past. My education was incomplete, I had no skills or training for a good job and I was living with a woman who disliked me. I didn't even have the gumption to hate her back. I just suffered numbly and hoped, unconsciously probably, that she would suddenly turn into a warm, loving mother-figure.

She hated everything I stood for and she talked all the time about her hates and her own virtues. She was totally disinterested in me except as a recipient for her outpourings. She snubbed me and she made me obligated to her by not allowing me to help with the housework. "You are a guest," she would say, "and I do not allow my guests to work in my home." And down she would go on her knees and scrub the floor in front of me. She threatened to commit suicide if Earle married me. [When he returned to Vancouver in May] he told her to go right ahead. She also pulled off pretty convincing heart-attacks when she could not get her own way.

She was a pillar of the church and had a reputation for being kind to the sick people in the neighbourhood. I drew some comfort from the fact that she seemed to like showing me off to her friends, although she once accused me of having a "snobby" English accent. She, being Scottish, would have a natural antipathy to an English woman—add to it that I was Jewish, divorced and had lived "in sin" with her son·in England and you can see how she objected to my presence.

She had a wife picked out for Earle—a telephone operator who crocheted doilies and went to church regularly—a pleasant, dull, conventional nothing of a girl. After six weeks of living with Mrs. Birney I became more and more internally agitated and depressed. However hard I tried to think of other things I continually found myself thinking that I was mad.

When Earle came to Vancouver... I told him of my anguish and he took me to a psychiatrist. He was kind and stood up to his mother when she tried to interfere. One day, however, he did suggest that as I seemed so ill and unhappy, perhaps our engagement to marry was a mistake and perhaps we should call the whole thing off. I was absolutely terrified. I felt the whole left side of my body drain of feeling—the side

next to Earle on the seat—it was almost as though I
had suffered a stroke. I was so reduced in psychic and
physical strength that I could not face leaving
Vancouver and returning to London. I was ashamed
to face my father and friends with yet another failure.... the psychiatrist had me move out of the Birney
home immediately.... No one with a strand of self-
respect and self-preservation would have remained
with Mrs. B.[3]

Martha's letters to her "Sonnie Boy" at the same time give a quite
different impression. "I find Esther a very kind sensible girl," she
wrote, "and [she] seems to have a good deal of common sense as
well as she will be able to help you in your work. She and you
will have more in common than any one I have seen yet. I only
wish this *rotten mess* your [sic] in could have been cleared up!
And that you could have been quietly married before you had to
go back to your fall work, wherever that will be! And I think she
will make a good wife providing you meet her half way.... Don't
worry about anything as everything is O.K. with us. Esther is so
good she helps with the house work and we are just waiting now
till it dries up so we can get out and cut the Lawns, its certainly
nice to have someone congenial to eat meals with and go around
with, only I am afraid its a bit lonely for her having no young
person around."[4]

While Martha—apparently at least—enjoyed Esther, and
Esther somehow endured the intolerable emotional climate she
had exchanged for an intolerable geographical climate, Birney
submitted his completed (and extraordinarily long) thesis of
some 850 pages on Chaucer's irony and subjected himself to the
rigors of his Ph.D. examinations. On 28 March, after passing his
written examinations on all periods of English literature, and
successfully demonstrating his ability in his minor subjects,
Germanic Philology and Old French, he reached the final hur-
dle, his oral examination by six English professors and eight professors from other disciplines.

"PASSED!" wrote an exhuberant Esther. "You'll have to introduce me to the Doctor. I won't know the Earle Birney who isn't

saying, 'I must go and work on my thesis' all the time. Keep well, darling & don't come home too much of a wreck. Love & kisses."

"My Dear Boy. Hurrah Hurrah Hurrah," wrote a proud Martha. "Good Boy. You have earned it. Now take a rest and don't worry any more. We have just got your letter and are so happy for you. Lovingly, Mother."[5]

But Birney himself took little pleasure in his success. What should have been the triumphant completion of a decade's study was, for Birney, a profound let-down. Though he passed "most brilliantly,"[6] he had nothing but disdain for the whole process, as his sarcastic description in an anonymous article[7] a year and a half later makes clear. In this article he dismissed scholarly research as fit only for the waste-basket and described scholars as "gleaners...engaged in a dull and snail-paced task" examining authors who are "pathologized, psychoanalysed, dissected, dessicated, and the parts of him hung to dry on the paling of the scholastic fence." The written exams seemed "dreary ruminations out of study outlines, reference books and professorial lectures, now regurgitated...in a green, slimy, unreadable mass" and the oral exam "almost a complete farce."

And, despite the fact that he had been jockeying for an academic position for years, Birney travelled rather disconsolately— and with a serious case of eye-strain—by train to Vancouver that May in the company of his old arch-rival, Roy Daniells, who had located a job at the University of Manitoba, disgruntled to be offered only a $2,200 lectureship teaching the pass English course to prospective teachers at University College on an annual basis (a quite reasonable job given the economic situation) rather than the more secure assistant professorship he hoped to find.

Birney's thesis, "Irony in Chaucer," was hardly scrap paper, however. In many ways it was an original scholarly work, outlining for the first time the tradition of irony in mediaeval literature—not only English literature, but Latin, Italian and French literature as well. Birney had been studying and writing about Chaucer's irony ever since G.G. Sedgewick had assigned him the topic for his graduating essay at UBC in 1925. As Sedgewick had realized, Birney was nothing short of brilliant intellectually. That brilliant intellect had now resulted in a deepening and refinement of his understanding of Chaucer, an expansion of his earlier ideas, and the powerful exposition of his views. Drawing on the vast reservoir of critical works on Chaucer's irony he had read in the British Museum and elsewhere, Birney argued that a romantic concept of irony had distorted Victorian and contemporary attitudes to Chaucer at the expense of Elizabethan criticism. Meticulously, he detailed all Chaucer's uses of irony in his works: its forms, its sources, its developments. Birney took a fresh look at several points of scholarly debate (such as the dating or interpretation of works) in Chaucer, offering new interpretations on the basis of his knowledge of irony. That he had accomplished this while deeply engaged with his Trotskyist activities was astonishing.

There was much in Chaucer that resonated for Birney. The range of class experience represented by the Canterbury pilgrims was one he was uniquely suited to appreciate since he himself felt as comfortable among road workers and carpenters like his father as he did among the wealthy young Zates he had known at UBC and Berkeley. Like Chaucer himself, his range of emotion and experience made him as receptive to the courtly tradition of knightly honour as it did to the bawdy vulgarity of the *fabliau.* He too could switch from the manners of the politest of gentlemen to the coarse obscenities of the illiterate. The notion of "pilgrimage," too, and the joys of travelling in the company of others while telling stories, was one Birney readily understood.

These elements—already echoes in Birney's earlier work on Chaucer—were now deepened by his political convictions. In his Ph.D. thesis, unlike his graduating essay, Birney focused on class issues. His analysis of Chaucer's irony was no longer a purely aesthetic exploration of Chaucer's literary devices. It had become explicitly Marxist. He now saw Chaucer's irony—or "ambiguous satire" as he called it—as the direct result of the poet's ambiguous class position. "What is particularly potent," Birney argues in his introduction, "and at the same time clearly decipherable— though hitherto neglected in Chaucer criticism—is the direct influence upon Chaucer's literary expression of the ambiguous class position in which Chaucer found himself, his middle-class origins, his courtly connections, his responsive interest in the new vigorous world of the bourgeoisie, and his economic and social need to reconcile that interest with the duties of a courtier. It is with a discussion and exemplification of this life-long contradiction in Chaucer, and its resulting irony, that much of the present study will be concerned."[8]

Though Birney's interest in irony was scholarly, it was not disinterested. It was an attempt to come to terms with the darker truths about his own nature; in particular, the ways crevasses seemed to open up between different sides of himself, alienating him not only from others, but from himself and inducing excruciating guilt. The ironist, went his long-considered definition, "is a man who *prefers*, for various reasons, to make a show of concealing his satiric thrusts. Like all satirists he is concerned with a lively presentation of certain selected realities placed directly against professed ideals of which the realities fall far short. Unlike the forthright fulminators, the ironist succeeds, by his indirectness, not so much in softening the blow—often quite the contrary—but in removing himself from clear responsibility for the attack."[9] Professed ideals, realities that fall far short, concealed satiric thrusts in order to avoid responsibility. This was not only the Chaucer Birney saw—a cautious and guarded poet who got away with attacking church and state because he was clever enough to use irony—it was Birney himself. His thesis was a justification of subterfuge.

With the successful completion of his thesis and the appointment at Toronto for at least the coming year, however, it seemed as if Birney was finally set on a path that would make secrecy unnecessary by integrating his many separate lives and selves into one impressive whole. From the vantage point of the Toronto lectureship, he was well situated to apply for jobs elsewhere, and his life with Esther promised ongoing work for the Trotskyist cause and freedom from the search for women, not to mention assistance typing and filing his work. And, as if to make up for all the frustrations of years of being overlooked, he was invited in the fall of 1936,[10] after returning from teaching summer school at UBC, to become literary editor of the Toronto left-wing journal *The Canadian Forum*. He was, he recalled, "flattered."[11]

Indeed he should have been. *The Canadian Forum* had established itself as the main vehicle for the new CCF party commentary, articles on the arts, and avant-garde fiction and poetry. It was Canada's version of the American *New International.*

Though there was no need for Birney to conceal his Trotskyist views from the board of the *Forum,* they made it clear that the journal itself followed the CCF line taken by political editor Frank Underhill, the outspoken Toronto professor of economics, and by contributor Frank Scott in Montreal, the civil rights lawyer and poet who, with Underhill, had been instrumental in founding the CCF. Indeed, Birney's Trotskyism served him well, since, like the CCFers, he was anti-Stalinist—an odd alignment Birney credits Underhill for perceiving. Birney seized the opportunity "to apply Marxist aesthetics" not to Chaucer but to contemporary literature. "I [would] have freedom to apply my own concepts of 'historical materialism,' to the literature I discussed," he recalled. But if he wanted to express his political views directly, he would have to do so elsewhere under a pseudonym. His role was to develop the literary side of the magazine, which was not as good as the other sections: select critical articles, poems and short fiction from the manuscripts that came their way and assign books to reviewers; but more importantly, to contribute regularly himself and actively recruit contributions.

Canadian literature was at a crossroads at the time Birney assumed his new position. Although the move to modernism was just under way in Montreal, with writers such as F.R. Scott, A.M. Klein and Leo Kennedy, and, in Toronto, Robert Finch and E.J. Pratt, the vast majority of poetry was still Victorian: an eclectic British pot-pourri of pretty musings on nature, sentimental wallowings and philosophical clichés. While the world writhed in the agonies of social and political conflict, poetry had somehow fossilized into formula. In a way parallel to Canadian political attitudes, Canadian literature was balanced on a fulcrum that pulled it with almost equal force back into this polite idealism of Victorian England and forward into a forthright North American realism.

As literary editor of *The Canadian Forum,* Birney found himself in a position of cultural power such as could scarcely have been imagined. It wasn't long before he began to exert that power in ways that inexorably shaped Canadian literature. As a lecturer at the University of Toronto, he was at an important nexus of like-minded former professors and new colleagues who could assist with reviews and articles, or even poems and stories, such as E.J. Pratt—the primary literary figure at that time whom Birney had met in Vancouver just that summer while both men had been teaching summer school; Northrop Frye—whom he had known at Toronto's graduate school in 1927; Herbert Davis, E.K. Brown, R.S. Knox, J.R. McGillivray, Norman Endicott, Gilbert Norwood and Louis MacKay, all professors of English; and professors of other subjects, Barker Fairley, Hermann Boeschenstein, Robert Finch and Gordon Andison. Beyond that, he could draw on his long experience in journalism—as editor-in-chief of *The Ubyssey*, as reporter for the *Point Grey Gazette*, as ad salesman and *Maclean's* subscription canvasser and as writer for the Trotskyist *New Leader*—to recruit and assess the value of manuscripts. With Esther enthusiastically typing his correspondence, he tapped into his own diverse networks: his university friends from UBC, Berkeley, Salt Lake City and the University of London. And he had no qualms about approaching writers, such as Christopher Isherwood (who declined), whom he did not know. It was not long before he had marked the literary section of the *Forum* not only with his taste for the best emerging writers in Canada, but also with his own international sensibility through contributors as diverse as Dr. Norman Bethune, who sent a lyric from the Loyalist lines in Spain, American realist novelists Sherwood Anderson and James T. Farrell, and Scottish poet and philosopher, Hugh MacDiarmid.

Within a year, Birney had also raised the technical standard of the magazine from one that regularly had typos and errors to one that was fully professional. To do so, he had employed his irritable temper constructively for once, tendering a letter of resignation to Frank Underhill on 29 December 1937 not for "political considerations" (though that was a factor, since Underhill was concerned that Birney was slipping his Trotskyist views into one of his *Forum* articles), but because "at least two stupid and entirely unnecessary mistakes occurred in the editing of two

Spanish poems.... [a] blunder I am held responsible [for] again, as for mistakes made this summer."[12]

More importantly, he had tipped the balance of literary taste in Canada by attacking sentimental verse and favouring the more direct social and political themes of contemporary poetry.

Birney's view of what literature should be informed his May 1937 article "Proletarian Literature: Theory and Practice."[13] In clear, direct prose, Birney reviewed three new works by left-wing writers (Ralph Fox, Arthur Calder-Marshall and Ernst Toller) with an eye to formulating the characteristics of good proletarian writing. Looking back over the history of the novel, he lists those whose fame seems most permanent: Cervantes, Francois Rabelais, Daniel Defoe, Henry Fielding, Leo Tolstoy, Honoré de Balzac and Thomas Hardy, and agrees with Fox that the common denominator is the courage to philosophize. Birney seems to agree with Fox that twentieth-century fiction has "retreat[ed] from epic breadth and realism" into "art for art's sake" novels. As for the proletarian novels of the thirties, Birney cites Fox, who claims that—except for John Dos Passos, Herbert Ernest Bates, André Malraux and Erskine Caldwell—there are many ways in which Marx would disown them.

> The Worker is not simply incoherent, passive, as in Hemingway's stories; he is not Elmer Rice's mechanized man; nor can the varied world in which he lives be exhausted in the stock types of the villainous Boss, the Idealistic Intellectual, and the Good Strike-Leader. The proletariat is not revealed either by photographing the cross-section of an individual on the slide of a Freudian microscope or by assembling the Masses "in the grip of inexorable economic forces." All these methods may be used in the socialist epic but they will be fused by the genuinely Marxist view, which is that each man has both a personal and a social history and that in their interplay lies the essential meaning of history.

Birney singles out Ernst Toller's play *Look Through the Bars* as a "testament... of his artistic loyalty to the working class" and formulates his own definition—reminiscent of Trotsky's—of good proletarian art:

> Proletarian art...must...be in the first place art, with its roots in personal experience, and its problems the eternal problems of mankind; it should not be designed to perform the work of party-resolutions, for that is the job of the the party, nor should it be a sectarian rejection of the bourgeois form for rejection's sake. Nevertheless, it should not forget to be proletarian; it should be written out of the ranks of the workers and in a speech they understand—written for them, for the "purging of their passions." ... [the proletarian artist] is not afraid to ennoble the revolutionary, whose fight is that of all civilization for survival. But that battle is not yet won, and if the artist is to help in the winning of it he must not sentimentalize.

In assessing these works, Birney incidentally raised a question pertinent to himself. In an era such as this, was art actually the most important pursuit? Wasn't it more important to devote energy to the great unwon battle for the survival of civilization? His answer was clear. Art must take second place. It was no more than "a lucky incident in a career primarily devoted to the more direct and urgent tasks of political argument and political struggle. It is the paradox of that struggle that the worker-writer must be ready to sacrifice his own artistic fruition in order that the heritage of past cultures, bourgeois among them, may be rescued and preserved and a finer society attained.... A Marxist should scarcely expect the literary revolution to precede the economic." Yet, despite this caveat, Birney's clear pronouncements on the nature and importance of proletarian art set as "contemporary" the magazine's literary tone, and alerted contributors to the standards against which their contributions would be measured.

In a scathing review of Nanaimo, B.C. poet Audrey Alexandra Brown's second collection, *The Tree of Resurrection*, for the August 1937 issue, Birney also made it clear that sentimental literature was unwelcome at the *Forum*. He pictures Brown as "[sprung] from the collective foreheads of the Victorian poets...fully-armed with the plaudits of Canadian authors' groups and of their attendant ladies." The "clamorous echoings in her verse of the nineteenth-century Great [poets] were welcomed as 'traditionalism,' as proof that even in its new greatness Canadian literature, like Canadian politics, condescended to remain loyal to the Empire."

> The title poem, somewhat diffusely Tennysonian, asserts a faith in personal physical immortality. There are other verses assuring us that beauty dies not, death is kinder than life, God exists. There are more anti-macassar embroiderings on Greek legends, and "delicate raptures, fragile ecstasies" upon Nature. The forests of British Columbia continue to yield for Miss Brown daffodils and no dogwood, halcyons not woodpeckers, innumerable oreads but never a logger.... Of the forty-two poems, only one mentions so local and ephemeral a being as a miner; he is a naughty fellow, who is punished for his amorousness by a creepy supernatural death in a folksy sort of mine.... Elsewhere Miss Brown speaks of war only in terms of silver trumpets and gold adornings.[14]

The juxtaposition of these two articles clearly reveals the poles of desirable and undesirable literature as far as Birney was concerned. "Good" literature showed man's personal and social history, touched on universal problems, was written in the language of ordinary people, and somehow contributed to the great revolutionary battle of the time without being strictly sectarian. "Bad" literature was purely aesthetic, removed from or indifferent to contemporary social problems, was written in the airy-fairy diction of British nineteenth-century romantics like Wordsworth or Victorians like Tennyson, and was idealistic, religious, sentimental or—worst of all—all three at once.

Given this frame of reference, it is perhaps surprising that Birney, as one of three judges (Bertram Brooker and Morley Callaghan were the other two) of a short-story contest he initiated in order to attract contributors to the magazine, awarded the prize to Luella Creighton (wife of historian Donald Creighton) for her story "The Cornfield."[15] The story, which topped sixty-five entries, dealt with the subtleties of an ordinary young girl's emotional life, despite the fact that the majority of the entries were attempts at Depression literature. In his "Short Story Contest—A Report,"[16] Birney sarcastically describes the shortcomings of some of the more "proletarian" entries ("One contestant allowed his dying freight-hopper to gaze at his dismembered limbs, from which the blood poured like fountains, and then calmly and lengthily to review the economic causes, the 'slump in the prices of agricultural products,' etc., which led to their dismemberment."), and explains that Creighton won though her story was "less ambitious in theme" because it was the best written. Despite his political convictions, his dedication to excellence in art carried the day. What Birney stood for was a contemporary sensibility *and* artistic excellence.

This was not to say that Birney was any the less committed to the Trotskyist cause. He had agreed with Underhill to keep his Trotskyist political doings apart from the *Forum*, except for his endorsement of contemporary literature, and a column he wrote in the *Forum* on current events called "Another Month." "Another Month," as Birney describes it, was "a regular tabulation of world news, in the Dos Passos manner, presented without commentary, but selected and arranged with an eye to the contradictions of capitalist society."[17] For this column, Birney used the pseudonym "Rufus," the name of a popular comic strip character with red hair like his own, but also one that carried forward the notion of "Matchstick," the childhood nickname which suggested both his skinny, carrot-topped frame and his inflammatory temper. Typical entries went as follows: "Canadian union official promises no sit-downs in Canada and American union ditto praises the peacefulness of the Canadian class struggle... 200 Sarnia workers strike in a foundry, are clubbed out with crowbars by a scab mob which half-lynches a union organizer and runs up the Canadian flag over the foundry;" or "Each English duchess is paying $2,000 for a 17-yard velvet court gown... York township women record that it takes a year to get

one housedress and a pair of stockings out of the relief authori-
ties."[18] It took only three months for "Rufus" to inflame Frank
Underhill. In the April *Forum*, "Rufus" ran an extra column[19]
that described the Guelph Reformatory riot in a way that
Underhill (who was himself so politically controversial that he
would soon be involved in a serious attempt to have him dismissed from the University of Toronto)[20] "expressed anxiety"
about the association of Trotskyist views with the *Forum*.
Though Birney focused not on this political knuckle-rapping in
the letter of resignation he sent Underhill, but on the technical
sloppiness of the magazine, "Rufus" was replaced by "Rufus
II"—the new business editor, Mark Farrell.

Though he could not air his political views in the *Forum*, Birney
was deeply engaged in Trotskyist activities. One of the first people
he contacted on his return from England was Joe Hansen from
his Utah days, the carpenter who had been an important member
of the Trotskyist group there, and at whose workshop full of
coffins The Sparks had sought refuge when one of their meetings
was broken up. Hansen had brought him up to date on the
American political scene. And he had also contacted his comrades
in Vancouver and met with them later during the summer after he
completed his Ph.D. while he taught summer school there.
Drawing on the expertise he had gained in underground political
activities from the Johnstones in Toronto, then in Vancouver,
Utah and London, and still using his pseudonym "Robertson," he
had set up in Toronto a Trotskyist group—called the "Socialist
Policy Group" in imitation of the English "Marxist Group in the
ILP" which he and Esther had belonged to—with hopes of developing it into a significant support for the Fourth International. In
a document called "Thesis Adopted by the Executive Committee
of the Canadian Bolshevist-Leninists for a Fourth International:
National Political Perspective," dated May 1938 and signed
"Robertson," Birney outlined the Canadian economic and political scene from a Trotskyist perspective and described the group he
and Esther had initiated as a cell within the CCF.

1. The Socialist Policy Group was formed in April this
   year as a legal organization within the Ontario CCF

under cover of which the 4th Internationalists in the CCF carry on their activity. Originating as an educational group, the SPG has gradually changed its character into a militant left-wing which is now in the process of:

(1) Adopting revolutionary positions on every question of national and international importance.

(2) of waging a relentless political struggle against the reformist bureaucracy.

(3) of exposing the reactionary politics and opportunist tactics of Stalinist stooges within the CCF.

(4) of publishing fortnightly an international mimeographed organ, the Socialist Action, bringing our point of view to the membership.

2. While the SPG has as yet attracted few revolutionary elements to its line, nevertheless it is felt that as the inevitable fight with the bureaucracy gets underway, all genuine left wingers will be drawn into the struggle in our support, although in the end they may not follow us out. It would be futile to attempt to set a date for leaving the CCF: this will be determined by the course of events, the tactics of the bureaucracy and the influence of the SPG in the membership. So long as we are allowed complete freedom to propagate our revolutionary ideas among the members and thereby spread our influence, unnecessarily provoking our expulsion would be pointless. On the other hand any paralysing curtailment of our freedom in the CCF, the outlawing of the SPG or banning the Socialist Action e.g. would premise a political struggle culminating in the formation of an Independent section of the 4th International.

3. Until recently the SPG was confined solely to Toronto where most of our forces lie. However steps have already been taken to transform it into a national tendency by the formation of a similar group in Vancouver, B.C. The tempo of our work in Toronto or Vancouver would not be hampered by developments

in either city owing to the nature of the national CCF
as a loose federation of practically autonomous provincial organizations. Under such circumstances the
expulsion from the CCF of our comrades in Toronto
would not exclude our Vancouver group remaining in
the CCF until local conditions warranted a split.[21]

Under pseudonyms too, he published articles in radical left-
wing American journals using radical left-wing rhetoric. In the
September issue of the *New International,* for example, he published a long statistics-ridden article situating Canada's economic
and political position in a global context called "The Land of the
Maple Leaf Is the Land of Monopoly: Canada and World
Politics."[22] In it he argued that there was "no other country in
the world where finance capitalism is so centralized." And,
despite his position at the *Forum* with its CCF orientation, he
took direct swipes at the CCF. "The 'Socialist' CCF," he fulmi-
nated, "has in its five years of existence reflected the same
national ambiguity, playing ball both with isolationists and with
collective security. Because it is still a loose federation its followers are treated to the spectacle of its seven federal parliamentary
representatives alternately supporting pacifism and the hypothetical wars of the League [of Nations]."
And wherever he could, he slid his political views into his
classes. And whenever he could, he slid his political views into
his classes. Birney was widely appreciated for his dramatic readings of Chaucer—especially the bawdy *fabliaux.* But he would
often digress. One of his students at the time, David Hayne, who
took his Anglo-Saxon course, and later became a professor at the
University of Toronto, recalls not only that Birney had a remarkable ability to read old English, but that "he regaled us with
many anecdotes about his working his way to England on a
freighter. The main point of all these anecdotes was that he was
not an ivory tower pedant, but a man of the people who had
seen the world and worked with his hands."[23] And Birney also
found ways of orienting his students to the left politically with
essay topics like "Changing Attitude to the Poor: [in] [Elmer]
Rice, [Erskine] Caldwell, with reference also to [George Bernard]

Shaw, [Walter] Greenwood, [Clifford] Odets, etc."[24]

Like water finding its level, Birney had initiated and seized the leadership of the Social Policy Group and had simultaneously risen at the *Forum* to the central position of literary influence in the country. If only he could also secure a university position, he would have felt that he had at last assumed his rightful place. To this end he had begun immediately on his return from England to employ his academic network not only on behalf of the *Forum*, but also in the interests of his career as an academic. Sedgewick continued to look out for him, of course, but came up with nothing. A job at the University of Alberta in Edmonton which opened up in 1936 went to Clarence Rupert Tracy, a Toronto B.A. and a Yale Ph.D. His old Berkeley friend, Merritt Y. Hughes, kept an eye open for a job at Wisconsin in 1937, and in 1938, Herbert Davis, one of the English professors who had examined him for the Ph.D. who was now Head of English at Cornell University, helped him apply for a position at four New York City colleges—Queen's, Hunter, NYC at Washington Square and Sarah Lawrence—but there were no openings. In his letters of application, Birney made it clear that he would actually prefer a job in the United States, where salaries were higher. By the summer of 1938, the strain had begun to show. Not only had his chronic eye trouble flared up, but his stomach was troublesome.

Sedgewick, who kept a steady and benevolent eye on his protégé gently queried both Birney's sense of persecution and his temperamental inability to settle down anywhere. "You are not being held back by anything but the circumstances that hold back others," he wrote in the summer of 1938. "The place [you now have at Toronto] may not be much, but it has a dignity & it looks as secure as most things are in these strange times." Sedgewick advised him to be sure of whatever "landing place" he chose after Toronto, but added, with remarkable insight: "But there comes to me—who have known and loved you a long time—the last bars of Schubert's Wanderer: *Dort wo du nicht bist, dort ist das Glück.* [literally, 'There where you are not, there is happiness.']"[25]

On Sedgewick's advice, Birney worked away at transforming

his Chaucer thesis into publishable form to make himself a more attractive academic candidate. To speed things up, he had typing help from Esther, who had failed to gain entrance to the university (despite an impassioned letter from Birney to the registrar on behalf of his "fiancée"),[26] and had—with the help of Birney's UBC fellow-Zate Dal Grauer—entered the School of Social Work. In July's issue of *The University of Toronto Quarterly*, in the driest pedantic prose, he published the chapter "English Irony Before Chaucer."[27] Next he began polishing "The Beginnings of Chaucer's Irony" for the prestigious American journal *Publications of the Modern Language Association*. Like many scholars before and since, he made the pilgrimage to Columbia University in New York City for the Christmas meeting of the Modern Language Association in 1938 in the hope of making contacts that would lead to a job. And he worked away steadily on a monograph which would be the book form of his whole thesis.

In February 1939, after returning from his futile trip to the MLA in New York, the prodigious work involved in his *Forum* editorship, the apparent futility of his Trotskyist activities with the Social Policy Group (which he described as "a voice crying in the wilderness"),[28] the long hours of preparation and marking for his English courses, and the meticulous preparation of his thesis for publication pushed Birney's frustration to an intolerable level.

In a letter that fairly seethed with hostility, Birney ingeniously confronted Blanche Colton Williams, Chairman of New York's Hunter College English Department. His letter consisted of questions and answers that had *not* appeared on the official job application form he had filed. The effect is one of outraged self-justification. To the question "Why do you think you are worth $3,000 [a year]?" for example, Birney answered: "Because I have spent the thirteen years since my graduation teaching and studying under widely varying conditions, because I have a Ph.D. from a university that rates fifth in the [world], because, as I think my recommendations and publications will demonstrate, I am a successful teacher and scholar in both mediaeval and modern fields and basically because my published articles show that I can write, and that I have something to say."[29]

Not long after, his frustration fanned by learning from Williams that he would have to be an American citizen in order to apply for a job at Hunter College (a virtual ban on Canadians, who would have to have the job and residence in the U.S. *in order* to obtain citizenship), Birney, who was usually sensitive and tactful in rejecting contributions to the *Forum*, lashed out at Paul Potts, a Vancouver writer whose poems were unacceptable in a double-edged letter that attacked the *Forum* at the same time as it attacked the poet. "You haven't yet learned some of the elementary jobs of your craft. Your punctuation is so lousy it's sometimes impossible to follow what you are trying to say. About ten years ago it was a fashion to follow E.E. Cummings and ignore things like that. The fashion's dead, & Cummings almost.... Your verse, 'The Nerve of the Bitch,' could, with a little polishing, punctuating, and strengthening of verbs, be quite effective—but I couldn't print it. The *Forum* sells mainly to a bunch of middle-class Canadian social-democrats who rush to cut off their subs[criptions] as soon as I print a word like 'bitch.' Personally, I want to go ahead and do it all the same, but the rest of the editors look at it differently.... I suggest you...send it to a journal less hog-tied with prudery than ours."[30] Though Birney's letter was unprofessional, even Ned Pratt agreed with its sentiments. "Your remarks" to "the buggar Potts," he wrote, "are the most incisive criticism I've seen in this country. True as geometry and much more interesting."[31]

Birney's temper spilled over onto Esther too, who was every bit his match. One student remembers her—complete with dyed red hair—coming to the closed door of the class where Birney was lecturing them and beating on the door and shouting obscenities at him. "He differed from the other professors in age and in rage," Mary Fowler, who took his Chaucer class in her second year, recalls. "He was always unhappy or unstable. I think he disliked teaching what he had to teach. He would come in very distraught and therefore never gave of himself to the lectures. We all thought he was quite odd. I remember one day he got livid. We were supposed to have looked something up and we hadn't. He went completely off-topic and went round the class shouting about all the illegitimate children of Robert Burns.

He was under stress having his wife or girlfriend coming after him. No other professor's wife waited around outside the classes the way she did."[32]

Despite his frustrations, Birney persisted in his search for a job throughout 1939, enclosing the article on Chaucer he had published in *PMLA* in September.[33] His former UBC friend, Mary Duncan, tried to locate something for him in Los Angeles, and he applied for a job he heard about at the University of Oklahoma, which did not even acknowledge his letter. He tried Syracuse and Northwestern in Chicago. Sedgewick wrote of a job at UBC, but advised him not to take it because it was "hack work" beneath Birney's talents. Finally a possibility opened up for a position in advanced creative writing through Herbert Davis, who knew A.H.R. Fairchild, the Chairman of English at the University of Missouri. "I mentioned a name or two here and said they would not be what he needed," wrote Davis, early in 1940, "then I went out for you and stressed your connection with the *Forum* articles and modern lit, etc. ...I said that you were on the Left, but stressed your anti-Communist feelings. I did not feel you would want to go anywhere disguised. I pushed very hard for you."[34] Birney thought it prudent to explain: "I ought in fairness to mention to you the fact that I have been for some time a socialist," he ingenuously wrote to Fairchild.

> I have always been an opponent of the communists, however; in England I was associated with the Independent Labour Party, and in Canada with the parliamentary socialist group, the Co-operative Commonwealth Federation. I have of late, however, allowed my membership to lapse as I have become convinced that politics is no field for me to work in. I find seeds of bureaucracy in even the mildest socialist group, and until that evil can be eliminated, there is a danger of any socialist state developing into the hell that Russia has become.... I'm interested in literary work almost exclusively now...your university need have no fear they would be importing a "red" if I joined your staff. I think the socialist ideal a better one

than the capitalist ideal, but I don't know how the change should be brought about, and I shall have to let other people bring it about for me. I shall always stand, however, for democracy, civil liberty, and the right of the worker to the fruits of his work. perhaps I'm only a Jeffersonian Democrat after all.[35]

Nowhere did he mention Leon Trotsky. Ironically, the secretive Birney was undone by even this degree of openness. Though Missouri showed enough interest in him to write to University College Principal Malcolm Wallace for recommendations, the job went to Henry Noyes, a candidate proposed by Roy Daniells. Birney later gathered from E.K. Brown that it had indeed been his politics that had undone him. "Missouri has decided I am too subversive for them," he wrote Davis in bitter disappointment. "As soon as I learned from you that you had mentioned my Left leanings to the dean, I knew I had to make a statement for myself. The statement was acknowledged politely by Fairchild, with a word of praise for my 'honesty' but no assurance that my ideas (mild, and mildly stated) would not count against me.... he did not dare appoint anyone at the moment who might take sides one way or the other on the current battle about admitting negroes to the state university. It appears the blacks pay taxes and have a quaint notion they ought to be allowed to go to the white man's college."[36]

Though Birney claimed to be well rid of such a job, his sense of rejection was profound. If he learned anything from this painful experience it was that honesty did not pay. His attempt to draw his secret lives up into the light and integrate his various energies had exacted a fierce price. In a letter that virtually wallowed in self-pity, he pulled out all the stops in an appeal to Principal Malcolm Wallace in hopes of a raise. "My wife has just been taken to the hospital," he wrote,

she is not in any danger, but she may lose the child we had hoped to have born to us this summer. If she loses it, it will be because she tried to keep on working at the job which she had taken in order to add to my salary....

If I were a young man, fairly green at my job, I would feel differently. But I will be thirty-six this summer.... Daniells, whose sophomore papers I corrected when I was an instructor at B.C. is now a department head. Younger men with half my background and a quarter of my teaching experience, are now being recommended equally with me for the vacancy at Missouri. What is the reason? ...I have no doubt that prejudice against my private political opinions has had something to do with it—even in a country which may shortly be calling upon me to die for "democracy."[37]

Though Birney's description of his political position seemed dishonest rather than "mild" in his letters to both Fairchild and Wallace, it was actually close to the truth. Trotsky's support of Russia's invasion of Finland in late November 1939 appalled Birney and dealt the final blow to his confidence in the ideals he had held for almost a decade. As he wrote to Wallace and several others,

I have been for many years a bitter enemy of Stalinist totalitarianism, and an active opponent of fascism everywhere. I once praised some of the opinions of Trotsky as opposed to Stalin, but now that Trotsky too has shown himself a defender of Russia against Finland, I have broken completely with his ideas and with any of the communist aims. I believe that some form of socialism is needed in the world to save us from the terrible slaughter and waste of war, and to cure unemployment and depression. But I believe that socialism must come democratically. For that reason, I oppose not only the various communist parties but even the bureaucratic tendency within the CCF. My only organizational affiliation is with the Civil Liberties League.[38]

About a month before, in January 1940, he had written an elaborate criticism of Russia's aggression on the basis that it was "a clear violation of an elementary Leninist principle, the right to self-determination of peoples."[39]

It was his last article as "Robertson." And in some essential way, it was the belated and abrupt end of his youth. "Our old days, when we were in Toronto together," Roy Daniells wrote in a letter late in January thanking Birney for giving him a reading list of proletarian novels, "have acquired a kind of glamour 'with the years,' but they weren't so very happy or fruitful, on a candid retrospect, and I'd rather be in my later thirties than ten years younger. It's at least less painful. And you?"[40]

"There is no news, except to report two miscarriages," Birney starkly replied.

> One was Esther's; we had hoped to have an heir in July, but the little fish was incomprehensibly eager to get into this world of woe, and Esther had to spend the last two weeks in the hospital. The doctor said the reason was simply that Esther had worked too long and hard in her social welfare job (Child welfare work, ironically enough). It's another of these vicious circles—in order to have money to have a child, Esther works, and loses the child... The second miscarriage you probably know about. Missouri.... I've no doubt you feel these times happier and more fruitful than our last student days. But behind those days, for me, were periods when I taught better, had more fun and better pay than I have now. After creating a very ungentlemanly uproar this year, I got an increase—but I'm still down in the failure class.[41]

✍ *12* ✿

WILLIAM AND DAVID

"**W**hat I am really truly glad about," Garnett Sedgewick wrote fondly to his irascible protégé on learning that Birney had "broken with the [Trotsky] boys" early in 1940, "is the news that you can now find time for writing. Without doubt you are better fitted for scholarship and writing than for politics. And I hasten to say that I don't mean the writing must be 'scholarly' or 'scholastic'—tho' it could be if you wished to have it so. And for God's sake," he teased with fatherly concern, "wherever you are, don't try hard to wear yourself down by roasting more than a dozen irons all at once. I am all for 'leisure for writing': give leisure a chance for a change. If it's a novel that is being gestated, give it due pre-natal care. For instance!"[1]

Birney was perfectly situated to respond to Sedgewick's advice and to fulfil his own declaration that he intended "to take a long rest, in which I will luxuriate once more in skepticism and political idleness, and try, if it is not too late, to do some real writing instead of the weekly political hack work I've devoted my spare time to for the last eight long bitter years."[2] He finally had an academic position in a major Canadian university and reason to believe it secure. As literary editor of *The Canadian Forum*—whose circulation was about 2,500[3]—he simmered in the very

180

crucible of Canadian literary life. Over the previous two years, he had helped forge contemporary literary standards. His knowledge of the best that was being thought and written in Canada, as creative writing moved away from colonial romanticism towards a tougher North American realism, could hardly have been exceeded. Straddling the two worlds—academic and literary—situated him at the very centre of literary power in a nation whose literary output was dominated by university men. So small was this community then, and so centralized its English writers in Montreal and Toronto where the publishing houses, many of the literary magazines and the main chapters of the Canadian Authors' Association (CAA) were located, that Birney knew most of the writers and critics of the day personally.

Among these, E.J. Pratt—or Ned, as he was known—stood above the rest. Birney had first met the convivial feisty Ned in Vancouver where both men were teaching summer school at UBC in 1936. They had taken to each other at once, and now, four years later, were colleagues at the university—Pratt at Victoria College, Birney at University College. And it had been Pratt, who was himself editor of the CAA's *Canadian Poetry Magazine* (circulation about 300)[4] who had recommended Birney to the *Forum*. Birney had only stated the obvious in the summary of "recent and good Canadian literature" he wrote in response to a request for information he received at the *Forum* in the summer of 1939 when he singled Pratt out as the most important and best poet.[5] Not that there was much competition. His roll-call of Canadian writers, since he overlooked Montreal poets such as A.J.M. Smith, A.M. Klein and F.R. Scott, was predictably meagre—poets Leo Kennedy and Dorothy Livesay and in fiction Morley Callaghan, Frederick Philip Grove and Luella Creighton—and included a number of writers virtually unknown later.[6] His correspondence shows he knew many others too: not only the Montreal group, but Raymond Souster, Anne Marriott, Alf Bailey—his old graduate student friend—Harry Cassidy's wife, Carol Coates, and Bill McConnell. In fact, Canadian poetry was about to take a quantum leap forward. Both Ralph Gustafson and A.J.M. Smith were busy compiling anthologies: the former for Penguin's 1942 *Anthology of*

Canadian Poetry (English); the latter—funded by a prestigious Guggenheim Fellowship—for Oxford's 1943 *The Oxford Book of Canadian Verse*.

Pratt deserved his uncontested status. In 1940 he was at the peak of his career, having published several of the major narratives such as "The Titanic" and "Fable of the Goats" which ensured his centrality in the early Canadian literary canon. It could be argued that he was poised at the summit of his poetic endeavours with "Brébeuf and His Brethren" in 1940. Certainly Birney, who reviewed this dramatic narrative—about the seventeenth-century tragedy of the Jesuits martyred by the Hurons— for the September issue of the *Forum*, offered extravagant praise for what he called "the Canadian poem of the year."[7] Earlier, Birney had dropped a note to his friend congratulating him on what was "obviously the literary event of the year" and expressing the hope that "the Americans will realize it is an event in narrative poetry on this continent, not just in Canada."[8] Now, officially, he praised Pratt's "narrative verve and dramatic intensity," his "flexibility of line," his "flashing imagination and panoramic eye," his "enthusiasm for mankind in its moments of courage, endurance, comradeship and self-sacrifice," his "restraint and a simplicity which are comparatively new." "Bigness of deed and character," he observed, "is not made merely spectacular or grotesque, but is heightened into the grand." "With this volume," he concluded, alluding to (and expanding on) Pratt's own observation two years before that "though there are no peaks in Canadian poetry there are at least a few foothills, and the mountains come to birth out of the foothills,"[9] "Mr. Pratt's own achievement continues visibly to rise into what may be the first of our Rockies."

As he turned from politics to poetry, Birney did not have to look far. His model was right there. He had already copied Pratt academically: on discovering that Pratt had a creative writing class in poetry, Birney began encouraging his students in the history of the short story to submit an original short story in lieu of one of their essays. Now he would see if he could outdo Pratt poetically.

As Sedgewick had recognized, Birney was perpetually in danger of being pulled in too many directions at once. And, though his decision to take a long rest and focus his energies on creative writing was serious, he underestimated the vacuum left by his abandonment of politics. He said he intended to "luxuriate" in "skepticism and political idleness." In fact, the key word in his letter to Sedgewick was "bitter." Birney's abandonment of the idealism that had sustained and invigorated him for almost a decade left him not only skeptical but dangerously close to cynicism. His loss of faith in Trotsky and the Fourth International tolled the death of Earle Robertson and marked in some profound way the end of his youth. In the absence of that galvanizing vision, he experienced a crisis that bordered on existentialism. What was life for? To what could he dedicate his talents and energies?

That fall, he fretted that at thirty-six he was too old for poetry: "I'm afraid I'm starting about fifteen years too late," he wrote to critic Lionel Stevenson.[10] With this fear in mind, he hedged his bets. He flailed about trying to recover his lost sense of purpose. He sought other kinds of jobs; notably, what he thought of as "propaganda work" to promote Canadian patriotism and incite the public against fascism.[11] He wrote Ira Dilworth, B.C. Regional Representative of the CBC and manager of radio station CBR in Vancouver, in hopes of radio work. And he contacted Major Gladstone Murray, general manager of CBC in Ottawa, offering his services and proposing a program on the history of religious tolerance in Canada.[12] And he appealed to his old Zate chum Bruce Macdonald, now with the Canadian Shipping Board, to help him approach John Grierson at the National Film Board for a job in Ottawa. Grierson was interested enough to request a sample script. But Birney's proposals on Religious Tolerance and Mother's Allowances"[13] (suggested by Esther, who had been working with welfare children by day and with refugee children at night) were both turned down. Though Birney's search for a job in radio and film work could be seen as a continuing commitment to socialism and democracy—certainly not "luxuriating" in political idleness—some of his other initiatives were far from Marxist. He wrote his UBC friend Dal Grauer that same fall, asking for a business job at B.C. Electric, where Grauer was secretary.[14]

Meanwhile, as if these irons were not roasting in the fire at all, Birney joined the university's officer training program (COTC) as a cadet (and cautioned a friend in Vancouver not to tell his mother),[15] a commitment that entailed two evenings and an afternoon each week. "I have joined the army," he, who had once thought teaching purposeful, wrote bitterly to Dal Grauer, "so what future I have will be settled without my having much to do with it.... Now that I've burned my bridges, this last year of academic life is distinctly pleasant... I don't give a damn about building up courses for the next year, or being pleasant to the Dean of Women."[16] To his former Utah room-mate Herman Singer, who was at a far enough remove to encourage honesty, he wrote candidly that being a cadet would provide "protective coloring" for his political past—a comment made with his colleague Frank Underhill's current public ordeal in mind.[17] He, at least, would not be pressed to resign from the university.

In November he resigned from the *Forum*. He claimed—to the editor of *World News* where he unsuccessfully sought paid reviews or a column—that he was "tired of working for nothing, and for a sloppy magazine."[18] But he may also have been piqued that the experience at the *Forum* which he had often cited proudly, had failed to find him work elsewhere.

In this morass of indecision, Birney tried to focus on creative writing. His method was to revive poems he had published and resubmit them and to go back to notes he had made in the 1920s and 1930s for poems he had wanted to write. Whether this was the cause or the effect of a sudden and profound bout of homesickness is unclear. But in his crisis that fall, Birney's bitterness focused strongly on the loss of his youth, a loss symbolized for him somehow by the loss of the western landscapes in which he had once been young and hopeful and free. Those were the landscapes of the earlier poems he had written or had planned to write. In reviving these now, Birney brooded upon the tragic passage of time.

With almost frantic haste, Birney sent off his poems in every direction, waiting anxiously for the judgements he was more experienced in delivering than receiving. *Partisan Review* in the U.S. had rejected "Hands" in June; three were returned by

Sewanee Review in August; two came back from *The New Yorker*.
But in August, Ned Pratt responded effusively to "Dusk on
English Bay" and promised, as editor, to publish it in the
Canadian Poetry Magazine along with two or three others, if
Birney could send more: "you write in the most richly imagina-
tive manner. This Dusk is a pippin: it's totally free of cliches! It
abounds in original concentrated metaphors and similes."[19] And
Evelyn Caldwell, a family friend of the Birneys, arranged for
"West Vancouver Ferry" to be published (for $3.00) in *The
Vancouver Province* where she worked as a journalist and editor.
But these were friends. Birney wanted to prove himself on the
strength of his work alone—preferably in the U.S. where there
could be no hint of favouritism. In January, Ralph Gustafson
took "Slug in Woods," a whimsical descriptive poem conceived
in 1928 and already published as a space-filler in the *Forum*, for
his forthcoming anthology. But Birney felt the sting of rejection
more strongly than the glow of acceptance, and he festered in
spite of his successes.

   In January, he was disgruntled to learn that he had placed fifth
in the *Canadian Poetry Magazine* competition. His poem "Eagle
Island" expressed his bitter mood at the time.

> I've had enough of this inert
> Ontario, this eunuch sea
> And pastured fenced nonentity
> I'm off to where a seafresh sun
> Slants golden warmth at dawn across
> Dwarfed Jurassic woods of moss…[20]

Here and elsewhere there is evidence of Birney's intense dislike
for Ontario where he felt emasculated and confined and his
equally intense longing to return to the invigorating landscapes
of his youth. "I shall always hate the complete lack of horizons in
this part of the world," he typically wrote to Herman Singer in a
declaration with symbolic as well as literal import.[21] As he wrote
to his mother—accounting for himself, as usual: "Esther was disappointed I didn't get 'first' but at least I came 'fifth' out of
450—and the joke is that my poem was a comic 'attack' on the

dullness of Ontario and its scenery, and a wish to be back in British Columbia… Eagle Island (where we spent some days in a summer cottage with the MacPhails—remember?)."[22]

By the end of January, Esther, who had quit her job in the fall, knew she was pregnant again. Her earlier pregnancy had prompted Birney to fix the seal on his disillusionment with Trotskyism by marrying Esther.[23] He had obtained an annulment of his marriage to Sylvia on 14 June 1937 on grounds of her inability to consummate the union (with Wilfred Judson, an old poker pal who later became a justice in the Supreme Court of Canada, as his lawyer). With no ceremony whatsoever and with the presiding Presbyterian minister's wife as their witness, he and Esther had been married by Samuel Lundie on 6 March 1940 at Port Credit just outside Toronto. "I had been divorced by Israel Heiger since 25 July 1938. We got married for the sole purpose of giving a child legitimacy," Esther recalls. "We both thought marriage was a bourgeois institution having to do with property and possessions. We had had a Marxist beginning and set out to live according to *The Communist Manifesto*. We believed you don't possess people. For this reason, neither of us objected to affairs."[24] Certainly Birney must have had doubts about the commitment of marriage. Not only was he dejected and unsure of himself generally, but during the summer of 1940 when he was on his own in Vancouver because Esther had been obliged to return to her job after driving with him to Banff, he had had an affair with Betty Carter McTavish—the stepdaughter of his old UBC girlfriend Mary Carter—whose husband was overseas with the British armoured division. He had managed to see her for a weekend in Montreal in early October, and she and her two-year-old son (whose rowdy antics he had objected to) had visited at Christmas. Like other women with whom Birney had been involved, Betty noticed his emotional detachment. And with brittle cynicism, Birney had conducted the affair in a spirit that encouraged Betty to befriend Esther as well.[25] Now Esther's pregnancy (along with Betty's growing anxiety about her husband's feelings) dampened the relationship. Birney turned his attention to painting the flat at 40 Hazelton Avenue and to earning more money for Esther's imminent medical costs by delivering off-campus lectures and writing articles for popular magazines such as *Saturday Night*.[26] He had succeeded the year before in pleading for a salary raise; now he tried again. This time, he not only got a raise of $200 (his salary was now $2,500 a year), but also a promotion to Assistant Professor—a triumph he greeted with what Sedgewick called "lugubrious melancholy."[27]

During those first months of 1941, while Esther was gestating the baby—whimsically called "Beowulf" in deference to Earle's interest in Anglo-Saxon literature—who was eagerly anticipated because of her miscarriage a year and a half earlier, Birney was gestating his first major poem, as if reminded by Esther's pregnancy of Sedgewick's advice to give his creative work "due prenatal care." Significantly, he announced its completion not to his poetry colleagues like Pratt, but to his mother, as if to assert a more important mother–son duo. "I've just finished a long poem about mountain-climbing," he wrote just after Easter when she thanked him for sending her a new Easter hat. "I've been working on it off and on, in spare time, for a couple of months. Now I'm wondering if I can get it published. It's hard to get a poem of 200 lines published these days."[28]

The poem was "David." In late April Birney began sending it off anywhere he could think of with carefully composed letters peppered with allusions to his work on the *Forum*, citing his awards and Ned Pratt's praise for the poem and pretentiously signed "Earle Birney, Ph.D., Assistant Professor," which suggested he had much at stake in having it accepted. Oddly, though, as if to defend himself in advance against rejection, his letters were also self-deprecating. (He also bolstered himself by sending off simultaneously his short story about the impact of the Great War on Banff children, "Mickey Was a Swell Guy," to *Story* magazine in New York.)[29] First he tried the American journals. "I doubt myself if ['David'] is up to your standards," he wrote *Atlantic Monthly*, "but there's nothing like trying the best. The poem is a story of mountain climbing in the Canadian Rockies and has at least the merit of material so far neglected by other writers. The form is a five-beat line, basically anapestic, in assonantal stanzas, abba. In working it out I have been influenced

by MacLeish's *Conquistador.* I write in deliberate opposition to
the prevailing cult of the obscure and the didactic, believing still
that the best poetry is 'simple, sensuous, and passionate.'"[30] To
New Directions he wrote,

> it's my belief that the really new directions in literature
> are *away* from the metaphysical, contorted, the spitless
> intellectualism, the clever-clever allusiveness to a mis-
> understood Marx or an illdigested [sic] Vico and
> *towards* a new colloquial gusto, the reassertion of heroic
> values (even at the cost of some romanticism), and a
> fresh, sensuous and emotional appraisal of the lives we
> live…if it isn't new, it's certainly unfashionable.… The
> material [in my narrative about mountain climbing] is
> strange to an easterner, and the west has no maga-
> zines…nobody has, apparently, written in that form,
> so it's out. And the damned thing tries to be under-
> standable and tragic and pictorial, and nobody but a
> duffer would want to read that kind of thing these
> days. Well, if you want to, I'll send it for your rejec-
> tion, together with a 100-line tetrameter couplet affair
> "On Going to the Wars," …[which] talks about a new
> direction I'm headed for, soon, I hope—England, in
> the guise of a second lieutenant of infantry.[31]

In succession, "David" was rejected by both these journals, and
by *Queen's Quarterly, Penguin New Writing, Twice a Year, New
World, National Magazine, University of Toronto Quarterly,
Kenyon Review, Horizon* and *Sewanee Review. Poetry* (Chicago)
hinted that they might consider printing the first eight sections
of the poem as an extract, but Birney declined. Finally, the poem
was accepted after close to half a year of submissions and rejections, by the journal he had resigned from less than a year before:
The Canadian Forum. As for most of the other poems he circulated unsuccessfully for publication in any but journals where he
had "pull" that year,[32] it was a pyrrhic victory. His rancour overflowed in a letter to Frank Wilcox: "Most of my verse, as you
might guess, stinks, and I have no desire to send it to you. Some

of it is even so bad that I put it out anonymously.[33] One of the effusions that I acknowledge will appear in the *CForum* next week, but I doubt if I will send it to you. It is a piece of ornate melodrama, and I would have you think better of me than that I published it."[34]

"David"'s first readers, like readers ever since, wondered whether the tragic events that befall David and his friend Bob had actually happened. Birney's response was secretive on this question. David was partly himself, as he wrote to Dorothy Livesay, "me at 19 when I was as romantic as hell."[35] But he opened up to poet Kenneth Rexroth, an experienced climber to whom the *New Directions* editor, James Laughlin, referred Birney for advice about where to publish his poem. Rexroth had not only climbed extensively in the Cottonwoods near Salt Lake City and in the Rockies, he had run into some of the students Birney had politicized at Utah in the 1930s. Rexroth challenged Birney's poem on technical grounds—that the rock at the peak would not splinter and that a fall of forty feet would not be enough to kill a man. As if to an old friend, Birney responded. He agreed that the rock probably would not splinter, though he pointed out that he had had in mind "the peaks on the north of the Bow Valley above Banff, particularly Mount Louis (Conrad Kain's favourite, or one of his) and its companion Edith, which *is* like that," but disagreed about the fall itself.

> This was an uninterrupted fall by a man falling backwards, landing on his back. Ten feet, landing on a rock-prong, might be enough. I changed it to fifty, for a rounder guess-number, but, boy, I'd hate to fall forty straight on to rock. Most falls which aren't fatal are not straight. As a matter of fact, part of the story got into my skull as a result of a fatal fall of *twenty* feet that happened to a friend of mine in the B.C. Coast Ranges. He is the model for David—a loveable young amateur, whom I'd always thought too cautious ever to get hurt. He was climbing a very ordinary mountain with one companion—no rope. I never felt that his companion's story was very coherent about the

exact reason for the fall, and I suspected something like I described in the story. The real David's back was broken and punctured by a sharp rock-rib and, as in the story, he was paralyzed from the neck down but conscious. His companion didn't push him over, of course—there wasn't any particularly [sic] cliff beneath him anyway. He went for help and David died of exposure and blood-loss before they could get back. I'm afraid it's a morbid story, for mountaineers; what I started out to give was the special happiness one gets in climbing, especially when young, and innocent of disaster—then the revulsion of feeling in a naive follower and hero-worshipper.[36]

The "real David" was David Cunningham Warden, an exceptional UBC student of Classics whom Birney had known well, since David worked with him for three years on *The Ubyssey*. In fact, Warden—whose main interest was literature—had been a close contender in 1926 for the position of editor-in-chief, which Birney narrowly won. Unlike Birney, Warden was conventionally handsome—tall, athletic (he played defence on the second soccer team) and intelligent. Kaye Lamb, a fellow UBC student who would later become Dominion Archivist in Ottawa, describes him as having the qualities of a classical Greek youth: "David was devoted to the outdoors and aesthetics; he was a big, very good-looking chap and made to be somebody [important]."[37] In the matriculation examinations, Warden had the highest marks in B.C.; he headed his class in first year; in the second and third years he won scholarships for character as well as standing. According to Kaye Lamb, Warden and Birney were both favourites of Sedgewick's: "There was a link there through Garnett Sedgewick. Sedgewick had what today would be called a preference for boys. Like Earle, who was two years ahead of Warden, David was Sedgewick's top English honours student. His death temporarily crushed Sedgewick; to lose him suddenly like that was pretty tough on him."[38] Warden's accident in the summer of 1927, while climbing in the coastal mountains north of Vancouver with Wilbur Sparks, shocked and disturbed the entire university community. Sparks, whom Birney would also have known, since he was assistant business manager of *The Ubyssey* in 1924 when Birney was a reporter, was a Science student described in the yearbook as "an incurable optimist."

David Warden's horrendous death (he fell fifty feet, not ten; lay where he fell for twenty-four hours; and died in Vancouver General Hospital two days later on 19 September 1927) prompted a poem by R.E.S. (Ralph Stedmond) in *The Ubyssey* that could be seen as the forerunner to Birney's, if it were not notable more for its sentimentality than its literary merit:

To David Warden

Dead! Can he be dead, he who was a man
  So young and strong, so clear of eye and mind!
  How dead? Can that broad current unconfined,
And tide so swiftly set that in him ran
So soon he stayed and from the sky's bright span
  Of his horizon be so soon declined?
  The common course of moon and stars assigned
A deep and fuller flow. By what dark plan
  Or motion of the spheres
Is this incoming wave so headlong fled?
  There shall no sign be given: nor to these ears
Come any answer from the empty bed
  Of Time's wide sea.... What virtue is in tears
When so high promise ends, and he is dead.[39]

But the horrible, gut-wrenching death of David Warden was only one of Birney's sources for his poem. Perhaps Pratt's comparison of Canadian literary efforts so far to foothills and of masterpieces to the Rockies triggered Birney's "western nostalgia"[40] and prompted him to locate a western equivalent to Pratt's heroic narrative of Brébeuf. Certainly, by his own admission, Birney had two other literary models in mind—Archibald MacLeish's Pulitzer Prize-winning saga of the conquering of Mexico by Cortes *Conquistador* (1932) and the mediaeval chivalric narrative *Song of Roland*.

Though Birney took the idea of conquest from MacLeish (possibly having in mind also the striking image of Cortes "silent upon a peak in Darien" from John Keats's famous sonnet "On First Looking into Chapman's Homer") and was influenced by many techniques of poetry from *Conquistador,* the more important elements that make "David" a classic of English poetry can be traced to his unlikely source for a contemporary poem, the Old French "*chanson de geste,*" *Song of Roland.*[41] Though there are many technical similarities between the two poems, the most striking aspects of *Song of Roland* are its setting in the Pyrenees, which is adapted to the tone and temper of the heroic military events during the Crusades that take place, and its dramatization of what was called *compagnonnage,* a relationship defined by one translator of the poem as follows:

> Two young men, not related by birth...might freely pledge to each other loyal comradeship and brotherhood in arms. Their pact was not necessarily formal; but its effect was to link the knights' destinies as firmly as any feudal tie or even blood connection...neither history nor legend offers any more illustrious pair of [such] companions than Roland and [his friend] Oliver.[42]

According to another expert on heroic poetry, such a friendship—involving ethical questions, loyalty to the death and shared ideals—is "a partnership of a special kind... The participants share both dangers and glory, and the honour of one is the honour of the other... A hero's love for his friend is different from his love for his wife or his family, since it is between equals and founded on an identity of ideals and interests."[43] There is more than a hint of such *compagnonnage* between David and Bob as they climb up and away from "the ruck of the camp" into a shared idealism. And the violence and horror of David's death equals the waste of splendid young manhood when Roland and Oliver die. And, as in many heroic poems, the hero must make an agonizing moral choice.

Though Birney was not on the climb with David Warden and

Wilbur Sparks, he had climbed many a mountain with friends himself. But more important, he had just lost faith in a crusade he had undertaken with Ken Johnstone when the two "brothers-in-arms" had sworn their allegiance to Leon Trotsky among the mountains of Norway. His abandonment of these ideals in January 1940—just before he began writing 'David,' constituted a wrenching disillusionment. "I have broken with POLITICS," he wrote a friend at the time,

> For a while I carried on a fight against the Old Man's Finnish policy—he wanted the Reds to win, at the same time piously "condemning" the invasion. But I finally had to face a lot of ugly facts I had been forced to admit for along [sic] time: that the Old Man's organization is growing as bureaucratic as the next one, that up here [in Canada] the whole organizational approach is quixotic and suicidal... I still think the ultimate choice is socialism or barbarism. But as for me, I've spent more than eight year's [sic] leisure time, and sacrificed more than I care to think of, for [a cause] that seems pretty futile now... My spare time, if I can find any, is going to be writing, and not political writing...you know me well enough to know that a break like this doesn't come easy, nor without a lot of thought.[44]

It was out of this clear turning point—a fall from hope and faith —that "David" and most of the other poems that would eventually be collected in his first volume *David and Other Poems* were forged. Like Bob, Birney now faced carrying on in a real world of moral ambiguity which was no longer uplifting, but diminished and ugly.

The interplay of Birney's real sources—David Warden's death, his own remembered exhilaration from the old mountain-climbing days, and the fall from political idealism into repellent moral relativity—and his literary models—Pratt's heroic narratives, the chivalric bonding of two young men in *Roland* and the sense of historic west-coast conquest in *Conquistador*—was a heady mix.

But its publication in the December issue of the *Forum* was upstaged by the birth on 1 September (Labour Day!), not of Beowulf or Magnus or Laurenson, but of William Laurenson, so-named for Birney's father and his mother's mother, despite the fact that the baby most closely resembled Esther's maternal Polish relatives. And meanwhile Birney was dickering with the Macmillan Company and Lorne Pierce at The Ryerson Press in the hope of publishing a small book of poems in which "David" would figure prominently. Surely it was not coincidental that the birth announcements the Birneys sent was in the form of a publication announcement that fooled many of their friends:

ANNOUNCING!
The publication of the first
work by the authors
EARLE and ESTHER BIRNEY

WILLIAM

This is a deluxe edition (8lbs. 3oz)
handsomely bound in pink kid,
limited to one copy

DATE OF RELEASE
SEPT. 1 1941

PRIVATE PATIENTS PAVILION
TORONTO GENERAL HOSPITAL[45]

As the year drew to an end, Birney had generated a flurry of activity that suggested he was covering all possible angles. He was teaching his courses, keeping, as he said, just one lecture ahead of his students. Whenever he could, he lectured and wrote articles for extra cash. His literary offspring proliferated and he was almost frantically pressuring for publication both as a poet and short-story writer. He completed two more sections of his thesis on Chaucer: one of which Roy Daniells had accepted for the *Manitoba Arts Review*,[46] the other of which was taken by the distinguished *Journal of English and Germanic Philology*.[47] In imitation of A.J.M. Smith who had won a Guggenheim grant to compile his anthology of Canadian poetry, he had concocted an application for a Guggenheim to do a study of the Canadian short story from 1835 to 1942 and was severely irked when E.K. Brown, who was about to leave Toronto to become department head at Cornell, refused to support him because A.S.P. Woodhouse was applying at the same time. And—as if he intended no future at the university—or in Canada at all, for that matter—he was ardently pursuing military advancement. Having passed exams at Christmas, he became a second lieu-tenant (infantry) after spending two weeks from 8-21 June in training at the army camp at Niagara, turned down an invitation to apply for a commission in the RCAF as "one of those poor buggers who teaches pilots how to fly on the ground in a dummy cockpit,"[48] and accelerated his on-campus activities as a drill sergeant.

Yet like a lone high note ringing out far above the welter of Birney's convoluted life came the voice of Lacey Fisher at 10:15 p.m. on Monday, 4 January 1942, as he read over the national CBC radio the poem newborn in the December issue of *The Canadian Forum*, the poem that began:

> David and I that summer cut trails on the Survey,
> All week in the valley for wages, in air that was
>   steeped
> In the wail of mosquitoes, but over the sunalive
>   weekends
> We climbed, to get from the ruck of the camp, the
>   surly
> Poker, the wrangling, the snoring under the fetid
> Tents, and because we had joy in our lengthening
>   coltish
> Muscles, and mountains for David were made to
>   see over,
> Stairs from the valleys and steps to the sun's retreats.

Right through to its spellbinding end,

I said that he fell straight to the ice where they
    found him,
And none but the sun and incurious clouds have
    lingered
Around the marks of that day on the ledge of the
    Finger,
That day, the last of my youth, on the last of our
    mountains.[49]

"Sonny Boy," age four.

With his mother and
father before Will
went overseas,
Banff, 1916.

With his mother and
father after Will
returned from
the Great War,
Banff, 1917.

"The Woodpecker,"
written and
illustrated by Birney
at Banff Public School,
c. 1915.

Birney in his Creston Valley
days, 1918–19.

Mountain climbing, 1922.

Jessie MacPhail, Vancouver, mid-1920s.

William George Birney and Martha Stout Robertson Birney, c. 1925.

David Cunningham Warden,
model for "David," 1927.

With Barbara Barrett (extreme left) and Berkeley friends
at the beach at Carmel, California, 1928.

Garnett "Doc" Sedgewick in the mid-1920s.

Corinne Hagon, inspiration
for "The Hazel Bough."

Catherine Fisk, Salt Lake City,
Utah, 1932–33.

Herman Singer, model for Van
Bome in *Down the Long Table*,
Salt Lake City, Utah, 1932–33.

Martha Birney and Sylvia Johnstone in Martha's garden
in Vancouver, summer 1933.

Roy Daniells in front of Tom Thomson's shack in Toronto,
summer 1933.

Esther Bull Heiger at about
the time she met
Earle Birney,
London, England, 1934.

Margaret Crosland, London,
England, mid-1940s.

The young Trotskyist,
London, England, 1935.

With Esther and "Barnacle Bill" at
45 Isabella Street, Toronto, before
going overseas, spring 1943.

Carlotta Makins,
England, 1944.

With Gwethalyn "Gwen" Graham and E.J. "Ned" Pratt
at the CAA conference in Toronto, June 1946.

Gabrielle "Gaby" Baldwin,
Montreal, 1946–47.

Einar and Muriel Nielson,
Bowen Island, summer 1948.

At Bowen Island, summer 1948, left
with Elizabeth "Bet" Campbell.

A.J.M. "Art" Smith and Malcolm and Margerie Lowry
at Dollarton, late 1940s.

The professor-poet.

❧ *13* ❧

OVERSEAS

On 5 May 1943, a week before his thirty-ninth birthday, Captain A. Earle Birney, Personnel #B904195, left Toronto for England to serve in the Canadian Armed Forces as a personnel selection officer. "My dear Birney," wrote James Wreford Watson, a geography professor at McMaster University in Hamilton, Ontario, a shy Scot who wrote poetry himself and had met Birney after sending him a long letter of fulsome praise for "David":[1]

> It must have been a big step to take to leave your call-ing and connections at the University, in which you had made so many advances and met with such suc-cess, and to break with Esther and Bill to whom you were so evidently attached, for a way of life that seems, on the face of it, so strange to you. And yet, without knowing you any better than our slight acquaintance-ship will allow, or than your verses will permit, I feel that you have done something essential to your idea of living and I cannot help but envy you your clear vision and straightforward action....
>
> Actually, you seem to have a great deal of the spirit

of David in you; with his same desire to top the top-
less heights; his eagerness for untrodden ways; his
claustrophobia in the constriction of human pettiness,
and the small and ever smaller human round; and his
love of action. Perhaps you are nearing the hook of
your Finger now.[2]

A photo of the Birneys in the duplex at 45 Isabella Street they
had moved into at the end of 1942 confirms this conventional
view of the soldier on the eve of departure. At the centre stands
Birney in his uniform, jaunty in his military cap and well-
groomed sandy moustache. In his arms is little "Barnacle Bill," as
he sometimes called him, wearing only a diaper, his head a mass
of brown curls, clutching in his hand his father's swagger stick.
Beside him is Esther, winsome in a flowered frock, her thick
chestnut hair casual and wispy, her face open, her smile warm.

On the surface, Birney's decision to enlist (almost forty, he was
too old to be conscripted) did seem to be the "straightforward"
result of "clear vision." It was anything but. Though he still
firmly opposed fascism, his reasons for enlisting were a tangled
complex that could not be explained as simple patriotism. His
numerous letters reveal few comments on the Allied cause. By far
his most extensive comment—one that was a far cry from his
former political idealism—was addressed to Frank Wilcox:

> we all swore we wouldn't fight if another war came
> along, unless it was a People's War. Well, what do you
> think? I'm damned sure [Anthony] Eden and Duff
> Cooper and [Winston] Churchill aren't fighting a
> peepull's [sic] war, and their crowd stand a good
> chance of staying on top...if we lose, too. I agree, on
> the whole, with Stephen Spender (do you read
> *Horizon*?) that the war has to be fought to prevent it
> being impossible to have social progress in our genera-
> tion—one can't put it more positively than that. On
> the other hand we've got to learn a lot from the fas-
> cists, to make reforms. I still think some kind of
> socialism the only answer, and Stalinism the great

long-term enemy of socialism. The best we can hope
for on this continent, whatever happens in Europe, is
a strengthening of the benevolent-dictator aspects of
the Roosevelt regime.[3]

Compared to the letters he wrote at a time when he espoused
the Fourth International, his letters now were almost entirely
devoid of political observation, let alone engagement. Fear was
not a deterrent to enlisting. He was too old to be sent into active
combat; so he had no sense of putting his life on the line. He was
glad to take a leave of absence from the university: he had complained bitterly about the burdens of teaching all year. And
although he occasionally wrote that he regretted leaving Esther
and Bill, there was no trace of the aching tenderness and soul-
wrenching desolation that had overflowed into his own father's
letters when he had left Martha and "Sonny Boy" for the Great
War almost thirty years before.

Whatever his inner reasons, Birney seemed intent on positioning himself publicly in the conventional role of noble martyr to
the great humanitarian cause. That was the stance he took in his
poem "On Going to the Wars"—a frankly autobiographical
address[4] (that owed much to John Donne) by a soldier to the
pregnant Jewish wife he is leaving:

> I do not go, my dear, to storm
> The praise of men: this uniform
> May shine less gay in gas and mud
> And be medallioned but by blood,
> While lips that know your lips will turn
> Uneasily to harlot worm.
> . . . .
> I, too, let's say, a travail owe:
> So that our son, who curls within
> The womb, may wake to brighter earth,
> I must not shrink from giving birth
> To death.
>
>   I go that he may stare

Blue-eyed into Canadian air
Unhaunted by the charnel birds
That drop their excrement of death.
I go that he may draw free breath

. . . .

I march that he may learn from grass
And rose what we have missed, the pass
To quiet life, and never set
The rendezvous my father met
In vain.

. . . .

My dear, I'll not survive to see
You bricked within a ghetto slum
In Canada, by booted scum...[5]

But Birney wrote this poem in April and May 1941, when Esther was pregnant, their child's gender unknown and there was as yet no question of his going overseas. And he published it at first in October's *Dalhousie Review* (it was rejected by *Harper's*, *New Directions* and *Canadian Home Journal*) under the pseudonym "Richard Miles," lest it become an embarrassment to him if he were never posted abroad.[6] The pseudonym was telling: "rich" was what he hoped to become (his chief grievance at the university was the low salary), and "miles" was not only the Latin for "soldier," it also suggested the distance he longed to put between himself and all that cramped and restrained him.

Later, Birney acknowledged authorship. He read the poem on Mavor Moore's CBC program, "Our Canada—the Arts Grow Up," on Sunday, 3 January 1943, a program that elicited so much mail that Moore was "surprised...at the volume and calibre of our listeners."[7] Birney's highly publicized departure overseas (an event marked publicly by an article in the the *Toronto Daily Star* that revived his 1935 contretemps in Berlin with the Nazis)[8] enhanced the poem's status. Bill Deacon, literary critic for *The Globe and Mail* saluted it as "the great Canadian poem of the war...the inspired word that speaks for us all as 'In Flanders Fields' spoke for us in the last war."[9] Even the grand old man of

Canadian letters, Sir Charles G.D. Roberts, wrote: "I am consumed with envy! It is 'top notch'—just right—I have almost said 'perfect'—but I don't want to be eulogistic in my language."[10] But Birney thought little of the poem ("a pseudononymous effusion of mine which I now regret publishing," he wrote A.J.M. [Art] Smith[11]) and admitted that it was "a little glib in parts...that what we believe in and hope for can't be expressed quite so simply."[12] And he confessed irritably to Art Smith: "I must revise ['On Going to the Wars']. The first stanza to go out completely. The rest to be tightened; it goes flat in utterance... There is a conscious echoing of [Wilfred] Owen, and several of [Richard] Lovelace. I think [Rupert] Brooke will disappear here with the first stanza."[13]

Most perplexing was Birney's indifference to the implications of his overnight success with "David." Quickly established as a literary landmark, the poem elicited excited reviews and extravagantly complimentary letters. Patrick Anderson of *Preview* and John Sutherland of *First Statement*, for instance, both sent copies of their journals from Montreal, where modern poetry was burgeoning, and asked for Birney's comments and contributions.[14] Despite the uncertainties of wartime publishing, Lorne Pierce of The Ryerson Press brought out a volume of twenty-two of Birney's poems, *David and Other Poems* in July 1942. Many reviewers praised Birney's "originality" and "freshness." Several thought the volume—"David" in particular—marked a new era in Canadian literary history. "It is something to find a Canadian poet for whom there is no need to apologize," ran a *Winnipeg Free Press* review. "Set Earle Birney's title poem, 'David,' beside any contemporary Canadian or American verse and it will not suffer from the juxtaposition."[15] Others, like Sedgewick, who was quoted on the cover with Pratt and UBC classics professor and poet, L.A. MacKay, detected an essentially western Canadian voice: "at the core of ['David'], giving it power, is a spirit that can be born of Canada only—of Canadian mountains and mountain air."[16] A Hamilton reviewer traced the poem's power to its masculine orientation ("this booklet of poems...is strictly a man's book").[17] Dorothy Livesay commended Birney's ability to be "popular and yet a poet."[18] In his review article of A.J.M. Smith's new poetry anthology, *Canada and Its Poetry* for the end-of-year issue of *The Canadian Forum*, Northrop Frye used "David" to illustrate what he considered to be "the central theme of Canadian poetry: the riddle of...'inexplicable life.' It really is a riddle of inexplicable death: the fact that life struggles and suffers in a nature which is blankly indifferent to it."[19] And Philip Child, novelist and professor, in his summary of "Letters in Canada: 1942" for the *University of Toronto Quarterly*, singled out Birney's collection as "the most notable" book of poetry all year: "there is authentic originality; he owes nothing at all to earlier Canadian writing and scarcely anything—when he is fully himself—to recent verse anywhere else. He has a harsh and intense sensibility which makes his pictures and rhythms fresh and living, and his technical accomplishment is brilliant, at times bewildering."[20]

Birney had every reason (and every encouragement) to build on this unparalleled success. He had worked out his own poetic theory "with conscious avoidance of the 'clever-clever metaphysical' image and the carefully obscure allusion...which has plagued England for a year and now plagues this continent,"[21] claiming he wrote "in conscious opposition to the momentary fashion of obscurity."[22] In particular, Birney disliked T.S. Eliot:

> When Eliot set the fashions the poets abandoned the people to talk to themselves, and the people have revenged themselves by giving up the reading of poetry. There won't be a renascence until ordinary people are won over to the reading of verse, as they read it in Victorian England. I don't mean that we need to write like [Alfred] Tennyson again. Even if someone in this country were writing like [Robert] Frost or [Edwin Arlington] Robinson or [Robinson] Jeffers or [Archibald] MacLeish—i.e. writing significant narrative in contemporary language—we would have a Canadian poetry and a Canadian audience. Pratt alone has been doing it... The younger crowd of Canadians, those who are any good...are still being intentionally obscure and ornately witty and darkly vegetational à la *Golden Bough*.[23]

And he negotiated the business aspects of publication with the aplomb of an experienced contract lawyer—anticipating for instance, that "David" would be anthologized for schools.[24] He insisted on sketching the mountain he had in mind ("a cross between Rundle, a peak on Bourgeau, and the Black Tusk in the Garibaldi country")[25] for Thoreau MacDonald, the artist who designed the dust-jacket for the book, modelling it on the iceberg he had used for Pratt's book. And he kept a close eye on reviews,[26] insisting that Pierce prod the sluggish *Vancouver Province* into action when no review appeared there.[27] He already stood at the centre of several large interlocking networks of those who were involved in cultural life in Canada and beyond: academics, poets, other writers, a few musicians and painters, CBC radio folk and magazine editors and subscribers. He quickly mobilized his considerable practical skills in a publishing world he knew well through his editorial experience and—with Esther's assistance (he dedicated the book to her at the last minute)—compiled a list of almost 350 names for Lorne Pierce to use circulating *David*. Those names included writers across Canada such as Ethel Wilson, Frederick Philip Grove, Anne Marriott, Dorothy Livesay, Raymond Souster and F.R. Scott; Alan Crawley, editor of the poetry magazine *Contemporary Verse*; old school chums like Mary Duncan Carter, now a librarian at the University of Southern California in Los Angeles; and Hilton Moore of Wall Street, New York; former colleagues at Utah; his old political comrades like Ken Johnstone; Toronto colleagues like Harold Innis and Frank Underhill; W.E. Gladstone Murray, CBC's director in Ottawa; the editors of all the journals who had rejected "David"; even a few judges and military officers. Not surprisingly, the first edition of five hundred was soon sold out. So was the second printing launched on 16 December. By 30 June 1943, a third print run of five hundred copies was delivered. That same month, though he was overseas by the time the announcement was made, Birney garnered the Governor General's Award for poetry. Had he stayed in Canada he could not have hoped for a more felicitous position from which to build a literary career.

Birney's curious situation reflected that of Canadian literature as a whole. The onset of the war skewed the natural evolution of Canadian letters and introduced extra-literary criteria and standards for the arts. Birney's western voice—along with the new west-coast poetry journal *Contemporary Verse*—had just rounded out the region-by-region unfolding of Canadian letters which had begun in the Maritimes with Charles G.D. Roberts and Bliss Carman. Simultaneously, new contemporary voices—organized notably, but not exclusively, in Montreal with the *Preview* and *First Statement* writers—were supplanting the traditional romantic idiom of the Confederation poets, and their imitators like Audrey Alexandra Brown. Had there been no war, these developments might have led in the direction of further technical experiment, new subject matter that centred (like P.K. Page's "The Stenographers") on urban rather than rural subjects; and narratives like Birney's "David" that developed Pratt's seminal work by taking different attitudes to nature and worrying ethical and moral dilemmas in a secular world. Both A.J.M. Smith and Ralph Gustafson were engaged in anthologies that they hoped would reflect a contemporary Canadian literature worth consideration abroad. The new voices were many, varied and competent: in addition to Smith and Gustafson themselves, they included the *Preview* group of poets, such as Patrick Anderson, A.M. Klein, P.K. Page and F.R. Scott; those of the rival magazine *First Statement*, such as John Sutherland, Miriam Waddington, Louis Dudek and Irving Layton; Robert Finch and Raymond Souster in Toronto; prairie poet Anne Marriott; and left-wing social activist Dorothy Livesay.

But the war interrupted this incipient process of literary development in a way that was dramatically represented in Birney's own career. Instead of focusing on the subjects that really engaged them, and experimenting technically, their attempts to locate unique national and contemporary voices were subsumed in the subject of war. Pratt, in "Dunkirk"—a poem Birney had praised "perhaps too enthusiastically" (he later said) in the *Forum*[28]—had adapted his great Canadian epic themes to the suddenly gripping subject of military conflict. Birney followed suit. The war did him a disfavour by encouraging the public to focus unduly on the war poems he quickly began writing instead of on those poems like "David" in which he was struggling to say something much more personal and complex than his war poems communicated. Bill Deacon's influential *Globe* review began with "On Going to the Wars," rather than the infinitely superior "David." And the subsequent adulation Birney received for this sentimental, "glib," derivative and essentially false poem steered him away from the subjects that engaged him more deeply. His decision to join the war effort and the coincidence of his being posted overseas at the very moment his first collection of poems was so successfully launched symbolized the interruption of a nation's literary development, just as it marked an untimely and unfortunate hiatus in the contribution Birney's special talents might have made. His academic friend Bill Robbins's inclination to "round...out the trinity" of war poets for his English course (adding Birney's poem to Rupert Brooke's "The Dead" and Wilfred Owen's "Strange Meeting") was typical. Robbins reported that Owen's poem ("the greatest to come out of the last war") was outdated: "it wasn't saying to these people in 1943 what it said in 1939. But I got them with 'Going to the Wars'—this was their language."[29]

Birney himself recognized that the new focus on war poetry did no favour to literature. In a February *Canadian Forum* review article of the anthology of war poetry *Voices of Victory*, he had argued, "No faithful anthologist will attempt to constrict poets around the "war effort" or any other effort... The challenges to Axis brutality are hurled chiefly by ladies in cities several thousands of miles from the bombings, or by gentlemen who owe part of their literary prestige to the fact that they are several decades older than any conceivable draft-age."[30] Despite this, the poems he next wrote were war poems.

What appealed to Birney about army service in the first place? Many men of his age—indeed many of his acquaintances such as Northrop Frye and Roy Daniells, for example—did not enlist. And why did he exhibit more excitement than regret at leaving Canada?

It was clear from Birney's letters that he loved his work as what he called a "Personnel trouble-shooter" in the army, "sorting out morons and neurotics, malingerers and asthmatics, among the clean corn."[31] He was part of a team of psychiatrists, doctors and Selection of Personnel Officers (SPOs) like himself who tested recruits for intelligence and mental and physical fitness, and made recommendations for their allocation. Such tests (first the F.H.3 Test, later the F.H.R. Test) had been introduced for enlisting soldiers in the winter of 1940–41, and the results sent by commanding officers to psychiatrists. Because the system was at first haphazard, the Directorate of Selection Personnel had been set up in July 1941, and a year later the General Service Corps Intake scheme was introduced. The aim of this comprehensive effort to test incoming military personnel was to identify individuals suitable for specific military positions by using the knowledge available through advances in psychology and psychiatry. "The psychologists main task in this Directorate," according to a 1947 report from the British Privy Council Office,

> has been to improve methods of selection. They represent the viewpoint that in man-power planning, quality as well as quantity must be given proper weight. They are responsible for setting up a means of classifying personnel for training in such a way that the Army's demands can be met with the best available supply of men. In doing this they have to take account both of the speed with which men can absorb training in an emergency and of the eventual level of efficiency which they can attain.[32]

The training Birney had undergone in Canada to prepare him for his role as an officer working with psychologists and psychiatrists making such assessments of Canadian soldiers had consisted of the psychological background of vocational selection, army trades and non-trade employment, the nature and uses of selection tests, problems in assessing educational achievements and employment experience, and techniques of interviewing. Men and women entering the army would not only be tested for physical fitness. They would also typically undergo a battery of tests for intelligence, mechanical comprehension, mathematics, verbal skills and comprehension of instructions. They would be interviewed for the double purpose of getting information about their history and qualifications and of gauging their temperamental fitness to cope with various aspects of army life, from the tedium of repetitive tasks to the increasingly well understood stress of what was called "combat reaction"[33]—a polite term for the nervous breakdowns often suffered by soldiers undergoing the horrors of war firsthand in a mental state dominated by the ever-present threat of pain or death.[34] After such tests, a report would be made recommending their assignment to some suitable position (or, in some cases, to one of Britain's twelve military psychiatric hospitals). Some idea of the volume of personnel passing through the Selection Centres under the aegis of the Directorate can be inferred from the fact that between March and October 1943 alone—the period during which Birney arrived to take up his post with the Selection Centre at Ash— 10,901 men were referred to army psychiatrists as a result of the tests done in the Selection Centres.

Before being appointed a Selection of Personnel Officer, Birney himself had had to undergo similar tests. The assessment the army made of him indicated that he was an exceptional candidate and that they prized his talents:

> An unusually well-balanced mind—well informed— dependable—forceful and very stable. Would make an excellent DPS officer, possessing fine qualities to be used in this service.[35]

Certainly, he had quickly "wriggled and wrangled and rangled my way up from the wranksome wranks,"[36] as he put it. He was manifestly suited to his new work, better suited to it than to the teaching which had become increasingly burdensome and unrewarding to him. "I've been around with the army for over two years now and it gets more and more interesting," he wrote Hendrie Gartshore with whom he now had more in common since Hendrie had become a psychiatrist in San Francisco.

> After getting my active commission I...worked for a month on officer selection. Then I was used as an

interviewer at the District Recruiting Depot. After
another month I was put in charge of personnel selection of active recruits for the depot in this military district...from Niagara Falls to James Bay, and so [my
job] embraces every type of Ontarian. The work was
intense but fascinating. I had the usual troubles—
insufficient staff, inadequate quarters and supplies,
staff sickness. But we managed to pull through the
worst time. I had a staff of thirty (interviewers, clerks,
stenographers, mainly) and we allocated about 700
recruits a week. The routine includes setting an army
aptitude test, as a preliminary assessment, interviewing
each man, and interpreting the findings in the light of
quota requirements for the different arms, medical rat-
ings, psychiatric reports, etc. There was considerable
time pressure as we had to keep pace with the recruiting centres... Working under conditions of constant
change, uncertainty and multitudinous recording...
[are] what makes army life at once exasperating and
spellbinding.[37]

Birney clearly preferred the open-ended excitement and uncertainty of wartime conditions to the restrictions and predictability
of the life he had been leading as a professor. At the same time,
he relished the rigidly defined hierarchy in which he had a greater
chance of advancement than any professor had in academe.

And he enjoyed bachelorhood. For a year, since the fall of
1940, he had been involved on and off with Betty Carter
McTavish, whose husband had been posted overseas, leaving her
and their small son behind. "When you say that our relationship
is unspoiled by inhibitions," she wrote to him from Montreal,
where she lived, "I think you are wrong. It is—not by mine, but
by [my husband's]...only by shutting him from my mind
entirely...can [I] enjoy myself with you. That, and knowing that
I'm not trespassing on Esther's territory. And I will have to see
her again to believe that, even though you have assured & reassured me."[38]

Not only was he disinclined to give up womanizing, unlike

Esther, whom one friend described as "a besotted mother,"[39] Earle often felt cramped and irritated by his son. He complained about the frequent interruptions to his sleep and was dissatisfied in particular about Bill's lateness in speaking; at eighteen months Bill was still chattering in what his father described as "exclusively his own language, which I find to be profuse in Slavonic consonants and Chinese in cadence, but quite unintelligible."[40] He cheerfully sent Esther and Bill off by train to Vancouver in mid-April 1942 to visit his mother, planning to join them in July. A young graduate student Ernest Sirluck moved in with him to share in the free existence Birney relished. "I'm definitely enjoying brief bachelordom," he wrote Herman Singer, the old room-mate from Utah days with whom he had first shared the delights of "batching it." Sirluck, who respected the amiable Birney's scholarship and sympathized with his difficulties as a left-leaning, experimental teacher in a conservative institution, recalls that "Birney was a creative writer in season and out. He saw his life as a kind of drama. He was living a life that deprived him of the exercise of his imagination, so he had to embellish life." Sirluck remembers one incident that was typical of that summer:

> I was asleep after a party I had left earlier than Earle. In burst Earle after midnight, ablaze with anger. He had been drinking a little. And behind him was Arthur Smith, who was in town doing something connected to his new Book of Canadian Poetry. Arthur had been attracted to one of the women at the party, which had excited the resentment and jealousy of Steve Hart, a professor of anthropology, who was a hard-drinking, hard-loving man. Hart insulted Arthur. Earle knew these girls very well and felt he was called upon to defend Art. He and Hart had exchanged hard words and soft academic blows. So Earle was waking me to get me to serve as his second in a fight with Hart.
>
> I had to spend the rest of the night getting Earle to simmer down. He was very romantic about certain

things—male honour, responsibility to one's guest, courage as essential to manhood, and the manifestation of courage in physical form. He remained youthful longer than most.[41]

Meanwhile on the west coast, Esther escaped the inevitable conflicts with her irascible mother-in-law by taking a job she soon found at the Vancouver Welfare Agency, leaving Bill in his grandmother's care. That summer Birney savoured his freedom and was happy to communicate by letter with the two women who, in person, often provoked him to irritable outbursts. His advice that spring to Bill McConnell, a lawyer and aspiring novelist friend in Vancouver who was about to marry, was telling: "You'll probably like marriage, though it's always impossible to know how much more fun you would have had if you'd remained single. Vice versa, of course, which is the catch."[42]

Army life structured and gave direction to the welter of mutually inconsistent options Birney had continued to juggle: "what future I have will be settled without my having much to do with it," he had written almost in relief to Dal Grauer when he joined the Canadian Officers Training Corps (COTC).[43] Those close to him recognized that his tendency to be pulled in several directions at once stemmed from a profound neediness. "I was very bucked by shamefast [sic] admission that you really liked 'David,'" he wrote Sedgewick. "I expected you to damn [it] with a long and noisy silence. It touches this young heart it does.... I *have* had a gratifying lot of remarks about it, though, which were absolutely necessary for me before I could get going on anything else.... All this was good, however, after twelve tantalizing personal letters of rejection from the leading journals of both hemispheres."[44] And Dorothy Livesay wrote to both Birneys, "I think it is splendid though that Earl [sic] pushed the thing through. He *needed* to be in print."[45] Approval and admiration felt like love to Birney. And he was pained and furious when these seemed to be withheld. When G.H. Clarke, editor of *Queen's Quarterly*, wrote him a congratulatory letter despite the fact that he had rejected Birney's poems so far, he vented his spleen to Art Smith: "The most amusing communication I've had lately is from George Herbert Clarke...repeating a good deal of his QQ review, and listing the verses he liked best. Among the seven he lists are four which he had previously rejected, under his own signature, for the QQ. He has either a bad memory or singular mental flexibility. He has never published a verse of mine in his life—and now he wants to use 'On Going to the Wars' in an anthology, without paying for it. I told Pierce to charge him double, the old hypocrite."[46]

Army life also promised to provide Birney with material for his "long-promised novel."[47] Not only did he delight in the work itself, the long reports he typed about recruits and their life histories were deliberately intended as rough drafts for fiction he would write later. "My army job will give me, daily, material for a novel—I'll have to keep mum about it till after the war is over," he wrote to Ralph Gustafson.[48] An elaborate report in January 1943, for example, about the court martial of a military medical patient who slit his wrists when he learned that he and the man in the next bed were married to the same woman, would later be the basis for a 1946 radio play "Court Martial."[49]

It was typical of Birney that at the very point at which he was acclaimed for his poetry, he should be turning his attention to fiction, just in case the poetry should fail. Ever since he had been writing his thesis on the Devon coast with Esther in 1935, he had hoped to write a novel.[50] That hope lay behind his determination to start up the Creative Writing course on the short story which would parallel Pratt's on poetry. He also ran a small workshop called—somewhat pretentiously—the Scriblerus Club (the name was taken from the group of eighteenth-century satirists that included Jonathan Swift and Alexander Pope) for ladies from the Junior League. For both groups, he generously contacted *Maclean's*, *Saturday Night* and *Liberty* in the hope of placing their best work. Through reading, discussion and assessment in these classes, he wanted to hone his own craft as a fiction writer. He had been delighted when Smith put his name forward early in 1942 to Whit Burnett, editor of *Story* magazine in New York, to edit a special Canadian edition.[51] Quickly he rallied the major short-story writers for contributions: Morley Callaghan (who was "skittish" at the notion of writing a "Canadian" story),[52] Ethel Wilson (who predicted hers would be too "feminine"),[53] Sinclair Ross (who agreed that Birney could change the age of his boy in "One's a Heifer" from eleven to thirteen),[54] Emily Carr and Hugh MacLennan, among others. But Whit Burnett cancelled the project before Birney had even received most of the manuscripts. It was a blow. As was the news from the Guggenheim Foundation. E.K. Brown's favoured candidate, A.S.P. Woodhouse, had been successful, but Birney had failed to get a grant to compile the short-story anthology which was to match Smith's poetry collection.

Even "David" had reflected Birney's interest in fiction, for it was a narrative involving character, setting and plot. Now, in mid-June, while he languished with a broken ankle in Brockville Military Hospital after he and several other officers-in-training were injured when they were mistakenly ordered to jump off a defective ramp—an episode that he used later in his novel *Turvey*—it was not poetry he wrote but a short story called "Hospital Day," which began and ended with a soldier in bed dreaming of the sultry brunette movie queen Hedy Lamarr.[55] Finally, in July, the *National Home Monthly* accepted his old Great War story "Mickey Was a Swell Guy" for $125, despite the fact that Birney refused to tone down the language.[56]

Poetry? Fiction? Scholarship…editing…teaching…creative writing groups? Life in the army interrupted this plethora of possibilities for Birney and raised the possibility of even more. His old mentor, Sedgewick, knew how difficult it was for his "utterly subversive" surrogate son to establish priorities and stick with them. "Please Earle," he pleaded in one of his rare serious moments once Birney was established overseas,

> think long and long before you leave teaching for other employment whether in the Civil Service or in industry. I know that the far bigger money is hard to resist both on your own account and your family's. I grant that promotion at Toronto is stupidly tardy & sometimes not forthcoming at all. But I do know also that you can teach, that the fact is recognized at Toronto, and that your scholarship is respected

there... And that's what I am most concerned
about—for, obviously, it is the thing you most want to
be at: without being at it, you will feel continuously
unsatisfied and thwarted. You're a restless soul by
nature; and, consequently, if you can't get your hand
in at the job you most like, you're running the risk of
being desperately unhappy.

...I have only two things in mind myself: I want
you to go on writing, I want you to be as happy as
possible.

Mother & I love you.

Garnett.[57]

Sedgewick rightly sensed that army life was seducing Birney
into a limbo in which he had no need to fix his path, resolve his
contradictions and choose from the bewildering options his
many talents and unflagging energy made possible. Once he
arrived overseas on 24 May 1943 and established himself among
his new colleagues engaged in liaison with British personnel
selection officers, he claimed he never felt better. Far from family
and university, he seemed to revert to a simpler, happier, more
boyish life. He bought a bicycle, just as he had in Banff as a boy
after his father left, and cycled with an army buddy out into the
lovely English countryside. He courted women. He sent off long
letters to his huge acquaintanceship in several countries. He
loved getting care packages from Esther and his mother, who
kept him supplied with khaki socks, shortbread, cakes (including
one for his birthday with paper-wrapped dimes hidden in it),
olives and lobster. "I keep very fit," he typically reported in one
of his weekly letters to his mother.

> Physically I haven't felt so well for several years, full of
> pep. Maybe it's the vitamin pills. I think it's also
> because the work isn't too hard at present and I have
> few worries that I can do anything about—the sol-
> dier's life is a curiously sheltered one.... The batman
> looks after my laundry and cleaning, makes sure I'm
> out of my bed in time, & that the bed is made, &

even gets my stamps and puts my shoes in a neat row under the bed. Somebody else is responsible for seeing that I eat regularly and get paid regularly. So long as I do what I'm told, nobody bothers me, nor I them. A nice life if you like it! [58]

Perhaps, as Wreford Watson had observed, there *was* something "essential to living" in Birney's decision to free himself from his settled, successful life in Toronto. Certainly, there was "a great deal of the spirit of David" in Birney, especially in his "eagerness for untrodden ways" and his "claustrophobia in the constriction of human pettiness" and his "love of action." As he wrote to an old UBC friend, Gerry Kerr, who had written like many others to congratulate him on *David,* "sometimes I wonder if I can ever fit into the measly little professorial world again."[59]

If Birney's "On Going to the Wars" was a false step in his development as a writer—as were the elegies "Joe Harris: 1913–1942" and "For Steve" which followed[60]—what was his true voice? What had he been struggling to say when those western Canadian poems gripped his imagination in the winter of 1940–41 that followed his disillusionment with Trotsky and the Fourth International?

Though he did not give their observations the special credence they deserved, Sedgewick, who loved him, and Dorothy Livesay, who didn't, and whose ideas about Birney's work never blurred into agreement, admiration or sexual attraction, both singled out the poem in *David* that came closest to expressing what Birney most wanted to say. And Sedgewick chose the "magnificent and profound" "Vancouver Lights" to read for his fifteen-minute CBC radio program on Canadian poetry in early February 1943. "Imagine yourself standing on the high ridge of Grouse Mountain," he said to put his listeners in the mood, "looking down on that amazing spectacle on some night last year."[61]

About me the night, moonless, wimples the
                    mountains,
wraps ocean, land, air, and mounting
sucks at the stars.[62]

With intensely sensual, indeed sexual, images, Birney set his macrocosmic stage. On it he set microcosmic man—"a spark beleaguered by darkness," "a unique glowworm"—alone atop the "brutish forehead" of the mountain in an overwhelming, indifferent universe of "primal ink" (the black ocean). Much in the poem resembles Pratt's *tour de force* "The Truant," and—as Birney's poem was published before Pratt's—may indeed have influenced it, probably because the two writers discussed their ideas on numerous occasions and read each other's works in progress.[63] Certainly "The Truant" impressed Birney deeply as a "celebration of the unique spirit of man, the one 'truant' in a world which science tends to picture as blindly mechanical," for it was the only poem he chose to read in a short BBC broadcast he did after he arrived in England.[64]

These lines of Birney's

> These rays were ours
> we made and unmade them.

may have anticipated Pratt's

> We flung the graphs about your flying feet;
> We measured your diameter—
> Merely a line
> Of zeros prefaced by an integer.[65]

But Birney's poem is darker and deeper than Pratt's. For Pratt, man's courage and intangible moral strength is glorious, redeeming him from the degradation of natural law and making him an endearingly quirky anomaly in the universe. But Birney's poem—like the final section of "David"—is suffused with self-disgust, stark terror and a suspicion that man is headed for self-destruction as he pollutes and destroys the planet. The "spark" of human life, like the firefly, the glowworm, Phoebus the sun-god and the red star Aldebaran which is the eye of Taurus (Birney's astrological sign) are as nothing in the vast blackness of night, the ocean, the "murk" presided over not by a male God, but by the sinister "black Experimentress."

On this mountain's brutish forehead, with terror of
   space
I stir, of the changeless night and the stark ranges
of nothing, pulsing down from beyond and between
the fragile planets. We are a spark beleaguered
by darkness; this twinkle we make in a corner of
   emptiness,
how shall we utter our fear lest the black
Experimentress
never in the range of her microscope find it?

. . . .

In the fathomless heat of our dwarfdom, our dream's
   combustion,
      we contrived the power, the blast that snuffed us.
      No one slew Prometheus. Himself he chained
      and consumed his own bright liver. O stranger,
      Plutonian, descendant, or beast in the stretching
         night—
   there was light.

The reference may be to Percy Bysshe Shelley's poem
"Prometheus Unbound." If so, Birney's position is diametrically
opposed to Shelley's. Whereas Shelley believed in the perfectibility of man, Birney articulates a darker twentieth-century vision
of man's inherent destructiveness. As such, the poem may be a
statement of the profound disillusionment Birney had recently
undergone in relation to Trotsky. He had abandoned Trotskyism
not only because social perfectibility seemed unattainable, given
the breakdown of political organizations through internal bicker-
ing, but Trotsky himself—the epitome to Birney of the visionary
male leader—had succumbed to aggressive avarice. What was left
was the principle of female power represented not by humanist
vision but by scientific investigation: the remote, unfeeling
"black Experimentress." Dorothy Livesay shrank from the bleak
vision of this poem. Her philosophy, she explained, was a distinct contradiction to Birney's ("I want to find poetry that
declares the opposite, that points to man working with
nature."[66]). None the less, she understood and engaged with

Birney's ideas: "You picture men as everywhere destroying and betraying nature. That is your philosophy." In reply, he paid her the great compliment, "Your remarks about 'ideas' are the most stimulating I've had." As he further explained:

> I am interested more than in anything else, in the nature of this dualism between man and the other forms of life & energy. As for my "philosophy" I think you are more certain of it than I am, or more conscious. I have not tried to present a philosophy and in only one case have I tried to write a meditative poem—"Vancouver Lights." There the meaning I intend is definitely not that "man is everywhere destroying & betraying nature." What I want to say, though I grant I may not have said it, is something much more complicated and tenuous—that man has now reached a stage in his development in which for the first time he has created the conditions for his own destruction—or at least let us say civilized man. It seems unlikely that the race will kill itself off, but society may easily reduce itself to the point where the highest level is represented by, say, Franco's Spain—to which perhaps the Papuan would be preferable. On the other hand, we may go on to great ant-like achievements such as communism.... Such a goal will demand...men who will work with nature.... A favourite illustration used to be literally "moving mountains"—building bigger and better canals. All this, of course, will simply speed the day when man has destroyed virtually every other form of life on the earth in order to populate every corner of it. Food can become wholly synthetic, we know already. Uncultivated vegetable life has been reduced to a fraction of itself just in our lifetime in this country. It can disappear, & then, the cultivated will die in its turn, as we eat sunbeams or something. Loony? Of course, but not impossible. The point is that socialism, etc., the best political path, may lead faster than ever to a mere

vulgar triumph of our single limited species in a barren world. Not a contingency worth the sober concern of any politician—but just the kind of thing that gets in the road when you try to track down the sources of contemporary emotion.... Your child comes into it. The next generation, even when you didn't have children, came into it. And no one of us imagines that the next generation, communist or not, is going to have a better time of it—probably worse.... A tough time. Perhaps defeated. It may take ten generations to slick out the system. If we are worried about the tenth, why not the ten thousandth from now? The fact that we don't believe in Christ or Kant or anybody particularly on the subject of the future doesn't absolve us from facing up to the possibilities of the future....are you not also concerned (as a thinker—not, I admit, as an activist) with what may happen to man when the sun cools a little more & with what will happen to the rest of living things as man continues to "succeed"?[67]

These ideas, which Birney had struggled—somewhat awkwardly[68]—to express in "Vancouver Lights," were indeed "complicated and tenuous." They constituted an extraordinarily far-reaching and prophetic interrelation of thoughts and feelings that superseded trite sentiments about the current war, the clever adaptations of Anglo-Saxon verse Birney was also turning out,[69] any enthusiasm about Chaucer and other works of literature he managed to convey at the university, or even the conflict in the *Forum* between politics and poetry he had already noted.[70] Noted critic Elizabeth Drew offered extravagant praise: "I liked 'Vancouver Lights' very much. Birney is a true humanist in his conclusions—and more virile than Arnold in 'Dover Beach,' I think!"[71] As Wreford Watson had succinctly observed about "David," Birney was struck by "the inexpressible significance of life and the insignificance of men."[72] His was a colossal overview of life by a man whose mind was so far-ranging that it chafed at the least restriction. "To follow the quick enormous strides of Earle Birney's imagination," wrote Marcus Adeney, one of the few reviewers who grasped what Birney was driving at,[73] "it is necessary to share with him, first of all, the lonely, still timeless mood of one who waits upon night, the spaces and the stars. The reader [of 'Vancouver Lights'] should ascend... that hilltop above Vancouver—himself become... a contemplative."[74]

And what Birney urged the reader to contemplate was, as Philip Child had said, "bewildering" and terrifying. In "Vancouver Lights," as in the final section of "David," Birney teetered on the brink of existential nausea.

14

THAT SEA CALLED TIME

"Dear Captain Birney," ran a letter in delicate spidery handwriting sent to Canada House in London 27 April 1944. "My friend Wreford Watson of McMaster University told me some time ago that you were coming to England and suggested that I should get in touch with you."[1] The writer was Margaret Crosland, a twenty-five-year-old student at the University of London, whom Watson had deluged with love poems just before he left his lectureship in geography at London, then with love letters once he arrived in Canada. She had not succumbed. She found his behaviour "peculiar" and "strange."[2]

Margaret, whose dark hair softly framed a face of unusual sensitivity and candid intelligence, had come to London from the Lake Country in 1941, just after her father died, to study French and English. She was living in Earl's Court at a strait-laced boarding house dignified by the name "The Romney Club." The young women there nicknamed it "The Virgin's Retreat." The war had played havoc with Margaret's life. Her fiancé—a schoolmate—had returned from service in the airforce completely blinded in an ammunition explosion. "It was the first ghastly experience I had...[but] I didn't see why this should mean the end of our engagement,"[3] Margaret recalls. But the relationship remained vexed. Since moving to London, Margaret had fallen in with a lively literary group: poets, publishers and editors. She aspired to become a poet herself, and had already published a few poems that were complex and personal. "All I thought about was poetry," she recalls. "It was all very exciting, against the background of the war." Her April overture to Captain Birney invited him to "a long talk about poetry in Canada, England and everywhere."

Birney's state of mind at the time he received Margaret's letter was volatile. Though he was thriving on army life—a life both carefree and structured—the delights of bachelorhood had begun to pall. His ambivalence about the foetid domestic life that had closed down around him with the birth of Bill and Esther's all-consuming maternity had found outlets in other women. First had been Betty Carter McTavish in Montreal. He had seen her on occasional visits between Montreal and Toronto, and the two exchanged letters. One of these, three months after Bill's birth, implies that she had recently had an abortion and was recovering from a subsequent infection.[4] Birney's admiration for her pluck in undertaking this alone and his guilt about sharing neither in her grieving nor her costs was clear. But it was none the less an extraordinary predicament for a man of his age and experience in the midst of ambivalence about fatherhood. Despite his guilt, something about the conquest and impregnation of Betty seemed to have answered some deeper need.

Next had been Corinne Hagon, a stylish dark-haired woman who had married an English airforce officer in England before befriending Esther in Canada. Corinne, whose husband was still overseas, lived with her young son across the street on Hazelton Avenue, and she had cheerfully provided support to Esther at the time Bill was born. Judging from letters sent to Birney after he went overseas, they appear to have had a brief, light-hearted affair just before he left.

More seriously, Birney had also became involved with Gabrielle Baldwin, a vivacious dark French woman from Montreal whose husband, Dick, was soon posted overseas. He had met Gaby, as she was called, in February 1943 at the officer's mess at "King's Landing," an old house converted into military quarters in

Niagara-on-the-Lake. Gaby had fallen in love at first sight. "I remember the night you arrived in the Mess," Gaby would later write him,

> I was there a few minutes before going to play bad-minton and there was [sic] quite a few people. You wouldn't remember me, nor the night. To me it's as clear as a picture: I told Dick when we came home— "There's a new officer who looks as if he needed a good cod-liver oil tonic!..."
>
> I can see your head towering over the other ones, as you came into the room (the third time I met you) and can still remember Dick correcting me as I intro-duced you...as Lieutenant instead of Captain—we sat in the little pioneer room, you on the little sofa, me in one corner—you had two cups of coffee and ate more than anybody else! I talked to you almost exclusively and [another man] kept starting long tirades about his father, and I wanted to tell him to shut up, that I wanted to talk to this perfectly wonderful man (if the censor has seen your bald head and long neck, he'll think I'm insane!)....it's a pure case of attraction.[5]

Theirs was an affair more intense and passionate than the others, and both of them spoke seriously of being married someday.

Once overseas, with greater freedom and distance from domes-ticity, Birney's Canadian romances faded somewhat and he soon became embroiled with a high-strung German singer and actress on whom he had gazed out of an audience of soldiers and offi-cers at the Crown and Anchor Pub in Ipswich in September 1943. Carlotta Makins, the estranged wife of William Makins, an editor at *Horizon*, proved to be more than even Birney could handle. Her dark sensual beauty and artistic flair could not for long disguise the fact that she too quickly became emotionally dependent. The passionate Carlotta—who wept profusely when Birney read her "David"—was given to clinging behaviour and an array of minor illnesses, such as eye infections and headaches, on which Birney at first tenderly danced attendance. Carlotta enjoyed *Sturm und Drang*, and she quickly became dependent on the man she claimed was her "Beloved and only man of mine."[6] She besieged him with recklessly scrawled letters declaring her love, tucking in photos of herself endorsed with comments like: "You know the question in my eyes and that the right answer from you, my Earle, will make & keep me happy. Your Carlotta." "Mein Geliebter," she typically wrote:

> Now I can tell you *one* more reason *why* I love you so very much, why you are so absolutely *my* man: I've just taken the small bar of chocolate [you gave me] out to console myself—because my eye is very sore and ticks and pulses with fever of the torn tissue— there it said I love you, Carlotta, and, Oh Earle, a *wave* of happiness & gratitude came over me irrestibly [sic]—yes THAT is it. Your thinking of the little things which do so much to me, the warmth and gen- tleness with which you surround me in thought and action, Du, and to which you return having led us to a tower of proud—yet abandoned—passion.[7]

Carlotta could not understand Birney's focus on her art, since she would have abandoned her career at once for him. "The most important thing for you," he typically wrote her,

> is that you should succeed in your art and so *realize* yourself most fully and take the place in the world that you should have.... We are both no longer chil- dren; passion is as strong in us as ever, but we also have other passions of importance perhaps for the world, and certainly of prime importance for us as useful people in it. To be an artist some ruthlessness is imperative; ruthlessness with oneself.[8]

Nor could she understand his calculated attitude to sex. Elsewhere he admonished his "Lieblinge": "I made it clear how I felt toward Esther and my boy and told you that our horizon must be limited to our days together in England... I do not think it wrong for us to have a full physical relationship and to be companions to each other in these difficult days. Neither does my wife."[9]

Though Birney was flattered by Carlotta's fixation on him, he consulted widely—with Esther, Corinne, Gaby, and his closest army buddy, Gordon Aldridge, among others—about how to extricate himself from her clutches. (In fact, she would pursue him sporadically until her last attempt in 1948 to have him find her a job in Canada so she could be near him.)

It was partly because he found Carlotta's neediness repugnant that Birney's affection for Esther revived. If domesticity with Esther had once seemed stifling, Carlotta's demands to be "spoiled" and her exaggerated and obsequious protestations of love became even more cloying. In an idealized version of each of these narratives for himself, he began to take refuge from the other. "I am married, and happily married," he wrote Carlotta in mid-January 1944.

> I am not bound to Esther by the strong physical ties that I am bound to you; but I am bound to her by ties of long comradeship, loyalty together in times of stress, and by a boy whom I love dearly. If I left her I know it would be a blow that would hurt her all the rest of her life, and I have no intention of doing it. If I were two men, one of them would be yours for life if you wanted him; but instead I'm only half a man— the other half is in Canada.[10]

Birney's dissatisfaction with Carlotta and his disgust with the chaos of sexual relationships the war had fostered everywhere around him found an outlet in "The Levin Bolt," a cynical prose sketch about an encounter in a working-class pub.[11]

In even bleaker moments, he dreaded that life was somehow eluding him. A number of comments in his letters suggest that he was disturbed—possibly deeply disturbed—by the fact that he was about to turn forty. To Carlotta he wrote, "you have never understood that in some way I am an 'old' man, stubbornly set in certain ways of conduct."[12] He reassured his mother that same day, "I'm too old and feeble to be sent anywhere near the fighting."[13] An urgent sense of the passage of time lent an air of desperation to his consideration of his status in the world. He was impatient to become a major, and when early negotiations for promotion were delayed, he responded irritably. And when he received a letter from A.S.P. Woodhouse, now head of the English Department at University College, outlining the position and salary he could expect on his return ($2,000, which was only marginally better than that of a new appointee), he was so distressed he hinted broadly in reply that he might resign. Taking personally situations which reflected nothing on his merits and everything on wartime conditions generally, Birney nursed what seemed to him devastating grievances.

What, he wondered, did he have to show for all his efforts? For all his talent? When would he have the status he deserved, the income he was worth? And was he always going to need several women, each an adjunct to his different facets, each a refuge from the others? Was he never going to be really "settled?" At forty he should surely be a major. And the university owed him a better deal. Would he never take his rightful place in the world?

These were the thoughts that plagued Birney at the time he received Margaret Crosland's letter at the end of April. He responded at once. In the next mail off went a copy of *David* with a peevish comment that betrayed his general sense of worthlessness and invited the rebuttal that would bolster his spirits: "Nothing in it is really what I want to write, and a few I wish I hadn't written."[14] And with this small volume of poems, he enclosed an invitation to come and spend the next weekend with him to celebrate his birthday.

So it was that Margaret Crosland, like the incarnation of spring in her flowered summer frock, met Captain Earle Birney on his fortieth birthday. Chatting away about poetry, the war, the ins and outs of personnel selection work, the niceties of Old French and Anglo-Saxon poetry (both of which Margaret had studied), the difficult impasse Margaret had reached with her blind fiancé, whose parents had taken a dislike to her, the balding lanky Canadian with the "thin unsatisfied face," and the fresh young Englishwoman, whose accent reminded him of his mother, so eager for advice and experience, passed the day together. "I spent my birthday in London," Birney reported to his mother. "Had lunch in a Chinese restaurant on Piccadilly Circus and went to Kew Gardens in the afternoon for a walk with Charles Bruce [who joined them], the head of the Canadian Press in London."[15] Nowhere did he mention Margaret, though the euphoria of that first meeting in what he suddenly began calling "this wonderful country in May-time"[16] can be sensed between the lines. "Have you ever heard or read Alfred Noyes' poem 'Come down to Kew in lilac-time'?" he wrote his mother, "Well it is not only lilac time, but time also for azaleas, rhododendrons, hawthorn, laburnum & dozens of other flowering shrubs."[17]

Within days after Birney returned to the army camp at Ash about thirty-five miles south-west of London, Margaret wrote a response to the poems of the man she found "fatherly." Where Carlotta had wept, Margaret shivered. "I've just read 'David' and shivered. It's good fierce stuff. I like your work because it's full of strength and action. Your verse moves & lives in a way that Wreford's does not & probably never will. His has no physical life... I like 'Vancouver Lights,' and 'On Going to the Wars' very much... I feel very feminine and precieuse in contrast, & my horizons are so small."[18] She enclosed a poem of hers ("The Mountain")—written during night alert duty for bombers at her local fire station, the Light Rescue Service at the Adelphi Depot in Charing Cross, where she volunteered after long days as a secretary in the Home Office. Later she would recall her view of Birney's poems, "Earle had a great yearning to be macho. He wanted to be terribly tough. I think it was because of his physique, tall and thin, looking sort of perpetually undernourished. That strong rhythm business goes right back to some of the Old English poems. I was studying it myself. There was something very masculine about it and rather tough and I thought it was a rather Stoic quality which Earle tried to cultivate—this business of climbing mountains."[19]

Unlike Carlotta—who had little interest in Birney's advice about her artistic work—Margaret eagerly discussed her poetry and poetics in hopes of a future literary career. Within two weeks of their meeting, she paid Earle a three-day visit, taking a room at nearby Aldershot and spending her days with him in the large garden at Ash which was made more glorious than usual by a spell of fine weather.

Margaret's letter on her return makes it plain that the two had fallen in love, and that the common ground was poetry:

> My dear,
>
> When you had gone last night there was so much I wanted to say. How really wonderful the 3 days with you & near you had been, how close we were together, & yet how much closer I wanted to be in every way, & how pleased I was when you felt better and how sorry I was for the times I was mean enough to grumble or to disappoint you. I've got an idea for a terrific poem—a sonnet, I think, but I'll see. I hope to bring into it several of the things we talked about, including the uncharted lands of love.[20]

What followed was a sonnet that defined their situation and eventually marked the course of Birney's own poetry. "These are poor times for loving," her poem so fittingly dated "Earl's Court, London" began, because "the steely wars outride / our youth." None the less, the poem went on to say, private dreams are not altogether humbled by the context of war, since a "revelation" occurs. That "revelation" consisted of an elaborate compliment to Birney, resonating with the strong Old English techniques of alliteration, double-barrelled words like "sky-shiver" which were technically called "kennings," and the strong beats he himself favoured:

> He came, the vision-builder, with sky-shiver
> before him, Unknown Lover, glory-giver.[21]

In response to Birney's "masculine" poetic persona, his taste for strong rhythms and the deeper emotional life he awakened, Margaret tempered her "feminine and precieuse" work, expanded her "small horizons" and made rapid advances as a writer.

In what soon became a unique and "courtly" courtship, Birney responded with a sonnet dated "Ash, Surrey June 1944" which began: "We've lept into a land as wide as you"—an idea that more than echoed Wreford Watson's poem "War Generation" which began:

> She came to me simply
> wide as the sky
> deep as the ocean
> wanting as I[22]

But unlike Watson's poem, Birney's ended with a Middle English kenning, "mappemounde" (which Margaret would have recognized as "the map of the world") in the line: "and cry to chart our mappemounde of love."[23] It was an image that was also a pun on "mons veneris," and the need to "chart" their love, a secret code. It suggested Birney's intention of initiating the sexually inexperienced Margaret.

Back and forth flew increasingly passionate sonnets between these two who became lovers in July after Margaret took Earle's advice and broke her engagement. They could meet rarely. Birney had few leaves from Ash, where he had taken on more onerous duties after being promoted to the rank of major towards the end of May (officially in mid-June). And Margaret was seldom able to leave London because of her night duty there. "The first time we stayed together in London," Margaret recalls, "was at the Waldorf Hotel. We walked there, and on the way we passed a flower-seller. Earle bought me some lovely blue cornflowers. It was sort of a wedding bouquet. We asked the chambermaid for some sort of vase, which was probably a jam jar. I know that next morning I took a last look at those flowers. I hated leaving them."[24]

By October Earle expostulated, "Fifteen nights! What a pathetic little heap to rescue from a life-time without each other."[25] Those nights, more often than not, were spent out on the Sussex Downs making love under skies that occasionally flashed with distant flares or throbbed with the drone of bomb-laden robot planes headed for London. It was a situation that resulted in the discomfort of insect bites (which Birney reported to his mother without mentioning how he got them), but also inspired the images that haunted their sonnets. One of Margaret's conveys this atmosphere and illustrates her new sense that love, not war, can win the upper hand:

> We are god-like here, building to our height
> this temple of each other, where the porch is hewn out
> from desire, and where delight
> sparks urgent in the sacrificial torch.
> Around us wreathes the smoke-enclouded song
> into the penetralium of the soul,
> Then sweeps us proudly to the hills, along
> our subject sky, where beggar-demons roll
> their plaything meteors, and with such dice
> bargain for lesser hearts of mortal price.

As the summer wore into fall, Margaret's letters and sonnets became more and more passionate, as Earle—her first lover, and one she would always recall as wonderful—awakened her to full physical sexuality. "The poem is wonderful," she wrote of his September sonnet ("Your body is the bread"), "I think you have managed to express so much of the inexpressible...the whole thing burns me up—I'm on fire for you, dearest. I have ideas for another poem, but so far only the first line exists, which may turn out impossible: 'O flammenwerfer love, that scorches in my heart—.'"[26] This line, comparing her lover (who whimsically continued to pun on her London address, "Earl's Court") to a German flame-thrower,[27] ultimately became "You flammenwerfer love, now scorching through my flesh" in an extravagant tribute to her lover's power to free her from inhibition and arouse her to "body-burning."[28]

And in a November sonnet that expressed both lovers' sense that theirs was an almost mystic union of body and soul, Margaret wrote:

> This hour was for perfection; brief and sublime
> it compassed flesh and spirit with a still
> yet urgent radiance. No parting chill

nor passion-heat could penetrate the clime
of our September-loving. To us the chime
of planet and the word of cloud, until
our sky's Octobered, cannot coin at will
this living gold, the full-moon's wealth of time.[29]

By September, Earle had helped Margaret move out of The Virgin's Retreat and into a small flat he partly paid for on Vauxhall Bridge Road. And Margaret introduced him to her literary friends—most importantly, those editors and publishers who might publish his work.

But self-interest was not the mainspring for Birney's courtship. His love for Margaret far exceeded what he felt for Carlotta, possibly for any woman he had known so far. He told Carlotta to forget him and explained he had a "kind of literary partnership" with Margaret, whom Carlotta had met.[30] He and Margaret were physically enthralled with each other; they shared a love for the literary; and—as would be amply demonstrated later in her career (she went on after her B.A. in Honours French in 1941 to become a major feminist literary critic, editor, and biographer of several French literary figures)[31]—Margaret was his equal in intelligence and talent. Perhaps most important, Margaret mirrored back to Birney the youthful image of himself he needed in order to overcome his distress about the passage of time. Not only was she younger, but her approval of his poetry meant that he was keeping up with the next generation. Through her, he placed "For Steve" in an English journal *The New Saxon Pamphlets*. "Am rather pleased," he wrote to Ralph Gustafson, "as they are all a younger crowd inclined to be patronizing to anyone over twenty and their acceptance at least makes me feel I'm not getting entirely relegated to the Older Generation."[32] She clearly posed a challenge to Birney's marriage.

Yet, as he wrote to Margaret in September, when their love was at its peak, "Something [is] held in check by my loyalty to Esther and Bill."[33] As always, Earle had been open with Esther about his affair with Margaret, forwarding some of Margaret's letters to her, and relaying Esther's comments back to Margaret. "Earle told me at infinite length all about Esther," Margaret recalls, "and he would read her letters to me and he would read her comments on what he had written to her about me. What a start in life for me! I didn't know people did this sort of thing.... And [Esther] used to write such amusing letters!" On one occasion Esther wrote to friends of hers who owned a farm in Sussex and arranged for Earle and Margaret to spend a weekend there together. The friends were shocked, but complied.[34]

Had Esther forced Earle to make a choice between her and any of the others, things might have been different. But she had virtually given her permission—as he had given her his permission—to have freedom. It was unlikely he would ever find such freedom elsewhere. And since Esther, too, had occasional affairs, she was in no position to complain. None of their friends understood. "If you are both believers in sleeping with anyone who takes your fancy," wrote Peggy Todd, one of the few women to resist Birney's advances, "why does Esther say: 'I suppose your platonic relationship is best'?? I shall never understand either you or Esther."[35]

But there was more to the relationship with Esther than this mutual philosophy based on the Marxist disdain for ownership. Despite their frequent quarrels, Esther was an affectionate, amusing companion with whom Earle shared a great deal: a general political outlook based on a shared political past, a delight in social interaction with a large assortment of friends, and an interest in the literary world. When others, like his mother or Ned Pratt, sent Earle cigarettes or chocolates as a treat, Esther sent books like Gogol's *Dead Souls* or the five volumes of George Bernard Shaw. Although she was stocky and broadfaced, hardly one of the cool dark elegant beauties he preferred, she had the English accent—somewhat like his mother's—that would always attract him in women, and she was aglow with vigorous good health. "She looked very well indeed," Wreford Watson reported to Birney after visiting Esther, "In a moss-green suit, which entirely became her, and her hair done up in a gleaming upswept mass. Her talk was full of those pungent sayings of hers, and witty too, as she cut and thrust at communists and nihilists, the *Star Weekly* & *Preview* alike. She was full of [her] trip [with Bill] to the Island: of the frantic rush to pack things off, and then her friends turning up hours late, while Bill, meantime, was on tip-toe with mingled doubt & anticipation."[36] Moreover, Esther, who had always helped with the clerical side of his work, had readily become his literary agent while he was overseas, handling the royalties from *David*, typing and sending his new poems to journals, answering much of his correspondence and forwarding such information to him as the request from J.M. Dent & Sons to reprint "David" in a secondary school anthology. ("I said to Dent's that you probably would, but that I would have to ask you first. I think it's a Good Thing—good for Canadian youth to read real poetry. Told Dent's they would have to speak to Ryerson & pay the price asked. Then I spoke to Ryerson's and said they should make Dent's pay. OK with you?")[37] And when Birney's Governor General's Award for *David and Other Poems* had been announced in June 1942, it had been Esther—accompanied by Corinne Hagon—who proudly accepted the award (which Birney referred to disparagingly as a "tin medal" shared "with some wretchedly bad poets of previous years")[38] in his stead at a dinner at the Royal York Hotel. "Won't that be nice for me," she had written him, casting herself as a comical buffoon. "I'll have to practice curtseying for the next two weeks, & at that I'll probably fall flat on my face at the great moment."[39]

Birney's work as a personnel selection officer—a subject in which Margaret had no interest—also brought him closer to Esther. Back and forth went long letters full of case histories: Esther's from her social work assessing families for foster children, Earle's from his military reports. On one occasion, Esther sent along tests she had devised to determine educational status so that Earle could adapt them for the educational section of his personnel tests.[40] In fact, Esther had ambitions to become a writer too. Like Earle, she was saving all her case histories as "promptings" with an eye to future fiction.[41]

Birney had been truthful when he told Carlotta and Margaret—and no doubt others—of his loyalty to Esther and Bill. Part of him *was* deeply engaged in the role of loving husband and father. He often visited his in-laws in London—especially relishing the company of "Poppa Bull," who was very fond of him. Like his own father, Earle was fully capable of tender

regard for home and family, and many of his letters to Esther—
unlike his passionate screeds to other women—were gently solicitous in ways reminiscent of his father's letters home during the
Great War. "Dearest," he wrote her in mid-March 1944, when
he was still deeply embroiled with Carlotta, "I shouldn't like to
think what would happen to my heart if anything happened to
you, sweetheart. So look after yourself, won't you dear, E."[42]
Another letter about the same time closed, "The raid is over, &
the stars resume their proper place. Soon the moon will be up. I
think I shall go for a walk in the wind & return for the ten
o'clock cup of tea and beddy-by. I have to be up at 6:15 (Duty
Officer). Goodnight dearest, goodnight beloved Billy. Sleep
tight, both of you, & may we soon be together again."[43] When
Esther raised the thorny issue of why he was less irritable away
from her and also confessed her jealousy of Carlotta, he replied
(as Spitfires roared by at tree-top level) in a way that suggested he
was reflecting seriously on his own complex personality:

> Interviewing all these [candidates] has proved…to me
> [that most people don't change at our age]; most of
> them are fixed at 28–30; they learn more about other
> people but seldom about themselves. The brainy
> insightful person is likely to go on changing in his
> thirties though, & some psychologists say that one of
> the characteristics of "genius" is an ability to go on
> developing indefinitely throughout life. I meant my
> remark as a sober realistic one rather than a pessimistic
> one—it should emphasize the urgency of the present,
> the danger of hoping to change "later." And I don't by
> any means think that I lost my temper more with you
> because of anything in you; you're an exceptionally
> good-natured & patient lady. No, it's partly because of
> close & daily association—living *together* not just in
> the same house, as one does with other men.…the
> army has peculiar advantages for someone of my tem-
> perament.…the ordered disciplined sheltered life of
> the soldier not actually in the front lines has so many
> advantages that thousands of our soldiers want to stay

in the army for the rest of their days—no threat of unemployment, of sudden unfair dismissal or lay-off or wage-cut—clothes, meals, beds, always there, always free; promotions slow but eventual in time.... Of course, this isn't exactly my dish, but it does explain why I should be better-tempered, less of a worry-wart.... Darling, don't be jealous of poor Carlotta...because she's too damned serious and clinging and melodramatic & intense & eternally sensitive. It's very flattering, but I don't want it.[44]

Even when his love for Margaret blossomed into poems of breathtaking intensity and commitment in September, he was simultaneously writing urgent letters to his superiors begging permission (which was declined) for Esther and Bill to come to England so that he could see them again.[45]

As if to resolve the juggling act that was his emotional life in November 1944 by demonstrating that none of the women in his life was all that important, Birney had a brief affair with Jeanne Belford, a farm wife in Surrey whose husband was posted elsewhere.[46]

Then, suddenly, fate intervened to uproot him—at least temporarily—from the complexities of his life. On 23 November he got orders to cross the Channel to Holland where he "shuttled in a jeep over frozen flatlands along the Dutch-Belgian border as the officer in charge of personnel re-allocations for the Canadian troops in [Field Marshal] Montgomery's army."[47] Typically, he was highly stimulated by a new situation and he eagerly engaged with it by compiling detailed statistics about Belgian prices and wages for everything from butter and clothes to rent and prostitutes, and described the ethnic make-up of the Walloon and Flemish population. In descriptions of almost fantastic detail (like the economic statistics he had prepared for Trotsky), he wrote of the various places he was stationed—first an old chateau (from which he took and kept a scrap of brocade wallpaper),[48] then to an abandoned German camp in a frozen swamp, then as a billet in the comfortable home of an insurance agent in Nijmegen.

But the excitement of this new adventure soon lost its sheen. Birney's health proved vulnerable in the cold damp of the famous "winter of hunger." "So far I keep well enough," he wrote Dorothy Livesay on 20 December in one of the numerous letters he energetically sent off to his many correspondents, "but the strain of life in a 'theatre of operation' is wearying even in a sedentary job, when you are forty. One is never quite free from agues, dysentery, sinusitis; & nervous strain. I'm very lucky compared with the boys at Nijmegen, however, whose submarine foxholes I recently shared, thankfully not for long."[49] But like many other soldiers, Birney quickly came down with the "Belgian crut," and by mid-March he was so ill he was hospitalized in Ghent with dysentery. In a letter four months later to his old Utah room-mate Herman Singer, he whimsically poured out the woeful sequence of illnesses that had removed him from action on the Continent and sent him back to England, then invalided him out of the army back to Canada in mid-July 1945:

After three weeks of being cornholed with glass tubes, choked with stomach pumps, innoculated, blood-tested, purged, enemaed, X-rayed, vaccinated, I was pronounced unfit for the Western Theatre and shipped to England on a Dakota for convalescence.

My Colonel, god rot him, thought I looked too fit for idleness and, after a week, sent me back to duty at a Repatriation Camp in England. This being a pooling ground for all the diseases of Italy, and I being on the make for any bug, the result was diphtheria at the end of the second week [7 April]. I spent three weeks on my back with that in a hospital near London.

The medicos thought I ought to stay another month, to avoid post-diphtheria paralysis; but again my Colonel, god blast him, got me out and back to work [lecturing on 14 May]. After a couple of weeks of that it began to dawn on me that some "catarrh" I had was a palatal paralysis [a common after-effect of diphtheria]. So I'm back in another hospital, miles from anywhere, finishing a second week of another stretch on my back.

So far, the effects are confined to palate and larynx; I talk like a harelip and have a tendency to pour out my nose anything I try to put down my throat, even the beer I get for my appetite—not much of a waste, considering wartime beer. For a while they thought I had the works—"peripheral" paralysis began in my toes; but it's stopped, & if it doesn't come back in another month I probably won't get it. However, there are still lots of other things that can happen; my shortness of breath may increase to the point where I go into an Iron Lung or a Wooden Kimona; my wild cardiac neuritis may win the day against a very positive desire to go on living and fornicating.[50]

Birney's illness threw the elements of his life into a different perspective. Margaret Crosland, wearing a curtain ring as a wedding band, claimed to be his wife so she could visit him where he lay in an isolation ward behind glass at the hospital in Ash. (He told Carlotta that he could have no visitors.)[51] But, despite the fact that he still sponsored her flat, the romance could not survive such circumstances. Meanwhile, Esther reached a state of collapse, not only through worry about her husband, but also because she sensed his emotional withdrawal once the affair with Margaret blossomed, and she was fatigued with the strain of coming home after work to care for Bill who had a severe case of measles. Illness demoralized Birney. He became emaciated. The paralysis of his palate slurred his speech and muted his voice; the paralysis in his fingers and toes made writing and standing difficult; and—even with canes—he could not walk far without becoming breathless.

No longer did army life seem ideal. Anxious to return home, he wrote his colonel requesting "compassionate leave" after his twenty-five months abroad to return to university teaching, pleading his own illness and Esther's "nervous breakdown."[52] On 5 June he wrote his mother, "I long so much to see you & lie in the garden hammock (if you still have one!) and I am worried about Esther and Bill.... I have written enough verse for a second volume now and am trying to find a publisher over here for it before I return. I have dedicated it "To my mother and my father's memory," so I hope it is published soon and that you like it. It is nearly all verse rising out of my war experiences."[53] The title Birney had chosen for his book was "Trek From Progress," a title that was intended to convey his belief that the war had been a step backward, not a step forward, for mankind. Some of the poems—such as "Vancouver Lights" and "Hands"—had appeared in *David*. Others—like "Joe Harris" and "For Steve"—were, as he had told his mother, verse arising from his war experiences. What was perhaps most characteristic of the volume was its range of voices. Birney was as capable of the light-hearted word-play imitative of Old English poetry in "Anglosaxon Street" (a playful description of Hazelton Avenue, Toronto) as he was of the profound and philosophical "Vancouver Lights" or the tough macho effects of "Invasion Spring." The poems reflected the fact that Earle Birney could be several different men.

Nowhere was this more true than in the poems that were inspired by the different women in his life. To Esther he addressed "This Page My Pigeon," a poem dated "Portsmouth 1944" (where he had left for Belgium), which acknowledges the continuity, stability and sanity she provided in a war-torn world to a lonely man caught up in destructive behaviour. The speaker imagines the page on which the poem is written to be a homing pigeon which

> Says that your voice still waters my memory,
> your eyes are leads to the wide light
> that will be. Swears you are part of the rightness
> of hills, the saneness of music and hemlocks.[54]

Yet, despite this acknowledgement, there are darker hints in the poem. Although Esther is "my greenest past, my rivered future," images of growth suggest quarrels and change—a pertinent and vexed subject in the Birneys' marriage. And the final image of a "heart tendrilled tight with existence of you" suggests that her love has him in a grip that strangles or imprisons.

In "The Road to Nijmegen," written in the Belgian hospital where he had lain in mid-March, Birney recalls Gabrielle Baldwin—to whom he specifically dedicated the poem. Unlike "This Page My Pigeon," "The Road to Nijmegen" concerns the devastation of war more than the fun-loving woman who is remembered. Later, Birney would deny that the poem was a love poem, a claim which, though perhaps technically true (since it is Gaby's wonderful humanity the poet recalls) is none the less false to their intimate relationship which was maintained in his absence through correspondence. The poem, he would later say when introducing readings of it, was composed

> from recollections of a particular jeep-trip I had made [as major in charge of selection of personnel for the Canadian Army in the north-west theatre] the previous December (1944) from our base at Ghent to the front near Nijmegen.... The road described was the famous Maple Leaf Highway which went up to the tip of the Canadian salient between Nijmegen and Arnhem. The period is after our failure to capture Arnhem and before the spring break-through. It was one of the coldest winters in European history, and there was, in the narrow Canadian salient, almost no fuel. Behind the front the country lay virtually paralyzed—bomb damage went unrepaired, and added to gradually by wandering V-Ones and V-Twos. The country had been fought over and left behind. So, the occasional grouping of graves of Canadian soldiers, often with either a helmet or a billy-tin on top as sole memento—burned-out tanks, blown-up bridges. Inhabitants mainly the very old or very young; the rest were either fighting or still doing forced labour on the German side (men & women). The only civilian means of transportation was the bicycle along these parts, as the highway was set aside for military use. Most bicycles one saw were of course without tires & when ridden over the cobbled roads, they "tossed" like boats. Most civilians spent their time trying to find

extra food from our troops, or lining up for their own
rations, or hunting for fuel. The lombards were cut
down, the beautiful lombards of the Flanders plain,
for fuel for the State and the troops; old peasants
leaped on the stump of each tree as it was bared, with
kitchen knives, penknives, anything; they'd whittle the
whole stump and roots away in a few hours, stuff the
chips into old sacks and cart them off ten, twelve
miles to their homes. Children begged at the back
doors of our mess huts or sifted bits of gravel heaped
up from a bomb-hole on the road, or from a dump of
repair material, looking for bits of coal.

Well, all this to me was the Waste Land came true,
the Daliesque consequences of war. And, since this
was a time when we couldn't be sure how or when the
war would end, the whole atmosphere was pretty
grim. I tried to say, in this poem, that what often sustained soldiers in such times & moods was the sudden
casual remembrance of the face of a friend, of someone whom you *knew* was more good than bad; it
made you think there might still possibly be some
hope for & in the human race. So I wrote this to just
such a friend…to someone out in the real living world
from someone who felt in danger of being buried alive
in a dead world.[55]

It is the vision of Gaby's face which "assures" the speaker and
gives him hope and a "creed" in the face of senseless suffering
and death, offering a counter-balancing image of kindness in a
world in which bleak cruelty and guilt seem overwhelming on
"this road that arrives at no future."

Oddly enough, Margaret Crosland was convinced that "The
Road to Nijmegen" was about her,[56] either because Birney told
her so or because she assumed that any poem other than those
clearly intended for Esther must be. This is hardly surprising,
since the poem "Skeleton in the Grass" arose from his experiences with her and "On a Diary" was his reflections on the diary
she had kept since 1935 and lent him in September 1944. Her

"entries" for 1944 and 1945 which he appropriated and recast in his own words to distil these experiences to their essence: he singles out her choice of "the lonely craft" of poetry over marriage to "the maimed hero"; the achievement of "summer's womanhood" and "love Pacific deep."

> In Junetime a Dana steps clean from her tree to go
>   dancing
> at last through the curving pied landskip of life.
> There's a great moon at ease on a Sussex down
> and the gaudy ducks of St. James are moored in time's
>   end....
> Now let this frenzied century unloose
> what gales it may—here walks unbowed a woman.[57]

And to Corinne Hagon, who had occasionally written to him—inquiring teasingly about his love life and reporting her own doings back in Toronto—he sent off a poem in late May (just before his third bout in the hospital) as different from any of the poems in "Trek From Progress" as possible. "From the Hazel Bough" was a description as spritely and frivolous as their brief affair had been, with its sly allusion to Hazelton Avenue where they had been neighbours. "Thanks for the poem," Corinne had written back. "I thought it gay and sweet. It's so long since anyone ever wrote poetry to me that I felt quite youthful. I have kept it for my eyes only, you may be sure!"[58]

But the poem which came closest to expressing his inner thoughts and feelings was written on the hospital ship he boarded with Margaret Crosland's parting "Anniversary" gift of a collection of George Barker's poems inscribed as "a token 'against the innumerable grieving of the sea'"[59] on 25 July 1945. The ship was called *El Nil* ("The Nothing" or "The Void"). The name could hardly have been more fitting. "Mappemounde"—a reworking of the sonnets he and Margaret had exchanged—was a poem more dark and bleak than any he had yet written. Compressed to almost unbearable intensity, it drew on the old Anglo-Saxon idea of the wanderer or seafarer and used the techniques of Old English poetry to express the thoughts of a man sailing home in ambivalence, not only about moral and ethical questions, but also about the very worth of life itself.

> No not this old whalehall can whelm us,
> shiptamed gullgraced soft to our glidings.
> Harrows that mere more that squares our map.
> See in its north where scribe has marked *mermen,*
> shore-sneakers who croon, to the seafarer's girl,
> next year's gleewords. East and west *nadders,*
> flamefanged bale-twisters their breath dries up tears
> chars in the breast-hoard the dear face-charm.
> Southward *Cetegrande,* that sly beast who sucks
> in with whirlwind also the wanderer's pledges.
> That sea is hight Time it hems all hearts' landtrace.
> Men say the redeless, reaching its bounds,
> topple in maelstrom, tread back never.
> Adread in that mere we drift to map's end.[60]

Its tone is one of self-disgust and profound dread. What was life going to be like with Esther again? How was he going to relate to the son he had never bonded with and who would not remember him? Sometimes, he had confided to Margaret, he felt that he loved Bill, but at others he dreaded the prospect of returning to fatherhood "because he hadn't had time to grow up himself."[61] And was he making a terrible mistake leaving Margaret behind? "It's a wrench to leave England, a flat and a girl waiting for me in London," he wrote Herman Singer.[62] Could he have loved her and lived with her more happily than with Esther? Was he leaving behind the only chance he might ever have for happiness? Or was all love doomed to disillusionment?

These were the questions that lay behind "Mappemounde." In one of his narratives for himself, he was like Ulysses: Margaret (to whom he had given Joyce's *Ulysses* as sexual initiation) was a siren; Esther, the faithful Penelope. And yet the force of the poem—so much more powerful than any of his others—came from his union with Margaret. From their interchange had come the sonnetlike structure, the strong Anglo-Saxon kennings like "whalehall," "maelstrom" and "landtrace"; the vivid images of nature with which their love had blended—"the waterfalling of my life," he had begun one of his sonnets to her. He even owed to her imagination the great whale Cetegrande in his poem, for she had written, "In the great ocean of our love, whales / are the utterance to swing your being's tide." To her, too, he owed the sense of scale and scope that expressed the vastness of the world their love had created—"With you, dearest," she had written, "I've had my first real look at infinity."[63]

Now he stared into infinity himself and saw not love but possibly his own inability to love. He could be a "shore-sneaker crooning to the seafarer's girl next year's gleewords" (or, as Herman Singer put it more bluntly, "a tom-cat")[64] but something in him blighted love, something kept him from honouring his pledges, made him "redeless." The sea he was adrift on was both universal and personal. The map he had made of his world in flux was one of blasted hopes, moral ambivalence, suspect facility—a limbo without anchor, a hollow void. That sea was called time, and its passage pressed in upon him now with an urgency and suffering more desperate than before.

❧ *15* ❧

Where Is Here?

The Earle Birney who arrived at Union Station in Toronto in late July 1945 was far from being the same Earle Birney who had left two years before. "Bill and I went to meet him," Esther recalls. "I told Bill in great excitement, 'Your Dad's coming home!' Then we saw this tall, pale shadow coming towards us down the platform.

"We went home to our lower duplex on Isabella Street and we all sat down on the bed. Earle put his arm around Bill's shoulder, but Bill—now almost three—looked at him as if he were a stranger. Earle would have liked a more demonstrative child, one who appreciated his dad. But Bill was never very demonstrative. He was bright and handsome—very secure in his relationship with me, but he needed time to get used to his father. Earle immediately set up a hostility with that boy. He never put his arm around him again.

"After Earle had been home a day or two, I woke up one night and he wasn't in the bedroom. So I went out and found him sitting in the sitting room looking rather thoughtful. And idiotically I said, 'What's the trouble? Are you worried about Margaret Crosland?' Because even before he arrived home, one of those blue letter-forms arrived and I thought it was from him to me

243

and I opened it. It was a passionate love letter from Margaret Crosland to Earle, saying that even if he'd gone, she was still his and he was still hers, and a lot of crap. So this was very much on my mind. I thought he was missing her because he made no particular demonstrations of love on coming back to me.

"And he said, 'No, no it's the child. You've let him run wild. He runs in and he runs out.' I said, 'It's his home. He has a right to run in and run out. I'm very happy with him running in and out.' And Earle said, 'No. And he has a door open at night to his room and that should be closed.' He was full of enmity really, and he had no patience with this. Any other father would have been so delighted with this beautiful, clever child. I had worked for a number of years as a social worker, and I knew from my training and from every instinct that this was a fine child. I'd lavished a lot of affection on him. He was a great compensation for me. I'd rented a room to two nurses—they were lovely girls— who looked after him when I was at work. So he grew up in a very good atmosphere. But he got on Earle's nerves. I know Earle had had diphtheria, been terribly ill. But he had always had such tight, quick-reacting nerves anyway."[1]

Esther and Bill were not the only problems Earle faced on his return after being invalided out of the army. Other strands of his fragmented life pressed in upon him. As Gabrielle Baldwin wrote to him, after a visit soon after his return, "I felt awfully guilty after leaving your home; it was very cheeky of me to breeze in, monopolize you completely and almost ignore Esther. I was so glad to see you alive and quicking (if slightly battered) that I forgot how to be an endurable guest. I hope I didn't hurt Esther's feeling; I must have been especially trying inasmuch (that I don't doubt for one moment) that I came last of a long line of the great Birney's girl friends who all flocked to 45 Isabella to see the returning Major. What a man.... If I was your wife I'd be the one having nervous indigestion... Earle, Esther has been so kind to me while you were gone; she always made me feel welcomed, always. And, it was wonderful for me to have a home in Toronto where I could land anytime that it suited me. I'll never forget it."[2]

In the hope of hastening Earle's recovery and stabilizing their marriage, the Birneys retreated to a cottage in early August at Thunder Bay.

Birney's personal difficulties were pressing. But he was also beleaguered professionally. He was faced squarely with the need to position himself in a country in which he had already acquired acclaim, but in which he still felt slighted.

Throughout his two years overseas he had maintained a correspondence with the top literary figures. He had written regularly to A.J.M. Smith at Michigan State University, the poet whose *Book of Canadian Poetry* in 1943 was a landmark in the development of Canadian letters. He had also been in constant touch with Ned Pratt at Victoria College, whose new *Collected Poems* had boosted him to the widely acknowledged position of "Dean" of Canadian letters; and Ralph Gustafson in New York, whose Penguin anthology of Canadian poetry rivalled Smith's collection.

Now that Birney was back, he often exchanged letters with James Wreford Watson at McMaster University, one of the authors of *Unit of Five*,[3] thanking him discreetly for introducing him to Margaret Crosland and sharing ideas about the Canadian literary scene. He also heard frequent news of literary doings on the west coast from Dorothy Livesay, who was hitting her stride as a poet, and from Alan Crawley, Livesay's friend, the editor of *Contemporary Verse* (a remarkable feat, considering he was blind). Birney also kept in touch with Bill McConnell, then an ordinance clerk in the army in Ottawa who was writing fiction, and Bill Robbins, a literature colleague at the University of Toronto who got a job at UBC in 1944. Aside from these friends, Birney was also corresponding regularly with Canadian journal editors such as G.H. Clarke at *Queen's Quarterly* and B.K. Sandwell at *Saturday Night*, as he submitted new poems he hoped to publish. And he also kept in touch with Lorne Pierce, his editor at Ryerson, who was pleased with the success of *David* and broached other possible books with Birney.

It appears from Birney's relentlessly prolific correspondence that he was loath to close off any option that could—even remotely—catapult him to fame. There is much evidence to suggest that, despite his keeping a close watch on the Canadian literary scene, he might well have abandoned Esther for a literary

life in England with Margaret if he had had success finding publishers for his writing there. Certainly it was not for lack of effort
that Birney failed to interest the English literati in his work. He
had made contact with editors like John Lehmann of Penguin's
New Writing (with whom he had much earlier tried to place his
work from Canada) as soon as he arrived overseas. And Margaret
had introduced him to a wider circle of literary folk. He had had a
few nibbles, but no real bites. *New Saxon Pamphlets* had taken
"For Steve" in 1944; John Lehmann took "The Road to
Nijmegen" early in 1945. But more of his submissions were
declined than accepted. John Lehmann typically wrote: "I was
very much interested in ["Joe Harris"], and the Canadian country
atmosphere appealed to me, but I feel nevertheless that its very
markedly religious note might make it rather difficult to fit into
New Writing.... I would like to say again that I am very anxious
indeed to have some good Canadian stuff, and I am sure you
could provide it for me."[4] And Martin, Secker & Warburg refused
to bring out an English edition of *David* (which by the end of
1944 had earned Birney $150 in royalties), as did the two pub-
lishers Birney wrote to after obtaining their names from Ifor
Evans, the Chaucer expert who had been his thesis adviser in
London.[5] And Hughes, Massie & Co. rejected the manuscript for
"Trek From Progress" (*Now Is Time*) on the grounds that its chief
market would be in Canada.[6] (Birney later noted that the manuscript was rejected by John Lane, The Bodley Head, Hollis and
Carter, Routledge and Secker & Warburg.)[7] Nor could Birney
drum up any interest in his work at the BBC. Not only did they
decline to use his poems for a radio program, he felt they snubbed
him. "He went to see these people, the producer and so on,"
Margaret Crosland recalls, "and had a long talk with them. He
came out of this office, leaving the producer with a secretary there,
then halfway down the corridor and realized he'd forgotten something, so he went back. He said, 'I found they'd waited until I had
gone to make themselves a cup of tea.' He felt terribly excluded.
It really upset him. But I think that was due to his rather bristly
manner. You know, I think he would produce a sort of manner,
saying: 'All right, you don't want to give me tea, do you.' And he
thought we were a lot of half-witted layabouts in Britain."[8]

As prairie novelist and short-story writer Sinclair Ross had written after a brief meeting in London right after Birney arrived in 1943 (they did not hit it off), it was difficult for Canadian writers to publish inside Canada *and* difficult outside Canada. "I know how you feel about writing and their not knowing what to do with it," he wrote Birney from his army base after meeting him. "I am really in the same position. It sounds all right to say I have a New York agent, but he is always chasing me for 'slick' magazine material, and I just can't turn it out. I get horribly depressed at times—being 'doomed' to write what no one wants to read."[9]

As a ploy to get published, Birney had even impishly suggested to Crosland that the two of them somehow start a controversy: "I have often thought I should engage in literary controversy over here if only to get myself known," he wrote Margaret. "That's how I started in Canada, as a fire-eater in the *Canadian Forum*.... How about attacking each other, under pseudonyms?"[10] It must have irked Birney that it was much easier for Margaret to be published in Canada in such journals as *Saturday Night* than it was for him in England.

In a defensive letter to Ned Pratt, Birney rationalized his position:

> Am trying to get an edition published over here but I have little time or opportunity to approach publishers in the proper English way i.e. through letters of introduction, teas, mutual friends, club lunches, etc. I tried a shot in the dark with Secker & Warburg but they turned me down. If you have any contact with publishers over here would you drop me an Air-Blue about it?... I wish the English ignorance to you and Canada generally could be broken down; no Canadian stuff of any worth circulates here at all.[11]

To complicate matters, Birney had indications that Americans were just becoming aware of his work. In January 1945, the University of Buffalo wrote to ask if he had any original manuscripts to contribute to their library. He eagerly sent off drafts of six poems, including "Mappemounde" and "From the Hazel

Bough."¹² That same month, Oscar Williams, who was editing
an anthology called *The War Poets*, wrote him to ask permission
to include "On Going to the Wars." Birney found this invitation
to be in the company of such poets as Archibald MacLeish,
Robinson Jeffers and e.e. cummings immensely flattering and
replied at once from Belgium enclosing copies of his other war
poems and recommending Margaret Crosland's as well.
(Williams took "For Steve," but Crosland's poems arrived too
late.)¹³ He also learned via Carl Klinck, at about the same time,
that an article by Professor Henry W. Wells, Columbia
University, called "The Awakening in Canadian Poetry" in the
New England Quarterly mentioned him favourably. "It came as a
most delightful surprise," he wrote Wells (describing himself as
"a semi-paralyzed patient" from his hospital bed in Sussex,

> and I want to thank you for your generous words on
> my own work. I think you have been too kind to
> some of us, and certainly to myself, but in view of the
> previous rather general neglect of Canadian verse in
> the U.S. perhaps it will not hurt us to be kindly
> treated just once. I should be very interested to know
> what the reaction to your article was, in terms of
> American editorial interest. So far as I know, yours is
> the first mention I have had in your country, with the
> exception of some "plugging" by my fellow-
> Canadians, Ralph Gustafson and A.J.M. Smith. Most
> of the verse in my *David* volume went the rounds of a
> dozen American journals without a single acceptance.
> Since coming overseas in 1943 I have been quite cut
> off from American journals....
>   I am hoping to make another attempt to break into
> the American journals when I return to Canada...and
> I am taking the liberty...of enclosing a few recent
> pieces in the hope that you can advise me...as to pos-
> sible outlets.¹⁴

Certainly, as Birney saw, the literary sensibility in Canada differed from that in England. His award-winning *David* sold

widely in Canada, but couldn't interest British publishers who none the less seemed to want "good Canadian stuff," whatever that meant. Contrary to what seemed to be the case, the war had not erased national boundaries in the pursuit of a larger literary cause. There was no "international" poetry, only poems that called themselves "contemporary" because they were anti-Victorian and dealt with war themes. Yet British poetry sold well in Canada, a clear sign that colonialism lingered. And what of the Americans? Were Canadian and American tastes on the point of converging? Most important, how could he second-guess the literary map so as to position himself advantageously?

For Birney, who had chronically been unable to establish priorities anyway, this confusing literary scene was anathema. If only a fixed set of criteria would emerge, he could begin to play the game. But how could he focus his ambitions when he was hailed for *David* as the best poet in one country and unable to find a publisher for the same book in another?

The strongest message came from a range of Canadians who urged him to return to Canada and take up the role of poet laureate and critic which he had left behind two years before. Esther thought his greatest contribution would be made as a political literary critic.[15] Lorne Pierce urged him to produce a novel. Pratt did too: "I think you could give us a Canadian 'Grapes of Wrath' on your experiences in England," he wrote, "and I am delighted you are systematically taking notes. I am sure you have the great Canadian novel in your fist."[16] That was an appealing thought. As Birney wrote to Margaret, "Look here, we've *got* to write novels; do a popular one, just once, and retire to unhampered poetry for the rest of your life."[17] Dorothy Livesay suggested he apply his business acumen to making Crawley's *Contemporary Verse* "a solid venture."[18] Wreford Watson articulated clearly what many others signalled Birney over and over again:

> ...we shall need your voice again, and your direction.
> You know, possibly better than I do, the lack of leader-
> ship in English letters and learning here in Canada;
> and above all in creative writing. Aside from Pratt,
> who still grows young though growing old, there is no

one in Ontario who is really sympathetic to the great contemporary tradition in poetry, and at the same time is in a position to assist its development among students and writers.... the general public [are] altogether infused with the narcotic of the past, and cannot see much good in English poetry after [Robert] Bridges.

... The disparagement of what perhaps began in his time with Hopkins, and has gone on to Eliot and Auden to become one of the most vital and organic movements in English literature, is to me incredible.... the custodians of Canadian literature [Pelham Edgar, G.H. Clarke, Watson Kirkconnell] seem either to ignore it, or else to despise it....

Men like yourself are desperately needed here, if we are to grow into the full realisation of the modern tradition; and more, if we are to make our contribution to it. I have come across one or two of your students who have really grasped the significance of what I have taken to be your efforts...well that is a start. Undoubtedly, too, your editorial policy on the *Forum* helped...

[Creative direction] is what we need. The C.P.M. [*Canadian Poetry Magazine*] offers very little direction, and then only in a retrogressive manner. It is too embracive. On the other hand, things like *Preview* are too restrictive; they cannot fulfil the requirement of communicating poetry to the public; they simply express it for a clique. Some intermediate position is needed; and I think you were one of the men who took that stand, and helped to educate not merely the public, but the writer as well. It is my hope then, that you will come back encouraged, strengthened and enriched to help lead forward Canadian letters into the same enviable place which Canadian art has achieved.[19]

Certainly Earle Birney was going to write. It is clear that he couldn't *not* write. The endless case histories he sent back to

Esther, the lengthy letters he sent off to hundreds of correspondents, the poems he continued to craft after hours of hard work—even en route to the front, all bear testimony to his compulsion to record experience in words. He amused himself when billeted at the Belgian chateau with a description of a typical day.[20] Even when he lay weakened with dysentery in the hospital in Ghent, he not only wrote "Road to Nijmegen" but also a long description of what he could see from his window and what transpired in the hospital, and sent it off to his mother.[21] It was as if experience in words tamed and shaped the welter of experience that for him so often bordered on chaos.

Though Birney was unclear about where he should focus his many talents, he could scarcely have been better informed about the Canadian literary scene he was returning to. Those war years had coincided with the greatest surge of literary expression and critical analysis the country had yet seen. And many of the letters Birney received from those who were directly involved in this "awakening" of Canadian poetry, as Henry Wells had rightly called it, offered up-to-date insights and candid personal views on the literary scene.

There were still traces of the Victorian, sentimental school Birney had derided in his sarcastic attack on Audrey Alexandra Brown a few years before. These poets tended to be members of local branches of the Canadian Authors' Association and published in its journal *Canadian Author & Bookman*. Bill Robbins sent Birney an amusing account of a talk he gave in Victoria to this group when he reported on E.K. Brown's new book on Canadian poetry:

> Brown's new book...is good, though [in] his later chapters on "the great," after the earlier excellent critical survey, he occasionally goes off the deep end over specimens which strike me as likely candidates for the "Stuffed Owl." He gives you a good page, referring only to "David," but that in terms of unreserved praise. One slightly ambiguous remark refers to your "brilliant, at times, bewildering technical mastery." You old virtuoso!

I could do a Leacock on provincial Canadian culture, having lectured on "Poetic Imagery" to about 20
local members of "Can. Authors' Assoc." O God! O
Montreal! Are they *all* like this? The expressions
ranged from frowning intentness to droop-lidded
ecstasy, but as regards the substance of the talk, blank-
ness was all.[22]

Not surprisingly, Birney declined an invitation to join the editorial board of the *Canadian Author & Bookman* in November 1944
on the grounds that he was not "sympathetic" to much of the
material they published.[23]

Art Smith offered a serious summary as he contemplated "with
mixed feelings" the CAA dinner of "good Canadian authors" at
which Birney was to receive a Governor General's Award for
Now Is Time:

Poetry seems to be blooming and booming in Canada.
Dorothy Livesay's book [*Day and Night*] continues the
good tradition established by *David*—or at least half
of it does: the half omitting Day and Night, The
Outrider, and West Coast. These pieces seem to me to
be poster art, crude and sentimental, and very inferior
to the beautiful and intense poetry of Lorca, Prelude
for Spring, and Fantasia. It is about them that I have
my say on the dust cover. [Ronald] Hambleton, I suppose you have heard is editing an anthology of modernist verse, *Unit of Five* (Hambleton, Page, Wreford,
Souster, and Dudek) which he has bamboozled Lorne
Pierce into publishing. The verse is good, but the
introduction (which I saw and which I believe has
since been canned) was ridiculously sophomoric,
pedantic, and egotistical. The *Preview* group is doing
well, though there seems to be little group rivalries
and petty animosities springing up between Montreal
and Toronto and the West. The more literary questions at issue seem to be cosmopolitanism and metaphysical wit vs. nationalism and simplicity. Patrick

Anderson and D. Livesay have been sparring in the
Forum on this. Klein and Wreford have "joined" the
Preview group. Klein's satire "The Hitleriad" is just out
in the *New Directions* Poets of the Month series. It
looks and is very nice; though to attack Hitler now is
rather like beating a dead horse. Klein was correcting
the page proofs of a hundred page volume of
"psalms".... This is going to be a major achievement. I
sent you a copy of [my] *News of the Phoenix*.24

And Bill McConnell reported his views:

A.J.M. Smith's anthology of Cdn Poetry is better than
most previous collections, but still unsatisfactory. Am
trying to get copies of the First Statement's to send
you.... You are right re: [my] novel. It is unwieldy and
cumbersome but hope to trim and pare and tighten as
it progresses.

Sutherland and his crowd were visited in Nov.
[1943] They are young, enthusiastic as hell, impractical, hypercritical, and thoroughly delightful.
Sutherland himself is 26, an enthusiast of Lawrence's
work, excellent beering companion. You probably
know Layton, shrewd, meticulous craftsman (two
poems in American poetry this month), a hard man to
argue with. Dudek they call the "giraffe," lyric, over-
sensitive to criticism, seems to promise a great deal.
The rest are the usual camp-followers....

Dee Livesay has written some exceptionally fine
sonnets. Am enclosing "West Coast," which is ambitious, fails in spots, I think, but is fairly good....

Last weekend we went down to Montreal with some
Vancouver friends. I had several spare evenings so
phoned around and spent the first one with the Preview
crowd—P.K. Page, quiet introspective Neufville Shaw
and his wife, garrulous likeable Bruce Ruddick (a Pte in
the medical corps) and carefully-speaking Frank R.
Scott. They were so different in texture, enthusiasms,

outlooks from the First Statement crowd (seen the following day) that I could immediately see the difference in their magazines' inclinations and policies. The
Preview crowd seemed older, more introverted, diplo-
matic, careful, and settled, saying shocking things with
tongue in cheek and feet crossed apprehensively. They
seem more inherently conservative, more afraid of
laughter, more conscious of the delicate cross-currents
of opinion and reception.

Ralph Gustafson wrote from New York to say that
your work and mine has reached England...and
should be out in the Penguin edition in several
months.[25]

McConnell enclosed a copy of a proposal for a federation of
Canadian writers from the provisional committee in Montreal,
Patrick Anderson, Louis Dudek, A.M. Klein, Irving Layton and
Neufville Shaw. It proposed a Dominion-wide organization of
writers backed by the provisional committee and others present
(Audrey Aikman, Alfred Bailey, William Blissett, Bruce Ruddick,
F.R. Scott, Smith and Sutherland) which would lobby for government grants, secure radio time, launch a national literary
magazine, supervise sales for Canadian writers at home and
abroad, and protect copyright and so on. Birney disapproved of
this federation on several grounds, most significantly because the
membership was to be determined undemocratically on the basis
of "writers who have something new and meaningful to contribute."[26]

Birney may have been influenced in his rejection of the federation by Pratt, for Pratt's view of the younger Montreal poets was
far from flattering. "I am very much like yourself, in being fed
up with that bunch of conceited asses and decadents in
Montreal," he wrote Birney,

the Anderson, Shaw, Ruddick coterie. They think that
there was no Canadian writing before they appeared.
Anderson comes out here from Oxford—a self-adver-
tised President of the Union—and immediately puts

up his shingle metaphorically as the one and only specialist in poetry work recognition. He takes a look at a landscape in a Canadian train and at once becomes the "inside interpreter." They are now starting an association called the "Federation of Canadian Writers" with themselves as the Provisional Committee. You should see the bloody inanities they put into print—there isn't one live thought or emotion.[27]

These typical excerpts from personal letters illustrate the degree to which Birney was abreast of the Canadian literary times. So much so, that in March 1945 he penned a clever squib based on Chaucer's *Parliament of Fowls* called "Parliament of Canadian Fowls," and sent it off for Dorothy Livesay's amusement.

> Far too much sky about,
> else from our barnyard why
> so many flying out?
> Here is no shadow bigger than wren's
> to trouble the diligent hens
> unless it be Ned, the lost
> kindly albatross.
> Of course it's these modern chicks,
> quite unpredictable
>
> . . . .
>
> Remember those kestrels,
> Smith and Gustafson,
> what an upset till
> we pecked them off south
>
> . . . .
>
> Now too we're crazed
> with in-flying strangers,
> owlets from Oxford...[28]

In addition to the remarks of his friends, he was well aware of the flurry of articles about Canadian poetry that accompanied the publication of Smith's landmark anthology.

E.K. Brown, in his *On Canadian Poetry* (1943)[29] had clearly

demonstrated Canada's neophyte literary status and had identified three main obstacles that had blocked the development of a
national literature: the exigencies of a sparsely populated pioneer
society with a rudimentary economic network in which book
production and distribution was uncertain; public taste, within
this small market for culture, which was provincial due to
Canada's colonial status; and an ingrained puritan attitude that
was inimical to the arts.

In December 1943, Northrop Frye's review of Smith's anthology in the *Forum*[30] took a different line. Frye's careful reading of
the collection induced him to attempt to identify "an attitude of
mind, distinctively Canadian." He rejected the stereotypes (such
as poems about the maple tree) often assumed to be "Canadian."
He, like Brown, thought colonialism had hindered literature in
Canada by causing what he called "creative schizophrenia": a culture that toadied to British themes, on the one hand, and one in
which authentic soul-searching was the subject on the other. He
concluded that the attitude of mind most distinctly Canadian
was to be found in nature: that "nature's apparently meaningless
power" induced artists to consider "civilized values" somewhat
trivial and resulted in a sense of "moral nihilism." The season
most apt to convey this was winter. In Birney's "David," he saw
an example of this "moral nihilism" in action: it was, for him, a
poem about "the riddle of inexplicable death."

W.W.E. Ross picked up on Frye's idea of the importance of the
"wilderness" as a unifying aspect of the Canadian identity. He
noted the importance for poets of "localizing the poetic figure"
and felt that Birney was one of those who had successfully done
so (through his description of mountains and of Vancouver).[31]

For Ralph Gustafson, in his defensive article "Apropos of
Canadian Poetry," Brown's "excuses" for the absence of a viable
literature held true. He blamed economic problems for publishers, a small population, and ineffective literary criticism for the
fact that Canadians were unresponsive to their poets. "Canada
has needed a Sibelius to her Finland, or an Unset to her Norway,
or a Frost to her New England. Canada has needed a genius to
compel," he concluded.[32]

And Dorothy Livesay in "This Canadian Poetry,"[33] took

Smith's notion from the introduction to his anthology that there were two streams in Canadian poetry: the native tradition and the metaphysical or cosmopolitan tradition, and argued that "in the furtherance and broadening of this native tradition our hope lies." For Livesay—as for Smith, who placed Birney in the native tradition—Birney seemed representative of this trend because he, like Anne Marriott and F.R. Scott, dealt not only with specifically Canadian locales but also treated "the recent struggles for social change, the turn to war and the search for peace."

No matter how one looked at it, Canadian poetry seemed to be about to burst into a new exciting stage which, as Birney had argued in his short 1944 BBC programme on "Canadian Poetry," had been ushered in during the 1920s when "the new generation rebelled against what it felt to be a romantic and sugary preoccupation with nature or the merely adventurous in man, and set out, under the influence of T.S. Eliot, Hopkins, and the tradition of John Donne, to write poetry that was emotionally tougher, and intellectually weightier, and technically experimental."[34] Poets were enthusiastic; journals were being assembled and distributed; critics were tussling with the sudden influx of new material, trying to define and establish a uniquely Canadian literary establishment. And everywhere, the name of Earle Birney was touted as somehow central to this new tradition. He admitted that he regarded his interviews of young Canadian men for military allocation as a useful way of gauging the issues he must treat in his writing. "I've now talked intimately & privately, for anywhere from an hour to five, with over 700 young Canadians, and I know there is such an animal, subtly different from anyone else under the common sun, and not a bad type of humanity on the whole—naive but not gullible, buoyant but not trivial, with plenty of brotherhood under the individualistic conditioning, and lots of guts and stability, and above all a fine avoidance of the contrasting excesses of English & American temperaments—without perhaps the strong colours of either.... Every one...with a story...but a story that can only be told of a Canadian."[35] Perhaps, he may have mused, it was he who was to become the "genius" Canada needed to compel an indifferent public from its lethargy.

Yet in his darker moments he faced certain unpleasant truths about himself. "Damn it, I must get down to writing something," he wrote Livesay. "I don't lack ambition; I lack discipline, protracted creative energy, and I must plead that I also lack free leisure. At any rate, I go on taking notes of Canadian youth I meet, & thinking and planning things to write; perhaps I'll do something decent yet, but sometimes I wonder if I'm just kidding myself. If I can get a year free when this bloody mess is over, I'll find out about myself. I've never had much freedom to write with; always had to make money, or thought I had; or study; or do outdoor work for health reasons; or some damned thing. Perhaps it's just a long chain of rationalization."[36]

Birney was irritated at Smith's classification of him in the native tradition. "You should be more critical of Smith's dichotomy," he wrote Dorothy Livesay. "I refuse to be classed in a 'native tradition'; it doesn't mean a thing to me."[37] Still committed to Trotsky's notion of the artist as a social and humanist visionary above mere nationalism (and correspondingly suspicious of anything that smacked of Stalin's concept of the artist as an arm of the State) he saw himself as thoroughly international. If anything, he saw the arts in Canada as breaking with England and aligning with the U.S., being swallowed by the whale, as he put it.[38] "We differ about the future of Canada as an entity," Dorothy Livesay wrote him in response to this notion. "The break with empiah must be achieved, parturition unfulfilled haunts our culture—but you fear the whale's swallow? I used to think it inevitable, and that is why I once agreed with Smith that we must be cosmopolitan, not Canadian.... I now think differently: that we *can* achieve a separate nationhood.... We are going to resist the American whale! And outgrow the Motherland! And be what you already are—in your poetry!"[39]

Putting aside the question of where Birney might situate himself in the effervescent literary scene that he re-entered on his return from the war, he had the more pressing business to settle of where he would be gainfully employed. Birney had indicated to his Chairman, A.S.P. Woodhouse, in the summer of 1944, that he was displeased with the salary of $3,000 he could expect on returning to University College and hinted that he might seek employment elsewhere. A letter Woodhouse sent the following spring requesting a decision from Birney triggered a more serious dispute. Birney's reply (the day after his forty-first birthday) was icily subtle. He would only commit himself to a year until he knew more about his prospects. He effectively understated his diphtheria and almost tongue-in-cheek enumerated his "literary activities," including "a torturous discussion with M. le Recteur of Ghent University, in a mixture of French, German, English, and Latin, on the subject of American methods of dialect recording and their usefulness in the study of Flemish."[40]

Once he returned, the cat-and-mouse game went on: Woodhouse pressing for a commitment from Birney to return to his university post and offering a light teaching load; Birney pleading delay due to recovery from his illness (he was entitled to four months recovery time after his discharge on 5 September 1945) and asking for six months' leave at the outset of his university job. When Woodhouse (who refused to grant the leave) politely mentioned in a postscript that the CBC had been trying to reach Birney, he had no idea that he was contributing to his own distress. The call was part of negotiations Birney had begun with the CBC in the hope of locating a better-paying job with them.

He had been encouraged in this move by Dorothy Livesay, who kept telling him that radio programs were an important way of reaching the Canadian public. Nor did she care for academe: "I am delighted you think of radio," she wrote early in 1945. "I would do anything to persuade you to get away from that neutral limbo, the university. You must not get caught there—not til you've had your break and done your job. I still believe that Pratt's work is musty, unreal, because his life is so. I am a minority, I know, but I cannot re-read any of his poems with any excitement. Yours—or indeed P[atrick] A[nderson]'s, offer a continual freshness."[41]

Without informing Woodhouse, on 1 September Birney accepted the job at the Montreal CBC as Supervisor of the European Section of their International Service at a salary of $4,000 a year. He was to try the job for three months, then give notice if it didn't suit him. The CBC could do the same, if they felt he wasn't working out. Woodhouse's stuffy letter on learning of this in mid-November, after the classes he'd hoped Birney would be teaching were well underway, was politely furious. "It may be that, in my anxiety not to seem to put pressure upon you while you were ill, I did not make it sufficiently clear to you how great is the difficulty caused to the University and the Department by indecision indefinitely prolonged, or (and this is a word of the most friendly advice) how very unwise it is to antagonize the authorities by seeming carelessness of the University's interests if there is any chance of your wishing to return." [42]

On 5 September, while Esther prepared the move to Montreal, locating an apartment at 3745 Avenue de l'Oratoire with Miriam Waddington's help[43] near the great bulbous dome of St. Joseph's Oratory, just east of the mountain, Birney travelled west to Vancouver to spend some time resting at his mother's. Like the returning soldiers he described in his poem "Young Veterans," something intransigent at his core asserted itself:

> They return with new cells, old eyes,
> to their strange children and older wives.
> They try to be as they were remembered
> or to contrive how they are rendered,
> and failing are themselves again.[44]

Though Esther remembers that Earle headed off to see his mother "within a day or two" of returning to Toronto, it was actually just over a month. However, she is right that, despite his weakened condition, Birney soon involved himself in an affair with his mother's boarder, a pretty, dark-haired dress-store clerk named Ruby Sharp, a poorly educated girl with a fondness for beer and bowling. Her favourite song was "Dream of Love." The two smoked surreptitiously in Ruby's room, hoping that Mrs. Birney wouldn't notice. As Ruby would confide in her letters to Birney after he returned to Toronto, his mother was extremely difficult to live with. "Your Mum thinks I am putting it on [pretending to have a stomach-ache], I think & just ridicules me. She has suffered all the pain there is too [sic] suffer, so guess theres [sic] none left for us. Really, Earl [sic], I can't see that her holiday has done her much good as she seems more bitter than ever. I can't hold a conversation of any kind with her or she nearly blows a fuse over something. I just hate speaking of your Mum this way to you, pal, but you know how it is." After a New Year's Eve party she complained, "I didn't arrive home until 6:15 a.m. of which your Mum was very mad, even though I told her I would be home for breakfast. I just said nothing as I figure its [sic] none of her business. She would really have something to kick about if I came home drunk, but what's the use?" And elsewhere she reported that his mother got so impatient for his letters that she "bawled out the poor postman." "Really, Earl [sic], when she doesn't hear from you about every week, it gets almost unbearable & then as soon as a letter arrives she's happy again.... She got it [the letter] & told me your news that I knew so well already but I was very innocent & interested—oh my, if your Mum only knew—but what she doesn't know won't hurt her, eh?" It is clear from what Ruby called his "swell letters" that Birney complained in turn about his mother and lectured her about getting more out of life.[45]

He was too ill to stand Bill's ins and outs, Esther bitterly observes, but "he was well enough to start this love affair with Ruby. Once he was back, he asked me to post a letter to her. I opened it, and it was all about how he wished he could marry her and how he loved her and all this crap. I came back and I said, 'I opened your letter.' It was stupid of me really, but I thought, 'This is so bizarre.' But somehow I never did anything about it. I never rocked the boat. I guess I always thought, 'When we're over this one, maybe there won't be anyone.' I was so busy living my own life, fortunately. I had good jobs. And all the people I knew in Canada came indirectly or directly through him. I was popular, well-liked. And I made my life out of those substitutions."[46]

✥ *16* ✥

HOMEWARD, BOUND

On 21 April 1946, Earle Birney received his first letter of con-
gratulations for his appointment to the English Department at
the University of British Columbia. The writer was the tall,
gawky seventy-five-year-old Pelham Edgar, son of Sir James and
Lady Edgar and retired professor of French and English at
Victoria College, friend of Duncan Campbell Scott and Stephen
Leacock, founder of the CAA in 1921 and its poetry journal the
Canadian Poetry Magazine, and negotiator for the Governor
General's annual literary awards. "I knew the young war horse
would return to the University track again," Edgar observed to
his former graduate student and colleague. "Has the old war
horse retired, or are you his second in command?"[1] The old war
horse was G.G. Sedgewick, who had manoeuvred behind the
scenes since October 1945[2] to help bring his golden-haired boy
home. Everywhere there was the sense that in the wake of the
Second World War a new era had begun. And the young war
horse Birney—whom the press immediately idealized as "The
Soldier Poet"—was no exception. Despite the fact that Birney
limped badly, was almost forty-two, and his red-gold hair noticeably receding and thin, there was something fresh and youthful
in his energetic outlook that caused others to identify him with

the new postwar generation. "I'm one of the old men going out," wrote fifty-six-year-old Bill Deacon, current president of the CAA and literary editor of *The Globe and Mail,* in a letter imploring Birney to take over the editorship of the CAA's failing *Canadian Poetry Magazine.* "You are one of the new men coming in. You fellows can make [the CAA] anything you want."[3]

The experimental year with CBC's International Services had been a failure. Birney had hoped that in Montreal he would be in on the latest communication system, draw Canada closer to the international scene, hone his own language skills (he worked assiduously on his French that year), and be closer to what looked like the most vital centre for poetry in the country—that is, the two groups that had found expression in the journals *Preview* and *First Statement.* He favoured the latter. "I feel that yours is the only Canadian journal which attempts to select on the basis of artistic merit and at the same time pays its contributors," he wrote John Sutherland, its editor, enclosing "On a Diary," and asking about two of Margaret Crosland's poems which he had submitted earlier. "It was because the *Canadian Forum* would not accept this principle that I stopped being their literary editor some years ago." Birney went on to mention a criticism from Louis Dudek that rankled. "Dudek listed me among the academics 'who are out of real everyday contact with the main currents of contemporary life.'... you may assure Mr. Dudek that however often we took to shelters in Europe they were not the shelters of libraries." He signed his letter "Earle Birney. Maj."[4] And secretly, his move to Montreal was calculated to bring him close to Gabrielle Baldwin, the French woman whose lovely face had inspired "The Road to Nijmegen."

CBC would have been happy to keep Birney on with his colleagues Helmut Blume, Eric Koch and Stuart Griffiths, among others. He had started up a useful magazine called *Radio Times* listing programs and running short articles, and had effected a bold and innovative media coup by having German prisoners-of-war from Canadian war camps come onto the radio to talk directly to those they knew back home as a means of countering Nazi propaganda.[5] But by the end of the winter, Birney actively sought the post at UBC. He and Esther never really fit into the

Montreal literary scene, except for their friendship with Patrick and Miriam Waddington, a friendship based on Patrick's collegiality at the CBC, activated by the interest all four had in poetry, and cemented by the common base Miriam and Esther shared as Jewish women involved in social work. Something of the mismatch between Birney and the Montreal literarti can be sensed in an account of an evening spent at Art Smith's which he sent Alan Crawley:

> we met many Montreal celebrities for the first time, and notably Abe Klein, an intelligent and witty man. Frank Scott also there, very affable, and trailing clouds of First Statement behind him. There was John Sutherland, young and feckless but pleasant enough, and his wife (Audrey Aikman) & his wife's sister both very ladylike in long gloves which they refused to take off even for eating. Audrey read the New Yorker most of the evening but her sister, more definitely pretty and dumb, chattered in a West Indian brand of Colonial English. Arthur Phelps and wife (who were delighted to have your greetings) sat somewhat on the side most of the evening as the race was to the young.... Also present were Irving Layton (whose manners, as with most of these ferocious younglings, are much meeker in speech than on paper) & his sweetie (Sutherland's sister [Betty]), the Waddingtons (Miriam and Pat) both excellent folk; also Sutherland's oafish patron a Boris somebody who annoyed Esther by continually referring to her as of the older generation.... I am still trying to get the MS of "On a Diary" back from Sutherland; the bastard is sending it around to all the NORTHERN REVIEW editors, though it was not submitted to them, but to the now-defunct FIRST STATEMENT. I am determined to submit nothing to this gang for they have no editorial sense of responsibility or even elementary courtesy.[6]

Birney found the long hours of work exhausting. He disliked

the severe climate, and suffered flu three times that winter. Even the travel to and from his office was difficult because his foot disability made it impossible to walk more than a few blocks or stand waiting for streetcars without pain. He applied for priority listing to get a car, obtained it, but was told by numerous car salesmen that he would have to wait until at least July due to postwar shortages. His mother adamantly refused to move east, and put pressure on him to return west because her health was failing. Above all, Birney had no time or energy left for creative writing. "Am still far too busy to write verse or write anything except pompous memoranda, and dull letters," he complained peevishly to Dorothy Livesay.[7]

The need for his talents was brought home to him time and time again. Alan Crawley reported a groundswell of interest in Canadian poetry when he lectured in the ballroom of the Empress Hotel in Victoria to the Federation of Canadian Artists early in 1946:

> Started to talk at eight twenty and said the last telling words at ten to ten so they had a belly full. It really went well and I was for a wonder a bit pleased. Said [A.M.] Klein's "Autobiographical" and "The Provinces"; [Dorothy] Livesay's "Lorca," "Serenade," "For Spring" and "The Child Looks Out"; [F.R.] Scott's "Saturday Sundae," and "CAA Meeting" ["The Canadian Authors Meet"]; [Raymond] Knister's "Stable Talk," "Turn Over Plow," and "White Cat"; [Anne] Marriott's "Prairie Graveyard"; [Floris] McLaren's "No More the Slow Stream"; [P.K.] Page's "Stories of Snow," "Landscape for Love," and "The Stenographers"; [Bertram] Warr's "Winter Stalks," "Heart to Carry On" and "Working Class"; and ended with Birney's "Dusk on the Bay" ["Dusk on English Bay"] and "This Page My Pigeon" and "The Road [to Nijmegen"] and with a good heap of comment and there was great attention and I felt the audience of some eighty or so as thoroughly interested and taking it all in. Dorothy and Pat Page said it went well and

even my critical [wife] Jean was pleased.... about
twenty came up afterwards and talked and brought in
four subs for *CV*... The newspapers of Saturday had
good and fairly intelligent report and both of them
mentioned you and your book and one of them said:
"Earle Birney is evidently Mr. Crawley's choice of
modern Canadian poets."[8]

Birney was flattered by such comments, but he was also stirred
to despair by reports of some of the literary doings that suggested
the "maple leaf school" of poetry was far from extinct. "You may
have heard or seen of the great Ottawa poetry contest," wrote
Anne Marriott, who worked at the National Film Board there,
"results of which were announced last night."

I was one of the judges—an incredible chore. 1134
entries, of which at least 1000 were of a badness
inconceivable. Never did I believe so many people
would write so many bad poems and evidently think
them so good! Several of the prize ones had good stuff
in them, though—it was the most marvellous relief to
find something even remotely passable in that welter
of doggerel and banality![9]

And in March the National Advisory Council on School
Broadcasting made clear their idea of Canada's foremost poets in
their choice of poets whose lives would be "dramatized" and
poems read for Grades 6–10: Pauline Johnson, W.H.
Drummond, Robert Service, Bliss Carman and Marjorie
Pickthall (or Audrey Alexandra Brown).[10]

The imperative to write was made more urgent by the success
of *Now Is Time*.[11] Birney had intended this collection of twenty-
seven poems, including five reprinted from *David and Other
Poems* (which was now out of print), to be the ultimate in contemporary writing. "The poet must write for now and combat
the old lies again." His sense that the war had done nothing to
further humanity was reflected in his working title "Trek From
Progress," which Lorne Pierce, his editor at Ryerson Press, had

persuaded him to change. The dedication of *Now Is Time* to his mother and to the memory of his father had occurred to him as he lay in one of the hospitals in rural England near Hindhead where his father had been in the last war.[12]

Successful though *Now Is Time* indisputably was, it did not surpass—or even equal—his earlier volume *David*. Certainly, response to Birney's second collection of poems could not be blamed on low visibility. With acumen mustered from years of experience in the publishing world—as newspaperman, editor, experienced poet—Birney focused his considerable business skill to making sure the book was properly disseminated and reviewed. He sent lists of those who should have free copies and journals where reviews should appear to Ryerson Press. He watched carefully to track reviews, and prodded recalcitrant newspapers and journals to produce them. One of these was S. Morgan-Powell at the *Montreal Star* with whom Birney skirmished briefly (Morgan-Powell pleaded illness and Birney retorted that as a military invalid he knew what that meant, the implication being that if an ill Birney could write the stuff, an ill journalist could review it) before Morgan-Powell produced the most acid review the book received. ("Such a welter of unpoetical words, such as picayune, emulsify, osmotic and sussurration," he had written, and criticized Birney's "deliberate cloaking of metaphor," his "awkward form" and his "straining after an uncompromising form of realism in which there is more ugliness than is necessary.")[13] Birney fired off indignant responses to reviewers he thought were unfair, like the anonymous reviewer in *Canadian Poetry Magazine* who found the volume "disappointing" because "the style has gone to seed in contortions of metaphysical modernity."[14] He even had his mother drop in on the Vancouver bookstores frequently to see when orders arrived and to dispel Ryerson's claim that customers were asking for the book under the wrong title.[15] He urged Ryerson to launch a publicity campaign in Britain and the U.S., to no avail. Whatever could be done to bring his book the widest attention possible, Birney did.

The majority of reviews followed closely the squib Ryerson Press sent along as publicity: Major Earle Birney was "our most talented soldier poet," his writing was "original," his technique was "thoroughly disciplined," and the poet "invariably has something illuminating to offer." In short, Ryerson promoted the book and reviewers generally reviewed it with the focus on Birney's credibility as a military man to address contemporary issues. "Birney has produced in fragile poesy, all the moods of an informal history of Canadians at war," went one review.[16] Thus did Birney's image as a "soldier poet" obscure his real merits and defects as a creative writer. More discerning reviewers, such as E.K. Brown in *Poetry* (Chicago), weighed Birney's strengths and weaknesses more objectively, noting the poems' unevenness, irony and persistent self-analysis. "At his best," Brown wrote, "Birney is rewarding indeed. Such a poem as 'Hands' is a severe test of a poet's quality.... The poet's experience was so intense, so deeply an affair of his inmost self, and his possession of his craft so sure, that the worn theme is made to seem new and vivid. He drifts in his canoe along a Pacific inlet, trying to escape from the pressures of a civilization geared to mechanical warfare, in which hands have been degraded into the 'extension' of tools."[17]

Here were Birney's real merits in a poem not coincidentally written before he went overseas. It was not his authenticity as a soldier, but his authenticity as a human being deeply concerned about what man was doing in and to his world that made his poetry significant. And that world was most poignantly rendered in the awesome shapes and smells and feel of the west coast.

The most significant aspect of the reception of *Now Is Time* was the general sense among critics and Birney's friends alike that it was not an advance on *David*. "Perhaps nothing in this collection will make the appeal of 'David,'" went a typical review in *Echoes*, "but it is interesting to see this writer not content to repeat himself, but eager to reach out in further experiments."[18] "What I return to most often," wrote Dorothy Livesay, who had every reason to empathize instead with Birney's social and political work, "are those [poems] where you are least literary and most in love—with life or nature or woman, it does not matter which. Though the Diary poem I had not seen before and it is most moving, riding to a beautiful climax (almost shall I say Sir Walter Raleigh and THE CLOAK)."[19] "The advance in tech-

nique and in flexibility," Roy Daniells reported, "has carried you
into techniques which don't make for easy reading... I was put
off at first by expecting something different (things more like
'David' and 'A-S Street'), by being baffled as to meanings because
of your more artful imagery, and by looking for more obvious
rhythms than you employ."[20]

"This is *confidential* advance warning that *Now Is Time* wins
Governor General's Award for 1945. Congratulations!" wrote
Bill Deacon, chairman of the Awards Board, on official CAA
notepaper to Birney on 24 March 1946. On 13 April it was offi-
cial national news: "Vancouver Poet Proves Ability: Birney Has
Scored Again," ran the headline in the "New Books" section of
the 11 May issue of *The Vancouver Sun*, an allusion to the fact
that Birney was one of only two writers to have won the award
twice since its inception in 1937. Congratulations streamed in.
Pratt's was typical: "Vi greeted me with the announcement....
Both of us decided to celebrate your triumph with a good drink,
Vi with tea, Ned with a sailor's snort of navy rum, a concentrated
remnant from last summer. Boy, we are glad that you won it, and
that you are getting your deserved recognition somewhat earlier
in the game than would have been possible fifteen or twenty
years ago. I am glad that a double-header came your way. You
will probably have to put your port and starboard bows into a
sea of jealousy caused by a lot of adolescent farts down your way,
but ride above them all. There is no one in Canada whose success gives me more satisfaction as I have been with you from the
start, prodding you on to greater activity."[21] Along with the
other winners—Hugh MacLennan for his novel *Two Solitudes*,[22]
Ross Munro for his academic non-fiction war account *Gauntlet
to Overlord*,[23] and Evelyn M. Richardson for her creative non-fiction autobiography *We Keep a Light*[24]—Earle Birney was invited
to a black-tie reception on the 29th of June for their Excellencies
the Governor General & Vicountess Alexander at the Royal York
Hotel hosted by the CAA as the apex of their twenty-fifth annual
national conference. Record numbers of writers attended.
Newspaper photos of Birney on this occasion show an elegant,
well-groomed slim man, whose face now crinkled into attractive
smile lines, wine glass in hand, amidst conversation with other

writers such as Gwethalyn Graham (whose *Earth and High Heaven*[25] he admired), fully at ease among the peers he had bested. Birney was allotted an extra segment of time to address the association on matters pertaining to Canadian literature.[26] His speech—later published through Roy Daniells in *The Manitoba Arts Review*[27]—focused on the urgent need for publishers, editors and reviewers to find new ways of stirring up interest in poetry; as for poets, in a theory that possibly owed much to his political experiences as a speaker and, further back, to his mother's ambition for him to become a Presbyterian minister, he argued that their oral art should be restored to its original place in public halls:

> the challenge is to the poet himself. A lot of poets, including some of the most promising younger ones, that I have met in this country, are too contemptuous of their audience. Let them stop and think that there are hundreds of thousands of people in Canada who have been educated in this generation to enjoy good music, good acting, good fiction and to a certain extent good painting. Don't tell me they can't also learn to enjoy good poetry. But before they do, a few people have to risk a little money on the poets, a lot of educators and critics have to catch up with modern modes of art, and the poets have to pluck up courage and rent a hall.[28]

"I am immensely impressed," Bill Deacon responded, "with the part about poets should hire a hall and if they can't hold an audience, the fault is with the poet. THAT'S THE STUFF—the truest word."[29]

When Watson Kirkconnell, whose literary taste increasingly seemed old-fashioned, resigned from the editorship of the *Canadian Poetry Magazine* in May, Birney was the obvious choice as his successor.[30] In a confidential letter, Bill Deacon wrote: "In my belief there is only one man for the job. You stand midway between the old reactionaries and the young incomprehensibles, sympathetic with both, aligned with neither—just the

man we need."[31] The response of the national executive committee at the annual meeting on 30 June confirmed this. "Sixteen of
us were present, representing all parts of of the country and, I
would say, all shades of opinion," Deacon reported. "These people also felt that you are the very man for the job, and Miss Anne
Marriott said that your influence with the younger poets would
be of inestimable value. She saw now the one chance of uniting
the poetic interest in Canada. We were very glad to hear from
Miss Marriott because some of the rest of us are not younger
poets, as she is, and we could not gauge their feelings towards
you."[32]

The CAA gave Birney a free editorial hand, limited only by his
obligation to leave business matters to the lawyer who was the
magazine's current manager, A.H. O'Brien. Birney was to be
paid fifty dollars per quarterly issue, and his mandate was to
breathe new life into a journal which was slowly going under
(the CAA membership stood at 920; by Deacon's calculation,
1,000 subscriptions were needed to keep the magazine sol-
vent).[33] With almost magisterial authority, Birney set out to turn
the *CPM* into *the* national magazine which would unite the various literary cliques across the country and in so doing be professional enough to carry Canadian poetry into international
markets. His policy—though less "leftist" (some members of the
CAA feared Birney would be too leftist)[34]—had not changed
much from the old *Canadian Forum* days: "So long as I am editor we will have no hymn sections, children's corners or nooks
for CAA branches," he wrote sarcastically.[35] "I too am neither in
the camp of E.K. Brown (which is a bandwagon rather than a
camp anyway) or Bill Deacon (for whom all Canadian crows are
swans, so far as public utterances go, though I know he feels it
necessary to counteract the national inferiority feelings in lit.)."[36]
His criteria would thus veer decidedly from Kirkconnell's and
eschew "academic" poetry. What he was after was simply the best
contemporary poetry in the country. Immediately, he raised the
subscription fee from six to seven dollars, then to ten dollars. He
scrapped the prize system and instituted a payment-by-line policy in which poets would receive fifteen cents per line or about
five dollars per page. He ardently recruited regional editors for

the masthead, easily persuading Ned Pratt to lend his name for prestige, but also enticing Philip Child in Toronto to oversee page proofs and the other business of publication; Charles Bruce (a Nova Scotia newspaperman whose *Grey Ship Moving* had been a close second for the Governor General's Award) to set up interest in the Maritimes; Roy Daniells (who was leaving the University of Manitoba to join the English Department at UBC with Birney) to enlist support in Manitoba; Patrick Waddington in Montreal to woo the members of *Northern Review*, the journal which amalgamated *Preview* and *First Statement*; Floris McLaren in Victoria to find west-coast writers and pursue a liaison with *Contemporary Verse* (they declined); Anne Marriott, who was currently working at the National Film Board in Ottawa, to locate prairie poets; and P.K. Page, also at the NFB, to act as an Ottawa contact. Birney approached each of these writers individually in ways he hoped would persuade them (only Page declined, on the basis of her loyalty to *Preview*). He urged them to join the CAA, which all except Waddington and Page did (even Dorothy Livesay joined), and urged them to use whatever influence they had to obtain new subscriptions and donors. "The main thing," he wrote Anne Marriott, "is to develop a mental set."[37]

While Birney basked in the glow of compliments from all quarters for his triple success—the Governor General's Award for *Now Is Time*, his appointment to UBC, and his accession to the editorship of the *Canadian Poetry Magazine*, Esther slogged away packing their Montreal belongings to move west, and set out with Bill at the beginning of June to endure a stay with her mother-in-law while she began settling their household. "I am willing to pay a good deal in rent rather than live indefinitely with my mother and pay storage charges on our furniture, not to speak of the psychiatrist bills if my wife and her mother-in-law have to live together beyond a few weeks," he wrote his past and future colleague Billy MacDonald at UBC.[38] The only available housing Esther was able to find was one of the tiny army huts (about 24 feet by 24 feet) at Acadia Camp on the UBC campus which had been built for use during the war and were now renting unfurnished for thirty or thirty-five dollars a month. "A backsliding conversion…and everything in straight rows and mud," as Birney would later describe it.[39]

The future certainly looked bright. At last, it seemed, Birney had found his place at the zenith of the literary world, and the kaleidoscope of his many-sided personality looked as if it had finally settled into the best possible design. He would return home with the unassailable cachet of an invalid major to the west-coast seascapes he and Esther loved. Already he planned to build a house somewhere along the coast. Meanwhile he had snagged what appeared to be the perfect job among colleagues like Sedgewick, Stan Read (a wartime buddy), Bill Robbins, Bill MacDonald and Roy Daniells (who arrived that same fall), despite the fact that enrolments would be heavy for a year or two to accommodate returning military personnel. He would teach a section of Freshman English, a Sophomore Survey and—his favourite—an advanced creative writing seminar (Literary Criticism and Advanced Writing)[40] to no more than twenty students he could hand-pick himself. His summers, he was assured, would be his to use for writing. He had an important contact on *The Vancouver Sun* in his old friend and fan Evelyn Caldwell who was in charge of reviews. "I find your 'stuff' terribly real," she had written him, "and I marvel that you (1) see the things you do, and (2) express them so potently… It's brilliant writing."[41] Even his remarkable editorial and critical skills found a seemly place, not as the main enterprise in his life, but as a sideline most useful to himself, since as editor of *CPM* he would now be positioned at the hub of the first nationwide poetry journal, one which he fully expected would receive international acclaim. Nor had his brief radio experience in Montreal been amiss. His immediate response to university president Dr. Norman L. MacKenzie's offer of a professorship at the same rate as his CBC job ($4,000) was to propose that UBC begin a record library of poets such as Archibald MacLeish and William Carlos Williams reading their own work, Basil Rathbone reading literary masterpieces, lectures by Granville-Barker on Shakespeare and other British writers, supported by lists of available recordings and a detailed analysis of costs. Finally, at age forty-two, a happy, secure and settled life could truly begin.

~§ 17 §~

DAY AND NIGHT

With the winning of his second Governor General's Award for poetry in the spring of 1946, Earle Birney's public image as Canada's major poet was fixed in time like a still photograph plucked from a fluid film. But the distance between that public persona and the complexities of his life differed as day from night.

Following the ceremonies at which he received his award for *Now Is Time*, he carefully designed the script for a radio interview of himself, composing "most of the questions and all of the answers" in order to ensure accuracy and control his image with the public.

So it was that Canadians who heard this interview on Toronto's CFRB radio station when he was in Toronto at the end of June would have heard the voice of announcer Rex Frost who began with a short summary of the impressive career of the poet who insisted on being listed as Major Earle Birney.

REX In 1942 Earle Birney won the Governor General's poetry award with his *David and Other Poems*. Three years later he did it again...and is thus one of two Canadians [the other was Laura Salverson] who have twice earned this distinction in poetry. We are very glad to have this opportunity of bringing to you the voice of this Canadian author, whose poetry ranks high not only in the literary scene of the Dominion, but also in the world beyond our borders. Earle Birney was born in Calgary and by his own admission has moved around quite a lot.... part of his schooldays were spent in Alberta, moving on ultimately to take his Bachelor's degree at the University of British Columbia. That was in 1926. Between that time and his enlistment in the armed forces in 1942, he studied or taught in California, Utah, London (England) and Toronto...taking his final Ph.D. degree in the Queen City. But it is as the poet rather than as a student, teacher and traveller that Mr. Birney is with us at the present time and naturally I'd like to ask him a few questions about his writing.... Were your poems the outcome of your war experiences?

E.B.   The pressure of world events made me feel that there were things I wanted to say, and I didn't have the time to say them in any lengthier way...poetry has been for me a safety valve...an opportunity for blowing off steam occasionally...a spare time occupation.

REX   You had not written any poetry before the war?

E.B.   None that I would want to speak of... I was too busy teaching.

REX   In other words, you had more time to be alone with your thoughts during your army service?

E.B.   Yes, particularly in hospital beds... I had about six months of that.

REX   Was it during that time that you wrote most of your poems?

E.B.   Well I had time to work out my early drafts and do some polishing…and [stroked out: during those leisure hours I found time to gather old thoughts—and new— together and weave them into what ultimately became a cherished idea—a book of poems].

REX   As a matter of general interest…how do you go about writing a poem…after, for instance, you've got the inspiration on a certain subject or person?

E.B.   I suppose I generally start with an idea that is related to a particular scene…a symbol.

REX   Something that you have experienced personally?

E.B.   Yes, an emotion that results in—what shall I say—a sort of stomach [replaced by: interior] tickling…that irritates until something is done about it…and my personal cure [stroked out: for that itch] was to start putting the [replaced by: evoking my] idea into words…then I'd let it simmer for a while before the polishing up process [replaced by: final dishing out]… I'm not a fast worker… I like to play my idea into words…and out again if necessary before making the final decision…this is it.

REX   You suggested, Mr. Birney, a moment ago that you didn't have time to say many things in any lengthier way…do I take it from that you regard poetry as a condensation of thought or idea?

E.B.   Well partly…also to me the natural literary expression for one's most powerful [replaced by: deepest] moods and emotions, because it allows you to make use of rhythm and music in a more memorable way than does prose…it provides the opportunity to use word colour for accent.

REX   Could you explain again, Mr. Birney, how that worked out in such a case as "David," which I believe is your best-known poem? And incidentally your first Governor General's award winner?

E.B. Well "David" is really a short story, but I told it in verse because I was interested above all in communicating a mood of physical adventure and youthful excitement [replaced by: zest] followed by an equally sharp [replaced by: intense] mood of tragic disillusionment...and to do that I needed a long swinging melody, and I needed also to create a tightness of form to prevent the story becoming sentimental.

REX That in itself is a very interesting expression because I think perhaps a large number of people avoid poetry or do not enjoy this form of writing because they think it is unadulterated sentiment...in other words, that poetry lacks fibre and reality.

E.B. Yes, perhaps too much of the verse which we studied in schools, and which our children still study, is of a sentimental or effeminate type, although I wouldn't blame the schools entirely for the lack of Canadian interest in poetry.

REX Then you do think there is a lack of interest among Canadians?

E.B. Yes, but I think they can be made interested in poetry, and in talking with other writers of verse in this country, I have often found them in agreement with me when the man in the street gets a chance to hear contemporary Canadian poetry well read over the radio or from a lecture platform, he likes it and is stimulated by it. The difficulty is in bridging the gulf between the poet and the audience, in Canada.

REX What would you suggest, Mr. Birney, has created this gulf?

E.B.   A number of different types of people.

REX   Who, for instance?

E.B.   Well, it's my opinion that publishers in Canada start
with the assumption that poetry doesn't sell and fail to
give even their best volumes proper advertising.
Booksellers too are inclined to tuck Canadian poetry on
the back shelves under "Canadiana" and keep them out
of their front windows on the theory also that poems
don't sell. Secondary schools and even universities lag
behind in making their students aware of the best that is
being written.

REX   I take it that you had some difficulty getting your poems
published?

E.B.   As far as book publication goes, no. My publishers at the
Ryerson Press have done an excellent job of presenting
the more talented young Canadian poets. But like all
other poets in this country at the present, I still have difficulty in getting magazine acceptance of my work,
mainly because there is so very little space allotted by
Canadian editors to poetry, unless it is thoroughly traditional in form, or in the school of Edgar Guest. "David,"
which has since been my most widely reprinted poem,
was rejected by 14 Canadian and American editors
before it was published in *The Canadian Forum*, and I
got it in there because I was the *Forum*'s literary editor.

REX   Being an editor sometimes has its advantages, eh?

E.B.   Undoubtedly. But I don't want to throw all the blame for
the neglect of poetry in this country on the editors and
publishers. I think the poets themselves must share some
of the responsibility.

REX   It seems to me, Mr. Birney, that you must have the

courage of your own convictions…it's not every writer of poetry or prose who could take half a dozen rejections, much less 14, without losing heart.

E.B. Anybody who isn't obstinate shouldn't be a writer. Especially with poetry, which someone has described as the arrangement of words in their least lucrative order.

REX I presume that's why you are in the teaching profession?

E.B. And expect to stay… Seriously though, the modern Canadian poet has a challenge to meet in trying to break through the barrier of public indifference. Some of them, and I don't exclude myself, seem to write at times as if they didn't care if anybody understood them. I know one young writer who defined his method of writing to me, as "muttering to himself in the hope that he would be overheard." I think that attitude leads to obscure and often tedious writing and that it reveals an unjustified contempt of the intelligence of the reading public. This is no longer a raw pioneer country; there are thousands of our citizens who have learned in this generation to appreciate the best in music and painting and prose fiction. I don't believe that these citizens are incapable of appreciating good poetry, but the poet needs to get out and get himself known to the public. He must learn how to make use of the greatest modern medium of communication, the radio. There seems to be no reason why Canadian poetry should not be heard on the air as often as Canadian music. I think it wouldn't hurt some of us poets, and perhaps improve our poetry if we learned to read our poetry well…then got out on a barnstorming tour of Canada. Everyone else hires a hall in this country. Why shouldn't we? Bliss Carman and Sir Charles Roberts made themselves national figures, not by hiding in coteries, but by reciting their works in the village schools and the town halls across Canada. I would like to see those days return.

REX As a well-travelled man, Mr. Birney, have you noticed any great difference between the acceptance of poetry in different parts of Canada? Take the east for instance?

E.B. Yes, I think the most favourable climate for poetry in Canada is Montreal. French Canada has much to teach English Canada in regard to the general fostering of the arts. The only annual cash prizes for literature in this country are awarded by the government of the Province of Quebec and they are given to English and French language authors without discrimination.

REX You spent a number of your formulative [sic] years in B.C., Mr. Birney. What about the west in general?

E.B. There, naturally, art traditions are just starting but, as in so many other ways, the west is rapidly catching up with the east. In my opinion, the only good magazine devoted to verse in this country [*Contemporary Verse*] is published from a bus stop on the British Columbia coast, and I know of no part of Canada which is richer in material, still unexploited by the writer.

REX I'd like to take this opportunity, Mr. Birney, of congratulating you on your recent appointment as Professor of English at the University of British Columbia.

E.B. Thank you very much, Mr. Frost. In a sense it will be like going back home.

REX And of course you'll be writing an appropriate poem.

E.B. That depends on how well they treat me. [replaced by: I probably won't be able to stop myself.]

REX Incidentally, Mr. Birney, I haven't had a chance so far to mention your more recent Governor General's award winner NOW IS TIME, but glancing at the clock gives me a very appropriate reason to say Now Is Time to say au revoir to our friends of the air... Now Is Time to thank you also for your timely and valuable interpretation of the place which Canadian poetry holds in the Canadian literary scene.[1]

After the interview, Birney griped to his publisher about not being paid: "As a radio man I know that such affairs are usually paid for," he wrote. "I had to give up an entire (and very hot) afternoon in the midst of a busy week.... In the CBC we would have paid at least twenty-five dollars for that.... Certainly I would never do such a thing again without payment, as I do not think the publicity itself is sufficient compensation." Ryerson Press responded to this unexpected outburst from a writer they thought ought to have been flattered to be invited for a radio interview by insisting that such interviews boost sales.[2]

Within a month of this interview, on 22 July 1946, Birney sent a letter from Vancouver to Gabrielle Baldwin which revealed a private chaos completely at odds with the cool authority of his radio appearance.

My dear Gabie,

Last Saturday Esther and I started going through our Gethsemane. I told her about us, and many things about myself that I had tried to conceal from her and everybody including you and myself. I told her how I had always been bedevilled by sex, how, although I loved her dearly and still do, sexually I had been able to get only a brief physical slaking with her, never enough to keep me from pursuing other women, from masturbation, from a mental obsession with sex. I tried to show her, and she understands, how my irritabilities with her have gone on and grown partly at least out of this mental malaise, something so far uncontrollable although I had always hoped I could grow out of it. To try to talk about these things with complete honesty has been almost like trying to tear my own brains out, it is so difficult and painful and groping. I told her how I had come to believe I would always be like that, always looking at the nearest legs, daydreaming about every attractive woman I saw or even pictures of them in newspapers, getting myself into unwanted complications with other women who, too, did not end the ceaseless need for search, for variety and sensuality and conquest and sexual plotting. In the early days with Esther it didn't matter so much; there were no children, and we had come together with an understanding which gave us sexual freedom. Yet always underneath I *wanted* to be free of all this, to have the mental peace and the singlemindedness and lack of distraction that others seemed to have, that came from a physical as well as spiritual oneness with a wife.

Then I told her that Margaret had opened my eyes to the fact that I *could* achieve this, that I could be so sexually content, over a long period, with one woman that I lost interest sexually in others, or at least dropped to no more than a normal awareness of other women—and how that again made me slough off my irritabilities and restlessness and gave me a chance to think again. Margaret wasn't a solution but she was an illumination; there are other things I need in a wife that Margaret hasn't got and Esther has; and there was a continuing love for Esther and a sense of responsibility towards Bill which made it natural and inevitable for me to come back to Esther. I hoped, among other things, that the new stability I had got with Margaret would transfer itself to my renewed relations with Esther. But that didn't happen and although I never wanted to return to Margaret, knowing it was no solution, I found my old obsessions and sexual deviltry returning and crowding thicker and thicker into me.

And then I told her of my relationship with you, of how strongly we had been attracted by each other from the first meeting but that we had remained simply close friends and I went overseas with no thought that we would ever be anything else, though I knew that you loved me. Then, in Montreal, how we were drawn closer than ever, partly by chance and partly by mutual frustrations, and yet kept apart by loyalty and love for Esther, and then the dam broke when Esther left and you came to the flat and then to Rice Lake. And how, for the second time in my life, I got that blessed peace and lightness of spirit and calm that comes from sexual fulfillment only this time with someone whom I knew I could go on living with and loving indefinitely and who unreservedly wanted to marry me. And I tried to tell Esther how even there, at Rice Lake, we missed her and felt something lacking without her, how terrible and hateful it was to be deceiving her and of how it was I who prevented you writing the truth to her because I wanted to tell her in my own way when the right time came. I have made it clear that your leaving Dick was not precipitated or caused by me, that I gave you no promise I would leave Esther for you nor did you ask or expect any such promise because your incompatibility with Dick had been there before you met me and would have brought you to a break if I had never existed. I have told her that you did not come west, principally, because we agreed I must make one further trial to make a life with Esther and Bill and your presence would not make it a really honest trial—and I have made it clear that it was above all you who insisted on this. Then I told her how these obsessions have returned upon me, driving me into myself, making it impossible for me to write, to think consecutively, to be amiable or decent in my ordinary daily relations, how I want to control and end this devil and yet always seem to be beaten by it.

All these confessions began with a quarrel about the discipline of Bill and we have talked a great deal about the problem of my relation with him, but we have both agreed that it is secondary to the other problem and partly a result of it. I told Esther that it was true I had not really wanted a family but felt it was imperative that she have a child, that I had hoped that I would be a good father but now believed I wasn't and wasn't somehow capable of becoming one because subconsciously I probably resented the distraction he caused, the impingement on adult living; despite myself he irritates me and I feel helpless and hopeless about it—because, if I interfere in his guidance I do not seem to be able to do so without being harsh and unloving—and if I don't interfere he feels deprived of paternal interest and strength. When I say I am stern as a reaction to Esther's softness and excess of patience she says that her softness is a reaction to my hardness. And when I look into myself I feel she may be right— after all, my notions about bringing up a child, or rather my ways, were learned from my mother, who made a hell of a mess of bringing me up; so, I have no trust in my own judgement about how to be a good father, although I have plenty of habit-reactions about it; underneath I don't *want* to be a father of children, I want to be a father of books. I have plenty of feelings of responsibility about Bill and I know he is a superior child, a loveable and intelligent one; but I have a curious detachment about him that I can't shake; I'm not really feeling responsible about him as a person, only as a social unit; that is, I feel that if I help to bring a child into the world I should do what I can to see that he is socially beneficial not harmful; sounds cold, and probably is. The truth is I have no real talent with children; they bore me most of the time, and I them. These last days, my being around the hut all the time and Bill too, have intensified the difficulties in our relationship.

Well, what is the upshot of all this? Naturally, a great deal of grieving. Esther was shocked, hurt by feeling herself physically rejected, hurt by realizing that a friend as close to her as you are was also, objectively speaking, the threat to her marriage. We have had much tears though few reproaches. Esther is so tremendously understanding and generous and truth-seeking that we have made a good number of strides I think towards whatever the future is to be. And, above all, catharsis has brought a great sense of relief to us both, to me because at last I have been able to get words out to explain much that was tormenting me internally, and Esther because at last she knows, she can dismiss the false fears and grapple with the real ones. And we both feel a sense of freedom. We start now with the realization that we may not be able to make our marriage last but that we are genuinely still trying to and still have time—a winter, a year, to see how things work out. We make no claims on each other now sexually; Esther knows that you are the woman who alone brings me physical fulfillment, whom I love even though I haven't stopped loving Esther. She knows that my devil isn't beaten and probably won't be unless I go to you, or, if you fail me, I go to live alone. But in justice to her, to you, to all of us, we must give ourselves time to think and find out about ourselves.

You will come at Christmas, I hope, please; we both want you to; it will be so much easier now, now that we are all "in the clear" with each other. I feel now that there is nothing I need hide from Esther, I have not been able to keep silent for fear of hurting her— now she knows as much as you and I do about ourselves, about each other. Esther realizes now too that one reason we couldn't be frank with her before was the fear that she would tell someone else, Reva [Brooks] for example. But my own suppressed torture was such that I had to take that risk, and I do not think Esther will violate this confidence. I have told her things which only the three of us can ever know about me—and Esther knows also that your part in all this must be kept locked away from Dick, and so from everyone else just now.

There have been interruptions—people for tea—and I am losing my own thread; I do hope, dear, I am making myself clear. To be clear and utterly truthful is a very difficult combination. If this letter sounds coldly analytical at times it is because for my own mental healing—I am really in a state of mental confusion—I must analyze and analyze myself. Esther wants me to go to a psychiatrist but I believe I have enough insight and self-knowledge to know what I want and need; maybe I just want too much. I want you ceaselessly and you know that is not just a physical need though, because of the nature of my whole trouble, that is what I have had to emphasize in this letter. I want Esther too in the sense that I have a very different past with [her] than you have with Dick—I could not bear to part from her without a full understanding, without a sense that everything had been tried to avoid [ending the marriage].[3]

Earle

⋅≼ *18* ≽⋅

STRAIT AHEAD

At the end of his first year at UBC, Earle Birney was happy. The sociable lanky poet-professor with his cane was in his element on campus. He still wore his khaki army jacket—sometimes with a black academic robe draped off one shoulder—when most of the other vets crowding the campus had dispensed with their military clothing.[1] "Our Bill will soon be six," he wrote an old Toronto friend in the spirit of a fond paterfamilias. "B.C. agrees with him and he is a healthy, if skinny, boy, very lively and probably no more a hellion than the average, though certainly no less. Esther and I are both flourishing and are glad to be back on the west coast. I am so looking forward to my first really 'free' summer since I can remember. Will spend it vegetating out here. Having Roy Daniells here is a great joy, too, as well as many other old friends."[2]

But Birney's difficulty establishing priorities soon began to undermine this long-awaited happiness. Not only could he not say "No," except on very rare occasions, he was incapable of doing anything less than his best in everything he undertook. Although his salary of $4,200 was sufficient (and matched that of others of his age or academic rank), he had for so long scrambled to make money and pinched so carefully to save it that he was easily lured by opportunities to make even small amounts more. His deep commitment to advancing Canadian literature nationally and internationally lent an almost missionary zeal to any work he could do for the cause, and his generosity in helping fellow writers was virtually boundless. As for his own ambitions, he continued to juggle a number of alternatives because he was uncertain about how his talents could be employed most fruitfully.

Was his main contribution to be as a poet? Many thought so. E.J. Pratt, for example, wrote of a Toronto party at which he, Claude Bissell, Ernest Sirluck and B.K. Sandwell had discussed the future of Canadian poetry. "I claimed, as I have maintained for some years, that you were our white hope, that [there was] no one, particularly in the Montreal 'faction,' that was even within light years of your constellation."[3] But Birney's poems were still being rejected more often than they were accepted by the myriad magazines and journals he sent them to. What difference did it make to win awards and be anthologized in six collections[4]—two of which were British and two of which were American—if editors persisted in returning much of his work?

Perhaps he'd be better to turn to fiction. He had been drawn in that direction long before he had made his mark as a poet. As far back as 1936, when he and Esther camped in the south of England while they finished his thesis on Chaucer, he had begun a novel. He had three short stories (aside from his *Ubyssey* efforts) which he could polish. At least fiction was lucrative. Poetry was not.

Or what about radio? Now that the war was over, households across Canada were tuning in to a host of cultural and intellectual programs on CBC—radio dramas, book reviews, poetry readings and discussions of literature. These, too, could fetch reasonable payments. Because of his year in Montreal in the International Service, he knew the radio world. He had always wanted to be a people's poet and a contemporary one. He was on record as touting the importance of hearing poetry and recommending that Canadian poets rent halls to give public performances. He had long felt he could excel in radio writing. "After listening to 'Stage 6' on 13 January 1946," he wrote Dee Livesay,

"'Strange Mr. Smith' by Gerda Norton…was so incredibly dull & ponderous & inept that I am greatly stimulated—have just called up Mavor Moore…to *finish* our play…. I don't feel at all 'above' writing for radio."[5] The play (co-authored by Moore, whom Birney had met before the war and knew overseas, when both were later at the International Services in Montreal) was "Court Martial," which was broadcast on 3 October that same year. Was radio the wave of the future? The way to reach the masses? The best medium to choose to write for now?

The solution—typical for Birney—was to pursue all three at once. He continued to write poems and submit them to Canadian, American and British journals, and pressed Lorne Pierce at Ryerson Press, who had allowed both Birney's award-winning books to go out of print, to bring out a new collection that would combine the best of his previous poems with his recent work. He revised his old short stories and sent them off, and started to plan a novel about his experiences during the war. And he undertook several radio programs for CBC and two for the BBC in England. All this in the "spare time" left over from his UBC job and his editorship of *Canadian Poetry Magazine*.

To some extent, Birney's priorities were established for him. His teaching duties came first, duties which, for most academics, would have been a sufficient year's work, especially for someone newly appointed. One of his students, who would later become a professor himself, typically recalls that Birney was "a good teacher, voluble and easy-going."[6] Birney's favourite class was his hand-picked group of twenty budding writers, chosen on the basis of a sample of writing. His approach in this new course was revolutionary. Despite his age and status, he treated these students as equals. Occasionally he gave them assignments, but more often they simply brought their own work, read from it, and took part in discussions about each other's strengths and weaknesses. Before long, they had organized themselves under the punning initials "AA" for "Authors Anonymous" (but hinting at "Alcoholics Anonymous," since they met informally outside of class at each other's houses where drinks were expected). Where Birney most took the role of mentor was in passing on his practical expertise in publishing. He organized them at once to put together their own magazine, *Thunderbird*, which appeared three times a year. He also wrote to his many magazine and journal contacts recommending—and often enclosing—specific poems and stories by his students, a strategy that resulted in a few publications. He got them to subscribe to the main poetry journals. A short notice in the *Daily Province* (probably arranged by Birney) hailed the "unique" course and pointed out that "Students John Wardroper, Ernest Perrault and John Baxter have had their works selected by *Canadian Poetry Magazine*, leading publication in its field. Effie Smallwood and Mrs. Mabel MacKenzie have had short stories accepted by *The Canadian Forum*. Other students whose writings have been submitted to national publications are James Beard, Bill Galt, Norman Klenman and Bob Mungall."[7] Wardroper and Klenman—both of whom pursued careers in radio and television—still have nothing but extravagant praise for the teacher who launched them. Klenman, like most of the students Birney taught that first year and for years to come, is fulsome: "Personally, Earle was the teacher and the person who most influenced me, opened so many pathways."[8] Robert Harlow, one of the students he chose for his second year's class, clearly describes Birney's approach:

> Earle took [my] story from his in-basket, glanced at it as if it were only a mnemonic device and tossed it onto the desk. It was never mentioned during the rest of our interview. What he was interested in was what I'd been, what I was now and what I wanted to be so that he could judge whether it was a potential writer he was talking to.... It was scary. He wanted to feel in me, I sensed immediately, a long-term commitment, and I'd never committed myself to anything except staying alive during the war and having enough money...to get drunk on Saturday night. Earle finally leapt to his feet, said I was accepted and gave me his wonderful grin-cum-smile. That yes, based on what could only have been wild surmise, changed my life. I've not written every day since, but there have not been many days when I haven't thought about the

craft and the art and about my ambitions for both.…

The workshop gave me people to know and some to be in touch with for the rest of my life. It gave a centre to my existence.… and Earle said yes to the [stories] I showed him, seeing always what I wanted to do and, each time refraining from re-writing them, sent me on my own in directions that would make them better stories. I learned how to teach myself, because Earle didn't enunciate rules; he shared experience, one-on-one equals before the task of trying to create something worthwhile on paper. At the same time I also absorbed from Earle the absolute basis for working with inexperienced writers, because what he'd done for me I tried later to do in my workshops. I didn't become his clone. None of us did. He didn't go in for that. He loved his own uniqueness, I think, and also the uniqueness in everyone else he taught or met.[9]

Birney also began sounding out his American university contacts—such as Ernest Sirluck, then at the University of Chicago—to see if he could discover graduate programs in creative writing to which his students might apply.[10] This resulted in the placing of three of his second year's class (Bob Harlow, Jim Jackson and Paul Wright) at the University of Iowa, the only university at that time to accept creative writing in lieu of an M.A. or Ph.D. thesis, with financial support from part-time teaching jobs and various scholarships Birney discovered and arranged. Once they were installed at Iowa in the fall of 1948, he maintained contact with them in long letters that were as friendly as they were helpful.[11] Next he wrote to John Gray at the publishing company Macmillan for a list of literary agents they might try out (and wrote to one of them on his own behalf).[12] He could not have been more serious about launching his students as writers, nor more generous with his time and energy on their behalf.

Birney enjoyed teaching, but disliked some of his other academic duties. At the end of his first year, Sedgewick was replaced as head of the department by Roy Daniells. Birney's initial pleasure at this appointment soon soured, for unlike Sedgewick, who ran the department himself and rarely called meetings, Daniells involved the department in many decisions and delegated duties to newly struck committees. "We are suffering the benefits of Democracy after 25 years of Benevolent Patriarchy," Birney complained to his new radio playwright friend, Lister Sinclair.[13]

As for his editorship of *Canadian Poetry Magazine*—another job that might have fully occupied anyone else—Birney threw himself into "trying to make *CPM* into a decent woman," as he put it to Norrie Frye; in other words, to establish it as a verse medium of international standards.[14] Birney's own account of the arduous work he did on *CPM* is given in *Spreading Time*.[15] Assisted by Esther at the typewriter and files (they kept a shoe-box file on Canadian poets like the ones he had kept on his graduate courses and his thesis), he maintained a huge and steady correspondence with his regional editors and poet friends. He solicited poems from authors he knew and sought advice to widen his net (asking Louis St. Laurent, then Secretary of State for External Affairs, for example, to refer him to poets in French Canada; St. Laurent simply referred him to the French CAA).[16] He responded to each submission. He even gave detailed criticism to poets whose work he rejected. He wrote many of the book reviews himself (he claimed he did fifteen to twenty for each issue, even though some issues did not have that many reviews).[17] He strenuously recruited subscriptions and donations (his old UBC fraternity brother, Dal Grauer contributed fifty dollars), and asked his friends and associates to recruit too. Within months subscriptions doubled and continued to climb. He initiated "exchanges" with other poetry journals to make sure *CPM* was reviewed widely. He arranged a special exchange issue for March 1948—the first of its kind—with the English poetry magazine *Outposts*, edited by Howard Sergeant, in which *CPM* would feature British poets and vice versa. He obtained the official patronage of Vincent Massey for the magazine.[18] And just as he had done with the left-wing journals of the thirties, he personally placed copies of *CPM* with news-vendors and bookstores, and urged others to do the same.

The small, red December 1947 issue of *CPM* was typical of the high standard Birney achieved. It contained work by a wide range of poets: Anne Hébert, Anne Wilkinson, Malcolm Lowry (whom he had met, found "enormously attractive"[19] and instantly befriended the previous May), the young James Reaney, P.K. Page, Bertram Warr—even Audrey Alexandra Brown to whom he had apologized for the scathing review he had done in *The Canadian Forum* ("I made you the victim [for]…sentimental Victorian fetishists").[20] Under the pseudonym "Oliver Yorke," he included his own "Sonnets in Wartime"—a selection from the poems he had written Margaret Crosland. "I really *believe* in eclecticism," he wrote Pat Waddington that Christmas Eve, "it is not a manner forced on me by the paucity of 'contemporary' material."[21] The issue also contained ten book reviews, covering recent publications in Canada, England and the U.S.; and sixteen reviews of international periodicals (ten American, three British, two Canadian and one New Zealand) for the information of writers.

Birney accomplished the editorial task he set out to do, but it was a pyrrhic victory. Within six months he was complaining. "I am seriously thinking of giving up *CPM*…" he wrote Pratt in mid-January 1947, "because it absorbs *all* my spare time. I have not written a line of verse since I took it over."[22] Birney's many frustrations (including his dismay that Sergeant's Canadian issue of *Outposts* was four months late, whereas he had overworked to meet the deadline), especially resulting from the worries of dealing from Vancouver with a magazine which was actually published in Toronto, gradually focused on the Toronto business manager, A.H. O'Brien. In March 1947, Birney's request to Bill Deacon that the elderly and unwell O'Brien be replaced by a young business manager who could be enthusiastic about Birney's editorial policies was ignored. Birney seems to have been unprepared for the backlash against his imposition of contemporary standards. "They ganged up on me," he would later recall, "As soon as I put the freeze on their Itsy-Bitsy Ditties they organized a subscription-*withdrawal* campaign among their own members (CAA)."[23] Subscriptions among the old guard did begin to drop off, and by early 1948, Birney angrily resigned, taking his regional editors and many friends with him after the

June 1948 issue. "I'm going into a quiet corner and shriek with joy at no longer being an editor of anything," he wrote to Dr. Jacob "Marko" Marcowitz, a *CPM* manager.[24]

On top of his teaching, editing, radio work and creative writing, Birney also managed a staggering number of outside activities. He was active in the Vancouver Branch of the Canadian Civil Liberties Union, protesting restrictions on Canadians of Japanese origin and supporting a Bill of Rights for Canada; he was on the advisory board of UBC's Players' Club; he wrote three descriptive essays (on Kootenay Lake, Harrison Lake and Capilano Canyon) for the Standard Oil Company's *See Your West* ("the boys with the money-bags"[25]); he planned a collection of western Canadian material that was to include his friends like Bill McConnell and Dorothy Livesay alongside his students (it was declined); he thought about a poetry anthology for use in Grade 12 and freshman university courses (it didn't materialize); he was on the poetry jury for the Governor General's Award in 1947 and 1948; he gave public lectures at the University Women's Club and the Vancouver Institute; he undertook the long-term task of collecting and publishing the poems of Bertram Warr, a young RCAF pilot killed overseas ("the greatest poetic loss Canada suffered"[26]) and wrote to Warr's sister in England with advice on an English publication;[27] he wrote to defend *CPM* from criticism by a local newspaper; he wrote to defend his *Now Is Time* from a critical review by E.K. Brown in *Poetry* (Chicago); he even found time to respond at length to the daughter of one of his mother's boarders from Banff days with information about his life and his poem "David" for an assignment in her English class at the University of Alberta. He took part in a Round Table discussion on poetry at the CAA's 26th Annual Conference, 7–11 July 1947. And, with almost ferocious attention to detail, he managed his own literary business—jumping on Ryerson Press for royalties whenever he found out his work had been used in writing or on the radio, pressuring A.J.M. Smith (who was revising his *Book of Canadian Poetry*) to include more of his recent work and less of his earlier, and negotiating his contract with Ryerson Press for the next book (*Strait of Anian*, 1948) in lengthy correspondence that, with hindsight, seems justified in treating the company with skepticism about its competence (he noted, for example, that Pierce had neglected to submit books of poetry for the 1947 Governor General's Award, one of which was Livesay's *Poems for People* which eventually won the award).[28]

Thus, Birney's "first really 'free' summer" in 1947 was actually far from free. He had planned to do his creative writing at Acadia Camp or at his shack, but soon an even more attractive place to write poems and begin his war novel became available.

As if he didn't have enough to do that summer, Birney had taken on a two-week creative writing seminar for the YMCA Public Affairs Institute at nearby Camp Elphinstone. It was there that he met Einar Neilson, a stocky, open-faced truck driver who had an avid interest in the arts. "Sometimes," Birney recalled, using the term "brother" in such a way as to suggest that the loss of the brother he had replaced as a baby had left a vacuum he longed to fill, "one has an almost instant sense of friendship and brotherliness. We sort of really, truly clicked almost instantly. I think that I, perhaps, am programmed to like Scandinavians, being sort of dimly one myself... There was something about him that appealed to me: the way he talked, his straightforwardness, and there was a good masculine quality I also liked in him." Neilson lived on Bowen Island, a short ferry ride north from Horseshoe Bay, where he had bought a small, steep, thicketed ocean property between Scarborough and Eagle Cliff on the east side of the island about halfway between the ferry dock at Snug Cove and the northern tip called Hood Point. Neilson knew and admired Birney's poetry even before meeting him at Elphinstone. And Birney was drawn to the prospect of the outdoors life helping Neilson complete "Lieben," the place he was building out of driftwood near the bottom of the cliff overlooking the little cove that led to nearby Miller's Landing. "So it was more or less agreed," according to Birney, "that I would come over when I could and give him a hand... He had big dreams about the place. It wasn't just a place to live. He said, 'Elphinstone Camp is supposed to be like Couchiching of the east, with all the big shots coming in and giving lectures and courses. But... just for a couple of weeks. I want to make a place where artists can come from anywhere and stay as long as they want. Of course, they'd have to help. They have to build it because I don't have any money.'"[29]

Norman Newton, a precocious writer in his late teens who corresponded with Birney from Albion, about twenty-five miles east of Vancouver, and later joined "AA" briefly (and went on to an outstanding career as a writer and musical composer), speculates that "Einar may have been one of these people—Scandinavians, Finns or Russians—who came to Canada around the turn of the century and later. They were not well-educated, tended to be left-wing, had very interesting ideas and got involved as workers in the idea of art and talked a lot."[30]

Birney loved roughing it for the rest of that summer, rowing into the village for supplies, chopping wood in the nude, swimming each day and camping under a little shelter at night. And, for some part of each day, writing. The exercise was "just what I needed with my lingering illness from the war to get back into shape before teaching."[31] Without the amenities (and possibly in imitation of Lister Sinclair, for whom he also felt "a remarkable kinship of spirit"[32]), Birney grew a moustache and beard as he had in England in the 1930s—both decidedly red— and began to look like a vigorous young Viking. During the week, Esther continued to act as his agent, fielding his phone calls, checking his mail and sending him urgent messages by ferry. On the weekends, she brought Bill out to relax with him.

Birney's friendship with Einar was clinched when Birney helped extricate him from a relationship with a woman who had made off angrily with the deed to Neilson's property (Birney confronted her and intimidated her into giving it back). And during the following winter, Birney encouraged Neilson in his new relationship with Muriel, "a big, rather plain music teacher from Winnipeg with a beautiful character, whom Neilson eventually married."[33]

The Birneys' new friendships with Malcolm Lowry and Einar Neilson, whom he introduced to each other sometime in late 1947 or early 1948, was to alter significantly the literary climate on the west coast, making it much wilder and free-spirited. Although he could go for months without drinking, the stocky, barrel-chested Lowry with the "demonic glitter"[34] in his eyes was an alcoholic given to extreme and unpredictable behaviour. And Neilson was a hard-drinking man who believed in free love. Earle and Esther (who did not drink to excess, Esther because she disapproved and Earle because of his delicate stomach) were so taken with Lowry and Margerie Bonner, his beautiful wife (a former Hollywood starlet), that they rented a shack just down from theirs. Without Birney, it is doubtful that Lowry's poetry would have been published in Canada, for he was insecure about it and would show it to very few people and only when he was drunk. But he trusted Birney, who looked up to him as a virtual genius, and let him have a few poems for *CPM*, and others to send to journals such as *Contemporary Verse*.[35] More important, both the Lowrys and the Neilsons provided writers with off-beat places which were bohemian and uninhibited.

Once Birney's second year of "AA" got underway, meetings sometimes took on a much more dramatic aspect. Several of the students from that class—a very special class, according to Birney—recall vividly evenings at Birney's shack. According to Ben Maartman, one of the few veterans in that year's class (he had been a fisherman, was then a social worker and parole officer, then a free-lance writer for the CBC), "Lowry was always drinking. This was the trouble. He was an extremely shy guy, but a very egocentric man too, and when he drank he just dominated everything. He could actually talk poetry when he was drunk, and Margerie was the only lady I ever knew who could actually scream and rant all in iambic pentameter. Once my friend and I were carrying a stove down and Lowry was stuck up a bloody tree. So we climbed on the stove and got him out of the tree. Then he said he'd help us with the stove and all three of us and the stove went over the bloody bank. One time we had a drunken party and I passed out and when I woke up [Earle] had put a blue ribbon on my dong. I often wondered what the hell else went on."[36]

Norman Newton first met Malcolm Lowry (who had just published *Under the Volcano*) at an "AA" meeting at Earle's shack that year. "He was a very dramatic person in my presence, always performing. He had something of the style of the old Shakespearian actor.... His singing was quite unmusical, and he accompanied himself with a furious and rattly strumming on the ukelele which would have caused embarrassment at a YMCA picnic."37 The Lowrys' shack was familiarly known as "Hangover House," and when they were away—as they were in the winter of 1948— Earle and Esther looked after it.38

Hilda Halpin (who met and married Phil Thomas from that same class and later became a professor of English at UBC), recalls that these evenings were "too crowded with event for a young girl to absorb." She puts a different slant on the same events. "Earle would get very angry that Malcolm got so drunk. On one occasion when Malcolm was drunk, Phil had to help Lowry home by carrying him on his shoulders because the tide was coming in. Earle was not inclined to help. Instead, he shouted, 'Climb down off your cross, Malc!'" According to Hilda, who admired Birney's work greatly but firmly declined to become one of his women, "he read 'Takkakaw Falls' and asked me if I recognized the sexual imagery in it. I said yes, but that I saw sex in everything. Earle was radiant with an adolescent sexuality. He was a womanizer; he was predatory at some essential level. I remember his saying his mother told him he was very unattractive. That he had no chin, that no one could possibly love him. I think he was surprised that he was quite acceptable to the opposite sex. I think he was making up for his puritan youth, the repression of his adolescence."39

Esther did not attend these meetings unless they were at the Birneys. There the gatherings were more restrained, though still very jovial. "Esther was her usual sardonic self," Hilda Thomas recalls. "In a silence, she would make some loud remark, such as: 'Of course Earle was a Trotskyist.' This would make Earle furious because he didn't want it to be known. [In fact, in 1948 there was a "Red Scare" in which eighteen prominent British Columbians, including Birney, were named in the papers, but it came to nothing.]40 Esther and I had a problematic relationship. As one of Earle's young female students, I was a threat." In fact, Hilda found Birney "a male chauvinist" who more than once treated her coldly. "I remember a meeting of 'AA' at his shack there when he complained bitterly about my use of 'pitiful' instead of 'pitiable,' and said I'd written 'a dreadful poem.' He was aggressively critical. It was destructive. I felt so unhappy about it because I couldn't understand why. He was a bit of a stickler, perhaps because of his Anglo-Saxon training. He liked things to be precise, exact." And she also thought that Earle's treatment of Esther was "quite unconscionable. He was stingy with her. I remember her complaining about her crockery. I told her to get some more, but she said Earle wouldn't let her."[41]

The consolidation of Birney's personal literary network of students and writers was only part of a west-coast literary surge. "I think Vancouver has stolen the spotlight in Canada for poetry," Pratt had written him in March 1948.[42] In late October, *The Vancouver Sun* ran a long article publicizing Canadian Book Week (November 1–7). It pointed out that five of the last seven Governor General's Awards for poetry had gone to B.C. writers. And 1947 had seen a bumper crop of awards for B.C.: Dorothy Livesay had won the Governor General's and the Lorne Pierce Medal for the best book of verse; Margaret Ecker Francis had won the Canadian Press Women's Club award for the best piece of journalism; Kitty Marcuse had won the North American radio prize for the best juvenile series; Lister Sinclair won a double radio award for two plays; Roderick Haig-Brown won the Canadian Library Association's award for best juvenile book. "Most important to potential writers," the article observed, "is the milieu being created in the city of Vancouver through its various creative writing classes." It listed four classes a week and a weekly lecture on radio writing offered at a local high school, Dorothy Livesay's class in journalism, a UBC night course by Prof. Burt Hughes, and Birney's "useful, stimulating" writing class. The sixteen-member Authors Anonymous group, it went on, "has sprung to fame such names as Eric Nicol, author of *Sense and Nonsense*; Cy Torrin, winner of Western Canadian Theatre Conference award 1947–48; Jean Thompson, winner of this year's Governor General's Award for the best student essay; Bill McConnell, short-story writer, represented in a recent Canadian anthology; Ernest Perrault, information officer, UBC, author of two CBC plays produced this year."[43] The article noted that B.C. had yet to make its mark in fiction, but that the emergence of Malcolm Lowry, Edward Meade and Ethel Wilson, whose novels had seen international publication during the past year, was a hopeful sign.

As Birney worked that academic year, 1947–48, with Ryerson Press to prepare *Strait of Anian* for publication, he was focused more and more on what kind of writing he really wanted to do. Under pressure from Birney, who wanted above all to achieve success *outside* Canada, Ryerson had designed *Strait* with an eye to the international market. "We are doing all we can to find a publisher in the United States who will take sheets of your work. If necessary we will take the sheets from them. We will do our very best to place you in New York and next we shall try London."[44] Later, they assured him, they would bring out a longer version for Canada. "The general idea [of the collection]," Birney wrote A.J.M. Smith in a vision that anticipated the multi-cultural mosaic that would become central to Canada's ideology two decades later, "is to stress the varied elements of Canadian society as a preliminary to considering the still more varied elements of world society and the necessity for social cohesion despite that variety, in order to preserve it."[45] The book's title (which Lorne Pierce disliked because it was obscure) was an allusion to the strait, now called Bering, by which Sir Francis Drake hoped to make his way back to Europe, but never found. It suggested both Canada's isolation from Europe and the need for her to develop her own culture, as well as Birney's frustrations in making his own mark abroad. Birney was encouraged in his hopes by Lionel Monteith, editor of *Poetry Commonwealth*, who had written in the summer of 1947 to say that he was looking for "fresh and revitalizing blood" from all the Commonwealth countries to brighten the British poetry scene.[46] And *Harper's*, the prestigious American magazine, had taken his new poem "Pacific Door" early in 1948 for the handsome fee of fifty dollars, while *Mademoiselle* magazine in New York had bought his short story "Bird in the Bush" in February for three hundred dollars (after *Atlantic Monthly* turned it down). None the less, he continued to receive far too many rejection slips from British and American editors for his liking. Birney shaved off his beard and joked, "I hope [my new face] will trick a number of people into buying my new book," he wrote B.K. Sandwell, who had accepted one of his new poems "Canada: Case History" for *Saturday Night.*[47]

But even as he read the page proofs for *Strait,* Birney felt discouraged about his poetry. "The proofs look fine," he wrote back to Ryerson Press, "though I'm sick to death with the sight of many of these poems. Why I ever wrote them I don't know."[48] He was discouraged about poetry in general. Lionel Monteith had written to say that "curiously, established poets in the U.K. and all over the world tell me they are not writing any poetry at the present.... There is something to be said for writing novels—they are certainly far more remunerative for one thing!"[49] And Ned Pratt had made the alarming speculation that, since Frank Scott and the Montreal writers were now finding Robert Finch's poetry old-fashioned, he and Birney might be next to be rejected.[50] His fears were realized with the publication of *Strait of Anian* on 17 March 1948, after a long delay. Even an enthusiastic letter from Ned Pratt (to whom the book was dedicated) could not disguise the fact that twenty of the forty-six poems—almost half—were reprints (many revised, as Birney would continue to do frequently) from Birney's first two collections, and that the earlier work outshone his new material. In a letter that upset Birney, Brewster Ghiselin, one of his former Utah colleagues who was currently teaching creative writing there, wrote to tell him that he did not like his recent poetry and suggested he write more like those he wrote during the war.[51] And the editor of *Quarterly Review of Literature* had returned "Ulysses," one of the best of his recent poems, with the comment, "we are not sure that...the content equals the batter of sound.... We appreciate your irony, your bold strokes; but your rhetoric seems rather often extremely strong."[52] Even Sedgewick concurred: "You will not blame me," he wrote, "if I remain loyal to 'David,' 'Vancouver Lights,' 'Steve.'"[53] This impression was reinforced when "David" was read again over the CBC on 28 January 1948, not by Birney himself—whose rather light, flat voice was not well-suited to radio[54]—but by the west-coast actor Arthur Hill. Reviews were unremarkable, praising his Canadianness ("Canada's wild and gargantuan terrain"[55]) and his "lively awareness of contemporary issues."[56] But there was one recent poem singled out more than once. That poem was "Canada: Case History," a clever satire suggested to Birney by an article he was asked to write for *Chatelaine*, "Are We Growing Up?"[57] In it, Birney adapted the methods he had used in Personnel Selection (and that Esther had used in her social work) to give his report on a case after clinical assessment. The satire was deft and gave forceful vent to Birney's frustrations, but as poetry it could hardly compare to his earlier work:

> This is the case of a high-school land,
> deadset in adolescence,
> loud treble laughs and sudden fists,
> bright cheeks, the gangling presence.
> This boy is wonderful at sports
> and physically quite healthy;
> he's taken to church on Sunday still
> and keeps his prurience stealthy.
> He doesn't like books except about bears,
> collects new coins and model planes,
> and never refuses a dare.
> His Uncle spoils him with candy, of course,
> yet shouts him down when he talks at table.
> You will note he's got some of his French mother's
>   looks,
> though he's not so witty and no more stable.
> He's really much more like his father and yet
> if you say so he'll pull a great face.
> He wants to be different from everyone else
> and daydreams of winning the global race.
> Parents unmarried and living abroad,
> relatives keen to bag the estate,
> schizophrenia not excluded,
> will he learn to grow up before it's too late?[58]

The response to *Strait* confirmed Birney's own dissatisfaction with his poetry. "The new is drowned in the old," he wrote Floris McLaren, "[it] just depresses me to look at. However, I've

given up writing verse, so it's no real matter now."[59] His hopes
flared again when he received a complimentary letter from C.
Day Lewis offering to try to find a British publisher for *Strait*.[60]
And he heard that T.S. Eliot himself was considering the book
for publication with Faber and Faber in England, but C. Day
Lewis was unsuccessful[61] and Eliot's company rejected it, as did
the other English publishers with whom Ryerson Press had been
negotiating. The situation was similar in the States. Marion
Saunders, a New York literary agent with whom Birney began
negotiating in the hope of placing his work, advised him that
"poetry doesn't pay" and encouraged him to try fiction with a
Vancouver or west-coast setting.[62]

Birney signalled his sense that one stage of his career was over
by resigning from the CAA. His mood of frustration was
brought to a head by a routine request for his late dues. Since he
had never been paid his editorial fee of fifty dollars for the final
June issue of *CPM*, he was outraged, and suggested icily in a
long and forceful letter on 15 November that the dues be
deducted from that. Birney outlined his experience in the CAA,
how reluctant he had been to join in 1946, how he had been
unfairly pressured by Bill Deacon on the grounds that the awards
Birney had won were CAA awards.

> I felt that I could not in fairness judge the Association
> without becoming one of its members and working
> within it for a more liberal approach to literary art....
> I have worked to the best of my ability, and often to
> the detriment of my own writing, to promote the
> point of view that I held.... I have now come to real-
> ize that the attitude of the majority of the Association,
> or at least of the members who control its public state-
> ments, makes further participation on my part both a
> waste of my time and a compromise of my artistic
> principles.... The CAA, to my mind, is predomi-
> nantly a body of aging hacks and reactionaries.... I
> have come to feel that the CAA is actually a hindrance
> to the growth of a mature literary culture in this coun-
> try.... I think the time has come for the serious writers

in this country to break with the CAA and form a
guild of craftsmen.[63]

Nor was Birney's grudge entirely personal. Some credence is
afforded his position by a glance at the program for the CAA's
26th Convention in Vancouver and Victoria. Though there are
glimmerings of contemporary issues (such as Gwethalyn
Graham's discussion of authors' contracts), it had more than a
hint of old-fashioned doings—teas, a visit to Pauline Johnson's
grave in Stanley Park and a poem on the program that was
hardly twentieth century. It began:

> Fair Tempe's groves 'neath Grecian skies
> With shout and song re-echo still;
> And dancing nymphs and fauns surprise
> By rocky grot and foaming rill.[64]

Finally, nine months after the publication of *Strait*, Ryerson
admitted defeat on the international front: "Every overture we
have made in the United States has been unsuccessful. The history of our work on your book in the U.S., more than any single
thing, has driven us to work out some way of getting past the
barricade that has been raised against all but a very few novelists."[65]

Almost immediately, Birney's hopes flared yet again, for *The
New York Times* book review section reprinted "Man Is a Snow"
in their poetry column, "and murmured something about
[A.M.] Klein and Audrey [Alexandra] Brown and me being poets
who should be better known in the U.S."[66] And soon after,
Saturday Review of Literature in New York (to whom Birney had
urged Pierce to send a review copy) reviewed the book. "Yours,
and the notice in August *Harper's*," wrote a grateful Birney, "are
the first New York reviews I've had in ten years of writing and
publishing verse."[67]

But he stuck to his decision to give up poetry. In a gesture that
suggested that he "treasured the wounds his poems had suffered
as much as their victories," he began papering one wall of his

UBC office with the rejection slips he'd received.[68] "I feel somewhat of a fraud as a poet," he confided to Norman Newton, "since I have spent so little time at it; instead of sacrifice and dedication, as with the real poets, it has been for me an outlet of my middle years, and one that I have already let go dry, for a while at least... now I teach and go about my duties with only one thought in mind—how to find time to re-write the novel."[69]

❧ *19* ❧

EAST OF EDEN

*T*urvey: A Military Picaresque Novel set in 1942–45 was published
29 October 1949, the optimum timing for Christmas sales. As
Birney described his first novel to Marion Saunders, the American
agent he hoped would market it successfully in the States, it was

> a kind of modern picaresque novel with a slaphappy
> central character of the Good Soldier Schweik type,
> only smarter.... the main theme...is the tendency for
> everyone to find in Turvey the faults or virtues or
> lunacies that are in themselves. [It is] partly a satire on
> contemporary over-play of psychology, aptitude test-
> ing, personality interviews, etc.; partly a symbolic
> study of the average man, who is really unidentifiable
> because in him people see only distortions of them-
> selves; partly just a comic picaresque novel about the
> goofier side in any army.[1]

To Ralph Allen, editor at *Maclean's*, he explained further:

> There are several [chapters] with Canadian settings,
> several in England and the rest in Belgium or Holland.

[*Turvey*] is partly an attempt to picture the Canadian character, partly a vehicle for mild satire against army red tape of the new psychiatric kind, partly just a humble descendant of Tom Jones, Sancho Panza and the Good Soldier Schweik. Only they were created by *real* writers.[2]

Birney had used the expression "topsy-turvey" (to describe the technique of comic reversals) in his graduating essay on Chaucer's irony written for Sedgewick (who was a great admirer of Stephen Leacock's humour) in 1926.[3] Now his own Chaucerian novel featured Thomas Leadbeater Turvey, a grinning private nicknamed "Topsy," whose sole military goal is to join his buddy McGillicuddy in the Kootenay Highlanders of British Columbia. The only action Turvey sees is an episodic series of behind-the-front muddles.

No trace remains of the novel Birney began while he worked on his Ph.D. thesis in England in the summer of 1935, which is curious given his compulsion to save everything.[4] Certainly, it could not have been *Turvey*. But his yen to write a war novel took definite form before he went overseas. On 21 May he complained to Ralph Gustafson that being sent overseas meant that he would have no time to write. "The irony," he added, "will lie in the fact that my army job will give me, daily, material for a novel—and I'll have to keep mum about it till the war is over."[5] Certainly, the long accounts of his doings as a personnel selection officer and the hundreds of case histories he recounted to Esther in his long letters home were not only meant to amuse her, they were also deliberately intended as notes for his novel (just as her accounts of her case histories in social work—also intended as notes for short stories she planned to write—were meant to amuse him). He claimed to have written more than three hundred letters to her in the two and a half years he was away,[6] and even if this were an exaggeration, the letters she saved at his request bear witness to the thoroughness with which he recorded military foibles. In November 1944, he had written a paper evaluating the Word Association Test administered to recruits. On his own initiative he also analysed and reported on the results of intelligence tests, and even went so far as to evaluate the various psychiatrists on staff to Esther's delight.[7] He had already used one case history for his radio play Court Martial. Now he used others from those letters in his extensive revisions of his novel "to check details...such as when there was a full moon in July 44."[8]

Other letters he wrote while overseas and after his return make clear the bawdy nature of army banter. Major Gordon Aldridge, who would later become director of the School of Social Work at Michigan State University, was an ally in conspiracy. The two officers were as unalike as Mutt and Jeff: Birney tall, fair and skinny; Aldridge short, dark and stocky. They often dated together—Birney with Margaret Crosland, Aldridge with her friend Mary—calling themselves "the A's and B's" because they signed into hotels as married couples.[9] Sometimes they covered for each other on leaves. But always they swore and joked. "Earle, you old barstard..." Aldridge would write him. Or, "Ma cherie (or chere, or cherry, or else)—."[10] As for Birney, he sent Aldridge such items as a meticulous "official" personnel report (headed "PERSONAL, CONFIDENTIAL, and HIGHLY UNIMPORTANT) which was a satiric forerunner of the episodes in Turvey. The report described a case of double identity, a soldier who was "evidently a well-spoken young saxophonist, a social and athletic Thespian...who, though willing to serve in any unit and in any capacity, should immediately be considered as outstanding-infantry-reinforcement-officer-material." However, the report went on, he was "on the contrary,"

    (a) suspected of playing only on his own organ
    (b) athletically inclined only in respect to
       (i) nose-picking
       (ii) one-man route marches ending in what are
           technically known as railroad craps
       (iii) a combination of (i) and (ii)
    (c) about as sociable and well-spoken as a spinster
       librarian with the curse
    (d) possessed of abilities variously estimated by his
       commanding officers as follows:

(i) not worth a shit (Capt. Holloway)
(ii)   "   a pinch of coon shit (Lieut. Haynes)
(iii)   "   pushing into a pisspot even to see the
               pretty bubbles (Capt. Birney).[11]

The elements of parody, satire, wit, bawdiness, irony and earthiness characteristic of Birney's sense of humour were also the basis of Paul Hiebert's *Sarah Binks*, a comic satire on Canadian poetry which may also have suggested ideas for *Turvey*, since Birney admired the book greatly when it appeared in 1947, referred to it often, and would later take from one of Sarah's outrageous poems the title for his literary memoir *Spreading Time*.

Birney had begun his novel in August of 1947 on Bowen Island after completing his work on the poems for *Strait of Anian*. He completed a first draft in the summer of 1948 back at Einar and Muriel's "Lieben" (having rented the Acadia hut to Roy Daniells and his new wife, Laurenda), while Esther made her first visit home to England since 1936 with Bill, whom her family had never seen. On their return in September, he began revisions (many of them prompted by the feedback he got when he read it in sections at "AA" gatherings), which Esther typed during the winter. He completed a third and final draft for a July first deadline in 1949.[12] With a characteristic eye to maximizing the financial rewards for his efforts, he sent early chapters off for magazine publication, two of which—after the usual rejections—were accepted and published.[13]

For his novel, Birney changed publishers. Dissatisfied with what he considered Ryerson's mismanagement of his three books of poetry, he took advantage of the fact that they had first claim only to his poetry, to send *Turvey* off to McClelland & Stewart at the request of their editor Sybil Hutchinson, his former student and friend. To Lorne Pierce, a prim, religious man (Ryerson Press was connected to the United Church), who was taken aback at reading in *The Globe and Mail* of 29 June 1949 that Birney had a manuscript in the works, Birney wrote tersely: "I did not think that the material in it was of the sort that would be acceptable to your firm, as it is a rather frankly written picaresque."[14]

Even though Jack McClelland, then a young inexperienced editor in his father's firm, had served in the navy, swore broadly himself, and had an unusually tolerant outlook, there were battles over just how ribald *Turvey* should be. "I first met Earle in about 1947 at a Canadian authors' conference in Victoria," Jack McClelland recalls, "and we became friends and never looked back. I don't think there were ever any problems except with the editing of *Turvey*. At that time we could not have published *Turvey* the way he wrote it. There was a stronger sense of censorship then and we believed it would be a problem."[15] "Jack...wants some censorship in the interests of a best-seller." The instinct to use realistic language was hardly new to Birney: he had been aware in 1946 that the language in his short story "A Bird in the Hand" "debars it from the genteel journals."[16] Now he griped as he fought to retain as much accuracy as possible for his dialogue. "I'm willing to make some compromises, but I'm more interested in writing an honest book than in producing an emasculated best-seller. Canadians will read American novels with four-letter words (or some of them) in them but for some odd reason they jump on a Canadian book that uses them. M & S even object to "bugger" and "Jesus." I have agreed to change shit to shat, but not tit for tat... Cocksucker is out...and so even is cokesacker, corksocker, socktucker...but what can you expect of a Toronto firm."[17] Birney became preoccupied with censorship that year and next. Two of his several radio appearances were discussions of James Joyce's *Ulysses*, which was banned in Canada.[18] And he responded to a student complaint about the obscenity of some of the books on his survey course (such as *Gulliver's Travels* and *Joseph Andrews*) with a vitriolic two-page defence.[19]

Though McClelland & Stewart and Birney were somewhat at odds about censorship, they were of one mind about libel. Birney's "formula" had been to "make [each character] the physical and biographical opposite of the real-life character."[20] Even so, there was a risk. Birney had deliberately excluded Gordon Aldridge (who had provided him with *Turvey*'s list of occupations) from *Turvey* "for fear that he would overshadow *Turvey* himself."[21] But many of his characters were readily identifiable by position and incident, if not by appearance and biography.

Birney became preoccupied with this issue too, especially since it occurred to him after the book was out that he had named the character based on Margaret Crosland "Peggy," the name of another woman he knew overseas—Peggy Todd. In something of a panic, he wrote to warn her.[22] And when a painter who came to work for him and Esther that fall turned out to be named "Turvey," he worried about that too.[23] Birney sought the advice of "AA" fiction writer Bill McConnell, who had completed his law degree. Bill (who according to Birney joked that *Turvey* would be "more obscene than heard"[24]) advised him not only on his contract with M & S (Birney took issue with every clause[25]), but also on libel-related matters.

As he worked on his final revisions, Birney was wracked with self-doubt. "I'm in the state of mind where I'm sure I've failed to do anything with the material," he wrote Ralph Gustafson.[26] He thought Peggy was too "dull," and wrote to his former student Mabel Hunter Mackenzie, now working on a Ph.D. in Toronto, "It's pretty lousy; superficial, often corny."[27] *Strait of Anian* had sold only slightly more than four hundred copies.[28] He feared *Turvey* would meet the same fate.

But, as with "David," Birney need not have fretted. Within three weeks, *Turvey* had sold out its first printing of five thousand copies, and in the next six months would sell another two thousand. Birney basked in success:

> I'm a bull-throated frog in my small puddle, getting interviewed by the press on quite irrelevant matters, autographing at bookshop bees, collaborating on a CBC dramatization,[29] sitting for photographers and "profile"-writing freelancers, bargaining for second serial rights with magazines, jockeying for review space, speaking to literary clubs, and going through all the usual nonsense of being an author, even if a very little one. So far the reviews have been very kind; 25 out of 30 quite favourable, and only two downright nasty.[30]

Birney took objection to *The Vancouver Province* and the *Saskatoon Star-Phoenix* reviews. "Why a distinguished poet who

can curl your toes with his descriptive powers, should write a
288-page book about a burlesque soldier is still a mystery to
me.... when barrack room humour...is not his meat," went the
former; the latter criticized the book's "misplaced and overdone
ridicule" and observed that Birney was "torn between education
and creation, and the result is not always happy."[31] Other
reviewers, however, delighted in *Turvey*, and saw in it what
Birney had intended. He was especially pleased by a "marvellous"[32] review by Malcolm Lowry which claimed that "a classic
has burst into our midst" that "fills a gap" in Canadian literature.[33] And he was surprised to hear that Major-General E.L.M.
Burns, his Commanding Officer in Holland, had reviewed his
novel favourably and remarked to Ethel Wilson on Burns's "gen-
erosity and capacity to forgive."[34] Perhaps the most remarkable
thing about *Turvey* was something very few could have known:
that it skimmed lightly over the surface of his war experiences
without ever plumbing the depths or scaling the heights of his
emotional life during those years. Neither his philosophical angst
about man's predilection for war and unfaithfulness, nor his
ecstasy in Margaret's arms found a place in his fiction.

Instead, the novel played to the nostalgia and patriotism that
marked the years immediately following the war and confirmed
his public image as Canada's "Soldier Poet." He was swamped
with letters from friends and fans across the country and beyond:
soldiers, teachers, students, established writers, aspiring writers,
radio listeners, crackpots, hospital patients, immigrants, expatriates. Hugh MacLennan, who had supported Birney's resignation
from the CAA, wrote, "*Turvey* is one of the most utterly enjoyable books I've read in years.... The dialogue is marvellous and
so are the scenes.... it's a lot funnier than Schweik;"[35] Capt. Fred
Haynes, who had been with Birney in Belgium in the winter of
1944–45, sent his regards;[36] he had friendly letters from General
Burns and the former minister of defence, Milton Gregg, who
had been commandant when Birney trained at Brockville;[37]a
patient in the Vancouver General Hospital claimed to be healed
from reading it;[38] even Gaby Baldwin, his former love, who had
seen *Turvey* in a bookstore while travelling with her husband in
the Maritimes, wrote to say he should look her up if he ever

came east.[39] Though there were intimations of libel suits, including one from General A.G.L. McNaughton and another from
Colonel K.S. Bjorn (who had temporarily been commanding
officer of the #1OCTU Selection Centre at Ash where Birney
had served, and on whom Birney had based his character
"Augusto"),[40] Birney carefully followed Bill McConnell's advice
and none materialized.[41] Early in May, Birney was delighted to
hear in confidence from the chair of the board of the Governor
General's Literary Awards that, although Philip Child's *Mr. Ames
Against Time* had won the fiction award, *Turvey* had won the
Stephen Leacock Memorial Award for Humour. "I think *Turvey*
is lucky to get posted to an outfit with [former winners] Hiebert
and John Robins and with Leacock as the original C.O.," he
replied facetiously.[42]

His only regret was that one reader whose opinion he cherished
most would never read it. Garnett Sedgewick—to whom he had
dedicated his book—died just a month before *Turvey* was published. He was, Birney wrote Lister Sinclair, "the man of all men
who has stood nearest in the role of father to me.... in his palmy
days, [his] was an act requiring suspension of bluff, trigger-care
about vocabulary, the excitement of intellectual battle."[43]

Birney also dedicated *Turvey* to "the Einar and Muriel Neilsons
without whom it would have been so much worse." Birney not
only meant that the book would have been worse had the
Neilsons not welcomed him on Bowen Island while he wrote it,
and hosted meetings of the "AA" at which Birney read sections
of it, but also slyly alluded to the fact that the experience of writing it would have been worse without their cheerful acceptance
of Elizabeth Campbell who spent just over two weeks at
"Lieben" with Birney that summer of 1948.

Elizabeth Campbell was then a thirty-four-year-old technician
working on the development of vaccines at the Connaught
Medical Research Laboratories in Toronto, whose love of the arts
had induced her to take evening courses in English and French
at the University of Toronto. She was already an established hand
at poetry. Her first poem "Who Believes in Fairies?" was published in a newspaper when she was a ten-year-old farm girl in
Richmond Hill, just north of Toronto, and at fifteen her poem

"Explanation" (about being unable to resist writing a poem about the "worn out" subject of spring) was selected as the *Mail and Empire's* "Daily Canadian Poem."[44] By her late teens, her work was appearing regularly in *Canadian Girl*, a magazine for adolescents. Though her poetry was conventional, it was marked by a strong sensuality not unlike Christina Rossetti's. It could not have been better suited for the series on the months of the year or flowers or birds or crafts which *Canadian Girl* featured. By the time she met Earle Birney in 1946, she had published well over a hundred poems, had been anthologized in Canadian and British collections and had won a few prizes.

She met Birney—then *CPM* editor—at the June 1946 conference of the CAA at the University of Toronto where Birney was in his element as winner of the Governor General's Award for poetry and chief speaker. She had joined the CAA especially because she admired his work ("'David' seemed to speak to me, to reveal his whole mind") and knew he would be there. Her first glimpse of him was at Hart House, where he spoke with the sunlight that streamed through the leaded windows illuminating his hair. She liked his voice and the characteristic way he pronounced the word "poetry" ("poit-try").[45] His impact was explosive. "I simply backed away from you, mentally and physically, with my mouth open," she wrote him in July. "A lamentable tendency to become inarticulate at such important moments prevented my telling you of the enormous pleasure I felt at meeting you, of my deep and continuing admiration of your poetry."[46]

Birney had every reason to recognize the name-tag that read "ELIZABETH K. CAMPBELL." It was not just that she had placed fourth in the recent CAA poetry competition that spring, and had told Anne Marriott (one of the judges) that her favourite poet was Earle Birney.[47] Five years before, in the 1941 Dominion Poetry Contest sponsored by *Canadian Poetry Magazine* in which Birney had been so disgruntled to place fifth out of the 447 entries with his anti-Ontario satire "Eagle Island," Elizabeth Campbell had placed first. Her poem "Ski Patrol" was a seven-part tribute to the farm boys she knew who had exchanged their usual chores to serve on military winter patrols. Although this poem was still vivid with nature description, the

introduction of a more serious theme proved a counter-balance
to sentimentality. One of the sections had been anthologized in
the English anthology *Best Poems of 1941*; another appeared in a
separate school reader for Ontario.[48] Curiously, there were
almost uncanny echoes of Birney's work—mainly the feel of a
sensibility shaped by outdoors experience in a large landscape
and a fondness for alliteration—in some of this poem's lines:

> Down, down, down like a plummeting hawk he goes,
> With the cold, incredible speed of hardwood on
>   packed snows.
> Then up, and off, and out like an arrow, a soaring
>   lark—
> Oh, the perfection of poise in that bold unbelievable
>   arc!
>
> . . . .
>
> There shall be
> No marshalled minds, no tutored thinking here,
> Save in a stern pursuance of the right.
> Accepting no forced creed, no savage bars,
> They shall return, bard, peasant, hero, seer,
> Each his own man, emerging from this night
> As free and individual as the stars.[49]

Though it would always rankle that she had bested him in
1941, Birney could not have been displeased that this talented
young woman with the sweet face and girlish voice was also
wonderfully alive and attractive. Birney immediately assumed
the stance of mentor, wanted to encourage her as a poet and
continued the correspondence she had begun after their meeting. "Dear Elizabeth," he wrote in September. "Do you mind
very much my calling you by your first name?" He took her
poem "Notes on a Northern Journey" for the December issue of
CPM, but declined her "Poet's Broadcast," which glowingly
described one of his own radio appearances, for "personal reasons." Elizabeth, describing herself as "another eager disciple,"[50]
offered to assist *CPM* with typing, licking stamps, recruiting
new members, anything he asked. Overawed by Birney, she

wrote "Poet's Path," which was published in October by *Saturday Night.*

> I know you walked this grey and grudging street,
> Saw all the calm of city and sprawling lake,
> Knew the trim wood, the passive gardened earth:
> How can they bear no traces of your going?
> . . . .
> Yet have I found these tokens of your passing,
> As faces have turned to the sunlight of your name:
> I have heard salt-tides in the voice, seen eyes lift
> To some inner height; heard on a warm Pacific gale
> Echoes of words you have written and spoken here.

"Your 'Poet's Path' was far too flattering," Birney responded. "I'm really a very ignoble creature."[51] Their correspondence broadened and deepened over the next year and a half until Elizabeth was following his every move in print and on the radio, and he was telling her most of his doings and even confiding his views to her. By the summer of 1948, they were virtually soul mates: sharing information on the Canadian literary scene, writing poems themselves, exchanging photographs, swapping life's ups and downs. And always with Birney the mentor, Elizabeth the self-deprecating naïf. Typically, she responded to hearing "David" read over the air; it "brought on a new high-tide of hero-worship—which the snapshot of that lazy golden Viking certainly didn't cause to recede!"[52]

A week after Esther and Bill left for England on 21 May 1948, Birney, who had given up poetry in frustration, resented the fact that he was not going to England too, and felt miserable, lonely and trapped at the prospect of sitting still long enough to write a novel, invited Elizabeth to join him for her summer holiday from mid-July to early August on Bowen Island.[53] "Hurry hurry!" he wrote when she agreed, his mood buoyant again, "The spirea is blooming all over the mountainsides, and the wild orange blossoms.... Don't forget your bathing suit—though you don't need it off Einar's rocks.... You will be an independent guest at Einar's, with no commitments to me in any way."[54] "I want to spend every possible moment with you," she replied. "I only regret having so little to give in return."[55]

"I thought it would be just a visit, nothing more," Elizabeth recalls, "but it was a very, very high-octane experience. He met me at my train on 16 July, and we went over to pick up his stuff at Malcolm Lowry's cabin where he'd been living and working on *Turvey* (his first draft typed out on UBC examination booklets).[56] We made wild love almost at once. I remember him as being very sweet and gentle. Then we took the water taxi from Whytecliffe to Bowen Island. He took me to meet his mother (we brought her something); he took me to meet Dorothy Livesay (who was snippety and kept putting me down); but mostly we were boating and climbing. He liked me because I was down-to-earth; also because I was active and could keep up with him, whereas Esther couldn't or wouldn't. By the end of those sixteen days, he said, 'We haven't been more than *this* far apart all this time; like a piston in a cylinder,' and he grinned."[57]

After their holiday of "enchanted meetings" in the wild natural settings where they made love in abandon, sharing the little attic room in the tolerant company of the Neilsons who enjoyed the open-faced, dark-haired Bet, playing at tasks like fetching firewood, which Birney chopped and she stacked, they were both deeply in love. Photos show a radiant Birney whose beard, according to one friend, was "glorious, thick and red and piratical, with an Elizabethan bravado in its curl and texture,"[58] looking almost as youthful as his childlike Bet. Before parting, they bought matching rings cut from the same bloodstone.

In a letter he sent to Edmonton where her train stopped en route to Toronto, he wrote in a state he had not experienced since his time with Margaret Crosland, "O my sweetheart, my heart is too much in a chaos of love for you to write anything coherent. I love you passionately, truly—I must always have loved you. You are what I want, need, drown for.... Keep my letters, darling; if ever I do anything to make my life worth recording, I want you to be part of that record."[59] He both hoped and feared she might be pregnant, and reported he was "relieved and bereaved" when she wrote that she was not.[60] As for Elizabeth, when she received the pictures of herself naked in the lovely

wooded cliffs near "Lieben," which Birney had taken and his colleague Stan Read had developed in his darkroom at home, she
described it ecstatically as "me in the Garden of Eden" and
admitted she felt "quite shameless."[61]

Their correspondence, now suffused with words of love and
endearments, became even more prolific. "He could really court
you," she recalls, "romantic, wonderful stuff, all those books he
sent me with inscriptions like this quote from Conrad Aiken:

> Thereafter they are as lovers, who
> Over an 'infinite brightness' lean:
> 'It's Atlantis!' all their speech
> 'To lost Atlantis have we been.'[62]

It was pretty nice for a little old farm girl to get this stuff."

As usual, Birney was honest, explaining his attitude to women
quite fully:

> I know that if we were married and living together,
> your code would be mine, for I would need no other
> woman sexually. Perhaps my present attitudes have a
> lot to do with a physical rejection of Esther. But there
> were habit-patterns begun before I met her, patterns
> formed out of a delayed adolescence, perhaps, about
> sexual intercourse. As I once told you, between the
> ages of 16 and 24 my sexual life was highly unsatisfac-
> tory. First, perhaps, the shock of a prostitute, making
> me recoil into juvenile masturbation and, later, experi-
> ment with homosexuality, at the same time pursuing
> women to the point of intercourse and either muffing
> it or recoiling from the act itself. I think too I was
> unlucky for a long time in the women I met. Then
> something happened; my luck changed; I grew up a
> little more, and I found in normal sexual intercourse a
> terrific release, a building-up of my long-abused ego,
> the sluffing [sic] of many feelings of inferiority, intense
> companionships, and a knowledge of women as
> human beings, such as I could not possibly have got in

abstinence or frustration.... I have lived a very intense, varied and complicated life.... I find myself, at 44, longing with all my heart for the monogamous peace, the cessation of the eternal chase, that you gave me and that I had once before...with Margaret Crosland.... She and I both knew that [she was not the transplantable sort of Englishwoman] and long since put aside any thought of marrying. In fact, I never at any time seriously considered it even if I were to become free. You, Bet darling, are the one person, the only person in the world I would want to marry if I were free.[63]

He explained that his current affairs were over: one with "a rather dull little schoolteacher whom I once slept with" and another more serious and turbulent involvement with Hilda Browne, a breathtakingly beautiful radio hostess of CKWX's "Around the Town" whom Birney referred to as the "Prima Donna" because she unpredictably made herself inaccessible.[64]

Birney could not keep Bet in a separate compartment of his life, as he had been able to do with other women. He could not even refrain from talking about her. "I met a lovely child (well, she's 30-something) lately, on her holidays out here," he somewhat ingenuously—and condescendingly—wrote a friend a few days after she left, "Miss Elizabeth Campbell. She writes quite good verse, that occasionally slips by into *Saturday Night,* and she is a lab technician at Connaught... I want very much for her to meet you. Don't bark at her now, dear; she's shy, but intelligent and honest and gentle, and god what a lot of people aren't!"[65] Given this degree of infatuation, the return of Esther and Bill was traumatic. As he wrote to Bet after meeting their bus from Seattle, "They looked tired but well. Esther, on starchy English food, has put on far too much weight. Bill is in the front-toothless stage. We drove up to Mother's & talked excitedly for hours and then Esther got a headache and we put her to bed with aspirin and I slept fitfully on the couch, full of disturbing thoughts."[66] Within days he wrote again, "My dear darling,"

I have bad news for you. I am going to have to stop
writing you for a while and must even try to stop
thinking too much about you. Esther's return has precipitated a crisis. I found myself quite unable to have
sexual relations with her. This has forced a general
show-down... Esther saw [two letters from
you]...and demanded to know what our relations
were, and I told her. She still thinks she and I can
make a go of our marriage but only if I cut myself off
from relationships with women...we have talked and
talked for two days, neither of us can scarcely sleep or
eat. And of course the tension affects Bill. If we separate and Esther takes Bill from Vancouver, I think it
would kill my mother. And I'm afraid of what it will
do to Bill and to Esther, not to speak of Esther's
father.... We decided I should see a psychiatrist and I
have just come back from two hours with Haig
Gundrie, the City Psychiatrist and an old Army friend
of mine. Haig agrees that it is still possible to save the
marriage, and imperative to try. He also thinks I
should for the time being refrain from writing you
except as I would to any friend.[67]

Bet, in her typically self-deprecating way, accepted Birney's dic-
tum, but added, "my love will remain as deep and tender for
you, no matter whether we write or not."[68] To add to his
dilemma (and his expenses), Birney learned that his mother—
now seventy-two—had uterine cancer. In October, she under-
went a hysterectomy. That Christmas he sent Bet a scarf from a
Bowen weaver and pictures of himself she had taken at "Lieben"
which prompted the response, "you on our own peak...my dear
mountain man. The other picture is a bit sad-making, ...like an
unexpected glimpse back into Eden from east of the garden."[69]
As for his own family Christmas, he sounded despondent and
irritable:

we had Mother and the two...taciturn bunnies who
live with her. She threw herself into Xmas with great

zest, as if to prove to the world that she is well again.... We had a little tree, and Bill, when he went to bed, announced that it had been the happiest day of his life—which makes it all worthwhile, I suppose. He also enjoyed Pinnochio (sp?) very much; the Little Theatre put it on here and I took him. For an adult, it was a pretty deafening experience. And it took me two hours to drive home through a traffic jam.[70]

Though Birney was making a valiant effort to conform to family life, he could not resist occasional letters to Bet. As for Bet, she realized at times that it might be better for everyone if she withdrew, but found herself unable to do so.

By the next spring, Birney was torn apart with indecision. He had applied for the second time for a Guggenheim Fellowship on which he planned to live alone in New York, fifty miles from Rahway, New Jersey, where Bet was considering taking a job. In March, he learned that he was not awarded the fellowship.[71] All spring, he toyed with the idea of another summer holiday on Bowen with her and she reciprocated by offering to pay her way. His family life was "a series of tensions, hopes and despairs." In early February, Esther took charge. She would leave, and she began arranging to go back to her family in England. "But lately," he wrote Bet, as if Esther's decisiveness had brought him to his senses,

> I seem to have removed *her* reasons for separation; that is, I do what she wants about training Bill, never interfere, cooperate when *she* wants cooperation and stay mum when she doesn't; so there are no more open quarrels about that. And since I take care never to be alone in the company of another woman or betray the slightest interest of *any* kind in anyone of the female sex, she has little left to needle me about there except when she sees a chance to reproach me about the past. Also I force myself to give her the kind of casual sexual intercourse she wants. I endure all this because I know Bill would be harmed by the break-up of the

family; he likes me and, when we aren't interfered with, we get on very well. And I endure it for my mother, who is, apart from us, a friendless old woman (she has systematically quarrelled with every one of her friends and relatives all through her life and now pays the penalty of a lonely old age). She is violent and rootless enough to jump off the Lion's Gate bridge (as she has threatened) if we break up.... As for my own happiness, that is tied up with freedom to write, which I'll never have, and freedom from this kind of family life.[72]

Meanwhile, possibly in a panic at the thought of being left alone, he wrote to Margaret Crosland, whose recent poetry impressed him with its "new imaginative extension of her style,"[73] and asked her to come to Canada and marry him. But she turned him down in April:

I feel now darling that I can't come. In many important ways I don't think we have moved too far away from each other. But we have both changed. I feel that you are very restless emotionally, and I really think that marriage or prolonged living-together doesn't really suit you.... If I had lived with you after other men instead of before, it would have been easier now.... I must seek to express myself in a vague and uncertain way. I'm remembering so closely all our time together. It was a completeness which in a strange way doesn't allow itself to start again—as though we tied a knot in the thread and just went on.... Possibly I enjoyed the unreality of our life together. I didn't want you to leave Esther for me in 1945, and if things had been big enough between us then I suppose it would have happened automatically.... When Esther leaves—if she leaves, and if you don't find things too strong for you even yet—then I do feel you should have a period quite on your own to sort out your feelings and what you really want and need.... I couldn't

feel in 1945 that there was any other end except separation, and my thoughts since have developed logically
from that point—no, logically isn't the word, because
there's no logic here, but it was the inevitable and in a
way futureless separation that coloured them.[74]

And in April Bet also seemed to be slipping away from him.
Through her friend the writer Farley Mowat and his wife, she
had met Elford Cox, a wood sculptor and language teacher at
Upper Canada College, who soon began to court her. In May,
Birney encouraged Bet to send letters to his office, "never to my
house, as Esther is sure to rip into anything and then into me."
When he suggested renting a summer place near Einar's for July
and August for his family, he reported to Bet that two days later
Esther flew into a temper.

> Why didn't I tell her what I was really thinking? How
> could I plan to take a family cottage on Bowen when I
> really wanted to play around with other women, etc.,
> etc? I was amazed. I thought we had been getting on
> O.K. lately.... Apparently my sin had been to assume
> that she wasn't really going back to England.... she
> began raking up all the past, (all *my* past, that is!) and I
> went to bed to escape.... But she came into the bed-
> room, put on an hysterical act which woke Bill...and
> must have given the neighbours in *their* bedroom, the
> other side of the thin partition, quite a stimulating bit
> of listening. When I wouldn't talk back, she got so mad
> she pounded me with her fists...it was grotesquely
> comic.... I now for the first time say that she can go
> only without Bill, as I'll fight for his custody. And yet,
> the tragedy is she really loves me in a cuckoo way, and I
> keep on having a tender and protective affection for
> her, and a belief that holding the home together is still
> worth trying and trying if it kills me.[75]

In June, he applied for the chairmanship of the English
Department of Royal Military College in Kingston—another

move that would have brought him closer to Bet—but the job was withdrawn.[76] By summer, he had decided not to have Bet come out. Bet, who knew nothing of his proposal to Margaret that spring, was becoming more deeply involved with El Cox and more and more sympathetic to Esther.[77] She wrote to Birney: "It isn't the first time you have been through a crisis like this, is it—remember you did tell me a lot about Margaret, and I rather think I just reminded you of her and brought back old troubles. Is that true perhaps?"[78] So that summer, Birney rented a cottage on Thetis Island "full of sunshine and blackberries and Indians"[79] where he and Esther and Bill spent a fine holiday fishing, swimming and relaxing in the wake of finishing *Turvey*.

During all the emotional upheaval that year and next, Birney continued his myriad activities at a frantic pace that often left him exhausted and peevish. One of his main concerns was the Canadian Writers' Committee (CWC), which was developing as an alternative to the CAA. In January 1949, the Royal Commission on the Arts, Letters, and Sciences, which would result in the Massey Report, was struck, and although Birney declined to head the CWC early on in discussions about what he then imagined (possibly in memory of his father) as a craftsmen's guild, he was actively involved with west-coast writers in preparing the brief by the CWC (of forty-three members) that was eventually presented to the Massey Commission on 19 November 1949 by Claude Bissell, F.R. Scott, and Len Peterson. The brief advocated "a body not controlled by any poetic body or clique of writers" to dispense fellowships and grants to support writers. (This brief, among others, eventually led to the founding of the Canada Council, modelled on the Arts Council of Great Britain which Massey had had in mind in 1949.)[80]

Each year also brought Birney more and more students to befriend, to place in the next stage of their careers, and to correspond with. And the sociable Birneys acquired more and more acquaintances through those they already knew. Birney's obligations—professional and social—multiplied accordingly. He assiduously fired off letters of recommendation for students such as Mary McAlpine, for whom he found a job at Macmillan in Toronto (she wrote back that "the words Earle Birney substitute open sesame in literary circles"[81]), and Daryl Duke, whom he placed with the National Film Board in Ottawa. He kept in touch with Eric Nicol, now at the Sorbonne in Paris. He advised and assisted his *Turvey* editor, Sybil Hutchinson, who was no longer at M & S because of a personality conflict with Jack McClelland in May 1950. He began a correspondence with Jay Macpherson, a student at Carleton College who had won a poetry competition he judged,[82] and with Desmond Pacey at the University of New Brunswick, whose anthology of short stories had been one of the books Birney chose for his radio program "The Ten Best Canadian Books."[83] And he met the writer George Woodcock, who had just returned to Canada from England, knew his poetry and was referred by Howard Sergeant to Birney for advice about the Canadian literary scene.[84] Woodcock and his wife settled on Vancouver Island and were soon added to the Birneys' ever-widening circle of friends: UBC colleagues like Roy Daniells and Reg Watters, CBC folk like Bob and Rita Allen, local writers like Malcolm Lowry, painters like Jack Shadbolt, musicians like Jean Coulthard Adams, who had set Birney's "Quebec May" to music,[85] and her husband. Birney also sent off poems, spoke on the radio (including a major series, "The Poets Look at Canada"), served two more years as a judge for the poetry section of the Governor General's Literary Awards and kept in touch with a staggering number of people, including Ken Johnstone, his former brother-in-law, now working in theatre production in Montreal, and Everett and Helen Hughes, from whom he learned that Sylvia had remarried and had a son.

Here too, Birney seemed unable to establish priorities. If he came to Toronto to see Bet, he explained, "Trouble is I have too many friends there who would be insulted if I didn't see them. I would have to stay either at the Wolfes—Rosie and Ray, 1705 Bathurst, the Ontario Produce wholesale fruit lad—or the Hagons on St. Mary's near St. Mike's College. And I would have to look up Maggie Richardson, Sybil Hutchinson, Gertie Garbutt, Ryersons [Press staff], John Adaskin, Professors Knox and Bissell and Norrie Frye and Ned Pratt, and Paul Corbett at Gage & Co., and lawyer Felix Eckstein and Roger Guyet, and the [George] Grubes, and Jack and Marg Parker, and the Steve

Harts perhaps, and Robert Finch and Norman Endicott, and
MacLean of Trinity, and J.K. Thomas and Morley Callaghan and
Mary-Etta Macpherson and B.K. Sandwell, and so on and on."[86]

With gentle concern, Bet offered her common-sense advice to
no avail: "couldn't you give up some of the committees and
things, or the evening Writers' Group? ...wonderful as it is for
those young people to have you, your own work is infinitely
more important. The radio work takes so much time too, and is
so fleeting."[87]

By November 1949, Bet had cast her fate with El Cox.
Unexpectedly pregnant, she wrote that after contemplating suicide, and unable to find an abortion, "[I] decided to become an
entirely different person and go through with it.... I can give
him exactly what he wants, I think, and still keep a private
core.... I realized at last during the summer that though you may
never really go back to Esther you will never leave her. Please forget me now...and don't write me again."[88] On 19 November she
and Cox were married.

Hot on the heels of the publication of *Turvey* was another coup
for Birney: the visit of Welsh poet Dylan Thomas to UBC.
Birney had heard through his contacts in creative writing at the
University of Washington that Thomas was coming to Seattle,
and arranged to extend his trip to Vancouver for the 6th and 7th
of April. It was to be the only Canadian stop on Thomas's first
American tour of more than forty universities, schools and colleges from New York to San Francisco.[89] "Dylan Thomas's visit
was an incredible success here," he wrote George Woodcock.

> I have never seen so many people so moved by poetry.
> We had S.R.O. in the Auditorium—1300 students
> jammed in, sitting in the aisles, etc.—and tremen-
> dous applause. He really put on a remarkable show at
> this noon hour appearance and also at an evening
> appearance in the Hotel Vancouver which was sold
> out (400 seats) and some people turned away at the
> door. I found him personally a wonderful guy, and he
> left me...with a sense of exhilaration and poetic

motivation.... By the way Dylan behaved with admirable sobriety and the only noticeable drunks were the inevitable Malcolm Lowry and a certain undergraduate lion huntress who got herself blotto trying to seduce Dylan without success.[90]

Elsewhere, however, he was more candid: "My largest poetic thrill of the year was housing and shepherding Dylan Thomas," he wrote Howard Norman, who was at a safe remove in Japan, "he is a unique and blessed combination: fine poet, great reader. A ruddy Welsh bard, and a damned good drinking companion."[91] As for Thomas, he wrote his wife that Vancouver was "a quite handsome hellhole" which was "more British than Cheltenham."[92] Certainly according to Esther, Thomas *did* get drunk. Birney's former student, Hilda Thomas, recalls being upset that she and Phil were not invited to the private party for Thomas. When she complained to Esther that she was upset not to meet Dylan Thomas, Esther—who like Earle was impatient with drunkenness—replied: "You wouldn't have felt that if you'd had to hold his head while he vomited." "That," says Hilda, "was Esther at her acerbic best."[93]

With *Turvey* so successfully launched, Birney turned to radio plays for extra cash. He had failed to place his short stories with Robert Weaver of the CBC in Toronto because Weaver was unimpressed with the stories and only accepted unpublished material.[94] So Birney turned to adaptations. On 10 April, his radio version of "Beowulf" was such a success that he was encouraged to try other material. Things were not much improved at home: "Esther is a very jealous wife, but very," he wrote to a woman friend who confided in him about her marriage difficulties. "The fact that she no longer has cause doesn't seem to end her insecurity. She is even capable of rowing about affairs that happened back at a time when *she* was having them too. So I don't dare be anything but canny in her presence or within earshot."[95] But once again he rented a summer cottage for his family in 1950—this time on Savary Island where they swam nude and amused themselves by observing the local characters. He churned out several half-hour adaptations of short stories and a play, using Esther as critic, for CBC's "Fall Fare," for which he earned seventy-five dollars a piece: "The Last Griffon" (based on Frank Stockton's "The Griffin and the Minor Cannon"); "The Murder in the Pawnshop" (based on Robert Louis Stevenson's "Markheim"); "A Party at the Undertaker's" (from Alexander Pushkin's "The Undertaker"); Pushkin's "The Queen of Spades"; "The Case of Dr. Trifon" (from Pushkin's "The District Doctor") and "The Second Shepherd's Play" (from the mediaeval Towneley cycle).[96] Birney was so prolific that his producer friend Bob Allen quipped, "you can't get near the Island for the flood of scripts that are pouring out. Assembly-line techniques have a lot to learn. It's wonderful! But when do you eat?"[97] *Turvey's* success had brought Birney something between $500 and $1,000, which had kindled the hope that he might be able to afford a house at last. In July, he received a substantial raise at UBC (from $4,700 to $5,200), and somewhat apprehensively bought a house just beyond the edge of the campus at 4590 West Third, near Tolmie "with a wonderful view" out across Burrard Inlet to the mountains on the north shore.

Before he and Esther could settle down that September, Birney's mother's condition suddenly worsened. "I had to pack up my mother's house," he wrote to Louis MacKay at Berkeley, "sell it, move her in on top of us while our boxes were still underfoot; Esther and I nursed her till we finally got the goddamned hospital to find a bed, and now we visit her twice a day. She is dying slowly and painfully from cancer."[98] On 30 October Martha Birney died. "Though she was 75, and suffered much" he wrote his old UBC friend Helen Hughes in Chicago, "it was still a shock to lose her; she was such a vigorous and unselfish woman, and Bill's perfect Grandma. She was a difficult personality who liked to manage people as well as help them, and she made enemies; but in her last years the best came to dominate in her and she made a good death. I only hope I do half as well. I shall always be grateful that she, who had almost no formal education, gave me the spur and the chance to get a good one and, when that took me into worlds she couldn't follow, she still gave me her loyalty and love to the end."[99]

Birney hoped keenly that *Turvey's* success in Canada would

ensure publication in Britain and the U.S. He located agents in both countries to this end, expecting that the Canadian editions of *Outposts* (1948) and *Poetry Commonwealth* (1950), which he edited, and the fact that recently he had published more work abroad than in Canada, would make him better known than most Canadians.[100] But English publishers tended to find *Turvey* "too Canadian"[101] and suggested that it "ought to go well in America";[102] American publishers also thought it too Canadian, or they worried that President Truman's invasion of Korea and the threat of a third World War would kill sales.[103] In the end, *Turvey* was rejected by six British and seven American publishers.[104]

This disappointment affected Birney's future plans. "Supposing I'd written a novel revealing the Tibetan character," he wrote Louis MacKay in disgust, "or even, to take something less timely, Nigerian or Ecuadorian. Why they'd grab at it. It's only Canada which must, for the U.S. book trade, maintain an unbroken [series] of mounties, trappers and pious *habitants*. Curious. I suspect it has something to do (if it exists in fact, outside the fear-complexes of American editors) with the sanguine American hope that Canada will somehow without fuss be absorbed into the Great Republic, and therefore she should not, meantime, be developing anything awkwardly different in the way of a personality. Anyway, I shall probably put more Americans into my next one and establish a Bellingham mailing address."[105]

Not that Birney planned to restrict himself to another novel—with or without Americans. "There is a serious novel he wants to do," wrote his friend CBC movie critic Clyde Gilmour in the cover story for *The Vancouver Sun* magazine supplement for 5 August 1950 which featured a photo of the now clean-shaven Birney in suit and tie "relaxing" with his wife and son at home, "and a stage play; and a number of radio dramas…more poetry, but nothing likely to channel him in a rut…. He's still looking around."[106]

❧ *20* ❧

A Trial

"It's just a chance and I seize at straws now that I'm 48 and have been turned down by Guggenheim, Rockefeller, and all the rest of them," Birney wrote Ralph Gustafson, pitching his case for Gustafson's support of a fellowship application in September 1952. "My university doesn't give sabbaticals so I seem condemned to teach till I'm 65—I should live so long—before I get a year off to write."[1] He felt trapped. And he felt unappreciated. Early that summer he had coined the phrase "the barefoot Canadian author" for a talk he gave in June at the Canadian Library Association in Banff, a talk he was adapting for a *Mayfair* article in which he complained that no author could live by writing in Canada.[2]

A month later, he heard that he had won a Canadian Government Overseas Fellowship of $4,000 (in French francs) for a year in France with his family. "We've been bowled over this weekend with sudden unbelievably good news," he wrote in high excitement to Gwladys Downes. "I've won a Dominion Government travelling fellowship to write a novel...[and] I must stay in France.... Me a year in France. I can't even speak the damned language.... Help!"[3] He wrote at once to Gustafson and E.J. Pratt, to thank them for "perjuring" themselves on his behalf.[4] Dorothy Livesay, one of the many friends who flocked to congratulate him, wrote, "I really am delighted that you have slipped out of the noose. It gives the rest of us hope."[5]

The good news galvanized the already overburdened Birney into frenetic action. With only two months to extricate himself from UBC for the spring term—not to mention his many other obligations—he and Esther scurried to make preparations. "I'm glad of the fellowship," he wrote Livesay, "but there are many problems. My French is lousy; my feet are bad and I'm in no shape for travelling at the moment; to get away by mid-December means high financing, especially if I'm to create pounds of credit in England to support Esther and Bill [at a private school] there. I'll have to sell the car, rent the house profitably, speed up my courses, etc. I'd really rather take the fellowship at 4590 W. 3rd and settle down to write the required novel. France will be a waste, I fear, on a lame, aging *paterfamilias*."[6]

Birney had reported his foot trouble to the Department of Veteran's Affairs before hearing of his fellowship. He now had almost continuous pain in his left foot, shooting pains up to the knee and cramps in his toes and leg. He had to sleep with that foot in layers of socks stuck outside the bed, and he needed a cane to walk.[7] Travel, and preparations for travel, would be difficult.

It did not help that he had committed himself to too many projects, as usual. A year before he applied for the fellowship, the pressure was already building, and the word "schizoid" cropped up from time to time in his correspondence. "In most universities," he carped to his former student George Robertson, whom he had helped get a job at the NFB, "a professor capable of offering Anglo-Saxon and Middle English is left free from other courses so that he can keep up with the tremendous output of scholarship in a field covering a thousand years; or an author giving Creative Writing is regarded as a resident author and has little else to do. But I have to be both...and in addition a committee man (I think I'm in 7 this year), a public speaker (4 bookings for the next month already), and a pitcher-in to sophomore work and freshman planning. Also I'm editing a war memorial book for the university and trying desperately to find time to finish my own book of poems for Ryerson (too late for Xmas now), an anthology they want by February, and my novel (also wanted by McC & S for Feb.). It just ain't possible, and I'm depressed with the work piled on me."[8] Something of the urgency of that last month in Vancouver informs his accounts to Lorne Pierce, "I have been swamped with passport and visa routines, innoculations, lectures, public appearances during Book Week [in November], house inventories and renting, packing, gardening, and visits to a doctor"[9] and to Gwladys Downes, "We are loaded with maps, guides, advice, and baggage. Boat sails next Tuesday and boy am I longing for it."[10]

But by the time the tall, bearded professor leaning on his silver-knobbed cane boarded the French cargo ship *S.S. Wyoming* with his wife and son on 24 December 1952, he had managed to take on several new assignments—mainly future radio and magazine reports of his travels—without having completed the anthology he had begun over a year before. Though he had promised the Royal Society that he would work on his novel for the five weeks it would take to round Panama to Le Havre, he tutored Bill with his Grade 7 texts and turned his attention to finishing the anthology *Twentieth Century Canadian Poetry* that he hoped would make money as a high-school and university text, mailing it off to Ryerson Press from Los Angeles. He also wrote long, newsy letters to make sure his many friends had his address c/o the Canadian Embassy on Avenue Foch in Paris, composed poems which he had "ready to hurl from the Canal Zone at various editors,"[11] and—after an adventure in a taxi in Curaçao—wrote a short story with homosexual overtones,[12] "Waiting for Queen Emma," that he hoped was sophisticated enough for *The New Yorker*. (They rejected it, but *Maclean's* published it as "Enigma in Ebony.") But the novel remained only "a faint buzz in my head."[13]

At this point in life, Birney might have relaxed into his accomplishments. *Turvey* had been published in paperback by William Collins, earning him $250. And since then, he had enjoyed much recognition and success. In the time since *Turvey* first appeared, he had been sent in May 1951 as UBC's delegate to the Canadian Universities Conference in Montreal and won the $200 Borestone Mountain Award for the best English-language poem in 1950 from the American Poetry Association for his 1945 poem "The Hazel Bough" which, due to his strenuous self-promotion, had been reprinted in the New Zealand journal *Arena*.[14] ("It was such a windfall," he wrote later, "I decided to blow it on a stock tip, on Placer Development.")[15] *David and Other Poems* had become a collector's item worth ten dollars a copy.[16] In the summer of 1952 he had spoken at the Canadian Library Association meeting at Banff; was invited to lead workshops and give readings at the University of Utah's fifth annual Writing Worshop at Salt Lake City; and won the first President's Medal from the University of Western Ontario for the best poem written by a Canadian in 1951. The poem, "North Star West" ("a dramatic saga of flight by [North Star] passenger plane from Montreal to Vancouver"[17]), was written in exchange for free fare from Trans-Canada Airways to the 1951 conference in Montreal and appeared in their journal.[18] It was one of the new poems in his latest collection, *Trial of a City and Other Poems*, which had appeared on 11 October 1952 after a well-synchronized radio performance of the title poem, three days earlier on CBC. At the Book Week in Vancouver (during which he simultaneously hosted Oscar Williams, the British poet), he was a star, reading a "duet" from his new radio play with the woman heading the drama program at UBC to an enraptured audience of eight hundred.[19] As Pratt had aptly written in his fellowship recommendation: "as a combination of scholar and creative writer there is no one in Canada to surpass [him]."[20]

But Birney did not feel satisfied with success. There was something almost symbolic in the reading of "David" and other mountain poems which he gave on Mount Norquay for the librarians' conference in August 1952. Not only did he seem trapped in time as a poet, since his public persisted in associating him with "David" more than with anything he had written since, but there was also something forced, hollow, a bit unreal, about his own sense of himself as a writer. The group of librarians (and Esther, who had accompanied him for a holiday) "assembled at the foot of the Mount Norquay ski lift," he wrote Pratt. "The loud speaker boomed me against the scarps of Norquay and Stoney Squaw and bounced phrases up to overtake the refugees who had taken flight from poetry.... More echoes funnelled down Forty Mile ravine into the valley and were heard on the main street of Banff. I'll never have such a big voice again."[21]

And he was surprisingly insecure about the prospect of Utah's summer course—partly because Stephen Spender was scheduled for the second half of their program. "I am in awe of these efficient American Poetry Workshops," he wrote Brewster Ghiselin, the colleague who had invited him, "have never taught at one, the very name paralyses me.... do please brief me."[22]

Trial of a City, his fourth poetry book, was a mixed success. He knew that his 1948 mountain-climbing narrative "Conrad Kain," failed to match "David," let alone surpass it.[23] He had originally intended to write another narrative, "Kootenay Story," as the title poem for this collection, but found himself unable to write it even after he had assembled the few previous poems and several new ones that would make up the book. So "The Damnation of Vancouver," as his new title work was originally called, was written under tremendous pressure of time and, perhaps for this reason, fused two facets of his writing: poetry and radio play. Covering both angles, he hoped to score financially as well as in reputation from the same work.[24] He was careful to check the conditions of the Governor General's Award just in case, since *Strait of Anian* had been disqualified on the grounds that it was almost half reprinted poems. And he joined the Poetry Society of America in anticipation of winning their annual award of one thousand dollars for the best poetry collection. But Lorne Pierce had rejected some of his new poems (as had several journals) and "The Damnation of Vancouver" was, in his own words, "a turgid dramatic poem," "an experimental fantasy"[25] and "a trial-balloon."[26] Despite his assertions to the contrary (and despite the praise he received from Ethel Wilson after reading it aloud at an "AA" meeting in her house on his forty-eighth birthday),[27] he secretly suspected *Trial of a City* was not his best work. "I feel rather gloomy about this collection," he confessed to Lorne Pierce, "I don't think it's up to scratch after all."[28]

Birney got the idea for "The Damnation of Vancouver" from attending a public hearing, in August 1951 on Vancouver Island, into a government proposal to dam Buttle Lake. "For many years before that," he wrote, "I had wanted to make a satiric survey of Vancouver, using in part a *Piers Plowman* technique but it wasn't until this Hearing that I saw a way of binding Langland with other ghosts into a semi-dramatic form."[29] Just as Langland judged mediaeval London and found it based on profiteering, Birney put a future Vancouver on trial with much the same result. Captain Vancouver finds the gorgeous site he discovered now polluted; a Salish chief testifies that the white man has destroyed his people; Gassy Jack, a sailor and saloon-keeper, pleads that the materialism of twentieth-century Vancouver is far worse than his vulgar misdoings. Only a housewife in the end briefly pleads love and hope, shifting the case to another, more human, level.

But neither the ninety-minute radio play nor the collection advanced Birney's career, despite the fact that the radio performance elicited many compliments from the general public, friends and associates and the book sold out its one thousand copies within two months. He sent more than a hundred copies—one-tenth of the print run—at his own expense to friends and influential colleagues. Birney was so popular with friends and the general public that praise was, in many cases, automatic; his radio and literary fans would probably have bought his next book regardless. But "The Damnation of Vancouver" was so esoteric it could not be appreciated by the public at large. And even his more sophisticated listeners noted the fact that, as he put it, Alice Hill, the actress playing the important role of housewife, sounded like "a bitchy Wagnerian Valkyrie instead of just plain Mrs. Anyone."[30] More seriously, a number of people commented that, as one reviewer said in a review of the verse play (with the irrelevant picture—taken by Bet Campbell on Bowen Island—of the bearded poet captioned "Poet and Conifers—Earle Birney of Vancouver gazing amid the Rockies"), "the whole case is biased from the start against the city."[31] Lister Sinclair, who among Birney's friends knew most about both drama and radio, explained tactfully that the irony was external, "this dramatic poem does not carry *within itself* the life of its own drama."[32] And Birney himself admitted that he had put his case too strongly and had erred in having no witness from the past speak against the prosecutor, Gabriel Powers. As for the collection of poems, it was reviewed enthusiastically in Vancouver ("brilliant satire and humour and literary artistry"[33]) and politely elsewhere, on the whole. Sinclair also offered detailed criticism of his other new poems. He disliked "Restricted Area" (which "sprang out of a deep hatred of anti-semitic goings on at Thunder Bay, Ontario"[34]) and "Biography," and "Takkakaw Falls" (a poem intended "to convey the continual rebirth of life and beauty out of the basic 'sexual' violence of nature"[35] and influenced by Hart Crane's "Hurricane"[36]), but admired "Bushed" (which was "a study of an extreme distortion of a soul...who withdraws more and more into himself...[until] he finally shuts himself into the cabin of his own insanity").[37] Listeners and readers agreed on Birney's poetic skill in his play, but found plot and characters wanting. And some, like Alan Crawley, found this, his most cerebral work to date, lacking in deep emotion."[38] Northrop Frye in his year-end summary of Canadian letters for the *University of Toronto Quarterly* produced the most thoughtful analysis. Describing the play as "erudite," he praised its "virtuosity of language" (Birney used a different poetic style for each character) but located a serious problem in the fact that Mr. Legion, the typical Vancouverite and only defender of the city, represents the materialistic values Birney clearly demonstrates must be destroyed, thus undermining the play's denouement. *Trial of a City and Other Poems* did not look like a serious contender for the Governor General's Award, or any other.

Birney vented his anxieties about his merits and his irritation at the pressures he had largely inflicted on himself in a number of feuds. At UBC he needled Daniells about what he felt was an unfair teaching burden and pressed for a new appointment in Old English to relieve him of half his courses. He also campaigned for an expansion of creative writing courses against the traditional academics in his department who considered even his one course "an expensive frill."[39] Daniells (who held firm) tried to placate him in a letter he didn't answer: "I regret the contretemps

in which we are at present involved. I do not forget your many
kindnesses to me in past years, some very long past, and I look
forward to a future when we may remember only such things as
those and not at all our present unhappinesses."[40] Birney also
fought with Lorne Pierce and his staff at Ryerson Press: over several clauses in his contracts, over the title for his anthology, over
the inclusion of study notes (Pierce tried to drop them) and over
who should be in his anthology (Pierce wanted Audrey
Alexandra Brown and Wilson MacDonald in particular, but
Birney wouldn't budge). He took Pierce to task for errors (they
named him "Earl" and his book *Now Is the Time*) on the dust-
jacket of *Trial*), and angrily returned a defective copy a friend
showed him. He was especially incensed that the somewhat sanc-
timonious Pierce did not want the word "damnation" (which was
a clever pun on the Buttle Lake "dam" that inspired him and on
the "*dame*" who redeems the indictment of the city) in the title
of his radio play, even though when he proposed it, he had
acknowledged to Pierce that it might be "too startling." Though
Pierce insisted on *Trial of a City*, Birney persisted in using "The
Damnation of Vancouver" for the radio broadcast and saw to it
that *The Vancouver Sun* ran a story called "Birney Has Trouble
Selling Title for Latest Opus."[41] He got testy with *The Canadian
Forum* for their delay in reviewing or even listing *Trial of a City*
until after it was sold out.[42] He also wrote a scathing counter-
attack "Feinting With Praised Damns" (never published) against
Dorothy Livesay, whose review of his guest-edited magazines
offended him.[43] He refused to give permission to the Montreal
Drama Playhouse to stage "The Damnation of Vancouver"
because they delayed in answering his letter outlining conditions.[44] He harangued the staff at CBC Toronto about Ross
McLean who had interviewed him (among others) about
humour, but had not used his interview—or more important,
paid him for it—in the actual program.[45] He took issue with
John Sutherland over being categorized in the
December–January issue of *Northern Review* as one of a
"Western Group...the most clear-cut political group of the thirties" with Livesay, Anne Marriott and others on the grounds that
he had been so political then that he "regarded the writing of

poetry as a treacherous withdrawal of energy from the class strug-gle."[46] And he rose to the bait when poet Irving Layton (whom he had met only once briefly, a meeting that resulted in a poetic reference to Birney later as "the drunken poet")[47] threatened legal action and sent his "undying hatred" as a consequence of a jocular radio review on CBC's "Critically Speaking" that included Layton's work. Birney wrote John Sutherland (Layton's brother-in-law) questioning whether Layton (who wrote an even more scurrilous reply) was "mentally ill,"[48] as Layton's letters to Birney "seem to reflect an hysterical personality with some kind of paranoid trend."

It did not improve Birney's temper as he prepared to depart for France and his anthology was in its final stages that a similar anthology (*Canadian Poems: 1850–1952*) edited by Louis Dudek at the newly established Contact Press in Montreal sud-denly appeared. "I'm afraid it may take a lot of the wind out of the sails of my collection," he wrote Pierce. Dudek's selection forced him to reassess his own, remove eighteen poems and introduce five others.[49]

To add to his irritation, both his publishers let his books go out of print well before Christmas. Collins could not promise a second printing of *Turvey* (first printing 15,000) until April (it did not appear until July). And two days before leaving Vancouver, Birney dashed off a complaint to Pierce: "It always seems to happen to me just before Xmas. Are you printing a sec-ond edition yet?"[50]

Even when the freighter sailed off, his frustration continued because a storm "penned [them] in Gray's Harbour for a long stinking week,"[51] which meant he would not be in France on schedule to complete the financial arrangements he had made. "Christmas surprised us by the docks of a pantagruelian iron foundry near Tacoma," he wrote sardonically in one of his many letters. "The next night we had progressed to a sulphite plant in Hoquiam, near Gray's Harbour. But there we stayed a week, making a sortie daily as far as the harbour bar, and returning to the malodorous dock; beyond the bar a gale roared... New Year's was acknowledged with dubious bourbon in the company of a Republican supercargo and a pilot's psychotic wife." Things brightened when he could escape the ship in various ports. "Eventually we got to San Francisco, not without considerable heavings on the part of Esther, Bill and the ship (I am blessed with immunity to motion-sicknesses). Three excellent days with various old friends [including the Gartshores], fresh crab at Fisherman's Wharf, a visit to my old bachelor fisherman-shack on Telegraph Hill…and four days with Frank Wilcox, who…is now wealthy and retired, on the strength of his family's olive and orange groves."[52]

Birney had planned to settle Esther (who had taken to "fussing about being overweight, and dieting")[53] with her father, Emmanuel Bull, in Golders Green, in north London, so she could pursue courses in contemporary embroidery design at the Royal School of Needlework. Bill (now eleven and "lanky as his old man)"[54] was off to Burys Court School in Leigh, Surrey. And Earle was to pick up his new Austin and find himself a quiet spot to write in France. As he put it to George Robertson, he "would dump them both on English relatives and confine myself to the south of France and, o yes, Paris."[55]

Birney didn't waste a moment in England looking up old friends (including Bert Matlow and his wife, and Margaret Johns, their old Trotskyist comrades; Margaret Crosland and her husband Max Denis; and Esther's former husband, Israel Heiger, and his new wife, Lois) or trying to place his poems with editors there and getting his work to the BBC in hope of a reading on radio. But the BBC returned his poems even before he set off in his bright, new Austin for France, explaining that they could not afford to use them, much as they liked the work—especially "David."[56]

Birney, the carefree writer, set off for the south alone: "I had to 'do' Auxerre, Tournus, Lyon, Dijon, Orange, Avignon, Aix and Fréjus on the way," he excitedly wrote to Archibald Day, the Canadian ambassador whom he had quickly befriended at a dinner in Paris on the way.[57] But, despite his delight in freeing himself of his family and the obligations he had carped about for so long, Birney crashed once he got himself installed in an apartment in Juan-des-Pins on the outskirts of Antibes in the Riviera. "Everything is too much the way it should be for a writer," he complained to his cousin Rosemary Baxter, who had an interest in literature and had written him from Aberdeen.[58] "The Grand Palais was not grand," he wrote in dejection to Archie Day, it was "a dump. I am on the top floor back with a lot of broken crockery." "[Juan-des-Pins] was cold, windy, heatless, and mostly shut up," he wrote to Norman Klenman, now writing film scripts for the NFB. "Also I got a little dysentery [and] didn't know anybody." "I wired Esther to leave her embroidery courses and join me before I go quietly mad."[59] When Esther arrived a few days later, he wrote Bill, "Mother has arrived... I was certainly glad to see her. This apartment is too big and too lonely for one person, and I was fed up with batching anyway."[60]

Now even the apartment seemed charming. Reverting to their old, sociable ways, the Birneys invited Gordie and Jan Baker to visit for a month: we have "a wonderful view of the Mediterranean from both bedrooms and a view of the Esterel hills from... the kitchen... three blocks walk from one of the finest sand beaches in the Riviera."[61] When the Bakers declined, he invited his old Zate chum, Bruce Macdonald (now Canadian Trade Commissioner in Bonn, Germany) and his wife.[62] When they declined too, he and Esther moved into a busy, family-run auberge (Auberge Provençal) in Antibes, where they could socialize with local people and go to French movies. By the beginning of April, when Bill flew down to join them for his month of Easter holidays, Birney was further cheered by the "unexpected" good news from the Royal Society that he had won their Lorne Pierce Medal for his contribution to Canadian letters.[63]

But when Esther and Bill went off to Florence, a disgruntled and envious Birney stayed in Antibes, resisted the lure of the film festival in nearby Cannes, and got down at last to begin the novel called "Summer Rebel"[64] (*Down the Long Table*) which he expected to publish in 1953, even though he had only outlined it so far. "Gloomily I have decided that I have damned little talent," he wrote Clyde Gilmour in one among his constant stream of letters home and abroad, "and the only reason I get books written is that I have a lot of sheer obstinacy once I sit down to a typewriter, and flat feet which make me inclined to sit."[65]

It is clear from his letters that Birney hated being confined to write, but loved being free to travel. He "ground out" three chapters while Esther and Bill were away. "When they came back," he wrote to Klenman in a letter typical of his many detailed descriptive reports, "we climbed in the Austin and went slowly back to Paris, a thousand mile detour via Marseilles (Corbusier's unité d'Habitation), Arles, Nîmes, Les Baux, Montpellier, Narbonne, Carcassonne ("so mediaeval you get ready to duck archers"),[66] Toulouse, Montauban, Cahors, the Lescaux [sic] Caverns, Limoges, Blois, Chartres, Versailles.... Ah, those hill towns behind the Riviera.... St-Paul-de-Vence, Vence itself, or St Jeannet. That last backed up under a Gibraltar-sized cliff, a little Provençal song on three or four notes—the old-gold rust on every roof tile, the white crazy-box walls, the soft old-lady olive trees. And a whole arena of terraces in the valley below, swashed with carnations and roses and wallflowers. It was April, too, and the peach blossoms were definitely improbable. The whole valley was bursting with so much flower there wasn't room for a leaf.... Esther and Bill kept on going back to London, and I holed up in a little joint on the Rue Toullier, near the Panthéon. Meantime Esther is repenting her return and threatens to join me again next week."[67] Birney was agog, not just at the lush scenery, but also at the mediaeval architecture which, as an expert in Chaucer and Middle English, he was uniquely prepared to appreciate. "Ah, Carcassonne!" he wrote the Woodcocks. "We liked Montauban too. There's a market square there with a double cloister, mediaeval, running right around it, cool and sun-chequered....[and] those tremendous flying buttresses leaping right up from the old tile-roofed houses [in Narbonne]...[and] Catherine of Medici's library room [in the Blois Chateau] is something to see...mediaeval wall panelling at its most sumptuous."[68]

His novel "Summer Rebel" (*Down the Long Table*) was in many ways an off-shoot of "The Damnation of Vancouver." The onset of the McCarthy era in the U.S., with its persecution of Communists, reminded Birney of his experiences in the thirties. He had already been named publicly in the B.C. "Red Scare" in 1948. But now stringent immigration policies to keep left-wing sympathizers out of the U.S. had been instituted and one of the reasons he had wanted to take the freighter from Vancouver, instead of crossing the continent by train and sailing from New York, was that he wanted to avoid "U.S. border snarls."[69] He was outraged that one of his students en route to a graduate creative writing program at Indiana had had to swear that he had never been a member of the CCF.[70] For Birney, who was determined to crack the American market with an American subject, the parallels between the witch-hunts of the thirties and the fifties seemed *the* important contemporary topic. "I want more than anything else to wind my slingshot at that Goliath," he had written George Robertson, "not the U.S. herself so much as our own shadow writ large over there and our national capitulation already to the still unspoken Yankee threat—'like us or be destroyed.' By god we've got to stand up and say we aren't Yanks and won't necessarily ever be Yanks."[71] He had structured "The Damnation of Vancouver" as a trial much like those in kangaroo courts where the sentence preceded the verdict and which were the main instrument of McCarthyism. Now he drew on his experiences as a radical Trotskyist at the University of Utah in the thirties for a novel that featured a McCarthy-like investigation into the political history of a professor much like himself. As he wrote to Brian Elliott, "The present affair is very different [from *Turvey*], alas, serious, heavy, lost in mazes of experimentation and political exegesis. It's about being a Radical in the Hungry Thirties—scene shifts from U.S. to Toronto, to Vancouver."[72]

He wrote at length about his book to Herman Singer, warning him that he was the basis for Van Bome, one of his main characters. "No cause for alarm," he wrote, "he's about the only likeable bastard in the book…more amusing and admirable than my hero…a non-political character in a political novel…. So if anybody thought of you…you'd get a clean bill of health from McCarthy." Because he could not do other than re-create his own political stance, Birney began to realize that his book would not appeal to Americans. It "is extremely unlikely to get any circulation in the U.S. on account of the unheroic hero who is somewhat me, and is an unsuccessful but unsatisfactorily repentant red."[73]

And, indeed, his agent, Howard Moorepark, wrote to say that two U.S. publishers had returned the three chapters he had finished in May without a contract, but not for the reason Birney anticipated. Appleton-Century-Crofts felt—as some critics of "The Damnation of Vancouver" had felt—that "the author is too anxious to press his theme at the expense of character development." And Houghton Mifflin Co. thought that the book was "too much of a tract and not enough of a novel to be successful."[74] An early draft of the novel's plot, with characters Ron, Thelma and Z (in place of Earle, Catherine Fisk and Esther), corresponds in every detail with Birney's life.[75] Had his scholarly training made him such a stickler for accuracy that he was unable to invent things? Or was the more important question: could Birney really empathize with anyone but himself?

Though he had all he wished for, Birney detested the life of an expatriate writer. "I sit at my typewriter in a ragged hotel beside the Sorbonne," he wrote Ethel Wilson, after Esther and Bill left the Left Bank for London, "while the April rains darkens [sic] my light-well. The novel goes slowly; I've done four revisions on the first 20,000 words and will have to do others. However, one can only go on trying, sweating, living it, and resisting everything else in life because everything else seems to be a temptation *not* to write."[76] He spent a miserable birthday on 13 May alone in his room in the Hotel Soufflot. Only an unexpected letter from Gabrielle Baldwin relieved his depression. "This morning was my forty-ninth birthday, a gloomy morning; grey light filtering through the dirty window of my pocket-sized bedroom, several floors up and back, in a run-down hotel, in a backstreet on the left Bank," he wrote in reply. "I had a bad taste from smoking too many cigarettes last night. I went downstairs; the parcel Esther said she was sending me for my birthday had not arrived. The only item of mail was a little envelope from Montreal almost entirely covered with French chiffres de timbre taxe—so many they were in double layers. Le patron was standing by to make sure I paid him for them—the staggering sum of 1221 francs. The letter had gone to Vancouver, to Paris, to Antibes, and back to Paris, all by air. This is too much, I thought. I will give up having birthdays. Then I opened the letter, and the sun burst through the window and birds sang in the eaves, and I was talking to Gaby. Wonderful, wonderful, to hear from you and at last to have an address to write. Because there was none before I felt I could write you safely."[77]

To assuage his loneliness, Birney wrote several other letters that day. One to Neal Harlow, UBC librarian, to say his novel was going "with agonizing slowness. God how I hate writing a novel. Why did I ever think I could?" Another to Bill McConnell ("my free lawyer")[78] to say "[I] begin to doubt [my novel] will ever get an American publisher—too pink." Another to his student Ernie Perrault with the advice, "Take it from an old man of 49 (today, god help me!) and don't delay your year in France. You get to be my age and all you do is sit drinking a citron presse and watch the lovers kissing all over the sidewalks. Somebody ought to stop this business of growing old." Another "in a sombre birthday mood" to Herman Singer, telling him that he was "Pushing fifty, by god, I felt almost too old to get up and dawdled in bed finishing [a book]." As if he were close to death, Birney instructed Singer "to send any of my letters to the UBC Librarian, who is to have most of my papers when I shuffle off."[79] And a few days later, he wrote to Floris McLaren about the termination of Alan Crawley's *Contemporary Verse* with its thirty-ninth issue after twelve years of publication, identifying himself with the magazine's rise and fall. "My own versifying life has synchronized with the magazine. So long as *CV* was there, I felt in accord with a tradition.... Now I wonder if my own drying up as a poet isn't geared also with *CV*'s demise.... The ideas still come but the sense of isolation from a significant audience increases."[80]

More than ever, he felt a kinship with Don Quixote. With Esther at his side, like a stout, merry, down-to-earth Sancho Panza, he had "detoured to see Daudet's windmill. I'm glad to report," he wrote Neal Harlow, "it is still standing...on a completely barren stretch of what I take to be black lava rock; a fat round white building with a dunce-cap roof and sails big enough to send Quixote charging at them."[81]

Certainly he felt ill at ease alone in Paris. The famous cafés of an earlier era, like the Vendôme, no longer sported literary lions. His favourite spot was "a bistro [Café Tournou] a few blocks away from me on the Boul' Mich' where you can hear a succession of bawdy chansonniers for the price of a beer, and there is a plaque to Verlaine on the wall."[82] Even so, Birney admitted his

French was not good enough to catch the jokes.

He cheered up when Esther rejoined him a week after his birthday for a trip to the Pays Bas via Rheims and the Ardennes to revisit places where he had briefly served during the war. They visited the family "straight out of Breughel"[83] near Ghent who had billeted him in 1945, the Van Heules, now wealthy through the insurance business. There, while England and her Commonwealth celebrated the coronation of Queen Elizabeth II on 2 June, they enjoyed "five days of champagne and lobster and six-course dinners and a powerful mixture of Cointreau and *Picon*, and yachting on the Schelde and motoring to Bruges ['most genuinely and unselfconsciously mediaeval'] and lunching in Brussels like great bloody nabobs. It is very hard on the digestive tract." And they went on to visit a rebuilt Nijmegen "to look for old haunts that had disappeared."[84]

Back in Paris in "this damnable freezing June,"[85] Birney turned his attention from his novel to proofreading the galleys for his anthology, fuming because Ryerson Press had neglected to include the manuscript to check them against. And he began the lucrative travel articles he had promised *Saturday Night*. Soon he succumbed again to the temptation to travel. He and Esther were back in Paris only a couple of weeks before they left on a five-week jaunt to Brittany. There they stayed at "a broken-down hotel in a sardine port" called Trinité-sur-mer, which they thought was so wonderful they phoned Lois Heiger to join them to keep Esther company while Birney was "slogging at the novel."[86] "No—not what you think," he wrote Gaby Baldwin, who had attributed his grumpiness and depression to his being between love affairs. "Lois and Esther have a big room downstairs and sleep together... I have a little upstairs room.... I do not have love affairs any more. I have grown very middle-aged."[87] But Lois Heiger recalls that she did have a brief fling with Birney then.[88] And to Herman Singer, Birney presented himself as quite other than a sedate, middle-aged *paterfamilias*. "I find that I feel much younger than I did in 1942—but partly because I avoid competitive situations with young men, except where young women are concerned, where age, not as yet having hit me below the belt, can be contrived to look like an asset. No

doubt this feeling is an illusion of my menopause, but it is nevertheless an illusion that brings me much pleasure."[89]

At Trinité-sur-mer, Birney (who had had to back out of his
commitments to Robert Weaver for radio travel talks)[90] put aside
his novel once again to continue writing articles for *Saturday
Night:* one about the trip over, one on Paris, and four sketches of
Brittany.[91] Once Esther left in early August, he travelled with
friends Brian Elliott and his wife Pat to Bordeaux (where he saw
the international El Greco show), to Biarritz and Urrúnaga, a
Basque hill-village (where he worked on his novel), and into
Spain to Bilboa before returning to Paris for a month.

On 14 October the anthology he knew was "almost my sole
proof that I didn't spend all the year in the Moulin Rouge"[92] was
published. As usual, he sent Ryerson Press a long list for complimentary copies (including copies to Canadian ambassadors
abroad), but instructed them not to send review copies outside
Canada, as he wanted to handle that himself. Partly because
Ryerson were charging four dollars for the book (double the price
of Dudek's), partly because he knew it would not be "a landmark
in Canadian Literary History,"[93] he was not sanguine about its
success. "I'm dubious about the anthology," he wrote George
Robertson, "it will probably be damned by both the Dudek-
McGill highbrows and by the conservative educationalists."[94]

By the time he returned to Vancouver for New Year's, his fears
were realized in a "real stinkeroo"[95] CBC radio review by
Margaret Stobie on "Critically Speaking," a program for which
he himself had done many reviews. Stobie confirmed one of
Pierce's criticisms in lamenting the omission of Audrey
Alexandra Brown. And she found Birney's thematic arrangement
of poems "confused." (He had arranged poems in groups under
headings like "Earth, Sky and Water.") The collection was
unlikely to appeal to students since it was "80% tepid and
mediocre" verse and therefore lacked "vigour, intellectual or
emotional." In a contrast that stung Birney sharply, she found
Rolfe Humphries's edition of *New Poems by American Poets* "altogether a delight."[96] And, as other reviews came in, he realized
that, although the majority were favourable, "the unfavourable
ones were in prominent places... I did not please the highbrows

[such as Desmond Pacey and Claude Bissell] who were judging me by what I was not trying to do. And I didn't please some of the Teachers' Mags—one of them ridiculed the very notion that Canadian Poetry could be seriously put forward for classroom study."[97] To add insult to injury, he soon also discovered that Lorne Pierce was busy revising the much more comprehensive *Canadian Poetry in English* he had edited with Bliss Carman, including an introduction by V.H. Rhodenizer which would blame "leftish" professors and critics for "the unhappy state of Canadian literature" and made pointed allusion to a poetry medal that "went to a leftish poet on the decision of three 'leftish' judges."[98]

As his year abroad drew to an end, Birney had little sense of accomplishment. In a long complaint he need not have wasted time on since it went unanswered, he detailed all the shortcomings of the fellowship program for French officials and made numerous suggestions for their remedy.[99] News that his UBC salary had risen to $6,800 didn't cheer him. The death of Dylan Thomas depressed him. He learned that Norrie Frye and Alan Crawley were now heading a poetry series for radio with Robert Weaver in Toronto for which he was expected to be a mere contributor.[100] And Ethel Wilson's words of encouragement—"you *have* the goods"[101]—seemed far from true. His efforts to have "The Damnation of Vancouver" and his radio script for "Gawain and the Green Knight" translated into German had come to nothing. He found an agent, but she reported that translators found both works "untranslateable."[102] Once he was back in London (which he disliked) for a last month and a half "helling around with old friends, seeing plays, galleries—and packing"[103] with Esther, he sent an unusually fawning letter to T.S. Eliot in an attempt to have Faber & Faber take his anthology: "Forgive this imposition; my only excuse is that in my own country, Canada, I am thought to be a poet—though I do not flatter myself that you have therefore heard of me." But Eliot turned it back immediately with the cool comment, "I am afraid that the market for anything in the way of regional anthologies is now almost negligible."[104] Worst of all, he was far from completing his novel, and he was convinced that it would be a failure. "[I have] a feeling that the novel, after a fair start, is going badly," he wrote George Robertson a couple of weeks before boarding the *S.S. Liberté* at Southampton on 5 December to return to Vancouver via New York (where he spent four days tracking agents, publishers and friends) and Toronto (where over two weeks at Christmas he did five TV programs (shaving off his beard because "my wife got tired of it")[105] that paid the flight back to Vancouver).[106] "I'm about two-thirds through, but bogged down, writing painfully, drearily, stubbornly. Behind lie a couple of really rather good chapters, one slightly Joycean, one Greenian…and some occasional flashes and passages; but much of it is, I'm afraid, damned dull. And it gets duller. Part of the trouble is the distraction of being in Europe."[107]

Typical of those "distractions" was a visit he recounted to his friends, Vancouver painter Jack Shadbolt and his wife, to an exhibit of the *societé des artistes indépendants*. His fascination with detailed lists and tabulations informed his report that there were "3072 exhibits of which just about 72 were worth…regarding."[108] "I really saw Paris—street by street, almost," he wrote later, "and put 10,000 French miles on the car."[109] With a wry sense of humour, he acknowledged just how "distracted" he had been, how eager to miss nothing of what might be his only trip abroad. "Have been exposed to, I should think, 300 churches, 50 museums, 40 forts, 30 art galleries, 2 grottos, hundreds of cafes, bistros, restaurants, hotels, charcuteries, parks, sens uniques, bidets, queues in bureaux de postes, zoos, belfnois, detours, and—Esther adds—thousands of lost man-hours waiting for l'addition in restaurants. I hope some of this sticks and I will be practically cultured at last."[110]

But Birney seemed to have no difficulty in weighing and judging the merits of writing versus travel. He had given the role of expatriate novelist a fair trial, and readily pronounced sentence. "I hope now to get [my novel] finished by [next] May," he decisively wrote to Gwyn Kinsey, his new editor at *Saturday Night*. "Then I want to head back to France and Europe generally for next summer, with no novel to be written, and write a series of travel articles."[111]

Publicity shot for the publication of *Turvey*, 1950.

Birney pinning rejection letters on the wall of his UBC office, 1950.

From left to right: Earle, Esther, an unidentified friend, Esther's
brother Donald, Lois Heiger, Max Denis and Margaret Crosland
as photographed by Israel Heiger, London, England, 1953.

Pauline Ivey, 1955.

Brian Merrett

"Four Generations of Canadian Poets"—Earle Birney, E.J. Pratt,
Irving Layton and Leonard Cohen, Toronto, June 1957.

Elizabeth "Liz" Cowley, 1959.

Alison Hunt, 1968.

Ikuko Atsumi, Vancouver, 1965.

William Birney and Marsha Taylor, 2 September 1967.

At the Love-In in Queen's Park, Toronto, 25 May 1967.

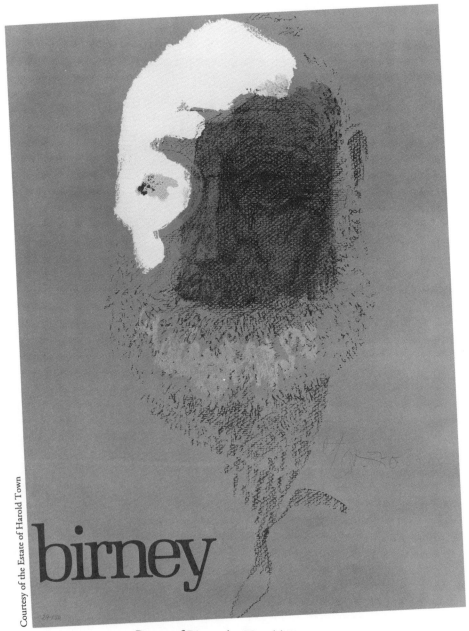

Poster of Birney by Harold Town, 1970.

Being interviewed by "a beauteous young Swede girl" in his study
at home in Vancouver, fall 1970.

With Wailan Low, 1973.

With grandsons Christopher and Earle, Jr., 1976.

Accepting the Vancouver Award for Lifetime Achievement,
Friday the 13th of March, 1987.

~§ *21* §~

IN FLIGHT

Two hours after he turned in his final grades on Sunday 8 May 1955, Earle Birney raced to board a plane alone for Mexico. He looked haggard and ill. His rapidly thinning hair was now almost entirely grey, and his doctor had warned him that he had an incipient duodenal ulcer. He had wangled a free return ticket from Canadian Pacific Air Lines Ltd. by offering to write articles on his trip that would refer to their company, and—since the airline planned to open a new Mexico–Toronto flight the next fall—they were happy to comply. As for the articles he would write for *Saturday Night*,[1] he needed the money to cover other expenses. Money had again become a serious problem. Though he kept it a secret from his friends, he was leaving Esther.

Once aloft, he relaxed into what he felt certain would be the beginning of a new, much happier, stage of his life. Taking notes assiduously for an article on the sudden transition from Canada to Mexico ("Mexico in One Jump"), he gazed down on the arid mountainous landscape he would duplicate for his editor in an aerial photo obtained from the Mexican Tourist Bureau. A room with a typewriter awaited him 150 miles north of Mexico City in San Miguel de Allende (described in *Time* magazine as "a centre for America's most active and wealthy communists")[2] at the spacious house of his old friend, the painter Leonard Brooks. Brooks had taken flight eight years before from Toronto, where he had had to teach at Northern Vocational School for $1,800 a year in order to survive. In Mexico, he was able to support himself and his wife, Reva, by teaching more informally and selling paintings in Mexico City and Los Angeles. Reva had become a close friend of Esther's in Toronto during the war. These two, and Miriam Waddington, who shared a duplex with the Brookses on Boswell Avenue not far from the Birneys, met frequently while their husbands were overseas. As Jewish women married to non-Jewish men with jobs in the arts, the three found they had much in common. Miriam and Esther were both social workers; but, more important, all three were themselves interested in the arts. Esther had aspired to write short stories, Reva would develop into a first-class photographer with work in the permanent collection of the Metropolitan Museum in New York, and Miriam was an established poet, whose work Birney had selected as an editor on more than one occasion. "Esther and I got along so well," Reva recalls. "I loved everything about her. She had a philosophical sense which influenced me in a helpful way. And she had a wonderful, husky laugh. She always spoke with such warmth of her family, and she was very hospitable and friendly to all sorts of people. She was very frank about sex, which was horrifying to me because I was secretive and a prude. She used to refer to Earle as "the goat" and joked that "he had the biggest penis, that was for sure." But Earle was [emotionally] cruel to Esther. She did so much for him. She bolstered him. He was ruthless really, though not in an inhuman way. He had an overabundance of sexual drive. He never could give himself over to a pure loving relationship. The pressure inside him drove him so."[3]

While Reva and Esther passed the time sociably in Toronto back then, Leonard, who was an official wartime artist with the navy, had seen Earle from time to time overseas, sharing occasional leaves in London, where Leonard had his studio. They had spent D-Day together, celebrating in the streets and watching the parade from a balcony of the war office where, according to Brooks, "we heard Churchill give a great speech that made us so emotional we almost fell off."[4] Leonard and Reva had often invited the Birneys to visit; now—possibly envious of George Woodcock's rhapsodic accounts of the previous summer he spent in Mexico with his wife, Inge—Earle had decided to take refuge there from what amounted to a physical and emotional crisis.

Nothing seemed to have gone right since his return from what he had taken to calling that "*annus mirabilis*"[5] in France. "He has had a difficult year since we returned from France," Esther had written Miriam Waddington. "His health is quite poor and his state of mind rather cast down and sad."[6] After what he recalled only as the delights of Europe, he found wet, foggy Vancouver a come-down "as provincial as ever"; he was, he wrote, a "bad case of uprooted provincial finding home soil stony."[7] "We do have a few people still trying to write hereabouts, thank god. But it's not exactly Paris or London here yet."[8]

Parachuted into the university mid-year, he found himself out of touch. He immediately focused blame on Roy Daniells, whom he saw as conspiring against him in his absence. Earlier he had been critical of Daniells for introducing time-consuming democratic procedures; now he took the opposite stance. "Our department head has, over the years, been quietly eliminating whatever democracy was inherent in our departmental set-up. I returned from a year's leave to find all the senior men cleverly isolated, power shared with a crop of new faces, kids with a couple of years' experience, imported by the Head to be henchmen of the New Order. It made things bad for us, especially for me. The Head has a particular grudge against me; he applied for the same fellowship I did and didn't get it. Also he is by way of being a poet who resents the fact that his executive duties interfere with his own writing. In fact, he wallows in executive detail to escape from the challenge of trying to write. Sooo, he's determined *I* shan't have time to write either."

Birney was furious that his courses had been rearranged in his absence: he had been given freshman and sophomore surveys, both of which involved onerous marking ("designed to punish me chiefly for winning a scholarship"), but, worst of all, his beloved Creative Writing course had been given to a young woman instructor and "slated for the ashcan next year." Birney wasted no time in gathering the senior professors into something remarkably like a Trotskyist cell, and, in his own words, they "had to organize a coup d'état and take dictatorial powers from the...Chairman." "Power has passed to a Committee of Senior Professors, the Head reduced to a nominal Chairman," he gleefully reported to Herman Singer by Easter.[9] "We had a revolt of the full professors," he would later say, taking clear responsibility for fomenting it, "which I led."[10] Birney claimed that he had been offered the chairmanship, but—realizing the time involved—declined. He wanted Daniells replaced by someone from outside.[11]

To that end, and in many other ways, Birney worked behind the scenes to make the changes he wanted in his department. Fearful that he would be "stuck for life"[12] with the senior Old English, History of the Language, and Chaucer courses (his one senior course was Old English that year and Chaucer the next), he kept in touch with M.H. Scargill at Alberta, who very much wanted such a job, and pressured Daniells to hire him. He insisted on a marker to help with his large courses. He continued his own very public activities, sharing a reading, for example, with American poet Theodore Roethke at the Vancouver Art Gallery—an occasion made possible by the fact that he had established close contact with Paul Engle who taught Creative Writing at the University of Washington where Roethke was visiting and the fact that his good friends the Shadbolts were in charge of many gallery activities. (Roethke—a big, blond, Swedish-looking man, whom Birney thought a "terrible" performer who did "a kind of shaggy bear dance"[13]—won the Pulitzer Prize two months after this visit.) He even took part in "a grotesque evening"—a spin-off from the free ticket to Montreal with Trans-Canada Airways that had resulted in his award-winning poem "North Star West" a couple of years before—when he sat at the head table of the Northwest Pacific Aviation Conference dinner in honour of "Mr. Helicopter." There he read his poem "to a puzzled mass of aircraft moguls and an impatient guest of honour who plainly wanted to get on to his own speech."[14] The next fall—having retrieved his Creative Writing course from both the young instructor and oblivion—he arranged a visit for W.H. Auden ("a fine poet...immensely knowledgable... A superior piece of fruit, but fruit none the less")[15] much like the Dylan Thomas visit and just as successful. During the summer—in which he peevishly settled down to complete his "abominable novel" "Summer Rebel"[16] (*Down the Long Table*)—Roy Daniells made the mistake of asking Birney to act as Head while he was giving lectures and readings in New Zealand. "I had fun exercising power," Birney impishly wrote Herman Singer, "...fired the departmental secretary and hired another from Paris, a honey; hired an American poet, Melvin La Follette...; hired Peter Marchant [from] Cambridge...bought new office furniture; chiselled a small scholarship out of certain Bookstore profits; and generally played hare-and-hounds in the general faculty paperchase."[17] Having accomplished most of his goals in the department within six months, Birney decided to remain aloof: "I will withdraw as much as I can from deptl. affairs to devote myself to what I want to do, which is to teach and to do my peculiar kind of research."[18]

More than ever, Birney felt that worst of all feelings for him: the feeling he was trapped. "Life is once more a round of fresh-man essays, sophomore essays, and mediaeval literature essays," he griped to Frank Wilcox. "However, I've only sixteen years to go to retirement."[19] He now felt captive to his image as Canada's "Soldier Poet" and decided he could not decline to edit and write an introduction for UBC's *Record of Service in the Second World War*, an account of UBC's work during the war years, and a list of those connected with UBC who served in the war.[20] And he felt captive to his public image as the author of mountaineering poems and other early work. When Frank Scott asked permission to include three of these ("Anglosaxon Street," 1942; "West Vancouver Ferry," 1940; "Eagle Island," 1941) in the collection of satiric Canadian poems he was co-editing with A.J.M. Smith (later published as *The Blasted Pine*[21]), Birney replied, "I'd rather you gave me the go-by entirely...or else consider more recent stuff."[22] He listed six more recent poems (published from 1946 to the present) and added a new one, "Mammorial Stunzas for Aimee Simple McFarcin"[23] (1959). Scott dropped "Eagle Island" and took "Mammorial Stunzas," "Anglosaxon Street,"

"Restricted Area" (1947) and "The Monarch of the Id" (1947).[24] Even *within* the genre of mountain poems Birney felt trapped. Nothing he had written since had yet drawn the attention of "David," a poem for which he received (and would continue to receive) countless fan letters[25] and many requests to read it. And, in the fall of 1954, it was included in the English curriculum for senior matriculation in Ontario (though it was taken off after a year because of a Catholic lobby against it as a poem advocating mercy-killing).[26] This sense that he had peaked too early was confirmed when "Bushed," unlike "The Hazel Bough" and "North Star West," failed to win one of the Borestone Mountain Poetry Awards (formerly the Poetry Society of America Awards), placing only among the top seventy finalists;[27] and *Trial of a City and Other Poems* did not win the award for best poetry book, though it was among the top ten finalists. He had the over- whelming sense that he was "growing gray in harness."[28]

The "harness" he most chafed against was domestic. Now that Bill was an adolescent, his activities and friends intruded more, especially by contrast to the previous year when he had been away at boarding school. There he had been unusually success- ful—academically (especially in math), athletically (playing cricket and riding horses) and socially. As for Esther, once she had Bill settled in school and the house in order, and once she had given the inevitable parties for much-missed friends, she felt free to take a job after Christmas as executive secretary for the Community Arts Council, which sometimes involved working nights to arrange such events as a visit from the National Ballet. The whole family resumed attendance at the Unitarian Church—a concession Earle had made a few years before when he realized that Bill knew nothing of Biblical tradition. The Unitarians' emphasis on ethical, social and political issues, as well as their interest in comparative religion, appealed to Esther and to Earle, who had had his fill of Christianity in childhood, and he gave the occasional talk for them. But he was far from happy in this structured family life. He felt tied down, smothered, imprisoned. And neglected: "I fear a vista of cold suppers,"[29] he wrote a friend when Esther began her job. And it was not long before he complained so much that Esther reduced her work to half-time (she went back to full-time on realizing that half-time merely meant doing the same work faster). Eventually, at his prodding, she quit: "now I'm taking her off salary [work] and putting her at free-lancing—an embroidery column for *Canadian Home Journal*," he asserted.[30] As for Esther, she unburdened her feelings to her friends. "I hope he never, never gets started on a novel again," she wrote Miriam Waddington. "I don't think my nerves would stand it!... Has given up smoking—almost, and has put on 15 pounds which suits him. He's the same mixture of a generous souled sensitive interesting man and a tartar to live with at times. However, I'm no longer the door mat I was and clamp down on too much temper and irritability."[31] Elsewhere she commented, "Earle remains Earle and we get along like a pair of old cats too tired to fight and becoming reconciled to the patchy fur and sour tempers that life has left us with."[32] He also complained relentlessly about Bill's decision to take up the tuba in the fall of 1954, a decision he blamed on Esther: "Our boy Bill was persuaded by his ever-hopeful mother to 'take orchestra' at High School. She, I suspect, dreamt of him playing first violin; I hoped he'd be given something small and soft like a flute. So he comes home with a ruddy big brass tuba, looking like the intestines of Chaucer's stede of brass. Practises every afternoon in the house; you can hear him all the way down to sea-level. And guess what his first tune is—Jingle Bells. On the Tooba. I now work in the office late late in the afternoon."[33]

Although the pressure to earn extra money was eased by the fact that the mortgage on the house (in Esther's name) was paid off in February 1954, and his total income for that year (not including Esther's $200 a month) was $7342.22,[34] Birney continued to accept "hackwork" in radio, TV, free-lance writing and consulting. He took valuable time away from his academic tasks and his novel, for example, to earn $200 for a 500-word descriptive piece (signed Earle Birney: Canadian Poet, Educator and Mountaineer) about Lake O'Hara for a Standard Oil Company travel guide. It began in a florid style he would have scoffed at in his days as editor of *CPM*: "Not on castle walls nor on the quilted farmlands and bridled lakes of older worlds falls this splendour. Here, tremulous with opal fire, the ceremony of dawn breathes down over summits older than story, over scars hewn by the endless besiegings of wind, of ice, of sun, and over battlements towered by the unimaginable power of the wrinkling globe itself."[35] The feeling that pennies must be saved and that poverty was just around the corner had become ingrained. And Esther's tendency to spend more than he would have irked him. Though his irritation and outbursts of temper might well have been traced to the impossible pressures he put on himself, Birney was convinced that they were caused by the expectations and demands of others.

This was especially true of the "cursed" novel "hanging around my neck like a mouldy albatross"[36] which he had never enjoyed writing and which he finished in its first draft just before resuming classes in the fall of 1954. The occasion was marked by an article in *The Ubyssey*, "Birney 'Browned Off' Over Writing Novels" in which Birney said that he was "glad to see the end of it."[37] He sent it off to Jack McClelland over Christmas and finished revisions on 28 March 1955. Birney had been acutely aware since beginning the novel that it was not good, and said so frequently. He was "not at all happy about the title."[38] He was even skeptical that McClelland & Stewart would publish it: "It's a heavy soggy mixed-up depressing novel which I doubt will get published," he admitted to John Wardroper.[39] This was a distinct possibility. According to Jack McClelland, the book was not up to company standards. "I had the policy of publishing authors, not books. And if they came up with a novel that we didn't think was the greatest thing that we'd ever seen in print and they really wanted it published, my attitude was to publish the bloody thing. I still think *Down the Long Table* should not have been published, but I didn't want ever to tell Earle that it was a piece of junk."[40] Birney also realized that U.S. publication was unlikely. "I'm pretty certain however, that whatever I do with it, it won't be taken by a New York publisher, for at least three reasons," he wrote his agent, Howard Moorepark, "it's too experimental in overall form (technique varying from chapter to chapter); it's too honest in its subject matter; and it's not well enough written from the standpoint of sheer lively dramatic writing."[41] Elsewhere he speculated, "Doubt if it will go—except locally.... Really, the book is a shambles." "It's lousy, though, in an undelousable sort of way, I'm afraid."[42] He felt that his creativity was exhausted, and that his domestic situation—possibly even Esther herself—was to blame. "I have fallen away in my ability to write in recent years," he concluded, "for reasons that, I think, have to do with domestic difficulties, which have been increasing."[43]

Once Birney sent off his novel in March, he took stock of a number of things. The fact that he tabulated his free-lance radio work to date suggests he was at least recognizing how overworked he had been, if not considering the possibility of reducing it: he had made more than one hundred radio appearances and done about thirty plays. He made a thorough list of the names and addresses of his ever-increasing correspondents—a staggering 1,200 names, many of which were couples—in seven countries.[44] He decided to forego the return trip to Europe he and Esther had carefully planned over the two years since they returned from France, and go instead to Mexico alone. According to Esther, it was his reading her diary that triggered the final separation. "I said, 'Earle, you had no right to read my diary, and I had a great need to express somewhere the anger and rejection that I experienced from you all the time, and I have a perfect right to put it into my diary and then I get rid of it that way.' But he said, 'No, I'm going.' And I kind of begged him to stay and said things could be different and all that stuff. But he left a couple of days later for Mexico."[45]

Because leaving Esther meant two households and greater expense (such as the car he bought her), and because he felt hard-done-by at UBC anyway, he wrote a four-page letter to the president of the university, Norman Lawrence (Larry) MacKenzie, whose service on the Massey commission and as one of the first Canada Council members made him sensitive to the needs of artists and a natural ally of Birney's, and asked for a raise. In his letter he exaggerated what he had accomplished on leave: most of another novel (true), three short stories (he wrote one), eight articles (he did six) and a dozen poems (no previous mention of these anywhere). He applied pressure by stating that the universities of Oregon and Washington had sounded him out for jobs (the result of his giving lectures through colleagues in both places within the previous two months). In conclusion, he compared himself to Daniells: "To be quite frank, I have for some time resented the fact that my salary is so far below that of Daniells…it is my understanding that Dr. Daniells' much lighter teaching load is, and rightly, his compensation for his extra duties.… though I have great respect for Dr. Daniells as a teacher and a scholar, I do not think that his record or reputation in these matters surpasses mine."[46] Two weeks later, Birney's salary leapt from $7,200 to $8,000, making him the highest paid senior member in the department of thirty-one professors and instructors by about $1,000, aside from Daniells, whose salary was somewhere between $8,000 and $8,500.[47]

None the less, since Birney had made no effort to keep up with Chaucerian scholarship, and had done no research or publishing in his academic field since 1942, he felt something of a fake when he learned that he had been elected a fellow of the Royal Society of Canada. With more than a hint of self-deprecation, he reported that he would go to Winnipeg in May—just before leaving for Mexico—to become, "a certified stuffed-shirt."[48]

After reaching Leonard and Reva's in San Miguel, Birney for once sat still. "I'm down here alone for part of the summer, resting after finishing my novel," he wrote his "Coz" Rosemary, who had just graduated in English from the University of Aberdeen, "out to this lovely mountain town to stay with artist-friends. Sun, frangipani blooms, cardinals in the pepper trees, lilies, fiestas, siestas & lots of plain sitting."[49] Birney fell in love with Mexico. According to Leonard Brooks, he adapted quickly to the leisured life, sitting happily on their patio simply turning his chair bit by bit to follow the sun and admiring their small green parrot "Pablo," or loping along the cobbled streets, endlessly curious about everything from local customs to the flora and fauna. In imitation of Reva, he bought himself a German Agfa camera and took up photography with such enthusiasm he returned with two hundred slides. And—once he recovered his strength—he felt free at last to behave as he wanted to: drinking the inexpensive liquor and having fun. "I think it is only a strong physical aversion of my stomach to more than a moderate amount of liquor which has saved me from becoming a local *borracho*," he admitted.[50]

"I took Earle to meet this beauty queen from Texas," Brooks recalled of a typical evening. "Reva was away in Mexico City. I thought Earle would like to meet her. She showed him the garden and he climbed up a tree—he was always climbing things—and he recited poetry. We left him there and went inside. Suddenly, he came running through the living room in his underwear, covered with mud, shouting, 'Where's the shower?' He had gone into a pool of what was practically sewage to cool off. 'Never mind,' I told the girl, 'He's just a Canadian poet.'" Birney's own account of this event at the time gives a good indication of his sense of release that summer. "Then there is the sexy blonde wife of a San Antonio oilman. Her husband, a lugubrious character who is allergic to drink (and perhaps to sexual intercourse?), spends most of his time, fortunately, back in Texas playing polo. Last week, during one of the polo-flights, I got happily drunk on tequila in her house, climbed a jacaranda tree, and went swimming alone in what I thought was her swimming pool but turned out to be an over-flow from the wash-house."[51] Brooks and Birney soon began "bachelor" jaunts together to local spots—like the busy little market town Pátzcuaro or the splendid sun-drenched beach at Manzanillo—which Birney later wrote about. While Birney took notes for his travel articles, Brooks would sketch or paint in the hope of providing illustrations. At night, they'd go into dingy sinister cantinas like those Lowry described in *Under the Volcano*. Birney later recalled one brush with death: "Once I came close to the real thing in a cantina in the brothel district of Morelia, when a drunken vaquero came in waving a pistol and looking for gringos, because his brother had just been shot wet backing across the Rio Grande."[52] "In those days, like most veterans who'd survived bombs, we thought we were invulnerable," Brooks recalls. "We'd go into these places and talk to local guys. We thought no one could push us around, but we were completely wrong. Once we were nearly shanghaied. Earle got into an argument which got pretty edgy. I got him by the scruff of the neck and said,

'Let's go!' He was drunk, but insisted on driving. I thought we'd
had it. He went around a curve in the mountain road and it was
only by a sheer second that we didn't go over. We were real
adventurers."[53]

Not only did Birney fall in love with Mexico, he fell in love
with Pauline Ivey, the daughter of the wealthiest of the Ivey
brothers of London, Ontario, who lived in a big apartment in
Mexico City. She had come there to be near her Aunt Ethel—a
violinist—and her Uncle Charles, who were friends of Leonard
and Reva's. "She was tall and willowy and fair-haired, a lovely
artless woman," Reva recalls. "She came from a very privileged
and wealthy background. She was lonely here. She wanted to be
in another ambiance, like the one she'd been raised in. She was
unattractive in a way, embarrassed, tentative, always a little awkward; and there was something craggy about her face. But she
was so generous and so good. She was the kind of woman Earle
used to get—orphan-like. He was not attractive as a man; he was
actually rather unattractive. But Pauline fell flat. She was overcome with joy that Earle would pay attention to her so
quickly."[54] Though Birney claimed he could never fall in love
with a girl simply because she was rich, Pauline's wealth was
important. "I can never marry again unless the girl's rich," he
wrote a friend later, in distress at the costs of living separately
from Esther, "Oddly enough, there is such a girl, but I'm not too
sure...."[55]

Courting Pauline did not prevent Birney from corresponding
at length with Elizabeth Cox while he was in Mexico. Bet had
written him a pathetic letter three years before, after hearing one
of his talks on CBC to say that "so much love can't be submerged
all the time." She was hurt to learn from others that he had been
in Toronto without calling her and reported that her marriage to
El left her miserable, since he treated her merely as cook, housekeeper and mother. She had, she wrote, been close to death more
than once. She had entirely stopped writing poetry. Birney, who
was trying to work things out with Esther then, had replied tenderly, but in a fatherly way, advising her to leave El and go back
to her job. "As for me," he told her in 1952, "I've effected a middle-aged compromise, live in reasonable happiness with my wife,

who is really a good woman, and have ceased to expect anything more sexually out of life; at my age, it doesn't matter so much." None the less, he added that he wanted her to write again.[56] He had not heard from her again until he visited the Neilsons on Bowen Island in October 1954. Because Einar, now a carpenter, had become rougher, more sardonic, and quite alcoholic, the friendship had waned and it was the first visit Earle had made there in two years. Now, Muriel, who was the island teacher, showed him a letter Elizabeth had sent her which asked after Earle and included photos of her two little daughters. "'The peery bonny tings,' as my Shetland aunt would say," Birney wrote Bet, adding, "it's better you should remember Lieben as it was." Her reply saddened him. El, who was gaining a national reputation as a sculptor, was completely absorbed by his art and indifferent to her: "he and I have very little emotional rapport now."[57] After that, she and Earle had continued a friendly, but desultory correspondence over the winter.

Now, in Mexico, he felt free to confide in her. On his fifty-first birthday, he sent her a maudlin letter filled with his sense of failure. *Maclean's* had turned down the serialization of his novel, a crushing blow, for he had expected to have the five thousand dollars they would have paid. He lamented the decline in his ability to write, and blamed this on troubles at home and the university responsibilities which had "got more intrusive." "My own [marriage] is on the rocks," he explained "for your private ear only" in his next letter. "The fault is mine, but I can't remedy it, and I had to get away to preserve my physical and psychic being. Esther is taking it very badly, and has apparently talked Bill out of writing me anymore." About a month later, Bet's own marriage went into crisis.

Earle was sympathetic, advised her to leave El, and offered her money. It is clear from her letters, despite an "awful doubt" that she might have failed with Earle the same way Esther had, that Bet still hoped he might marry her. But he backed off. "How I long to feed that 'famished spirit' [you write of]. But I cannot. My whole life is in a mess now, Bet, and I must not tangle any more people up in it, most of all you, the loveliest finest human being I have ever known."[58]

Birney turned instead to Pauline, to hours of letter-writing to his huge circle of friends and to his work. Before leaving Mexico, he gave a poetry reading (the first by a Canadian poet), arranged by Leonard and his friend Douglas Cole, the Canadian ambassador, under the auspices of the Anglo-Mexican Institute, an event that was covered in English and Spanish on the front pages of Mexico City newspapers.[59] And, with the image of Brooks's artistic and financial success on moving from Canada to Mexico in mind, as well as the fact that there was more popular interest in poetry there, he bought "a barren lot in a fly-haunted alley, for almost no money"[60] in San Miguel and engaged labourers to build a wall around it as the first step towards a permanent residence. Despite inevitable bouts of "the Aztec two-step," he intended to return as often as possible.[61]

Esther, meanwhile, had been taking a new direction in Montreal. To earn money, she had taken in a boarder, John Pearson, who, according to Birney, was "her boy-friend, who lives in the basement and whom she is 'curing' of homosexuality and alcoholism."[62]

Birney left Mexico earlier than he had planned because Frank Scott invited him to take part in The Canadian Writers' Conference financed by the Rockefeller Foundation at Queen's University in Kingston the last four days in July. There, among about a hundred literary people—poets, novelists, publishers, editors, critics, librarians—and members of the public, Birney took part in discussions on writing and the problems of reaching a public in Canada, subjects on which he had developed strong opinions because he was unusually sensitive to slights and easily felt excluded. As the conference demonstrated, it was impossible to determine the degree to which these opinions were idiosyncratic or justified, because his sense of being neglected was shared by fellow novelists and poets alike. "Canadian painting has arrived, is widely recognized, and is fostered by the state-supported National Gallery," Scott observed in an article on the conference for the *University of Toronto Quarterly*. "Canadian drama has its festivals and awards, and now the stimulus given by the annual Stratford performances. Music has also made important advances. Writing," Scott contended, "though equally entitled to attention, is largely ignored.

> Only two "little mags" exist in the entire country for experimental work, one university quarterly publishes and pays for short stories, but there does not exist in Canada a literary magazine of the type of *Partisan Review, Hudson Review* or the *Sewanee Review,* where a coterie of writers and critics maintain a constant watch for new talent and subject writers generally, both old and new, to an informed criticism. Indeed, it was remarked that criticism of Canadian literature scarcely exists at all; that few universities and schools give Canadian literature courses, and if they do are hard pressed to find copies of the books the students should read; that the Governor-General's Awards, though well-intended, are a somewhat hollow gesture since they carry no money prize and the recipient is expected to pay his own way to wherever they may happen to be given out each year. When to this we add...the plight of Canadian libraries, there being considerable areas of the country where the public has literally no access to books at all, and...figures as to the paucity of book-stores, the picture seemed inexcusably black.[63]

Since such subjects as average book sales (3,000 copies of Canadian novels, about three times the sales for British or U.S. authors) and the role of media, especially television, which had only within the last three years become widespread in Canada (generally encouraging to Canadian writers) were discussed by experts, the conference provided an important overview for Birney of the literary situation in Canada, as it did for other writers. It also gave him a chance to see friends and associates again: old friends like A.J.M. Smith and Dorothy Livesay; acquaintances like Morley Callaghan and Anne Wilkinson; professionals like Robert Weaver and John Gray; others such as his chairman, Roy Daniells, and his publisher, Jack McClelland; even former students, like Phyllis Webb and Norman Klenman.

On the social side of the conference (which he described as a "small amount of sleep and...large amount of rye"),[64] he continued his Mexican-style adventuring with his former students. Norman Klenman (who was leaving the NFB to write free-lance in Toronto) and his wife, Daphne, took him for a spin in their racy Sunbeam Talbot roadster: "it wasn't a pleasant experience," he wrote his son Bill, now fourteen, in one of the kindly, but awkward, letters he sent him that summer, "because the driver, who was taking some of us to a party, was somewhat drunk and was trying to show us that he could do 100 miles an hour; I was in the back seat, and the convertible top had got stuck half-way down, so my head was wrapped in canvas and bumping against the steel braces most of the time. The driver got so bad we forced him to stop and took the wheel away from him; but then we had more trouble because none of us had driven a Sunbeam Talbot and it takes some getting used to."[65] He also got himself into difficulties with Phyllis Webb, to whom he had continued to give affectionate professional advice and detailed criticism of the poems she sent him ever since she had been his student because he greatly admired her work. He had been especially pleased to learn the previous spring that she had dedicated her poem "Standing" to him.[66] Somehow he found himself involved at Kingston in a triangular situation with Phyllis and Frank Scott. "I'm sorry if my switch of bedrooms embarrassed or disappointed or shocked you," Phyllis wrote him right after the conference. And when Birney replied that Scott was "possessive," Phyllis wrote that it was she, not Scott, who was the possessive one, adding "now you know what my poems are all about."[67]

Right after the conference Birney went to Toronto, where he met with Jack McClelland to make last-minute changes to his book (Jack wanted to cut the newspaper columns, but Birney refused) and see other friends. This time he made confidential arrangements to meet Bet for lunch. He gave her a pair of abalone earrings and Mexican dolls for her two "pint-sized Bets." "Toronto is beautifully and sadly haunted," she wrote him after he left. "I shall never go through the Rosedale Station without a stab of memory, someday I shall go to the Wellesley station especially to sit on that trashcan for a moment. Darling!.... One lovely moment…when you came quietly stepping through that CBC door (as I have seen you step along a forest path) and turned to me with the smile I dream of."[68]

Before returning to Vancouver via Toronto—where he did a couple of radio quiz panels ("Court of Opinion" and "Now I Ask You") and two TV shows ("Fighting Words"), travelled overnight to Stratford with Bob and Rita Allen to see *Julius Caesar* and *A Merchant of Venice* and lunched again back in Toronto with Bet—Birney was off to Montreal for a week to arrange some short-wave travel talks to be broadcast in Spanish to Latin America by CBC International Services.[69] And he took a look at the Stephen Leacock papers, the first to do so since Leacock died eleven years earlier, waxing so excited at finding unpublished manuscripts and letters that, as if he had no other obligations, he planned to edit them.[70] But he had other reasons for the visit. "There is a girl here, and she has a car and a cottage on a lake up in the Laurentians," he wrote Herman Singer.[71]

On his way back to the Vancouver apartment he arranged to share with architect Bill Tassie, Birney spent four hours in the airport "trying to talk sensibly to my estranged wife and son."[72] "Young Bill is more reconciled now to the separation, but Esther [who had changed jobs and was a social worker at the provincial Tuberculosis Hospital] is still begging me to come back," he reported to Herman. "I find it highly expensive to stay separate, but highly peaceful, by contrast, too. What will come of it all I don't know. At the moment I feel somewhat depressed."[73]

But what depressed Birney most on his return to Vancouver was not his separation, but the reception of *Down the Long Table* which was dedicated "To Leonard and Reva" and published on 15 October. He was already annoyed that McClelland & Stewart had changed his title "Summer Rebel" because it was "too sexy and too summery."[74] Had critics welcomed it enthusiastically, he would have been in high spirits, especially since he had now entered into a prolific and passionate correspondence with Pauline in whom he was investing his future emotional security. And he was well able to fill his time. He showed his Mexican slides to 125 people, in small groups, that fall and threw himself into the stage reading–production of "The Damnation of

Vancouver," in which he read the part of Gabriel Powers, whose "Joycean double-talk" he had intended to stand for "the sinister judgement the future may pass on us."[75] ("We had a packed house & a good one, and it was fun—but a lot of work. I am not cut out for acting, but I love the atmosphere of theatre.")[76]

But despite his continous assertions that his novel was not very good over the three years he took to write it, he was indignant at his treatment by reviewers. Though the book appeared at the ideal time for Christmas sales, it was not reviewed widely until the new year. "Only four so far," he wrote on 2 December, "two favorable (*Ottawa Journal, Tor[onto] Star*), one so-so (*Montreal Gazette* [which termed it, to Birney's chagrin, "the apologia of an egghead"]), one panning (James Scott, in a syndicated column I saw in *Victoria Times*). Local reviewers silent, except a columnist, Mamie Moloney, who likes it.... Sales are O.K. but not spectacular."[77] Even the strictly political review in *The Workers' Vanguard* by Ross Dowson, the Canadian Trotskyist who was later to initiate the revolutionary League for Socialist Action, condemned the book: "Anyone around the movement those days will recognize...many of the main characters... Birney moves from superficial appearances, misunderstandings, to distortions, to monstrous and malicious caricatures. Jack MacDonald, pioneer organizer, Maurice Spector, leading theoretician of the Marxist movement of those days, along with a host of lesser figures, are presented as melancholy partisans of a lost cause, cynical self-seekers, egomaniacs, neurotics and psychopaths. The only truth...is the picture of the dilettante world of the petty bourgeois student, Gordon Saunders, the half-world of the campus, the twilight world of the professor lost in study of mediaeval literature."[78] He learned from Howard Moorepark that E.P. Dutton and Harcourt Brace had both turned it down, which meant American publication was remote. And Margaret Crosland and her husband, who had been trying unsuccessfully since he left England at the end of 1953 to place *Turvey* in England again, had no better luck there. Birney knew that his huge network of friends and associates were primed to assist in any way they could. "Hurry up and finish the novel, Earle," Norman Klenman, who had just filmed an excerpt from Hugh

MacLennan's *Each Man's Son* prodded him the previous February. "Maybe we'll get the NFB into a sensible line of work, and film at least a piece of you. *Turvey* was on the consideration list last year, but the dolts were genuinely frightened of doing anything humourous, human or lusty."[79] But what good were such offers when the novel itself had been declined for serialization and did not excite reviewers?

The combination of depression about his novel, financial worries and a general sense of being "bogged down" in his work made Birney more receptive to Esther's pleas. "What is the way out of this impasse?" he wrote in a long, rambling letter to her in October. "I was *not* happy living with you, my health was going to pot, bodily and mentally. I don't have the belief that you have changed that much…in the ways that…led to unhappiness between us, anymore than I believe that *I* have changed in my fundamental attitudes. To go back and live with you would be to give up all the health and peace and wholeness I have gained in the last few months.

"But my dear, so much of the present problem stems from the fact that you are working, working long hours. *This you don't need to do.* Why do you say you 'worry ceaselessly about money'? We have agreed, I thought, on money. You have enough [$225 a month] and you know you will always get more from me when you need it, for yourself and for Bill…. You are working because you want to, because you want extra money, presumably to go to England or somewhere…. All these months have been for me sad too, and lonely; but I too have been determined to have the courage to be, at last, the person I am, not what you wanted me to be and I couldn't be. For one thing, I must, must be honest, emotionally as well as intellectually honest, with you, with everybody…. I have been happier, healthier, more energetic, younger-feeling, more able to work, since I have been alone than I have been for years before…. You made me feel that I was a tyrannical and unjust and unloving father and husband, even when I was trying my best to be otherwise. You watched my every move, recorded them, often judging me wrongly and unjustly, and you talked about me behind my back, to Bill, to Lorna, to the ever-present psychiatrist…. Love isn't enough; two people so different can't be made over in the likeness of each other. You are strong-willed and managing, and so am I, and we pull against each other. Moreover we are poles apart in our attitudes to sex, in our very approach to it. Do you really think you and I can live a life of peace, dignity, and self-respect, with all this between us?

"Something else I must face up to, in myself, is that I am tired to death of money problems. All my life I have wanted to be an artist, a writer, and I have been frustrated at every turn, and still am, by having to earn a living so arduously that I can't do the real things I can do, that are more important to me and, I think, to others. Quite bluntly, I need a wife who has money, some money, enough to help me get quit of a university and just write. Yes, even at my age. I certainly won't marry a woman for her money, but I won't marry one who hasn't any.... O, Esther I know all this is terrible. You know I care. You know the twenty years means so much to me too. Maybe there *is* a way back... Give me more time. Give me till the New Year. There's no point at all in forcing back into the home a captive father, is there?"[80]

In December, Pauline arrived in Vancouver to see him, en route to Toronto to spend Christmas with her parents. According to Esther, "he phoned and said that Reva Brooks' friend, Pauline Ivey, was coming to town, and Reva had said so many nice things about me that she was very anxious to meet me. Could he bring her over the next day?"

> I'm very fond of Reva, and I said, "Well, okay." And so this nice woman, gentle, blonde, tall, slim, quite nice-looking, well-dressed, about 30, came with him and we chatted a bit about Mexico. And then they left. I thought she was leaving the next day to go east to her family. After he'd left the house with Pauline, he came running back and said Pauline and he were giving a cocktail party that night and would I come? And I said, "No, thank you. I'm not standing by as a guest when I've been the hostess." For a poet, Earle had so little understanding about the way people could feel. So he left, and I didn't see Pauline Ivey again. But Bill came down. He would have been about fourteen then.

He was either around and met them, or heard what was going on, and he came in to me and said, "That girl is his girlfriend." And I said to him, "Don't be silly. She's a friend of Reva's who wanted to meet me." But I did pretty soon learn that she had come to Vancouver to arrange for her marriage to Earle.[81]

Earle and Pauline had become engaged. "My darling, Back to letters again!" wrote Pauline on reaching her family home in London. "And back in the old familiar surroundings of London again, I have to sit down quietly, feel the ring and see your picture to convince myself that it wasn't all just a dream."[82] "Darling…I am only the empty shell, the husk, the hollow tin can of a man; the contents went away on the plane with you. And I am sad, and very much alone," he was writing to her at the same moment.[83] "There was a poignant moment when I picked up the kitchen gloves by the stove and smelled a wisp of your perfume still clinging to one of them somehow," he wrote in his next letter, "your presence is still everywhere in the flat, the office, and in my heart."[84]

Birney continued to feel responsible for Esther and Bill, especially for those jobs he knew neither of them could handle. In mid-November, for example, he was at the house helping with the garden, which had "gone to pot when I left," spreading compost over the flower beds in preparation for winter. And in response to a frightened call from Esther, he hurried over to help her cope with John Pearson who "went off the cure… I got food into him (he's been on a 10-day vino bat) & got him to sleep, but I'm afraid I've got to get him into the psychiatric vet's ward."

Finally, Christmas—that notoriously emotional season—weakened his resolve. "When I read your letter this morning I wept," he wrote Esther two days before the holiday. "I felt so deeply your love for me, and your patience and forgiveness…. I would like very much to have breakfast and present-opening with you both…. And I want to go to church with you and hear Bill read the lesson." By 30 December, he had virtually succumbed, self-indulgently musing at great length—and with many inconsistencies—upon his own perplexing nature. "Certain things in myself

I should be happy to change; I *want* to be far more tolerant, patient, and good-humoured and outgoing than I often am. My failures in these regards I certainly can lessen, and must, though some of my frettings and fussings undoubtedly stem from over-burdens of responsibility and work, and fluctuate with my general health.... I do not have, so far as I know, a general reputation for being intolerant and bad-humored, though I don't think anybody would single me out as an model of patience in any way.... I get on best with people who do not expect any-thing very much from me, don't make demands, who accept me as I am, who give me the freedom to go my own way that I am always willing to give others.... I am more at ease with quiet, even unaggressive people, not because I want to dominate them but because they give me a sense of relaxation and of being free.

"This word 'free' keeps popping up. Is it an obsession with me? In some ways, yes. I am a writer. This is a fixture in my tempera-ment. It makes me want to roam, to experience, to be alone often, to be unencumbered by worries so that I can summon the energy for artistic concentration. It makes me drive myself to hoard up time and money so that I can get away from and free of my job long enough to create something. Now none of this is very rational, especially in someone who is plainly not of the first rank as a writer. But it seems that most of the first-rankers are so much more hag-ridden by their daemons than I am that they practically destroy themselves and others. So at least there are compensations all around for being only half an artist, so long as the other half can earn a living and keep the artist-half within the bounds of health and sanity. But what I'm getting at is that this half-artist in me I won't give up; and when you try to change cer-tain things in me you run up against the terrific unconscious resistance of that half. I don't want to equate art with sexual infi-delity, but in me there must be a connection somewhere. There is some deeply rooted thing in me that not only desires other women's bodies, but that makes me spill over with very genuine feelings of tenderness and affection for more than one woman. I don't even think this means that I love my wife less; I don't think there is just a fixed quantity of love in a human system; I think loving is also a philosophy and a kind of substitute art. In the fourteen long years of my first bachelorhood, though I was often very starved sexually, I went to prostitutes on only three occasions, and I could never conceivably go to one again, nor to any woman with whom there could not be some kind of love-relation. I must agree with you that sexual fidelity makes for a far more stable and happy marriage, and that the other thing brings risks and deceptions and all sorts of unpleasant things…yet I cannot really in my heart believe that my relations with several women we could both name have been a bad thing. On the contrary, I know full well that I brought genuine love to those women which is still with them and which they draw some strength from to this day.… I brought you a sense of insecurity, perhaps, but my feeling is that you already had this, and that you created it unnecessarily in yourself because you wanted my love of you to be a possession which excluded other loves.… There was really nothing wrong with [our physical relationship], except that I subconsciously resented the sexual act with you because you had made me feel that there was a 'price' for it, the price of sexual fidelity which, however hard I tried to pay it, I simply could not.… Frankness is essential. Lack of it destroys me, because when I can't be frank without hurting, I deceive in order not to hurt, and then I hurt and despise myself, and quarrel with you out of resentment because you have made me deceitful!

"[As for Bill], I feel very much now, as you have felt all along of course, that he needs more of me than he gets. Of course, when I was at home, my life is [sic] so crowded that I am not at all a normal satisfactory father in the amount of time I can devote to him. Here again, the artist problem comes up—especially the artist who cannot support himself by his art. I live two complete lives and put out as much energy and thought and time on them as a lot of men do on one life. Yet I *must* do this; in my nature, this comes before anything else.… when I was in the depths of unhappiness about our marriage, I kept saying: stick it until Bill is sixteen. Then came the frightening symptoms of collapse, and I knew I must run away, get out, or I would be physically and mentally wrecked.

"Let us say," he proposed, despite the fact that he had claimed "if I return, it will be as a prisoner"[85] and had warned Esther clearly that he could not and would not change, "[that] we will both make every effort in our power to make the next two years into a happy marriage for Bill and for us. If we succeed, naturally, we would have no desire to part at the end of that time."[86] For Esther, however, the Trotskyist ideology of non-ownership which had been the basis of their marriage was worn thin. "I only learned later," she would write, "that Lenin and Trotsky were against promiscuity and that it was a vulgarization of their views to treat sexual need as one did the thirst for a glass of water."[87]

Within days, Birney had moved back home, where Bill had exchanged his tuba for the supposedly quieter bassoon. "I have heavy news for you," he wrote Pauline, now back in San Miguel. "I have agreed to go back home, to try again, at least on a temporary basis. The first, most urgent thing I want to say, is—don't desert me, my dearest, don't stop loving me, don't cut me off from you. I could not bear it, I couldn't go through with it if you did. I have gone back, though it is you I love with all my soul and in all my bones, because I cannot stand to see the consequences of my own act of leaving them. Bill, especially.... He is frightened and miserable, because, if I don't come back, Esther is going to sell the house, which represents the last bit of physical stability for him."[88] Magnanimously, Pauline politely replied, "Somehow I guess that I have known all along that it wouldn't be possible for me either to seek happiness for myself at the expense of wrecking two other lives nor would it be any use to have you with me only to see you tormenting yourself."[89] From his office—without telling Esther—Birney continued almost daily letters to Pauline in Mexico; his weekly letters to Bet ("God, I wish I could live with you in Mexico!"),[90] occasional letters to Gaby Baldwin, Margaret Parker and Phyllis Webb and even once—as a result of coming across an old postcard of hers from their wartime trysts—a letter to Carlotta Makins which went, "you are as fresh and living in my memory as on the last day that I saw you."[91] By May he wrote to Phyllis Webb, "Things are immensely better. I don't regret leaving, nor coming back either, as the results on Bill alone [who was heading his class with straight "A"s] have been very salutary."[92]

Now he took out his frustrations professionally, in vehement letters to the papers that had ignored *Down the Long Table*. "The editorial policy of your paper in regard to book-reviews stinks," he exploded to *The Vancouver Province*, "my novel was sent to your paper in *early November*, in plenty of time to be listed, at least, for the Xmas book-trade, the only open season on books in Canada. The *Toronto Star* was able to review it by Nov. 12; long before December, the *Ottawa Journal* featured it as the best English-Canadian novel of 1955 (along with novels by Gabrielle Roy and Roger Lemelin).[93] The local *Sun* and *News-Herald* have reviewed it long ago."[94] To the publisher of *The Globe and Mail*, H.G. Kimber, he expostulated, "your book-review editor [Bill Deacon] does not consider my novel among the 125 books worth reviewing in the course of his year's labours…. [yours will remain] one of the most parochial and disorganized and trivial book-pages in Canada so long as you keep your present book-editor."[95] He was especially miffed that Robertson Davies did not review the novel in *Saturday Night*: "I don't mind being slammed so much as being ignored or boycotted, which is what both *Sat[urday] Night* & *The Globe & Mail*, to mention only two, have done to the book."[96] Even his friends were unsure: though Ethel Wilson, Clyde Gilmour and E.J. Pratt enjoyed it, Claude Bissell and Desmond Pacey did not.[97] And not one reader recognized his clever structure, a sure sign it had failed: "I tried to arrange a sequence of techniques from sect[ion] one to 18," he laboriously explained to André Sacriste. "18-19-20 are a pivot, and the book then repeats the techniques in a reverse order—to get an over-all double spectrum—as if you started with blue and went through to red, then red and back through to blue…. This sounds horribly involved and calculated, but in practice it was simply a guiding format, dictated by the Senatorial framework and the swinging of the book in the centre around the freight-train episodes."[98]

Not surprisingly, *Down the Long Table* was not taken up by either British or American publishers, despite a fawning letter from Birney to J.B. Priestley (whom he had hosted at UBC in the spring of 1956), asking him to refer the novel to his British agent.[99] He failed to locate a French translation, despite the fact that his friend André Sacriste translated the book and had an "in" with Galliard.[100] Nor did it win any awards. Birney had no intention of trying to write another novel; he wanted to turn instead to the stage play in verse he'd had in mind since "The Damnation of Vancouver," more plays for the exciting and powerful new medium of television and, for the first time since he was hired at UBC a decade before, some scholarly writing. "I intend to concentrate on some critical-literary and academic work for a while and by next May I should be in shape to spout," he wrote Brian Elliott in Australia, where he hoped to go some day.[101] "I don't expect to try the novel form again," he stated bluntly to Bet.[102]

Fast though he could move, Birney felt the hot breath of the next generation of Canadian poets at the back of his neck. He continued to give each new crop of Creative Writing students whatever help he could: in 1955, for example, his efforts resulted in the publication of a poem by Lorna Cameron; a story in *Maclean's* by Heather Spears (who would go on to publish extensively),[103] and the appearance of Ivan De Faveri's story "Maurice" in *The Canadian Forum*.[104] Meanwhile, a new group of poets—some his former students—were basking in the literary limelight. "Phyll Webb is hugely thought of in Montreal," he wrote early in 1954.[105] When he read her "Skywriter" and Jay Macpherson's "Cold Stone" and "Ordinary People in the Last Days," in Seattle[106] in early March 1955, among works by other poets (Scott, Klein, Smith, Anderson, Page, Reaney, Waddington, Wilkinson, Dudek and, of course, himself), Theodore Roethke and others singled out Webb and Macpherson as the best. I prefer Macpherson and Webb, like Roethke, Birney was soon claiming.[107] He asked Jay Macpherson (to whom he had awarded second prize—out of eighty-five entries—in a Toronto Varsity poetry contest in 1954) to send him *Nineteen Poems* and *O Earth Return* for his reading in Mexico.[108] "Seems to me," he wrote Miriam Waddington, whose "Lovers" and "Erosion" he had read to audiences in Seattle and Oregon, "the women are the Hope of Can[adian] Poetry in the Fifties. (You can infer that I don't share some regional enthusiasm for the Laytonesque.")[109]

This, too, was the theory he put to two young poets who had

written him in 1955. "I wouldn't be surprised if Jay Macpherson and Phyllis Webb turned out to be the best Canadian poets yet." The young men addressed him in a manner completely unlike anything he'd seen before. They were neither stiff and formal like many of Birney's contemporaries, nor tough-talking buddies like others, nor playfully respectful like his former students. Admitting that they were drinking wine, these men wrote with a forthrightness that bordered on playful insolence. "[We] think you are the greatest poet in Canada today. Better than Pratt, A.J.M. Smith, Klein, etc., and almost as good as Birney," they wrote. "[Y]ou will never be known outside the confines of Canada, at least I don't think so," wrote the more dominant of the two, who explained he was a thirty-six-year-old poet who expected to become famous some day. "[A] book has to be published outside of Canada in order to receive critical acclaim. It would seem we are still a colony therefore. I regard [it] as a special tragedy that such poems of yours as 'David,' 'Slug in Woods,' 'Vancouver Lights,' 'Mappemounde,' 'Reverse on the Coast Range' and others should not be known and acclaimed as the very best.... The world will lose much richness because it knows not Birney.... [Y]our later stuff is just ordinary.... *Trial of a City* was uninteresting to me.... The tragedy is that you could still write great poetry under certain conditions and locale."[110]

The sender's name—which Birney and the rest of Canada would see long into the future—was Al Purdy.[111]

Though this letter, and much else, confirmed Birney's sense that he was a failure, he was successful in thwarting his department's attempt to terminate his Creative Writing program. Through the Fine Arts Summer School, he was able to expand it by initiating three workshops (drama, poetry and fiction) for the 1956 summer session. Ultimately, he hoped to incorporate these as courses in the winter sessions of the English Department: "we are planning an actual Major in Creative Writing," he wrote Lister Sinclair behind the scenes, "a sort of sub-department—and that's why I raise the possibility [of a permanent position] with you.... We would have the only real school of it in Canada... Mind you, there are still plenty of die-hards in my dept. who aren't happy about what's happening."[112]

Come summer, Birney was off again to Mexico, but this time he sped south with Esther in their new Chevrolet, stopping en route in Washington to see the Woodcocks (Earle had success-fully recommended George for a position in the English Department at the University of Washington), in San Francisco to see Hendrie and Barb Gartshore, and in Los Angeles to pick up Frank Wilcox, who joined them for most of the trip. They had rented their house (complete with John Pearson) to Toronto professor Ken McNaught and his wife, and left Bill behind with his friend Chris Eades for a time, after which Bill would go to the Lucky Strike Ranch on Bridge Lake for the summer.

This time Birney would do things right. He had audited Dr. Paul Arriola's Spanish class all year at UBC. He would include Esther, and he would only commit himself to short weekly travel columns for *The Vancouver Province* ("getting down to the bot-tom of my own literary barrel")[113] and an adaptation of Langland's *Piers Plowman* for Robert Weaver's CBC radio series, "Wednesday Night."[114]

In the first week, he worked on his articles ("grinding out some corn").[115] But soon he was off with Leonard for a four-day "bachelor holiday" over the mountains to a raunchy port near Vera Cruz.[116]

Hardly had he got back when he heard that Bill had been involved in an accident that had eerie echoes of "David." "Bill and Chris went on a hike alone together in the wild woods near Vancouver," he later wrote André Sacriste, "they were qualifying for their First Class Scout badge, which necessitated their living 'on their own' in the woods for 48 hours. On the afternoon of the first day, Chris struck his head on a rock and fractured his skull. Bill had to leave him (he was unconscious) after giving first aid, and go three miles through the forest looking for help. Fortunately he came across two men fishing and brought them back. The two men carried Chris a half-mile to an open spot where a helicopter could land; then one of the men went to find a phone and summon the air-rescue squad, while Bill and the other man stayed by Chris all through the night. The helicopter took Chris off at dawn, and Bill then had to tramp ten miles back to the highway and home. He was unharmed and has come through the experience well, and the local newspapers of course have played him up as a 'hero'. [In fact, Bill was flown to Ottawa later and awarded a medal by the Governor General "for meritorious conduct for aiding critically injured Patrol Leader Christopher Eades after Eades had fallen 35 feet during a Scout test hike."][117] We are very glad he remained cool and did what he could, but we have been in great anxiety about Chris, who lay unconscious for another fifteen days, and had developed a head infection.... he is slowly regaining his powers of speech and memory and the doctors expect a full recovery."[118] Birney took offence at *The Vancouver Province* account of the rescue, which drew parallels with "David," as if his poem had been autobiographical. "The only permanent sufferer," he commented after Chris recovered, "is the reputation of my poem."[119]

Once Bill was at the ranch, Earle, Esther and the witty Frank Wilcox drove about, seeing local towns with their fiestas and museums and craft markets, visiting spots from Lowry's *Under the Volcano*, climbing the ancient pyramids of the Zapotecs, swimming the same day in the warm Pacific at Salina Cruz on one side of the isthmus and in the Atlantic at Vera Cruz on the other.[120]

But on their return to San Miguel, their happy companionship was suddenly shattered. Esther found out about Pauline Ivey. After a terrible show-down, she took flight by train back to Vancouver.

In a panic, Earle responded see-saw fashion as he had in the past. When *he* wanted to leave, Esther wanted him to stay; but when *Esther* left, he begged her to return. "I am continuing to plead with her not to separate," he wrote John Pearson, who was trying to console Esther at home. "I offered at the last, in San Miguel, not to see the lady in Mexico at all, and to become a single minded husband at last. I think I can be this to her, and I want to be. And I am most anxious that we keep together...at least till Bill no longer needs a unified home. But Esther seems to have lost all heart for the marriage, to want independence, and especially freedom from having to live with me. I don't blame her... Esther wants me to leave my home, set up as a bachelor again...sell the house and buy [her] a smaller one."[121]

"She is not a well girl, [and] talks a great deal about some operation and that she hopes she will not pull through it, etc.," Pearson replied. "[S]he wants a real home and a real family life— not just to be a cook and housewife.... You may never find anyone as warm and vital and intelligent as Esther."[122]

But Birney stayed on with Pauline, working away at the Brooks' and teaching the first class (fifteen students, mainly American) on the writing of poetry at the Art Institute. Before leaving, he shared a poetry reading of English-Canadian works at the Instituto with a Spanish doctor who read Lorca and modern Mexican poetry in Spanish. They sold out the hall's hundred seats at a dollar each, and donated the money to the Children's Library.[123] "I left Mexico, with enormous reluctance, on August 15," he wrote Frank Wilcox, whom he asked for advice about how to use the hallucinogenic peyote he had brought back from Mexico. "I had promised Bill to pick him up on the 25th at his Bridge Lake ranch and get him down to Vancouver in time to absorb the Pacific National Exposition before school overtook him.... but it was a long dull trip. Except for the first few days, when Pauline was with me. We drove up through Aguascalientes (where we chanced into the liveliest fiesta I've ever seen) and Zacatecas, a wonderful crumbling old mining town, and up to Juarez. On its outskirts, I very nearly lost Pauline to the police. She, being a Mexican citizen, had planned not to cross the border but to take the plane back at the Juarez airport. However, the border is now a defence-in-depth, and the airport lies north of the visa-line, which we had innocently crossed without knowing it. She was suspended in official limbo unable to go forward, and I unable to drive her back (since my Mexican visa had simultaneously been taken away from me irrevocably). As you will have guessed, the bureaucratic knot was severed only by the edges of several peso notes. She got to the airport, and I to the Caribou, via Colorado, New Mexico (Taos, an over-rated tourist trap if ever I saw one), the Grand Tetons, the Grand Coulee Dam, the Grand Thompson Canyon, etc.

"It was a sad and tender parting with Pauline, believe me. Knowing that there was an amorous Frenchman determined to marry her if I didn't, and having decided I was already married for life, I kissed her and her riches good-bye with dramatic finality. In a letter I got last week she tells me she has already announced her engagement to her family, and plans to take the fortunate Frenchman on a two-year honeymoon in Europe."[124]

Sad though Birney was, he had, as usual, another iron in the fire. Don Harron, a Canadian war veteran who was now a scriptwriter and actor, had written him in San Miguel to propose turning *Turvey* into a musical comedy and had reported that he had convinced Mavor Moore, now head of Canadian Players, to put it on in Toronto after Christmas. At the very thought of all the money such a show could bring him, Birney was flying high. "I am keeping my fingers crossed.... *Turvey* may be taken on a tour of Canada by a professional company," he wrote excitedly in October, "and even perhaps to the U.S. and Broadway. There are two Broadway producers nibbling at the bait, and a Hollywood agent..."[125]

❧ 22 ❧

CIRCUMFLUENCE

The Earle Birney one person knew was not the Earle Birney known to another. He had mixed in three different countries with many types: from burly construction workers to effete Zeta Psi fraternity brothers. He numbered among his many friends academics and carpenters, diplomats and truck drivers, poets and politicians. He was as comfortable with students in their twenties as with the senior statesmen of universities, and as easy with Jews as with Japanese.

Though his main study had been Chaucer, his minor was in Linguistics and Philological Studies. His facility with Old and Middle English was so ingrained that he often quipped in phrases or lines from early literary works. He had briefly flirted with scholarship in this secondary field in 1954 with a paper for the Canadian Linguistic Association in early June on the techniques of indicating levels of spoken "Canadian,"[1] and toyed for a time with the preparation of a dictionary of Canadian English.[2]

Most of his readers were unaware that "David" owed much to the technique of Anglo-Saxon poetry, even though other poems at the time—notably "Anglosaxon Street" and "War Winter"— drew attention to his experimentation with such models. *Turvey's* success stemmed in large part from the humorous juxtaposition

of dialects —from "Canajun" to cockney—which Birney per-
fected through the interviewing notes he had meticulously
recorded as a personnel selection officer, and through reading his
manuscript aloud to Esther, the Neilsons, Bet and his "AA"
groups. Several reviewers noted especially his adenoidal character,
Clarence, the Night Orderly, who said such things as "You godda
rest that aggle."[3] Behind *Turvey* lay such stories as "The Levin
Bolt" (1944)[4] in which a French whore says "serty" for "thirty,"
and a Scottish sailor remarks, "Jerry doesna forrget us." And after
Turvey, Down the Long Table elicited praise from some reviewers
for its display of dialect: "phonetic vernacular," wrote one, "[is]
reported with a scholarly precision that would have done credit to
Professor Higgins himself...."[5] Birney's gift for gab made him an
excellent adapter of stories into radio plays. But it was partly
because of his scholarly facility with dialects in "The Damnation
of Vancouver"—from William Langland's to the Salish Chief's—
that the play was too cerebral for most listeners, a *tour de force*
that was better read than heard or seen. Since 1946, when he had
pleaded with poets in his speech to the CAA to become wandering minstrels, renting halls and reading aloud so the great "oral
tradition" would engage the masses, he had been an exacting
critic at the readings of others at UBC and elsewhere. He was as
keenly disappointed with Auden's performance as he was ecstatic
about Dylan Thomas's. Though, unlike his friend Lister Sinclair,
he had a flat voice unsuited to radio or acting, he took note of
what worked and began honing his stage skills for the future.

Birney's talent for turns of speech had long served him well.
Through it he had overcome the pain of unpopularity at school,
where his Banff classmates had scoffed at the sissified politeness
his socially ambitious mother demanded at home. To fit in, he
had learned, you mimic the coarse stories of survey gangs, the
twenties' slang of classmates, the jargon of military psychiatrists
or the pompous phrases of academe.

Though different styles are generally understood to be appropriate for different occasions, Birney had raised linguistic adaptation to an art, positioning himself readily—at times with careful
deliberation—to communicate with others. Like an ever-shifting
kaleidoscope, he assumed an astonishing range of vocabularies

and speech patterns to accommodate an ever-increasing circle of contacts who helped him get what he wanted or cushioned him against any possibility of agonizing exclusion. For those who did exclude him, he had other linguistic strategies: though his love letters were suffused with sentimentality, those he fired off to his critics were searing; and to Roy Daniells, the friend he felt betrayed him, he was icily insinuating.

Within the span of a year, he could write as if he were a plethora of personalities. To his old friend E.J. Pratt, who had heart trouble, he could write affectionately:

> My dear Ned,
>   Yesterday I heard from Dudek that you were ill "with a serious heart attack." I hope to God it is not "serious" and that you are already well on the way to recovery. Esther and I are deeply concerned and anxious for news. Please don't try to write yourself but perhaps Vi could find a moment to send us a postcard. You are very dear to us, as you are to all who know you, Ned, and we don't want anything to happen to you. Get well soon, and take our love and our concern, meanwhile. And to Vi and to Claire.[6]

Or he could joust as a ribald fellow-poet with Irving Layton, with whom he had made peace:

> Epitaph for any Canadian Writer
>
> He tried to lay the world
> but the bitch said "mañana"
> Content to let him masturbate
> Some more Canadiana.[7]

And, with paternal concern, he could placate Phyllis Webb, who was upset at his views on capital punishment:

> Phyl dear,
>   I'd no intention of angering you, and I'm most sorry

it happened. I intended to provoke you to argument, to giving me your thoughts, since you had obviously been doing some thinking on the subject. As for me, I don't really think it's a simple problem, mainly because I, personally, would prefer to be executed than to be kept forever in jail or, alternately, to be remade into some psychiatrist's image...[8]

When he approached those he looked up to, such as Lionel Trilling, Tyrone Guthrie or Stephen Spender, he was obsequious. To Edmund Blunden, the English poet, now Chairman of English at Hong Kong University, he wrote:

Dear Professor Blunden,
I am ashamed not to have expressed to you earlier my delight at receiving your book with the manuscript poem included. Your *Poems of Many Years* will be one of my treasured books for as many years as I may have.[9]

Sometimes he lapsed into strict military address, as in this letter to Prime Minister John Diefenbaker:

Dear Mr. Prime Minister,
I feel that I must call to your attention, sir, and appeal for your aid in correcting, an unjust refusal of the Passport Office to grant a passport to my wife...
If this had happened in the years of the previous government, sir, I would have put it down to the arrogance and indifference of a regime too long in office. That it is happening today, that a Canadian citizen and wife of a native Canadian, can be suddenly deprived of one of the rights of her citizenship for reasons that have to do only with red-tape, I can explain only by the assumption that you, sir, and your government, are unaware of the dilatory and arbitrary habits which the present Passport Office seems to have inherited from its past...

I am, dear Mr. Prime Minister, yours

Sincerely,
Earle Birney, Ph.D., F.R.S.C.[10]

At other times, he regressed into the verbal sparring of his frater-
nity days, with friends like Bruce Macdonald, now Commercial
Counsellor at the Canadian High Commission in New Delhi,
India, with whom he was plotting a visit in 1958:

> Bruce,
> Are you serious about this? Cards up, man, because
> I am thinking of blowing my accumulated royalties…
> on a ticket.…
> The BIG Question is how in hell to finance it with-
> out feeling I am being an utter heel in relation to
> Esther and Bill.… However, I may get a fair propor-
> tion of my salary from UBC…how much, depends on
> how good a sales-talk I can put up to Larry
> MacKenzie, who might increase the proportion if he
> feels my Indian Summer has some tie-up with UBC
> prestige. So I need badly some shred of evidence that
> some Indian university is ready to invite me to give a
> lecture or two on Canadian literature.…
> So what say, Brucey? I'm getting steamed up about
> coming. It would be wonderful to sweat out the sum-
> mer with you.… By gad, this is calling your bluff.[11]

He could be a model of manners—often echoing Esther's
English accent and phraseology—as he was with Miss Beatrice
White, the British mediaevalist at Westfield College in London
and editor of *YWES*, from whom he obtained the crucial reference that gave him a Nuffield Fellowship in 1958:

> Dear Miss White,
> You will think it extraordinary that I never replied
> to your kind letter and lunch invitation. The truth is
> that I took your letter into a phone booth, tried to
> reach you, failed, & left the letter in the booth… My

abject and ashamed apologies. I will try to restore
myself in your good graces in October...[12]

But he could also be earthy and vulgar with people like Frank
Wilcox or Herman Singer, for whom he routinely added a
bawdy joke (such as "They say the smallest balls in the world are
mothballs")[13] at the end of his letters:

Dear Herman,
  I plan to leave about June first for India, where an
old drinking pal is now Canadian Commercial
Counselor... [H]e has air conditioning and free
drinks and number one boys, and offers vague
promises of nautch girls, so maybe it's as good a place
to risk cholera as anywhere.
  I have been farting around in the east lately....[14]

He knew how to approach a truck-driver friend of Einar
Neilson's in Banff, where he wanted a summer job for Bill:

Dear Mr. Crosby
  I was, in fact, one of the small fry that used to hang
around Mathers Rink and dream of being a speed-
skater, and watch you go soaring by, with envy and
hero-worship... Einar Neilson...advised me to write
directly to you. I know you are a busy man but I hope
you wont mind my writing you, as an old Banff
boy...[15]

But try as he might, he could not quite find the right words to
connect with Bill himself, who at eighteen was about to enter
UBC with three scholarships as a result of having stood second
highest in the province:

Dear Old William,
  It was wonderful to get your air mail card today
...[and] to know that you had won a scholarship... I
hope it is even more money than the Legion one. So

you've been hiking up mountains. What a long walk uphill Rundle is, eh?... Couldn't do it now! I'm glad you're getting the feel of the nearer mountains while you have a chance there in Banff. I suppose Tunnel was the first "mountain" I climbed, when I was seven. Often used to go up after school, especially in the spring to pick crocuses....[16]

Even his letters of recommendation varied according to his relationship with his students. For his student Heather Spears—whose "Asylum Poems" he admired—he would write to the Canada Council grants program:

I am happy to support the application of Miss Heather Spears for a Junior Arts Fellowship... A few years ago Miss Spears was a member of my senior course in Creative Writing. At that time and since, I have continued to follow her writing, particularly in poetic fields. I can say honestly and without hesitation that she has the greatest talent as a poet of any student I have ever taught in thirty years of teaching.[17]

But his tone was quite different in recommending Betty Lambert whom he described elsewhere as "a physical as well as cerebral asset"[18] and with whom he was on such familiar terms she planned to fly with him to a conference in 1957. He had sent a short story of hers to the American magazine *Liberty* on the grounds that "Canadians are too puritanical to print it." Now he referred her for a scholarship, fellowship or assistantship at the University of Oregon, and sent a brusque follow-up letter when this one was not answered within a month:

Mrs. Lambert is the best writer in my class this year and one of the most promising fiction students I have ever had... She is twenty-two, married, without children, and with a husband whose own work is of the sort that allows him to move about freely, so that she has no domestic problems in relation to this application. She is a personable girl, with a good sense of humour, a lively mind and a mixture of sensitivity and reality in her work and in her attitudes to life, which I find rather refreshing... I would be grateful therefore if you could let me know at your very earliest convenience if there is any possibility...as her husband's income is not large.[19]

Though Birney certainly reciprocated generously to those who helped, or might help, him—offering hospitality to one and all, doing favours both personal and professional—his verbal adjustments to others were part of a manipulative attitude which could be seen in the advice he gave others such as Stuart Kirby, his old Trotskyist comrade, now an economist at the University of Hong Kong, who wanted a job at UBC:

So far as I can see, the people who will really decide...are MacKenzie, Andrew Deutsch, Dore, Soward and Chant (somewhat in that order, I suspect) though of course with McFee, Holder of the Academic Purse, not to be neglected. If I were you I would keep in touch with whichever one of these you feel closest to... In your position I should certainly ask for a full professorship; I think if you made them feel you would drop rank to come they would regard you as too eager... I would make sure UBC knows what your salary, your real salary, is, in terms of perquisites and costs of living, and hold out for as much as you can get...write to whatever contacts you have at likely U.S. institutions, tell them of your temporary appointment at UBC and apply for a Summer School job for 1960. If you landed something good like that it would both impress UBC and make them fearful they were going to lose you. Nothing succeeds like bargaining at UBC, when it is circumspectly arranged not to appear to be bargaining.[20]

Birney's linguistic agility was also one facet of his general restlessness. He had tried to settle down to scholarly writing in the fall of 1956, but it was a full twenty years since his degree and the challenge was formidable. He had abandoned the idea of publishing his 1936 thesis on Chaucer in a fit of pique that the University of Toronto Press "refused to consider [it]."[21] He had also claimed that, because of the many printer's errors (more than fifty) in the 1941 Chaucer article Roy Daniells had arranged for in the *Manitoba Arts Review,* he had "lost interest in getting further material published."

Now there were sound reasons to return to Chaucer. The continued preference of critics and anthologists (notably Desmond Pacey, who was preparing his *Ten Canadian Poets* in 1957)[22] for Birney's early poems over his recent ones, confirmed the fears he had had for a decade that he was drying up as a poet.[23] "'David,' it's true, is my best known poem, alas—as I think I've written better," he complained.[24] His frustrations with *Down the Long Table* and his failure to find British or American publishers for either of his novels, made him abandon all thought of writing another.[25] Don Harron's stage production of *Turvey,* which opened the week of 7 January 1958 at Mavor Moore's Avenue Theatre, had folded after five weeks and lost $15,000, despite good reviews. It seemed unlikely to go to Broadway, partly because the Canadian Players production had been amateurish broad farce, and partly because *No Time for Sergeants* (a play with a similar theme) had captivated New York. Even the radio version of *Turvey* seemed doomed. Although CBC bought it in January 1956, it was still not scheduled for production in April 1957, despite protests from Birney: "this letter is conveying...an author's wail of frustration at not seeing his baby christened."[26] And the ninety-minute adaptation of *Piers Plowman* for a radio program the last Sunday in May 1957 also discouraged him from further dramatic work because it had been "a fiendish job, and...the labour-pains showed."[27] The final blow would fall when officials for B.C.'s Centennial in 1958 declined to include his "Trial of a City" (unless he replaced the bawdy saloon-keeper, Gassy Jack, with a noble pioneering type)[28] along with some of his B.C. poems in their anthology of B.C. writing,[29] and Pierre Berton at *Maclean's* paid him a kill fee rather than print the "obviously hurried" article he wrote attacking the Centennial, not because of its content, but because it lacked Birney's usual "charm and urbanity."[30] (Birney sent it instead to *The Canadian Forum* who published it, and he wrote Bet that it was "too controversial" for *Maclean's*, and that it "isnt possible right now to tell the truth about this stinking Centennial.")[31]

The list of the Canadian poetry books "that might command international respect" which he sent at the request of the Canadian Library Association in 1957 were: Phyllis Webb's *Even Your Right Eye*[32] ("the best book of verse by a young poet"), Irving Layton's *The Bull Calf*[33] ("most original...best-known in the United States"), Leonard Cohen's *Let Us Compare Mythologies*[34] ("generally considered by the reviewers as the most important new voice in Canadian poetry for many years"), Dorothy Livesay, *Selected Poems*[35] and F.R. Scott's *The Eye of the Needle*.[36] He did not try to suggest that his own work belonged in this company.

Not only was Birney doubtful about any future as a creative writer, there were also pressures to update his academic credentials at UBC which he couldn't ignore. Enrolments had leapt from 7,000 in 1956 to 10,000 a year later. By 1959, the English Department was no longer a small clique, but a many-faceted assortment of ninety-three. The department now offered graduate courses, for which professors were expected to be actively engaged in research and up-to-date with new scholarship in their fields. Pressure fell directly on Birney because the first Ph.D. candidate they would graduate, Beryl Rowlands, had chosen a mediaeval subject, and Birney was to be her adviser. In the fifties postwar boom, salaries had risen dramatically—his own from $8,500 in 1956 to $10,000 in 1957. And since his free-lance income from royalties, radio work and permissions fees for anthologies had never been high (in 1957 it was a meagre $557.43),[37] there was little financial incentive to continue outside work. For all these reasons, he focused on the English poet who, like himself, encompassed all classes and styles, his favourite, Chaucer. His project was a book whose subject applied more than he may have realized to himself: "Chaucer's Hidden Ironies."

Although Birney had enormous talent for research and scholarship, he hated the solitude of tomblike libraries. None the less, in the fall of 1956, he disciplined himself to research and by 8 March 1957 had a 10,000-word paper on the "Friar's Tale" to read at one of the department's fortnightly "open seminars." Esther appreciated the change. "Earle is much improved," she wrote her friend Miriam Waddington while he was out preparing this paper at the library, "much kinder and more patient— faithful and affectionate. Of course, all this happened when I finally said, [Y]ou don't matter in my life, get the hell out. He is looking much older and has a somewhat beaten-by-life air which is sad. He never made the great international success he longed for and couldnt settle for simpler goals. What a mess most intellectuals make of their lives when their talents are real but small."[38]

When classes ended, Birney drove off to the annual meetings of various Learned Societies in Ottawa, then on to the University of Toronto with a $1,500 UBC grant to do three weeks of research on Chaucer (where his former University College colleague, artist Barker Fairley, did "one of his dourer sketches" of him),[39] and returned by way of the universities of Iowa and Montana, where he gave talks on Canadian poetry. By August, he was back for a holiday with Esther, salmon fishing and writing up his research, on Galiano Island, while Bill worked his summer job at Bella Bella, a Haida community on the north-east coast of Vancouver Island.

By the time classes resumed in 1957, Birney was fit to be untied. "I've done no imaginative writing at all this summer," he grumbled to Irving Layton, "having several academic or critical articles heavy on my back to unload."[40] He claimed in his research report that he had drafted a 5,000-word article which would be ready by January, and completed 6,500 words on aspects of his theme.[41] That fall, he faced two new courses: an honours seminar on Chaucer and a graduate course on mediaeval literature. But the scholarly life cramped and vexed him. To Frank Scott, who had pressed him to attend the Ottawa conference, he complained that he felt "trapped...in the learned societies' funeral [sic] celebrations" and dared him to compose a satire in the same vein as "The Canadian Authors Meet" to be called "Royal Society of Canada Meets."[42] And, although at

Montana he enjoyed "bourbon, dancing, poker, every damned night—and then rainbow fish over the weekend," his visit to Iowa was "Christly hot and poorly organized."[43] As Esther had observed, submission to scholarship seemed to age him. He complained to Frank Wilcox of having "whiter hair and a blacker disposition, the general aging process in one of my make-up."[44] "[T]he academic chains are almost crushing," he wrote John Wardroper, "and I have written nothing of a creative nature for nearly four years since I finished *Down the Long Table*. Perhaps it's been partly reaction to the critical reaction to that book, which at least two of the influential Canadian critics [W.A. Deacon and Robertson Davies] refused even to review, and most of the others were snooty about."[45] Accustomed to the quick publication of commercial magazines and the instant gratification of radio shows, Birney chafed at the slowness of academic articles. It took at least two years for publication in *Modern Language Quarterly*, he was told when he submitted his article "'After his Ymage': the Central Ironies of the Friar's Tale," and at 8,000 words it exceeded their maximum length of twenty pages in any event.[46] When Charles Allen Smart sent him a copy of *At Home in Mexico*, which Birney had helped him revise in San Miguel in the summer of 1955, he wrote back fervently, "God how it makes me want to go back there again."[47]

Birney was nearly desperate to fight free of academe again. Ironically using his year of scholarship as leverage, he applied for a Nuffield Fellowship to go to London and complete the book on Chaucer. The same day he applied, he wrote in a letter of resignation as chairman of the committee of graduate studies (one of many he left that year): "There seems to be plenty ahead for me to do in either the Creative or the Mediaeval field, but…it will become quite impossible for me to keep up a background and competence in both.… The latter is much nearer to my present personal interests and activities."[48] In the application itself, he claimed to have worked "from time to time" on his book (by which he could only have meant his 1936 thesis, sections of which had been published in various journals between 1937 and 1942), and explained that the fact that his research "[couldn't] be done anywhere but [the British Museum, Oxford and

Cambridge]," was "the main reason my book has not been completed before now."[49] Though the "main reason" Birney had not completed his book had nothing to do with the location of materials and everything to do with the fact that he had put his creative writing and other activities first for years, he was able by careful wording to skirt these issues and make a convincing case for the completion of a book that would add a few more chapters on Chaucer's irony to those he had already published. Although the application forms for Nuffield Fellowships stated that fellowships were normally awarded to applicants aged twenty-five to thirty-five, Birney—now fifty-four—obtained one.

Having arranged for Esther to travel by "a more orthodox route" eastward over the Atlantic to London and set up their "Nuffield Flat" on Prince Albert Road, and having arranged for Bill—who was class valedictorian—to work at Banff before entering residence as an honours chemistry and maths student at UBC, and having arranged to sell the house on West 1st, and having arranged—through his friends abroad and *their* introductions to others—for a series of hosts (and a few paid lectures) that would ensure "I won't be merely a lonely tourist...at the other end,"[50] Birney slipped free of his "crushing academic chains" for a trip alone westward across the Pacific and around the world.

With a little green notebook crammed with the addresses of friends to whom he had given in return a series of forwarding addresses, he was off 30 May 1958 for Honolulu. As if he were still eleven, when his mother had insisted he maintain a daily journal as they travelled by train to visit relatives in Calgary, Birney labelled his little green book "My Trip." His arrival in Honolulu, where he was greeted with leis, luaus and "real Hawaiians [sic] grand-dames" and spent two luscious days at the Hawaiian Village Hotel "soak[ing] in the surf,"[51] prompted a parody of the Twenty-third Psalm:

"Twenty-third Flight"

Lo as I pause in the alien vale of the airport
fearing ahead the official ambush

a voice languorous and strange as these winds of Oahu
calleth my name and I turn to be quoited in orchids

. . . .

o implausible shepherdess for this one aging sheep

. . . .

O nubile goddess of the Kaiser Training Program
is it possible that tonight my cup runneth not over
and that I shall sit in the still pastures of the lobby
whilst thou leadest another old ram in garlands past
  me,
and, bland as papaya, appearest not to remember me?
And that I shall lie by the waters of Waikiki, and
  want?[52]

While Bill—whose weakest subject was English[53]—was giving his valedictorian address with his mother beaming in the high-school audience, his father was flying on to a week in Japan, where he gave lectures arranged by Howard Norman, brother of Herbert, the late Canadian ambassador to Egypt, at the Canadian Embassy in Tokyo and at Norman's Kwansei Gakuin College in Nishinomiya, near Kyoto. He toured Tokyo with free guides and a chauffeured car provided by International House where he stayed. "Got to a kabuki in Kyoto, to a girl's opera in Tokyo, and to the headquarters of judo," he wrote the Wardropers. And to a select few he added, "there seemed no point in trying to tell the little maid [at Kyoto's Japanese inn] not to undress me each night."[54]

Next he was on to Hong Kong, where he stayed with his old Trotskyist friend, Stuart Kirby. Another four days in Bangkok followed (where he flatly refused to pay for drinking water in his room at "The Erewhon") during which he toured temples, *klongs* (canals), the palace, and "met quite a few people...through the British Club, the British Council and the University." Again, a select few also learned that he scouted out low life as well as high life: "Got to know a young Thai working at the World Travel Bureau who insisted on taking me, free guiding, to the non-tourist night places, including an enormous working-class opium den and naked girly show and some odd night markets."[55]

Tired of "temple-trotting" and sore with sacroiliitis, he batched it for a month with Bruce Macdonald, his old Zate friend, in New Delhi. In blistering heat, they took a chauffeured car over 130 miles of "incredibly confused roads" to Agra and saw the Taj Mahal and the Red Fort, "both by moonlight and by very hot sunlight." But the highlight of his stay in India was "six dream-like days" in Kashmir with Bruce. "I lived on a gargantuan houseboat moored in a lotus bed opposite the Gardens of Shalimar—you know, pale hands. [We] had 5 servants plus 2 boatmen, guiding service, three excellent meals a day, a sort of gondola to go places, three bedrooms, etc., everything furnished in walnut, all for $5 a day."[56] (On his return, *The Vancouver Province* reported of his around-the-world trip, "Kashmir he found hard to get into.")[57]

Another highlight was Athens, where Birney arrived after going to Damascus (which was supposed to be sealed) via Teheran "by a most devious and illegal route...on an Arab plane that left in the middle of the night with anti-aircraft mountings and me (only passenger)."[58] Athens, he wrote several friends, was the place he wanted to retire in "some little Greek seaport" or "some Ionian cove,"[59] and he stayed on an extra couple of days to visit museums, take a bus to Delphi and swim in the Ionian Sea "under glorious sunshine, clean mellow air, and a perfect sea-temperature."[60]

From Athens, he stopped for "a few touristy days in Rome" (where he dined with a woman friend of an acquaintance—"an expensive dish... [and] a silly bitch"),[61] then "a long sleep in Zurich" and a brief stay in Paris, where he missed his London plane because he located "one of my old loves" to spend the evening with.[62]

Birney arrived in London to take up his Nuffield Fellowship officially on 1 September, exhilarated from his circumnavigation of the globe. The trip had been "the most concentrated piece of education I've ever had in all my life of 'courses' and books," he wrote Bill McConnell.[63]

After the sybaritic splendours of his summer, London seemed "a grimy great ugly city" where "the old class-lines [seem to be] sharper than ever."[64] In terms that were oddly reminiscent of his peripatetic father's long-ago prospecting for gold, he pictured himself in the British Museum as a miner "chipping away at the granite wall of Chaucer criticism, in hopes to mint something, even if only fool's gold."[65] Despite restful weekend jaunts with Esther in their new—and fourth—Austin to visit such friends as Margaret Crosland, who had developed a fine career of her own as the biographer of Colette and Cocteau, a translator of French literature into English, and—ironically—the editor of an anthology of marriage proposals *The Happy Yes*,[66] who now lived with Max Denis in "a curious 30-room Edwardian country house in East Sussex,"[67] or Canadian artists Bruno and Molly Bobak, who lived in Somerset, Birney could work no longer than three weeks. His intensive survey of the books, monographs and serials containing Chaucer criticism since 1934 (underneath which he concealed chocolate bars to nibble)[68] affected his eyes—"never my strongest organ."[69] "I didn't get established into work," he wrote his "Coz" Rosemary, whom he planned to visit, "until mid-September...and then, after three hard weeks' work, I came down with a recurrent eye-strain that has plagued me all my life."

Birney had to stop reading. Eventually, by following the advice of a Harley Street specialist, he could do "a modified day's work...by dint of switching through three pairs of spectacles."[70] By the end of November he wrote Bill, "My eyes are considerably better and I manage to get a fairly decent day's work in at the B.M., but the long enforced rest has put me miles behind in all my letters, and answering them consumes my evenings. Esther gets out more, to movies and plays."[71] In one of these many letters, he wrote in frustration, "the year, with its wonderful release from lecturing and administration, is flying away on me."[72]

During what he was convinced would be his "last fling," Birney did not want to spend his days "chained to my desk" with a surprising number of Canadian colleagues around him: his former student, now a Milton scholar at Chicago, Ernest Sirluck; Bill Blissett from Saskatchewan; UBC colleagues John Hulcoop and Geoff Hall; Millar MacLure, a Shakespearian from Toronto; and Gwladys Downes, who was working on Mallarmé's symbolism.[73] Tea with his sponsor Beatrice White and her colleagues was *not* his idea of fun: "I...beheld assembled University of

London professors and their wives," he wrote his colleague Dick
Fredeman at UBC, "a sight even drabber than similar functions
at UBC, perhaps because all the men wear the same clothes, are
the same height and never laugh out loud."[74] Nor did he want to
spend his nights at parties "that might as easily have happened in
Vancouver" with the same people he spent his days with, or with
other Canadian expatriates such as Dorothy Livesay, Phyllis
Webb, Daryl Hine, Graham McInnes, Heather Spears, Norman
Levine and (once and briefly) Mordecai Richler, whom he
described rather enviously as "in the plush, writing television
scripts."[75] Sometime during that year, he managed to slip away
for a holiday on the Continent with Margaret Crosland, during
which, according to Margaret, he somewhat illogically was "pro-
prietorial" towards her.[76]

Paradoxically, the writing Birney now wanted to do was creative. Jack McClelland had promised a *Selected Poems* to be
jointly published with Harcourt, Brace or Knopf in the U.S. and
Abelard-Schuman in England,[77] and he wanted Birney to produce some new poems and locate a distinguished American poet
to write the introduction.[78] As early as October, Birney reported
he was writing verse again. And he also allowed himself to be distracted from his research by Lorne Pierce who wanted a revised
and updated version of *Twentieth Century Canadian Poetry*.
Content with nothing less than his best, Birney "cut out a good
number of pieces by very minor figures and strengthen[ed] the
representation from the more major ones," adding such poets as
Irving Layton, Phyllis Webb, Jay Macpherson, Fred Cogswell,
Charles Bruce, Elizabeth Brewster, Daryl Hine, Heather Spears
and George Johnston, and rearranged the poems from thematic
groups to chronological order.[79]

In other ways, too, Birney refused to be tied down to his
Chaucer project. He had always been fond of Elizabeth
Cowley,[80] who though she had never been his student, was
friends with the special class of '48 that included John
Wardroper, Eric Nicol and Norman Newton. He had first
encountered Liz in a long playful poem she sent him in 1946 as
a student in Victoria College, B.C. asking advice about moving
to UBC:

That studes write odes to patient profs is rather dis-
concerting,
A pseudo-sage might wise be gauged were he to term
it flirting

. . . .

Alumnae know I not by name
Except he in the light of fame

. . . .

So please can *you* suggest a hovel
Or must I needs go forth and grovel?

. . . .

Write soon (in poetry or prose), to one the world so
little knows
Then best my friendship you relinquish
Because I'm majoring in English.

Signed in the depth of tribulation
By one who dreams of graduation—[81]

Now Liz had become a producer with the top BBC television
interview show "Tonight," was a friend of the Wardropers, and
naturally fell in with the expatriate group the Birneys saw
socially. The ebullient, attractive Liz (he referred to her as "pneu-
matic Liz of the BBC")[82] was unlike other Canadians whom
Birney described as "the practical pimps and the spiritual virgins
of the continent" with their "demi-vierge air in all sexes... [that]
says, 'I know the scene, Jack, but I ain't goin to lose my maiden-
head.'"[83] By February 1959, Earle Birney was in love.

While Esther spent some time with an old school-friend at a
reducing resort in Torquay on the Cornish coast, trying to lose
weight,[84] Earle flew to Nice in the south of France where he
stayed with Art Smith and his wife in their apartment near
Cannes. He installed himself in a fine bed overlooking sunny
sands and palms and didn't get up for a week, "having brought
the English flu bug along. However, this worked out well" he
wrote Bruce Macdonald candidly,

Lib [Liz], my sweetie, had insisted on spending the first week skiing in Switzerland, a sport I no longer enjoy… [S]he joined me for the second week, which we spent in a nearby hotel under the understanding and benevolent eye of Art & his wife, with which went the use of their car for jaunts up to Provence to see [Ken] Rexroth, and into the various hill-towns. It was very early spring there, and charming—but it did not subvert my loyalty to Greece. Lib was most loving and, despite a sly campaign by my pal Art, remained faithful; I say this with some confidence because I didn't give the bastard a chance to test her defences in private. We flew back via Geneva, where we saw an excellent show of contemporary Canadian non-representational painting, and wandered hand in hand by the chilly lake. We managed to arrive back in London and go our separate ways without detection, and to see each other frequently, though by no means as often as I would like. Esther, who suspects, has apparently decided to avoid asking awkward questions.…

Lib…is getting another holiday very shortly and proposes to spend it largely with me. After my failure to attract anyone into bed with me last summer, I feel faith returning, glands swelling, cells rejuvenating. Life is still wonderful.

There are…little problems. Lib, who is 32 and unmarried, has lately taken it into her head that she should undergo the experience of wedlock and motherhood, for which she is certainly magnificently equipped [and]…thinks…I should be the partner in this venture.… I have no desire to go through fatherhood again. Until I depart in September, however I am careful to see that she meets only my happily married male friends, and to keep a strict eye on them too, since she has another defect…in that she seems automatically to arouse forthright lust in other males, unaccompanied, I feel, by the spiritual exhaltations of my own more aging passion.

However, thanks to her, I have just reached 55 without a tremor, and feel younger daily.[85]

In a whimsical squib "To Think of It"—a doggerel verse quite unlike the elegant passionate sonnets he once sent Margaret Crosland—he reasoned with Liz that marriage was out:

Think of being married to a man who chomps
and seldom romps;
who likes to stay awake till two
and gets up early too;
. . . .
lacks words to praise whatever pleases
but, for what doesnt, pours out a jumble
of bitter boredom and of jealous grumble;
. . . .
who tries, at fifty-five, to be precocious,
and is enraged to find his tennis now atrocious;
who blames the world because his books are flops
and yet will go on writing till he drops;
whose head is bald and teeth are yellow;
who grows more crabbed with the years instead of
    mellow;
whose clothes are out of style and seldom clean,
eyes weak, feet flat, shoulders too stooped and lean,
. . . .
too large an ego and too small a head,
a sheep in company and a goat in bed.
. . . .
Think of this super-sensitive and jealous oldster,
suspicious even of your bolster,
think of this man, cantankerous and crinkled—
and leave him quick, before you too are wrinkled.[86]

With the same mischievous sense of humour, Birney wrote a fan letter about Liz to the BBC under the pseudonym "Mr. Cottingham-Ross."[87]

By way of placating Esther, Birney took her on a ten-day trip to Scotland, where he found the Scots much more to his taste than the English with their "eternal game of oneupmanship." "We drove via Durham & the Border country [where he visited Hugh MacDiarmid, who was preparing a lecture on Burns [for Bucharest and Sofia] to Edinburgh where I got involved in a prolonged party [hosted by Bingo Mavor] with several Lowland nationalist poets [Sydney Goodsir Smith, Norman MacCaig, Russell Grant and Alexander Reid, editor of *Saltire Review*, who took some of Birney's poems] and several bottles of international Highland whiskey, the fine almost-white stuff you never see in the south. Then we drove in and around the Highlands as far up as Sutherland... Looked up some of my own clan, the Robertsons, in Aberdeen, and was lapsing into brogue before I left."[88]

In Aberdeen, Birney finally met his "Coz" Rosemary, to whom he had been writing since 1953. "I remember taking them [on] a tour of Aberdeen," Rosemary recalls, "and that Earle was not as I had expected. He was very quiet—rather sad looking. I felt that I disappointed him. With hindsight, there might have been stress between him and Esther, who did most of the talking.... I don't think we wrote after that visit—until 1962."[89] And Birney also paid for a month-long trip Esther took in May and June with Alice Frick (a CBC producer who was buying television scripts and studying theatre) to Scandinavia, while he "[stayed] on in London to slog out some Chaucer papers at the end of May"[90]— and see Liz.

Batching it in London brought new frustrations. "After a somewhat sleepless night and now a day in which I cannot work for thinking of you, I feel I must write," ran the long, self-pitying letter he sent her after seeing far too little of her.

> I must pocket all shreds of pride and appeal to you to help me with all the love you have left for me. I have had to steel myself to the prospect of an inevitable and no doubt final parting from you at the summer's end, and I have been able to face that only by the hope and the plan that at least, now, there would be a unique fortnight when I could devote myself completely to

you…even to pretend for a moment we were married.

…Yesterday you came for supper and a play, but you were tired and it was a rush between eating and napping and "Tonight" and playgoing. If afterwards you had said…"stay the night, and we can have break-fast together"…[it] would have made me feel that you wanted more than the usual hurried sex.… But it wasnt that way, and tonight is to be devoted to another man, and Friday night to "Tonight," and Saturday and Sunday to relatives. That leaves perhaps only one week before Esther returns—and how many of those nights will I be longing and lonely for you? Darling, darling, don't do this to me!

…I go, at 55, from you to a loveless, sexless and increasingly lonely old age with a wife who wants only the security I give her and a child who is cold and indifferent to us both. I suppose it has all been of my own making, but that thought doesn't make it any eas-ier to bear. You have given me a brief Indian summer; don't let the north wind blow on me a week earlier than it has to.… Love me now, darling, as much as you possibly can; I am drowning without you.[91]

While Esther returned to Vancouver at the end of August to rent a house at 4584 West 1st, not far from the one they had sold—a beautiful one, large enough for Bill to join them, with a magnificent view of the whole Pacific coast and a basement apartment she could rent to students—Earle spent his last ten days abroad sporting with Liz on Ile de Porquerolles in the Mediterranean off Toulon. It was, he said, "one of the few ves-tiges of the Old Riviera, vintage 1910. Dirt roads, a few bicycles, no motor vehicles except two ancient affairs the two rival hotels use to ferry baggage up from the pier."[92]

Before he became involved with Liz that winter, Birney had reflected on an observation of Irving Layton's that "the more dis-ordered (the poet's) personal life is…the richer his art will be." "I don't know whether I agree with you," he wrote back, "I *hope* it isnt true, as personally I'm always wanting to put my life in order. Isnt it rather that the poet is the sort of person who has to make an order but is never content with it, must change it for another order, a new place, a new belief, a new girl, or just a new metric? It is this appalling need for new emotional experience that has always disturbed my life, taken time away from the actual writing.... [D]o you mean, for example, that the poet imposes order only *through the poem*, leaving his life as chaotic as before, or does he learn, from the act of creating a poem, a way of coping with the disorder in his life that helped to produce the poem? In other words, is there a real purgation of agony or sorrow, or not? One doesn't write consciously to improve one's own life, god knows, but it would help if it did."[93]

The issue was a serious one. Certainly Birney—like Layton—courted emotional upheaval. But, unlike Layton, Birney's attachment to the conventional life Esther represented was as strong as the appeal of anarchy. In a short explanation for Liz called "Consolation for the Stillbirth of a Marriage," he summed up the great divide in his nature with considerable insight:

> His nature would have been divided; one half of him wanting Europe, the excitement of London and a professional career, the world of Entertainment and the Public, youthful things, youthful friends, the continuation of adventure through loves, jobs, journies, celebrities;

> the other half wanting North America, the excitement of writing and reading, of pedantry, the world of students and scholars, concentration on the one love and job, journeys into wilderness and quiet, away from the Public, fishing, thinking, growing old, vegetating.[94]

The pain of leaving Liz behind was so intense that he began a letter to her as soon as she disappeared from view, which began: "Sweetheart, I looked for you to wave to from the bus but you had dropped out of sight in an eye-blink, was it into the 'dead vast and abyss of Time'? If so, I will wander in it forever or till I find you."[95] Two months later, he was still "psychically back on the island of Porquerolles...sunning and swimming...and general lazing."[96] He continued a lengthy and passionate correspondence with Liz from Vancouver for a full year, seeing her briefly in July when she returned to see her dying father.

Somehow, despite eye-strain and other health problems, despite the time spent away from his research travelling, despite his forays into creativity, despite the time he devoted to favours for friends (such as looking for flats for Art Smith, Ken Rexroth, Bob Allen, Dick Fredeman and a friend in California),[97] and despite the turbulence of his emotional life with Liz, Birney managed to complete the enormous research task (working "like a proper mole")[98] which he had set himself. By the end of his year in London, he had four papers on Chaucer's irony placed in journals ("'After his Ymage'—Structural Irony in the *Friar's Tale*" for *Mediaeval Studies*, "The Squire's Peacock Yeoman" for *Review of English Literature*, "The Franklin's Sop in Wine a Hangover Remedy" for *Notes and Queries*, and "The Inhibited and the Uninhibited: Ironic Structure in the *Miller's Tale*" for *Neophilologus*), two others ready to submit ("The Ironies within the *Summoner's Tale*," which was soon accepted by *Anglia* and "The 'Gentil' Manciple and his Tale," accepted by *Neuphilologische Witteilungen*), and he expected to have more done (including one on the *Reeve's Tale*) by Christmas.[99] "Congratulations, Earle, on the...splash with which you're re-entering the academic, as distinct from creative, field," wrote Ernest Sirluck on his Christmas card that year. "You must be feeling a euphoric glow—and should."[100]

But if Birney was feeling a euphoric glow it was not on account of the scholarly work that was part of what he called "the academic squirrel-cage."[101] He was pleased to find Roy Daniells on leave ("almost as good as being away oneself")[102] and his old friend Bill Robbins the interim chairman of English at UBC. But what he was really euphoric about was the resurgence of his creativity.

"Sometimes I think of the Birney of 'Vancouver Lights' and wonder where he is," wrote Al Purdy, who wanted a reference for a Canada Council grant. "The same? No, of course not. Or *Trial of a City*, or 'Mappemounde'? All the goddamn Birneys wander

over the globe looking for poems."[103] Although the two poets
had still not met, Purdy looked on Birney as a model. As Purdy
had told Montreal poet Ron Everson, "I look at Birney's poem
"Bushed" as an example of somewhere near the way I'd like to
write. Behind that poem is a whole universe of meaning waiting
for the reader, as also in many of Yeats's poems."[104]

Birney had unequalled facility with words and was a stunning
craftsman, but his poems were sometimes superficial because
they lacked the moral conviction and personal emotion of poems
like those Purdy mentioned. His best works were those in which
he faced the deeper questions: "Who of us," he had written Alan
Crawley, "has a convincing argument, a good intelligent one,
that is, for going on living...hoping for something other than
disaster and annihilation?"[105] He had been sobered by the death
of Malcolm Lowry on 27 June 1957, and by the suicide of
Esther's friend John Pearson the following year. Now, after the
stimulus of his travels through Asia, the Birney of his almost
existential early poems reappeared. "I am finding being in the
middle of one of the world's largest population-bombs to be
both exciting and appalling,"[106] he wrote Howard Moorepark
from New Delhi. And to another friend he wrote, "My travels,
since India, have been most satisfying and, I hope, educative.
The common reservoir of good-will in the world is really very
ample for human needs, if only the conduits flowed freely.
Teheran I found not so happy a place to be—Americans in the
saddle and hated, the sense of everything working towards an
Iraqui solution, if toward any, the overlays of fanatical Fatimi
Muslimism and corrupt Mogul-like royalty.... I liked Syria and
the Syrians and found Damascus a living history book."[107]

Once he was back in London, the "stimulus of knocking about
Asia"[108] was augmented by thoughts of how difficult he found
"personal" poetry. Those thoughts were triggered by the book of
poems (*A Laughter in the Mind*) Layton sent him: "I am most
moved by some of your..."personal" poems.... For me they
would be the hardest to write."[109] As the events of the summer
took hold of his imagination, it was their "appalling" side rather
than their "exciting" side that gained ascendance. "I don't think
anyone could ever be the same person again after a few weeks in

India, or in the Arab world," he wrote Ethel Wilson.[110] "As for cruelty, malevolence," he wrote Betty Lambert, "the world has much of it; I saw it directed more nakedly against helpless children in the streets of Cairo and Teheran.... But you must go to India to see people dying unaided in the gutters of busy streets; and to start thinking all over again about the value of human life in a grotesquely over-populated world."[111] And to Heather Spears he confessed, "[T]o choose between verse and prose...is a problem for me. When I was in Mexico I tried only prose travel sketches, as I felt I wanted 'to get everything down' & get it straight. But this summer, seeing so much of the world so quickly, I got a different reaction. It seemed to me there was too much ever to say, and most of it said and said before, and that what mattered, if anything mattered even for me personally, was to catch those moments when the strangeness of scene fused with the familiarity of recognition of people, and I suddenly felt as clearly one-and-close-with some human being with whom I couldn't even pass greeting in words, some leaping sympathy out of the common misery and horror and love and mystery of being alive together with them. So I've been thinking, anyway, but when I try to make poems, it all goes slowly, as ever. Perhaps I've grown too old to write what I should have written when I was your age. Be warned!"[112] In other words, the best vehicle for his recent experience was poetry. Or, as he wrote Ralph Gustafson, "After six years of rotting or whoring with prose, I've started trying verse again."[113]

As he had maintained to Esther, there seemed to be a connection between his conquest of new experiences or new women and his creativity. This equation of creativity and virility was something Art Smith (who sent his regards to both Esther and Liz) also seemed to recognize: "Your creative activities—scholarship, poetry, criticism—to say nothing of your other successes, make me feel more and more like a eunuch."[114] The best poem that took shape in the spate of verses Birney began formulating that year of Asia and Liz, was "Bear" (later titled "The Bear on the Delhi Road").[115] It was the only poem he wrote on holiday with Liz. "You may just recall," he wrote Bruce Macdonald, "that when we were driving up to Chandigarh we glimpsed a

Himalayan bear by the roadside being switched by its trainers. The sight, so quickly passed, stuck in my mind and came out in a poem (which was written in a grape arbour on Porquerolles):"[116]

> Unreal, tall as a myth
> by the road the Himalayan bear
> is beating the brilliant air
> with his crooked arms.
> About him two men, bare,
> spindly as locusts, leap.
> One pulls on a ring
> in the great soft nose; his mate
> flicks, flicks with a stick
> up at the rolling eyes.
> . . . .
> If far on the Delhi way
> around him galvanic they dance
> it is merely to wear, wear
> from his shaggy body the tranced
> wish forever to stay
> only an ambling bear
> four-footed in berries.
>
> It is no more joyous for them
> in this hot dust to prance
> out of reach of the praying claws
> sharpened to paw for ants
> in the shadow of deodars.
> It is not easy to free
> myth from reality
> or rear this fellow up
> to lurch, lurch with them
> in the tranced dancing of men.[117]

Here was a moment glimpsed, a quite literal "leaping sympathy out of the common misery and horror and love and mystery of being alive." In that moment Birney captured a situation as grotesque as the over-population that appalled him. And it was invested with his own feelings; even "Himalayan bear" might have been a pun—conscious or unconscious—on "him a'layin bare." Like the bear, he was a natural creature made to amble freely in woods, not to be trained for someone's amusement in captivity. The bear, like Don Quixote, is "tall as myth"; he makes a figure at once noble and ridiculous. And the "spindly" men who prance around him, caught in the hopeless task of civilization, are ironically more pathetic than the bear. This poem, informed by Birney's wisdom in middle age, more than any other, illustrated the quality Purdy recognized: "Yours is a more personal way of thinking, to me anyway, that aims at a deeper fulfilment of the individual, a breaking out from national boundaries, a sadness at our violence, etc. Anyway, that's part of what you are to me.... One thing about the poetry we're writing now is that it has nothing in it...that bespeaks the feeling and longing of your *Strait of Anian*—there is no clear and easy road [back] to Europe."[118] Or, as Ralph Gustafson put it, "The two poems I have read of the lot you brought back from the Far East make me certain that a new, wonderful book of poems must be coming from you...a beautifully resolved poetry."[119]

"Ellesmereland," "Wake Island," "A Walk in Kyoto," "Bangkok Boy," "Flying Fish," "Wind-Chimes in a Temple Ruin"—these and other fine poems appeared that year. Not surprisingly, they were snapped up by journals in England, Scotland, the U.S., and Canada. *Atlantic Monthly* took "Ellesmereland." But even greater recognition awaited him: "*The New Yorker* surprised me by taking ['The Bear on the Delhi Road']," he wrote Purdy excitedly. "Maybe this means I'm slipping, but at least it's nice to slip on a fifty dollar bill rather than a one dollar."[120] "For the first time in the twenty years I've been dribbling out verse," he wrote Wilber Stevens, "I begin to feel the Great Barrier of the 49th parallel is cracking for me. Though the all-important American edition of the [selected] poems is still delayed, I am getting a few things into magazines and recently clicked with *Atlantic, Colorado Quarterly, Northwest Review, Ladies' Home Journal*, and now *Inland*. Have things coming out in half a dozen of the smaller mags in Britain now too. All this encourages me to get back to verse writing whenever I can free myself from academics."[121] Six months later, he wrote in elation that he was "pushing out the poems still" and had "added *Arizona Quarterly, Antioch Review* and the *New Yorker* to my scalp collection."[122] Even by the fall of 1960, Birney was still drawing from "a writing vein," "whacking out a dozen or so poems which had been nagging me for the last year"[123] in the week before classes began. One was an incisive satire dashed off as the answer to a question from John Ciardi, editor of the New York journal *Saturday Review*. Ciardi had asked why Canada had no Dickinson, no Whitman, no great body of poetry; to which Birney had replied in lines that would later be titled "Canlit.:"

> Too busy bridging loneliness to be alone,
> We tried to reach in railroad ties what Emily wrought
>   from bone.
> Sir G.D. Roberts, Carman, could not see
> For all the goddamned woods a mythopoeic tree.
> We French, we English, never fought our civil war,
> Or maybe we endure it still, a bloodless civil bore,
> No wounded lying about, no Whitmans wanted.
> It's only by our lack of ghosts we're haunted.[124]

A month later he sent off several more serious poems to Bob Weaver for CBC, adding "[T]here are, I hope, more on the way to being born:"[125] "State of Sonora," and "Francisco Tresguerras"—his start on a "Mexican Suite"; his group of Asian poems, to which he had added "Twenty-third Flight"; "First Tree" (later "First Tree for Frost")—the first in a group he planned about childhood in the Alberta bush; a haiku, the first of others he had in mind; "Captain Cook" (which took off from a line in "Pacific Door") and "Vitus Bering"—from a group he envisaged on west-coast exploration; and three individual poems, "Aluroid," "Prayer" and the best of this later group, "El Greco: *Espolio*,"[126] a moving and ironic poem based on the painting he'd seen with Esther at the El Greco exhibit in France in 1953, which pictured a carpenter making the cross for the crucifixion of that "other carpenter's boy," Jesus. As with the bear and his trainers, the poet is both. Here, in intensely compressed form, were Birney's reflections on craftsmanship versus conviction, even a glimmer of his Trotskyist view that the working-class man has an innate dignity, though unconscious of the larger issues. In a profound reflection on the personal implications of this painting ("The Despoiling," meaning both the gambling for Christ's belongings and the challenge of crafting the cross without spoiling it), Birney touched on the problem at his own heart's core:

> To construct with hands, knee-weight, braced thigh,
> keeps the back turned from death.[127]

As he had once confessed to Bet, "all this work keeps me from thinking too much."[128]

Birney's encompassing of the world confirmed his commitment to internationalism. He had dabbled—very successfully—in translation: a Hungarian poem of Attila Jozsef's, "Nobody's as Poor as a Poor Man"; and two poems of Mao-Tse Tung's, "Midstream" and "Snowscape from a Plane,"[129] for which he had done a free translation to accompany his UBC colleague Ping-ti Ho's literal one. In his speech to the National Federation of Canadian University Students in the summer of 1959, he argued that "one of the basic 'needs' that should be discussed at a conference [on Education and the Needs of Society] is education for *world* society.... Canada has a chance to be a great independent force for the pacification of the world, but Canadians, to help us seize that chance, must not be ignorant of the world, of its peoples and problems, nor ignorant of their own history, their own heritage and culture."[130]

By the end of 1959, Birney was happier than he'd been for some time, despite delays in his next book. He loved the house Esther had rented, especially the attic room that gave onto the inlet where he sat typing naked on hot days. Bill had finished first year with 87 per cent and was proceeding in Honours Physics; Roy Daniells was on leave; and Liz was supplying him with the romantic correspondence he craved. In letters during the year that followed, despite his customary self-mocking tone, he sounded positive: "I am still a scatterer of energies, an unpredictably-tempered husband, and an uneven teacher who can sometimes be so dull he bores himself. As a father I enjoy my son hugely, but at a puzzled distance, since he is now, at eighteen, plunged into second-year of honours mathematics and chemistry, a scholarship student with the articulation of a pugilist and the vocabulary of a beatnik. Esther is well and keeps her youth, or what we have of it, better than I do; she is a part-time social worker in the field of subnormal children."[131] He even acknowledged that the publication delay was partly his doing: "My *Selected Poems* is still hanging fire, partly because I keep tinkering with the old stuff and wanting to shove in new, partly because the London edition has been held up by strikes, and the American by the resignation of an editor who liked my stuff and the appointment of one who thinks it stinks."[132]

He had every reason to expect his poetic renaissance to continue, and he kept himself as alert as a barometer to the literary climate—especially in the U.S.

It was Joe Langland of the University of Massachussetts, whom Birney had engaged to teach the UBC summer school poetry course for 1960, who raised a subject that would become crucial. "Robert Lowell comes into Amherst to read from and discuss his new book, *Life Studies*, a radical departure from his *Lord Weary's Castle*[133].... He says that the first book was an acquired voice which he mastered. Now he is trying to see what his own 'voice' is. After having won the Pulitzer prize and international acclaim for an 'acquired voice,' this should be of some moment, and probably of some artistic and aesthetic importance. It may even be something of what Paul Shapiro says has to happen to all modern poetry. Should be a lively decade."[134]

❧ 23 ❧

ANOTHER CURVE OF TIME

On 5 March 1958, Earle Birney sent Irving Layton a photograph taken in Toronto the previous June called "The Four Generations." It marked an occasion engineered by Birney at Layton's request to introduce Layton and his friend, the young poet Leonard Cohen, to his old friend Ned Pratt. He playfully remarked on the fact that a hairdresser's sign was legible behind them: "We're all pursuing the impossible, trying to make waves permanent, neither hair nor the symbols for sound will stay forever kinked." But when he had first seen the photo, his comment had been more ominous: "The girl you dragged out of Diana Sweets to photograph the Four Generations," he had written, "managed to get only 3 1/2 in the picture. You three are in plain view, only my left half. I try to believe this is not symbolic."[1]

Perhaps that half-representation of Birney *was* symbolic. Pratt, who had earned the epithet "the Grand Old Man" of Canadian literature, was seventy-five; Birney, fifty-four; Layton, the Wild Man of Canadian Poetry entrancing and shocking audiences everywhere, was forty-six; and Cohen, whom Birney and many others considered "the most important new voice in Canadian poetry for many years,"[2] was twenty-five. With only eight years

411

between them, Birney and Layton might well have been considered to be the same generation, but Layton (who coined the concept) was eager to disassociate himself from the establishment and align himself with rebellious youth.

Since at least 1959, Birney had sniffed a change in the literary wind. He had described Ken Rexroth after his visit to the south of France that spring with Liz Cowley as "the Daddy of Beat poets." He was intrigued on visiting Rexroth again in Cornwall, England, with Esther that summer to find him dictating his autobiography into a tape recorder. His intuition was confirmed in the spring of 1960 when he travelled to give a poetry reading at the San Francisco State Poetry Center, which had been established in 1953 to foster the "new point of view"[3] of beatniks who had gathered in the coffee houses of North Beach.

It was a coincidence that Birney was among the first Canadians to read there. He had not been sought after, but, in his usual way, had contacted the head of the Center, Ruth Witt-Diamant, because she was an old teaching-fellow friend from his Berkeley days. He returned from San Francisco somewhat puzzled. Bob Dylan's popular "Ballad of a Thin Man,"[4] which was released five years later, described his bewilderment perfectly. The half-haunting, half-jeering line "Something is happening and you don't know what it is, do you, Mr. Jones," could have been written for him.

"San Francisco is certainly lively now," he reported to Dudek,

> with about six poetry mags, and cellar readings, with and without combos, going on somewhere or other practically every night. I was in one with Mel La Follett [an American who taught Creative Writing whom Birney had brought to UBC], who was reading some new stuff of his.... Rexroth is Big Time now; is speaking his autobiography, without notes or script, over a local radio station, and New Directions is to bring it out, if Laughlin agrees to pay what Kenneth wants, which is a lot. He is also going on a reading tour of the U.S. this month, alternately on campuses and night clubs, at $350 a crack. I wrote Irving suggesting you

boys might know of a Montreal patron or fund or something that might want to pay Rexroth up there.[5]

He reassured Louis Dudek that "the alleged academic [versus] North Beach beat feud was largely in the newspapers."[6] He told Ruth his readings—for which Rexroth was his chairman—went well: "a far larger and appreciative audience than I anticipated"; but elsewhere blamed her poor organization (due to illness) for one quite small audience: "I started with a dozen, after waiting twenty minutes. Another two dozen wandered in, by ones and twos, throughout the rest of the hour."[7] He noticed Layton's latest book *A Red Carpet for the Sun* displayed in North Beach and saw that poets there were reading him. But he did not notice anything incongruous about the mixture of people—some invited by his request—at the reception hosted by his ex-student, now Canadian Consul, Douglas B. Hicks, which included his old friends Hank and Bobbie Gartshore; L.A. MacKay, the Canadian professor and poet; and the young San Francisco poet Lawrence Ferlinghetti, whose poems went like this description of poet as acrobat:

> For he's the super realist
>
>   who must perforce perceive
>   taut truth
>   before the taking of each stance or step
>   in his supposed advance
>   toward that still higher perch
>   where Beauty stands and waits
>   with gravity
>   to start her death-defying leap
> And he
>   a little charleychaplin man
>   who may or may not catch
>   her fair eternal form
>   spreadeagled in the empty air
>   of existence[8]

Birney seems to have regarded the San Francisco scene as a

temporary quirk, though he was savvy enough to allude to it. "Why be a poet?" or "Poetry with and without beat" were the titles he suggested for a talk at the Idaho State College Conference on the Humanities the following month. "I decided to strike out fresh and pick a subject that would allow me to talk about poetry from both a writer's point of view and a teacher's, and to bring in a little bit of beat in the process," he explained.[9]

Birney could not help noticing changes in his new crop of students. "The delicate little beauty," he wrote in mock astonishment, describing a girl commenting on T.S. Eliot, "[says,] 'Like who reads him. Shit on that kind of crap.'"[10] He was hardly shocked. He had been an outspoken critic of censorship since the banning of *Lady Chatterly's Lover* and *Ulysses* (a battle he would continue in 1961 by defending Henry Miller's *Tropic of Cancer*);[11] had long delighted in Chaucer's ribald *fabliaux*; had fought for freer language in *Turvey*; welcomed the loosening of literature in such books as *The Naked and the Dead* (1948), *Catcher in the Rye* (1951) and *Lolita* (1955); and appreciated daring new foreign films such as *La Dolce Vita* (1960) and *Last Year at Marienbad* (1961). But he had the sense that he might become redundant when he realized that some of his students of creative writing, "followers of the Black Mountain group, are bringing out a poetry sheet which they have called *TISH*,[12] which they are careful to explain is an anagram."[13] Foremost among these was Franklin (Frank) Davey, who had earned a first in Birney's Chaucer course in 1959–60, and by 1961 was asking to submit poems instead of a thesis ("probably on the [Charles] Olson, [Robert] Duncan, [Robert] Creeley, [Denise] Levertov, and [Larry] Eigner school")[14] for his M.A. (Birney recommended a thesis.) Jack Hodgins was in his 1959–60 class; the 1960–61 group included other writers of future fame—George Bowering, Daphne Marlatt, David Bromige and Rona Murray; and Lionel Kearns enrolled in 1961-62.

Birney's sense that his generation was being supplanted was reinforced by the rebellion of his own son—now nineteen and six feet four—in the winter of 1961. "My boy left home this winter to live in residence as a result of an argument with me over whether or not he should help me wash some dishes he and

I had just had breakfast on (which I had cooked, his mother being out),"[15] he confessed to Bruce Macdonald. To add insult to injury, as far as Birney was concerned, Bill did not perform well enough in his third-year exams to meet honours math standing "largely because he was busy building himself fame as the top poker player on the campus."[16]

It was clear by the 1950s that American poets had superseded their British counterparts. John Crowe Ransom, William Carlos Williams, Wallace Stevens, e.e. cummings: these were the names to know. What was not so clear was the direction the North American mainstream was taking. The Beats and Black Mountain poets shared certain anti-establishment traits: they stood for spontaneity, revolution, experimentation—even anarchy. Their informal coffee-house readings and alignment with music had accomplished something Birney had once yearned for: the return of poets to their oral and popular roots. But in stark contrast to this literary movement which dramatically expressed the beginning of a full-blown social revolution, another group— heavily influenced by the archetypal literary criticism of Northrop Frye at Toronto—were writing mythopoeic poetry loosely based on Jungian concepts of universal symbols and myths. This poetry—associated in Canada with Daryl Hine, Jay Macpherson and James Reaney—was closely connected to intellectual exercise and seemed cool and élitist by comparison with the Beats.

Though there were many exceptions, oral and popular poetry expressed the immediacy of personal experience—often in loose colloquial form. In contrast, mythopoeic poetry reflected extensive education, was more disciplined, and therefore associated with academe. One was Dionysian, physical, expressive and personal; the other was Apollonian, cerebral, reflective and detached. Out of this fundamental clash of attitudes arose the question of whether or not universities fostered or smothered creativity and, beyond that, whether creative writing could or should be taught. In a questionnaire about the poet and the university circulated among Canadian poet/academics in 1956—the results of which were published in January 1957—there was a wide range of opinions. Eli Mandel thought the university was the best home for poets; so did James Reaney, who claimed "academic obligations have had a really restorative effect on [my] imagination." Both Frank Scott and Alfred Bailey thought their university jobs gave them more free time than they would have had in any other job. Louis Dudek thought the university tapped energy and creativity, but also provided "valuable book knowledge" and, eventually, "more ease and leisure." Only Wilfred Watson and Birney felt that their university work was completely detrimental; and Birney was by far the more forcefully negative. Watson argued that university life was too "sheltered," and "hound[ed] [the poet] into the decencies and conformities…[and] surrounded him with the debauching enthusiasm of student minds," offer[ed] him academic promotion…which he knows he shouldn't want," and "eats up his time, and, especially his idleness." Birney's blast was familiarly personal: "Academic obligations have *hindered* me in writing poetry. I delayed writing, when I was a graduate student, to devote all time and energy to achieving my doctorate. That gained, I had to delay several more years till I had mastered the teaching problems of a great variety of courses, including graduate ones, which I was required to teach at the University of Toronto. Summers, and many evenings, went in extra teaching because the salary I was paid was not even at subsistence level for myself and family."[17] No mention of Trotskyist politics; no mention of radio, television, and other extra work after his salary increased to a comfortable level around 1953; no mention of generous grants for travel.

For Birney, who had, as he put it, "juggled all three balls" for decades—at times the Chaucer scholar or expert on Canadian literature, at others the poet, and at others yet the mentor of students of creative writing—the issue was serious. If these various activities were diametrically opposed, he was self-cancelling, more or less his own worst enemy. When he described the university position—teaching creative writing, giving lectures and readings—which he negotiated at the University of Oregon for March through June 1961, he called it variously "Visiting Professor," "Writer-in-Residence" and "Poet-in-Residence," depending on who he was writing to. But how long could he manage to hold these facets of himself together if debate centred on how antagonistic they were?

The case was well-put by poet Robert Bly, the American poet (who would later write the male self-discovery tract *Iron John*[18]), then one of the editors of a Minnesota magazine called *The Sixties*, who responded indignantly to Birney's 1960 ad for UBC's Creative Writing program:

> There is something horrifying about the assumption that every editor of a literary magazine must have a battery of "instructors in Creative Writing" working under him. This is a revolting idea. There is something revolting also about the whole idea of courses in "creative writing" and "Majors in Creative Writing," which you, as a serious poet, must well understand.

Birney wrote back at once, pointing out that Bly had been in the Creative Writing school at State University of Iowa:

> we are both trying to find and to encourage the young writers of "The Sixties" and after; [my job] operates in a more restricted field and at a lower level [than yours], but without the work of 'serious poets' in universities during the Forties and Fifties, the level of writing in the journals of the Sixties would, I suspect, be a good deal lower than it is. And this you, as a serious editor, must well understand.

But Bly, an essentialist who thought academe muffled creativity, snapped back,

> I still think there is something revolting about poets teaching creative writing, and no amount of reasoning can do away with it. There is some degradation of the poet involved. I was at the Iowa Workshop, directed by Paul Engle, which was a grotesque farce, but I also took part as an undergraduate in some creative writing courses at Harvard under [Archibald] MacLeish, for one. They were directed by serious men, but they were

absurd. The whole atmosphere of a university is the
exact opposite of the delicacy of poetry.... Most creative writing courses do much more harm than
good.... Poetry and the classroom are incompati-
bles—a poet can teach, but he should not cage himself. I do not agree with your idea that the level of
writing in the journals of "The Sixties" is higher than
before, partially because of the work of serious poets
in universities during the Forties and Fifties. The level,
at least in America, is much lower... than it has ever
been, and for the major part because poetry has
become domesticated in the universities."[19]

Certainly, Bly's opinion echoed aspects of Birney's own views.
Hadn't he often complained of being "caged" or "chained" or
"trapped" or "tied down"? Weren't his difficulties with Esther
(with whom he now cohabited in a "housekeeping arrangement")[20] and with Bill, partly a result of his resistance to being
domesticated and constrained? On the other hand, the university
paid him well (he asked for and got another raise in 1961) and
the long summers free of teaching gave him ample time to write.
Without that base and those qualifications, he would not be
invited for lectures or qualify for travel grants—like the
Dominion Government Overseas, the Nuffield, and now the
Canada Council Senior Fellowship he was awarded for the
1962–63 academic year. Where *did* Birney fit into this new
debate? What side was he to take in what he called "the curious
civil war going on in North American poetry"?[21]

He hated the burdens of university teaching. But the life of an
indigent poet was too insecure to contemplate. He liked neither
the mythopoeic "school" nor the Beats and Black Mountain
group. On the one hand, he agreed with Al Purdy that "poetry
[was] in danger of being taken over by the Macpherson-Hine
school."[22] And when he was overlooked in the selection of six
poets to read at the Humanities Association of Canada meetings
in mid-June 1959, he rationalized bitterly: "I would love to have
[gotten] in on [it], but...the gulf between east-west in Canada

[is] much greater than between west Canada and the U.S. No poet west of James Reaney rates in eastern Canada nowadays."[23] But on the other hand, he thought even less of some of the other poets: "I cannot discover that Olson taught anybody anything," he would later write, "his greatest fans stumble into the same incoherence for which he is so well-known, whenever they try to explain his magic. 'Yuh gotta git withit, Yuh gotta.' Creeley, I have much evidence to tell me, was an extraordinarily narrow-minded and intolerant teacher... widely ignorant of literature, and interested only in making little Creeleyites."[24]

Any sense of urgency about these matters was superseded late in 1960 by the failure of McClelland & Stewart to get *Ice Cod Bell or Stone* out in time for the 1960 Christmas sales. Birney withdrew his manuscript angrily to wait a year. He turned instead to help Margerie Lowry, who had come from Hollywood to publish the work of her late husband, Malcolm. It was a gesture that was typically gallant towards Margerie (who needed money) and reverent towards the writer he thought a genius. "Some of the manuscripts were in chaotic condition," Birney observed, "having been rescued from the beach near Vancouver when the squatter's shack...was bulldozed into the sea in his absence."[25]

For a start, he agreed to edit the two trunkfuls of disorganized Lowry writings, place poems and stories in paying journals and arrange publication of collections and books, and, by January 1961, was "very busy" doing so. He arranged for the sale of the Lowry papers to the Special Collections branch of UBC's Library "so it's there for the future M.A. and Ph.D. thesis writers, biographers, debunkers, editors, etc.,"[26] read Lowry's poems for a two-hour radio progam in late February 1961, and scripted a television show about Lowry for CBC's "Explorations" on 21 June 1961. By that time he had prepared a Lowry bibliography, edited a book of Lowry poems and was sending them round individually to journals in advance, as well as helping Margerie collect and edit Lowry's short stories for a book to be published by J.B. Lippincott in the United States.[27]

Though eventually Birney would accomplish the astonishing and generous feat of placing more than one hundred Lowry poems in journals and small magazines, his *Selected Poems of Malcolm Lowry* (published in San Francisco by Ferlinghetti's City Lights Books) has since proved unreliable. As a later scholar Kathleen Sherf has shown, Birney took such liberties with Lowry's manuscripts that "critics who use [the texts Birney published] as the basis for their comments on Lowry's poems are not really commenting on Lowry's poems at all."[28] By unbinding four of Lowry's manuscript notebooks, Birney mixed up the sequence of entries; his annotations in ink on the manuscript obscure Lowry's punctuation; his "silent emendations" (he reduced one 114-line poem to 51 lines and split it into stanzas) alter the poems dramatically; and his imposition of Lowry's "Lighthouse" structure on all his poems, instead of the early work it was meant for, plays havoc with Lowry's intentions.

Birney's effort to help Margerie and immortalize Malcolm did not go unrecognized. Although Margerie eventually proved fractious and unappreciative of his help, *Hear Us O Lord from Heaven Thy Dwelling Place*, the collection of Lowry's short stories he helped her prepare, won for Lowry the 1961 Governor General's Award for fiction and for Margerie the $1,000 which now accompanied the award.

As for his own poetry, taken up in relief after Margerie left for Hollywood, Birney was both in and out of the early sixties' picture. His liberal attitudes—especially about freedom of expression and sex—were, in the word of the day, "groovy." So was his interest in other ethnic groups. He would continue to do translations and warmly befriend many sorts of people. In a heated correspondence, he took Bruce Macdonald to task for his disapproval of his daughter's involvement with a West Indian man.[29] He denounced in letters and a poem ("Turbonave Magnolia")[30] the racism he witnessed aboard the Spanish freighter *Begoña* in 1962.[31] And in the fall of 1963 he introduced the black American writer James Baldwin at a Vancouver meeting of Civil Libertarians.[32] Birney's enthusiasm for experimentation was also "in," as was his youthfulness of spirit. "On my 57th," he wrote to Bet 13 May 1961,

I feel profoundly lucky and grateful for being alive,

and feeling no older than I did at 47 except for a bursitic knot in one shoulder [from attempting tennis] and a tendency to sciatic hips. In fact I think I felt older at 37, marking U. of T. exams and glumly shining my belt buckles to go down to hated army camp at Niagara, with an end to peacetime work in sight and the end of the war unknown. And certainly I feel more chipper and hopeful and more outgoing than I did at 27, with a lonely demanding mother, and a fiancee breaking off the engagement, and the threat of being fired at the U. of Utah because of the depression.[33]

"Or even 17 (when I was broke and jobless and had decided I would never get to a university)," he added to another friend, "If I can manage to live to 97 I should be really peppy and ready to start living."[34] Fred Cogswell, editor of *Fiddlehead,* expressed feelings others shared when he wrote Earle, "If I could envy any man anything, I'd envy you your youthfulness. It is an inspiration."[35] Certainly there was something endearingly boyish about Birney's search for a kaleidoscope while he was in San Francisco and his delight when one was found: "It's a passport to the Abstract," he exclaimed.[36]

But Birney was not young, and he had difficulties other than bursitis and sciatica. His retreating hair was white, and his face had wrinkled into character. In June 1961, though he would joke about it, his eyes weakened again, and he needed two sets of new glasses: "Seems one eye wants to roll in and up, the other in and down. If this keeps up I could go on vaudeville maybe," he wrote his son, Bill.[37] At Bowen in the late summer of 1961, while collecting oysters off-shore at Lieben, he slipped on a stone and broke his ankle (he claimed the stone moved).[38] Later on, he damaged his esophagus when he "went kind of mad, racing up on the top deck and diving into the blessed cold waters off a friend's power boat."[39] Despite his adaptability—socially and linguistically—Birney could not quite keep pace with change. The girls he seduced were getting younger and younger by contrast, and the powerful feeling of conquest was undermined by the freeing of sex from taboos. Language that was second nature to

Birney was "square" to young listeners. Although he quickly mimicked the jargon of a new Americanized generation, he described himself travelling to the University of Washington with Esther as "this strolling minstrel and his wench"[40] and his letters were still peppered with words (often British) like: "motorcar," "batching," "hack," "snooty," "rather," "stuffed shirt," "fortnight," "stinkeroo," "rascal," "welched," and—significantly—"oldster."

His poetry, too, was both in and out of the sixties' picture. He was experimental and interested in other cultures, but he was also reflective and often detached. With "Six-Sided Square: Actopan," "Appeal to a Lady with a Diaper," and "Njarit" he had begun to experiment with visual effects—curved lines on the page, jumbled type and various graphics, such as italics and capital letters.[41] But reviewers of *Ice Cod Bell or Stone*, in which these poems appeared in the spring of 1962, were—aside from Louis Dudek whom Birney had just hired to teach summer school at UBC—lukewarm. "The poet is obviously trying to put another dimension into poetry, a living poetry—the project fails," wrote one under the heading "Tendency to Gimmicks." To another, these experiments "to suggest the swaying of a bus or the wind over the barranca…seem like ingenious trickery rather than poetry." Another disliked his poems in broken English, saw his "Joycean experiments" as a "dead end," and was "irritated at the confused typography." Others noted that Birney's poetic trip around the world looked "outward, not inward." The influential *Globe and Mail* review with the headline "Birney Brings Cool Pity," observed, "Despite the pity, many of them give the impression of aloofness. They are possibly more impersonal than much of Mr. Birney's other work in verse." The review that finally drew fire from Birney simply emphasized these criticisms. Robin Skelton, a young English poet, critic and professor at the University of Manchester who was teaching summer school at Victoria College, B.C. and had never heard of Birney, praised his liveliness, wit, descriptive power and rhythmic strength, but went on to say, "I was…positively alarmed at Dr. Birney's cleverness. If it is dexterity that makes a poet, his place among the Immortals is irremovably reserved…. [his poetry] is never dull—

it is, if anything, galvanically hip—in the cleverest and most stylistic way.... I could not find any one poem which really moved me. The book struck me as being a piece of monumental cleverness calculated to impress those who can be impressed by cleverness.... it is almost as if, for the ten years spent compiling this book, Dr. Birney has been terrified of ever, for one second, talking straight. He should be more self-confident."[42]

What reviewers praised, when they did praise, was Birney's philosophical bent. Robert Weaver found the collection "quieter...the most mature and disciplined" yet.[43] The *Globe and Mail* review admired his humour and his wide scope. Seen against the strobe-lit, drug-enhanced backdrop of the sixties, Birney's work—despite his attempts to be trendy—had more in common with the great Victorians like Matthew Arnold, Alfred Tennyson and Robert Browning than with his younger contemporaries. His satires, such as "Mammorial Stunzas for Aimee Simple McFarcin," were merely clever squibs, whose appeal was limited and temporal. His best work was also facile, but it was reflective, poignant and philosophical as it agonized over the human condition. Though Birney had rebelled against the artifice and sentimental prettiness of Canadian imitators of the Victorian tradition like Audrey Alexandra Brown, his mature work had a majesty of movement and profundity in the contemplation of man's ethical dilemmas that was reminiscent of the great nineteenth-century poems like "Andrea del Sarto," "Dover Beach," or "The Lady of Shalott." His poetic lineage could be traced back through Pratt in Canada and Frost in the U.S. (whom he acknowledged in "First Tree for Frost") to those who thought and felt the difficulty of being human.

He outlined his view of the purpose of poetry in a letter to the English Speaking Union member who organized a talk for him in New Orleans in the fall of 1962. He wanted, "[to drive] home some points about the necessity for imaginative reaching-out to other peoples and tolerance of difference, and understanding of the effects of mass poverty, if we are to keep the peace."[44] In jottings for a lecture topic he offered to the Humanities Association of Canada, which selected him to make a tour of nine eastern universities from Newfoundland to McGill in February 1962—

"Some Reasons for Writing Poetry" (or in jest "Some Unreasons
for Writing Poetry")—he explained: "the nature of the poetic
process as I see it myself. Emphasis on both the anarchic and the
social impulses behind writing; poetry as free play and exploration, and poetry as humanist affirmation."[45] The notion of
poetry as "free play and exploration" harmonized with the era,
but the rest of Birney's theory was about to be superseded, or
perhaps already had been. Irving Layton had told him his poems
were "full of bounce," and reassured him that he had "lost none
of your vigour." However, he went on, pinpointing a crucial difference between his own work and Birney's, "I miss the 'I' loving,
retching; the intense personal note that comes out of involved
living. There's a roving camera eye, sensitive and quick. [But]
poets are not rivers but pools, and their wisdom should go deep,
deep into their own native soil."[46]

Frost had observed in a speech at Bread Loaf, Vermont in the
summer of 1961, "I don't like loathesomeness in a poem. I'd just
as soon step into something nasty on the street."[47] But for
younger poets like Lionel Kearns, whose "Stacked Verse"[48]
evolved from Charles Olson's "Essay on Projective Verse," the
treatment of such subjects was the whole point:

> Lesson
>
> "Fish bladder"
>   the old man said
>   but the kid
> fished it out with a stick
>   and read:
>   "For the prevention of disease
>   only"[49]

Younger poets embraced the loathesome and the anarchic;
Birney—like Frost—preferred to keep such thoughts at bay. "We
all have to have wombs to crawl into," he wrote Einar Neilson in
an earnest moment, "because it's not us that's mad but the cock-
eyed world; the madness is a collective thing and we can only
keep individually sane by keeping as much out of the...bour-

geois-collective society as possible."[50] His eight-program radio series called "At Random with Earle Birney," were far from the randomness being espoused by the next generation, even though he tried to update his material with titles like "The Pride Before the Fallout: Brinkmanship in Chaucer and Today."[51] Though Birney had an "in" with Ferlinghetti through their personal meetings and the Lowry publication, Ferlinghetti turned down *Ice Cod Bell or Stone:* "because I continue to look for the truly *boulversant* and *apocalyptic* in poetry."[52]

It was not surprising that Birney's manuscript of "Selected Poems" could not find an American publisher, but it was not surprising either that it came tantalizingly close. Wesleyan Press considered it along with sixty to eighty other poetry manuscripts in 1961, declared it "not modish" and wrote back: "a more serious problem arose in connection with your selection. The poems as a whole seemed too uneven in achievement, even though we recognized you as a true poet. We liked the ones we cited and wished there had been more of that quality."[53] Although Birney's poem "Christmas Comes"—one of seventy finalists—did not win a Borestone Mountain Poetry Award in 1961, there was a good chance *Ice Cod Bell or Stone* would get the Governor General's Award. "This is such a good book," wrote poet and old Icelandic scholar George Johnston, who admired everything about the new book, "and everyone knows you and just think, it will get another GG's award and a thousand bucks to go with it."[54]

Although a cynic might have observed that Birney, anxious not to be left behind, courted the popular Irving Layton in order to keep abreast of new trends and take part in what one writer called "The Golden Age of Canadian Poetry,"[55] it was in character for him to do so. Almost always generous and encouraging to students in a way that respected their unique abilities, accustomed for years to close contact with the best writers across the country and beyond, and happier by far in the company of friends than alone or in his family, unshockable Birney naturally encouraged controversial Layton—whose fans included Creeley, Williams and Olson and whose *A Red Carpet for the Sun* had won the Governor General's Award for poetry in 1959.

In the spring of 1962, after learning that he had been given a Canada Council Senior Arts Fellowship to travel, write and lecture on Canadian poetry for a year, Birney asked Layton if he would like to replace him at UBC for the year, perhaps to stay on in the program.[56] Since "the bearded angel"[57] Robert Creeley was coming on staff in the fall, a Canadian writer was needed to "balance" the Creative Writing program. As it was, all the Creative Writing teachers except Birney were American or American-trained: Jake Zilber, Tony Friedson, Warren Tallman, Jane Rule and Helen Sonthoff. When Layton responded enthusiastically, Birney replied, "This is wonderful! If only we can pull this off, we really will have not only the unquestionable focus for young writers in Canada, we'll have the foundation for a leading CW centre in North America."[58]

Birney's dreams were explicit:

> This week a San Francisco agent flew up to see me and meet some of our students; Last week the western editor of Doubleday, Doran, did the same thing. Yesterday, the Head of Fine Arts, who has just moved into a fine new building in the centre of the campus, told me that if CW can get free of the English Department, they plan to include us in an extension to his building: our own offices, seminar rooms specially designed, recorded poetry playback room, magazine and reading room, etc. This year our students have been placing stories in mags across Canada and poems in U.S. mags; they've been winning NFCUS awards, CBC prizes; one girl has an experimental Beckett-type play in a downtown playhouse which she wrote in Friedson's playwrighting course; the TISH group have bought a press and are planning a series of poetry chapbooks, first one already out (Frank Davey). Jake Zilber is starting a new mag., on PRISM funds, which will be mainly for far-out satire. I want to see us expand in courses, sections, students; design a tape and maybe even disc library of northamerican poets; publish and make CANADIAN LITERATURE open up

to take Canadian Literature; use our students to raise the level of the campus radio station (a very expensively-equipped one), break into more tv programs downtown (CBC is building a $6 million new centre in Vancouver), take over the Van[couver] Poetry Centre and bring top poets and other writers from all over the English-speaking world; make lumber barons fork out the expenses for all this if necessary. Sure, I'm getting manic about it, but Hell we've got the basis for <u>anything</u>. When Ferlinghetti read poetry at noon hour on the campus this winter, 1100 crowded into the auditorium and hundreds were turned away. Creeley got almost as many. Robert Duncan was so surprised at his good reception he came back and just hung around on his own for another two weeks... I've just persuaded Walter Koerner, the pulp man, to found an entrance schol[arship] to bring the best creative writer from high school here.[59]

Birney brought his considerable talent for political strategy into play on Layton's behalf, advising him in detail about applying (he suggested getting three references, one from Frank Scott). Birney's Creative Writing Committee of Jake Zilber, Warren Tallman and John Hulcoop backed him, as did the four teaching assistants, George Bowering, Lionel Kearns, Frank Davey and Phyllis Webb. But when during a telephone conversation Roy Daniells, still Head of English, hung up on him abruptly on 18 May, he knew things were going wrong. At the meeting on 8 May between the Creative Writing Committee (which considered and approved Layton's application) and the departmental Appointments Committee, Daniells had said that there was no money to hire anyone, to which Birney had replied that Daniells must request money from the dean. When Birney learned Daniells had not gone directly to the dean, and he saw the dean himself and was told he would have to wait as the dean was going away, he wrote a long, carefully worded letter on 14 May to his friend, UBC President Larry MacKenzie. Birney was furious that Daniells put off going to the dean; Daniells was enraged that Birney had gone over his head to the president, without sending him a copy of his letter. What ensued was a cat-and-mouse game that was unworthy of both men, in which they allowed the issue of Layton to fan into flames the sparks that had smouldered between them for years.

According to Birney, who wrote long, defensive letters to several of his friends, as well as to Daniells and other colleagues, Daniells stalled in the hope Birney would have left UBC on his Canada Council grant on 1 June, at which point he would see to it that Layton wasn't hired. Avoiding an irate Earle Birney could hardly have been easy, but Daniells managed to do so. According to a six-page blow-by-blow letter Birney wrote Daniells (with copies to MacKenzie, Dean S.N.F. Chant, the Creative Writing Committee and the department's Executive Committee) a month later, he tried several times on 12 May to talk to him:

> Although my office was ten yards from yours and we were both on the campus every day that week, you left me no message and, when I saw you in the hall and started toward you, you turned abruptly and hurried down the far stairs....
>
> May 17 I again attempted to see you, having observed you in our common hallway. However, you retreated anxiously into your office, locked your door, and did not answer my knock....
>
> May 18...faced with a three-day holiday, I phoned your home.... In a voice more suited to one of Franco's generals rebuking a corporal, you... demand[ed] to know if I had written to the President. When I innocently confessed to this military crime and [was] about to explain it was at the Dean's request, you bark[ed]: "Then there is nothing further to discuss," and bang the phone in my ear....
>
> May 22 I received a note from you, dated two days earlier, in which you tell me...you are "turning over Layton's file to Dean Chant [who]...will give his opinion direct to the President." A professor in another department...later reported to me that he

observed you elaborately tip-toeing down the empty
hall and silently fixing this note on my door (while I
could be heard typing inside) and tip-toeing away
again. Such poltroonery would be laughable if you
were a teaching fellow, but you are, God save us, a
department head, dealing with an important question
of appointment. Are you merely a coward, or in need
of psychiatric help? ...Meantime you affix to your
office door a printed notice: "Looking for Someone
With a Little Authority? I Have as Little as
Anyone."...mute evidence of your sham humility and
a public display of childish petulance...

May 25 you wrote a note in which you said that
"there were, I think, three letters" in support of
Layton, but that they were with the Dean... Also, that
your Appointments Committee "was unable to recommend" Layton.... you evidently felt you should deliver
[this note] personally but in disguise, to my office.
Two colleagues in other departments separately
reported to me that they saw you once more tip-toeing to my office door while I sat working and waiting
inside; this time, although it was a sunny day, you
wore a raincoat buttoned up, a scarf around your chin,
a hat pulled down over your face. I will spare you their
speculations about your mental health. Later that day
a senior colleague...informed me that you had
approached him...for advice about hiring two new
staff.... you had lied to me and my committee from
the start when you said that you had no money.

May 30 [finding the Dean] out of town...[and
commencing] my year's leave in two days... I had no
alternative but to go to the President...[who] asked
me to return to the Dean...and advise him that I was
to see the file. This I did...only to be told that (1) you
had not put into writing any of the reasons why
you...turned Layton down, and (2) that you had
marked the Layton file "Confidential" with...specific
instructions that no one in the department was to

have access to it. The Dean...[showed me] the letters
in support of Layton.... they turned out to be highly
complimentary. Layton's colleagues both in McGill...
and in Sir George Williams...considered him not
merely a good teacher but, in the words of his department head, a "great one" whom they were loath to
lose.

    There was...a large part of the Layton file which the
Dean ([whom you had convinced] that Mr. Layton
was a writer of obscenities...) reluctantly told me you
had requested should not be shown me.... when you
had been too busy to write me or even to speak to me,
it appears that you had been...writing letters to literary personalities in Canada whom you thought
might...supply you "confidentially" with unfavourable
opinions of Layton.... it appears that these gentlemen...sprinkled so much praise between the blame
that you were unable to use any of them...[60]

Birney was right that Daniells had solicited three extra letters
immediately after the 8 May meeting of the two committees,
and he correctly concluded after glimpsing one of the signatures
upside-down, that Desmond Pacey was one of them. But he was
wrong in speculating that Daniells had chosen only "persons
whom [he] knew had engaged in controversy with Layton...or
who had reviewed his work unfavourably" and he was wrong to
think the letters were too positive to serve Daniells's purpose.
Desmond Pacey was, in fact, a close friend of Layton's as well as
an admirer. His letter praised Layton's lecturing and his "warm
personal interest in students as individuals"; but he summed up
by saying "He would lend some lustre, though he might occasionally cause some embarrassment." The second letter was from
Northrop Frye (whom Layton had attacked in print), who none
the less took the time to consult with a couple of Layton's colleagues at Sir George Williams. Frye also praised Layton as "a
most valuable teacher," though he added "especially for students
who would be 'disciples.'" He remarked that Layton was experi-
encing "a rather difficult adjustment to middle-age," that he

"might be confused at UBC as to where his partisanships should be" (e.g., whether to attack *Prism* or *Canadian Literature*), and predicted that he "will show little real development from now on." The third letter, from Harold Files, Chairman of McGill's English Department, was (aside from routine praise for Layton's teaching) unremittingly virulent. Files described Layton as "fantastically self-centred" and thought (as Birney himself once had) "the love of fame and greatness...made him very imperfectly sane." He predicted that if Layton went west, "the world will soon be informed that the centre of culture has shifted far to the West." Furthermore, he considered him "not much of a scholar." He went on to say that Layton "lacks humour, perspective, or any decent restraint," and that (as Layton himself had told Birney)[61] "Sir George Williams has lately refused to give him the status and tenure he had hoped for largely (as I have been told) because Irving lacks the power or disposition to stem a flow of lowly Billingsgate and reckless assertions when people fail to please him." As for McGill, Files commented, "no one [here] has ever suggested hiring Layton."[62]

Suspecting the worst of letters he would never see, and as furious that "Buggernuts Daniells"[63] had out-manoeuvred him as disappointed that his dreams for the best Creative Writing centre in North America might not be realized, Birney lashed out with decades of pent-up rage.

> You have lost our respect in the eyes of writers across Canada and in many literary centres in the rest of the world where Irving Layton's name is known and respected. You have proved yourself...the intolerant and sectarian Puritan you were when I first met you thirty years ago and which you have secretly remained. You do not like Irving Layton, nor me, nor anyone who is seriously engaged in the writing of literature, because we are life-loving, not life-denying, because we are not as concerned with respectability and mere academism as you are, because we effervesce and write and publish, while you remain critically superior and intellectually sterile....

As an alumnus and a longtime senior staff member
of this university I denounce you as a man unfit to
hold administrative office, as a man whose humanism
is a sham, who stoops to deceit, lie, and trickery to
gain his ends—in sum, a moral and intellectual coward.

You will not have Irving Layton in your department
next year. Neither will you have me. I have endured
your misleadership of our department for fourteen
years but this final piece of stupidity, arrogance, trickery and plain falsehood is more than I can take.[64]

A month later, after an angry letter from Layton, President
Larry MacKenzie, who along with Dean Chant, had stepped
down from administration, wrote to Birney saying that he was
sorry Layton hadn't "held his fire," since he had been in the
process of getting further opinions from Claude Bissell, Frank
Scott and Cyril James.[65] He expressed the hope that Birney
would return to UBC, but it was too late. Birney was writing to
one and all that he had resigned.

Having sent off forwarding addresses in all directions, Birney
drove off with Esther, heading for San Miguel where they had
rented Allen Smart's house not far from the Brookses for three
months. Esther, having quit her part-time job with retarded children, had rented the house now too big for the two of them to a
family of eight and found a wonderful bright, rambling flat on
English Bay behind the Sylvia Hotel, two blocks from the lovely,
wooded Stanley Park. "I have a bedroom one end of the flat, E.
the other," she wrote Miriam Waddington, whom Earle had successfully recommended for a Canada Council grant that year,

We meet to eat, are cheerful and companionable in a
remote sort of way. Neither really knows what is going
on in the mind and heart of the other and I for one
never intend to reveal what is going on in mine. We
talk of the news and literature and people...it seems
to suit both of us and this way we sail over the reefs of
each others real personality. It never fails—if I say

what I'm really thinking about anything—even art or
the news—it leads inevitably to quarrelling. I think E.
must be the most irascible man that mortal woman
was ever tormented with…the quick, hot temper, the
childish uncontrolled rejoinder pops out. Oh the joy
of having been able to master the rejoinder of
silence.[66]

Once term ended, Bill would join them to see Mexico—a
twenty-first birthday coming-of-age present from his father.[67] In
San Miguel, Birney would study Spanish three hours a day and
give occasional lectures and classes at the Instituto Allende or
"menopause manor" ("ancient Republican gringas taking art
courses and younger gringas from Wellesley [the American
women's college] hoping to lose their cherries to Latin lovers")
and the new Academia Hispaniola-America, neither of which he
considered serious academic institutions.[68]

Birney had argued in his application for the grant—backed by
his most influential friends, University of Toronto President
Claude Bissell and Bruce Macdonald, now at the embassy in
Athens—that Canada needed cultural ambassadors to supplement their diplomats and economic emissaries.[69] Typical of his
presentations—which he took very seriously—was a reading of
"The Damnation of Vancouver," at the "El Centro Universitario
de Teatro on 17 de Agosto a las 19 hs." in Mexico City. P.K.
Page, who was now painting wonderful canvases, and her husband Arthur Irwin, the Canadian ambassador to Mexico, threw
an elegant cocktail buffet for him. Birney also consulted with the
film director Luis Buñuel, who was planning a film of *Under the
Volcano* ("I didn't feel B[uñuel] had much of a clue himself as to
what he wanted to do with it"),[70] and worked with Raul Ortiz,
who was translating the novel into Spanish, not only on Lowry's
book, but on his own poems which he was translating himself
"with the help of maestros, maestras, friends, dictionaries, the-
sauri, and bottles of tequila."[71]

On his 1958–59 trip, Birney had felt sure that travelling quickly
and catching glimpses of events stimulated his poetic imagination. But he had had doubts about the process after flying to

Toronto for five days from Oregon to Toronto in May to read at
the Canadian Conference of the Arts at the O'Keefe Centre. He
had spent twenty minutes talking with Esther in the Vancouver
airport on his way back to Oregon. "This kind of travel speed
renders everything one does into a kind of uneasy dream," he
wrote Bet afterwards, unhappy that he had not been able to
spend a night with her, as he had (in the "sterile" surroundings of
the Royal York Hotel) in February on his Humanities
Association tour.[72]

Uneasy dream or not, Birney was determined to slake his
appetite for experience on what he was sure would be his last
leave.[73] No sooner had Esther and Bill left, than his Oregon student Judith Bechtold ("that rarity: a good-looking girl who can
make firsts in Chaucer and also in a writing class")[74] arrived. It
was not an auspicious visit: "I'm getting over a strep throat," he
complained to Kate Simon, a San Miguel friend who had left,
"while coping with a 22-year-old ex-student...a sweet pure
Catolica from Portland, Ore. who has come down here alone
against the wishes of her Parents and the warnings of Friends, for
a 20-day vacation in Mexico.... She is so introverted it's worrying. But no doubt I'll weather through this episode...which
could fit into...a *Lolita* rewritten for circulation by the
Propogation of Christian Knowledge."[75]

In letter after letter—typed with his eight-pound Olivetti
portable on various hotel stationery with exotic headings—to
friend upon friend, Birney recounted his whirlwind travels as he
raced from place to place, checking at every stop for letters which
he began to personify as if they were Furies pursuing him round
the globe, fretting when those he expected failed to appear, complaining of the pressure to reply when they did. "After Mexico I
was in New Orleans and Baton Rouge for ten days," he wrote
student David Bromige, who had won a Woodrow Wilson scholarship to Berkeley, "lecturing on Chaucer, Can. Lit., etc. at various universities and even to the Rotary":

> Then Miami, Lima (2 universities), Santiago (ditto),
> Buenos Aires (sightseeing), Santiago and Lima again
> for more lectures, Colombia (rotting in a river swamp,

[mainly in Cartagena]), Curacao (swimming until a jelly fish bit me), Trinidad (lecturing, "one of the most percussive islands I was ever set throbbing in"),[76] Jamaica (lecturing, drinking, partying, mountain-hiking), Caracas (fast rubbernecking), then a long slow Spanish ship [the Turbonave Begona] to Vigo ("I kept comparatively sane by hammering out 25 letters")[77] and a ditto train to Madrid for a Christmas with two ex-UBC students of mine [John Whittaker, at Madrid's Canadian embassy, and his wife] en famille, with a day ferreting out El Grecos through the windy streets of Toledo, and peering at hundreds of Goyas and Velasquez through the dimlit mortuary-cold air of the Prado. It was bloody cold in Spain and on Boxing Day I flew here, only to arrive in time for what is apparently going to be the biggest snowstorm of the Age or something. I sit huddled on the rug by the gas-fire pecking this out with a kink in my neck in a friend's flat on Old Brompton Road.[78]

Though Bromige and others may have felt sorry for Birney, who had given thirty lectures by the end of November, they needn't have. By "spreading myself thin over the landscape"[79] he had managed to get to many exciting places, his favourite being Machu Picchu high in the Andes, and though he was unlucky in the weather, he was fortunate in other ways. The London flat he was huddled up in belonged to Liz Cowley. And the title of Layton's new book *Balls for a One-Armed Juggler* prompted him to write: "My balls have disappeared into my scrotum... This afternoon, however, a delicious and almost-young Sussex lady poet is being lured to this apartment, while my flatmates stay carefully away, and I am hoping to have the essential round twins tickled down into proper position again."[80]

In a grand gesture that implied a great deal about his state of mind, Birney imported a sleek red Volvo P-1800 sports car ("a small red devil much too young for me")[81] from Copenhagen in February, and having lined up friends to visit, headed south as soon as he had broken it in. In his zeal to enjoy what he called

"Birney's last travel fling before settling down into the race between death and retirement,"[82] he seemed to have forgotten that he had complained on reaching London, "I've been moving far too fast for my own good."[83] "Haven't done much writing lately," he wrote Layton,

> too much travelling. But then, I never expect to be back in Europe, and am belatedly seeing what I should have tried to see 30 years ago, when first I came to Europe (and had no money to see it). I set off from London the beginning of March, with an old English girlfriend from wartime days [Margaret Crosland, the "almost-young lady poet"], and drove to Florence; after a week, she had to get back to London because of a book she was writing on assignment to a deadline. But I met up with an old Canadian girlfriend, of more recent vintage [Liz Cowley, whom he had invited in a letter from Jamaica][84] and we carried on through Italy to the boot at Brindisium [sic], over by car ferry to Patras, and into a fishing village in the Peloponnesus. Weather was still coolish, though, no swimming possible, so we went to Athens to see Ken Hanson, the Portland, Oregon poet (Reed College, on sabbatical). Went north through Jugoslavia to Venice, Verona, through France to Andorra, down to Barcelona, and into another fishing village [L'Ametlla de Mar],[85] Catalonian variety. After two weeks, up to Madrid, where the girl went back to London and my wife arrived by plane from Vancouver. More wandering: Toledo, Cordoba, Seville, Algeciras, Gibraltar, Granada, Valencia—and into a Tarragonian-Moorish fishing village, where we now are. But when June comes we're committed to joining Esther's two brothers in a house on Majorca. In July, Esther will go to England; I'll probably hole up in yet another fishing village.[86]

In fact, by the end of 1962, his leave half over, Birney had done no writing: "I've seen a great number of places [he had now visited eighteen countries], slightly improved my Spanish, lectured about 40 times on various subjects of no great importance, probably, to small and sometimes uncomprehending audiences; written numerous diary notes and letters and postcards, met hundreds and hundreds of people—and that's it. No real writing done at all."[87]

Birney did not last long with Esther's brothers David (a dentist) and Donald (a script-writer and film producer he had tried to relocate in Canada unsuccessfully) at Fornlutx, Mallorca. They were "ganging up on me" and had, he complained testily, "uncharming foibles." "One of my brothers-in-law," he griped to Layton, "[is] an arrogant selfish prick who wouldn't let anyone else drive [his car]."[88] Birney left by bus (his Volvo was in London) and settled in with a rented car at the other end of the island on a high cirque below the highest mountain, Puig Major, where Esther soon joined him. There he finally began to write, contemplating, among other things, Death.

He had good reason to do so. Not only was he increasingly preoccupied with aging, retirement and his own mortality, he had lost a number of important friends. Herman Singer, the carpenter who had been "closer to me than many brothers"[89] (Birney called him, inaccurately, "my oldest correspondent"), had died of a heart attack in June 1961. The following month, he lost three more friends: the forty-six-year-old wife of Ken Johnstone, his old Trotskyist comrade and former brother-in-law; Dal Grauer, his old UBC and Berkeley Zate chum who had been secretary at B.C. Hydro and was UBC Chancellor when he died of leukemia (Birney gave his commemoration address, referring to him also as "far closer...than most brothers");[90] and most tragically, the sixteen-year-old son of Jan de Bruyn, one of his three UBC colleagues who founded *Prism*, who fell to his death mountain-climbing (Birney's poem "Climbers" was read at the funeral). Now, as he lay tanning and eating oranges on fine Mallorca beaches, poet Ted Roethke ("a fat psychotic drunk")[91] died of a heart attack in a Seattle swimming pool. The following month, Herman Singer's son committed suicide. "Yes, maybe there are absolutes, after all," Birney wrote Layton in response to the preface to *Balls for a One-Armed Juggler*, which he much admired, "death is one, for any organism that can conceive of death, and death for the race is now a negative absolute."[92] When *Turvey* appeared that year in a McClelland & Stewart New Canadian Library paperback with an introduction by George Woodcock, he reported, "it makes me feel like dead to look at it."[93] His sense of impotence deepened when he learned that the 1962 Governor General's Award he hoped for, and that others like Dudek, Souster, John Robert Colombo and Ron Everson expected him to win, had gone, not to his *Ice Cod Bell or Stone*, but to James Reaney's *Twelve Letters to a Small Town*.[94] (It was Reaney's second Governor General's Award for poetry, and he also won the award for drama in 1962.)[95] "Frye-Reaney-Macpherson...are an academic in-Group in Canada just now," he wrote Ron Everson. "It would seem that the colonial time lag still operates a bit; just as Jung is getting his well-deserved debunking in Europe, his poetic followers become fashionable in Canada." However, he added, "Roy Daniells [is]...the real nigger in the GG Woodpile."[96] To his Oregon writer friend, Ralph Salisbury, he joked bitterly, "I've decided I'll be discovered After Death or Never." As for the new book of poems he was "trying with genuine desperation to shake...out of my dusty podskull"[97] and for which he knew McClelland & Stewart were not eager, since they wanted another money-making novel like *Turvey*, he wrote, "I call [it]...'Last Poems,' a sinister title, but I don't intend much more than that. I hope to switch to short stories and an autobiography of my early years.... The trouble is that nobody reads poetry any more." "When I'm depressed," he wrote elsewhere, "I call it LAST GASP... I put nothing on the ms so it's come back in the contract as...'Untitled'—and maybe that's the best one yet. Or 'Unentitled to Liberties.'"[98]

Despite the fact that he had completed about "120 pages printed" of poems (including "Beyond False Creek Mouth"—later "November Walk Near False Creek Mouth"—which would provide the title for his next collection), Birney's return to UBC in the fall of 1963 deepened his depression. He was, he told Bill, who had graduated first class in Honours Mathematics and won two scholarships to the M.Sc. program in Computer Mathematics at the University of California in Los Angeles, that he would not want to drive him south because he was "rather saturated with travel."[99] He had put 13,000 miles on his "honey of a car" in seven months.[100] "Now," he wrote resignedly, "I expect to wither away in Vancouver, all voyages over."[101] While abroad, he had successfully negotiated his dream to separate the Creative Writing program from English (partly by lining up a job at Oregon and using it as a lever without mentioning that the salary there was much lower than UBC's) and Dean Chant (whom he referred to as "Dean Shant," "Dean Cant" and "Dean C _ _ T")[102] had met his conditions: that he administer the new separate program, teach what he wanted and have no classes in the English Department.[103] As "proof of whether I've won or not," he intended to have Layton on staff.[104] But since the replacement of his friend Larry MacKenzie, who supported the arts, by the new president, J.B. Macdonald, who had been a dentist, Birney no longer had the leverage he was accustomed to. Layton was not approved for appointment, and other plans to bring American poet friends to UBC were also thwarted by the Canada Council policy that only Canadian writers be sponsored.[105] Though he was having the usual difficulties placing his new poems in magazines before they came out in book form (he prepared a target list of 166 periodicals publishing poetry in 1963),[106] "David" was still being anthologized, but for Grades 9 and 10, instead of senior high school.[107]

More seriously, by being away for more than a year, Birney had lost touch. It had been Warren Tallman who set up the summer poetry conference with workshops, readings, talks and informal gatherings by Olson, Creeley, Duncan and many others in the summer of 1963 which galvanized many young writers. "[It was] one high-water mark of Tallman's influence, and the impact of the U.S. writers on campus and in Vancouver generally," recalls Tom Wayman, a young poet who had attended UBC readings since 1962 and entered second-year Honours English the following year,

> I was working as a reporter for the *Vancouver Sun* that summer, and so could only attend the evening readings. I was curious about these writers since articles

about them often appeared in the *Ubyssey*'s literary
pages, and in campus literary magazines like *Raven*,
and many references to their work would be provided
by the student writers whose readings I so faithfully
attended."[108]

Wayman sided with Birney (and loved the senior Poetry
Workshop he took in 1964–65 which culminated in a collection
of student poems called "From the Earle's Court")[109] in what he
perceived as "a schism in the approaches to contemporary poetry"
at UBC with Birney representing and promoting "the modernist
tradition in Canada (Scott, Smith, Layton, Livesay, Purdy and so
on)" and Warren Tallman…originally from the U.S.,

> [having] a particular interest in a group…loosely
> called the Black Mountain School: Charles Olson
> (who had been a teacher and and eventually rector at
> Black Mountain College in the U.S. South, 1951-56),
> Robert Creeley (and through him Denise Levertov),
> Allen Ginsberg (and by extension, the Beats), Robert
> Duncan (and through him the San Francisco renais-
> sance—including Lawrence Ferlinghetti, Gary Snyder,
> Lew Welch, Jack Spicer)…[for whom] the basic text
> was Donald Allen's anthology *The New American
> Poetry*. What was heady about these authors…was
> that…[they] wrote a lot about writing—about their
> own writing, about intricate theories of poetic compo-
> sition, about the place of literature, in society, in a
> human life…. Our Canadian authors seemed a pretty
> dull, staid, uninformed, taciturn lot in comparison.[110]

Peg Robertson, another student who attended the full conference as a CW course, would more typically recall: "Besides the
informal atmosphere of the summer campus and the casualness
of the poets present, there was a sense of excitement which per-
vaded all the meetings, discussions and readings…. There was
the sense of being present, and right in the middle of what was
happening. Creeley was back from New Mexico, Olson was up

from New England, Ginsberg flew in from India. Philip Whalen, Denise Levertov, Margaret Avison, Robert Duncan, were all present from time to time. What happened in the exchange of ideas and opinions was electrifying."[111]

Birney had written in March 1962 that he was not "lukewarm about Creeley,"[112] and he protested to David Bromige that he did not attend the "summer clambake" not because he "disapproved" of it, but because he had to wait to qualify for exemption from paying duty on the Volvo and stayed in Toronto to "cash in" on various radio, television and magazine assignments and read at a poetry gathering at John Robert Colombo's with a group of Toronto poets.[113] But he wrote to Layton,

> Tallman (who was largely responsible for pushing Creeley into UBC) is [Daniells's] pal and [the conference] his pet dream. I am taking care to stay away till it's over because, though I think it's a good thing and some of the people invited to it are good...the general set-up reflects a kind of lop-sidedness in Warren's literary judgements, esp. when it comes to picking teachers.[114]

To Ron Everson he added later, "[The] solid phalanx of Black Mt. hillbillies...did a good job in their way.... But they introduced cultism in its extreme form. Anything written unlike what they were writing was dubbed not just inferior, but Anti-poetry. How the Puritan mind is reborn in every new movement! Christ = Creeley, and anti-Christ = anti-Creeley."[115]

Scarcely had Birney reacted to the conference, when he was stung by a piece he had missed while away in the April *Canadian Forum* by Peter Dale Scott, Frank's son: "You give your game away," he lashed out,

> when you talk about "our poetic elders"...in contrast to "the newer poets".... If you could read a poem of mine like "Captain Cook" without this initial jaundice of the Rebel Youth you would...see...that the final lines are prepared for in the opening lines.... For

God's sake, Scott, why don't you grow up? Father-rebellion is something we all had to go in for, in adolescence. You can't make a critical credo of it. Smith and Layton and I are not necessarily worse poets than you and your pals because we are older.[116]

He was even more angry when the editors of *El Corno Emplumado* (The Plumed Horn), a Mexican journal which had accepted work by two of his students (George Bowering and Lionel Kearns) turned down all thirteen of his poems in Spanish translation because they "didn't seem exactly what we want for future publication...though there are a number of good things in all the poems." Further, "the translation was largely very poor," Margaret Randall de Mondragon wrote. In his scathing rejoinder, Birney accused her of being patronising, and suggested the Canadian postmark did him in.

> It happens that one of the poems I sent you, as a sort of test...was one that took first prize a few years ago in the annual Borestone Mountain awards, and has been reprinted, since its first appearance in an American quarterly, at least ten times and in four countries. It is really too well known a poem for you to have taken— but you wouldn't know that, would you? I've no doubt that a certain amount of unAmericanism in my poems wouldn't go over well with the patrons on the U.S. side.... As for the "translation being largely poor," I've no doubt some of it was. But the translation of the poem I'm referring to, "From the Hazel Bough," was made by Raul Ortiz, whom most intellectuals in Mexico would recognize at once as the translator into English [sic] of Lowry's *Under the Volcano* (or haven't you heard of this book?) and as one of the top educators at the national University of Mexico. He is perfectly tri-lingual. And who in hell is your husband, what has he achieved in the realms of translation, to sneer at the translations of people like Prof. Garaiz, himself a Spaniard, a Mexican...a poet and a linguist?

Submit again?—you and your husband know what you can do with your plumed horn.

Mondragon—no doubt shaken—wrote back immediately.

> In the history of [our] correspondence, we've never received as rude a letter as yours... We are two young poets and our decisions are based purely on our own likes and dislikes.... I believe that two people who pound their typewriters and walk the streets daily in order to obtain the 25,000 pesos needed each time they go to press have the right... to decide what goes into their magazine.... Your mention of the Canadian postmark... is simply ridiculous! Proof of our warm feeling towards Canada should be found in the fact that we have published Lionel Kearns and will soon publish George Bowering, among others from your country. And our latest issue carries ample coverage of the exciting recent poetry seminar at the University of Vancouver.... But perhaps the most incredibly childish of your accusations is your mention of the "antiamericanness" in your poems.... If you are at all familiar with... our magazine, you'll note that we have published Communists and Catholic monks... and that one of our aims is to carry the torch of brotherhood above and beyond either politics or state lines.... I am very sorry that this obviously hurt you to the point of writing a letter that does not at all befit a poet and professor.[117]

That fall, Birney was puzzled to learn two of his ninety Creative Writing students were convicted on marijuana charges.[118] And he was alarmed that Avo Erisalu, the first student to hold the Creative Writing entrance scholarship he'd solicited from Koerner, was rumoured to be advising students not to enrol in the program.[119] Though he tried to make light of it to friends like Art Smith, Birney knew he was losing his hold: "It's really Far Out to be writing poetry at our age, so far out it may yet be IN again, who knows?!"[120]

For reasons other than these, Birney felt that his fledgling program was not getting off the ground as he'd imagined: "Creative Writing, after the first frenzies of liberation is in the doldrums," he wrote Beryl Rowlands, who had finished her Ph.D. thesis and placed several sections as articles in journals, "chiefly because Dean Chant has still six months to go to retirement, and refuses to do anything about anything… We aren't yet legally a Dept., but we aren't anything else—so I have the responsibility without power or money." Birney's budget for his "School" of Creative Writing (the same status as Theatre, and—when they began—as for Music and Fine Arts) consisted of the three salaries of those teaching in it, plus one hundred dollars for supplies. Although Birney knew in advance it would not be a "department," and did not think to negotiate what his title would be, he was as angry that he and his program lacked the trappings of power, as he was that they had no money to expand as he had planned. He was quick to note that his school was the only Canadian institution included by MCA in its graduate scholarship scheme for writer-students in the Entertainment Arts, and that the publishers, Macmillan, had doubled their prize money for student competitions. But the new president and the dean both refused to budge. The dean, he wrote Bet, "has really double-crossed me."[121]

As if this "Low Crisis"[122] weren't enough, Birney had a pressing personal crisis to deal with. Bet Cox had finally left her husband and moved in with her sister in Duncan, Vancouver Island. In the summer of 1961, she had brought her two daughters out for a July holiday on Bowen Island and had visited "Uncle Earle" with them at "Lieben," where Birney was living alone, except for weekends when Esther brought friends over. He wrote Einar, who was working in Banff as a bus line manager, that he had been "making up for thirteen years lost time, since my old love has returned to the island. It is really like old times in more ways than one. H[ilda Brown], who gave me a bad time of it running interference in 1948, is having to be fended off again in 1961."[123] Bet's husband joined her later, met Birney briefly before they headed back east, stopping en route at Takkakaw Falls: "the falls meant so much of you to me, as it battered the brown throbbing thighs of its mountain," Bet wrote on her return.[124] That summer, she had published the eight sonnets she had written Birney (in frank imitation of Margaret Crosland) for his forty-fifth birthday in 1949 in *Fiddlehead*.[125] The similarities to Margaret and Earle's wartime interchange—and to "Mappemounde"—could easily be seen in Bet's poem about Bowen Island, even though her sensibility was much less intellectual and her rhythms more gentle:

> Fall whirled us off, the maps half-made. Now lest
> The essence of our green adventure fade
> To legend, drifting in a lotus shade
> With Cythera and dim Isles of the blest,
> Let us in exile learn cartography,
> Bend to our pens in these our disorient days,
> Knowing so well that vanished shoreline, trace
> The rock, the tree, and where our treasures lie.
>
> . . . .
>
> So by this lonely, long, convinced exertion,
> Filling out maps, we'll yet believe things certain.[126]

She hoped they didn't embarrass him: "I ought to have used a pseudonym, but oh hell, who cares." "I embarrassed?" he wrote back, "Good god, I would be proud if anyone identified me with them."[127]

Now—at a point when he could least pay attention to her—Bet was nearby, sweetly reminding him of their wonderful times together, and he felt pressured. "Dearest I think we *will* live together, some time," she had written. She was not only poor, having only a low-paying job with a dentist in Duncan, but she was "terribly depressed." "I am not near enough to see you," she wrote, "only near enough to make you nervous about my trying to—oh darling, if I could just have a note once in a while."[128] But now that Bill had left home and he could with relative ease leave Esther (who had a new job helping unwed mothers with the Children's Aid Society) to move in with Bet, he unaccountably held back: "I still love you, you know," he wrote with cynical insight that probably resulted from sorting through masses of his old files of letters in the Special Collections at UBC's Library "to decide what I should preserve for a dubious and hypothetical and probably indifferent Posterity," "and I begin hoping again. But I am so old now, and bitter and sterile. I don't even know if you'd like me... I want to live with [your girls]—and you—but can I leave Esther without wrecking her?... I'm all in a tail-spin."[129]

So great was the tailspin of Birney's professional and personal life that he developed a stomach ulcer (which he worried might be cancer), and had to give up many foods and liquor. "All this winter I've been trying to repair the liberal-minded dikes, re-introduce concepts of tolerance and variety into all the minds of the brainwashed students from last summer's seminar," he wrote Ron Everson as 1963 drew to a close.

> Creeley got more money from... New Mexico and is no longer on our scene; but Tallman is here, and Skelton over in Victoria. Between them they are try-ing to divert students away from our program to Victoria. Daniells helps them out... However, we still have...seven courses, with three instructors—by far the largest set-up in Canada.... Am really trying to decide whether to quit teaching... Don't like to leave Vancouver but I know I can't freelance from out here, so I'll decide something soon.... My new book is due out March but...I want to revise it—cut it down to size, make sure it's not too goddamned "clever." ...It will be my last, except for a Selected Poems I want to bring out someday, but not while the [Robin] Skeltons and the Franklin Daveys and the like are the critics in influential journals.[130]

As for Bet, he insisted she meet Esther (one friend responded "Oh! Bet! Esther would go right over you like a steamroller!").[131] in what looked like an attempt to neutralize any fantasies she might have about his leaving the marriage. "I really feel if she once met you," he had argued, at the same time as offering Bet his room and making it clear he would sleep elsewhere, "she would love you. No doubt she has feared you in the past, when she had a possessive attitude to me. Now all that is gone; she wouldn't stand in the way of anything you and I wanted to do.... She is a social worker with a big heart, once female jealousy is out of it."[132] By Christmas, while Esther was in Los Angeles with Bill, Birney was resting in an attempt to recover before the next term began. On Boxing Day, he invited Bet and her daughters, Kathy and Sally, to Vancouver to see the Moscow Circus, and paid their fares from Duncan. This was the first time he and Bet had had a chance to be alone since she had arrived in B.C. in July. Birney helped her find a job in the Bacteriology and Immunology Department at UBC (in mid-February she stayed overnight for her interview and met Esther), and he located a small flat for her. He tried to explain his various dilemmas with very little concern for hers: "I think with some longing of the possibility of living alone and slowly going mad in a shack some-where—but I don't even have enough income to support myself alone in a shack," he wrote of a fantasy that curiously resembled his poem "Bushed" and seemed oblivious to the fact that he now earned more than $12,000 a year while she earned $300 a month. But by May, despite Earle's words, "Don't despair. Don't say we are never going to live together,"[133] Bet gave up. In what amounted to a farewell letter, she backed away from a fight he instigated over her landlady, complained mildly that he was the only person who called her "helpless," reminded him that she lived in what he thought were "squalid" conditions because, hav-ing lost fifteen years out of her career, she was underpaid, and gently said goodbye to him for a while.[134]

The new academic term brought more aggravations. Robin Skelton had criticized Birney in the autumn issue of *Tamarack Review* for "aggressively globe-trotting," a criticism that was close to the bone and drew a sarcastic reply. Far worse was an article in *Canadian Literature* by the director of Carleton University's Institute of Canadian Studies, Robert MacDougall: "The dodo and the cruising Auk." Birney fired off a rejoinder, taking issue with MacDougall's "advising young Canadian writers to stay away from our universities and so escape the contamination of us older hacks."[135] Esther, who liked Bet, believed Earle's health problems were the result of their incompatibilities and frankly advised him to leave her and go to Bet. He explained his ill-health (which his doctor thought was "psychosomatic")[136] and appealed successfully to Dean Chant, who promised to see the president about taking Birney off all administration without increasing his teaching duties. (Birney had another job lined up at the new Simon Fraser University in Burnaby, in case this failed.)[137] When he was unable to get Ralph Gustafson a job, he was "disgusted with the whole damned university.... I like to deal in telegrams, fast decisions, long distance phone calls, etc. But I have to work with a horse and buggy budget under a stage-coach Dean."[138]

As always, Birney had turned to women—usually gleaned from his creative writing classes and often vulnerable because of marital or financial difficulties—to comfort himself. He had been involved with Betty Lambert for a time, writing his "Villanelle"[139] about an occasion on which she stood him up at Bowen Island ("villain" "elle"). But he quickly turned his attention from Betty to Rona Murray, a lovely, elegant woman separated from her husband. She somewhat resembled movie actress Vivien Leigh and had a precise English accent from her early schooling in India.

"I was one of the women he trapped," recalls Rona, who began sitting in on Birney's classes after deciding to switch from drama to poetry. "Before I met him, Gwladys Downes and Phyllis Webb looked at each other and laughed. They said, 'You're just his type.' It was amusing in a way.

"He invited me and another woman poet to ride down in his red sports car to a poetry conference in Eugene, Oregon, where Birney was admired by the poets—all male—who were associated with the university. Earle was a 'biggie' so the huge auditorium was packed. Robin Skelton was there. Earle had never forgiven him for the nasty review he once gave him, so the two of them were avoiding each other. Earle got up there and gave a wonderful and very funny speech. He spoke chiefly to the students, and said they must feel like horses being put through their paces in harness. 'Don't think that you're the only ones,' he said. 'It goes on even until my age. There is someone in this auditorium who

gave me a very critical review. It is a very meretricious piece of
work. I'm going to read it to you.' And he read Skelton's review.
Everyone loved it. There was tremendous clapping. It was Earle's
revenge, of course. He did carry these things around. He never
forgot a putdown. He used to tell me about the trouble he had
with his adviser at Berkeley [Tatlock]. The way he told it was
that this man disliked him very much, and when a professor
from Harvard or Yale or somewhere asked him during his oral
examination if he had read a certain thesis and he hadn't (and
couldn't, since it wasn't in the library and Earle had no money to
go elsewhere to read it), his adviser was embarrassed into agree-
ing that this showed Earle had no interest in the topic. He was
pretty bitter about it. Holding grudges was one reason, I think,
that although he had many friends, he didn't seem to have close
ones.

"In Oregon, without my knowing it, he was courting me. He
was pushing me forward [as a poet]. I was shy and insecure. And
then this other woman poet went home by bus or train. In the
hotel elevator he took my hand and kissed it, and said, 'Will you
spend the night with me?' It was so awkward. He seemed so old
to me, sort of a father-figure. He was physically not very attractive—very white, pale skin; he would sit in his office looking like
an old tortoise. But he was vain. Photos were very important to
him. He had a little mirror where you couldn't see it, but he
could. It jutted out from his desk. I had known him perhaps not
as long as a year. He had been charming to me; told me where to
send my poems (they were all taken); I didn't want to affect my
marks; and I wanted to get my marks on my own merits. He was
hanging onto his youth like mad."

Rona Murray's relationship with Birney took place largely on
Bowen Island. "I went over quite often while I was writing my
thesis, a collection of poems (later published as *The Enchanted
Adder*, which won an award).[140] He was not really interested in
teaching, but, as my adviser, he was very patient with me and
didn't try to impose his views. He was a naturalist. I admired that
about him. At one time he was experimenting with shellfish or
plants, watching to see what they did. He was like a little boy in
some ways. It used to embarrass me. He loved 'Lieben' and was

very relaxed there, but he'd sit in the kitchen sort of staring at me with this lovelorn look. He loved to play the piano, but he played very badly. I think he was a very lonely man. There was this rebound thing: he was always scrambling to fill that void. He needed a woman, but he didn't really like women very much. He could be marvellous and was fun, but he wanted a payment for it. He had very little use for women who weren't his lovers."

Rona was put off by Birney's anger over politics and people. "He loathed Roy Daniells; he did not like Malcolm Lowry, thought he was a bad writer and didn't like his drinking; he loathed Auden because he was homosexual (he said he saw Auden pay a boy); he was very, very anti-lesbian and homosexual and had no time for writers like Jane Rule. In some ways, he was quite puritanical. I was a feminist, and Earle was not, though given his generation, he can hardly be blamed for that. But when I was a Teaching Assistant for him and for the English Department I learned rather a lot about the network. I was really appalled. Letters among male academics and poets which I had to open and handle for *Prism* would say things like: 'I'm delighted with your protégés.' or 'I see your bed-partner's published.' Quite a lot was published not on merit, but on who you knew. It was all men in power positions. Chairs, the choices of readers, 'I'll bring you in; you bring me in.' There was an incredible network around the Governor General's Awards, the CBC, all those aspects of the arts.

"Probably unwisely, I said I was through. I told him I couldn't take my Ph.D. there. I had applied for a Canada Council fellowship. He wrote a letter that made it impossible for any university to accept me. He thought I was a poet, not a research academic, which was quite valid. (Eventually I did get my doctorate at the University of Kent in England, and obtained a position at Selkirk College in B.C.) I used to play tennis with him, and cut that off. He was very difficult and very nasty about that. He really was affected by it. But I was very glad to remain friends with him, and not for ambitious reasons."[141]

By the end of a frustrating academic year, Earle was working with Jake Zilber and others to find his successor,[142] having justified the program (and soothed his spirit) with the many testimonials that flooded in to UBC after he circulated a request as part of a brief for the new dean, Kaspar Naegle.

"You taught us how to discipline our flair." Yvonne Agazarian[143]

"I learned to do a lot of writing…and changed from a person who thought about writing, to one who wrote every day." George Bowering[144]

"What affected me a great deal was the meeting others who were involved with writing." Daphne Marlatt[145]

"Profound benefit… [I] published my first poems, works which were the direct product of this class." Lionel Kearns[146]

"It familiarized me with the larger literary picture; it alerted me to the existence of a body of contemporary literature; it gave me immediate access to professional standards." Norman Klenman[147]

"I was allowed to *talk* about writing with people who were as avidly interested in it as I was." Betty Lambert[148]

"Enabled me to find in my other more orthodox courses a new dimension and a depth which might otherwise have escaped me." John Baxter, assistant professor of English[149]

"Excellent… [met] Marianne Moore." Rosemary Kent-Baxter, Editorial Dept., *Vancouver Times*[150]

"The most enjoyable and the most useful activity…at the U. of B.C. …I have retained friendly relations with a surprising number of that small class." Tom Franck, Professor of Law, New York University[151]

"[I learned that] revision [is] an inevitable discipline in writing." Peg Robertson[152]

"Dr. Birney's dispassionate and careful critical attention to my work has been of incalculable value to me as a poet." Marya Fiamengo[153]

Just before Easter 1964, Birney finally realized that what he had first glimpsed in San Francisco four years earlier was no literary quirk but a social and literary revolution as significant as the political upheaval he had fervently joined in the thirties. But this was a revolution in which he could not fully take part. Leonard Cohen had arranged the McGill reading on 13 March, lent Birney his black beret for the event, and put him up at his mother's Westmount house. But there was something comical—even poignant—about what happened when he returned there after his reading. "Two carloads of [Westmount cops] tried to prevent me entering your mother's house," Birney wrote, as if he had been in an episode from the Keystone Kops or back leading his Utah students to investigate a strike or in Berlin defying Nazis. "The Allisters said the cops were suspicious because I was wearing a beret (I think, by the way, the beret is yours, however, I have become attached to it. Can I send you a cedar-bark hat in exchange?)... I made a dash for the door, key in hand, and established my residential rights.... The cops were reluctant to enter I suppose without a search warrant."[154] Birney—far removed from the Quiet Revolution—did not understand until later that he was suspected of being an FLQ terrorist planting bombs in Westmount mail-boxes.[155] But he sensed there was a difference between Cohen's visits to his Hydra Island house in Greece and his own embassy-hopping; between Tallman's summer '63 conference and his plans to bring a Trinidadian playwright and steel drummer next summer;[156] between Cohen's open romance with the lovely Marianne and his secretive assignations with women like Gaby Baldwin, whom he saw while he was in Montreal that March. There was something about the poetry reading he could not quite put his finger on that excluded him: "the audience was full of poets: Layton, Cohen, Dudek, Eldon Greer, Henry

Moscovitch, etc.," he reported, with no idea of what "flower children" were. "The last-named came, with his Charles-Adams [sic]-
like slinky darkhaired girlfriend, attired in sombre black but with
brilliant mauve silk bands around their foreheads and bearing yellow tulips in their hands. They entered late, of course. I gathered
it wasn't a gesture directed at me in particular, simply
Moscovitch's way of keeping up with the competition for attention in the jungle of Montreal poets."[157] In one of the polite conventional thank-you notes he had been brought up to write after
favours, he wrote Cohen that it had been "my first and probably
my last reading in Montreal. Now that I am back here, Quebec
not only looks far away again in space but, this time, it seems on
another curve of time. I will have to be reborn with Laurentian as
my native tongue to be an acceptable poet in the Montreal of the
near future. However, I think you will survive."[158]

It was a promotion tour dreamed up by Jack McClelland to
launch four M & S poetry books in the fall of 1964 that made
clear which generation Birney belonged to. It had begun as a tour
for Layton's *The Laughing Rooster*, but "McStew," as his writers
called Jack, thought that publicizing Birney's *Near False Creek
Mouth*, Phyllis Gotlieb's first collection *Within the Zodiac*, and
Cohen's *Flowers for Hitler* as well in a series of joint readings in the
last week of October (for which he could get Ontario government
funding) would appeal to the media and public and sell more
books than separate tours. Birney enthusiastically cooperated: "I'll
be on a kind of four-man vaudeville team touring [six] eastern
Canadian universities,[159] two shows a day, each on a different
campus," he excitedly wrote a friend. "Layton, Cohen, Gotlieb
and Birney. Sounds like a New York firm of Jewish lawyers with a
junior goy partner thrown in to get the carriage trade. We will read
our poems, autograph our books, appear on panels, be attended
throughout by a film crew from the National Film Board."[160]

The "Peripatetic Poets," as one headline termed them, travelled
in cars provided by the Ford Motor Company, and gave readings
against backdrops designed by Harold Town to packed audiences, often to standing room only. "Do you dig contemporary
poetry?" went one advance notice. "Maybe not, but undergrads...will have the chance to experience it first hand this week

when four leading Canadian bards, competing directly with The Frug, and The Watusi, with folk singers and even The Rolling Stones, set out on a poetry reading tour." For an audience not quite ready for the "neurotic affiliations" and "reeling despair" of Cohen, it was Layton who stole the show. "Famed for his forthright use of four-letter words and his defence of free-wheeling sexual activity, Irving Layton probably was the most eagerly awaited of the quartet, and it was good staging to save him for the last," wrote one journalist. "Layton comes on as the burly, sloppy, bon-vivant, ready to indulge in good Rabelasian, scatological jollies," wrote another.

Birney (whom journalists still associated with "David") read first, choosing his 1942 poem "Anglosaxon Street" and some from the new collection, including "For George Lamming." He was described variously as "distinguished professor," a "Westerner," "too much the Creative Writing teacher" and "prosaic": even his friend Louis Dudek was critical, "Both [Birney and Gotlieb] are examples of highly-polished professional workmanship, a sort of professional writer's poetry. Their very defect is that they lack the subjective energy of Cohen or Layton: they are too cool and capable."

To a new generation wearing "corduroy, denim and leather," acutely aware of changing dress codes, the four poets represented clear-cut differences: the thirty-eight-year-old Mrs. Gotlieb, whose poems concerned "suburban domesticities," wore a demure white blouse, a black gabardine skirt, and pearls; Layton, whose long thick hair waved back over his ears, wore a crumpled suit with a sprig of parsley in the buttonhole, his tie askew; Cohen had a Caesar haircut and wore a black leather jacket over a dark shirt and mismatched tie; the almost bald Birney, who now had a thick white beard, wore an immaculate dark suit over a white shirt and tasteful tie. "Hipster, romantic, gentleman and mystery": that's how Don Owen the young NFB film producer summed them up. As far as the youthful audiences were concerned, the gentlemanly Birney was "square."[161]

By the time Don Owen had edited his footage, the film had become a documentary exclusively about the writer who would surpass the other three and gain the international reputation

Birney had so arduously sought: "Ladies and Gentlemen: Mr. Leonard Cohen." Even Birney singled out Cohen in retrospect. "'Portrait of a Genius' will always remind me of both you and Leonard," he wrote Layton on stationery he took from The Inn on the Park where the "screwiest week of 1964" began, "and his fabulous freewheeling preludes to [our readings] and of the other good times when [Laytoncohenbirney] were drawn together." Ironically, Birney, too, had known the despairing anarchism Cohen espoused. But the time had not been quite ripe for him to break free of convention and follow the existential instincts he expressed in such poems as "Vancouver Lights," "Mappemounde," "Bushed" and "Bear on the Delhi Road." It was Cohen in his poems, novels and songs, who would "free myth from reality,"[162] not Birney, who had drawn back from the void[163] like the lovers in "The Hazel Bough," who "winked when they met and laughed when they parted, and never found time to be broken-hearted."

Though Birney had forgotten all about the "Four Generations" photograph seven years before, the passage of time had proved his premonition prophetic. The death that affected Birney with "the sadness of great loss"[164] more than all the others that troubled him was the death of E.J. Pratt in June. Ralph Gustafson was the only poet at the funeral. "I flew up to Ned Pratt's burial," he wrote Birney. "Not a poet there to lower Ned into the soil. I thought Trawna was lousy with poets? Or I suppose they thought Ned didn't rate."[165]

It was the end of an era. With the death of Pratt, the ascendancy of Layton and the imminence of Cohen, Birney would never be fully in the literary picture again. As Esther would sarcastically remark in her version of the 1964 tour and the film that resulted, Birney was "The Face on the Cutting-Room Floor."[166]

~§ *24* §~

ESCAPE ARTIST

Esther Birney remembers meeting Ikuko Atsumi clearly. It marked, she would write ten years later, "the last time... I spoke to Earle in a completely trusting way."[1] "I had been working that day with the Children's Aid when I answered the phone a little past six. To my surprise it was Earle. His pleasant voice and his affectionate tone aroused reciprocal feelings in me."[2] "He was a bit late, so I said, 'Oh supper's ready, what's holding you up?'"

> He said, "How's your day gone?"
> And I said, "Oh, I've been picking up neglected children as usual"—something like that.
> And he said, "Oh, I've got one here—one of my students."
> Ikuko had come into his office weeping and said that the night before her husband, a handsome young Japanese [computer] engineer on a year's exchange, had beaten her. I, who always encouraged Earle to bring home his students or other friends, said, "Well, bring her home."
> So he arrives with this little Japanese hippie in her mid-twenties—very ordinary-looking, but with lovely

456

skin—who could hardly speak English at all. Earle was most insistent that we do what we could for her. He arranged for her to stay the following week with Dorothy Livesay who had a large house in Kitsilano. Meanwhile she stayed with us.

She'd been with us four or five days when we had a kind of a dinner party which she had cooked for us all—what's the famous Japanese dish... all sprouts and mushrooms...that you do at the table?[3] It was very successful. Everything was fine. But when Earle went to bed, she went to bed. (I had my own room; Earle had his room. My room had two beds in it and she was in one and I was in the other.) I was quite a while putting the dishes away, but finally I went to bed and she woke up and said something about how he had asked her to go to Bowen Island with him. And I said, "Well, it's a nice place. You might enjoy being there."

And she said, "You don't understand. We're in love."

And I said, "Oh, has he been pestering you? Don't let it bother you; he does that with all the pretty girls," or something like that.

She said, "No, no, you don't understand. We're going to get married." And she ran out of the room down to Earle's room and I heard them talking quite a long time. Meanwhile I turned out the light.

And then the door opened and Earle was standing in the doorway with his arm around the little Japanese girl, and he said, "It's quite true. We're in love and I want a divorce."

And I said, "Well, I can't do anything about it tonight. Please go away." And so he and she finished the night in his room.

The next day I was so outraged and so furious. He said he was going to take her to Bowen Island and I shouldn't worry. That she was very upset and he would help her until she met another young man. That he didn't for a moment think he could take the place of a young person. That she needed to be free of

her husband and find another man, and that's what he
wanted to do to help her, but there was nothing very
serious intended.

Later he phoned from Bowen Island and said, "This
is nothing serious." And more or less conveyed the
feeling that it was a passing episode that would soon
be over. I didn't say, "Look, what's all this about
divorce?" I knew Earle would have said, "Oh, I just
said that to please her." So she came and spent the
night and we had a kind of *ménage à trois*.

The next day I was still so outraged and furious that
I called a friend and together we went round to look
for a flat for *me*. My friend, who was another social
worker, said, "Why are *you* leaving the house? You've
done nothing to merit this. You stay in the house and
let *him* go. That afternoon I called a psychiatrist
whom I'd been seeing—not at that time, but not very
long before, because I'd had various kinds of obsessive
and miserable anxiety feelings—and he said, "Tell
them to leave at once. That's an intolerable situation.
You shouldn't be in that situation."

So when Earle came home (by that time he'd moved
Ikuko to Dorothy [Livesay's]), I said to him, "I must
ask you to leave. I don't want any more of this nonsense going on."

Earle's temper flared and he said, "You and I have
talked about this before, and you said I could stay till
the end of the year."

And I said, "Yes, but I've changed my mind." And
he was so furious that he took off the heavy winter
boots he was wearing and threw them right across the
room—not at me, fortunately.

But he packed a couple of bags and left and went to
live with Ikuko in a flat a stone's throw from my place
on Comox. I'm not sure who told me—either
Dorothy or Earle—that when I had been so compla-
cent about their going to Bowen while they were getting into Earle's car, Ikuko had said to him, "Esther

will win because she's taken this all so calmly, she must be feeling very comfortable." And she had the nerve to come to me later on and complain that Earle was coming home too much!

I don't know what was going on in Earle's mind. I don't know how much he cared for this girl. I suppose it was another conquest, and he went ahead with it. And that little woman had plans laid out from the first moment she arrived here, and Earle fell in with them like the fool he was about girls. She had been auditing his poetry classes and of course he had noticed her. He had set her up in a flat before I met her. Her husband had spied on them, and I seem to remember she even came to the house to tell me how upset she was about that. But Earle was still very much in touch with me. He was trying to live two lives really. He was corresponding with Claude Bissell about coming to work in Toronto. He was looking everywhere for someone to take his place in the Creative Writing Department. He was really closing off his Vancouver life altogether. All this was going on behind my back. It's really like a comedy. It was all so crazy.

One day after he finished teaching and exams I came back from work and found a note from Earle saying he'd gone to Seattle to meet John Wain, the British novelist, and that he would call me later, or something like that. I had a phone call that night from Ikuko's husband asking if I knew where his wife was. I said, "You're darn tooting I know where you wife is. She's gone off with Earle Birney somewhere." So he came over with a bottle of wine and we had a very nice time together.

Then I started getting letters from Earle. He'd taken his big, red sports car, his big red Volvo sports car, and her, and their luggage, and motored right across Canada to where he had a part-time job Bissell found for him at the Scarborough branch of the University of Toronto.[4]

Birney had dropped Rona Murray, the poetry student with whom he'd been having an affair that spring and summer, because, he said, she had wanted to marry him.[5] (Rona said it was Earle who wanted to marry, and took her to see his lawyer to try to figure out how to divorce her estranged husband.)[6] Esther was wrong. Earle did love Ikuko and believed she loved him. He helped place her poem "A Bough Breaks" in *Alaska Review* in December 1964, and two months later (suffering from continuous indigestion and another threatened ulcer) confided to Irving Layton, whom he could count on not to condemn him, "I'm in a hell of a state these days, under the surface."

> Have to carry on, the Square Bearded Prof, but my private life is operating at a temp. very close to steam. Any moment there may be an explosion which, if it comes, will cost me my job, and probably send me eastward as far as possible, and on the bum and the lam both.... I've had a lot of crazy and perilous amorous adventures in my life, 95% of them unknown to anybody but the girl concerned—but this turmoil I'm in now is farther out than a Burroughs novel. Man you wait till your [sic] sixty—the best is yet to come, even if it cant last. The best and worst all rolled together. I'm going through the greatest, most beautiful and, no kidding, the most passionate sexual experience of my life (and I've no complaints about the past ones). The girl is 24, Japanese, an art school model, a poet (in Japanese), & becoming one in English. Her husband, also Japanese, is dangerous, and has suspicions.... I cant confide in a damned soul in this town. The outcome will be something melodramatic: elopement, or death, or both. I'm certainly Yeats' paltry thing, "A tattered coat upon a stick" but by god this scarecrow's soul is clapping its hands. If only I could sing like Yeats! I can't even sing like myself, just now, too busy living the crazy melodrama. Please dont mention all this to anyone. It's important we keep under cover till the term ends, at April's

end—which may well be mine too. But please, please write me. The girl really loves me—that's been all too well tested—and wants to marry me! Did you know I was really such an old fool?[7]

Reporting a Freudian slip that must have made Birney's stomach churn, Edith Shiffert, *Poetry Northwest's* Far Eastern correspondent, who had recommended Birney's course to Ikuko (whom she described as "a brilliant young woman...two books of poetry published...highly respected here"),[8] wrote from Kyoto to say that the Japanese translation of Birney's "Haiku to a Young Waitress" (which he had sent her) had been mistranslated as "Haiku to a Young Mistress."[9] And surely he meant more than it seemed when he wrote to Alan Crawley "how Oriental contact enriches our traditions."[10]

As Esther later realized, Birney had been looking around for someone to replace him as head of the Creative Writing program, which—now that he had freed it from Daniells's English Department—no longer challenged him. Ralph Gustafson, Dorothy Livesay, Jack Ludwig, Charles Israel—and, of course, Irving Layton: these were the names he considered. In the end, it was Robert Harlow, his former CW student, who got the job. Dorothy Livesay agreed to teach his poetry writing class. And with all the hush-hush caution of his early Trotskyist subterfuge, he had written widely (at times lying outrageously)[11] to try to find a job for himself and admittance to graduate school for Ikuko in an Ontario or Quebec University. As for Daniells, he was given the highest honour UBC could bestow on a professor. He was made the first Professor at Large, with a large salary and no duties other than to be on hand in case he was wanted to lecture in any department.

By describing such posts in the U.S., common since Robert Frost served as "a poetic radiator" at Amherst from 1916 to 1938,[12] Birney had persuaded Claude Bissell to set up a writer-in-residence position for him at the still-incomplete Scarborough College, where, by curious coincidence, his office faced Bet Cox's lab. Meanwhile, he was to use an office at 49 St. George Street on the main campus where he was to be available for students of creative writing to drop in and discuss their work. He was also to give a series of public lectures and a few readings through the year. In return, he was to receive a half-salary, which he immediately began to supplement with free-lance assignments. And he began negotiations for the sale of his massive hoard of letters, books and other memorabilia to the University of Toronto Library in 1966 for the equivalent of a year's salary.

Ikuko was admitted to the University of Toronto graduate school. Birney's old friend Ernest Sirluck, then Dean of Graduate Studies, recalls how Birney went about arranging her admission. "He did something I really didn't like," Sirluck recalls of the man he none the less felt warmly towards,

> though I mustn't blame him too much. He wrote from Vancouver that he was coming back and would like to see me. I wrote back, full of enthusiasm. He arrived and phoned and we made a date. He chose to see me in my working hours, not for lunch.
>
> He came into my office at 63 St. George St. and I told my secretary not to interrupt us for an hour because I was very keen to see him. He came in and I greeted him and we sat and talked for half an hour or more, just catching up and so on, and *then* he said, "There's someone I want you to meet." And he gave me her name.
>
> I said that I'd be glad to meet her. And he said, "She wants to enter the graduate school. She's just outside."
>
> I said, in surprise, "You mean you've kept her waiting outside?" I was annoyed that I'd been a party to keeping her waiting. And I was even more annoyed that that was the object of Earle's visit. What he really wanted was for me to relax the entrance requirements or arrange for her to meet them in some suitable way. If he'd called me up and said, "I've got this woman, my student, who doesn't have all the requirements for graduate school, and I'd like you to help her meet them, that would have been fine. In the end, that's

escape artist 463

what I did. But I didn't like the indirect approach. That, under the guise of the reunion of old friends, he was getting his girlfriend into Graduate school. She was a very attractive young Japanese woman, I remember, and later Esther was really amusing on the subject of Earle's China dolls and Madame Butterflies.[13]

Letters at the time suggest that, contrary to Esther's recollection, Birney did not leave her a note when he left Vancouver because he did not want Ikuko's husband Sato to trace her.[14] "O Esther dont hate me for not writing or for leaving Vancouver without a message to you," he wrote on 27 April as soon as he reached Toronto. Concealing the fact that Ikuko was living with him, he recounted at length his trip, his living arrangements ("she is in a furnished room…[I] got a small furnished flat"), news of their Toronto friends, his health ("I'm feeling immensely better, no stomach troubles, sound sleeping") and their finances (he generously sent three hundred dollars for her to have a trip to Mexico and was more than fair in his proposals for property division). "I wonder if you know how often I have thought of you," he added affectionately, "sometimes with worry and sadness, but always with respect and love. And yet I do know absolutely that this parting is the right thing for us both. I want desperately to be free, to be able to re-shape what is left of my life in my own way."[15]

At first, Esther had her lawyer (and friend, since he had boarded with her during the war), Felix Eckstein in Toronto, write Birney. But after a couple of phone calls—one from Earle, one from herself—she softened sufficiently to write: "What you could not have known was…the hours of weeping, the letter of despair written but never posted, the feelings of hopelessness…. And from that evening on, the days of anxiety and puzzlement, the depression, the total inability to understand your actions."[16]

By mid-May, Earle and Ikuko had visited Layton and Aviva in Montreal, found an old flat in Toronto's élite Rosedale district at 35A Chestnut Park Road, and Birney had sent off some of Ikuko's poems to Fred Cogswell ("she will become one of Canada's most unusual and important writers"),[17] who enthusiastically accepted

"Soaring" for the November 1965 *Fiddlehead*. Supported by such friends as George Bowering, the Gustafsons and George Johnston ("it does me good to see you so creatively restless"),[18] Birney was flying high himself: "I am happier than I ever thought a man could be, now that we are together after so many battles with the Great Square World."[19]

But almost at once the consequences of his bid for freedom from Esther and academe and Vancouver bore in on him. Ikuko set out to "improve" him by trying ointments to lighten the freckles on his skin. And without Esther, social life was difficult. "It is slow sorting out old friends here into those who can be included in my strange new life, and those who cant," he wrote Layton,

> even those who accept, and remain close, are preoccu-
> pied. And Ikuko doesnt make friends easily. She's
> frightened, of course, of scandal that would affect her
> acceptance into the grad school here (it is not yet offi-
> cially through). The ones she has accepted here are
> Bob Allen (CBC), Steve Vizinczey [author of *In Praise
> of Older Women*, with whom Birney had dealings over
> Vizinczey's short-lived Montreal magazine *Exchange*],
> and his wife Gloria (ex-wife of Don Herron [sic] the
> actor).... We go up to Souster's Friday night (her
> birthday) but I fear the conventional exteriors of Ray
> and his wife may throw her into one of her dark silent
> moods. She is, must be, lonely for Japanese voices &
> faces, & for good literary conversations. We will prob-
> ably go up to Morley Callaghan's this weekend—and
> again I go in doubt. Meantime she slaves away at
> [Edmund] Spenser, 1 1/2 hrs a day with me, more
> hours alone at it. And the rest of the daytime has gone
> largely in settling-in and buying supplemental furni-
> ture. I have been disrupted, anxious. It is probably a
> thousand to one against my dreams surviving—the
> differences in culture, ambitions, the inability to be
> entirely open about living-together. Well, I must keep
> courage and love and patience, and so must she.[20]

Esther, knowing nothing of these goings-on, had issued an ulti-matum: "I remain in cold-storage in Vancouver waiting for you to come back when you grow tired of your next girl-friend.... All you seem to want is to have me at your disposal," she wrote on 7 July, after learning from a friend that Earle had seen a psychia-trist about his guilt and did not want to proceed with a divorce.

> Such continuous suspense... is unendurable. I must know where I stand. It is for you to make the decision and it must be *either–or*. From now on I want you to be *either* a real husband to me or we will part for good. If you refuse to be a husband to me—I will agree to a separation or divorce (whichever you pre-fer), provided all financial matters are finally settled. I will not ask for anything unreasonable. But the terms must be fair. Unless we arrive at such an agreement in the near future I have decided to come to Toronto in the fall as your wife. *I mean your sole wife.* I will not tolerate any rival in our home, be it Ikuko or any other girl-friend of yours. In the past I have closed my eyes to a great deal because I felt you wanted me to be your wife even though you had other intimate associa-tions.... You will now have to convince me by *behav-ing like a real husband.*

Even Bill had had enough and had cut off all communications with his father. "I asked him to answer your letters," Esther wrote, "but he was furious with you because you wanted to sacri-fice me, his mother, to a little girl like Ikuko.... what example have you set him with regard to his feelings and mine? For you nothing existed but your 'delirious happiness'.... If you paid any attention to the feelings of others you could have foreseen that you might lose your son as well as your wife."[21] Earle found this unjust and complained to Irving Layton, "My reward [for giving Bill love and sacrificing more than once my inner happiness in order to maintain a stable home for him and financing him through to where he is now] is to be so utterly rejected it sounds unreal. For when I finally left Esther, he (in Los Angeles) decided

I was 100% wrong without hearing my side of it, refused to answer my letters or acknowledge birthday gifts, & engaged himself actively in trying to prevent a reconciliation between his mother and me... This, apparently, is all done on grounds of high morality, while he lives with a girl he's no intention of marrying, in a better house than I can afford, on the Santa Monica beach, enjoying a bigger salary than mine, driving a big new sports car, on a salary I helped him achieve. (In his third undergraduate year he got taken in a professional poker game, had to have his debts paid by me [Esther says this claim is "rubbish."], then flunked out [in fact, merely did not get honours standing and took the year over again to win a scholarship], & it was I who cajoled him back to college and into his present career as a computer mathematician.) He has, in other words, become a real Square who rejects me because I'm not."22

But by July 25, Ikuko had left in a panic for Japan. As Birney would later explain to George Bowering:

> So I got Ikuko into the Grad School at U. of T., paid her fees, set us up in a really swell pad in Rosedale, in the one decaying house in a kind of British Properties surroundings. That is, there are huge elms, curving streets; quiet; expensive neighbours, but our house is part of a minute re-zoning area and is divided into six broken down but huge flats with catsmells in the corridors and a young tart upstairs & happy drunks across the hall. We had a good month here.... I have some sets of friends here...Al Purdy before he went up to Baffin; other poets, CBCers, etc. We got around; took her to...the coffee joints...a couple of cocktail parties (at one she almost conquered Harold Town). Made a trip to Kingston & stayed in Reg Watters' river-house on the St. Lawrence; & in Al Purdy's shack at Ameliasburg (wrote a poem about this, coming out in *Tamarack*); went to a few shows, a lot of art galleries. Also spent a lot of time at home, especially in bed. All in the past tense now. Deserted husband complains by letter to Japan Mom, who threatens to fly here. (Fear

of Immigration.) Husband threatens to fly here. Wife refuses to divorce. Ikuko loads up with guilt feelings, fear. God speaks to her in a dream the night before I arrive back from Calgary [25 June; Birney was addressing the Alberta Society of Artists]. "You must get a room by yourself at once." So she gets it. With what I have given her, she has enough to last through summer school…just before she was to write her final exam in her Summer School course, she got a cable from Tokyo & a one-way plane ticket. Cable said her mother had died suddenly. So she took off the next day….she left me a note…. Then a week later I heard from my wife, who evidently couldnt resist writing to tell me, that it was all a plot. Her mother is alive and well, and probably was waiting for her at the Tokyo airport. The plot involved husband Sato and another Japanese prof at UBC and, of course, the mother…. I havent heard anything from her…. Rashomon is a kid's story to what really goes on in Japanese culture patterns.[23]

When he received Ikuko's note, Earle was heart-broken. "I'm one of God's loneliest men right now," he wrote Layton. "I've been very depressed, lonely, abandoned—no kidding," he wrote his fellow-translator, Juditte Sarkany-Perret, "Romantic words, but they still can have meaning."[24]

After exchanging more anguished letters with Esther, meeting her at the University of Alberta in Calgary when he received his first honorary doctorate on 13 November 1965, and again in Toronto on 27 November for a week, Earle and Esther were reconciled in February 1966. Though Birney had been cold and remote during their two visits (in Calgary, according to Esther, the only time they were alone for dinner, "he brought a newspaper to the table and searched it for items about himself!"),[25] he suddenly changed after she said she was returning from Toronto to Vancouver. "He treated me as he never has in his life before— like a loving appreciative husband—guess he was so pleased to get rid of me, eh?" she wrote her father.

He begged and implored me to stay; he made every conceivable promise; he admitted he was wrong and had been for years about everything. But I refused to change my mind and came back and signed the divorce papers last week. I still have two months to change my mind if I decide he really has changed. He has written me pitiful letters about his guilt and his loss and he has phoned and begged me to come back, but I just can't tell whether it is because this time he knows he has gone too far, or whether he has really changed. He sent me $100 for Christmas and said it was a first payment on a new engagement ring as he would marry again if I went through with the divorce! It's all a bit funny isn't it.[26]

There was much truth in Esther's conviction that Birney was "a man who is terrified of getting older and he equates still getting women with keeping young."[27] After all, Birney (whose main complaint about Esther was that she talked about his misdeeds to her friends and her psychiatrist behind his back) had written to her: "I must have the home and the atmosphere of tolerance for the young writer even with all the attendant problems they bring, in the way of, perhaps, late parties, some wildness. I will not settle into old age; it must force me to my knees. I still have enormous energy—for work, love, physical exercise, parties."[28]

Birney had become, as he said, the "oldest young poet in Canada."[29] He announced to Esther that he was writing in a new way. "Even Frank Davey, who was the one student in the Tallman crowd who really never said anything but bad about my work, has recently published an article about the new 'Black Mountain' poetry of Canada in which he talks of my 'regeneration' as a poet in my last two books."[30]

Birney's adroit play with language aligned easily with the methods of the latest fashion: "concrete" poetry. One of the first things he did as writer-in-residence was study recent articles on contemporary poetry in the avant-garde journals he had picked up in London when he read at the Commonwealth Arts Festival (for which "The Mammoth Corridors" had been commissioned) at the Royal Court Theatre in September 1965: two issues of *The Times Literary Supplement*; George Dowden's "Poetry of the Deep Image" in *Series: an Eleventh Finger Book*; "Concrete Poetry" in the *Glasgow Review* (summer 1965); the summer number of *Extra Verses*; and an account of "Between Poetry and Painting," an international exhibition of visual and concrete poetry held by the Institute of Contemporary Arts in London during October. Birney's notes outline the main ideas that were to influence his next stage. "Concrete poetry (so-called because it is 'real,' that is, visual and tactile) is made up of squiggles, pictures, curliques or... typewriter letters arranged in unusual patterns," said bpNichol, the twenty-two-year-old Canadian poet whose "poetry kit" *BP Letters Home*[31] was the last word in innovation. According to Marshall McLuhan, concrete poetry "has no message." But Birney disagreed. To him, concrete poetry had an element of fun, and presented a challenge because "it requires both a full knowledge of language as such and a sense of the multiplicity of meaning and a respect for the ultimate mystery of communication beyond the rational, beyond fixed symbol into the eternal flux."[32] To some extent, Birney was influenced by Edwin Morgan and Ian Hamilton Finlay, both Scots[33] who were backed by Americans Jonathan Williams, Robert Creeley, Robert Duncan, Louis Zukofsky and Charles Olson. According to Creeley, concrete poetry "has to do with the accumulated effect of words *as seen*, not heard." Critic Barbara Smith of Bennington College wrote, "In concrete poetry letters and junctures retain their own physical identities and become elements of a visual rather than an auditory design. One might say that poetry here aspires not to the condition of music but to that of spatial art."[34] This was a roundabout way of saying that new poetry somehow reflected such modern phenomena as advertising, in much the same way as Andy Warhol's pop art Campbell Soup cans or Lichtenstein's blow-ups of comic-strips, and connected with the daily lives of ordinary people. In another way—as Birney was quick to realize—concrete poetry was a revival of such seventeenth-century "shaped" poems as George Herbert's "The Altar."

An example of concrete poetry was offered in an article Birney clipped from the American skin magazine *Cavalier* that

September. Lowell Conway, a bearded "dungareed" ex-copy-writer from Greenwich Village, explained the stages of his development into a "poet of the commonplace, almost of the banal" using this poem, among others:

Traffic Meter

insert coin
turn handle to

Right
(as far as possible)

60 minutes

10 cents[35]

Birney had already written the same sort of thing without realizing it a decade earlier. For Christmas 1955, he had sent Rosemary Baxter two whimsical paper spirals to hang on her tree that carried a message handwritten in a circular fashion: "Dear Coz—You must revolve either these twin worlds, or yourself, if you are to untangle me. Whichever you pick, I hope that the result will be just the right amount of gentle giddiness for the Yuletide" and so on.[36] The first concrete poem Birney deliberately wrote followed the same model. Ikuko had explained to him that the ideograph for "eddy" was a rock in a stream.[37] "Like an eddy" was drafted in this ideograph provided by Ikuko and took several forms thereafter. Its best-known version was handwritten and circular, working from the outside inward and ending with the single strong word "ROCK" at the centre of its spiral: "Like an eddy my words turn about your bright ROCK."[38] And like the card-decorations he had sent his Coz which were meant to hang on her tree, Birney had the poem made into a mobile by Rosemary Vaughan, who had contacted him after hearing him discuss concrete poetry on the radio. Birney seized every chance to advance such poetry in his readings and talks. "I find the U. of Toronto fantastically corpse-like so far as literary creativity is concerned," he wrote an English friend, "so I'm starting a one-man Putsch.... I'm reading my own stuff, carefully selected to show anti-academic bias, in about eight places in the city [recently established York University; four of the U of T colleges; the Beaches Library; the Bohemian Embassy; Hamburger Joint; the Women's Press Club][39]...and I'm giving a public lecture on the anti-creative role of Canadian universities, the need to abolish degrees, English depts., administrators, and all the other doors of imperception."[40]

It had not escaped Birney that many of the best younger poets, such as Al Purdy, Milton Acorn and Joe Rosenblatt, whom he had personally "rescued" from a blue-collar job with the CPR, were high-school drop-outs—a fact that was a clear indicator of the times. The revolutionary attitudes of the sixties—especially on university campuses where sit-ins, and other sorts of idealistic and rebellious protests were sweeping North America—made traditional poetry—even poetry as "modern" as Birney's own best recent poems—seem square. That side of Birney which was proud to be working-class, at odds with academe, and inclined to be Marxist, surfaced with almost visionary zeal and certainly with few qualms about downplaying his academic career: "he was a logger, farm labourer, sewer man, salesman, seaman and labour organizer, amongst others" ran the blurb in the program for the Vietnam Peace Concert—where he blasted Canada's "holier-than-thou apathy" at Eaton Auditorium in May 1967.[41] In March 1965 he had signed a petition urging the Canadian government to protest American intervention in Vietnam; he had utter disdain for "the rich culture/vultures who subscribe to *Vancouver Life* and *About Town*"; he spoke out in favour of the legalization of marijuana and confessed publicly that he had smoked pot in Mexico; he contributed one hundred dollars to the defence fund for bill bissett, a young Vancouver poet charged with marijuana-related offences in 1968; he picketed officials from the Dow Chemical Corp. (who were believed to be manufacturing chemicals used for napalm in the Vietnam War) when they were recruiting engineers at the University of Waterloo; and he contributed to the defence fund for *The Golden Convulvulus*, an erotic magazine in England that had been charged with obscenity.[42]

Birney thrived on the new ideologies of the sixties which had swung society much closer to his way of thinking. His sensual love of nature prepared him for flower children; he had been "doing his own thing" for years; as a former Trotskyist he detested bourgeois pretensions and the unimaginative conformity of what was now called the Establishment; he had always been "groovy," an eccentric "swinger" who opposed "squares." Long before Timothy Leary articulated it, he was ripe to "turn on, tune in, drop out."

Birney deliberately wooed young writers, and was astonishingly responsive and helpful when they sought his help. Some were his students of creative writing at various stages of their careers: Tom Wayman, whom he recommended successfully for a Woodrow Wilson Fellowship that took him to the University of California at Irvine; George Bowering, whom he cheered on as he rose to win a Governor General's Award in 1966; Lionel Kearns, with whom he compared notes about concrete poetry; Rona Murray, whom he eventually helped get a Canada Council grant to do research at the British Museum;[43] Phyllis Webb, whose papers he helped sell to the University of Saskatchewan in 1967. But many others approached him out of nowhere, and he gave every one his full attention and support. John Newlove, whom he successfully referred for a Canada Council grant; Joe Rosenblatt, whom Birney mentored, befriended and eventually helped to gain a Canada Council grant and national recognition as an experimental poet; Gwendolyn MacEwen, whose application to the University of Toronto he supported so she could study the Egyptology that would inform her novel *King of Egypt, King of Dreams*[44]; Judy Zacharias, a hippie from Albuquerque, whom he advised about coming to take Creative Writing in Vancouver (which she did); John Robert Colombo, to whom Birney gave a quote for the back cover of his book of William Lyon Mackenzie poems; Austin Clarke, the Barbadian immigrant broadcaster and writer whom he supported for a Canada Council grant; Kirby Congdon, an American poet ("that blackangelic poetmadman")[45] who edited *Magazine* in New York State, with whom he exchanged views on literary and practical matters; Michael Ondaatje, on whose behalf he asked the Canada Council for money to make a film version of one of his poems; David Cronenberg, whom he supported for a Canada Council grant to do a screenplay and a novel; bill bissett, whose *blew ointment* he considered "the only genuinely experimental/contemporary mag in canada" and for whom he also supported a grant.[46] The headline in a 16 December 1966 *Varsity* article was the simple truth, "Birney Encourages Aspiring Writers." And because he was situated in a powerful position, not only as a literary representative on the Canada Council's Advisory Arts Panel but at the hub of a literary wheel that spun outwards through all ranks and over three decades of the Canadian literati and, beyond that, into the United States and Britain, and, even beyond *that*, into such remote spots as Mexico, Peru, Greece and India, Birney's advice and support was as close to being a guarantee of success as was humanly possible.

He used this influence to make his old dream from as far back as 1948—to establish a sort of craftsman's guild for poets—come true. Although he refused to assume office in the organization, he was the driving force that recruited many members and formulated the policy and structure of the League of Canadian Poets which got underway in 1966.

Like a modern version of Don Quixote, noble in his black turtleneck and jacket festooned with a fresh daffodil, yet also somehow grotesque as he energetically took on the causes of the sixties, the spindly Birney happily joined 4,500 guitar-strumming, prayer-bell-tinkling, incense-burning, flower-casting hippies in Oriental robes, fur vests or striped ponchos from as far away as San Francisco in Queen's Park for Toronto's first Love-In on 25 May 1967. Flaunting his white side-burns (his "side-Birneys" or "muttonshops," as he liked to call them), he read his poems along with Buffy Sainte-Marie, Leonard Cohen and various folk and blues bands, for a generation he could relate to much better than his own.

With childlike delight, Birney soon adopted the no-capitals writing style made fashionable by e.e. cummings and used it whenever he thought it was appropriate. Somewhere along the way he had forgotten that he once derided the e.e. cummings school of non-punctuation and lower-case letters as a "fashion" that died around 1930.[47] Now he agreed with popular media guru Marshall McLuhan (with whom he did not become friendly at U of T) who was saying what he himself had always known: that the medium was the message. To the Canada Council, he still wrote the stiff conventional references he knew would be effective, but to the writers themselves, he was more likely to say,

> for the record   youve really been turning me on   why
> havent i bn reading you all this time
> your hearts furious involvement
> your blood that doesnt lie   is all people
> man you shd have that cc grant without asking
> anyway i can help   let me know…

> dont break yr back/neck w cpm woman
> they almost did it to me in 2 yrs those caa ghouls
> roberts pratt amabelking me kirkconnellugh bourino-
>   tobroin
> and now you   maybe youll be the one
> to burn the corpse   send us
> send us up some good strong ghat smoke
> get it up into the road of the space capsules

> but you may need allthat yorkville lingo
> its what even they think/write in lavs
> those canlit profs[48]

Birney was relieved to have burst free of academe. He resigned from the Royal Society of Canada ("the Hothouse Home of all the Canadian Paceys & Daniells, Conrods & Kluncks… I gave a paper once, attended a second year, but couldn't take it")[49]; though he still gave the occasional lecture when asked and supported the scholarly work of his former student Beryl Rowlands, now a professor at York University,[50] he announced he would never return to Chaucer criticism;[51] he refused to do reviews or prefaces. Except for his ongoing editorial work on Malcolm Lowry, which he hadn't thought of for months, he seemed to be abandoning the authoritative role of the scholar.

But he was outraged when he received a copy of a skit (which began with a news item using his name) that was performed the year he left by a group of M.A. students (all married women) for the English Department party at UBC. Though the author of this and other skits about academic life, Irene Howard, who had taken Birney's Chaucer course and a graduate seminar in Middle English literature, wrote to tell him about it before he read it, he staged an angry tirade:

> the [Professor] of your skit is made out to be one of [Anton] Chekhov's venial & self-deceiving fools, who is really leaving for an extra $3,000, to go to a worse place... My Alberta remarks [alluding to his speech on the occasion of his LL.D. about universities stifling creativity][52]...become ridiculed—the doubletalk of a posturing and unhappy demagogue... Nobody knew...that I had taken a *drop of $6,000*, not an increase of $3,000, to get away from the repressive hostility which I was encountering from the husbands of many of these same English Department Wives. Nobody knew...that if I had never won a Guggenheim, it might be because I had never applied for one, not because I wasnt really "a professional."[53]

Birney backed off when an apologetic and explanatory letter came back from Howard (who says she knew little, if anything, about his life outside the classroom) describing the skit as "an innocuous satire on the academic life which would apply to everyone in the Department."[54]

Having made his bid as a creative writer (he did a series of radio talks on the subject which were published by the CBC as *The Creative Writer* and hired himself an agent, Matie Molinaro) and made it clear that he despised the universities—except as venues for him to give paid readings or crusade on behalf of his new causes—Birney was also inflamed at some of the reviews of his *Selected Poems* illustrated by his old friend Leonard Brooks, which finally appeared on his sixty-second birthday, without the simultaneous American publication he and Jack McClelland had done their utmost to arrange. Birney wrote a "snide" preface[55] to the book, stating that it contained "half my poetic cinders sifted from the slag of dead periodicals and six out-of-print-and-out-of-mind books"; they were, he said, "signals out of the loneliness into which all of us are born and in which we die, affirmations of kinship with other wayfarers" and he wrote them "to talk to another man within me, an intermittent madman who finds unpredictable emblems of the Whole in the trivia of my experience."[56] Robert Weaver described his work as "expansive, masculine, even heroic." And George Woodcock considered him "one of the four most maturely vital poets writing in Canada today."[57] But in *The Globe and Mail* Miriam Waddington noted the absence of women and children in his work and argued that Birney wrote his best poetry when he stayed home and wrote of what he knew: she thought his "tough, spacious, witty and ironical, but…also cold and melancholy" poetry "should be read for northness, to find out what the Canadian spirit is really like." Birney fired off a long point-by-point reply which ended "it is foolish for someone who is as good a poet as you are to get yourself involved in this kind of journalistic critical-quickie…. You would spend your time much better writing more poems." Later, he added a note to his letter, "She never answered this! but made many malicious complaints about this letter to Esther and others."[58] John Robert Colombo, editor of *Tamarack Review*, offended Birney even more. He called him to discuss their problem with a negative review. Not wanting to offend either their reviewer, American writer Hayden Carruth, or Birney, Colombo agreed to look at a review by Kirby Congdon of *Magazine* (a young black-leather aficionado who was now recruiting poems for a special issue on motorcycles) which had sent Birney "out on a narcissistic cloud"[59] for possible simultaneous publication. When Colombo printed only Carruth's review, Birney was convinced he had been the victim of a deliberate "hatchet job."[60] Nor was he pleased to read in the *Winnipeg Free Press* that, apart from Birney's usual extensive revisions to all but eight of the ninety-nine poems, Chester Duncan found "little evidence of a general 'progress' in poetic artistry" and thought "not everyone succeeds by being daring in a modern way. There is a place for tight little islands of traditional expertise, especially if they are supported by the warmth, learning, and compassion of a Birney. What's the point of being second to Cummings if his way, because of its uniqueness is an end?"[61] And he was incensed when Barry Callaghan (whom he later recommended for a grant)[62] commented in the *Toronto Telegram* that he had "added nothing fresh to what he was doing ten years ago."[63] Perhaps the most perceptive review came all the way from Athens: Hugh McKinley, the Irish poet, saw Birney as engaged in "the Newer struggle with the Demon of the Establishment...when we find that each windmill tilted at is also loved, we begin to understand the depth of penetration his experience has effected."[64]

But Birney cheered up almost at once as he sped east with Esther (who was on holiday from her job at the Ontario Mental Health Centre on Queen Street) in his "little red Vulva"[65] to visit friends on the way to the second annual Charlottetown Festival of the Arts in Prince Edward Island to act as a paid consultant for the musical comedy *The Adventures of Private Turvey*, which was alternating with *Anne of Green Gables* and Mavor Moore's *The Ottawa Man* in the summer of 1966. Birney was under strict orders not to interfere directly, but to report any suggestions he had to Don Harron (script-writer), who in turn would discuss them with the artistic director, Mavor Moore. He and Esther were "faithful but silent attenders...a couple of old crocks on the sidelines while splendid youth literally occupies the stage" for the rehearsals, during which Birney jotted down lists of suggestions and complaints, chief of which was his objection to Turvey's singing a sentimental song by Norman Campbell, librettist, called "Starbright."[66] To add injury to insult, during one of the rehearsals, Birney somehow managed to crack two ribs when he fell into a winch-shaft at the back of the movable stage during a black-out, an accident which meant no swimming.

But *The Adventures of Private Turvey* opened 25 July 1966 to a sell-out premiere that ended with a standing ovation lasting twenty minutes, and local papers raved about the performances of Jack Duffy (Turvey), Barbara Hamilton (a nurse), Don Harron (a padre) and Kate Reid (in two cameo roles). The army ballet, in which ten privates took their assault course drill, never failed to make audiences roar with laughter. For the rest of the season, which ended 3 September, the show drew near-capacity crowds of seven to eight hundred. But although there was talk of a winter season at Toronto's Royal Alexandra Theatre, and a cross-Canada tour, even a Broadway production, it was *Anne of Green Gables* that toured Canada the following year and would endure as a classic.

Behind the scenes, however, "The Private Adventures of Birney" were more dramatic than anything on stage. He had found his promise of fidelity to Esther impossible to keep. Even when he was begging her to join him in Toronto, he had already replaced Ikuko with Alison Hunt, a teacher at Riverdale Collegiate whom he had met at a reading in the Beaches Library. "Meantime, of course, I don't live without loving," he had written to Irving Layton.

> A widow in her early thirties, a London woman who was a journalist there, married a Canadian, came to Toronto, stayed on after her husband died. She gives me love and serenity, a love of poetry…and of bed, without wanting marriage or anything much at all from me except my love… She teaches high school, and has a 5-year old boy."[67]

Alison was a striking vital woman with the dark hair and English accent that so often attracted Birney. He admired her teaching ability and loved her "tolerant and sunny temperament"[68] and continued to see her "with the usual furtiveness i hate but cant do anything about so long as esther has the attitudes she has."[69] "I came after the Japanese girl," Alison recalls:

> It was depressing. His heart was broken. I think he got a lot of excitement out of all this stuff, trying to rescue her, rushing around and shaving off his beard and running around, and driving all over. He told me she said, "I hate your skin. It goes all blotchy." I thought that was heartbreaking. We went and stood outside the classes that she went to so that we could give her

her mail. That was the excuse.

So when I met him, he swoooooped. He wanted a lover and he had this rather nice place in Rosedale. I found Earle exciting and he was a super lover. He's much the best lover I've ever had. He was so creative in the way he cared about you. I mean for that time and [considering] his age, I thought that was great. I mean he was concerned about giving pleasure as well as [receiving it].

It was the flower child time then, and we used to do things. It used to be lots of love-ins and things, terribly exciting. [We'd go] to coffee houses and down to Yorkville. He was great. He took me around. He didn't hide me. I remember going to parties at Barbara Frum's, once wearing a silver paper dress, and meeting a really nice Rosedale couple—Bob and Rita Allen. They were all very nice to me.

He was always telling me how great he was at speed-skating, and I remember going with him and my son to a lake in Scarborough where you could skate out of doors, and there'd be coloured lights and music. It was lovely.

Oh, he was difficult at times, but there were lots of things about him that intrigued me. He used to tell me that he dreamed in colour and that he could plan his dreams. Not the first one, but if he had an interesting dream he could plug back into it. It always worked. I was fascinated by the way his mind worked. He really liked physical activity, which I did, as well as being such a fount of wisdom and intellectual life.

I think he enjoyed clandestinity. He was so furious that he wasn't made the Master of Massey College and [Robertson] Davies was. He used to say, "What has he got that I haven't got?" Once I went to the wrong place at Massey. I went to this social gathering at Robertson Davies', and after I'd taken the first sip of sherry I realized I was at the wrong place. So Earle said, "Let's get out of his office, and go to mine and make love on the carpet." Then later, when he was at Waterloo, that was hysterical. He was billeted in this sort of apartment, which was really nice, but one end of this building was just full of female students, and so he'd be sort of sneaking upstairs, that sort of thing.[70]

"He was particularly remote from me that summer," Esther recalls,

because he was having a long torrid affair with Alison... I represented some kind of stability, and dear, dear Esther never really complained because she had a Marxist beginning with him.... I never objected to the affairs because this was the Marxist interpretation of the communist manifesto that marriage, bourgeois marriage, is a marriage of possessions... So here you have [in Birney] someone who couldn't let go of Mom—that's where I was.

We were going to a reception at the [PEI] Premier's [Walter Shaw]...and so we were checking our watches to be sure we were on time. And I said to him, "Gee, it's so-and-so time," and he said, "No it's not." So later I got dressed and came down, and because I am an aimiable person, I said, "You were right. My watch was wrong." And he said, "Yes, but you had to win."

Now the last time he'd done that, I'd said, "Earle, if you ever say that to me again I am just going to walk away and you'll be lucky if you see me again. It's not a war and I don't have to win anything, I just have to try and talk to you."

And so I turned on my heel and went into the house. He went as white as that teacup. His eyes were starting out of his head. He started screaming and ran upstairs to his room (we had twin rooms on the landing) and threw himself on the bed and seemed to be having convulsions. I was terrified. He's capable of these berserk rages. He was a three-year-old having a temper tantrum because Mummy wouldn't let him do so-and-so. I've never seen him so upset, except once when he said, "I've got my gun upstairs. Let's go and finish all this."

I gave in completely like the mother with the child who's turned blue. I just stood there and stroked him and said, "You're right, you're right, you're the best, you're the best. No, no don't misunderstand me, we'll go now, we'll go."

And after that, we went, both of us so shaken we could hardly get to the place. He wandered around those rooms looking absolutely beside himself. But I put a good face on it. I sat next to the Premier on a sofa and told him I'd never sat that close to a Premier, and he said, "Make the best of it, the election's tomorrow and I probably won't be returned," which he wasn't.[71]

Birney spent much of his time that summer with the students he was hired to teach in a four-week Creative Writing course at the Atlantic Summer School of the Arts (he was touted as "Canada's leading poet") in the new Prince of Wales University in Charlottetown. Though the American and eastern Canadian tourists who strolled through Charlottetown were scarcely ready for it, Birney started "the first cabaret/coffee house style poetry readings in this benighted island."[72] One of these events provided what for Birney was the high point of the summer: "One of my biggest thrills ever as a poet," he wrote Kirby Congdon, "was reading some of my stuff against the noise & sullen opposition &/or hellraisin drunks, & getting control—except against one fullback-sized Texan who would have clobbered me for real (esp. as I was getting over a double rib fracture at the time) if he hadnt been smothered under a half a dozen nimble musical comedy dancers—all because I read a poem of mine with a crack about American foreign policy in Vietnam. I really reached that guy, & it was a pity, in a way, that I wasnt big enough & fit enough to have carried the argument on with his weapons."[73]

Birney seemed blind to the inconsistency between his condemnation of the Vietnam War and his deep involvement with *The*

Adventures of Private Turvey. Given his political views, musical comedy about war was almost a contradiction in terms, a throwback to the sensibility he had had years ago when he himself was a military officer. He disapproved of having Turvey sing a sentimental ballad without recognizing that sentimental ballads were stock-in-trade for the genre. He was convinced that a musical could be anti-war without seeing that if it were truly so, it would cease to be a musical comedy. Had Birney turned the script over completely to Don Harron and Mavor Moore, it might have been shaped into a successful musical. But when the time came later to discuss rewriting for further productions, he stubbornly refused to budge: in a seven-hour meeting, the script-writer, music writer, the director/choreographer and his lawyer, Birney's agent and Birney "argued mainly about whether it was to be an anti-war musicale or just a light-hearted nostalgic treatment of world war II, canadian version   i was for the anti-war attitude, & finally won my point   however, i had to allow a compromise: the actors depicting soldiers can say only 'buck you, sergeant.'"[74]

This was not Birney's only blind spot. He was oddly out of step with the cultural nationalism that had been building in Canada since Glenn Gould began to record and give performances in 1950; the Stratford Shakespearean Festival pitched its tent in 1951; the new medium of television ran Canadian programs like "Front Page Challenge" and "Hockey Night in Canada"; Painters Eleven, an informal association of artists such as Jack Bush, Harold Town and Jock Macdonald, took shape; and the M & S New Canadian Library Series of paperback reprints of outstanding Canadian publications edited by Malcolm Ross got underway in 1957 with its first reprint, *Over Praire Trails* by Frederick P. Grove. In part because of Birney's own efforts, the infrastructure for Canadian publishing and book sales was much more fully established, and more than one generation of students had been taught some Canadian writing through the new books— especially the anthologies—that had proliferated since the 1940s. He was aware of this, since a number of anthologists sought his permission (and paid the fees to which he now usually had exclusive rights, since many of his books had gone out of print). By 1966, for example, "David" had been anthologized twenty-three times and his copyright permission fee was three hundred dollars. But to him the nationalistic Margaret Atwood (who joined the League of Canadian Poets from the outset) was not so much the brilliant feminist poet and fledgling novelist as she was simply another young poet who had submitted thirteen poems to *Prism: international* in 1964 (he kept three) and had visited his UBC poetry class in November the same year. Judging from his letters (which scarcely mention Atwood), he was much more *en rapport* with younger male writers, and his attitudes and views, not to mention his behaviour, were ill-suited to the feminist movement which—like cultural nationalism—had begun gathering momentum in the early sixties.[75]

Birney had never even heard of the 1961 protest led by Robin Mathews and James Steele against the American draft dodgers who had taken so many positions in Canadian universities, and even if he had, he (who had hired a number of Americans at UBC and depended on several American academics to arrange readings and lectures for him) would have disagreed. "Personally, being an internationalist," he wrote poet Fred Candelaria at Simon Fraser University, "I prefer the kind of citizenship which permits me to move freely in other countries."[76] As he had amply demonstrated since he took over the editorship of *Prism* in 1963, and changed its name to *Prism: international,* his philosophy of the arts had remained broadly eclectic. And he thought it a matter of little importance that he did not find time to write something for Al Purdy's anti-American collection *The New Romans.*[77]

Cultural nationalism reached fever pitch in the lead-up to Expo '67 and the World Poetry Conference that was part of the Montreal celebrations. Birney gladly accepted the position of Centennial Writer-in-Residence at Waterloo University, having spent a second year at the University of Toronto (1966–67) in the same position for full rather than half salary. (He enhanced his income cleverly by such means as selling a substantial portion of his library of books and periodicals to the Toronto Public Library.)[78] But he showed little interest in the national birthday party, which he dismissed as "the Centennial Circus" or "the year of Canada's Official Narcissism," observing wryly that he was "in some demand as a sort of Centennial Survivor, old enough maybe to have been around at Confederation."[79] Birney joined the gung-ho spirit that year only in so far as he was doing what he had always done, "hop[ping] around between campuses" giving readings for no less than $150 a shot, plus expenses. By mid-April 1967 by his own detailed calculations, he had travelled 20,000 miles by plane since the New Year and expected to do another 5,000 before the end of May.[80] As for the World Poetry Conference, which he left early because he had the flu, he enjoyed George Barker's remarks and admired Rina Lasnier, but otherwise thought it a silly sham.

Birney's reaction to Expo '67 and perhaps even his flu might have resulted in part from the strain of attending Bill's wedding. For months before, he wrote with deceptive casualness that he might not "be able" to go. Bill had not communicated at all since the Ikuko episode, and had remained close to Esther, who returned with him to Port Angeles, Washington, to prepare for the wedding. Birney's pain came through in offhand sarcasm: "Bill is getting married to some Methodist country schoolteacher in northwest Washington—don't ask me why," he wrote Ralph Gustafson.[81] "As the Wicked Parent, the loose-living ancient beatnik, I remain uninvited to the wedding," he wrote Phyllis Webb.[82] Bill's fiancée, Marsha Taylor, persuaded Bill to send an invitation, and the night before the wedding, Earle appeared. "I was giving a dinner for the bridal party," Esther recalls, "and Earle turned up, and Bill threw his arms around his father and all was peace for awhile." They were married on 2 September 1967, the day after Bill's twenty-sixth birthday. Within a year, they moved to Vancouver.[83]

Birney disliked his stint as Centennial Writer-in-Residence at Waterloo, which he began in the summer of 1967 while Esther travelled around Scandinavia and Europe with a friend, then visited her father with Bill for what would be the last time before he died. He was predisposed to like Waterloo because he had admired the student publication *Chiaroscuro* edited by John Robert Colombo, which Colombo had sent him in 1957. But much as Birney loved young people, his tolerance had limits. When the students arrived back in September, their partying near the Student Village dormitory, where he had chosen to live in a don's suite in the girls' residence, provoked him to write a seething letter to Warren Ober, the Chairman of English who had hired him:

> It's a few minutes from midnight. Yielding to what may prove to be a regrettable impulse I am about to get dressed again, pack up my books and half-finished drafts of letters, and set off for Toronto.... The incredible noise, the vacuous yelling, screaming, blowing of trumpets, ringing of cow-bells, shrieks, trompings, blind throwing of footballs, still goes on outside my window.... the sophomores have, apparently, been given a week's license to indulge in a thinly-disguised sadistic Saturnalia. There is something much worse going on...than all the "marihuana [sic] orgies" and long-haired love-ins many professors...are so morally exercised about.... For any thoughtful and sensitive person, it is a disgusting show....
>
> I like to be in full possession of my faculties when I give lectures or conduct seminars.... The guard on the phone laughed and said this "would probably go on for a couple of days...they've called a bonfire for 2 a.m. near one of the residences & it wont be quiet till after that."... Please cancel my first class. I hope to be catching up in sleep when its members show up at three tomorrow.[84]

By the end of the year, Birney expressed disappointment with his year there: he was upset that there was so little socializing among professors, let down by the meagre turnouts at his readings and remarked to a student reporter, "I don't know, maybe I haven't made a dent at all."[85] But the stint had served its real purpose, increasing his income while reducing his expenses. By the end of the year, his careful calculations of his assets showed that he was worth approximately $64,000. Feeling fairly secure about money at last, he was certainly glad to drive off to take up the Regents' Professorship he had been honoured with at the

University of California at Irvine, California in late March: "I got off from the University of Waterloo, forever I trust," he wrote a friend.[86]

Birney arrived at Irvine to find that Esther had rented them a gorgeous cliff-house overlooking the Laguna Beach, half an hour from the little campus of 2,700 students. "Would like to hear you reading [your poems] sitting on our beach," he wrote Peter Stevens, the young poet and professor at the University of Saskatchewan in Saskatoon who was preparing a study of Canadian poetry from 1940 to 1960,[87]

> under the flowering cliffs, & in the sound of surf, etc. All the California baloney, it's here, plus Reaganism, the 100,000 Irvine ranch (on the edge of which is our campus), oranges, surf-bobbers, power-yacht-basins, army heliports, abalone divers, and a few bearded poets lost in a sea of vacuous female californian pulchritude. Down here you'd *need* examinations to meet your students for the second time (first being registration—in between they're 20 miles away on the beaches, tanning or surfing or skindiving).

The Regents' Professorship was "a soft touch."[88] All Birney had to do during his three months was give half a dozen public lectures and be available for those who wanted to consult with him. "We live," he wrote, "immersed each morning in seafog, drowned in sun by midday, burned in improbable raddled sunsets at evening. I don't know much about the night as I go to bed around dark & get up to work & swim with the dawn. A nice life if you could settle down to it."[89]

But Birney could not settle down to it. He had complained frequently that being a Writer-in-Residence had kept him so busy he had little time to write (ironically, the main purpose of such a position). Certainly his carefully itemized reports on his activities at Toronto and Waterloo show that he took his job more seriously than almost anyone else would have. "You have invariably made contributions above and beyond the call of duty,"[90] Warren Ober had written him with thanks. But now that he had leisure to spare for his poetry and a climate he loved, he chose to do other things. Despite the fact that he had put almost 200,000 miles on his Volvo since he bought it in 1962, in addition to his extensive plane trips, he was itching to travel, this time to Australia and New Zealand. As he had written to Einar and Muriel Neilson a year before, "the older I get the less I need stability."[91]

Tom Wayman, who was studying at Irvine that year, noticed a profound change in his mentor from just three years before: "My earlier experiences of him as a teacher had been that he was deeply interested in what the *student* was working at expressing, in whatever form the *student* had selected. At Irvine, however, Dr. Birney was very impatient with what the students were writing. He declared that concrete or shaped poems were the forefront of poetic endeavour, and was rather dismissive towards other approaches to the art (as practised by virtually all the poetry students there at that time). It was as if he had given up being a teacher, and was functioning as an artiste: here's what I, as a master of the art, am currently absorbed by and if you want me to respond meaningfully to your work, it better be along the lines that fascinate *me*. I don't know whether this change was due to the shock of life in Southern California, or to living with Esther as a family (their son William was...working in Los Angeles—about thirty-five miles north of Irvine—and I think they saw him from time to time). I know I was quite disappointed in Dr. Birney's behaviour, because prior to [his] arrival at UCI I had been singing his praises and my fellow grad students found little to relate to when [he] did show up. [He] gave a series of talks on campus on poetries in English other than English and American, which covered Australian, Canadian, African, West Indian, etc. writers.[92] I remember, though, missing at least one of his talks...something I never would have done at UBC... The Birneys did entertain at their fabulous house in Laguna; I remember being present along with other grad student writers. But it was as if Dr. Birney had burned out on giving all to his students, or as if he had a chip of resentment on his shoulder that after so much effort he was not as famous, or honoured, or rewarded as he felt he deserved. In any case, our friendship cooled after the UC Irvine experience."[93]

Birney spent most of his spare time at Irvine setting up his trip Down Under. No Royal Tour could have been attended to with greater care. He wrote all the journal editors (enclosing poems for possible publication) and anyone anywhere he thought might have contacts there. Then he wrote each of them in turn, outlining his itinerary and asking them not only to set up readings and lectures, but obtaining from them lists of writers and works—especially contemporary ones—that were considered the best. Using these lists, he read and read Australian and New Zealand writers and began consolidating his knowledge by preparing lectures. His early public lectures at Irvine were on subjects he had addressed over the past three years, such as "Concrete Poetry," "Shaped Poetry," and "Poetry of the Sixties"; but by the end he was lecturing on "Poetry: Australia and New Zealand."

By the time he left for Australia from Vancouver carrying several copies of the modified "Selected" *Memory No Servant* which John Gill brought out as the first production on his printing press in June ("my FIRST publication in book form in the usa... it's some kind of a bitter triumph for me, after 25 years of trying"),[94] he was a virtual *Who's Who* of Australian letters, and had readings well set up, as well as social events arranged from receptions in Canadian High Commissions to student beer fests.

Birney's trip was financed by a special Canada Council Medal and Award of $2,500 which he was given in a special ceremony in Ottawa on 2 May 1968. He had known of this well in advance, because he had been asked to resign from the Canada Council's Art Advisory Panel to avoid conflict of interest. The award—for outstanding cultural achievement—also went to A.J.M. Smith, painter Jacques de Tonnancour, and architect Eric Arthur. His Excellency, the Governor General Roland Michener, made the presentation for which Birney (dressed very conservatively in dark suit, white shirt and tie) was described as a "forerunner in Canada of recent issues in the visual aspect of the poem and ceaseless teacher and promoter of young poets." Ironically, Birney's success was mixed with failure, which may have been the main reason he accepted the award but declined ("threw back," as he said) the medal that was presented with the Canada Council Award.[95] At the same time he was hailed as the "forerunner" of visual poetry, M & S and the new Coach House Press turned down his visual poems (tentatively titled "Though I Die Old"[96] or "Ten Kins" or—when angry—"Screw Yew McStew"[97]) and he resorted to having bpNichol produce the book *PNOMES, JUKOLLAGES, and OTHER STUNZAS* through his *grOnk* series.[98]

Birney's trip to Australia was a final "last fling" before retiring somewhere near Vancouver—possibly Bowen Island—to a house with a garden and a cat."[99] He had no intention of taking Esther, who stayed in Vancouver at a sublet flat near Stanley Park to start in at yet another job in social work; she "isn't as fond of rapid travel or of tropical weather as I am," he told others.[100] He had told the Australians and New Zealanders he contacted that he was "most keen about meeting younger poets."[101] And he wanted to dress more youthfully now, in one of the currently fashionable Nehru jackets, and dark shirts. But above all, he wanted to travel with Alison Hunt, for whom he had written one of his new poems "i think you are a whole city."[102]

"That's what I liked about Earle," Alison recalls of the trip on which she was "extra baggage," "he was always ready to try new things, new experiences."

> He was very game. We went off into the desert with an aboriginal guide who made a campfire and put these dreadful grubs and insects and maggots into it. He eat [ate] them. He'd eat anything.
>
> We stayed at some places like Canberra and Melbourne and Sydney where we'd be billeted in these cottages. And usually he'd be in one end of this long dark corridor and I'd be miles down at the other end. And we used to giggle an awful lot and run about and it was cold. I think he enjoyed that sort of thing. It's sort of funny. From one day to the next you never quite knew how he would get up in the morning. There were times on the trip when it would be a gorgeous day, and what would he be doing? Wearing dark glasses, having spent the night wearing these stupid black eyeshade things. I thought they were terribly

unromantic. Then he'd turn around the next morning and you'd wake up and he'd say, "So okay, where are we going?"

One thing I found very strange. Wherever he went he had like 500 people to woo who'd written to him and he'd written to. And the Big Link to Earle was the American Express. He'd go in there three times a day whenever we were in the big places. And there'd be this great pile of mail. I had this idea that a poet sat around and looked at things and read books all the time. But he was always writing what I thought were long, sort of business letters. He'd be bitching and signing all these lovely things for people to get their Canada Council grants, and all this support for about a hundred thousand poets. And a lot of it seemed to me an awful lot of busy work. He loved that. He'd get up at seven o'clock in the morning and be writing letters for four hours. Sometimes he'd pull the curtains, put on dark glasses and spend all day writing letters to the editor, to the publisher, saying things like "You pisspot McClelland" or "You piss me off, Jack." It was like an intravenous transfusion for him, I think.[103]

Judging from his letters and the remarks quoted in various Australian and New Zealand newspapers, Birney was exhilarated to have wriggled free not only of Esther but also of the preconceptions he encountered in Canada, free to reinvent himself. "The sprightly 64-year-old poet—whose bristling sideburns and Nehru jacket reflect his youthfully non-conformist approach to life—still had plenty of energy left to talk about the need for a greater literary exchange between countries of the Commonwealth," went one account. He has read and studied all [our writers] from Katherine Mansfield through half a century to Janet Frame, Allen Curnow and James K. Baxter... "I'd like to meet Frank Sargeson, the writer," [he said] "I've been reading his novels and short stories for years." "A man should wear what he likes, and not what his wife chooses—I am married," he was quoted as saying. "Wonder what kris wrote you about that weirdo party at taylor's," he wrote Richard Tipping, a concrete poet he met there. "i remember that kris was about my only defender against the incredible conservatism & de gaullism of mine host the Taylor   kris & the taylor boy's pet wombat were my friends." [104]

By the end of his trip, Birney had "read Canadian poetry, especially the under-30 poets, in about 40 different places from perth to dunedin & alice springs to samoa,"[105] but had found Australia and New Zealand too conservative for his liking, and complained on his return of "the dismal human landscape of both countries."[106]

The return to Vancouver in November—especially after snorkelling on the Great Barrier Reef and holidaying on the beach at Apia in Samoa on the way back—was a shock. "Masses of mail awaited me," he wrote his new Toronto friend, Jack Jensen, a handsome, adventurous Danish bachelor who was a buyer for Coles Book Stores Limited and—like Birney—was devoted to the good life,

> & more has slid in, delayed, following me around new zealand & australia and all those boxes arriving [of material Toronto didn't want], each to be lugged up...& all of them, plus the ones already here, to be sorted, catalogued to sell to U. of Calgary, price-guessed...at least i have resisted social invitations, become a complete recluse, except that i haven't yet got tough enough to refuse entrance to people who make the effort to come to me knock...i have a largish bedroom (esther has her own)[107]

One social invitation Birney was delighted to accept before becoming a "complete recluse" came from Pierre Elliott Trudeau. On 20 November at a private dinner in Trudeau's residence in Ottawa, he savoured an evening with Paul Almond and Genevieve Bujold, Alfred Pellan, Harry Somers and Barbara Chilcott, Ian and Sylvia Tyson, Roger Rolland, Renée Claude, and perhaps a dozen others.[108]

Birney was determined to finish the work he had started on Malcolm Lowry several years before. "my ambition," he wrote his friend Stephen Vizinczey, author of the controversial *In Praise of Older Women*, "[is] to produce the fullest, honestest, thoughtfullest book by-and-about lowry."[109] But he could not resist arranging a triumphal Canadian reading tour for himself in the New Year. He left on 16 February for Selkirk College in Castlegar, B.C., where Rona Murray was teaching and had arranged his visit. Then he was off to Georgian College in Barrie, Ontario; then to York University, where Beryl Rowlands arranged a Chaucer lecture ("that abortive effort," he would later say)[110] and Victoria College at the University of Toronto; then he was on to McGill, where he stayed with Louis Dudek, and next the Université de Sherbrooke and Bishop's University, where he stayed with Ralph and Betty Gustafson, in Quebec's Eastern Townships. Later he would complain, "each place arrang[ed] its own sort of weather hell for me. It wasn't necessary to convince me I don't like eastern Canada."[111]

He swung back through Toronto in March, over to the University of Wisconsin and, finally, Michigan State University, where he visited Art and Jean Smith. "theres a new generation compared even with 3 years ago," he wrote excitedly to Louis Dudek on his return. "i felt it when i got those lovely blunt questions at mcgill ('are you married? what is your position on student power? why do you write?' etc.   i love 'em, & wish i had been like them when i was their age)"[112] Birney was embarrassed to realize that somewhere on his tour he had lost the stainless steel ankh which Esther (who was now amusing herself taking a drama production course and working in Gestalt therapy) had given him to wear around his neck at readings. He wrote to all his hosts, and eventually got it back from Doris Baulch who had set up his Barrie reading. The whole tour earned him $900 ($350 of which was Wisconsin's honorarium),[113] not enough, he thought. "I doubt if I'll ever do it again," he wrote a friend, "in addition to the discomforts, the fees I can get in Canada are negligible...and I am bored with my own voice, with my now-stale poems."[114] Not only that, he felt unappreciated. James Barber, the entertainment editor for *The Vancouver Sun*, reviewed the reading he gave at Simon Fraser:

Earle Birney is looking younger and sounding older...
mechanical gimmicks...stuffs his readings with
accents and impersonations...begins to sound like a
quarulous [sic] dabbler in whimsy. Birney in the past
has tried to be Cummings, Leacock and even Irving
Layton, but experience does not yet seem to have
taught him that...raising the voice an octave style,
lowering it to indicate significance, are performing
arts..., not the creative ones of the poet.[115]

Esther agreed that he had "turned himself into a clown."[116] But
Birney now *was* an entertainer, and—after twenty-three years of
experience—he was a good one (though not as good as Ginsberg,
who was drawing crowds of 1,700).[117] His best reading poem
was "Billboards Build Freedom of Choice," which he read with
an American accent (the poem had been suggested by billboards
he had driven past in Oregon) and with his head turning back
and forth as if he were a driver actually reading the billboards as
he passed. It was vintage Birney—social commentary, pawky
humour, precisely rendered dialect, thought-provoking puns:

Yegitit?
Look see
    AMERICA BUILDS BILLBOARDS
so billboards kin bill freedoma choice
between—yeah between billbores no
    WAIT
its yedoan hafta choose no more between
say like trees and billbores lessa course
wenna buncha trees is flattint out inta
    BILLB—
yeah yegotit
youkin pick between well
    hey!   see!   like dat!
    ALL VINYL GET WELL DOLLS $6.98
or—watch wasdat comin up?
    PRE   PAID   CAT?
PREPAID CATASTROPHE COVERAGE

yeah hell youkin have damnear anythin
   FREE 48 INCH TV IN EVERY ROOM
   see!   or   watchit!
   OUR PIES TASTE LIKE MOTHERS
yeah but look bud no chickenin out
because billbores build
   AM—
yeah an AMERICA BUILDS MORE
buildbores to bill more—
sure yugotta! yugotta have
   FREEDOM TO
hey! you doan wannem godam fieldglasses!
theys probly clouds on Mount Raneer
but not on
   MOUNT RAINIER THE BEER THAT
   CHEERS[118]

Back in Vancouver, Birney finally got down to finishing his annotated version of Lowry's "Collected Poems." He worked almost without interruption of any kind (with Esther "grinding out lowry commentaries on the typewriter"[119] for him), and by the end of July (a month past his deadline) was finished. Finished, but miserable. "wd have written you long ago," he wrote to one of the many correspondents he had neglected, "but got really bogged down in the malcolm-lowry-swamp   yesterday i airmailed 225 pp. of my edition/collation of his Coll. Poems & i still have to do a 20-p. intro.   it's been killing me, ruining my summer (one of the best vancouver's ever produced) & losing me all my friends (including any lingering respect i even had for myself, that i ever took on the bloody job)."[120] As always when he forced himself to sit still and concentrate on intellectual work, his whole self rebelled. He vented his spleen by writing another—more cynical—version of "Canada: Case History," which *Saturday Night*[121] accepted. Feeling trapped triggered fantasies of escape: towards the end of April, his thoughts turned to Margaret Crosland, and he wrote to see how she was faring; a week later, after reading *Harpoon in my Hand*, he wrote the author Olaf Ruhen, "[I] often envied you your life—not that mine has been dull for me, but I never really fulfilled my longing to be a proficient self-reliant man of the sea, and to know the wide Pacific, the way you have been and have done."[122] It was bad enough to be "chained," "tied down, "imprisoned" doing scholarly work, but worse still, he was alone. "Esther dear," he wrote in a letter that echoed with emptiness,

> I worked on letters last night, and was up again early this morning & put in another 6 hours at UBC collating. Would have finished today, but my eyes were too tired.... my stock of friends, either tennis-playing or not, is kind of low at the moment... What I'll do, I think, is just go over & bang on the tennis wall in the courts in the early mornings.... The only phone calls are, of course, all for you.... [the flat] is very empty and lonely without you...it was good exercise for me to do the carpets in your room & mine & the living room-dining room, & wash up my dishes & plan what i'm cooking for today, the regular little housewife...the flat has been silent as the tomb all morning & probably will continue this way.[123]

Birney referred to the flat as "my monkish cell," felt as if he were "chained to the ghost of malcolm lowry," portrayed himself researching as "one of the droopywhiskered dribbly old men haunting public libraries & looking evilly at little girls," and finally—having resorted to Valium to help him sleep[124]—lashed out in frustration, "its been this fucking lowry stuff   i hate him now."[125]

Much more to his liking was playing with poetry in ways that were as fey as any flower child. He loved

> working with a kid [Andy Suknaski, in his late twenties] who is a good visual artist esp. with woodsculpture & plastics, also sand-candles & ornamental kites so we are doing (a) kite-poems, about 6 ft long, made by folding up 10 ft long "concrete" poems of mine which he has run off as monotypes from a huge slab of

glass he paints backward we are accumulating kites for a Big Day next month when we get on the beach in the city and fly them, letting them go to come down in some bewildered suburban backgarden (b) sand-candle-pomes, with the little verses inscribed in the wax, & the candles set burning at low tide on some lonely beach.[126]

Birney was almost beyond himself when he learned that the sacrifice of his summer, his correspondence and his friends had been for naught. An editor at Jonathan Cape wrote that the notes and introduction were too long, and Margerie Lowry, who had dropped contact with Birney for years, now said she would not approve Birney's edition because he had omitted some of Malcolm's poems.[127]

As soon as he mailed off the finished manuscript, Birney sat down and wrote thirty letters straight off.[128] Then he proof-read the small inexpensive paperback version of his *Selected Poems* that M & S were bringing out (to launch their new NCL series) for the high-school and university market. Next he wrote an introduction for the collection of Bertram Warr's poems he'd intended to publish for twenty years and planned a textbook (*The Cow Jumped Over the Moon*) for Holt Rinehart and his autobiography ("so little time left for life and strength").[129] Then he was off to Toronto in October to tape readings of some of his poems for former student Earle Topping's *Canadian Poets on Tape*—an assignment for which he was paid $850, and one which enabled him to spend an ecstatic night with Bet Cox.

On his return, partly to rest his eyes, he was off on 24 November with his friend, UBC professor Tony Kilgallin, for a month's holiday skin-diving in Fiji before tackling another reading tour of Canada and the U.S., despite his outburst that he never would again. But after ten days in Fiji, he had another of the accidents that seemed to plague him: "I got caught by a sudden comber," he wrote Bet in an affectionate letter, "& rolled against the reef-edge. Got a lot of cuts & some coral poison & so we came over to a tiny island 60 miles from Suva, by boat, where I can stay off my feet till the cuts heal.... You would be amused to see me at this moment, sitting in bare skin except for a breech-clout and a scattered decoration of bandages & bandaids on my rump and necklacing my ankles—in the porch of a Conradian bungalow on a jungly hillside where they ate the last missionary over 94 years ago."[130]

The affair with Alison was over. But not before she had become pregnant. "I was pissed off by that, but he thought it was a great big giggle," she recalls. "I thought he was boasting—here I am Big Daddy—Pablo Picasso has nothing on me—that sort of thing. He thought Irving Layton would know of a good guy to do an abortion, but he didn't. I didn't want the child, and I'm sure as hell he didn't. So there was nothing problematic. I didn't have any of this angst or nonsense. But I did realize then that I wanted a father for John, and Earle never seemed to be interested in children. Esther used to say, 'My God, he's much nicer to Joe Rosenblatt than he is to Bill.' And it's true; he was.

"We didn't have a row or anything. He encouraged me to go back to U of T to get my M.A. and wrote a letter for me. We just split up after that, and I remarried in 1969. But he always kept up an interest in me. I liked that about Earle."[131]

Though Alison was no longer in his life, Bet was an important part of the plans Birney took up on his return to Vancouver just before Christmas. Their October meeting had been so felicitous ("I found you much happier and lighter," she wrote),[132] they eagerly planned another weekend together when he went to Toronto right after New Year's 1970 for his long script conference for a new version of the musical of *Turvey*. Though he would be busy that Saturday, he asked her to meet him at the Park Plaza Hotel on Friday, and hoped she would join him at Jack Jensen's vacant flat on Sunday.

She was also to meet him on the reading tour to augment the $93,000 he was now worth[133] which he had arranged around the Bishop's University Arts Festival at the end of January 1970 in Lennoxville. On his way, he was to visit the University of Saskatchewan in Regina from the 11th to the 13th, then the University of Calgary, the University of Saskatchewan at Saskatoon, and St. John's College, the University of Manitoba, in

Winnipeg. He had written his former students, poets Seymour Mayne and Frank Davey at Sir George Williams, to set up a reading there, and also got in touch with Gaby Baldwin (who had asked him to spend her teacher's holiday in mid-February in Toronto with her)[134] to make sure he saw her in Montreal. He would see Bet first, as he passed through Toronto. "i'm living pretty well by myself now," he wrote Judy Bechtold, who had written him she was divorcing her husband just before he left, "partly in toronto, partly travelling around—i was in the fijis all through november, then in toronto; tomorrow i start on a poetry reading tour of canada; in march i do another one across the u.s.... you know i've carried my kind of love for you ever since you were in my class   it would be fantastic if you would agree to take that "trip to someplace very beautiful" with me...dont write me to the barclay st address as that's esther's address...the best address...is c/o Jack Jensen, 19 Isabella St., Toronto. I'll be there soon."[135]

But on Monday night 25 January, as he sat chatting to the Toronto taxi driver from the front seat he preferred, heading home to Jack Jensen's flat through a sleet storm, out of nowhere skidded a Cadillac that rammed into the taxi head-on. In a flash, Birney's face smashed against the window, fracturing his upper jaw, and breaking his nose. The next day, he was to have left for Montreal.[136] Two days later, the telegrams flew far and wide:

IN HOSPITAL FOR REST OF WEEK, REGRET CAN'T COME, PLEASE INFORM ALL CON- CERNED.[137]

☙ 25 ❧

A Dry Season

"I liked the [Harold] Town portrait that is postered," Al Purdy wrote to Earle Birney, whom he regarded as his slightly older counterpart,[1] in March 1971, "you're fading out of life and into death, and death to life, dunno which."[2]

But Birney knew which. As he approached seventy, he felt time running out. Much as he would like to have dodged the truth, he was old. The birth of his two grandsons, Christopher John on 18 September 1970 and the red-haired William Earle (Earle, Jr.) on 28 August 1971, nudged him a notch closer to death. As he felt the life cycle wrench forward, Birney's mind kept wheeling back, surveying his life as if from a vantage point high above. He seemed to want to hover over his experiences, probe more deeply into their meaning, and—with Jack McClelland and others urging him to write his memoirs—he began sporadic forays to gather material. "let me know in advance where & when [you come out to the rockies]," he wrote Ralph and Betty Gustafson in 1970, "because i want to get back to banff & environs sometime again soon, to get the memory moving back to the 1910's there when i was a schoolboy."[3] And early in 1971 he made the "sentimental journey" to what is now the Glenbow Archives in Calgary where he taped poems, was interviewed by J.H.R.

499

Thomson of the Riveredge Foundation and researched his family's history;[4] gave readings in Red Deer and Lethbridge, and made a stopover for a long reminiscing interview and taping session with Jon Whyte, the nephew of one of his former schoolmates, who was now in charge of the new Archives in Banff which housed, among other things, old issues of the *Crag and Canyon* which documented his early exploits, and some Birney family photos and documents.

Over time, Earle and Esther ("Canada's most-with-it grandparents," as Bill called them)[5] had evolved an arrangement convenient to them both. Though they still shared the same apartment on Barclay Street in Vancouver, they had not shared a bed for more than ten years and one or the other of them was frequently travelling or out with friends. Esther, Birney wrote, was "very busy with gestalt therapy communes, etc. all the fashionable yakyaks...[and] i'm living pretty much by myself now, partly in toronto, partly travelling around."[6] In Toronto, he stayed with the Allens or with Jack Jensen, sometimes in their absence, and sometimes for several days or weeks. As for his travels, he arranged and undertook as many reading tours as he could, and cheerfully joked about "birney's annual farewell tour."[7] On one of these, his Washington, D.C. reading at the Canadian Embassy was upstaged by the October '70 crisis in Montreal. "The embassy's security head wanted to have my reading cancelled, & refused to have it take place in the embassy for fear of bombing," he wrote Bill,

> a prof. at johns hopkins u. got his u. to offer me shelter for the reading—this offer then shamed the canadians into coming up with their own solution, which was to hold it in the can[adian] cultural offices rented in one of the U.S. Govt's. Intercommunication buildings it seemed everybody was willing to risk blowing up *that* building (nothing makes sense when a flap is on) the rumours & alarums lost me over half the audience (85 invitations had been accepted, 35 people showed) but there was a good response & lots of extra food & drink, so no sweat[8]

With old age, Birney found sexual conquests somewhat more difficult, but seemed to be resigning himself to the inevitable. He had a brief affair with Maria "Puci" des Tombes, whom he had met in New Zealand, and who came to Canada to visit her daughter Anna (soon to be Anna Porter, later publisher of Key Porter Books), who was now his editor at McClelland & Stewart. Despite a plea to come back to Canada and live near him ("I am quite sure that you and i could find a great deal of happiness, and perhaps the permanence we both desire, and stability, and mutual love and fun and trust," he wrote, offering to pay her fare),[9] she decided otherwise because of Esther. Soon, however, Birney set his sights elsewhere: "this french chick [Catherine Broustra, who nursed him for days after his accident] who is supposed to be writing a book about me for the univ[ersity] of bordeaux has been living around (& off) me (never on me, dammit," he wrote acquaintances in San Miguel, "but i shd really get reconciled to monasticism at 66 anyway) shes been here nearly 10 days, & distracting me from work—i'm trying to organize another poetry-reading tour, this time thru u.s., starting April Fool's Day (that's me)."[10] In a line for one of his new poems, which Purdy found deliciously comic, he wrote "Sideburns have been sapping my strength."[11]

But though Birney adopted a self-mocking stance, describing himself as a "tottering troubadour,"[12] he was far from happy. He was disappointed that Esther was often away when he wanted company and that she did not always put his comforts ahead of her own activities, which now included frequent visits and babysitting with the grandsons she doted on. Nor did he like the fact that when he wanted her to travel with him, she maintained firmly that she disliked hot climates and the stress of constant travel for long periods and refused to go. "She likes the *idea* of travel," he complained to Ralph Gustafson, "so we talk a lot, & then I take the trip."[13] He was bothered too by physical problems: his eyes were developing cataracts; his finger joints frequently ached with arthritis, as his mother's had; and he had not fully recovered from his collision in the taxi. His fractured jaw, which had been wired shut for almost two months, had almost healed and he had gained back the fifteen pounds he had lost on

a straw-fed liquid diet, but his dentist, Dr. Murray Frum (broadcast journalist Barbara Frum's husband) in Toronto, could not be
certain for another two years whether or not his upper teeth
would survive: "half of them act dead the other half act like sting-
ing hornets…it's just the nerve damage that plagues me now."[14]
Worse, after a dental session at the end of April 1970 in which
eight fillings cracked in the accident were replaced, he developed
an infection that closed his jaw and spread into his neck, so he
had to return to "the weary round of doctors, antibiotics, clinics,
painkillers, liquid diet, vitamins, this time with the addition of a
Water Pik"[15] and make sure he was not getting meningitis before
heading back to Active Pass on Galiano Island to have a holiday
fishing and writing poems while Esther nurtured him. Worst of
all, he felt blocked whenever he tried to write. He even had to
"help get the steam up" for writing the ever-present letters by
addressing the envelopes first.[16] He knew with a sinking heart
that the few poems he did manage were not good.[17]

   Birney's fuse was understandably shorter than ever. His explo-
sions of resentment increased and he found himself engaged in a
number of otherwise inexplicable feuds. He complained of difficulties with McClelland & Stewart who were preparing his next
collection, titled *Rag & Bone Shop*[18] after the phrase in Yeats's late
poem about the disappearance of his ability to write poems,
"The Circus Animals' Desertion":

> Now that my ladder's gone,
> I must lie down where all the ladders start,
> In the foul rag-and-bone shop of the heart.

Of these new poems he wrote, "some of them so new they may
need to be banged to start breathing but half of them are just old
collected things rubbed in fresh spit":[19] "ive been distracted by
the daily fuckups arranged by mcstew," he wrote Purdy, adding,
"you really think we shdnt let the yanks take over publishing?"[20]
And he was irked generally by M & S, complaining about his
contracts, puzzled that he could sell his books on tours but often
couldn't find them in local bookstores, and blaming his lack of
creative momentum on "a growing despair about what happens

to my poems after they are first printed—the mistakes in reprints etc. still going on."[21]

Despite the fact that he had now read for many American universities (and more than once in several of them), he was miffed that he could not arrange a reading in New York City: "it's dog-eat-dogging in the alleged poetry world there," he griped to his friend, New York writer Dave Markson, "(there isnt a first rate poet living in the city, to begin with—mostly small coteries of 3rd-raters lording the scene in pseudo-psychedelic pubs)—& since i consider myself an average 2nd-rate poet, & i just concentrated on seeing all the painting, sculpture, intermedia shows, that were happening i found myself being coldshouldered, in fact barred, from reading my poems to anybody in the whole fucking city."[22] And to his protégé Joe Rosenblatt, who had arranged a reading there, he wrote that he was "treated like a country hick," "i've never had anything but snubs from New Yorkers whenever i've been brash enough to think a few people down there might be interested in hearing me."[23] His resentment even spread to John Gill, the one American who had been willing to buy a press and learn how to use it in order to publish *Memory No Servant*.[24] "he published a very limited edition—cd never find out how many, 500 perhaps," he wrote Purdy, "& then advertized it in [no] more than one *Canadian* mag—& took orders from Canada (book-collectors, libraries, anybody wanting to 'collect' me) this of course defeated the whole purpose...which was to reach maybe a few thousand American readers, by the only way open to me."[25] Even Birney quickly realized how unfair this complaint was, and recanted: "i said some silly things about john gill," he wrote Purdy two days later,

> i want you to forget about them   above all dont quote me to him...his edition of my poems was 'limited' but i knew that in advance, that was the deal & he may have taken only a few orders from Canada, & only before I asked him not to & the advt. he placed (i saw only *one*) could have been done before he realized that i wanted the edition to circulate only in the US...how could i expect so small a publisher to afford

a distribution system?　i dont know what was wrong
with me when i wrote you...bitching that way about
john he has been a good friend to me, even though
he didn't include me in his anthol. of the 16 best can.
poets—i guess that was what was sticking in my crop
[sic], & suddenly came out.[26]

Birney was no more pleased in retrospect with his career in
Canada. "i [don't] think the gg awards are worth a fuck except
that now they have money," he sounded off to George Bowering,

> when i got them they didnt even have that & the
> "prestige" was a bloody albatross or Canada Goose
> around my neck for years afraid this new "service"(!)
> gong or whatever it is is as bad i threw one back at the
> govt. 3 years ago but this time i decided i dontcare
> (there's still no money in it of course) & when you get
> to my age they'll make a square pigeon of you to be
> shot down anyway whatever you say.[27]

"Myself, i've had as much shit thrown at me as any Can. poet
ever had, & most of it by college profs," he expostulated to
Purdy in an attempt to gain perspective, "i've generally tried to
ignore it, just as i ignored the roses i got too, because neither are
relevant to *me*; i know my own faults & virtues better than they
do; & i write to please myself first, & reviewers last. True, once
in a while i get mad, when i feel a *personal* attack, & i fight back.
It lets off steam but nobody wins these battles, & time-energy is
drained off from what might have been real word-work."[28] But
he reacted, as always, to the reviews of *Rag & Bone Shop* (which
received several good reviews and quickly went into a second
printing): "the yankees have been doing hatchet jobs on my book
here (andreas shroeder in PROVINCE) & one Michael Finlay in
SUN, real slimy personal-attack jobs" and basked predictably in
the sympathetic attention of "a beauteous young Swede girl, a
free-lancer" who interviewed him (while Esther served them tea)
in his study at home for a *Sun* article (which pictured the laid-
back, white-bearded Birney in a trendy striped shirt and leather

boots, and concluded, "Not everybody grows old.")[29] and in Jack Webster's lively radio "Hot Line," on which he defended himself "for not believing in God, the Bible, & Wacky Bennett."[30]

Birney's complaints ranged far and wide. He complained about the Creative Writing program at UBC ("narrow and bureaucratic")[31]; about George Woodcock's preface to the NCL *Turvey* ("solemn & harmful")[32]; about "Kitchmas" ("the summation of all the woolyminded hypocrisy of christians...a huge selling plot of big business... i wont cooperate i wont send present or xmas cards i give my friends presents when I want to");[33] about an NFB film version of "El Greco: *Espolio*" ("ignores El Greco & rewords my poem");[34] about the mail that invariably awaited him on his return from reading tours ("an appalling Dump... And yet a fascinating one that you must scrabble through, looking for nice letters...cheques, offers from British publishers, etc. & finding duns, rejection letters from British publishers, time-elapsed requests to help milk the CanCow, circulars, large folders of doggerel from never-to-be-published ladies (& some gentlemen), etc....");[35] about the fact that a British poster advertising his reading described him as American;[36] about lending Bill money to buy a house in 1971 (he generously lent $17,000 at 4 1/2% instead of the current 8 1/2%), "i keep on working at least it leads to money and my son likes to borrow that so i still have a little usefulness";[37] and, perhaps most of all, about the fact that his beloved red Volvo was wearing out.[38]

But his most serious wranglings by far were those with Frank Davey and Dorothy Livesay. Davey had already tangled with Birney in 1966 when Birney took issue publicly with Davey's defence of a statement by Gwladys Downes in her review of his book *Bridge Force* that Davey's poetry was like "watered-down Birney." Davey responded that—given Birney's recent experiments with poetry—it was more a case of Birney being "watered-down Davey." Downes reaction to this was a letter of explanation in which she quoted Birney as saying that he and Davey had little in common except red hair and the desire to be poets. Davey enclosed a clipped lock of his light brown hair in his rebuttal to Birney.[39] Since then, however, they had become friends. Davey had now begun a short biographical-critical book on Birney for Copp Clark at the same time as Richard Robillard had with McClelland & Stewart.[40] Though his own publisher had asked him to assess Robillard's manuscript (which he did), Birney had immediately taken Davey's "side" in the matter, as if the situation were a competitive one rather than the natural development of critical books on his career. He gave him permission in advance to use any quotes from his poems for free and speculated, "i am on your side... i doubt [Prof. Robillard's book] will be able to 'compete' with yours."[41] But when Birney received Davey's first draft four months later, he turned on him. He began fairly objectively by listing typos and correcting errors in the bibliography, then moved on to take issue defensively with various aspects of the content (such as Davey's summary of his dispute with the CAA and his omission of his Regents' Professorship at Irvine), and finally descended into a personal attack on Davey.

> You exhibit considerable snobbism here as well as ignorance of the economy of even a full professor's life in the immediate post-war years... we (me, wife, son) lived in half an army hut... to save money in hope of making a down-payment on a house (this was not mere bourgeois ambition, but... constant pressure from the university on senior professors to... let the new staff in)... i had to maintain a small house in south van my mother owned but could not keep on her sole income, a world-war-one-widow's pension— & i had to pay a psychiatrist for monthly, sometimes weekly, visits my wife had to make to him... so i grabbed at every chance to make money by writing, & you ought to know nobody pays anybody for academic articles on Chaucer—so, yeh, sure, i "squandered what little free time" i had—dont you think it went against the grain? ask yourself what *you* would have done, though i doubt you could imagine yourself into such a situation, you are so thoroughly a smug product of the prosperity years.[42]

A month later, in two further "epipseuds" or "episads," as he insultingly called his critiques for Davey, Birney was utterly ruthless. "You always seem to assume that my inventive powers are weak, so if anything seems especially lively it must be because it's drawn directly from some one person in real life this is the characteristic english-prof-syndrome, based, i think, on a good deal of jealousy of the creative person…sorry you found *Turvey* 'unexciting' for a whole 100 pages this is purely a subjective judgement which, however, you state as a fact wouldnt it be more modest of you if *even once* in the course of your (*to me*) not very exciting 128 pages, you used a phrase like 'to me unexciting'? or would that destroy your authority as an omniscient professor?" Davey's assessments of *Down the Long Table* (which Birney himself had always thought was poor) drove him to even greater extremes: "Your own naivety as a critic has here led you into writing defamatory rubbish about me, earle birney, the author. Since you cant distinguish between an author and his heroes or his anti-heroes, you must assume that I indeed treated some woman the way Gordon Saunders did [he seduces a married woman who dies after an abortion]… I will, of course, have to consult my lawyer about this."[43] "God, I've been amazed by the pettiness and ingratitude of your recent letters," Davey wrote back to Birney. "I have written the most complimentary account of your work to date, and concluded it with an appraisal of an extravagance even I worry about—and you think you need a lawyer. More likely I need a psychiatrist." Birney, not to be outdone, slammed back, "what a predictable letter! you publish a book which sets out to damn most of my published work—and then you want to weep on my shoulder… It's nothing to my regret that you ever sucked me into helping you get started on this malicious little piece of pseudo-criticism…stop pretending to be my impartial biographer and my artistic judge-and-jury; the role is a little too big for such a small and malicious little twerp as you have turned out to be." Davey's response was as simple as it was final:

dear Earle:
Go to hell.
Frank[44]

Birney's quarrel with Dorothy Livesay was even more inflammatory. Nothing much had ruffled their friendship for almost half a century. In fact, Birney had recently sent her a solicitous postcard commiserating with a problem she had with her leg, and had graciously accepted her request to act (with her children) as her literary executor.[45] But when he read her article "The Documentary Poem: A Canadian Genre" in *Contexts of Canadian Criticism*, edited by Eli Mandel in 1972, he saw red. "Earle Birney tried his hand at the narrative poem," Livesay had written,

> But he also sought to adapt it to documentary patterns. It is true that *David* conforms closely to the narrative style, but there is proof that this was no imaginary story. Birney's companion on that fatal mountain climb was a *real* David. His death was due to a rock slide.[46]

Birney wrote a stiff letter to Dorothy, advising her to read his "refutation of this calumny" in his recent short book vindicating the creative over the academic ("the writer-teacher-student tangle in poetry")[47] on creativity and academe, *The Cow Jumped Over the Moon*,[48] and demanding that she "acknowledge the untruth publicly, both in print, and to the next meeting of the Learned Societies, where you originally made your statement:"

> your statement is not only false and grossly misleading for your readers and mine, but it is libellous. You specifically identify me by name as the other character in my story, the character who commits what in Canada is an act of murder. Moreover, you imply that I covered up my "crime" by giving a false account of a "rock slide." This is grotesquely untrue.[49]

Livesay responded awkwardly, pleading ill health, expressing the wish that he had given her a chance to defend herself, and explaining that she had heard the version she printed from members of Warden's family. She argued, unconvincingly, that her sentence could be taken to mean that David was Earle's companion at UBC, not necessarily on the mountain with him. Dorothy wrote to Eli Mandel to warn him of the situation, and to tell him that her lawyer advised that Birney had no case for libel. She admitted that she ought to have checked the version Warden's cousins told her, that she was doing so now, and offering her defence (that Birney had quoted her out of the wider context of her article). She also wrote to Birney's UBC contemporary, Sadie Boyles, to ask her help in clarifying the situation. Sadie—who knew David well—confirmed the date and place of Warden's accident (after mid-September 1927 at Granite Falls on the North Arm of Burrard Inlet) and recalled that Wilbur Sparks was with him and that Birney definitely was not. Meanwhile—despite the attempts of friends to calm him down—Birney engaged Toronto libel lawyer, Julian Porter (M & S editor Anna Porter's husband), to press his demands for retraction.[50]

Behind the fury Birney directed at both Frank Davey and Dorothy Livesay lay guilt and fear. To Davey, he adroitly focused on the *death* (which *was* invented) of the professor's wife, Anne Barton, in *Down the Long Table* ("you have no evidence or reason to link the death of the fictional woman in my book with me") to divert attention away from the abortion Catherine Fisk actually had—and for which he was responsible—in 1932. Similarly, although he was entirely right to protest that he had not been on the climb with David Warden (and it was also clear that Wilbur Sparks did not push Warden off a cliff, since Warden lay alive for roughly twenty-four hours while Sparks went for help and did not die until three days after the accident), Birney focused his outrage on Livesay's inference that he was a *murderer*. The exposé he really feared and felt guilty about lay concealed in the off-hand remarks Livesay made to Mandel simply to "prove" that Birney knew Warden. "I do know that Warden was closely associated with Birney when Birney was editor and then Editor-in-Chief [of the *Ubyssey*], before his graduation in 1926. They were both doing Honours English under Sedgewick, who was also the 'sponsor' of several hiking trips on the North Shore."[51] Sedgewick was homosexual, and David Warden—like Birney—was one of his favourites without being lovers. But it had been at UBC in 1925–26 that Birney himself had briefly (and unsatisfactorily) sampled homosexuality with the flamboyant young professor Frank Wilcox, who remained his friend. Leonard Leacock, one of Birney's Banff climbing friends, was also homosexual. It was the closer examination of *these* relationships (which, incidentally, might have thrown more light on "David" with its phallic images of "The Finger," "squelched slugs" and "obscene toadstools")—just as it was the closer examination of his taboo affair and the resulting abortion with Catherine Fisk—which threatened Birney and triggered his anger. Davey and Livesay had cut too close to the bone.

As Birney cast his thoughts back over his life, he turned once again to Bet. He had backed away from the opportunity to leave Esther for her when she had spent the year with her daughters in Vancouver, but now, awash with nostalgia, knowing that the girls were grown up and Bet had no love interest elsewhere, he wondered if he hadn't missed out on the love that would bring him happiness. When his mouth infection interfered with a visit they planned in the summer of 1970, he wrote describing the cottage Esther had rented on Galiano Island and regretted his indecision in the past: "no neighbours within sight, lovely quiet woods for miles behind, a baldhead soaring around, as well as humming-birds on the porch, and deer coming up to the door practically quiet, with a fireplace, even a tv, perfect   i should have bought something like that when i first met you & kidnapped you into it."[52] Bet sent him a love poem she wrote after hearing him read from *Rag & Bone Shop* on the radio on 27 February 1971 ("manna for a gaunt season") which ended:

> How I lay listening as you dived, swam
> Impossible oceans, assaulted fabulous heights,
> Then, drained, spilled your last exhaustion of words
>
> ·
>
> As I have seen you, spent, on attained shores;
> Or some utter, gasping peak; or after love.
>
> I slept, then, as on our first island.[53]

He was moved, as he had been when she sent him poems twenty-three years before; more so, he imagined, because her mind, like his, was circling back to the past. "thank you my dear, my very old-young-dear... i wanted a letter too to tell me how you all are & what plans are ahead i think you were planning to come out here again this summer yes?"[54]

Birney's own plans included a whirlwind reading tour for April through June in Britain which he had set up around an invitation from the London Poetry Society in Earl's Court, where Margaret Crosland had once lived. He was awarded a return airfare by the "CanCow," used it to buy a cheap charter seat and used the rest ($400)—supplemented as usual by honoraria for his readings—to pay his expenses. As always, he found such jaunts exciting. He was "surprised and pleased," he reported in one of his frequent bulletins to his Coz, who had set up a reading at the Aberdeen Arts Centre and gave him a party afterwards, when his old friend Wreford Watson arranged a reading in the University of Edinburgh Staff Club Chambers as an after-dinner entertainment for a group of geographers.[55] "i had a grand time in dublin," he wrote her later from Margaret Crosland's country home where he was relaxing over Whitsun,

> stayed with an IRA lad, & had a big reading over Sinnott's pub...and was given a special welcome by 2 Irish pipers playing an ancient greeting-tune to a visiting bard! since then ive had good readings in newcastle...young & hippy "geordies" & a more sedate but very hospitable group in chesterfield (derbyshire) & ive read to a tiny & unresponsive group in Westminster Library (london) & to a goodsized & very responsive leftwing group in a more working-class part of london (islington—the Tribune Magazine group) & then 2 days ago to a big circus-tent full of english poets, intellectuals, snobs, & some fine young people too, at the Bedford Square bookbang... i have also had a weekend in Bordeaux, & read to 150 students of English there...it seems i was liked, & certainly i was entertained—far too well—too much

wines & rich foods for my old stomach—i had to
come back to england to save my liver[56]

Later, he continued his saga from London, where he expected
Esther to join him any day, "Last night was great—about 20
[Oxford] undergrads, all groovy, none of them snobs (what a
change at Oxford!) & most proletarian & 'provincial' in
speech—also in rebellion against the Establishment in all ways.
They dug my reading & took me into a tutor's digs in one of the
450-year-old colleges for a hash party."[57]

On his return, Birney eagerly awaited Bet's summer visit, as she
did too. She wrote on 20 July, "Twenty-three years ago today I
first woke up on Bowen Island. It was the birthday of my life,
the day my true love came to me—I have always thought of July
19 as my true & only anniversary date & hope in a couple of
years to think of it as our silver wedding."[58] As for Earle, who
felt devastating loneliness once Esther left for a three-month trip
to Australia, it seemed to him that "the brief times with you
make up the reality of my life   i shall be alone until i see you
again   please make it soon   call me as soon as you get to vancouver   and write me meantime."[59] But before Bet could leave
for what they both hoped would be an ecstatic reunion in B.C.,
she discovered she had uterine cancer and had a hysterectomy on
20 July. "i wake up thinking of you," Earle wrote

> i'm in a strange state   a writers' block, a real one,
> about my book   i can write down things of no impor-
> tance & pay bills but i cant write my book [*The Cow
> Jumped Over the Moon*] & personal letters are very
> hard   i think maybe i've been working too hard at the
> preparations for writing the book, after the heavy
> reading trip in britain   then i still have tooth trouble
> $170 worth of it last week alone & much more to
> come   had to get another book, not really one—a spe-
> cial selection of poems for an imaginary british pub-
> lisher who never materializes my epitaph   but why
> aren't i immensely happy   i have my health   if only i
> could bring you back yours... are you being properly

cared for my dear dear bet? ...i just stay in my flat trying to work   sometimes i go out in a corner of the little park...and do very simple yoga exercises... are you
going to come to your cottage? ...it is very difficult to
know what to do ever isnt it about anything i
mean...can i send you fare money?[60]

"He came out to the little cottage I called 'Sea-Level' at
Mission Point on the Sunshine Coast which I had bought when
my aunt left me a small inheritance," recalls Bet. "He was so
kind to me. It was only four weeks after my operation, so he
spent three days there, sleeping in his sleeping bag on the living-
room floor. He set up a little table outside so he could write in
the sun."[61] "i forgot my blankets and pillow—a perfect Freudian
forgetting," he wrote her on his return to Vancouver, "and so i
will come up on Friday, unless you say nay, stay over night, and
bring you down Sat... i loved every moment of being at
Mission Point with you even the ones when i was arguing with
you."[62]

By the end of December, on learning she was not yet fully
recovered, Birney wrote and offered her money so she could quit
her job and invited her to go with him on the three-month reading tour of Asia and Africa he planned for the winter and spring
of 1972. He wanted to believe that they could salvage something
together, but he wasn't altogether sure. "i come alive when i'm
with you (or think i do   maybe you dont think so?!) because you
are alive and loving and sensible and enduring and kind i love
you   please stay well."[63] But Bet did not quit her job, nor would
she agree to go with him on his Asian-African tour. She had
already sensed how unalike she and Earle were, and wondered—
understandably—to what extent "secrecy and deceptions...added
spice and excitement to the affairs—a well-known psychological
facet, of course." "I am old now," she had written, taking the risk
of offending him,

and perhaps becoming a bit reactionary, & not afraid
to be so—and I think the old "middle-class virtues"
are also a form of doing one's own thing & not to be

scoffed at… I am really so unlike you, I wonder you have loved me so long—and I really do believe you have (although, my dear glorious over-powered poet man, the trouble with having a number of lady-friends is that finally they are all mixed up in your memory!) but that surprising elastic bond between us has made my life real. Lost poet I may be—but I was touched & loved by you.[64]

Birney spent an evening with Bet in Toronto in mid-February before he left for Africa (he typically fitted in readings in London and Ottawa en route), asked her to send him "masses of letters" to the thirty countries he was to visit, and—since one of Bet's daughters now had a child—his last written farewell was an unromantic "keep well, gramma, love, E."[65]

Birney's African-Asian trip (for which he "milked the Cancow" for $2950) was the most exotic and frenetic since his first "last fling" almost two decades earlier in 1953. "I had a ball," he wrote Ralph Gustafson on his return, ranking his stop-offs like a boy listing flavours of ice-cream:

Didnt regret a day, or wherever I went; but some places my average stop of 3 days was enough. Other countries deserve a year, perhaps another lifetime: the Uganda-Tanzania-Kenya world; Ceylon, Singapore & Malaysia, the Philippines. Favourite towns: Kampala, Mombasa, Dar-es-Salaam, Nairobi, Kandy, Singapore. Favourite campuses: Ibadan (U. of Nigeria), Peradeniya (U. of Ceylon, or Sri Lankar as we have learned to write it now—near to Kandy), Kuala Lumpur (Malaysia), Cape Coast (Ghana), U. of Singapore, U. of Hawaii, Honolulu.…

I agree with you about H[ong] K[ong]—dreadfully deteriorated since 1958, when I was first there. Then there were only hundreds of thousands of starving refugees. Now all the bloody refugees have motor cars.… I bypassed [Bali]… because I distrust & dislike the regime, having read of the fine writers, poets, rotting in their jungle concentration camps; but if you have enough political qualms you couldnt go anywhere (or stay in Canada either, for that matter).[66]

Birney may have been sensitive to the political compromises he might appear to be making because he was contemplating a trip to Russia, knowing that Margaret Atwood (whose books *Surfacing* and *Survival* that year had enhanced her status as Canada's literary star) had refused to go on political grounds. And he might have had the odd twinge of guilt—despite the cultural work he was doing for Canada—at the lush holidays that were also part of his trip. "i'm sitting in the equatorial sun in a bathing suit," he wrote his Coz from Moen Island in the Truk District (a group of islands in the Carolina Islands of the South Pacific) with a sensual appreciation of natural beauty that had—if anything—increased as he aged,

> swathed in coconut oil over a fairly deep tan, as i write—i have about 150 [degrees] of lagoon in front of me, the water is every shade of green & blue reflecting the various depths—grey green for coral sandbanks, bright green for coral reefs, blue for the deep lagoon water (300 ft.)—invisible underneath lies what's left of the Japanese Sixth Fleet—hundreds of supply ships, & many destroyers, submarines, etc.... the lagoon is actually sea-water filling the crater of a volcano thrust up from the sea floor & the islands are the tips of later subsidiary volcanoes that emerged out of the old crater... the reefs are crowded with tropical fish, hundreds of different species & colours & sizes, from tiny bright blue ones like butterflies to big groupers & sand sharks   soon i'll put on my mask & fins & snorkel & have a look at what's out swimming today—tomorrow i will team up with 3 norwegians in a boat trip 30 miles to the outer reef for some more exciting swimming maybe
>   But all this ends in 2 days, when i must get back to civilization, i.e. on to Honolulu, where I give the last

of my readings   sweat is preventing the ink from
marking the paper![67]

Despite his plea to Bet, Birney did not receive a letter from her
until he reached Honolulu on his way back, but he kept in touch
and dedicated *The Cow Jumped Over the Moon* to her. Though
he tried to see her again in November 1972, she was in hospital
when he called, recovering from a car crash which was as dreadful as his own had been. It would be months before she recovered from her many bruises, strained right wrist, scalp wounds
requiring many stitches, and the loss of her four lower front
teeth. So the possibility of living together—felt but never
stated—gradually subsided once more into friendship. "It was
great to get my copy of the book," Bet wrote at the end of 1972.
"And how touched I was to see the dedication—I feel I have
attained a tiny bit of immortality. And the book is most absorb-
ing—like listening to you talk."[68]

After the euphoria of his Asian-African trip—on which he had
given an incredible forty-three readings—levelled out, and he
had dealt with the mountain of correspondence that awaited him
on his return, Birney felt depressed. He had never been able to
adapt to the electric typewriter which was too fast for him, and
now, after pecking away with four fingers as usual, he had developed "acute inflammatory sinuvitis" in his wrists, had one arm in
a sling, and could not type at all. He had written a cranky introduction to *The Cow Jumped Over the Moon*, which he defiantly
called an "anti-textbook." And he, unlike Bet, was decidedly
unenthusiastic about it. "about the only people who'll ever read
it are those i send copies to," he griped to Joe Rosenblatt on a
postcard that reproduced a Jack Shadbolt painting called—
appropriately—"Remnants of a Dry Season," "like it's never
appeared in a bookstore yet to my knowledge, & i cant get extra
copies by ordering even, & nobody has reviewed it."[69] And he
began referring to the autobiography he had looked upon with
sentimentality as an "anti-autobiography."[70] That Christmas of
1972, with Esther visiting friends in Toronto, and Bill and his
family off with Marsha's parents, he handwrote a long, lugubrious letter to his Coz:

i stayed here & batched & nursed my sinovitis & an
unceasing cold, & shuttled back & forth in the teem-
ing rains to feed my son's 2 siamese cats   they were as
abandoned as i was over the holidays... we had a
record rainfall—Xmas Day was 43/4 inches, the most
we've ever had on Xmas Day[71]

In an attempt to cheer himself up, he kept on the move with
readings and did his best to get Esther to come back to Asia and
Africa with him. By mid-February 1973 he reported to Ralph
Gustafson that, despite the fact that she disliked "heat, bright
suns, being in the same room or plane or bus with people who
smoke, swimming in waves, hiking, climbing, crowds,"[72] she had
agreed:

i'm off on another reading tour starting next week: u.
of washington (seattle), edmonton, saskatoon, regina,
winnipeg, north bay, south porcupine, barrie, peter-
borough, toronto, & perhaps other ontario places
would have gone on to quebec but nobody wants me
there any more—will get back to vancouver by april in
time to start on a trip to asia & africa with esther, who
hasnt been to those continents & has finally given in
to my urges that she sample them with me.[73]

But not even the British publication of his selected poems *Bear
on the Delhi Road* by Chatto & Windus cheered him up. "You
sound gloomy with that 'washed up' bit, but dont think you
should be," wrote Al Purdy, who tried to lighten Birney's mood
by congratulating him on the British collection. "I think
[English publication] was bound to happen, even if you didn't
think so. This may work out to a 'second career' or something,
stimulate you to write like hell.... As you well know, poems
come at odd times when one doesn't expect it."[74]

❦ *26* ❧

DEATH TO LIFE

Earle Birney was jogging when he had his heart attack. His daily runs were part of a lifestyle fashionable among the young, which included yoga and vegetarianism and promised not only good health but a longer life. He had just returned a couple of days before—elated and relaxed—to the Vancouver apartment he shared with Esther from a reading tour in the east which would have knocked out a much younger man. Though he was sixty-eight, he had given eighteen readings in seven weeks, and as if even the university audiences he once found "groovy" seemed now too old for his taste, proclaimed on 10 April 1973 to poet and professor Elizabeth Brewster who had hosted his reading at the University of Saskatchewan, "what I really dig these days are the high school audiences anywhere."[1] But now as he loped lightly along the lane like a curious bearded stork towards the corner to pick up the morning paper, he suddenly came to as if from a bad dream, face down on the hard ground. Finally, he thought, gasping for breath, pain shooting through his chest, this is the end.

But after a few minutes he managed to drag himself up on his knees, then slowly—like an ancient infant—crawled part-way down the lane, then painfully pulled himself up onto his feet and made his way shakily back to the apartment. "Fortunately," he wrote Ralph Gustafson, as if he'd escaped a fate worse than death, "nobody noticed, or I'd [have] been packed off to hospital in an ambulance... [I] phone[d] my doctor... [who] being a young doc... doesn't like hospitalization much more than i do, so he's kept me free, if tottery."[2]

A few days after his accident, Earle received a call from Lily Low who had just arrived in Vancouver. Lily, a twenty-three-year old graduate student, had met Earle in Toronto through Tony Kilgallin, the friend he'd gone skin-diving with in Fiji. Kilgallin, a UBC professor who was working on a book about Malcolm Lowry,[3] had been her supervisor for the undergraduate thesis she wrote on Mordecai Richler. Knowing she had decided to complete an M.A. in English at the University of Toronto, he suggested that Earle might give her a call when he was there to do some readings for CBC. On 7 March 1973 they had met for coffee and apple pie at Manny's Delicatessen around the corner from the apartment at 30 Charles St. West where Lily was living with her boyfriend while taking graduate courses from Robertson Davies and Marshall McLuhan, among others. "It was funny," Lily recalls in her quiet matter-of-fact voice.

> He told me on the phone that he was going to Peterborough to give a reading and asked me to have dinner with him when he got back. He must have had second thoughts about dinner. We had a three-hour chat at Manny's instead, mostly about Marxism and teaching and books—stuff he had tried to do. I was a serious student in those days. We got along well. He walked me back to my place and asked me if I'd like to see him again, and I said, "Yes." A few days later he called and asked me to come with him to Bob and Rita Allen's country place near Uxbridge. I agreed to go and spend a weekend. It was the acid test, exposing me to his friends and his friends to me. We had a very good weekend, and it just never stopped. I saw him every day after that. He was very subversive.[4]

Lily's parents were Cantonese who had left South China in 1949 for San Francisco where they caught a train to Victoria on Vancouver Island. Lily spent her first six years in Victoria's Chinatown ghetto, where her father ran a gambling joint. Despite the inevitable racism, she recalls with understated humour that she had "a great childhood."

> I was very conscious of being Chinese. I went to Chinese school every day for two hours, and, since Chinese was my first language, the culture sank in. My father had three wives in the old-fashioned way. That was quite acceptable. My mother was the second one. He was sixty-nine years old when I was born. So I have one full brother who is thirteen years older than me and a number of half-siblings.
>
> Because my father worked nights, I spent the day with him. When I was two, they must have thought I was uncivilized because they sent me to a church nursery school where I went for four years. They tried to train me to be Christian, but it didn't work. I was born with a heathen nature, I guess.[5]

When Lily learned that Earle had had a heart attack, and that he had not told Esther who (having apparently overcome her aversion to hot climates) was holidaying in Hawaii for a month, she moved into his apartment to take care of him. With cheerful tenderness and a no-nonsense air, she spent several weeks there cooking delectable meals to help him gain weight, walking along slowly with him in the bright blossomed spring air, and loving him with a steady devotion that astonished him. "He's just such a loveable person," she explains, "a wonderful human being."

By the end of June—with Lily gone to her family in Victoria and Esther (who noticed nothing amiss about his health) back from Hawaii—he had fallen in love with Lily. "He gave his red Volvo to Bill, all his marijuana to a friend, and returned to Toronto," she recalls. "It was symbolic. He was cutting himself off from a whole part of his life."[6]

Birney took a room at the Andorra Hotel on Charles St. East, close to Lily's apartment, and began researching for his "anti-autobiograhy" with Lily's help at the Thomas Fisher Rare Book Room in the University of Toronto's Robarts Library. It was not long before he had moved into her apartment. "My boyfriend of four years was on the way out anyway," Lily recalls.

> He was a museologist whose first tour of duty was an apothecary shop in Niagara-on-the-Lake, so we parted amicably at that point. When Earle left Vancouver, he decided to make another big sale of his papers to U of T; so when he moved in he had about thirty-five cartons of books to store. He brought his other worldly goods too: his camping stool, knife, gun, swimming fins and goggles, his old shaving mirror, his fifty-year-old sleeping bag and all his clothes. So we spent the next two and a half months on Charles St. with all these cartons in that small apartment.[7]

Even by early July, Esther knew only that Lily was Earle's research assistant. But on 5 July, Earle wrote a long letter (which was largely myth, according to Wailan) in which he gradually worked up to telling her of his decision. "dearie," the letter began, "so far as the Ottawa Reading is concerned, you were wise not to come... Lily came with me since I had 2 reservations." After much chit-chat, including the information that Lily had had a separate room at the Elgin Hotel, he broached his real subject:

> esther ive been keeping back the most important thing to tell you because ive found it so hard to say, & because i wanted to be sure what it was i should say   i think it only honest to tell you that lily is living in this flat with me for the present   at my age & in my physical condition this news hasnt much sexual significance but it does mean that we are "co-habiting," *though with no promises to each other beyond the moment*   it's something i've drifted into, out of loneliness and by chance   my relationship with her, as you know, began as a professional one & we had expected

to keep it that way... lily was committed to the summer here, both because of one last course not yet completed for her M.A., & because of her agreement to
work for me at the RBR during July & Aug.—then
the girl-friend she was to live with this summer, also
got a job out of Toronto [like her boyfriend], & Lily
was faced with finding another place to live or keeping
up a higher rent than she could afford alone   sharing
this flat, where most of her books & possessions are
anyway, was a more sensible arrangement in any case,
or at least in *this* case, since we were working together
& liked and respected each other   i have my own
small bed (with my old sleeping bag in the little
porch, for hot nights) in the living room & she still
has her bedroom-workroom—ive my own desk and
bookcases   she does the cooking & shopping, in
between working at the RBR with me, & on her
course...

　　i cant help it if this news hurts it hurts me to send it
too because my feelings for you havent changed at all
& among those feelings is a desire never to see you
hurt & especially never to be the cause of your being
hurt   but i feel so close to the end of my days   my
hold on life, on wanting to live, is so tenuous, that i
must do what keeps me alive, or go completely under
i live from day to day not knowing if the next sharp
pain is the prelude to renewed invalidism, or death, or
just another passing bit of angina   & my will to live
is tied in, as always, with wanting to write, & being
able to write... i need a closer companionship than
you and i were able to give each other in these later
years...

　　i dont think it serves much purpose to judge whose
"fault" that was—the fault of Father Time, maybe, our
society, or even the "virtue" of our giving each other
freedom to develop ourselves in our own ways—you
towards group work & the special friends you have
made through those channels   and me to writing &

those friends   friends we shared up to a point (and
there's where ive been much to blame, for not finding
the time and interest to give to *your* friends, to the
same extent you always cheerfully gave to mine)...

i cant plan far ahead—but within the immediate
present i want steady & loving companionship, someone who gets their pleasure out of looking after me,
cooking, shopping, letter-writing, researching for me,
learning from me, & so on...

perhaps i will be alone again   or perhaps you will
still want me back   i wont blame you if you dont
you have a longer life ahead & it is your right & perhaps your necessity to find a steady fulltime companion of the sort ive never been   in this letter all my
egoism shows   because i'm admitting it   i'm out in
the open, as a dying animal, trying to find the best
way for me to finish my self-appointed career as a
writer[8]

Esther replied in a short, almost numb letter, expressing her
appreciation that he had explained so fully and giving him the
birthday dates of Bill and his family: "It is my intention to think
well of you and to speak well of you...if you ever need me I will
be there to be with you. I mean any kind of an emergency... I
have said absolutely nothing to Bill & Marsha and have no
intention of doing so. Your wish to live near the literary scene
should be sufficient."[9]

In mid-August, Lily decided to approach Esther directly. In a
letter written amidst the confusion of readying herself to move
with Earle into a bigger apartment on Alexander Street near
Maple Leaf Gardens, she said,

I have wanted very much to write you for many
weeks, but have been prevented from doing so by
what I recognize now as a foolish desire to have something cogent and "proper" to say. I should have known
all along that I had only to look into my heart, and
write.

...I believe in circles that include, that generate human contact and draw us to our greatest potentials as beings capable of knowing and loving.... I suppose that it is sisterliness that I feel, on a rather basic level, but more than that too. Estrangement is so senseless, such a waste. I have had too much quarreling and bitterness in my life to willingly and knowingly allow any more to happen around me without my trying to create peace and harmony.... I believe that our union is right, fit; I know that we're making each other very happy, and that in itself is precious. But we don't live in a vacuum and we don't live outside of time, hence I feel guilty that you have been hurt. I suppose the greatest injury is that of being kept in the dark. To me, at least, that would be the greatest injury. I am sorry. It was wrong.

I wish that I could say that I'll be good for Earle and good to him forever and ever. But I made that kind of promise to a young man four years ago—not very long—and broke it. I can't make promises now that I don't know if I can keep. Earle's age and his health are forcing me to live one day at a time when, by instinct, I am one who plans and dreams. But young and old together have to temper dreams with reality, and it's not very romantic. I've not many illusions. Some days I am tortured by Earle's past and by the thought that I may be only one more, though perhaps the last, of many women whom he has loved as intensely as I believe he loves me now. Very foolish of me to be affected by it that way because the alternative is only ignorance, which is not bliss. But enough of that.

I realize that it may be awkward for you to accept me, in whatever form, but I still do hope that we can be friends.[10]

Esther did not reply.

But Earle and Esther continued to exchange affectionate, analytical letters, Esther sensing that—like Earle—she was making a break from a vexed past: "When I count my blessings, and how many I have to count," she wrote in September, "I number you among them. I have some very dark memories and many dark, sad feelings, but as Adler says, we write our own 'scripts' and I certainly wrote myself a humdinger."[11]

From the outside, it looked as if Birney at sixty-nine were off on another fling. Al Purdy, who had been dazzled by Birney's prowess with women ever since Birney had taken him along to visit one of his girls and talked her into leaving her boyfriend's bed to come and sit on his knee,[12] wrote to congratulate him on acquiring yet another beautiful woman. And Bet—who was usually placid—jotted on the back of the envelope of the last letter he had sent her before she heard his news,

Spring '73
Summer '73   — end: EB began to live with Lily Low
             aged 24—City Park Apts!!![13]

As if it were an apocalyptic cleansing force marking the end of an era, a fire swept through Esther's apartment on 26 September while she was out. She moved into the Sylvia Hotel nearby and wrote at length to Earle about insurance claims for things of his—or theirs—that were damaged by fire or smoke. Finally, after two weeks in the Sylvia, Esther's anger surfaced. "And again I cant sleep—Damn it!" she wrote at 5 a.m. 7 October to Earle.

> Your letters are full of affection & thoughtfulness & caring but they never allude to the big main situation——me alone, me lied to, me deserted for a young woman, my forty years of wasted effort and devotion, my life investment.
>
> OK you don't want to deal with that—OK. Then don't talk of how much you care & don't run to my friends to ask them to cope with "poor Esther." I've coped before & I'll cope again. But I'll do it with my eyes open to the real situation. Go in peace—if you can. It is not my intention to harry you in any way. But for Christ sake stop telling me you care & then

invite me to share your home with your mistress. Jesus, you've even perverted her into this mad kind of sadism. We haven't advanced far from Ikoku [sic], have we when Esther, whom you love so much, was asked to be an onlooker while you shared an ineffable happiness.

If you knew in Jan. you were going to leave why didn't you leave instead of remaining a frozen, locked away presence lying daily about your relationship. Wasn't your "great love" worth taking a chance on & being honest about instead of lying & lying & deceiving me—& that whole Ottawa mess—everything could have been avoided. I would probably have moved out in Feb. if I had known about Lily & perhaps the fire would never have happened. And anyway I resent bitterly your old terrible habit of making assumptions about how I would behave. I wouldn't have hung on to you then as I don't propose to hang on to you now. It would have clarified your coldness, your disinterest in me & my friends—it would have made sense. If you think back it was always the "discovery" that I had been lied to & made to feel duped & fooled as well as unloved—Pauline Ivey (a letter) Alison Hunt (a letter) Gaby, Ikoku—your whole bloody harem—I was always lied to.... What kind of a de-sexed mouse was I—to burn & suffer & go on... Don't torture me by telling me I am "always with you" that I am always your loved Esther. I'm not. I am your deserted, lied to, unloved Esther & I have been for years, since you came home after the war with your affections given to Margaret Crosland—till the next one came along whoever she was. I must read your autobiography to find out.... I should have shared my anger back, back, back—thru all the Lilys & Ikokus & Alisons, the Gabys & Bettys.

And now you can show all this to the present reigning queen & prove about her being the true love of a beleaguered man. Oh yes, she thinks she's the last—

maybe she is—after all you're not as young as you were. But at least she'll know of my sadness & bitterness & to hell with the pretense & the invitation to come & be a guest on your comfortable hide-a-bed—& when do I get sent home—when do I start to "smell" & receive intimations of not being welcome—in fact, when does reality set in?

Don't bother to write me letters about how "impossible" marriage has been with me. I can write better ones, believe me. What is unbelievable is my acquiescence in it. There's nothing to return to.

But somewhere there is an Esther who was in your mind when you wrote "This Page My Pigeon." And my Earle wrote it before he disappeared. That's the two people who would rebuild a shattered marriage. Shattered not in Jan. 1973, but at the end of the war when you came home... Would to God I could have been in touch with my feelings long, long ago.

And now for a letter from you giving me an untold number of reasons for not trying again. Too bad to put you to all that trouble. Well, go ahead. It will be the last one in which you catalogue my deficiencies as a wife. I could add to them, believe me & they would read—condoning, enduring, accepting, allowing you to be cruel to Bill & terrible to me. And for myself—being a mouse, hanging on to you, hoping when there was nothing to hope for...

Dear old love—don't flinch from what I have written. For me it is the first strong rung in a new way of being. If I'm alone at the bottom, so be it... I accept what life dishes out to me at this time. And if I never see you again I will be glad that you know how I felt at the end.[14]

And with that, Esther was off for a holiday in Tahiti until her apartment was repaired.

As soon as Earle and Lily had their new apartment on Alexander St., they wrote friends inviting them to stay. "We offer

indoor and/or outdoor sleeping facilities and hot and cold running water," Lily wrote to Bob Sward on behalf of them both.
"Come, stay with us, and share our joy."[15] And joy it was. "i'm
living with a young Cantonese girl & brought her with me on
this reading tour i'm doing in Britain," Birney wrote to Dave
Markson, sounding lighter at heart than he had for years, "any
chance you might visit Toronto? ...i got a coronary so i'm
slowed down now for a while, on the wagon (well, almost) &
counting the chorestorol [sic], but finding life more wonderful
than ever (all of which is probably a description of senility)."[16]

The London trip centred on the launching of *The Bear on the
Delhi Road: Selected Poems*[17] by Chatto & Windus—a short edition of selected poems, which had prompted reading invitations
from the Poetry Society and others. It was a triumph—one that
might have been meaningfully shared with his English wife
Esther, who had first shown him the town, typed and sent off so
many of his poems to British magazines, later helped contact editors for him there, and accompanied him on numerous trips to
visit her family. But it was Lily who shared this long-awaited
glory, and—in a reversal of roles—Earle took the keenest delight
in accompanying her around to all the sights she had never seen
before, explaining everything he knew about them.

On their return, Birney faced poor reviews for the collection he
had finished before meeting Lily *what's so big about GREEN?*[18]
"You should see the shit thrown all over me in [the] Waterloo
Chevron, by an English Dept. teaching fellow (age 26) named
Gale McCullagh," he wrote Purdy:

> "Birney has made Canadian poetry a bad joke... he
> has traded in...nonsense...token rubbish...refusal to
> lie still now that the Muse has deserted him for a
> younger generation...should not be allowed" [ellipses
> Birney's] let the buyer beware, etc. or an equally
> vicious flinging of dung by some bastard named
> Blacky in the Carleton student newspaper or
> "Professor" Garry [sic] Geddes, who so recently was
> coming to me for help, advice, comfort for his own
> lousy scribbles, is now publicly re-writing my poems

in the Globe in order to show how easily they could be made to sound better or your friend Dennis Lee, who actually likes the book, it seems, but can only say so in a sentence which puts down everything else ive ever done   i'm getting pasted for "my lengthening locks" (as McCullagh so politely puts it), which i cant do anything about, except at a barber's...off with the old, or the recognizably good—on with who-ever-is the reviewer's little bedmate of the moment   criticism means exactly nothing, al, never did, never will[19]

Birney seemed to have forgotten that he once criticized the kind of poetry he was now writing himself. When he had toured England in 1959 he had disliked the experiments of poet Chris Logue, "[Logue] is with...coldbloodedness writing beat verse and chanting it with a four-piece jazz band that effectively drowns out the words," he had written Wilber Stevens. "Fundamentally it is...the expression of a kind of death-wish about the word."[20] Now he was doing the same thing himself. One of the more enjoyable occasions with Lily in the first few weeks they had spent in Toronto, before he returned to Vancouver in April 1973, was a successful evening jam session at York University's new Burton Auditorium with the American expatriate percussion combo Nexus. Birney had already experimented in Toronto coffee cellars and elsewhere with multi-media performances, but Nexus—with its three-hundred-odd instruments—seemed to provide just the right sound environment for his poems. With tinkling yak bells and throbbing temple gongs, mysterious sounds from odd kitchen implements such as jello moulds, and ingenious manoeuvring of wires and tools, they provided a dramatic background to Birney's intense semi-sung readings. But it was true that the new pieces in *what's so big about GREEN?* were far from Birney's best work. These concrete poems (which had titles like "messyjests for a kinageing kitchmess" and "today's your big pubic reading") had sprung not from the heart, but from the head. They were cerebral and glib, cynical and cold.

Just as his affair with Liz Cowley had brought to life the emotions that found expression in "Bear on the Delhi Road" and "El

Greco: *Espolio,*" Birney's intense engagement with Wailan—as
Lily began calling herself now, reviving her Chinese name which
meant "reward" (wai) "orchid" (lan)—had the same effect on his
poems. It was his first parting from her—when she left Toronto
to pay a Christmas visit to her family in Victoria—that triggered
the deepest feelings he had felt for some time. "here i am sitting
alone with a flat-full of room, beds, etc," he wrote Purdy in
abject loneliness on 30 December 1973 in a letter that analysed
in minute detail Purdy's new collection *Sex and Death.*[21] "wailan
decided to have a dutiful xmas with her victoria fambly   a decision she is living to regret, from what she says in her letters   anyway ive been batching it for the fortnight (she'll be back new
year's eve, d.v.).... Come to town & talk with me."[22] And out of
these deep feelings of abandonment came a poem for Wailan:

>   NO BODY
>   (coming home from the airport)
>
>   i walk home in snow-slush
>   plodding alone imagining
>   the leap of pulse
>   under your graywool glove
>
>   snow slants down
>   an endless flock
>   of tiny bird-flakes
>   over me they wheel
>   and for a while move upward
>   having nowhere to fall
>   since you went away
>
>   the flat's not real
>   like a room "restored"
>   in a Pioneer Museum
>   exact but unconvincing
>   where is the being
>   who gave the armchair meaning?
>   i do not think

the TV will turn on

your small slippers
wait by the chesterfield
they do not move
something arranged
by a slick director
they lack the feet
which are human and complete
with minuscule calluses

i water the yellow chrysanthemum
silent as a photograph
nothing drinks
the armchair
stiff with air

only the bed grows
and is heard
it is twice as big already
and noisily empty
and yet an imitation too
a stuffed animal
nothing warm under the fur
no
body[23]

This was a poem that tapped the universal well of loneliness with its simple negatives "nowhere," "nothing," "no body." And in its references to small, childike details ("tiny bird-flakes," "small slippers," "minuscule calluses," "stuffed animal") it suggested Birney's theory that "It is the persistent child in the adult that makes the enjoyment of poetry possible."[24] "Yes I like [your poem] 'For My Green Old Age,'" he had written Irving Layton years before. "[I'd like] to be an old man as Chaucer was   or made out he was   like a leek with a hoar head and a green tail the tail standing up."[25] Now, with Wailan—or "Lan," as he affectionately called her—he had come alive as if reincarnated into this ideal. There was something spiritual about Wailan's presence, and something about her graceful, compact body and subdued voice that had the aesthetic qualities of a perfect poem. He had had a similar response to Ikuko, but his bitterness at her betrayal had kept him from publishing his poems to her.[26] "There Are Delicacies" (Scarborough 1965), which was written for Alison Hunt, anticipated the classical simplicity of the poems he now began to write for Wailan:

> there are delicacies in you
>> like the hearts of watches
> there are wheels that turn
>> on the tips of rubies
> & tiny intricate locks
>
> i need your help
>> to contrive keys
> there is so little time
>> even for the finest
>>> watches[27]

Now he had so mastered his craft that not a word was wasted in these poignant tributes to Wailan. It was now that his experiments in concrete poetry and dickering with gimmicks served a purpose greater than facile play. The use of lower case letters, the fondness for alliteration, onomatopoeia and Anglo-Saxon kennings, the tight shaping of poems that might earlier have sprawled awkwardly into longer lines, a lilting musicality reminiscent of "The Hazel Bough," the careful control of everyday images to allow each simple word to carry its own weight without straining for melodramatic effects like those in "David": with these techniques Birney crafted some of the most touching and true love poems ever. His first poem to Wailan on 27 January 1974 delicately conveyed the unique qualities of their January-May love and was a classic of its kind:

> SHE IS
> (for wai-lan, on her 24th birthday)

she is
a little spruce tree
fresh & every way
herself
like a dawn

when warm winds come
she will move
all her body
in a tremble of light

but today she stands
in magical stillness
she has clasped
all my falling flakes
from the round of her sky
and wished them
into her own
snowtree

through the cold time
she holds me
with evergreen
devotion
she bears up my whiteness

o so light may i press
letting each needle
grow in her own
symmetry

for i am at peace
in her form
after whirling
and faithful to all
her curves

but when warm winds come

we must stir from this trance
she will lift living arms
to the sun's dance

i will slide then
in a soft caress
of her brown sides
and my falling will end
somewhere in her roots

may my waters then
bring her strength only
help her hold trim
and evergreen her being
with suns and winds
for o many and many
and happiest years[28]

Al Purdy—suddenly sobered into grammatical formality—was not the only one to note the excellence of these poems: "The Six for Lan are the best love poems I've ever seen of yours," he wrote. "As if some bars to being personal had dissolved in yourself, and I think you have had such bars. But these, now, are lovely and delicate, they care about what they say. I am struck by the differences between my own love poems and yours. I am wildly romantic, at least to myself; but you are delicate and tender, with an overlooking sort of love."[29] And Birney replied, "your praise of the Lan poems is very generous & warming to me   it's so easy to muff any kind of love celebration, and seemingly impossible not to be laughed at for claiming mutual love, when the age difference is 46 years (not to mention the presumed race-gulf)   it's only because it's really true, this relationship, that i can get up the nerve to write about it at all—& of course i'm just writing around the rim of it."[30] Even Bet Cox found the poems inspired by Wailan immensely moving: "I love the poems he's written for Wailan," she says, "they bring tears to my eyes every time I read them."[31]

At first, relieved to have finished her M.A., Wailan went along with Earle on his readings and speeches in Newfoundland,

Halifax, Texas, Kingston, Windsor, Toronto (at Ryerson Polytechnical Institute where Alison now taught and had arranged his visit) and Banff "for the ride and to sell copies of his books." Clearly amused at the business aspect of selling books on such readings, Wailan observed, "we try to do a wilson macdonald at the end of every reading. i take a substantial commission of course!"[32] Then, by April, she took a job at McClelland & Stewart as a manuscripts editor while Earle did "some housekeeping, & some fiddling with the idea of an autobiography,"[33] spurred on by numerous friends such as Ralph Gustafson, who wrote "We need your life by *you*."[34] But after four months, she quit. "when I took the job, i expected something of an apprenticeship as a maker of books, but i spent the whole four months…reading most of canada's worst attempts at creative and other kinds of writing," she wrote George Johnston in Ottawa with wry humour. "now i am free, only to be earle's galley slave rather than jack mcclelland's. the working conditions are better, though."[35]

His tender, solicitous and intellectual relationship with Wailan ushered in a time of happiness such as Earle had never known. All his friends noticed the transformation and commented in genuine amazement that—unlikely as it seemed—Earle had finally found a true mate. Only Esther refused to accept Wailan. Soon he had several projects enthusiastically underway: not only his "impossible autobiog[raphy],"[36] as he now called it, but his collected poems, a volume of his political writings, and an unexpurgated *Turvey*. As if that weren't enough, M & S were preparing a new NCL paperback of *Down the Long Table*. "he is always trying to do half a dozen things at once, and gets himself into ruts," Wailan commented affectionately, "but he's feeling quite strong, and is in much better health than he was a year ago."[37]

As for Wailan, after her disillusionment at M & S she had decided to become a lawyer. "got to do something useful with my life," she wrote to George Johnston in one of the many letters she either jointly wrote with Earle or wrote on his behalf, "so i decided to try to get into law school. it seemed socially worthy and intellectually challenging enough—also, i have never met a lawyer who starved. i wrote the entrance exam, came home and wept bitterly in earle's shoulder for an hour, and decided that my legal career was over before it even began. but miraculously, i didn't disgrace myself after all, and was accepted by osgoode hall, at which point earle told me that he had to take me around the world."[38]

"yes," Earle added in the same letter with more readings and yet another literary project in mind—a "global village book" based on a comparison of this trip with his notebook entries from previous trips,[39] "round we're going, & when we get back i'll be broke & wai-lan will have to wait table or something at Osgoode to pay the fees—& then support me in my dotage.... our voyages will be superficial—a week or less in a score of places: paris, vienna, prague, budapest, dubrovnik, athens, cairo, nairobi, seychelles, sri lanka, bangkok, saigon (where wai-lan has an aunt), singapore, bali, djakarta, timor, darwin, port moresby, new hebrides, fiji, tahiti—& then a settling down in mexico for a few months (if we've survived all these other places!)."

Largely because of Wailan's healing presence, but also because of his daily yoga exercises, slow walking and vitamins, Birney's health had improved. Little by little his bitterness subsided and he began to let go of old grudges and unrewarding obligations. He lost interest in the tangled legal case with Dorothy Livesay and Eli Mandel over "David," and the lawyers involved agreed to let sleeping litigants lie.[40] His cantankerousness over the reviews of *what's so big about GREEN?* moderated into an acknowledgement that—on the whole—they were "pretty good." And, although he knew that it was partly due to the efforts of his friend Jack Jensen that the book was among those chosen by "Books Canada" (headed by Jensen) for U.S. distribution, he was none the less pleased to see the first shipment of two hundred sent off.[41] He said the paper on Malcolm Lowry he gave at a Lowry conference in Austin, Texas would be his last, and resigned himself to the fact that "Bitch Margerie"[42] was unlikely ever to give him permission to publish the annotated collection he had worked so hard to assemble. The conference at Banff on Canadian Cultural Identity would also be the last of such occasions for him. Nor would he continue to engage himself in the League of Canadian Poets, whose policies now seemed to him indistinguishable from those of the CAA.[43] He still indulged in lengthy diatribes, but even these were far less vitriolic than in the past—more verbal ventilations than felt grievances:

the 2-vol. COLL. POEMS…will no doubt be the signal for all the smartass Canadian reviewers to close in for the kill   theyve been telling me i should be "restrained" from publishing my bad poems (i.e. everything since "David") & such defiance as a Coll. will really trigger the Andy Wainwrights & Clare MacCullaghs & Schroeders & all the other riffraff the LCP has now cluttered itself with   well it'll be the last of my bones to throw them… UBC wont invite me at all (i got to read there once, since i left in 65, & only as a surprise substitute for Frank Scott) & [Robin] Skelton is one of my most vicious & consistent attackers   the "English" Dept ("American" they should call it) at SFU wont invite me & I've read there only because Lionel Kearns has managed to smuggle me in via the Student orgs or the Dept. of Sociology… my only travel plans for this year are a 2-day trip to Manitoulin Island to read to some Indian students[44]

He quickly backed away from a confrontation with Desmond Pacey over errors in Pacey's "scalplock collection"[45] *Selections from Major Canadian Writers*,[46] when Pacey explained that he had had a rough few years and now had cancer. He even acknowledged some spectacular errors of his own: "who am i to be self-righteous about misquotings?" he wrote Pacey, "i who not only misquoted a charming poem of Herrick's in my *Creative Writer* but assigned it to Ben Jonson!"[47] There were no anguished letters sent off on his seventieth birthday 13 May 1974; only a pleased response to Esther (who had become president of the Vancouver Fabric Arts Guild and was also learning about Transactional Analysis) for sending him a card that arrived that day. And when he sold the last batch of his papers to the University of Toronto, he generously gave the full two thousand dollars to her.[48] "my health, ever since the attack, has been a bit unpredictable, up & down, but in general gradually more up ive had to learn to live with less blood circulating around & am conscious of being older & different & maybe in some ways a less difficult person," he wrote her.[49]

With Wailan, Birney had recaptured his youthful spirit. Their days passed happily in the most ordinary activities. "It is hard to describe happiness," Wailan observes. "We were happy just doing nothing much of anything."[50] At home, they read or watched their new colour TV together; Earle played the small new piano he bought to replace his Vancouver one; he and Wailan both tended the plants they enjoyed. Weekends they were out to see friends, or off to Uxbridge to wander around the Allens' place; Earle chopping wood when it was warm, Wailan cooking in the rustic kitchen. In bed, Earle would read to her, sometimes playfully testing her by reading bits from famous poems to see if she could guess which ones. "The most important thing about Earle to me," Wailan was later to say, "is his humanity and his conscience. It's those things that informs [sic] our lives together, and I think informs his work as a writer. He has enormous ups and downs but that sense of social responsibility is always there; his love of people is always there. It's what keeps him alive, and, keeps me interested in him."[51]

Earle and Wailan loved to talk, planning and dreaming of trips they could take together. It was with the enthusiasm of his own first trip abroad that he dashed off one of his comic lists to Gustafson: "we are in a chaos of packing, storing, planning, credit-finagling, winding-upping, all for our flight to London." He seemed at last to have put the sense of imminent death behind him: "The 'business of staggering deaths' is something i have wanted to write, and couldnt," he admitted, "and dont need to now—at 70, one's old friends are dead or dropping on all sides... i'm looking forward most of all to showing Wailan Athens (& Crete, if there's time & money)."[52] At last Birney seemed able to spend money freely. Though his trip around the world with Wailan would cost almost $11,000, only $1,650— the cost of his own air ticket—was paid for by the Canada Council on the understanding he would give readings and write poems as he went.[53]

Earle had never been happier travelling—so happy he didn't

even think much about his two-volume *The Collected Poems of Earle Birney*[54] which was published by M & S in his absence. His letters to friends fairly brimmed over with delight as he visited old friends like the John Wardropers, the Stephen Vizinczeys, Garrick Hagon (Corinne and Bill's son, now an actor in London), the Bert Matlows and George Johnston (spending a year away from Carleton in the Cotswolds with his wife and "multitudinous & multiracial" children) and met interesting people like Rusty Grant, "the tough Scot doctor-saint of St. Pancras, who sees scores of non-paying slum patients daily—& Dennis Enright, the melancholy Jacques among the English poets"[55] and, later in New Zealand, the poet Alan Curnow.[56] Without the pressure to earn money or fill his empty times, Birney enjoyed his occasional readings. But best of all was showing the world to Wailan who could not have been more appreciative. "this is Wailan's first sight of a really dirty city where the life expectancy is still in the thirties, the milk only half-pasteurized & the butter a half-mixture from the dubious teats of water-buffalo," he reported from Cairo, "& she is properly conscience-stricken."[57] "This is a marvellous city to be in love," Wailan wrote of Vienna.[58] Birney generously arranged for her to go on when he flagged: "2 hours of proxy-smoking laid me too low to do anything the first 3 days after [from Athens to Cairo] but lie about, while Wai-lan went off, at my urging, with the good doctor Farid, dutifully to see the pyramids & bazaars & the Arc[heaological] Mus[eum] & all (which i'd seen in '58)."[59] On Christmas 1974 he wrote George Johnston from Colombo, Ceylon, where he gave a reading and went with Wailan "on a 3-day wandering, mainly by jeep, in the sri lankan jungles, looking at unearthed ruins, monkeys, & so on": "we'll hunt down a decrepit taxi & rattle over to the Canadian High Commissioner's Residence for a Canadian-Turkey-Xmas-Dinner, flown in from Ottawa—we will pass a few cypress trees here & there, brought down from the high hills & decorated with strangely Hindic baubles for the tourist eye."[60] In Bali, where, according to Wailan the dances "are totally authentic and indescribably beautiful,"[61] they had more adventure than they wanted: "we had an ugly triangle-headed serpent in our bedroom at midnight,"

Birney wrote, "hot night, we were still awake, lying naked on our twin beds—wailan started for the bathroom & the snake came through the door as she opened it—she jumped several feet back on her bed—the snake coiled aggressively at the foot of it & i decided that my shoes and cane were less easy to reach than the telephone—eventually a houseboy came with a bamboo pole, about 6 foot—he took one look at the snake, pronounced it venomous & ran for reinforcements—these materialized (after an interminable wait, the snake holding his prepared position unwinkingly) in the shape of a bigger houseboy with a ten-foot pole, with which he managed to slay the dragon by pounding it into the corner wall—the hotel proprietor next day gave us a more expensive room off the ground floor, at the same rate, & we kept agreeably quiet about the incident."[62] Then it was on to Castaway Island, Fiji, for a day of sun, reef-swimming, and good food on Wailan's twenty-fifth birthday: "We celebrated it with a Maori fish-breakfast in Auckland, & an Air NZ 2nd breakfast on the plane to Nandi, & some excellent raw marinated Fiji fish for lunch here in Lautoka, & a late supper of something like shark-fin followed by ice-cream smothered in passion-fruit & guava juice."[63]

It was not only the adventures Birney could share with Wailan, but also his political and social observations: "it's a troubled global village now," he observed.

> in Kenya the university was closed by administrative lock-out of rebellious students—in Athens the students were locked out by the govt. because [they] wanted to have a mass *grave* investigated (it contained leftish students bumped off by the army during the Cyprus war)—in the Seychelles Islands ("Eden of the Indian Ocean") we sat on the airport runway for 2 hours while all the baggage for a full Viscount was unloaded again, in a tropical downpour, looking for a bomb—here in Ceylon the unemployment is 12%, a good section of the rice farmers are making soup from jungle leaves to keep alive till the next harvest, & all the universities are closed because the education

students stole *all* the keys & struck for guaranteed teaching jobs (at $35 a *month*).[64]

Finally, they reached Mexico, where they rented a car so Birney could show Wailan all the sights—Mexico City, Puebla, Fortin, Villahermosa, Campeche, Uxmal, Mérida, Chichén Itza, Chetumal in Quintana Roo, Palenque, Tuxtla Gutiérrez, Mitla, Monté Alban, Oaxaca, Cuernavaca, Taxco, Toluca, Morelia—before settling into San Miguel for a visit with Earle's old artistic soul mate Leonard Brooks and a rest "a very young Joan with a very ancient Darby, to write, sleep, eat, by our little manzanita fire up a burro's alley on the cobbled hillside."[65] His only mishap in San Miguel was a sprained toe, the result of jumping from a tree he had climbed to get in a window because Reva's bedroom door was jammed shut.[66]

"Earle could be his best self with her," Reva Brooks recalls of their stay nearby that summer. "Wailan had the most marvellous figure. She used to sunbathe in a bikini on the patio and he would be in the corner out there typing away. He celebrated her in every way: sexually and spiritually. He would flutter around her like a mother, looking after her as if she were a delicate little thing. If she had a pain in her toe, he was so solicitous. She was allergic to insect bites, and he would watch out for her when she was outside. And Wailan was yielding and docile, attendant to his every wish. After all these women, she was extremely open and reacted in the most feminine way possible. She was practical: an excellent housekeeper and cook. She loved to be in the kitchen making him—and us—these wonderful meals. It was the first time in his life he was really happy."[67]

From his new perspective, Birney's view of humanity and the world widened until it was synoptic without sacrificing intimacy. "There is so much & so little to say about being alive, at seventy, & still 'with all my imperfections on my head' & few of whatever perfections i ever came close to when young and spanking. But i too rejoice in the bouncing, undeserved health of my balls & the stubborn images still forming in the brainpan—but i am too greedy of life to concentrate as i used to—i grab each passing moment & postpone the slow hard work of the poemaking—

this is partly what senility is about, i suppose   i'm incredibly lucky in my love   wailan is the dearest, gentlest, most understanding of creatures & endures everything with patience & laughter, even in Prague, where everything went wrong, or almost."[68]

Earle and Wailan had been back in Toronto less than two months, most of which had been spent happily setting up their new apartment on the twenty-second floor at 200 Balliol St., overlooking Mount Pleasant Cemetery, when on 1 July 1975 their serenity was shattered. They had been planning the coming year—Wailan off to Osgoode at York University in September, Earle away in October or November to the USSR for a 3-week tour,[69] and making the most of what little time was left. "we were holidaying at [the Allens'] country house near uxbridge ont," wrote Wailan in obvious distress ten days later,

> three wonderful days had passed, a sort of second (or third) honeymoon for us, just the two of us out there—when earle decided to do some pruning at the top of a large beech tree overhanging the house... [he] fell 30 feet out of [the] tree and fractured his hip.... Fortunately there was a telephone in the house, and the ambulance came amazingly quickly. the resident doctor at the local hospital took one look at the xrays and sent earle off in the ambulance to the scarborough centenary hospital, which is the closest one to uxbridge with a resident bone specialist.... earle is in the hospital now, and will be for another 7 weeks. his hip was dislocated as well as fractured into 3 pieces, so he's in traction, flat on his back, and miserable with pain. he's also had a pulmonary embolism which has me frightened. that's less painful to him, but a greater threat to his life...unfortunately [the hospital is] out in deep scarboro and it takes me an hour and a half to get there by subway and bus. a chore, but i'd go twice as far if i had to to be with earle. what distresses me most is his pain. the doctors say that he is doing well, that he's on the mend, but as far as i can see, he gets

worse and worse every day. because of the pain, he can't read can't write, really can't do anything. i go and sit with him for the larger part of every day, but i feel utterly helpless to do anything for him. no matter how many times i adjust his pillows and padding, the pain continues. he has drugs, which he is understandably loath to use, and when he does, he naturally drifts off into a drugged state, which is a relief to him but probably not very good for him

i'm afraid this is a rather depressing letter. but that's not the way either of us feel. earle's spirits are actually fairly good. i am anguished and frightened.[70]

"The only consolation is that he's having the pains of healing, and not the pains of dying," she wrote George Johnston, "I'm so grateful that he's alive after that fall, though sometimes a wave of terror sweeps over me—the way i felt when I found him at the bottom of the tree... I'm answering his letters, unfortunately not nearly as entertainingly as he would himself."[71]

Birney did not return to their Balliol apartment until early September. At a scant 120 pounds, able to walk only with crutches and a boot brace, he was still in perpetual pain. He began hypnotherapy to try to wean himself off codeine, and looked into acupuncture as a possible cure. He could write nothing. "the 7 weeks chained to a hospital bed," he wrote Johnston on 6 September, "& now 2 more lying about trying to get sleep & to become human again have made me incapable of writing even letters to good friends. It is my dear Wailan who has kept me going at all, & continues to be the source of my hopes and morale."[72]

As for Wailan, she had begun the training at Osgoode which would ensure her financial independence in the future, and loved it: "I am becoming known for imagination, if not for brilliance, and am making new friends. Contrary to my expectations, I haven't yet met anyone I don't like at Osgoode—no sharp dealers, no cut-throats. It promises to be a good year if I can just keep my head above water."[73] Earle (who often said he thought she should take lovers since he was so old)[74] was also pleased: "it gets her back into circulation with young people again, at a competitive level," he wrote George Johnston,

> something she has missed since she finished her M.A.
> at U. of T. and she *likes* hard work, savors any challenge to her memory cells, & so accepts the long
> evening homework, the 15-hour a week lecture schedule, the 1 1/2 hrs of bus & metro travel each way five
> days a week… & on top of that she has to come home
> & cook my supper & do some of the housecleaning
> chores that cant be done on crutches   so i sing her
> praises, to what i hope is an indulgent ear, for i owe
> her the will to survive & begin coping again—during
> the 56 days i was in a Scarboro hospital… wailan (not
> yet at Osgoode) kept my mail uptodate & the flat in
> shape, & yet was at my bed by one in the afternoon of
> every day & stayed till darkness & the end of the visiting hours   i have never had such devoted and understanding love   even my defective character has
> improved living with her   tell this to any 25-year-old
> who thinks sex ends with forty or that the generations
> cannot really understand each other![75]

Birney cancelled his Russian trip, but by mid-January was well enough to travel to Kingston for a reading at Queen's University; then (shepherded by Jack Jensen) on 9 February to others at Loyola College campus of Concordia University and John Abbott in Montreal, and two more at Carleton University and the University of Ottawa the following day, before being helped home by Tony Kilgallin.[76] "i love the readings, & the audiences are still really responsive," he wrote Purdy, "but what kills me is wading on crutches thru slush & snowbanks, or trying to walk with them over sheets of ice, or up stone academic steps & thru revolving doors… i *must* get mellower soon, or i'll end up a really ungrand old creep… if it werent for Lan, i'd choose to die with it (the pain, that is)   at 71 i can roll with the punch of being a semi-cripple permanently, what is permanence at 71? but pain that never ceases & gets worse with the exercise needed to

keep the leg from stiffening up entirely, is a different matter—
the drop-of-water torture, waking daily with the same pain i
finally killed at 2 a.m. with booze & codeine, no fun   but i do
love love, and still can make it, so what the hell, archie, as
mehitabel so poignantly put it."[77]

Almost as a jest, Birney was thinking of collecting his love
poems, "but wailan wont let me put any in that were made for
other girls   women are really possessive, even about the past
they couldnt have affected, not being around   well i hope soon
to have enough made just for her   she's worth as many poems
as a man could write out of love."[78] Instead, he would write the
poem which would provide the title for his next collection of
poetry: "Fall by Fury":

> ...So I threw the last snag down
> and the locked saw after
> turning and shifting my grips
> to descend to Wai-lan
> when something   my Hubris
> some Fury of insect wing and sting
> drove its whining hate at my eye
> One hand unloosed convulsive to shield
> and I slipped
> forever from treetops
>
> Caught in a yielding chair of air
> I grasped and grasped at a speeding reel
> of branches half-seized and wrenched away
> by the mastering will of earth
> The next bough surely—
>   my hard mother
> crushed me limp in her stone embrace
> stretched me still with the other limbs
> laid my cloven hip and thigh
> with those I had cleft....[79]

Birney's fall soon became mythic. Purdy mocked it as "showing
off for Wailan"; and Tom Wayman, his former student, was

inspired to write a poem "My Old Master," in which the old
master deliberately enacts the Biblical story of Adam plucking
the apple for Eve while a skeptical crowd below warns of danger
and pronounces him an old fool just before he falls:

> But to my old master, the sensations he was experiencing
> were not as awful as those below him
> hoped and feared.
> "For some reason, this tree
> has taken off like a rocket
> leaving me suspended in midair,"
> my master observed to himself as he travelled
> now upright, now head over heels.
> "This is more than a little thrilling
> except I'm being beaten black and blue
> by the limbs flying past.
> Lucky I got as far as I did
> before this extraordinary event occurred."
> And sure enough, in a few more minutes
> the watchers on the ground could see
> that whatever position his body assumed
> in its tumbling, painful descent
> my old master continued to grin triumphantly
> as he clutched in his outstretched hand
> a perfect apple.[80]

A low point in Birney's long, long recovery was the party for
Books in Canada in April 1976 at which he hoped to see Al and
Eurithe Purdy, since Wailan had stayed home to study. "they had
to unlimber a rope-haul freight elevator to get me up [to the
fourth floor] & then somebody (jack jensen probably) had to
find a chair, a real chair, & carry it over the heads of the standing quackery of editors/reviewers/artists/bums so i could sit
down in a corner," he wrote Purdy in a self-mocking vein later,

> have you ever had to sit in a corner looking ninety—
> of course not—i felt already dead, observing from the
> unseen spirit world with perhaps only a sinister aura

just visible enough to warn anybody approaching to make a deviation around my chair, eyes fixed elsewhere   true, some of these kids even knew i was a poet, or rather that i look a bit like one of the Original Canadian Poets, long dead, but that wasnt their responsibility...i exaggerate, as always   there were little angels of both sexes who brought me cheese (no, that was jack again), & the EDITOR IN CHIEF himself brought me a beer, & i managed to keep my foot tucked under my arm (or maybe the chair arm) so it didn't get trampled hard enough to split up & just as i was leaving a bright little girl told me she was the art editor of the Can Forum & just loved "David" & even followed me out & down the freight elevator to make sure i didn't break in two on the premises, & just then a beautiful lady arrived alone in a taxi & i helped her out & she told me she had just left her husband and...but anything more would be betraying confidences, as well as lying[81]

But by September 1976, he was back on the reading circuit with a new bootbrace and two canes, looking like "a stooped comma moving between two exclamation points,"[82] and gave seventeen readings in ten days, mainly in centennial or community colleges and larger high schools, but also at three universities. While in B.C. he visited Bill and Marsha and reported on "my marvellous grandsons, i mean they look marvellous, being six & five respectively & healthy." "i enjoyed it thoroughly," he wrote the Johnstons on his return, "lugged my books on my back, and sold literally hundreds."[83] Next it was Montreal, Sudbury, Windsor and Chatham. So high were his spirits now and so full of life was he, that before leaving with Wailan for a Christmas in Cuba, he sent round copies of the Toronto Public Libraries bookmark advertising "Experience Canada!" which featured his photo above his poem "Can.Lit." with the scribbled comment "just a bookmark now   earle."

↢ *27* ↣

NOW IS TIME

It was Friday the 13th of March 1987 when Earle Birney received his Lifetime Achievement Award, the plum of the third annual Vancouver Awards. Canada's Elder Statesman of Literature (as he was called in the ceremonies that evening) had been flown to Vancouver for the televised presentations in the newly renovated Commodore Ballroom of the Hotel Vancouver.

Earle Birney at eighty-two was a man changed and not changed from the Earle Birney who had leapt from one life to another in 1973, and had fallen by fury three years later. He had plumped out a little; his face glowed with vitality; he looked seasoned and serene, as if he inhabited his whole self. His full white beard and tuxedo made a striking study in black-and-white, as if to proclaim that the divisive extremes in his personality no longer pulled him apart, but had attained balance at last. The years with Wailan had brought him a joy of such breadth and depth it remained inexplicable. They had been, she knew, the fifteen happiest years of his life.[1] "I credit myself with improving his temperament," she says. "He was so hot-tempered when I first met him, but we were soul mates from the first, and gradually he mellowed. We only had half a dozen fights in all that time, which, considering Earle's temperament, is pretty good. It was just so easy. He always fascinated me. He has that creative genius which is endlessly interesting."[2]

With Wailan, Birney's wanderings continued to lure him to youthful adventure, to see the world afresh through her eyes. With her he shared exotic experiences and obscure observations, passed on his many-layered knowledge of the world, and earned the full acceptance from his friends scattered across the globe of the special qualities Wailan brought him. Somehow for Wailan, they puzzled, he had found a patience he had formerly lacked. Though he could be subversive in luring her from her studies to watch television with him, or listen to him read Chaucer or Dickens in the evenings, he helped and encouraged her legal training, and urged her to fulfil herself through the career she wanted. And every year, despite the loneliness that ravaged him when she left, he supported her annual two-week visits west to her family.

Holidays had to wait for Wailan, but when they finally arrived they were filled with delight. In June and July of 1976, they had holidayed in the Canary Islands, where Birney found swimming in the warm salt water and lurching along the sand on the canes he needed after his accident immensely restorative. The following summer, they had gone to visit friends in London, Ireland and Scotland—dropping in on Earle's Coz and her family in Aberdeen and renting a student flat at the University of Stirling where he had written poems and a preface to *Ghost in the Wheels: Selected Poems* while Wailan cooked for him and made day trips to Pictish ruins and other sights. For Christmas, they had travelled to the Brookses' in San Miguel. In the summer of 1979 they were back in Scotland for five weeks, and Birney introduced Wailan to his relations in Shetland. That Christmas, they were off to California, seeing "some pals of 50 y[ea]rs ago."[3] After Wailan was called to the bar in April 1980 (she had articled with Julian Porter, the lawyer who had represented Birney in his libel dispute with Dorothy Livesay and whose mother-in-law was one of Birney's former loves), travel had become even more difficult. But in the spring of 1981, they had gone back to San Miguel "loafing in the Brookses' hacienda, drinking good tequila again with old friends around the Jardin, listening to a lot of strings, getting an itchy ass from lovely [spicy] food."[4] In 1983 it had been back to London; in 1984 they had sought the sun in Manzanillo, but found it changed so much for the worse that they had fled to San Miguel; in 1985, it was London again, and Paris, Rome, Florence and Venice.

On this strenuous itinerary, anxious ambition no longer spurred Birney on. His experience centred on Wailan and was suffused with her presence. Even a temporary separation from her in 1984 (he immediately phoned Bet Cox who helped him move into a flat on Church Street, which he called his "office"),[5] that had resulted from Wailan's deep involvement in her demanding professional life had been soon mended. They had bought a silver Mazda, a "selfish 2-seater sports job"[6] in 1983, and with the reckless abandon of a newly licensed sixteen-year-old, Birney had delighted in driving at unholy speeds and an array of bad driving habits around the back roads with Wailan. No longer was he scrambling desperately as if he had to scale impossible heights. He had arrived, and found life delicious. "ive been wanting to do something, maybe an anti-autobiography, for a long time," he confessed to writer Patrick Lane, not in alarm as he would have in the past, but quite philosophically, "but life, living, keeps getting in the way of it & who to write it to? who for? what for?"[7]

Meanwhile, he had proceeded, finally, to settle his affairs with Esther, who had gradually come to realize that Wailan was somehow different from his other women. Esther had halted the divorce she had initiated when he had fled Vancouver with Ikuko in 1965. But now she had begun another suit, petitioning for divorce in December 1976 on grounds of adultery (the papers specifically noted that there had been no "sexual relationship at all [between herself and Earle] for the past 15 years"[8]). The divorce confirmed financial arrangements that had been worked out informally between them in the months and years following Birney's desertion: that the income from their three mortgages (Bill's, and two others from properties at 4542 West 10th Avenue and 3449 West 27th Avenue which they had bought with the proceeds of the sale of their large house in 1958) would be Esther's; that she would have their belongings, save his books and his car, as well as some of his investments; that he would pay for the divorce; and that the beneficiary of his $10,000 life insurance policy would be Esther, not Wailan.

It had been Friday the 13th of May 1977, Birney's seventy-third birthday, that their hapless, troubled marriage officially ended with the decree nisi. In a poem called "Decree Absolute," Birney expressed both his solicitous hopes for Esther's future happiness and the recognition that he had been hurting her from the very beginning:

> we remember strangely the first hurts from love
> the young are pierced through by their passions
>
> you must not grow ancient poor dear
> but quickly old enough to forget
> this last aggression
>
> it will be enough to carry
> to our separate deaths
> the memory of the first time
> i stung you to tears
>
> young and loving and alone with me
> while beyond the window of our train
> all Kent was singing with appleblossom
> shaken by the bees.
>
> Canterbury 1935—Toronto 1975[9]

"Decree Absolute" was only one of the poems that continued to flow from Birney during his years with Wailan. Once the debilitating pain of his accident had subsided and he shook the addiction to codeine which followed, he had exuberantly taken on project after project. The whimsical little collection *Alphabeings & Other Seasyours* and *The Rugging and the Moving Times*[10] both appeared in 1976. *Ghost in the Wheels: Selected Poems* and the New Canadian Library edition of *The Damnation of Vancouver*[11] (with an introduction by Wailan) appeared in 1977; *Fall by Fury*

& Other Makings[12] ("absolutely…my last collection of poems"[13]) in 1978. That same year, he had managed to have six books by six different publishers underway, and acquired a three-year Canada Council Senior Arts Grant to support this work and further projects: in addition to *Fall by Fury*, he had assembled ten prose pieces (fiction, reminiscences, essays) for Mosaic/Valley Press—*Big Bird in the Bush* (1979); he was working with editor Bruce Nesbitt and Allan Safarik of Blackfish Press to collect his political prose, "Conversations with Trotsky"; Simon Dardick at Véhicule Press was editing his memoirs—*Spreading Time: Remarks on Canadian Writing and Writers,* Book I: 1904–1949, (1980)—a partial autobiography that disappointed many who expected to find the drama of his life portrayed (Purdy, for instance, had hoped to glimpse the "more colourful Birney" he knew);[14] another American collection *The Mammoth Corridors* the same year for Stone Press in Michigan; essays on Canadian literature, "Echoes from the Beaver Swamp"; essays on world literature "Malcolm Lowry and Dylan Thomas in Vancouver"; a book of his own comments and counter-comments, "My Serve, Your Serve"; a biography of his father and grandfather; a personal war memoir (about which he was wary because of libel); a book on his early life; a collection of his radio plays; and—despite the fact that his academic work was long out of date—his essays on Chaucer's irony.[15]

Only three of these projects would be completed: four sections of his proposed "Coming of Age in Erikson B.C." appeared in *B.C. Outdoors* (1980),[16] then *Words on Waves*[17] in 1985 and *Essays on Chaucerian Irony*[18] (finally published in 1985 by University of Toronto Press, who had turned down his thesis manuscript in 1936 almost half a century before). And, despite his certainty that *Fall by Fury* was his last collection of poetry, he would bring out a small chapbook *Copernican Fix*[19] with Jack David's ECW Press in 1986, and planned another to be called "One Muddy Hand" (published in 1991 as *Last Makings*). While Birney joked affably of "my inability to stick to one book at a time"[20] and complained tongue-in-cheek "i'm working hard on another book though i wonder why,"[21] friends—like George Bowering—cheered him on: "I see you have another half-dozen books out. Way to go!"[22]

In between the happy days spent with Wailan—evenings watching television or reading, weekends at the Allens' Uxbridge cottage, bicycle rides in Mount Pleasant Cemetery, plays and art shows—Birney had continued to give readings, especially to high schools near Toronto, many of which were arranged by the League of Canadian Poets, whose listed rates had risen from $430 plus expenses in 1977, to $600 plus expenses in 1979. In 1981, he had commuted to London on Mondays and Tuesdays to be "writer-in-resonance," as he called it, at the University of Western Ontario. There he had met John Cage in the Faculty of Music and worked with him on joint performances. In 1981, he made three recordings with Nexus (Wailan designed the jackets and he wrote the notes). In 1983—at almost eighty—he gave more than twenty-five readings, and toured Lloydminster and Grande Prairie in Alberta and Whitehorse in the Yukon. The following year, he had spent a week even further afield giving readings and classes in Fairbanks, Alaska: "[it] was great even though it went down to -60 F," he wrote George Johnston on his return, "i had an 8-day program that involved being up by 6 and being driven or sledded to various one-room schools on the tundra as well as doing a Rob[er]t Service gig in a pipeline workers saloon something new every day i live everybody grateful i came at all, hospitable, energetic, tough, sentimental, gutsy, and independent as hell   i loved them all."[23] And somehow he had found time to fit in many extras: on-site work for "Seeing Ourselves," a CBC TV show directed by his former student George Robertson in 1977; a fortnight in England in the fall of 1978 to promote *Fall by Fury* ("poor weather...and sparse & often unresponsive audiences");[24] two D.Litt. degrees (at McGill in 1979 and University of Western Ontario in 1984); consultations for the 1981 NFB sixty-minute documentary of his life "Portrait of a Poet" produced by Tom Daly, written and directed by Don Winkler, and narrated by Mavor Moore ("Birney disliked it, as did *Vancouver Province* critic Michael Walsh, "depressingly superficial...a portrait of the poet as eccentric");[25] a CBC radio concert with Nexus on 30 January 1983; and an introduction for an award-winning animated film version of "Villanelle,"[26] the love poem he wrote for his former student, Betty Lambert, by Elizabeth Lewis in 1985.[27]

The tribute to Earle Birney at the Vancouver Awards,[28] not surprisingly, centred on poems that reminded his audience that he had put the Canadian west on the world's literary map: "Vancouver Lights" and—of course—"David." As he himself had written of the new generation of literary critics who were chronicling Canadian literature, with a cantankerousness he kept well-concealed at the Vancouver Awards, "what a laugh all this re-making of history is, especially when done by the babies of the time, now suddenly so knowledgeable. The history of the development of contemporary writing in Vancouver, from 1946–60, is pretty largely a one-man show, and that man was me."[29] Though Birney over-simplified, there was much truth in his claim. With "David," the heroic narrative that fixed his image for all time as a masculine mountaineer whose down-to-earth language struck a chord in the hearts of ordinary men, he transformed the epic geography of the Rocky Mountains into Canada's imaginative myth. In other poems too—"Vancouver Lights," "North Star West," "Bushed," "Pacific Door," "The Damnation of Vancouver," "November Walk Near False Creek Mouth," even his early whimsy "Slug in Woods"—he introduced a sense of colossal space and a profound bonding—both affectionate and disturbing—with a unique territory.

And there were other ways he had developed contemporary writing in Vancouver. He initiated Creative Writing courses at UBC, he recruited writing prizes and scholarships there, and he stubbornly persisted in expanding the range of courses for winter and summer sessions until he had established a full-fledged Creative Writing program. He not only fostered the work of local students, but also provided them with a living model of the practising poet no young person would hesitate to emulate, and inspired by his example many who would never have considered a career in the arts. For twenty years, Birney enthusiastically engaged in literary debate with young writers, many of whom went on to contribute to cultural life in Canada and elsewhere, and most of whom found life deepened and enhanced by one man's conviction that the arts truly matter. Birney's wide-ranging approach to Creative Writing was astonishing: the intense critical sessions; the focus on developing each individual talent; the social gatherings (not to mention the wild binges at Malcolm Lowry's, Einar Neilson's and elsewhere) that made clear a few things about the literary life; the many readings at UBC by poets like Dylan Thomas, Theodore Roethke, W.H. Auden, and Charles Olson; the effort made to place students in American graduate programs of Creative Writing; and the hundreds of letters of encouragement and concern and friendship that followed them there and throughout their careers; the skill with which he edited (and trained students to edit) an extensive series of literary magazines, the friendships he maintained with other west coast writers like Dorothy Livesay, Ethel Wilson, Roderick Haig-Brown, Malcolm Lowry, Phyllis Webb, Andy Suknaski and his two favourites, George Woodcock and Lionel Kearns. And the energy with which he kept all these strands of the Vancouver literary community intertwined was the driving force behind a burgeoning contemporary literary community in a once-parochial city where being a poet had meant being sentimental, arch and effete, a literary community that did not collapse later, but continued to grow and flourish.

Ironically—perhaps doubly so for one who was an expert in irony—the public images that propelled Birney into fame were not an accurate reflection of his aims or the content of his writings at the time, and they ultimately obstructed any clear understanding of the best of his later work. He was acclaimed not for the internationalism he passionately espoused, first through his Trotskyist endeavours and then through his avowed literary allegiances, but for the western regionalism that only partly motivated his early works and for the patriotism of the war years that seemed (despite much evidence to the contrary) to inform works such as "On Going to the Wars," "For Steve," "Joe Harris," "This Page My Pigeon," "The Road to Nijmegen" and *Turvey*. To his public, Birney moved quickly from being Canada's Western Poet (an image that had a distressing tendency to slip into The Hayseed Hick) to take up the role of Canada's Soldier Poet. It was hunger for the expression of western regionalism and wartime patriotism in Canada that won for him the Governor General's Award for *David and Other Poems*. It was patriotism that won for him the same award for *Now Is Time*. And it was patriotism that helped him win the Leacock Medal for Humour for *Turvey*—a black comedy that slicked over the surface of those deeply troubling years. The zenith of his career was 1946, when he won his second Governor General's Award. After that, although he won both overall awards, such as the Lorne Pierce Medal for his contribution to Canadian culture, and specific ones, such as the Borestone Mountain Award for "The Hazel Bough," he failed to win the major book awards which he coveted.

Had these powerful public images dissolved, it might have become clear that Birney's best poems—"David," "Vancouver Lights," "Mappemounde," "Bear on the Delhi Road," "El Greco: *Espolio*," even the apparently light-hearted "The Hazel Bough"— were probings of the human condition in the mid-twentieth century that bordered on existentialism. But Birney could not resist using these images when it seemed advantageous. Even at the Vancouver Awards, he thanked his audience for "rescuing me from exile in Toronto"—a sly poke that did not fail to prompt an affectionate response from the crowd in the Hotel Vancouver ballroom. His fall from the innocent idealism with which he regarded Trotsky was a dashing-down as acute and dramatic as that in "David," the first poem to emerge when Birney leapt across a yawning ideological abyss from political commitment to a vindication of the aesthetic. Because of his political engagement, his poems were seldom art for art's sake. Like a latter-day Lazarus returned from an ashen world, he wrote to share his disillusionment, to register his frequently sardonic observations on life and to caution humanity at large against the future consequences of present actions. These probings owed much to a unique temperament and circumstances, a personal angst that was by chance symbolic of a contemporary secular world fallen from idealism, alienated from Victorian faith and morality, comforted somewhat bleakly by nature, and drawn by default to a biological construct of reality by the failures of love, politics, education. Had there already been a well-established western Canadian literature in 1941, "David" might have been heralded not so much as a glorification of western landscapes and exploits, but as a poem about the unsettling realization that life is lived at the expense of others. It was hardly a surprising insight for a man who suffered from profound loneliness and carried considerable guilt from the knowledge that he had replaced an older son who died; that his birth had injured his mother so she could have no other children; and that his sexual drives could not be channelled. With hindsight, his early poem "Slug in Woods" seems a prophetic allegory; the small green slug "himself his viscid wife," inching his way through the huge, dangerous, vaulted woods:

> Stilled
> is he—green mucus chilled,
> or blotched and soapy stone,
> pinguid in moss, alone.[30]

This sensibility lay behind Birney's best humanitarian writings. And it also lay behind his satiric squibs. These timely biting poems that took stock of the social and political pulse with impish glee include: "Anglosaxon Street," "Twenty-third Flight," "Billboards Build Freedom of Choice," "Mammorial Stunzas for Aimee Simple McFarcin," "Restricted Area," "Can. Lit.," "A Small faculty stag for the visiting poet," "To a Hamilton (Ont.) lady thinking to travel," "What's so big about GREEN?" and especially his various versions of "Canada: Case History." Most of these, like his satiric novel *Turvey*—no matter how clever and witty—have already dated, or will almost certainly do so as social and political conditions evolve. But in their day, they drew attention to a range of shortcomings in ways that were amusing and incisive.

Because the public images, so assiduously courted and sustained by Birney, warped the course of his career, his real merits as a poet were not reinforced. He was—even by his own assessment—not a poet of the first rank. He was hampered by the very cleverness that marked his verses. So eager was he for fame, and so talented at marketing himself and setting up journals, or organizing editors of other journals that would publish his work, that the test of merit seldom came into play. Even the Vancouver Awards were conducted by Birney's former students, now owners of the television station that awarded them, Norman Klenman and Daryl Duke, the evening's host, whose admiration and loyalty must have made Birney wonder whether it was these sentiments—not his lifetime achievement—that lay behind his selection. He had known the same ambiguity since "David," the poem rejected by so many editors in three countries, had finally been published in *The Canadian Forum,* where he had not long before been literary editor. If his work had been submitted anonymously to editors who were not his friends, who had never published in journals he edited, who had not sought recommendations for grants or who had not been his students, would it have been accepted?

The Vancouver Awards citation made no mention of Birney's scholarship. Certainly his impact on his academic field had been relatively slight. Though his thesis was brilliant and well researched and his potential for academic work was of the first order, he did not work with any consistency on his chosen field. His later research—conducted intensively during his year off in 1958—was remarkably productive considering it was a one-time blitz, but the publication of his collection of essays came too late to contribute anything more to Chaucer scholarship than the essays in separate journals already had. And, unlike major scholars who groom graduate students to carry research forward, Birney trained only one doctoral candidate, Professor Beryl Rowlands, who took a post at York University in Toronto.

Birney's scholarship made its most effective contribution not in the classroom or on the page, but through osmosis in his creative writings. His keen sense of irony, his comic flair, his comprehensive social observations, and his word play in such works as "David," "Anglosaxon Street," "The Damnation of Vancouver," *Turvey* and many of his concrete poems, owe their characteristic tenor and rhythms to Birney's linguistic training and agility.

Much has been said of Birney's craft as a poet, and there is evidence to suggest that he regarded himself as a craftsman like his father, the sign-painter and wallpaperer much in need of a craftsman's guild to assert his value and demand fair pay. His talent in crafting poems was, according to poet Al Purdy, "the really wondrous thing about Birney":

> He can take the most ordinary subject-thing and make
> it into a verse of nearly passionate interest. How?

Through juxtapositions, word play, enjambments, images, and endings that circle back to something said at the beginning, and thereby often make the whole poem meaningful. But that attempt to analyze his methods says very little, because, in the end, I don't know how he does it.[31]

Because of his interest in craftmanship, Birney was an inveterate reviser of his work and a ready experimenter. There was no form he could not master—lyric, sonnet, narrative, concrete, even the mediaeval villanelle. The linguistic twists and turns of English echo through his work from his studies of Anglo-Saxon and Chaucerian English, through the many Canadian dialects he encountered in the army, not to mention others he responded to first with his Shetland mother, then in a series of women from Britain—above all Esther—whose voices reminded him of hers, then with an enormous range of speakers he encountered on his travels around the world, right up to the groovy language of the beats and the jargon of contemporary slang. He never stopped listening and learning, nor ceased to delight in incorporating new idioms in puns and secret codes in his work.

In art, as in life, he was secretive, subversive and "crafty." One example from many can be found in his epigraph for *pnomes jukollages and other stunzas*.[32] "In Chauceres hazelwoode I walk alweye/ Ans never thynke out of his shawes ('woods') to streye." On the surface, this seems to mean that Birney never intends to stray from the path Chaucer took. But the allusion is to the section of Chaucer's *Troilus and Criseyde* in which Pandarus is persuading his niece Criseyde to become Troilus' mistress: "Ye, haselwoodes shaken!" exclaims Pandarus, using an expression which meant "You might as well shake hazelnut trees" (or something like "don't be nuts") as to waste time sending Troilus a ring instead of capitulating immediately.[33] There is another layer of meaning in the dedication because it alludes to Birney's own poem "From the Hazel Bough," in which an affair is described which is based on Birney's brief encounter with Corinne Hagon, his neighbour on Toronto's Hazelton Avenue. She and Birney both had hazel eyes. Given these complex allusions, the dedication actually means, "I have no intention of straying from the ways Chaucer described in *Troilus and Criseyde*, or from the 'hazel-woods' I described in my own poem 'From the Hazel Bough.'" In other words, Birney was saying: "I have no intention of giving up being unfaithful."

One of Birney's lifetime achievements was his genius for friendship. What Wailan calls "his ability to draw love out of others" may have stemmed from the deeply ingrained loneliness of an only child who knew he had lost a brother. But it transformed the Canadian literary scene over an extraordinarily long period of time. From a time when Canada's cultural figures were very few indeed, Birney was situated by happy accident among people—like his UBC mentor Garnett Sedgewick, his Zate fraternity brothers Hank Gartshore, Bruce Macdonald and Dal Grauer, his Trotskyist friends Sylvia and Ken Johnstone, and later his English friends Bert Matlow, John Archer and Esther Heiger—whose influence ensured a nucleus of the top political, intellectual and literary figures from all classes of society in North America and Britain. Through this international nucleus, he was able to widen his circle of friends until it included virtually all the important literary figures in English Canada, from E.J. Pratt and Dorothy Livesay in the 1920s to Leonard Cohen and bpNichol in the 1970s, as well as countless literary figures in other countries.

It was a happy accident, too, that Birney was positioned to take full advantage of the emergence of Canadian arts programming on CBC radio. His year with International Services in Montreal directly after the war put him in touch with CBC's decision-makers and, in effect, trained him in the dynamics of radio work. Though he saw his radio interviews, script-writings, adaptations and readings largely as a fortuitous venue for supplementing his income, his many appearances in the 1940s and 1950s consolidated and extended his influence on Canadians during a time of intense national spirit, an influence that broadened further still with the advent of television.

Birney's remarkable business acumen and organizational skills, combined with his outgoing personality, resulted in numerous editorial positions in the years after he was editor-in-chief of

The Ubyssey in 1925–26, which, in turn, kept him in constant
touch with the thrust of a rapidly developing literary scene in
Canada and with the writers themselves, as generation upon generation of writers emerged like a rapid sequence of time-lapse
photography. He never quite let go of the vision of himself as the
vendor of the exciting scoop, which had first thrilled him as a
newsboy on a bicycle in Banff during the Great War. Unlike
many others, he was willing to fight (or temperamentally unable
not to fight) for his principles: he was the first editor in Canada
to initiate guest-editing exchanges with other publications and to
insist that creative writers be paid, and, even though he had the
placement of his own poems mainly in mind, it was partly
through his personal research efforts that Canadian writers
became aware of the full range of national and international outlets for their writings and of the awards for which they might
compete.

In other administrative ways, too, Birney affected Canadian
letters. It was his idea to found a literary guild along the lines of
craftsmen's guilds that was finally realized in the formation of the
League of Canadian Poets in 1966. Though he himself soon
withdrew—as he often did when his pristine visions became
imperfect realities—when his scheme was adopted (he claimed
that the League was another CAA, the association against which
he had initiated the idea in the first place), the League itself continued to flourish. As one of the artists who helped prepare a
brief to the Massey Commission in the mid-fifties, and as a
member of the Arts Advisory Committee later, he helped shape
the policy of the Canada Council in ways that made it possible
for him to elude what he viewed as the entrapment of academic
life by securing travel and other grants, but he thereby benefited
many other creative writers and artists as well. Somehow he
always found time to write recommendations that conveyed the
special talents of each applicant, not only for his students and
friends, but for virtually anyone with potential, whether he had
met them or not. And when he received such grants himself, he
took them entirely seriously, positioning himself as a cultural
ambassador, promoting Canadian literature generally, and reading from the works of those poets he believed were Canada's

finest, all over Canada and abroad. As Leonard Cohen put it succinctly in the 1964 inscription he wrote in Birney's copy of his novel *The Favourite Game* (1963), "you keep a great network in repair."[34]

If it were possible to trace the careers of the hundreds of writers who learned to hone their craft from Birney—whether in formal classes, in workshops or through informal discussions or letters—and the careers of those of the next generation of students who were influenced in turn, it might also be possible to measure the extent of his influence on Canadian writing. As John Robert Colombo rightly commented, it might take twenty years [just] to assess Earle Birney's influence on young writers at the University of Toronto.[35] His overall influence can only be guessed at, sensed rather than known, by looking at a few examples. Though Birney was an indifferent father to his own son, Bill, he could not have been a more effective mentor to the young men who sought his advice for their writing. Sometimes, as in the case of John Wardroper, Birney opened the door for a person from rural B.C. to the cultural sophistication of a career as an editor for London's *Sunday Times*. He transformed the life of Joe Rosenblatt by helping him find funding to write instead of working on the railway, a literary career that led to a Governor General's Award for poetry for *Top Soil* in 1976. For Al Purdy, ultimately a more important poet than Birney, who began submitting poems to Birney at *Canadian Poetry Magazine* in 1947, he was a friend, a model and a mentor. Birney's cultural catholicism was such that he was able to encourage poet George Bowering when he won the Governor General's Award in 1969 for *Rocky Mountain Foot* and *The Gangs of Kosmos* at the same time as he donated money for the counter-celebration of "The People's Poet" Milton Acorn (also briefly his student), whom many thought ought to have won it. West-coast novelist Jack Hodgins (who won the Governor General's Award in 1979 for *The Resurrection of Joseph Bourne*) put into words what student after student felt about Birney: "I wanted to be a novelist more than anything," he says, recalling his trepidation at submitting a sample of his writing to Birney before entering the Creative Writing course in 1958–59 on which he would soon get "A's":

I found myself justifying my ambitions in what must
have been an almost comical combination of inarticulate shyness and awful pretention—sputtering words
about wanting to capture myths about the part of the
world I'd grown up in! He didn't laugh, or even make
me any more uncomfortable than I already was. He
said I had an eye for detail and an obvious interest in
style. He recommended that I read Ethel Wilson and
invited me to join the class.... I suspect I learned from
his manner more than his words. He treated our work
with respect, he honoured our ambitions (except an
ambition to write westerns), he was kind, he behaved
as though we deserved to take part in discussions
about serious literature being written by others.... he'd
encouraged and taught me by the model he was, if
nothing else; just the fact that he existed caused me to
want to be good."[36]

With his female students, Birney's success was less certain.
Though he encouraged and launched a number of these, like
Phyllis Webb, Heather Spears, Marya Fiamengo, Betty Lambert
and Rona Murray, who proved to have extraordinary talent, too
often his sexual attraction—or indeed his sexual involvement—
clouded his judgement, and he recommended others whose literary merits were doubtful. Because the meeting of minds
sometimes blurred into the merging of bodies, he was not able to
strike the same camaraderie with young women which proved so
inspiring to young men.

In the love poems his countless lovers inspired, he delineated a
subtle range of feelings: in "This Page My Pigeon" (for Esther)
the ambivalance of a man torn between the desire for the continuity of marriage and family and the claustrophobic sense that
marriage is constricting him; in "Mappemounde" (for Margaret
Crosland) the ache of irrevocable loss; in "From the Hazel
Bough" (for Corinne Hagon) the delicious sensuality of an affair
free of commitment; in "Takkakaw Falls" (for Bet Campbell) the
tremendous power of sexuality; in "Like an Eddy" (for Ikuko)
the visual representation of male and female principles; in "i

think you are a whole city" (for Alison Hunt) the awe of discovery through love; in "She is" (for Wailan) the tender protectiveness of the older lover for the young woman who must outlive
him.

The most genuine response the Vancouver Awards ceremony
evoked from Birney was the curious identification he felt with
his mother and her family. "I want in conclusion to thank my
grand-uncle Magnus Robertson," he said on accepting his large
V-shaped trophy, pronouncing the name with a rolling Scots
burr, and making the mistake of calling his uncle his grand-
uncle, "who was a sailor on a sailing ship in the 1870s. He
jumped ship in Nanaimo and went to work in the mines there,
in the coal mines, worked assiduously for about twenty years,
and by that time had saved enough money to send for his young
sister to come out and join him in Nanaimo. And that was my
mother."[37] It was a romantic image: one his Berkeley fiancée,
Barbara Barrett, had so long ago called "the up-on-the-top-deck
of the ferryboat you."[38] The red-headed Viking seafarer, Errol
"the wanderer," the name that was really his. The runaway, the
daring rebel, the working-class labourer. The man with the
vision of a better world and a heart generous enough to help others in the great quest to achieve it.

Birney returned from the Vancouver Awards to help Wailan
move in to the nine-acre property near Uxbridge named "Slough
of De' Pond," which they had bought a few months before. It
was true that he had written two years before to Esther, to
describe Corinne Hagon's funeral (at which he read "From the
Hazel Bough" and "managed not to cry till it was over"[39]) and
speculated that he might not last another summer; and for the
first time ever, he had cancelled at the last minute the conference
trip to Singapore he planned for June 1986 ("between my fitful
ticker, my sciatica, cataracts, etc., i had to face up at last to being
older than 60").[40] But he still had several literary projects enthusiastically in hand (including "My First Seven Years," which was
being typed by a part-time secretary, and his "really-last b[oo]k of
pomes, title "One Muddy Hand"),[41] and had recently been corresponding with Daniel Larden and Jon Whyte in Banff about
the possible designation of the little house his father built on

Squirrel Street as a registered historic resource. As he wrote poet John Newlove, the M & S editor he admired inordinately, "I'm still no nearer writing the poems, novels, plays, essays i was always going to write. But, hell, I've really enjoyed life & would love another 80 years of it if only I could keep my cock up long enough."[42] Or, as he wrote the following year to poet George Johnston, "life is too short… i need another 80 just to know better, and savour, the friendship of my friends."[43] And there was still something he regretted he'd missed in life: after being flown by a teenage pilot in a two-seater monoplane (the only available transport because of the Vancouver Expo) to the Seattle airport in July 1986 after doing a four-day stint at Harrison Hotsprings as what he called "floater-in-residence," Birney wrote, "marvellous trip, flying beside Mount Baker etc. I wish I had learned to fly."[44]

Birney spent the weekend on his return from Vancouver with Wailan at Slough of De' Pond to recover from his trip west. He excitedly looked forward to the "day that the snow in the woods will have shrunk enough so we can discover the perhaps mythical trail to 'our' river which the older natives swear was once detectable meandering thru the bog."[45] But there was still snow. While Wailan cooked, he shovelled paths here and there and chopped wood, as if he were years younger.

The following Thursday, 19 March, he was back in the city, consulting with librarian Debra Barr, who had begun compiling her guide to his papers in the Thomas Fisher Rare Book Room in 1986. "I called him occasionally [when I needed to identify correspondents, for instance], visited his apartment, and met him for coffee," Debra Barr recalls, referring to the journal she kept at the time,

> so it was odd that I had hesitations about meeting him for lunch [that day]. "I've rarely experienced premonitions, but was afraid that one day we'd be walking to lunch on campus, and Earle would have a heart attack and collapse on a sidewalk.
>
> He came into the Fisher a couple of times to sort through some correspondence with me, and, sure

enough, then suggested working for a full day and breaking for lunch at the Faculty Club. I couldn't think of any reason for refusing.

I kept my eye on him on the way over. No need to—he had his usual bounce. I stayed nervous for a while at the Faculty Club, since there weren't many customers or waiters around. The bartender seemed fairly stationary, though, so I settled down. I could always ask *him* to find a phone.

We stayed for a couple of hours. For the first time, since I was feeling that time was limited, I asked Earle some personal questions. Without being so crass as to ask him how he felt about dying! I nudged the conversation in a spiritual direction, enquiring first about his parents, his childhood, Sunday school.... His father was a religious man, but didn't like attending services. His mother, on the other hand, ran church schools zealously, and sometimes insisted that Earle go to services several times on Sundays. He'd "had his fill of it," and as an adult was uninvolved. He did allow, though, that he was no longer disinterested in the concept of life after death. This cheered me—he'd be willing to recognize heaven if he came across it soon.

I also asked about the war, and the women. He spoke of relationships that might never have taken hold had there not been a war to incubate them. Carlotta, whom Earle speculated had been a spy, and who later disappeared—she was "vulnerable," and "really did love me," he said, as if this might have been disputable. And Margaret Crosland, "shy," "not one to make advances," brought up by her parents "as a proper young lady." She had an aptitude for languages, and was working as a translator. Earle began to stay at her place during his leaves. She knew that he was married, and had a son, and would be returning to Toronto following the war. She made no complaint when he did, and went on to "marry a Frenchman—predictably." Their marriage didn't last—"also predictably."

Eventually Margaret and Esther, each always aware of the other, met. (During the 1960s? My notes aren't clear.) They met on warm terms (I think this was in London). Esther, who "wasn't much of a traveller," wasn't keen on carrying on to Italy, and suggested that Margaret go with Earle instead.

Earle said that of all the women he'd known, Margaret was the one whom he should have stayed with. Their temperaments were complementary. It had disappointed him when she'd sold his letters to her, and he hadn't written to her since. (I considered [this] a bit much, in view of the fact that he'd sold *his*.) He missed her, and didn't consider it right for two people to be out of touch "when they've meant something to each other."

We went out onto the sidewalk again after lunch. Earle seemed fine. We climbed a flight of stairs to the front office of the U of T Press, where some copies of a book were set aside for him. While we were waiting, I looked at the displayed publications, and picked one up to show Earle. I turned to him and saw him stiffening, a heavy body on dissolving feet. He started to fall, very slowly, toward me. I caught him calmly because I'd been prepared for this.[46]

It would be his last climb. Now was Birney's time.

> Now was the season...
> I was climbing the tall beech
> to prune dead limbs...
>
> Each grasp tugged at the old zest
> for a climb: the rock-fort a year back
> in Sri Lanka   and before   in my sixties
> up the yellow spines of the Olgas...
> at fifty-eight in cloud on the ribs
> of Huayna Picchu... at thirty
> inching down chalk on Lulworth cliffs

…twenty-one and over the icy necks
of the Garibaldis…and before that
the mountains of youth… Temple… Edith
all the climbings made in joy of the sport
and never with hurt

as now to the topmost vault
of the beechtree's leaves I rose
to the flooding memories of childhood
perched in my first treehouse
safe in its green womb…[47]

⚜ *Epilogue* ⚜

Earle Birney did not die after his heart attack on 19 March 1987. With the assistance of the scientific technology he had once personified as "the black Experimentress,"[1] his heart was artificially stimulated, and he survived.

Ironically, the man who hated to be trapped or caged or enclosed, the man who was in favour of capital punishment because he could never have tolerated incarceration, the man who chose the subject of mercy-killing for his major poem, was to be confined to the chronic-care ward of a hospital honouring the monarchy he despised in a city he disliked: Toronto's Queen Elizabeth Hospital. There he has proven to be a difficult patient, but one beloved by the bevy of old women who are his companions.[2]

Wailan has cared for him vigilantly, hoping to make a difference to what is left of his life as a brain-damaged patient. This is, she knows, no ordinary nonagenarian. She tried a hired nurse at their apartment on Carleton Street for ten months and took him for outings to Slough of De' Pond, but when even these efforts proved inadequate to deal with Birney's sudden impulses at unlikely hours to go out on his own, she had no alternative but to return him to hospital.[3] There he has held his final "Earle's Court" for many visitors, a role he fortunately could not fully grasp.

Birney has always feared aging and death. Rona Murray recalled that he was "horrified by old age." She remembers his

569

reaction on seeing a man with a walker. "'If I ever reach that stage,' he said, 'I want to be given something to finish it.' He definitely felt he would rather take a pill."[4] He would be almost ninety before Wailan realized what he had been trying to tell her when she had taken him half a dozen years earlier to their Uxbridge retreat. "He kept saying, 'I want to go over...go over'—something like that. Isn't that what David says to Bobbie in the poem?" And long before, when he had visited his dying friend Bill Hagon in hospital in the summer of 1969, he had written to Bill's wife, Corinne, and their sons in keen distress, "i guess it was when i couldn't feel anymore *what* bill was feeling or thinking about anything (which was the last two times i saw him) that he died, for me.... i couldnt know any longer what his response was and that upset me so much i couldn't even write directly to him anymore...since there seemed no longer hope of recovery, and communication was gone for me, i mourned him then, and cried for the loss of one of the best friends i ever had"[5]

Now it is Earle Birney's turn to drift to map's end. Drift, until the words chosen by him in the late summer of 1960 are read: "At my funeral, please read: Dylan Thomas's 'And Death Shall Have No Dominion.'"[6]

Endnotes

Introduction

1 G.G. Sedgewick, 15 Oct. 1927, Earle Birney Papers, Thomas Fisher Rare Book Library, University of Toronto.

2 Corinne Hagon, 22 Jan. 1944, Earle Birney Papers, Thomas Fisher Rare Book Library, University of Toronto.

3 The University of Buffalo Library, 23 Jan. 1945 and E.B. to the University of Buffalo Library, 8 Aug. 1945, Thomas Fisher Rare Book Library, University of Toronto.

4 E.B. to Elizabeth Campbell, 3 Aug. 1948, Earle Birney Papers, Thomas Fisher Rare Book Library, University of Toronto.

5 E.B. to Adam Hazard, [n.d., spring] 1966, Earle Birney Papers, Thomas Fisher Rare Book Library, University of Toronto.

6 This sum is based on the recollection of Richard Landon, director of the Thomas Fisher Rare Book Library, that E.B. was paid $16,000 for the first and largest collection; and various letters of E.B.'s that refer to a second payment of $2,000 later. The actual sum of the first payment is blocked out on the library records.

7 E.B. to Elizabeth Cox, 26 Aug. 1963, Earle Birney Papers, Thomas Fisher Rare Book Library, University of Toronto.

8 Pat Christmas to E.C., interview, Dec. 1991, Victoria, B.C.

9 See, for example, E.B. to Herman Singer, 22 July 1959, Earle Birney Papers, Thomas Fisher Rare Book Library, University of Toronto.

10 H.R. Ellis Davidson, as quoted by Kevin Crosley-Holland in *The Norse Myths* (London: Andre Deutsch, 1980), p. xxix.

11 Crosley-Holland, *Norse Myths*, p. xxix-xxx.

12 See Anna Birgitta Rooth (Lund: C.W.K. Gleerups Forlay, 1961), pp. 244-48.

13 The description of the Vikings given by Arab diplomat and diarist, Ibn Fadlan, when he encountered them on the Volga in 922, as quoted by Kevin Crossley-Holland, *Norse Myths*, p. xv.

14 See E.B. to Bruce Nesbitt, 3 July 1979, National Library of Canada.

15 E.B. to Heather Spears, 14 Jan. 1959, Earle Birney Papers, Thomas Fisher Rare Book Library, University of Toronto and E.B., "Chaucer's Irony," Graduating Essay, 1926, UBC, p. 18, Earle Birney Papers, Thomas Fisher Rare Book Library, University of Toronto.

16 E.B. to George Johnston, 28 May 1979, George Johnston Papers,

National Archives of Canada.

17 David Malcolmson, *Ten Heroes* (N.Y.: Duell, Sloan and Pearce, 1941).

18 Camille Paglia, "Speed and Space: Byron,*" Sexual Personnae: Art and Decadence from Nefertiti to Emily Dickinson* (New Haven: Yale University Press, 1990), p. 359.

19 Samuel Johnson, as quoted by James Boswell, "Part VII: 1777-78," *The Life of Samuel Johnson,* ed. Christopher Hibbert (London: Penguin Classics, 1986), p. 231.

20 I noted this dream at once on the paper I keep by my bed.

21 Gabrielle Baldwin to E.B., 26 Feb. 1945, Earle Birney Papers, Thomas Fisher Rare Book Library, University of Toronto.

22 *The Annotated Bibliography of Canada's Major Authors,* ed. Jack David and Robert Lecker, vol. 4 (Downsview: ECW Press, 1983).

Chapter 1: The Great Divide

1 William G. Birney to Martha Birney, 12 June 1916, Earle Birney Papers, Thomas Fisher Rare Book Library, University of Toronto.

2 E.B., "My Father," unpublished ms., [n.d.], Earle Birney Papers, Thomas Fisher Rare Book Library, University of Toronto.

3 *Crag and Canyon* lists. See W.G. Birney to Martha Birney, 29 Nov. 1916: "I am not going to take the bread out of the mouths of you and Earl [sic] for *any* Paint Company." Earle Birney Papers, Thomas Fisher Rare Book Library, University of Toronto.

4 *Crag and Canyon,* 14 Nov. 1914.

5 E.B., autobiographical notes for "Conversations with Trotsky," unpublished ms., p. 9, Earle Birney Papers, Thomas Fisher Rare Book Library, University of Toronto.

6 *Crag and Canyon,* 13 Nov. 1915, p. 38.

7 See E.B.'s short story on this event, "Mickey Was a Swell Guy," *Big Bird in the Bush: Selected Stories and Sketches* (Oakville, Ont.: Mosaic/Valley Press, 1978).

8 E.B., autobiographical notes for "Conversations with Trotsky," ed. Bruce Nesbitt, unpublished ms., p. 8, fond Earle Birney, Literary Manuscript Collection, National Library of Canada.

9 "Mickey was a Swell Guy," *Big Bird in the Bush,* and additional details from autobiographical notes for "Conversations with Trotsky," Earle Birney Papers, Thomas Fisher Rare Book Library, University of Toronto and taped interview of E.B. by Jon Whyte, 19 Feb. 1971, Archives, Whyte Museum of the Canadian Rockies, Banff, Alberta. The poem E.B. refers to is Browning's "How They Brought the Good News from Ghent to Aix," which describes the ride on horseback of a man who carries information that will save the West Prussian town of Aix-la-Chapelle—an imaginary incident.

10 William G. Birney to Martha Birney, 6 June 1916, Earle Birney Papers, Thomas Fisher Rare Book Library, University of Toronto.

11 William G. Birney to Martha and E.B., 9 Jan. 1916, Earle Birney Papers, Thomas Fisher Rare Book Library, University of Toronto.

12 William G. Birney to Martha Birney, 19 Dec. 1915, Earle Birney Papers, Thomas Fisher Rare Book Library, University of Toronto.

13 William G. Birney to E.B., 2 July 1916, Earle Birney Papers, Thomas Fisher Rare Book Library, University of Toronto.

14 William G. Birney to Martha Birney, 28 June 1916, Earle Birney Papers, Thomas Fisher Rare Book Library, University of Toronto.

15 William G. Birney to Martha and E.B., 23 Mar. 1916, Earle Birney Papers, Thomas Fisher Rare Book Library, University of Toronto.

16 Letter with E.B.'s verse not extant. William G. Birney to Martha and E.B., 10 June 1916, Earle Birney Papers, Thomas Fisher Rare Book Library, University of Toronto.

17 E.B., "Alfred the Great," unpublished ms., Earle Birney Papers, Thomas Fisher Rare Book Library, University of Toronto.

18 William G. Birney to Martha and E.B., 16 June 1916, Earle Birney Papers, Thomas Fisher Rare Book Library, University of Toronto.

19 "Diary: 20 Jan. 1916–29 Apr. 1916," 20 Feb. 1916, Earle Birney Papers, Thomas Fisher Rare Book Library, University of Toronto.

20 E.B., "My Father."

21 Charles W. Brown to E.B., 16 Feb. 1919, Earle Birney Papers, Thomas Fisher Rare Book Library, University of Toronto.

22 Esther Birney to E.C. and Wailan Low to E.C., numerous interviews.

23 William G. Birney to Martha and E.B., 9 Jan. 1916, Earle Birney Papers, Thomas Fisher Rare Book Library, University of Toronto.

24 This letter is no longer extant.

25 William G. Birney to Earle and Martha Birney, 6 June 1916, Earle Birney Papers, Thomas Fisher Rare Book Library, University of Toronto.

26 Birney, "A Camping Week," *B.C. Outdoors* (Dec. 1980), p. 34.

27 E.B., autobiography notes, unpublished ms., Earle Birney Papers, Thomas Fisher Rare Book Library, University of Toronto.

28 William G. Birney to Martha Birney, 10 June 1916, Earle Birney Papers, Thomas Fisher Rare Book Library, University of Toronto.

29 William G. Birney to E.B., 20 July 1916, Earle Birney Papers, Thomas Fisher Rare Book Library, University of Toronto. In fact, the anniversary was 17 August, but it had become synonymous in family ritual with Will's birthday on the 18th.

30 A holograph list of members, dated 11 Oct. 1917, can be found in Scrapbook No. 1, Earle Birney Papers, Thomas Fisher Rare Book Library, University of Toronto.

31 E.B., *Spreading Time: Remarks on Canadian Writing and Writers*, Book

I: 1904–1949 (Montreal: Véhicule Press, 1980), p. 6.

32 E.B., "Diary: 20 Jan. 1916–29 Apr. 1916," 1 Jan. 1916, Earle Birney Papers, Thomas Fisher Rare Book Library, University of Toronto.

Chapter 2: Lowlands and Highlands

1 E.B., interview by J.H.R. Thomson, typed transcript, p. 1, M4201, Riveredge Foundation, Glenbow Archives, Calgary, Alberta.

2 Sometimes E.B. refers to his birthplace as a log cabin.

3 Margaret Crosland wonders what his life would have been like had he been named Errol instead of Earle, the implication being that he might not have had such elevated ideas about his place in the world.

4 The name can be traced to 1261. According to E.B., who researched the matter, "my spelling [of Birney] is an English one, my father's folk being Bedfordshire for a long way back. I think the Irish spelling, or one of them, is Byrne, and the Lowlands Burney. Then there's Bernie, which generally turns out to be Jewish. I seldom come across my own spelling except in Americans from Virginia—a branch of the family went there with the Elizabethan colonists, I understand." (E.B. to Rosemary Baxter, 22 Jan. 1957, property of Rosemary Baxter, Aberdeen, Scotland.)

5 E.B., "My Father," unpublished ms., [n.d.] pp. 1-2, Earle Birney Papers, Thomas Fisher Rare Book Library, University of Toronto.

6 See newspaper obituary of William Birney, "Death of an Old Time Albertan," [n.d.], E.B. Scrapbook No. 1, Earle Birney Papers, Thomas Fisher Rare Book Library, University of Toronto.

7 See their wedding certificate in Scrapbook No. 1, Earle Birney Papers, Thomas Fisher Rare Book Library, University of Toronto.

8 Rosemary Baxter to E.C., interview, 3 Sept. 1989, Aberdeen, Scotland.

9 Rosemary Baxter to E.C., interview, 3 Sept. 1989, Aberdeen, Scotland; and Eva Leask and Annie Robertson to E.C., interview, 4 Sept. 1989, Lerwick, Shetland.

10 Rosemary Baxter, E.B.'s first cousin once removed, provided many papers such as family trees; a copy of Robert Robertson's eviction notice; an interview of Geordie Gair, a distant relation of E.B., by Brian Smith; as well as her own recollections in an interview, 3 Sept. 1989, Aberdeen, Scotland, and numerous holograph notes and letters to E.C., from which the details of this section are taken.

11 See the obituary of Rev. G.T. Manley, *Shetland News*, [n.d., probably 15] March 1962.

12 Rosemary Baxter claims that E.B.'s usual representation of his mother as "fleeing" from her home is "over-dramatised." See Rosemary Baxter to E.C., 24 Feb. 1994, property of E.C.

13 Transcript of an interview by Brian Smith with E.B.'s distant relation, Geordie Gair, [n.d.], property of Rosemary Baxter, Aberdeen, Scotland.

14 "Obituary 1936: Death of Mr Robert A. Robertson, Weisdale," type-script, property of Rosemary Baxter, Aberdeen, Scotland.

15 E.B., *Spreading Time: Remarks on Canadian Writing and Writers*, Book I: 1904-1949 (Montreal: Véhicule Press, 1980), p. 1.

16 Olaf Ruhen, *Harpoon in My Hand* (Sidney: Angus and Robertson, 1966). E.B. to Olaf Ruhen, 26 Apr. 1969, Earle Birney Papers, Thomas Fisher Rare Book Library, University of Toronto.

17 E.B. "My Father," p. 3.

18 E.B. to Elizabeth Brewster, 12 Feb. 1983, Elizabeth Brewster Papers, National Archives of Canada, MG 30, D 370, vol. 10.

19 E.B., *Spreading Time*, p. 1.

20 E.B. to Rosemary Baxter, 6 Mar. 1953, Earle Birney Papers, Thomas Fisher Rare Book Library, University of Toronto.

21 Edmund Morrison to E.C., interview, 27 Nov. 1990, Pender Island, Vancouver. Morrison remembers Birney telling him of this on several occasions.

22 E.B. to Elizabeth Brewster, 19 Apr. 1983, Elizabeth Brewster Papers, National Archives of Canada, MG 30, D 370, vol. 10.

23 For both a visual sense of Banff at that time and numerous anecdotes about local events see *Rocky Mountain Madness: A Bittersweet Romance*, photos chosen by Edward Cavell and prose selected by Jon Whyte (Banff: Altitude Publishing Ltd., 1987).

24 E.B., interviewed by Jon Whyte, 19 Feb. 1971, Archives, Whyte Museum of the Canadian Rockies, Banff, Alberta.

25 E.B. to Alan Crawley, 20 Feb. 1943, Earle Birney Papers, Thomas Fisher Rare Book Library, University of Toronto.

26 E.B., "Education—For What?" a speech for the National Federation of Canadian University Students Conference, "Education, Research and National Development," 30 Aug. 1960, UBC, Vancouver.

27 E.B., "Sketches done at Banff Public School"; poems, presumably hand-written elsewhere, have been typed at some later date onto the same page as the sketches.

28 E.B. to Elizabeth Brewster, 19 Apr. 1983, Elizabeth Brewster Papers, National Archives of Canada, MG 30, D 370, vol. 10.

29 Rosemary Baxter to E.C., interview, 3 Sept. 1989, Aberdeen, Scotland.

30 E.B. to Beatrice White, [n.d., holograph addition "Nov. 1960"], Earle Birney Papers, Thomas Fisher Rare Book Library, University of Toronto.

31 Rosemary Baxter to E.C., interview, 3 Sept. 1989, Aberdeen, Scotland.

32 E.B. to Heather Spears, 14 Jan. 1959, Earle Birney Papers, Thomas Fisher Rare Book Library, University of Toronto.

33 E.B., interviewed by Jon Whyte, 19 Feb. 1971, Whyte Museum of the Canadian Rockies (Archives), Banff, Alberta.

34 E.B. as quoted by Al Purdy in "The Man Who Killed David," *Weekend*

Magazine, 14 Dec. 1974, p. 17.

35 Newsclip, *Canadian Pictorial,* [n.d.] 1913, Scrapbook No. 1, Earle Birney Papers, Thomas Fisher Rare Book Library, University of Toronto.

Chapter 3: Down in the Valley

1 E.B. to graphologist, 26 Mar. 1922, *The Veteran,* Ottawa, Scrapbook No. 1, Earle Birney Papers, Thomas Fisher Rare Book Library, University of Toronto.

2 E.B., "A Chancey Venture," *B.C. Outdoors* (Oct. 1980), p. 32.

3 Details taken from E.B., "Hot and Cold," *B.C. Outdoors* (Nov. 1980), pp. 34-55.

4 E.B. to George Bowering, 3 Apr. 1966, George Bowering Archive, Contemporary Literature Collection, W.A.C. Bennett Library, Simon Fraser University. In fact, Birney was 14 when he moved to Creston.

5 Frances Hobart (Lyne) to E.C., [n.d., probably Nov.] 1990, property of E.C.

6 E.B., "A Camping Week," *B.C. Outdoors* (Dec. 1980), p. 35.

7 E.B., "Hot and Cold," *B.C. Outdoors* (Nov. 1980), p. 36.

8 E.B. to William and Martha Birney, 20 Mar. 1921, Earle Birney Papers, Thomas Fisher Rare Book Library, University of Toronto.

9 E.B. to William and Martha Birney, 23 Feb. 1921, Earle Birney Papers, Thomas Fisher Rare Book Library, University of Toronto.

10 E.B. to William and Martha Birney, 2 Mar. 1921, Earle Birney Papers, Thomas Fisher Rare Book Library, University of Toronto.

11 E.B. to William and Martha Birney, 23 Feb. 1921, Earle Birney Papers, Thomas Fisher Rare Book Library, University of Toronto.

12 E.B. was probably mistaken in this title and meant Ralph Connor's *The Sky Pilot: a Tale of the Foothills* (Toronto: Westminster Co., 1899), since he and his father shared great pleasure in Connor's works.

13 E.B. to William and Martha Birney, 23 Feb. 1921, Earle Birney Papers, Thomas Fisher Rare Book Library, University of Toronto.

14 Details taken from E.B. letters to William and Martha Birney, 1921, Earle Birney Papers, Thomas Fisher Rare Book Library, University of Toronto.

15 E.B. to William and Martha Birney, 23 Feb. 1921, Earle Birney Papers, Thomas Fisher Rare Book Library, University of Toronto.

16 E.B. to William and Martha Birney, 3 Mar. 1921, Earle Birney Papers, Thomas Fisher Rare Book Library, University of Toronto.

17 E.B. to Martha Birney, Earle Birney Papers, Thomas Fisher Rare Book Library, University of Toronto.

18 E.B., autobiographical notes for "Conversations with Trotsky," ed. Bruce Nesbitt, unpublished ms., fond Earle Birney, Literary

Manuscript Collection, National Library of Canada. I have rearranged the sentences in this quote.

19 John Archer to E.C., interview, 4 May 1989, London, England. Archer recalls: "He particularly remembered having met an Englishman who had come to Canada because he was a failure in England—as so many did—but had been to a public school, and who, after drink, recited choruses of Greek drama at great length. He impressed Earle very much. His project was to earn money in the summer and go to UBC in the winter."

20 E.B., autobiographical notes for "Conversations with Trotsky."

21 Details taken from "Reminiscences on Early Pest Control in Banff," *Crag and Canyon*, 14 July 1976, p. 5; and Dorothy Tefler to E.C., interview, 30 Aug. 1991, Rossland, B.C.

22 E.B., interviewed by Jon Whyte, 19 Feb. 1971, Whyte Museum of the Canadian Rockies (Archives), Banff, Alberta.

23 Graphologist to E.B., [n.d., prob. late spring] 1922, Scrapbook No. 1, Earle Birney Papers, Thomas Fisher Rare Book Library, University of Toronto.

Chapter 4: Social Climbing and Intellectual Heights

1 Mount Inglismaldie is 9,885 feet; Mount Girouard is 9,875 feet. See Eric J. Holmgren and Patricia M. Holmgren, *Over 2000 Place Names of Alberta*, 3rd ed. (Saskatoon, Saskatchewan: Western Producer Prairie Books, 1976).

2 E.B. to Desmond Pacey, 8 Apr. 1957, Earle Birney Papers, Thomas Fisher Rare Book Library, University of Toronto.

3 See Harry T. Logan, *Tuum Est: A History of the University of British Columbia* (Vancouver: The University of British Columbia Press, 1958).

4 "Record of Alfred Earle Birney in The University of British Columbia," 3 Oct. 1927, Earle Birney Papers, Thomas Fisher Rare Book Library, University of Toronto.

5 See news clipping in Scrapbook No. 1, Earle Birney Papers, Thomas Fisher Rare Book Library, University of Toronto.

6 See issues of *The Ubyssey* and *Totem* for 1922-23 in Special Collections and University Archives Division, University of British Columbia.

7 E.B., *Spreading Time: Remarks on Canadian Writing and Writers*, Book 1: 1904-1949 (Montreal: Véhicule Press, 1980), pp. 8-10.

8 E.B., *Spreading Time*.

9 E.B., *Spreading Time*.

10 E.B., *Spreading Time*.

11 Edmund (Ted) Morrison to E.C., interview, 27 Nov. 1990, Pender Island, B.C.

12 Sadie Boyle to E.C., interview, 2 Sept. 1991, Vancouver, B.C.

13 E.B., *Spreading Time*, pp. 10-11, 15.

14 Roy Daniells, "Profile of Garnett Sedgewick," CBC radio, 29 Aug. 1949, transcript in Earle Birney Papers, Thomas Fisher Rare Book Library, University of Toronto.

15 Sadie Boyle to E.C., 30 Dec. 1990, property of E.C.

16 Ted Morrison to E.C., interview, 27 Nov. 1990, Pender Island, B.C.

17 E.B., "Dormit Flumen," *The Ubyssey*, 18 Oct. 1923, p. 6.

18 E.B., "Shun!", *The Ubyssey*, 18 Oct. 1923, p. 7.

19 E.B., *Spreading Time*, pp. 16-17.

20 Sadie Boyle to E.C., interview, 2 Sept. 1991, Vancouver, B.C.

21 In *Down the Long Table* (Toronto: McClelland & Stewart, 1955), Gordon Saunders, the protagonist based on Birney, describes himself as a "go-getting twerp" "hawking advertising" during an equivalent summer. Gordon makes $1000.00 that summer by conning and bullying, a three-month income that is twice as large as the university fellowship on which he was supposed to live for a year (pp. 42-3).

22 E.B. to Dorothy Livesay, 5 Sept. 1944, Earle Birney Papers, Thomas Fisher Rare Book Library, University of Toronto.

23 Literary Editor [Bernard McEvoy, E.B.'s holograph addition], *The Vancouver Province*, 24 Sept. 1924, Earle Birney Papers, Thomas Fisher Rare Book Library, University of Toronto.

24 E.B., *Spreading Time*, pp. 14-15. The poem was the basis for "Vancouver Lights."

25 Ted Morrison to E.C., interview, 27 Nov. 1990, Pender Island, B.C.

26 Mary Morrison to E.C., interview, 27 Nov. 1990, Pender Island, B.C.

27 Though Birney's largely autobiographical character, Gordon Saunders in *Down the Long Table*, is not homosexual, he is suspected of being so: "those two sorority girls did [think I was a pansy] when I was an undergraduate," Gordon thinks to himself, "didn't know I heard them; and the campus pansies put me down for a swot—or merely afraid to try?" (p. 47).

28 Florence Kerr to E.B., [n.d., summer] 1924, Earle Birney Papers, Thomas Fisher Rare Book Library, University of Toronto.

29 E.B., *The Ubyssey*, 23 Sept. 1925, p. 2.

30 E.B., *The Ubyssey*, 3 Nov. 1925, p. 2.

31 E.B., "Editorial," *The Ubyssey*, 31 Oct. 1925.

32 Sadie Boyle to E.C., interview, 2 Sept. 1991, Vancouver, B.C.

33 See Edward Starkins, *Who Killed Janet Smith?: the 1924 Vancouver killing that remains Canada's most intriguing unsolved murder* (Toronto: Macmillan of Canada, 1984) for an excellent account of this crime; and James Dubro, *Dragons of Crime: Inside the Asian Underworld* (Markham, Ont.: Octopus Publishing Group, 1992), pp. 56-58, for the context of the Canadian Asian underworld within which it occurred.

34 Janet Smith.

35 Ted Morrison to E.C., interview, 27 Nov. 1990, Pender Island, B.C.

36 Ted Morrison to E.C., interview, 27 Nov. 1990, Pender Island, B.C.

37 Jessica Noble (MacPhail) to E.C., interview, 2 Sept. 1991, Vancouver, B.C.

38 Ted Morrison to E.C., interview, 27 Nov. 1990, Pender Island, B.C.

39 E.B. to Barbara Barrett, letters 1929–30, Earle Birney Papers, Thomas Fisher Rare Book Library, University of Toronto.

40 E.B., *Down the Long Table* (Toronto: McClelland & Stewart, 1955), p. 47.

41 Caption for Alfred Earle Birney, *Totem*, 1925-26, p. 12.

42 E.B., "Chaucer's Irony," Graduating Essay, 1926, UBC, 120 pp., Earle Birney Papers, Thomas Fisher Rare Book Library, University of Toronto.

Chapter 5: A Dying Fall

1 E.B. to Leonard Leacock, 20 June 1926, Earle Birney Papers, Thomas Fisher Rare Book Library, University of Toronto.

2 Kropotkin (1842-1921) was a Russian anarchist; Bakunin (1814-1876) was considered the activist founder of world anarchy.

3 Rose Macaulay, *Told by an Idiot* (New York: Boni and Liveright, 1923).

4 See Otto Weininger, *Sex and Character* (trans. from German), (London: William Heinemann, 1906). Weininger (1880-1903) was under 30 when he wrote this book. In it he draws on biological, psychological and philosophical sources to present a characterization of sexual types, such as "The Courtesan," "The Mother," "The Hysterical Woman." Weininger covers such aspects of sexuality as homosexuality, bisexuality and pederasty. Weininger's theories are overtly anti-feminist, if not misogynist. He considers women to be inherently unethical, soulless and dishonest; finds "genius" in music, painting, philosophy, religion, etc. to be essentially male; thinks men have more logic and better memories than women; thinks women are vain and disposed to polygamy.

5 E.B. to Leonard Leacock, 20 June 1926, Earle Birney Papers, Thomas Fisher Rare Book Library, University of Toronto.

6 Martha Birney to E.B., 7 Oct. 1926, Earle Birney Papers, Thomas Fisher Rare Book Library, University of Toronto.

7 G.G. Sedgewick to E.B., 12 Oct. 1926, Earle Birney Papers, Thomas Fisher Rare Book Library, University of Toronto.

8 This is Claude Bissell's description in *Halfway Up Parnassus: A Personal Account of the University of Toronto 1932-1971* (Toronto: University of Toronto Press, 1974), p. 5.

9 Bissell, *Halfway Up Parnassus*.

10 Martha Birney to E.B., 3 Oct. 1926, Earle Birney Papers, Thomas

Fisher Rare Book Library, University of Toronto.

11 Martha Birney to E.B., 7 Oct. 1926, Earle Birney Papers, Thomas Fisher Rare Book Library, University of Toronto.

12 It was Edmund (Ted) Morrision who suggested this connection. Morrison to E.C., interview, Pender Island, B.C.

13 Martha Birney to E.B., 17 Oct. 1926, Earle Birney Papers, Thomas Fisher Rare Book Library, University of Toronto.

14 Martha Birney to E.B., 8 Nov. 1926, Earle Birney Papers, Thomas Fisher Rare Book Library, University of Toronto.

15 Martha Birney to E.B., 2 Nov. 1926, Earle Birney Papers, Thomas Fisher Rare Book Library, University of Toronto.

16 Martha Birney to E.B., 15 Nov. 1926, Earle Birney Papers, Thomas Fisher Rare Book Library, University of Toronto.

17 Dal Grauer to E.B., 20 May 1926, Earle Birney Papers, Thomas Fisher Rare Book Library, University of Toronto.

18 Frank Wilcox to E.B., 24 Aug. 1926, Earle Birney Papers, Thomas Fisher Rare Book Library, University of Toronto.

19 Ted Morrison to E.B., 13 Nov. 1926, Earle Birney Papers, Thomas Fisher Rare Book Library, University of Toronto.

20 E.B., *Spreading Time: Remarks on Canadian Writing and Writers*, Book I: 1904-1949 (Montreal: Véhicule Press, 1980) pp. 24-25.

21 E.B. to Desmond Pacey, 8 Aug. 1957, Earle Birney Papers, Thomas Fisher Rare Book Library, University of Toronto.

22 Ted Morrison to E.B., 26 Dec. 1926, Earle Birney Papers, Thomas Fisher Rare Book Library, University of Toronto.

23 G.G. Sedgewick to E.B., 21 Nov. 1926, Earle Birney Papers, Thomas Fisher Rare Book Library, University of Toronto.

24 E.B. to Leonard Leacock, 21 Nov. 1926, Earle Birney Papers, Thomas Fisher Rare Book Library, University of Toronto.

25 E.B. to Martha Birney, 29 Nov. 1926, Earle Birney Papers, Thomas Fisher Rare Book Library, University of Toronto.

26 E.B. to Martha Birney, 3 Dec. 1926, Earle Birney Papers, Thomas Fisher Rare Book Library, University of Toronto.

27 E.B. to Martha Birney, 2 Dec. 1926, Earle Birney Papers, Thomas Fisher Rare Book Library, University of Toronto.

28 E.B. to Martha Birney, 3 Dec. 1926, Earle Birney Papers, Thomas Fisher Rare Book Library, University of Toronto.

29 E.B. to Martha Birney, 15 Dec. 1926, Earle Birney Papers, Thomas Fisher Rare Book Library, University of Toronto.

30 G.G. Sedgewick to E.B., 30 Nov. 1926, Earle Birney Papers, Thomas Fisher Rare Book Library, University of Toronto.

31 E.B. to Desmond Pacey, 8 Aug. 1957, Earle Birney Papers, Thomas Fisher Rare Book Library, University of Toronto.

32 E.B. to Leonard Leacock, [n.d.] Apr. 1927, Earle Birney Papers,

Thomas Fisher Rare Book Library, University of Toronto.

33 E.B., "Conversations in Knox College, 1927 (Dining Hall)," unpublished ms., Earle Birney Papers, Thomas Fisher Rare Book Library, University of Toronto.

Chapter 6: A Great Depression

1 See Barbara Barrett Papers, 1929, Earle Birney Papers, Thomas Fisher Rare Book Library, University of Toronto.

2 Barbara Barrett to E.B., Earle Birney Papers, Thomas Fisher Rare Book Library, University of Toronto.

3 Barbara Barrett to E.B., [n.d., holograph addition by E.B., "sometime later 29 April ?"] 1929, Earle Birney Papers, Thomas Fisher Rare Book Library, University of Toronto.

4 These three are characters in Thomas Hardy's novel *The Return of the Native*: Eustacia Vye, the intense, dark-haired heroine; Diggory Venn, the rustic "reddleman," who is covered with red dust from the red chalk (reddle) he sells to herdsmen to mark their sheep and is an unsuccessful suitor; and Clym Yeobright, the idealistic, bewildered protagonist.

5 Barbara Barrett to E.B., [n.d.] 1929, Earle Birney Papers, Thomas Fisher Rare Book Library, University of Toronto.

6 Barbara Barrett to E.B., Fri. night [n.d.] Aug. 1929, Earle Birney Papers, Thomas Fisher Rare Book Library, University of Toronto.

7 Barbara Barrett to E.B., Friday night [n.d.] 1929, Earle Birney Papers, Thomas Fisher Rare Book Library, University of Toronto.

8 Barbara Barrett to E.B., Fri. night [n.d., probably summer 1929], Earle Birney Papers, Thomas Fisher Rare Book Library, University of Toronto.

9 Barbara Barrett to E.B., [n.d., probably early May] 1929, Earle Birney Papers, Thomas Fisher Rare Book Library, University of Toronto.

10 See E.B.'s "Transcript of Record," University of California, 6 Mar. 1930, Earle Birney Papers, Thomas Fisher Rare Book Library, University of Toronto.

11 Details of course descriptions and professors' names are taken from "University of California Announcement of Courses of Instruction Primarily for Students in the Departments at Berkeley for the Academic Year 1927-28 [and 1928-29 and 1929-30]" (Berkeley, Calif.: University of Berkeley Press, 1927, 1928, 1929).

12 Barbara Barrett to E.B., [n.d., probably early May] 1929, Earle Birney Papers, Thomas Fisher Rare Book Library, University of Toronto.

13 E.B. as quoted by Barbara Barrett, Tues. night [n.d.] 1929, Earle Birney Papers, Thomas Fisher Rare Book Library, University of Toronto.

14 Barbara Barrett to E.B., Friday night [n.d., probably May or June] 1929, Earle Birney Papers, Thomas Fisher Rare Book Library,

University of Toronto.

15 E.B. as quoted by Barbara Barrett, Tues. night [n.d.] 1929, Earle Birney Papers, Thomas Fisher Rare Book Library, University of Toronto.

16 Barbara Barrett to E.B., 27 May 1930, Earle Birney Papers, Thomas Fisher Rare Book Library, University of Toronto.

17 Barbara Barrett to E.B., 25 Aug. 1930, Earle Birney Papers, Thomas Fisher Rare Book Library, University of Toronto.

18 Barbara Barrett to E.B., [n.d., probably summer] 1929, Earle Birney Papers, Thomas Fisher Rare Book Library, University of Toronto.

19 E.B. to David Bromige, [n.d., holograph note by E.B. "prob. Apr. 63"], Earle Birney Papers, Thomas Fisher Rare Book Library, University of Toronto.

20 Hendrie Gartshore to E.B., 4 Mar. 1929, Earle Birney Papers, Thomas Fisher Rare Book Library, University of Toronto.

21 Frank Wilcox to Prof. R.P. Utter, letter of reference for E.B., 12 Mar. 1926, Earle Birney Papers, Thomas Fisher Rare Book Library, University of Toronto.

22 E.B. to Leonard Leacock, 14 Feb. 1929, Archives, Whyte Museum of the Canadian Rockies, Banff, Alberta.

23 Harry M. Cassidy to E.B., 4 Nov. 1929, Victor W. Odlum Collection, National Archives of Canada, MG 30, E 380, vol. 2. Cassidy would later serve for five years as director of social welfare for B.C. and for five years after that as dean of the School of Social Welfare at the University of California. In 1945 he took a position as professor of social welfare and director for the School of Social Work at U. of T., a position he held until his death in 1951. His publications include: *Unemployment and Relief in Ontario* (1932), *Social Security and Reconstruction in Canada* (1943), *Public Health and Welfare Reorganization* (1943) and, with F.R. Scott, *Labour Conditions in the Men's Clothing Industry* (1935).

24 Hendrie Gartshore to E.B., 2 Feb. 1930, Earle Birney Papers, Thomas Fisher Rare Book Library, University of Toronto.

25 Dewart Lewis to E.B., 27 July 1929, Earle Birney Papers, Thomas Fisher Rare Book Library, University of Toronto.

26 Barbara Barrett to E.B., Thurs. night [n.d.] Nov. 1929, Earle Birney Papers, Thomas Fisher Rare Book Room, University of Toronto.

27 E.B. to Leonard Leacock, 14 Feb. 1929, Earle Birney Papers, Thomas Fisher Rare Book Library, University of Toronto.

28 Barbara Barrett quoting E.B. to E.B., Wed. night [n.d., summer] 1930, Earle Birney Papers, Thomas Fisher Rare Book Library, University of Toronto.

29 Barbara Barrett to E.B., 11 Aug. 1930, Earle Birney Papers, Thomas Fisher Rare Book Library, University of Toronto.

30 G.G. Sedgewick to E.B., 8 Dec. 1929, Earle Birney Papers, Thomas Fisher Rare Book Library, University of Toronto.

31 Barbara Barrett to E.B., Tues. afternoon [n.d., probably end of May] 1930, Earle Birney Papers, Thomas Fisher Rare Book Library, University of Toronto.

32 E.B. to Leonard Leacock, 14 Feb. 1929, Archives, Whyte Museum of the Canadian Rockies, Banff, Alberta.

33 Barbara Barrett to E.B., 28 May 1930, Earle Birney Papers, Thomas Fisher Rare Book Library, University of Toronto.

34 Barbara Barrett to E.B., 13 June 1930, Earle Birney Papers, Thomas Fisher Rare Book Room, University of Toronto.

35 Barbara Barrett to E.B., 11 June 1930, Earle Birney Papers, Thomas Fisher Rare Book Library, University of Toronto.

36 Barbara Barrett to E.B., 15 July 1930, Earle Birney Papers, Thomas Fisher Rare Book Library, University of Toronto.

37 Barbara Barrett to E.B., 11 June 1930, Earle Birney Papers, Thomas Fisher Rare Book LIbrary, University of Toronto.

38 Barbara Barrett to E.B., 8 July 1930, Earle Birney Papers, Thomas Fisher Rare Book Library, University of Toronto.

39 Barbara Barrett to E.B., 3 July 1930, Earle Birney Papers, Thomas Fisher Rare Book Library, University of Toronto.

40 Barbara Barrett to E.B., 1 July 1930, Earle Birney Papers, Thomas Fisher Rare Book Library, University of Toronto.

41 Barbara Barrett to E.B., 22 July 1930, Earle Birney Papers, Thomas Fisher Rare Book Library, University of Toronto.

42 Barbara Barrett to E.B., 18 Aug. 1930, Earle Birney Papers, Thomas Fisher Rare Book Library, University of Toronto.

43 Barbara Barrett to E.B., 13 Apr. 1929, Earle Birney Papers, Thomas Fisher Rare Book Library, University of Toronto.

44 Barbara Barrett to E.B., 2 Sept. 1930, Earle Birney Papers, Thomas Fisher Rare Book Library, University of Toronto.

45 Barbara Barrett to E.B., 26 Oct. 1930, Earle Birney Papers, Thomas Fisher Rare Book Library, University of Toronto.

46 Hendrie Gartshore to E.B., 10 Nov. 1930, Earle Birney Papers, Thomas Fisher Rare Book Library, University of Toronto. I have rearranged the sentences in this quote.

Chapter 7: Deserted

1 Hattie R. Graham, "Description of a Man," Scrapbook No. 2, 30 Mar. 1931, Earle Birney Papers, Thomas Fisher Rare Book Library, University of Toronto.

2 Anonymous and undated essay, Scrapbook No. 2, Earle Birney Papers, Thomas Fisher Rare Book Library, University of Toronto.

3 Birney's course descriptions and other related materials, Earle Birney Papers, Thomas Fisher Rare Book Library, University of Toronto.

4 These are Gordon Saunders' thoughts from *Down the Long Table* (Toronto: McClelland & Stewart, 1955), p. 49. They are identical to Birney's own feelings about teaching as a "useful" profession.

5 G.G. Sedgewick to E.B., 1 Nov. 1930, Earle Birney Papers, Thomas Fisher Rare Book Library, University of Toronto.

6 E.B. as quoted by Sedgewick to E.B., 1 Nov. 1930, Earle Birney Papers, Thomas Fisher Rare Book Library, University of Toronto.

7 E.B. as quoted by Sedgewick to E.B., 1 Nov. 1930, Earle Birney Papers, Thomas Fisher Rare Book Library, University of Toronto.

8 G.G. Sedgewick to E.B., 12 Mar. 1930, Earle Birney Papers, Thomas Fisher Rare Book Library, University of Toronto.

9 Barbara Barrett to E.B., 23 Feb. 1931, Earle Birney Papers, Thomas Fisher Rare Book Library, University of Toronto.

10 E.B. to Ray B. West (an M.A. student at Utah at the time), 13 July 1959, Earle Birney Papers, Thomas Fisher Rare Book Library, University of Toronto.

11 E.B., *Down the Long Table*.

12 E.B., *Down the Long Table*, pp. 43-45.

13 See correspondence between E.B. and Herman Singer, Earle Birney Papers, Thomas Fisher Rare Book Library, University of Toronto.

14 E.B., *Down the Long Table*, p. 23.

15 E.B., *Down the Long Table*, p. 21.

16 E.B., *University Chronicle*, University of Utah, 15 Dec. 1931, pp. 1-2.

17 E.B., *Pen*, University of Utah, May 1932.

18 This estimate is based on a passage in *Down the Long Table* in which Gordon thinks at his last meeting with Anne in the late summer of 1932 (also definitely the date at which Birney and Catherine Fisk were discussing their situation): "Christ, *after a year*, to be caught in the last meeting!" (emphasis added)

19 E.B. to Herman Singer, 8 June 1945, Earle Birney Papers, Thomas Fisher Rare Book Library, University of Toronto.

20 Catherine Fisk to E.B., undated letter, Earle Birney Papers, Thomas Fisher Rare Book Library, University of Toronto.

21 E.B., *Down the Long Table*, p. 43.

22 E.B., *Down the Long Table*, p. 43.

23 E.B., *Down the Long Table*, pp. 18-19.

24 Catherine Fisk to E.B., Mon. night [n.d.], Earle Birney Papers, Thomas Fisher Rare Book Library, University of Toronto.

Chapter 8: Sylvan Dreams

1 Roy Daniells to E.B., 17 July 1933, University of British Columbia, Special Collections and University Archive Division, Roy Daniells Papers.

2 Sylvia Johnstone to Ken Johnstone, [n.d., probably July] 1933, Earle Birney Papers, Thomas Fisher Rare Book Library, University of Toronto.

3 Sylvia Johnstone to Ken Johnstone, [n.d., probably July] 1933, Earle Birney Papers, Thomas Fisher Rare Book Library, University of Toronto.

4 Jean Barman, *The West Beyond the West: A History of British Columbia* (Toronto: University of Toronto Press, 1991), p. 247.

5 Jean Barman, *The West Beyond the West*, p. 252.

6 Description by John Herd Thompson with Allen Seager, *Canada 1922-1939: Decades of Discord*, The Canadian Centenary Series (Toronto: McClelland & Stewart, 1985), p. 232.

7 Jean Barman, *The West Beyond the West*, p. 254.

8 Margaret A. Ormsby, "Work and Wages," *British Columbia: A History* (Toronto: Macmillan of Canada, 1958, 1964), pp. 437-463.

9 "A Remembrance of Sylvia Easton: January 15, 1914 - October 26, 1990," [synopsis of Sylvia Easton's life], pamphlet distributed at her funeral, 26 Oct. 1990. Copy given to E.C. by Esther Birney.

10 Sylvia Johnstone to E.B., 8 July 1933, Earle Birney Papers, Thomas Fisher Rare Book Library, University of Toronto.

11 E.B. to Martha Birney, 16 Sept 1932, Earle Birney Papers, Thomas Fisher Rare Book Library, University of Toronto.

12 "Deals Self 13 Hearts Has to Discard Them," [unidentified newspaper, possibly *The Varsity*], [n.d., holograph addition by E.B. "20 Feb.? 1933"], Scrapbook No. 2, Earle Birney Papers, Thomas Fisher Rare Book Library, University of Toronto.

13 E.B., *Spreading Time: Remarks on Canadian Writing and Writers*, Book I: 1904-1949 (Montreal: Véhicule Press, 1980), pp. 25-26.

14 See "Tumbledown Shack...Or Art Shrine," *The Telegram*, Toronto, 6 May 1961, p. 20. The shack itself was moved to the grounds of the McMichael Canadian Art Collection at Kleinburg, north of Toronto, to become a Tom Thomson museum.

15 E.B., *Spreading Time*, p. 25.

16 E.B., *Spreading Time*, p. 26.

17 E.B. *Spreading Time*, p. 26-27.

18 *The Spark*, single issue published Nov. 1932 by the Student League of Canada, Earle Birney Papers, Thomas Fisher Rare Book Library, University of Toronto.

19 E.B., *Down the Long Table* (Toronto: McClelland & Stewart, 1955), p. 137.

20 Paul Axelrod, *Making a Middle Class: Student Life in English Canada During the Thirties* (Montreal and Kingston: McGill-Queen's University Press, 1990), p. 135.

21 Axelrod, *Making a Middle Class*, p. 130. Ten per cent of Victoria College

students participated in the SCM movement in the mid-thirties.

22 I am indebted for this quote to Charles M. Levi, doctoral candidate in History at York University, to whom Sydney Hermant, who was a classmate of Ryerson's at Upper Canada College, made the following statement in an interview, 22 Oct. 1990: "I knew him well. As a matter of fact, I remember once seeing Stanley Ryerson on the street, and I'd go over and talk with him, and he'd say, 'You'd better not spend too much time with me, I'm under observation by the R.C.M.P. If you're not careful, they'll take your picture and they'll think you're one of us too.' Nobody was mad at anybody, you see?...fellows like Morris Wayman and Stanley Ryerson, they were just students like us, nobody was mad at anybody. Different world altogether." (Transcript of SAC Historical Project Interview re: 1928-35). Ryerson would later publish several Marxist-inspired books on history and current affairs.

23 See Dorothy Livesay, *A Winnipeg Childhood (Beginnings)* (Winnipeg: Peguis Publishers Ltd., 1973); *Right Hand, Left Hand: A True Life of the Thirties* (Erin: Press Porcépic, 1977); and *Journey With My Selves: A Memoir 1909-1963* (Vancouver: Douglas & McIntyre, 1991).

24 This department was a forerunner of the Faculty of Social Work.

25 Dorothy Livesay, "The Author of 'Turvey'," ms. typescript, Dorothy Livesay Collection, MSS 37 [1950], Box 100, Fd. 19, p. 1, Department of Archives and Special Collections, University of Manitoba Libraries, Winnipeg. See also Livesay, *Right Hand, Left Hand*, p. 73.

26 E.B., *Spreading Time*, p. 27.

27 E.H. Carr, *The Russian Revolution, From Lenin to Stalin: 1917–1929* (London: Macmillan, 1979), p. 74.

28 Carr, *The Russian Revolution.*

29 See Leon Trotsky, *The Age of Permanent Revolution* (New York: Dell Publishing, 1955), p. 314-19; and *Leon Trotsky on Literature and Art* ed. Paul N. Siegal (New York: Pathfinder Press, 1970), pp. 36, 42-49, 93. For Birney's later discussion of the influence of Trotsky's theories on his work, see E.B., "The Writer-Creator in Today's World," *Earle Birney* ed. Bruce Nesbitt (Toronto: McGraw-Hill Ryerson Ltd., 1974). I am indebted to Mithili Kadambari for this reference.

30 Axelrod, *Making a Middle Class*, p. 135.

31 E.B. to Leonard Leacock, 20 June 1926, Earle Birney Papers, Thomas Fisher Rare Book Library, University of Toronto.

32 E.B.'s comparison of the Collective Swimmer, the Bathers, and the Greyboys and the Island to Trotskyists, the bourgeoisie, the proletariat and the communist Utopia, respectively, which is the substance of Gordon Saunders' speech to the Social Problems Club of the University of Toronto, is taken from Leon Trotsky and can be found in Leon Trotsky, John Dewey and George Novack, *Their Morals and Ours* (N.Y.: Pathfinder Press, 1986).

33 Frank Underhill was in his mid-forties, had been writing for *The Canadian Forum* since 1929 and was currently chairman of its editorial board. His publications would include: *Social Planning for Canada* (1935); *In Search of Canadian Liberalism* (1960); *The Image of Confederation* (1964); and *Upper Canadian Politics in the 1850s* (1967).

34 Thompson with Seager, *Canada 1922-1939*, p. 232.

35 Sylvia Easton to John Ayre, interview, 6 March 1980, property of John Ayre, Guelph, Ont.

36 E.B., *Spreading Time*, p. 27.

37 E.B., *Spreading Time*, p. 27.

38 John Ayre, *Northrop Frye: A Biography* (Toronto: Random House, 1989), pp. 71-72.

39 Roy Daniells to E.B., [n.d., probably summer], 1933, University of British Columbia, Special Collections and University Archives Division, Roy Daniells Papers.

40 E.B. *Down the Long Table*, p. 100.

41 Sylvia Johnstone to E.B., [n.d., probably summer] 1933, Earle Birney Papers, Thomas Fisher Rare Book Library, University of Toronto.

42 Rosa Luxemburg (1871-1919) was a leader of the Polish and German Social Democratic parties before World War I and later led the revolutionary left within the German party and was a founding leader of the German Communist Party (KPD) *Spartacusbund*. She was arrested on orders from the Social Democratic government in January 1919 and murdered in Berlin.

43 E.B. and Daniells would have been aware of both Chaucer's and Shakespeare's versions of this story. Literary scholars at this time, such as C.S. Lewis, sympathized entirely with Troilus, who dies for the love of the woman who betrayed him.

44 See Henry Wadsworth Longfellow, "Hiawatha's Wedding-Feast," Section X, *Song of Hiawatha*.

45 Roy Daniells to E.B., summer 1933, Special Collections and University Archives Division, Roy Daniells Papers, University of British Columbia.

46 E.B. to Roy Daniells, 10 July 1933, Special Collections and University Archives Division, Roy Daniells Papers, University of British Columbia.

47 E.B. to Roy Daniells, 15 July 1933, Special Collections and University Archives Division, Roy Daniells Papers, University of British Columbia.

48 Ken Johnstone to E.B., 30 Aug. 1933, Earle Birney Papers, Thomas Fisher Rare Book Library, University of Toronto.

49 W.L. MacDonald had taught Birney freshman English Composition at UBC (in this class Birney was one of only two students to obtain First Class standing); second year English Literature; English Literature of the 18th Century; and Chaucer. In all these courses Birney distinguished himself. See W.L. MacDonald, letter of reference to Prof. R.P.

Utter, Chairman, Department of English, University of Utah, 25 Feb. 1926, Earle Birney Papers, Thomas Fisher Rare Book Library, University of Toronto.

50 E.B. to Ken Johnstone, [n.d.] July 1933, Earle Birney Papers, Thomas Fisher Rare Book Library, University of Toronto.

51 E.B. to Roy Daniells, 10 July 1933, Special Collections and University Archives Division, Roy Daniells Papers, University of British Columbia.

52 Thompson with Seager, *Canada 1922-1939*, p. 224. Tim Buck quoted in *Saturday Night*, 2 (Feb. 1929), p. 1. Section 98 of the Criminal Code addressed "Promoting Changes by Unlawful Means," and specifically targeted "any association…whose professed purpose…is to bring about any governmental, industrial or economic change in Canada by use of force, violence or physical injury to person or property," etc.

53 E.B. to Ken Johnstone, [n.d.] July 1933, Earle Birney Papers, Thomas Fisher Rare Book Library, University of Toronto.

54 Sidney Hook, *Towards the Understanding of Karl Marx, a Revolutionary Interpretation* (London: Gollancz, 1933).

55 E.B. to Roy Daniells, [n.d.] July 1933, Earle Birney Papers, Thomas Fisher Rare Book Library, University of Toronto.

56 Sylvia Johnstone to Ken Johnstone, [n.d.] July 1933, Earle Birney Papers, Thomas Fisher Rare Book Library, University of Toronto.

57 E.B. to Roy Daniells, Thurs. [n.d.] July 1933, Special Collections and University Archives Division, Roy Daniells Papers, University of British Columbia.

58 Sylvia Johnstone to Roy Daniells, 25 July 1933, Special Collections and University Archives Division, Roy Daniells Papers, University of British Columbia.

59 Sylvia Johnstone to Roy Daniells, 6 Aug 1933, Special Collections and University Archives Division, Roy Daniells Papers, University of British Columbia.

60 Sylvia Johnstone to Ken Johnstone, [n.d.] July 1933, Earle Birney Papers, Thomas Fisher Rare Book Library, University of Toronto.

61 Sylvia Johnstone to Ken Johnstone, [n.d.] July 1933, Earle Birney Papers, Thomas Fisher Rare Book Library, University of Toronto.

62 Sylvia Johnstone to Roy Daniells, 6 Aug. 1933, Special Collections and University Archives Division, Roy Daniells Papers, University of British Columbia.

63 E.B. to A.M. Stephen, 30 Sept. 1933, Earle Birney Papers, Thomas Fisher Rare Book Library, University of Toronto.

64 Sylvia Johnstone to Roy Daniells, [n.d.] summer 1933, Roy Daniells Papers, Special Collections Division, The University of British Columbia Library, Vancouver.

65 E.B. to Ken Johnstone, 24 Sept. 1933, Earle Birney Papers, Thomas Fisher Rare Book Library, University of Toronto.

66 Sylvia Johnstone to Ken Johnstone, [n.d.] July, 1933, Earle Birney Papers, Thomas Fisher Rare Book Library, University of Toronto.

67 E.B. to Roy Daniells, 28 Aug. 1933, Special Collections and University Archives Division, Roy Daniells Papers, University of British Columbia.

68 E.B. to G.G. Sedgewick, 3 Oct. 1933, Earle Birney Papers, Thomas Fisher Rare Book Library, University of Toronto.

69 Newsclip in E.B., Scrapbook No. 2, Earle Birney Papers, Thomas Fisher Rare Book Library, University of Toronto.

70 Esther Birney's account of Sylvia's description to her in 1982 or 1983 of these events; Esther Birney to E.C., interview, Jan. 1991, Vancouver.

Chapter 9: A Burning Issue

1 Circumstantial comments suggest that the following were among these six students, or that they would have gone on this mission had their parents not intervened: Paul Anderson, Marge Anderson [she probably had another surname as Anderson is her married name], Ed Herron and Alice Langworthy. See E.B. to Kenneth Rexroth, 24 Nov. 1941, Earle Birney Papers, Thomas Fisher Rare Book Library, University of Toronto, which mentions these names in connection with E.B.'s political activities at the University of Utah and includes the comment: "one of the originals was a dreamy little blonde, Alice Langworthy, with a real flair for writing and as full of complexes as a hound dog with fleas."

2 Details taken from numerous descriptions in Birney's correspondence at the time, in particular, a letter to A.C. Cooke, 21 Jan. 1934, Earle Birney Papers, Thomas Fisher Rare Book Library, University of Toronto.

3 Details taken from the Salt Lake City *Progressive Independent,* 22 Sept. 1933.

4 E.B. to Harry Cassidy, [n.d.] Dec. 1933, Earle Birney Papers, Thomas Fisher Rare Book Library, University of Toronto.

5 E.B. to A.C. Cooke, 21 Jan. 1934, Earle Birney Papers, Thomas Fisher Rare Book Library, University of Toronto.

6 For more details on Swabeck and other contacts of E.B.'s in the U.S. Trotskyist movement, see James Patrick Cannon (who was himself one of Birney's contacts), *The History of American Trotskyism from its Origins to the Founding of the Socialist Workers Party* (N.Y.: Pathfinder Press, 1972).

7 E.B. to Arne Swabeck, 26 Dec. 1933, Earle Birney Papers, Thomas Fisher Rare Book Library, University of Toronto.

8 E.B. to James P. Cannon, 16 Nov. 1933, Earle Birney Collection, Thomas Fisher Rare Book Library, University of Toronto.

9 Arne Swabeck to E.B., 1 Dec. 1933; and E.B. to Arne Swabeck, 6 Jan. 1934 ("By this time you will have received the application forms of

three of us here. Two more should be on the way any time now."); and E.B. to Malvina [unidentified—possibly an agent in either New York or Los Angeles assisting with arrangements for Dr. Lorenz's tour. See Viktoria Lorenz letters], 30 Jan. 1934 ("I am a CP member under another name and am devoting as much time as I can to the cause, mainly as agit-prop."), Earle Birney Papers, Thomas Fisher Rare Book Library, University of Toronto.

10 Harry Cassidy to E.B., [Nov.] 1933, Earle Birney Papers, Thomas Fisher Rare Book Library, University of Toronto.

11 E.B. to Harry Cassidy, [n.d.] Dec. 1933, Earle Birney Papers, Thomas Fisher Rare Book Library, University of Toronto.

12 Jack MacDonald to E.B., 10 Sept. 1933, Earle Birney Papers, Thomas Fisher Rare Book Library, University of Toronto.

13 James P. Cannon to E.B., 13 Nov. 1933, Earle Birney Papers, Thomas Fisher Rare Book Library, University of Toronto.

14 Theodore Draper to E.B., 13 Jan. 1934, Earle Birney Papers, Thomas Fisher Rare Book Library, University of Toronto.

15 E.B. to Theodore Draper, 16 Jan. 1934, Earle Birney Papers, Thomas Fisher Rare Book Library, University of Toronto.

16 E.B. to Viktoria Lorenz, 10 April 1934, Earle Birney Papers, Thomas Fisher Rare Book Library, University of Toronto.

17 E.B. to B.J. Field, [n.d., Sept.] 1933, Earle Birney Papers, Thomas Fisher Rare Book Library, University of Toronto.

18 S.L. Solon to E.B., 24 Oct. and 20 Nov. 1933, Earle Birney Papers, Thomas Fisher Rare Book Library, University of Toronto.

19 Viktoria Lorenz to E.B., 18 March 1934, Earle Birney Papers, Thomas Fisher Rare Book Library, University of Toronto.

20 E.B. to G.G. Sedgewick, 3 Oct. 1933, Earle Birney Papers, Thomas Fisher Rare Book Library, University of Toronto.

21 E.B. to Ken Johnstone, [n.d.] Nov. 1933, Earle Birney Papers, Thomas Fisher Rare Book Library, University of Toronto.

22 Esther Birney's account of Sylvia's recollections in 1982 or 1983, Esther Birney to E.C., interview, Jan. 1991, Vancouver.

23 E.B. to Ken Johnstone, [n.d., Nov.] 1933, Earle Birney Papers, Thomas Fisher Rare Book Library, University of Toronto.

24 E.B. to Martha Birney, [n.d., probably Nov./Dec. or Jan. 1934], Earle Birney Papers, Thomas Fisher Rare Book Library, University of Toronto.

25 E.B. to Ken Johnstone, 20 Nov. 1933, Earle Birney Papers, Thomas Fisher Rare Book Library, University of Toronto.

26 E.B. to Ken Johnstone, 10 April 1934, Earle Birney Papers, Thomas Fisher Rare Book Library, University of Toronto.

27 E.B. to Viktoria Lorenz, 7 March 1934, Earle Birney Papers, Thomas Fisher Rare Book Library, University of Toronto.

28 E.B. to Viktoria Lorenz, 7 Mar. 1934, Earle Birney Papers, Thomas Fisher Rare Book Library, University of Toronto.

29 The lecture was on Granville Hicks's new book, *The Great Tradition*, a study of the American social novel which Birney also reviewed over the radio, possibly simultaneously, on 2 April 1934. In a letter to Donald E. Calvert, an Instructor in English at the University of Toronto, 24 December 1933, Birney wrote: "Hicks, unfortunately, is a Stalinist dogmatist, but he may have produced a good book nevertheless."

30 E.B. to Viktoria Lorenz, 10 April 1934, Earle Birney Papers, Thomas Fisher Rare Book Library, University of Toronto.

31 E.B. to Viktoria Lorenz, 10 Apr. 1934, Earle Birney Papers, Thomas Fisher Rare Book Library, University of Toronto.

32 E.B. to Ken Johnstone, 23 April 1934, Earle Birney Papers, Thomas Fisher Rare Book Library, University of Toronto.

33 Arne Swabeck to E.B., 3 July 1934, Earle Birney Papers, Thomas Fisher Rare Book Library, University of Toronto.

34 Kenneth Rexroth to E.B., 3 Oct. 1941, Earle Birney Papers, Thomas Fisher Rare Book Library, University of Toronto. Rexroth had heard of Birney's impact on the community from Ed Herron, Myra Tanner and Marge Anderson, some of E.B.'s followers at the University of Utah.

35 Birney writes in *Spreading Time* (p. 28) that he was told in the fall of 1933 that the academic year 1933-34 would be his last, but this is not substantiated by his letters during that year, which imply that the question of his reappointment was not yet settled. And in his final report to the Royal Society after a year in England working on his thesis, he states: "Just a week before news of the fellowship reached me I had been offered a renewal of contract at a salary markedly more than the fellowship covered." Pelham Edgar Papers, Thomas Fisher Rare Book Library, University of Toronto, File 12:1, pp. 4-5.

36 *Spreading Time*, p. 28.

37 Ed Herron to E.B., 28 June and E.B. to Justin Stewart, 20 July 1934, Earle Birney Papers, Thomas Fisher Rare Book Library, University of Toronto.

38 The result of E.C.'s *Privacy Act* request to the Canadian Security Intelligence Service was that there was no personal information concerning E.B. in the Security Assessments Information Bank (SIS-PPU-005) or in the Canadian Security Intelligence Service Records (SIS-PPU-015). Access to the Canadian Security Intelligence Service Records (SIS-PPU-010) was refused "pursuant to sub-sections 16(1) and (2) of the *Privacy Act* since any personal information, if it existed in this bank, could reasonably be exempted by virtue of one or more of sections 19(1), 21, 22(1)(a), 22(1)(b), 25 and 26 of the *Act*." See D.L. Outhwaite, Access to Information and Privacy Coordinator, to E.C., 31 May 1993, property of E.C.

39 E.B. to Maurice Spector, 4 Aug. 1934, Earle Birney Papers, Thomas

Fisher Rare Book Library, University of Toronto.

Chapter 10: Ripe for England

1 E.B. to Martha Birney, 26 Sept. 1934, Earle Birney Papers, Thomas Fisher Rare Book Library, University of Toronto.

2 Pelham Edgar to E.B., 31 Oct. [1934], Earle Birney Papers, Thomas Fisher Rare Book Library, University of Toronto.

3 E.B. to Martha Birney, 11 Oct. 1934, Earle Birney Papers, Thomas Fisher Rare Book Library, University of Toronto.

4 Catherine Fisk to E.B., [n.d.] 1934, Earle Birney Papers, Thomas Fisher Rare Book Library, University of Toronto.

5 E.B. to Martha Birney, 11 Oct. 1934, Earle Birney Papers, Thomas Fisher Rare Book Library, University of Toronto.

6 E.B. to Martha Birney, 1 Dec. 1934, Earle Birney Papers, Thomas Fisher Rare Book Library, University of Toronto.

7 The Plenum ratified the policy of the French Trotskyists entering the Section Française de l'Internationale Ouvrière (the French Section of the Second International, which was the official name of the Socialist Party). See Pierre Franck, *The Fourth International: The Long March of the Trotskyists*, trans. Ruth Schein and intro. Brian Grogan (N.Y.: Ink Links, 1979), pp. 51-52.

8 John Archer to E.C., 17 Mar. 1993, property of E.C. See also John Archer, "Trotskyism in Britain: 1931-1937," Ph.D. thesis, degree awarded by the Council for National Academic Awards (CNAA), Polytechnic of Central London, 1979. This thesis can be obtained through Inter-library Loan from the British Library at Boston Spa in Yorkshire, England.

9 John Archer to E.C., 17 Mar. 1993, property of E.C.

10 The other three branches were: Clapham, South Norwood and Islington. See John Archer to E.C., 17 Mar. 1993, property of E.C.

11 John Archer to E.C., 17 Mar. 1993, property of E.C.

12 Archer to E.C., 17 Mar. 1993.

13 *Ibid.*

14 John Archer, "Trotskyism in Britain," p. 133.

15 John Archer, "Trotskyism in Britain," p. 140.

16 John Archer to E.C., interview, 4 May 1989, London, England.

17 Archer to E.C., interview, 4 May 1989.

18 Margaret Johns to E.C., interview, 3 May 1989, London, England.

19 According to John Archer, the British Trotskyists could not sell their publications publicly, but could only circulate bulletins among their groups. Though Birney no doubt expedited the purchase of materials from the States, these groups had already been "supplementing their own publications with those of Pioneer Publishers in New York, consisting mainly of translations in pamphlet form of Trotsky's writings

and of the 'Militant.'" (Archer, "Trotskyism in Britain," p. 137.)

20 Margaret Johns to E.C., interview, 3 May 1989, London, England.

21 E.B. to Don Calvert, 24 Dec. 1933, Earle Birney Papers, Thomas Fisher Rare Book Library, University of Toronto.

22 Letters to Martha Birney, 19, 20, 21, 22, 23, 25, 26 Aug., and 3, 4, [n.d.], 10, and 27 Sept. 1934, Earle Birney Papers, Thomas Fisher Rare Book Library, University of Toronto.

23 E.B. to Martha Birney, 19 Aug. 1934, Earle Birney Papers, Thomas Fisher Rare Book Library, University of Toronto.

24 E.B. to Martha Birney, 11 Oct. and 11 Nov. 1934, Earle Birney Papers, Thomas Fisher Rare Book Library, University of Toronto.

25 E.B. to Martha Birney, 11 Nov. 1934, Earle Birney Papers, Thomas Fisher Rare Book Library, University of Toronto.

26 E.B. to Martha Birney, 1 Dec. 1934, Earle Birney Papers, Thomas Fisher Rare Book Library, University of Toronto.

27 *Ibid.*

28 E.B. to Martha Birney, 11 Nov. 1934, Earle Birney Papers, Thomas Fisher Rare Book Library, University of Toronto. John Archer notes that this flexibility of class was also an aspect of C.L.R. James's character. At the same time that James was playing a leading role in opposing Marxist Group members entering the Labour Party in 1936, he was earning his living by writing about cricket in the *Manchester Guardian* and working on his *Black Jacobins* which was staged as a play in a West End theatre. See John Archer to E.C., 17 Mar. 1993, property of E.C.

29 John Archer to E.C., 17 Mar. 1993, property of E.C.

30 E.B. to Martha Birney, 24 Feb. and 5 Mar. 1935, Earle Birney Papers, Thomas Fisher Rare Book Library, University of Toronto.

31 Archer, "Trotskyism in Britain," p. 147.

32 A full account of the "Kirov affair" and Birney's suspension from the ILP is given by John Archer, who attended the meeting in Archer, "Trotskyism in Britain," p. 147-151.

33 "A Personal Statement by Comrades Kirby, Patterson and Robertson in Defence of Party Democracy," Open Letter to members of the ILP, 27 Jan., 1935, Earle Birney Papers, Thomas Fisher Rare Book Library, University of Toronto.

34 E.B. to Martha Birney, 27 Mar. 1935, Earle Birney Papers, Thomas Fisher Rare Book Library, University of Toronto.

35 John Archer to E.C., 17 Mar. 1993, property of E.C. See also Archer, "Trotskyism in Britain," p. 154.

36 Archer, "Trotskyism in Britain," p. 157.

37 John Archer to E.C., 17 Mar. 1993, property of E.C.

38 E.B. to Martha Birney, 27 Mar. 1935, Earle Birney Papers, Thomas Fisher Rare Book Library, University of Toronto.

39 John Archer to E.C., 17 Mar. 1993, property of E.C.

40 E.B. to Martha Birney, 10 May 1935, Earle Birney Papers, Thomas Fisher Rare Book Library, University of Toronto.

41 E.B. to Martha Birney, 10 May 1935, Earle Birney Papers, Thomas Fisher Rare Book Library, University of Toronto.

42 Esther Birney to E.C., interview, 5 Aug. 1989, Vancouver.

43 Esther Birney to E.C., interview, 23 Apr. 1993, Vancouver. According to Esther, "Unfortunately, [Israel] lacked sex appeal and I should never have married him or I should have waited till he had developed such appeal for me." Esther Birney, "About Me and the Jews," unpublished ms., 1975, p. 7, University of British Columbia, Special Collections and University Archives Division, Esther Birney Papers.

44 Esther Birney, "About Me and the Jews," unpublished ms., 1975, p. 1, University of British Columbia, Special Collections and University Archives Division, Esther Birney Papers.

45 Esther Birney to E.C., interview, 5 Aug. 1989, Vancouver. Esther wrote her account of this incident as an introduction to E.B.'s poem "Joe Harris, 1913-42" in *Canadian Review of Music and Other Arts*, vol. 2, no. 9 & 10 (Oct.-Nov. 1943), p. 30.

46 "It may be that during their intimacy, and perhaps near the end of it, Earle may have told Esther some such tale, with the embellishment of the literary artist's invention about the coin added. I don't recall the event… Naturally, I was aware of Esther's existence; in that circle, I could not fail to be. But, if my memory is still reliable after nearly sixty years, I was looking elsewhere at the time. It may be that Esther may have wanted me to 'take her out.' We were all young then and eager for life." John Archer to E.C., 17 Mar. 1993, property of E.C.

47 Esther Birney to E.C., interview, Jan. 1991, Vancouver.

48 Esther Birney to E.C., interview, Jan. 1991, Vancouver.

49 Esther Birney, "About Me and the Jews," unpublished ms., p. 6, Special Collections and University Archives Division, Esther Birney Papers, University of British Columbia.

50 E.B. to Martha Birney, 10 May 1935, Earle Birney Papers, Thomas Fisher Rare Book Library, University of Toronto.

51 Esther Birney to E.C., interview, Jan. 1991, Vancouver.

52 E.B. to Martha Birney, 19 May 1935, Earle Birney Papers, Thomas Fisher Rare Book Library, University of Toronto.

53 W.H. Clawson, as quoted by E.B. to Martha Birney, 1 July 1935, Earle Birney Papers, Thomas Fisher Rare Book Library, University of Toronto.

54 E.B. to Martha Birney, 11 June 1935, Earle Birney Papers, Thomas Fisher Rare Book Library, University of Toronto. The manuscript is not extant.

55 E.B. to Martha Birney, 19 Apr. 1935, Earle Birney Papers, Thomas Fisher Rare Book Library, University of Toronto.

56 E.B. to Martha Birney, 19 Apr. 1935, Earle Birney Papers, Thomas

Fisher Rare Book Library, University of Toronto.

57 E.B. to Martha Birney, 2 May 1935, Thomas Fisher Rare Book Library, University of Toronto.

58 E.B. to Martha Birney, 11 June 1935, Earle Birney Papers, Thomas Fisher Rare Book Library, University of Toronto.

59 Pelham Edgar, quoting E.B., to E.B., 16 March 1935, Earle Birney Papers, Thomas Fisher Rare Book Library, University of Toronto.

60 E.B. to Pelham Edgar, "Final Report to The Royal Society of Canada," 5 July 1935, Earle Birney Papers, Thomas Fisher Rare Book Library, University of Toronto.

61 Roy Daniells to E.B., 16 Oct. 1935, Earle Birney Papers, Thomas Fisher Rare Book Library, University of Toronto.

62 C.S. Lewis to E.B., 24 Oct. 1935, Earle Birney Papers, Thomas Fisher Rare Book Library, University of Toronto.

63 G.R. Owst to E.B., 17 Jan. 1936, Earle Birney Papers, Thomas Fisher Rare Book Library, University of Toronto.

64 Archer, "Trotskyism in Britain," p. 134.

65 Margaret Johns to E.C., interview 3 May 1989, London, England.

66 Esther Birney to E.C., 5 Aug. 1989, Vancouver. John Archer has no recollection of these activities (See John Archer to E.C., 17 Mar. 1993, property of E.C.).

67 Leon Trotsky, *Writings of Leon Trotsky (1935-1936)* (N.Y.: Pathfinder Press, 1977), p. 150.

68 John Archer, "Trotskyism in Britain," p. 179.

69 E.B. to Martha Birney, 19 Nov. 1935, Earle Birney papers, Thomas Fisher Rare Book Library, University of Toronto.

70 E.B., "Conversations With Trotsky," ed. Bruce Nesbitt, unpublished and unpaginated ms., fond Earle Birney, Literary Manuscript Collection, National Library of Canada.

71 E.B., "Conversations With Trotsky."

72 E. Robertson [E.B.], "General Outline Canadian Situation," [n.d., probably Nov. 1935], Earle Birney Papers, Thomas Fisher Rare Book Library, University of Toronto. The outline, mainly listing statistics, gives information on population, the nature of Canadian capitalism, British and American interests in Canada (exports and imports), a description of the Canadian political parties, a description of the proletariat (estimated between 800,000 and 1,000,000 unemployed), a list of trade union organizations, a list of Canada's main industries, a lengthy description of the position of farming and farmers and a province-by-province breakdown of voting regarding "left" parties.

73 E.B., "Conversations With Trotsky."

74 E.B., "Conversations With Trotsky."

75 E.B., "Conversations With Trotsky."

76 E.B., "Conversations With Trotsky."

77 Letter dated Nov. 1935, "Trotsky's Writings: 1935-36," p. 197, as cited and further documented and explained by John Archer, "Trotskyism in Britain," Footnote 17, p. 206.

78 E. Robertson [E.B.], "Conversations With Trotsky."

79 Leon Trotsky, *Writings of Leon Trotsky: Supplement (1934-40)* (N.Y.: Pathfinder Press, 1979), p. 917.

80 *Writings of Leon Trotsky (1935-36)* (N.Y.: Pathfinders Press, 1977), p. 365.

81 Leon Trotsky, *Writings of Leon Trotsky: Supplement (1934-40)* (N.Y.: Pathfinder Press, 1979), p. 639.

82 *Writings of Leon Trotsky (1935-36)*, p. 378.

83 Ken Johnstone, "Return to Berlin," magazine article, [n.d.], E.B., Scrapbook No. 2, Earle Birney Papers, Thomas Fisher Rare Book Library, University of Toronto.

84 E.B., "Conversations with Trotsky."

85 M.H. Halton, "Two Youths Assaulted 'Didn't Salute Flag' is Only Explanation," *Toronto Evening Star* (3 Dec. 1935).

86 E. Robertson [E.B.], "Incident in Berlin," *New Leader*, 13 Dec. 1935. Copy in The National Library of Canada, Ottawa.

Chapter 11: Levelling Out

1 Esther Birney to E.C., interview Jan. 1991, Vancouver.

2 Esther here refers to the theories of Eric Berne, who defined three main roles that people assume when interacting: the parent, the child and the adult. See Eric Berne, *Games People Play; the Psychology of Human Relationships* (N.Y.: Grove Press, 1964).

3 Esther Birney, "About Me and the Jews," unpublished ms., 1975, University of British Columbia, Special Collections and University Archives Division, Esther Birney Papers, p. 8.

4 Martha Birney to E.B., 5 May 1936, Earle Birney Papers, Thomas Fisher Rare Book Library, University of Toronto.

5 Neither of these letters is dated, but both are in the Earle Birney Papers, Thomas Fisher Rare Book Library, University of Toronto.

6 W.D. Bonner, University of Utah professor of Chemistry, to E.B., 9 June 1936, Earle Birney Papers, Thomas Fisher Rare Book Library, University of Toronto.

7 [A Professor], "The Department Calves," *The Canadian Forum* (July 1937), p. 134.

8 E.B., Ch. 1, "Irony in Chaucer," draft Ph.D. thesis, p. 55, Earle Birney Papers, Thomas Fisher Rare Book Library, University of Toronto.

9 E.B., "Irony: Working Definitions," Notes for Ph.D. Thesis, Earle Birney, Thomas Fisher Rare Book Library, University of Toronto.

10 George Grube to E.B., 5 Nov. 1936, Earle Birney Papers, Thomas

Fisher Rare Book Library, University of Toronto.

11 E.B. *Spreading Time: Remarks on Canadian Writing and Writers*, Book I: 1904-1949 (Montreal: Véhicule Press, 1980), p. 28.

12 E.B. to Frank Underhill, 29 Dec. 1937, Earle Birney Papers, Thomas Fisher Rare Book Library, University of Toronto.

13 E.B., "Proletarian Literature: Theory and Practice," *The Canadian Forum* (May 1937), pp. 58-60.

14 E.B., "The Moon-wist of Audrey Brown," *The Canadian Forum* (August 1937), pp. 176-77.

15 Luella Bruce Creighton, "The Winning Story—The Cornfield," *The Canadian Forum* (June 1937), pp. 97-99.

16 E.B., "Short Story Contest—A Report," *The Canadian Forum* (June 1937), pp. 98-99.

17 E.B., *Spreading Time*, p. 37.

18 Rufus [E.B.], "Another Month," *The Canadian Forum* (April 1937), p. 22.

19 Rufus [E.B.], "Crime Club," *The Canadian Forum* (April 1937), pp. 10-11.

20 See Douglas Francis, "The Threatened Dismissal of Frank H. Underhill from the University of Toronto—1939-1941," *CAUT Bulletin ACPU* (Dec. 1975), pp. 16-21. I am indebted to Prof. William H. Nelson for drawing this article to my attention.

21 Robertson [E.B.], "Thesis Adopted by Executive Committee of the Canadian Bolshevik-Leninists for a Fourth International: National Political Perspectives," unpublished ms., May 1938, Earle Birney Papers, Thomas Fisher Rare Book Library, University of Toronto.

22 E.B., "Conversations With Trotsky," ed. Bruce Nesbitt, unpublished and unpaginated ms., fond Earle Birney, Literary Manuscript Collection, National Library of Canada.

23 David Hayne to E.C., interview, 13 May 1991, Toronto.

24 E.B., "Essays—English 4G—1939," teaching materials, April 4, 1939, Earle Birney Papers, Thomas Fisher Rare Book Library, University of Toronto.

25 G.G. Sedgewick to E.B., 29 June 1938, Earle Birney Papers, Thomas Fisher Rare Book Library, University of Toronto.

26 E.B. to Mr. Fennell, Registrar of the University of Toronto, 26 Feb. 1937, Earle Birney Papers, Thomas Fisher Rare Book Library, University of Toronto.

27 E.B., "English Irony Before Chaucer," *The University of Toronto Quarterly*, 6 (July 1937), pp. 538-57.

28 E.B., "Is French Canada Going Fascist," [*New International*],(Oct. 1938), in "Conversations With Trotsky," ed. Bruce Nesbitt, unpublished and unpaginated ms., fond Earle Birney, Literary Manuscript Collection, National Library of Canada.

29 E.B. to Blanche Colton Williams, [n.d., probably 1-10 Feb.] 1939, Earle Birney Papers, Thomas Fisher Rare Book Library, University of Toronto.

30 E.B. to Paul Potts, 27 Feb. 1939, Earle Birney Papers, Thomas Fisher Rare Book Library, University of Toronto.

31 E.J. Pratt to E.B., [n.d., probably early March] 1939, Earle Birney Papers, Thomas Fisher Rare Book Library, University of Toronto.

32 Mary Fowler to E.C., interview, 23 Feb. 1992, Beaverton, Ontario.

33 E.B., "The Beginnings of Chaucer's Irony," *PMLA*, 54 (Sept. 1939), pp. 637-55.

34 Herbert Davis to E.B., 5 Jan. 1940, Earle Birney Papers, Thomas Fisher Rare Book Library, University of Toronto.

35 E.B. to A.H.R. Fairchild, 5 Feb. 1940, Earle Birney Papers, Thomas Fisher Rare Book Library, University of Toronto.

36 E.B. to Herbert Davis, 29 Feb. 1940, Earle Birney Papers, Thomas Fisher Rare Book Library, University of Toronto.

37 E.B. to Malcolm Wallace, [n.d.] Feb. 1940, Earle Birney Papers, Thomas Fisher Rare Book Library, University of Toronto.

38 E.B. to Malcolm Wallace, [n.d.] Feb. 1940, Earle Birney Papers, Thomas Fisher Rare Book Library, University of Toronto.

39 E.B., "Defense of Stalinism vs. Defence of World Revolution," "Conversations With Trotsky," ed. Bruce Nesbitt, unpublished and unpaginated ms., [n.d., probably Jan.] 1940, fond Earle Birney, Literary Manuscript Collection, National Library of Canada.

40 Roy Daniells to E.B., 22 Jan. 1940, Earle Birney Papers, Thomas Fisher Rare Book Library, University of Toronto.

41 E.B. to Roy Daniells, 29 Feb. 1940, Earle Birney Papers, Thomas Fisher Rare Book Library, University of Toronto.

Chapter 12: William and David

1 G.G. Sedgewick to E.B., 14 Feb. 1940, Earle Birney Papers, Thomas Fisher Rare Book Library, University of Toronto.

2 E.B. to G.G. Sedgewick, 6 Feb. 1940, Earle Birney Papers, Thomas Fisher Rare Book Library, University of Toronto.

3 E.B. to George Dillon, editor *Poetry* (Chicago), 24 Nov. 1941, Earle Birney Papers, Thomas Fisher Rare Book Library, University of Toronto.

4 *Ibid.*

5 E.B. to King Gordon, 31 July 1939, Earle Birney Papers, Thomas Fisher Rare Book Library, University of Toronto.

6 Poets Gordon Leclaire, Alan Creighton, Louis MacKay (pseudonym John Smalacombe), Margot Osborn, Ida de Bruyn, William Robbins, Patrick James and Sheila Campbell; and fiction writers W.J. Brown,

John Ravenshill (pseudonym), Matt Armstrong and Mary Lowry Ross.

7 E.B., "Canadian Poem of the Year," *The Canadian Forum* (Sept. 1940), p. 180. Reprinted in *Spreading Time: Remarks on Canadian Writing and Writers*, Book I: 1904-1949 (Montreal: Véhicule Press, 1980).

8 E.B. to E.J. Pratt, 3 Aug. 1940, Earle Birney Papers, Thomas Fisher Rare Book Library, University of Toronto.

9 E.J. Pratt, "Canadian Poetry—Past and Present," *The University of Toronto Quarterly*, vol. viii (1938-39), p. 2. In fact, Pratt actually wrote, "the mountains come to birth out of the foothills and the climbing lesser ranges."

10 E.B. to Lionel Stevenson, 5 Jan. 1941, Earle Birney Papers, Thomas Fisher Rare Book Library, University of Toronto.

11 E.B. to Bruce Macdonald, 3 Sept. 1940, Earle Birney Papers, Thomas Fisher Rare Book Library, University of Toronto. Birney wrote: "I have a knowledge of labor politics which could surely be of some use in the shaping of governmental propaganda."

12 E.B., "This Freedom: Freedom of Religion," unpublished ms., [Sept.] 1940, Earle Birney Papers, Thomas Fisher Rare Book Library, University of Toronto.

13 E.B. to John Grierson, 24 Nov. 1940, Earle Birney Papers, Thomas Fisher Rare Book Library, University of Toronto.

14 Dal Grauer to E.B., 3 Sept. 1940, Earle Birney Papers, Thomas Fisher Rare Book Library, University of Toronto. Grauer told Birney to stick to academics: "Why don't you get that book on Chaucer out and then pull strings to get into the UBC?"

15 E.B. to Lionel Haweis, 9 Jan. 1941, Earle Birney Papers, Thomas Fisher Rare Book Library, University of Toronto.

16 E.B. to Dal Grauer, 21 Oct. 1940, Earle Birney Papers, Thomas Fisher Rare Book Library, University of Toronto.

17 E.B. to Herman and Bernice Singer, 9 Jan. 1941, Earle Birney Papers, Thomas Fisher Rare Book Library, University of Toronto.

18 E.B. to J.K. Thomas, editor of *New World Illustrated*, Toronto, 9 Jan. 1941, Earle Birney Papers, Thomas Fisher Rare Book Library, University of Toronto.

19 E.J. Pratt to E.B., 7 Aug. 1940, Earle Birney Papers, Thomas Fisher Rare Book Library, University of Toronto.

20 E.B., "Eagle Island," *Canadian Poetry Magazine*, 5, No. 3 (Apr. 1941), 41-42.

21 E.B. to Herman Singer, 24 Nov. 1941, Earle Birney Papers, Thomas Fisher Rare Book Library, University of Toronto.

22 E.B. to Martha Birney, Sunday aft. [n.d., probably Jan.] 1940, Earle Birney Papers, Thomas Fisher Rare Book Library, University of Toronto.

23 Certificate #K37905 issued 31 Jan. 1940. See letter to William Birney, 5 Aug. 1975, Earle Birney Papers, Thomas Fisher Rare Book Library,

University of Toronto.

24 Esther Birney to E.C., interview, 5 Aug. 1989, Vancouver.

25 See letters between E.B. and Betty Carter McTavish, [n.d., probably Aug.-Sept.] to [n.d., probably mid-Oct.] 1940, Earle Birney Papers, Thomas Fisher Rare Book Library, University of Toronto.

26 E.B., "Decorated with Anarchisms," *Saturday Night*, 12 April 1941, p. 33. Birney was paid $13.00 for this article on student howlers.

27 G.G. Sedgewick to E.B., 20 April 1941, Earle Birney Papers, Thomas Fisher Rare Book Library, University of Toronto.

28 E.B. to Martha Birney, [n.d., soon after Easter] 1941, Earle Birney Papers, Thomas Fisher Rare Book Library, University of Toronto.

29 E.B. to the editor, *Story Magazine*, 23 April 1941, Earle Birney Papers, Thomas Fisher Rare Book Library, University of Toronto. Birney admitted in this letter that he had been influenced by Sherwood Anderson's story "I Want to Know Why."

30 E.B. to the editor, *Atlantic Monthly*, 24 April 1941, Earle Birney Papers, Thomas Fisher Rare Book Library, University of Toronto.

31 E.B. to James Laughlin, *New Directions*, 24 Apr. 1941, Earle Birney Papers, Thomas Fisher Rare Book Library, University of Toronto.

32 E.B., "Waterton Holiday," "Reverse on the Coast Range," "Smalltown Hotel," "Eagle Island," "Monody On A Century," "Dusk On English Bay," were all published in *Canadian Poetry Magazine* where E.J. Pratt was editor. "Grey-Rocks" was published in *The Canadian Forum*.

33 Birney had in mind "On Going to the Wars," which he published that year in *Dalhousie Review* under the pseudonym Richard Miles because it described a soldier going overseas and Birney feared that he would be given a desk job in the army that would keep him in Canada. See E.B. to editor, *Dalhousie Review*, 23 May 1941 and 30 Oct. 1941, Earle Birney Papers, Thomas Fisher Rare Book Library, University of Toronto.

34 E.B. to Frank Wilcox, 20 Nov. 1941, Earle Birney Papers, Thomas Fisher Rare Book Library, University of Toronto.

35 E.B. to Dorothy Livesay, 5 Sept. 1944, Dorothy Livesay Collection, MS. 37, Department of Archives and Special Collections, University of Manitoba Libraries.

36 E.B. to Kenneth Rexroth, 24 Nov. 1941, Earle Birney Papers, Thomas Fisher Rare Book Library, University of Toronto.

37 Kaye Lamb to E.C., interview 3 Sept. 1991, Vancouver. Kaye Lamb, after consulting with Sadie Boyles, who, in turn, consulted with Ted Morrison, retracted this connection between David Warden and E.B. Sadie Boyles apparently convinced him that E.B. had not known David Warden. The combination of Lamb's account to me (which he offered authoritatively without hesitation or qualification), the fact that E.B. clearly stated at the time that he had had Warden's accident in mind when he wrote "David" and the subsequent retraction through

discussion with Boyles and Morrison (who were both also on the staff of *The Ubyssey* and would therefore have worked directly with both Warden and E.B.) is perplexing.

38 Kaye Lamb to E.C., interview, 3 Sept. 1991, Vancouver.

39 R.E.S. [Ralph Stedmond], "To David Warden," *The Ubyssey*, vol. X, no. 1, 28 Sept. 1927, p. 2.

40 E.B. to Frank Wilcox, 30 May 1941, Earle Birney Papers, Thomas Fisher Rare Book Library, University of Toronto.

41 For a full treatment of E.B.'s use of this source see E.C., "Earle Birney's 'David' and the *Song of Roland:* A Source Study," *Inside the Poem: Essays and Poems in Honour of Donald Stephens*, ed. W.H. New (Toronto: Oxford University Press, 1992), pp. 60-69.

42 D.D.R. Owen, trans. *The Song of Roland* (Bury St. Edmunds: Boydell, 1990), p. 11.

43 C.M. Bowra, *Heroic Poetry* (London: Macmillan, 1952), p. 65.

44 E.B. to Hilton Moore, 29 Jan. 1940, Earle Birney Papers, Thomas Fisher Rare Book Library, University of Toronto.

45 Copy in E.B. Scrapbook No. 2, Earle Birney Papers, Thomas Fisher Rare Book Library, University of Toronto.

46 E.B., "The Two Worlds of Geoffrey Chaucer," *Manitoba Arts Review*, vol. 2, no. 4 (winter 1941), pp. 3-16.

47 E.B., "Is Chaucer's Irony a Modern Discovery?" *Journal of English and Germanic Philology*, vol. 41 (1942), pp. 303-19.

48 E.B. to Frank Wilcox, 20 Nov. 1941, Earle Birney Papers, Thomas Fisher Rare Book Library, University of Toronto.

49 E.B., "David," *The Canadian Forum* (Dec. 1941), pp. 274-76.

Chapter 13: Overseas

1 For a more thorough discussion of this letter and of the genesis of "David," see E.C., "The Influence of the Scottish Long Poem on Earle Birney's 'David,'" *British Journal of Canadian Studies*, vol. 7, no. 1 (1992), pp. 59-73; and E.C., "'David' and the *Song of Roland*: A Source Study," *Inside the Poem: Essays and Poems in Honour of Donald Stephens*, ed. W.H. New (Toronto: Oxford University Press, 1992), pp. 70-80.

2 James Wreford Watson to E.B., 17 July 1943, Earle Birney Papers, Thomas Fisher Rare Book Library, University of Toronto.

3 E.B. to Frank Wilcox, 30 May 1941, Earle Birney Papers, Thomas Fisher Rare Book Library, University of Toronto.

4 E.B. wrote to James Laughlin, editor of *New Directions*, 23 May 1941, "On Going to the Wars" is an attempt to express simply the emotional complex which has driven me into volunteering for active service.... Curiously, it is not the kind of poem I could get published in Canada (except in Pratt's *Canadian Poetry Magazine*, circulation 200) because it

stresses the Jewish question. I am Anglo-Saxon but my wife is a Jewish Englishwoman, and that is why the poem is written the way it is. Most Canadian editors are, I find, quietly anti-Semitic." (Earle Birney Papers, Thomas Fisher Rare Book Library, University of Toronto).

5 E.B., "On Going to the Wars," *Dalhousie Review*, vol. xxi, no. 3 (Oct. 1941).

6 E.B. to editor, *Dalhousie Review*, 30 Oct. 1941, Earle Birney Papers, Thomas Fisher Rare Book Library, University of Toronto.

7 Mavor Moore to E.B., 12 Jan. 1943, Earle Birney Papers, Thomas Fisher Rare Book Library, University of Toronto.

8 "Once Nazi Victim, He's in Army Now," *Toronto Daily Star*, 26 June 1943.

9 William Arthur Deacon, "Canadian Poet in Wartime," *The Globe and Mail*, 7 Nov. 1942.

10 Sir Charles G.D. Roberts to E.B., 7 Apr. 1943, Earle Birney Papers, Thomas Fisher Rare Book Library, University of Toronto.

11 E.B. to A.J.M. Smith, 10 Nov. 1941, Earle Birney Papers, Thomas Fisher Rare Book Library, University of Toronto.

12 E.B. to Sir Charles G.D. Roberts, 18 Apr. 1943, Earle Birney Papers, Thomas Fisher Rare Book Library, University of Toronto.

13 E.B. to A.J.M. Smith, 24 Nov. 1942, Earle Birney Papers, Thomas Fisher Rare Book Library, University of Toronto.

14 Patrick Anderson to E.B., 4 Apr. 1942, and John Sutherland, [n.d., probably July/Aug.] 1942, Earle Birney Papers, Thomas Fisher Rare Book Library, University of Toronto.

15 Scrapbook No. 2, 1943, Earle Birney Papers, Thomas Fisher Rare Book Library, University of Toronto.

16 G.G. Sedgewick, radio talk CBC Vancouver, 1 Feb. 1943.

17 E.J.R., "New Poems," *Hamilton Spectator*, newsclipping in Scrapbook no. 2, Earle Birney Papers, Thomas Fisher Rare Book Library, University of Toronto.

18 Dorothy Livesay to E.B., 2 Feb. 1943, Earle Birney Papers, Thomas Fisher Rare Book Library, University of Toronto.

19 Northrop Frye, "Canada and Its Poetry" [rev. of A.J.M. Smith ed., *The Book of Canadian Poetry*.] (Chicago: University of Chicago Press), p. 209.

20 Philip Child, ed., "Letters in Canada: 1942," *University of Toronto Quarterly* (Apr. 1943), pp. 305-307.

21 E.B. to the editor, *Dalhousie Review*, 23 May 1941, Earle Birney Papers, Thomas Fisher Rare Book Library, University of Toronto.

22 E.B. to G.H. Clarke, 12 July 1941, Earle Birney Papers, Thomas Fisher Rare Book Library, University of Toronto.

23 E.B. to Lionel Haweis, 27 Jan. 1942, Earle Birney Papers, Thomas Fisher Rare Book Library, University of Toronto. E.B. refers here to the

work on "primitive" religion and myth by James Frazer, *The Golden Bough.*

24 E.B. to Frank Flemington, 9 Aug. 1942, Earle Birney Papers, Thomas Fisher Rare Book Library, University of Toronto.

25 E.B. to Gerry Kerr, 20 Feb. 1943, Earle Birney Papers, Thomas Fisher Rare Book Library, University of Toronto.

26 E.B. to Lorne Pierce, 22 June 1942, Lorne Pierce Papers, Queen's University Archives.

27 E.B. to Lorne Pierce, 15 Feb. 1943, Lorne Pierce Papers, Queen's University Archives.

28 E.B. to Roy Daniells, 22 Nov. 1941, Earle Birney Papers, Thomas Fisher Rare Book Library, University of Toronto.

29 William Robbins to E.B., 8 Mar. 1943, Earle Birney Papers, Thomas Fisher Rare Book Library, University of Toronto.

30 E.B., "Advice to Anthologists: Some Rude Reflections on Canadian Verse," *The Canadian Forum* (Feb. 1942), pp. 338-40.

31 E.B. to Gerry Kerr, 20 Feb. 1943, Earle Birney Papers, Thomas Fisher Rare Book Library, University of Toronto and E.B. to Lorne Pierce, 15 Feb. 1943, Lorne Pierce Papers, Queen's University Archives.

32 Privy Council Office, "Report of an Expert Committee on the Work of Psychologists and Psychiatrists in the Service" (London: His Majesty's Stationery Office, 1947), p. 29. Further details of the work of personnel selection can be found in this publication.

33 For a full account of the psychological implications of military service see the essays in *Military Psychiatry: A Comparative Perspective,* Contributions in Military Studies, No. 57, ed. Richard A, Gabriel (N.Y.: Greenwood Press, 1986). "Combat reaction" is discussed by David Marlowe, "The Human Dimension of Battle and Combat Breakdown," p. 8.

34 For an interesting overview of the relationship between psychiatry and the military during World War II, see Eli Ginzberg, John L. Herma and Sol W. Ginsburg, *Psychiatry and Military Manpower Policy: A Reappraisal of the Experience in World War II,* Graduate School of Business, Columbia University, Human Resources Study (Columbia University, N.Y.: King's Crown Press, 1953).

35 Excerpt from "'A' card, A. Earle Birney, 2/Lt.," 1 Aug. 1942, Department of National Defence (Army), See Scrapbook No. 2, Earle Birney Papers, Thomas Fisher Rare Book Library, University of Toronto.

36 E.B. to G.G. Sedgewick, 3 Apr. 1942, Earle Birney Papers, Thomas Fisher Rare Book Library, University of Toronto.

37 E.B. to Hendrie Gartshore, 29 Dec. 1942, Earle Birney Papers, Thomas Fisher Rare Book Library, University of Toronto. I have moved one sentence in this quote for greater clarity.

38 Betty Carter McTavish to E.B., [n.d., probably Aug. or Sept.] 1940,

Earle Birney Papers, Thomas Fisher Rare Book Library, University of Toronto.

39 Corinne Hagon to E.B., 10 Sept. 1943, Earle Birney Papers, Thomas Fisher Rare Book Library, University of Toronto.

40 E.B. to Gerry Kerr, 20 Feb. 1943 and E.B. to Hendrie Gartshore, 29 Dec. 1942, Earle Birney Papers, Thomas Fisher Rare Book Library, University of Toronto.

41 Ernest Sirluck to E.C., interview, 16 Oct. 1990, Toronto.

42 E.B. to William McConnell, 25 Mar. 1943, Earle Birney Papers, Thomas Fisher Rare Book Library, University of Toronto.

43 E.B. to Dal Grauer, 21 Oct. 1940, Earle Birney Papers, Thomas Fisher Rare Book Library, University of Toronto.

44 E.B. to G.G. Sedgewick, 3 Apr. 1942, Earle Birney Papers, Thomas Fisher Rare Book Library, University of Toronto.

45 Dorothy Livesay to Esther and E.B., 20 Dec. 1942, Earle Birney Papers, Thomas Fisher Rare Book Library, University of Toronto.

46 E.B. to A.J.M. Smith, 20 Dec. 1942, Earle Birney Papers, Thomas Fisher Rare Book Library, University of Toronto.

47 E.B. to Aunt Kate Birney, 15 Feb. 1943, Earle Birney Papers, Thomas Fisher Rare Book Library, University of Toronto.

48 E.B. to Ralph Gustafson, 21 May 1942, Earle Birney Papers, Thomas Fisher Rare Book Library, University of Toronto.

49 "Case of H 19121, GNR 'Davis, W.D.' (pseud.)," 26 Jan. 1943, and "Supplementary Hospital Reports," 10 Feb. 1943, Earle Birney Papers, Thomas Fisher Rare Book Library, University of Toronto. The half-hour radio play, for the CBC Vancouver Drama series, was called "Court Martial," and aired 27 Sept. 1946.

50 See E.B. to Martha Birney, 11 June 1935, Earle Birney Papers, Thomas Fisher Rare Book Library, University of Toronto. This may not have been the same novel, since no draft of a novel exists.

51 A.J.M. Smith to E.B., 23 Jan. 1942, Earle Birney Papers, Thomas Fisher Rare Book Library, University of Toronto.

52 E.B. to A.J.M. Smith, 12 Feb. 1942, Earle Birney Papers, Thomas Fisher Rare Book Library, University of Toronto.

53 Ethel Wilson to E.B., 10 Apr. 1942, Earle Birney Papers, Thomas Fisher Rare Book Library, University of Toronto.

54 E.B. to Sinclair Ross, 5 Apr. 1942, and Sinclair Ross to E.B., 15 Apr. 1942, Earle Birney Papers, Thomas Fisher Rare Book Library, University of Toronto.

55 E.B. "Hospital Day," *Blitz*, vol. 1, no. 5 (Sept. 1942), pp. 6-7.

56 E.B. to J.K. Story, 9 June 1943, and J.K. Story to E.B., 7 July 1943, Earle Birney Papers, Thomas Fisher Rare Book Library, University of Toronto.

57 G.G. Sedgewick to E.B., 11 Mar. 1943, and G.G. Sedgewick to E.B., 7

Aug. 1943, Earle Birney Papers, Thomas Fisher Rare Book Library, University of Toronto.

58 E.B. to Martha Birney, 6 May 1944, Earle Birney Papers, Thomas Fisher Rare Book Library, University of Toronto.

59 E.B. to Gerry Kerr, 20 Feb. 1943, Earle Birney Papers, Thomas Fisher Rare Book Library, University of Toronto.

60 E.B., "Joe Harris: 1913–1942," *Saturday Night*, 22 May 1943 and "For Steve," *The Canadian Forum*, Aug. 1944.

61 G.G. Sedgewick, radio script CBC Vancouver, Earle Birney Papers, Thomas Fisher Rare Book Library, University of Toronto.

62 E.B., "Vancouver Lights," *David and Other Poems* (Toronto: Ryerson Press, 1942), pp. 36-37.

63 Although it is not clear which poet influenced which, Birney's poem was first published in the June 1942 issue of *Canadian Review of Music and Art*; Pratt's was first published in the December 1942 issue of *The Canadian Forum*. It was at Birney's home that Pratt first read "The Truant" aloud at a stag party given for Ernest Sirluck on the eve of his marriage, 15 Aug. 1942. See David Pitt, *E.J.Pratt*, vol. 2 (Toronto: U. of Toronto Press, 1984), p. 299. Also see Northrop Frye's diary entry for 15 August 1942: "Ned read us a new poem: general theme of the conflict of Orc & Urizen. Swell poem too." However, Pratt apparently entertained his friends by reading them bits of poems in progress during lunches, and, since the first draft of "The Truant" is dated early 1942, it may be that Birney heard or saw parts of the poem before he wrote his. I am indebted to Prof. Ernest Sirluck for drawing my attention to this entry, and for speculating on the matter with me. Ernest Sirluck recalls that Pratt read sections of "The Truant" long before it was published, and it is probable, though not certain, that Birney heard at least some of these readings. (Ernest Sirluck to E.C., interview 19 May 1993, Toronto.)

64 Major Earle Birney, "Canadian Poetry," Calling the West Indies, BBC radio, Dec. 1943, Earle Birney Papers, Thomas Fisher Rare Book Library, University of Toronto. Birney also read Archibald Lampman's "Winter Evening," A.J.M. Smith's "A Hyacinth for Edith," an excerpt about dock workers from Dorothy Livesay's "West Coast" and his own poem for Esther ("D-Day") "from the deceptive quiet of Southern England on D-Day."

65 E.J. Pratt, "Extravaganzas," "The Truant," *Collected Poems* (Toronto: MacMillan, 1944), pp. 309-14.

66 Dorothy Livesay to E.B., 2 Feb. 1943, Earle Birney Papers, Thomas Fisher Rare Book Library, University of Toronto.

67 E.B. to Dorothy Livesay, 14 Feb. 1943, Earle Birney Papers, Thomas Fisher Rare Book Library, University of Toronto.

68 I find the rhetroic in this poem overdone. E.B. pointed out his main techniques in a letter to Desmond Pacey, 20 Apr. 1957: "["Vancouver

Lights"] is half-rhymed throughout…mainly assonantal couplets (flowing, oceans) with some half-rhyme (winking, ink) and some consonance (Phoebus, Nubian)." Earle Birney Papers, Thomas Fisher Rare Book Library, University of Toronto.

69 E.B. wrote on 3 Apr. to G.G. Sedgewick that he was editing an Anglo-Saxon reader for use as a university text with W.H. Clawson, J.D. Robbins and Father L.K. Shook. On 21 May 1942, he wrote Sedgewick again to tell him that he was working on "a modified verson" of Anglo-Saxon poetry "with some attention to kennings." Earle Birney Papers, Thomas Fisher Rare Book Library, University of Toronto.

70 E.B. to Dorothy Livesay, 13 Dec. 1943, Dorothy Livesay Papers, Queen's University Archives. Birney wrote: "Agree that the CForum's verse bears little correlation to its politics but don't quite know what the answer is. Publish verse only when good verse of the appropriate ideology is obtained? That would practically eliminate it as a literary organ. Or change its politics? The change might easily be for the worse. I used to think I knew the answers in politics but I'm damned if I do now."

71 Elizabeth Drew, as reported by Geoffrey Brun to E.B., 13 Apr. 1960, Earle Birney Papers, Thomas Fisher Rare Book Library, University of Toronto.

72 James Wreford Watson to E.B., 3 Mar. 1942, Earle Birney Papers, Thomas Fisher Rare Book Library, University of Toronto.

73 Marcus Adeney to E.B., 10 July 1942, Earle Birney Papers, Thomas Fisher Rare Book Library, University of Toronto.

74 Marcus Adeney, "Poetry," *Canadian Review of Music and Art*, vol. 2, nos. 9-10 (Oct./Nov. 1942), p. 7.

Chapter 14: That Sea Called Time

1 Margaret Crosland to E.B., 27 Apr. 1944, Earle Birney Papers, Thomas Fisher Rare Book Library, University of Toronto.

2 Margaret Crosland to E.C., interview, 5 May 1989, Upper Hartfield, England.

3 Margaret Crosland to E.C., interview, 5 May 1989, Upper Hartfield, England.

4 E.B. to Betty Carter McTavish, 25 Nov. 1941, Earle Birney Papers, Thomas Fisher Rare Book Library, University of Toronto. Birney writes: "most of all I worry about you. Is that infection cleared up? I wanted to talk with you more about the whole mess, but there didn't seem to be an opportunity. It's hard to tell you how I feel about the whole matter—partly ashamed, partly very grateful to you. I admire you beyond words for your toughness and unselfishness—you're deceivingly fragile, darling, it's always a shock to realize again how much silent courage you have. I know I wouldn't have gone through

the same thing without roping the responsible party in on the grief. I feel a great debt to you, that can't be repaid by money, but certainly I owe you that too as a minimum. The hell of it is I can't properly repay you for what you had to spend without letting Esther in on it, as we have a kind of joint account. She would be the first to want me to repay, and would have no ill-feeling about it at all, but I have so far respected your wish that I shouldn't tell her. Don't you think I should?... I'll never be able to recompense you for the pain and the worry."

5 Gabrielle Baldwin to E.B., 8 Sept. 1943, Earle Birney Papers, Thomas Fisher Rare Book Library, University of Toronto.

6 Carlotta Makins to E.B., 24 Oct. 1943, Earle Birney Papers, Thomas Fisher Rare Book Library, University of Toronto.

7 Carlotta Makins to E.B., 27 Oct. 1943, Earle Birney Papers, Thomas Fisher Rare Book Library, University of Toronto.

8 E.B. to Carlotta Makins, 16 Jan. 1944, Earle Birney Papers, Thomas Fisher Rare Book Library, University of Toronto.

9 E.B. to Carlotta Makins, 24 Jan. 1944, Earle Birney Papers, Thomas Fisher Rare Book Library, University of Toronto.

10 E.B. to Carlotta Makins, 16 Jan. 1944, Earle Birney Papers, Thomas Fisher Rare Book Library, University of Toronto.

11 "The Levin Bolt," ms., Jan. 1944, Earle Birney Papers, Thomas Fisher Rare Book Library, University of Toronto. The story was eventually published in E.B., *Big Bird in the Bush: Selected Stories and Sketches* (Oakville, Ont.: Mosaic/Valley, 1978).

12 E.B. to Carlotta Makins, 24 Jan. 1944, Earle Birney Papers, Thomas Fisher Rare Book Library, University of Toronto.

13 E.B. to Martha Birney, 24 Jan. 1944, Earle Birney Papers, Thomas Fisher Rare Book Library, University of Toronto.

14 E.B. to Margaret Crosland, [n.d.] May 1944, Earle Birney Papers, Thomas Fisher Rare Book Library, University of Toronto.

15 E.B. to Martha Birney, 16 May 1944, Earle Birney Papers, Thomas Fisher Rare Book Library, University of Toronto.

16 E.B. to Martha Birney, 24 May 1944, Earle Birney Papers, Thomas Fisher Rare Book Library, University of Toronto.

17 E.B. to Martha Birney, 16 May 1944, Earle Birney Papers, Thomas Fisher Rare Book Library, University of Toronto. The poem Birney refers to is "The Barrel Organ."

18 Margaret Crosland to E.B., 20 May 1944, Earle Birney Papers, Thomas Fisher Rare Book Library, University of Toronto.

19 Margaret Crosland to E.C., interview, 5 May 1989, Upper Hartfield, England.

20 Margaret Crosland to E.B., [n.d., 20-31] May 1944, Earle Birney Papers, Thomas Fisher Rare Book Library, University of Toronto.

21 Margaret Crosland, "Sonnet #1," *Strange Tempe* (London: The Fortune

Press, 1945), p. 30.

22 James Wreford Watson, "War Generation," *Of Time and the Lover* (Toronto: McClelland & Stewart, 1950), p. 52.

23 This, and the other sonnets—14 in all—exchanged by Birney and Crosland can be found in the Earle Birney Papers, Thomas Fisher Rare Book Library, University of Toronto.

24 Margaret Crosland to E.C., 27 Sept. 1989, property of E.C.

25 E.B. to Margaret Crosland, 10 Oct. 1944, Earle Birney Papers, Thomas Fisher Rare Book Library, University of Toronto.

26 Margaret Crosland to E.B., [n.d., probably late Sept. or early Oct.] 1944, Earle Birney Papers, Thomas Fisher Rare Book Library, University of Toronto.

27 Birney was briefly stationed at the Flame-Throwing Unit at Storrington, Sussex, in April 1945.

28 Crosland, *Strange Tempe*, p. 31.

29 Crosland, *Strange Tempe*, p. 32.

30 E.B. to Carlotta Makins, 5 Sept. 1944, Earle Birney Papers, Thomas Fisher Rare Book Library, University of Toronto.

31 Margaret Crosland would become a well-known translator of works by Cocteau, Colette, Pavese, de Chirico and de Sade. Author of *Colette: the Difficulty of Loving* (1963), which won the Prix de Bourgogne; biographies of Edith Piaf, Jean Cocteau, Louise of Stolberg and Simone de Beavoir; and two works on women writers: *Women of Iron & Velvet* (1976) and *Beyond the Lighthouse* (1981); and editor for volumes of Cocteau, Pavese, de Sade and Raymond Radiguet.

32 E.B. to Ralph Gustafson, 3 July 1944, Earle Birney Papers, Thomas Fisher Rare Book Library, University of Toronto.

33 E.B. to Margaret Crosland, 4 Sept. 1944, Earle Birney Papers, Thomas Fisher Rare Book Library, University of Toronto.

34 Edith and George Hillyer to E.B., 30 Dec. 1944, Earle Birney Papers, Thomas Fisher Rare Book Library, University of Toronto. "I have had a letter from Esther…making me call you names probably unwarranted. She mentioned that you had taken Margaret for something more than a literary friend, in fact that she has shared your bed. You would therefore welcome an invitation from me for a week-end…to get out of the hotel atmosphere. You both looked so damned respectable that I didn't for the moment think you had gone that far."

35 Peggy Todd to E.B., [n.d.] Jan. 1944, Earle Birney Papers, Thomas Fisher Rare Book Library, University of Toronto.

36 James Wreford Watson to E.B., 22 June 1944, Earle Birney Papers, Thomas Fisher Rare Book Library, University of Toronto.

37 Esther Birney in a holograph note to E.B. on letter from Dorothy Henry, J.M. Dent & Sons to Esther Birney, 13 Mar. 1945, Earle Birney Papers, Thomas Fisher Rare Book Library, University of Toronto.

38 E.B. to Catharine Gartshore (Hendrie's mother), 15 July 1943, Earle Birney Papers, Thomas Fisher Rare Book Library, University of Toronto.

39 Esther Birney to E.B., 2 Sept. 1943, Earle Birney Papers, Thomas Fisher Rare Book Library, University of Toronto.

40 Esther Birney to E.B., 6 May 1944, Earle Birney Papers, Thomas Fisher Rare Book Library, University of Toronto.

41 Esther Birney to E.B., 6 Dec. 1943, Earle Birney Papers, Thomas Fisher Rare Book Library, University of Toronto. "I hope to use these for my memory when I get the leisure to write stories about Canadian soldiers."

42 E.B. to Esther Birney, 17 Mar. 1944, Earle Birney Papers, Thomas Fisher Rare Book Library, University of Toronto.

43 E.B. to Esther Birney, 13 Mar. 1944, Earle Birney Papers, Thomas Fisher Rare Book Library, University of Toronto.

44 E.B. to Esther Birney, 13 Apr. 1944, Earle Birney Papers, Thomas Fisher Rare Book Library, University of Toronto.

45 E.B. to Colonel Line, 5 Sept. 1944, Earle Birney Papers, Thomas Fisher Rare Book Library, University of Toronto.

46 Jeanne Belford to E.B., 12 Nov. 1944, Earle Birney Papers, Thomas Fisher Rare Book Library, University of Toronto.

47 E.B., *Spreading Time: Remarks on Canadian Writing and Writers*, Book I: 1904-1949 (Montreal: Véhicule Press, 1980), p. 67.

48 This scrap of wallpaper can be seen in the Earle Birney Papers, Thomas Fisher Rare Books Library, University of Toronto.

49 E.B. to Dorothy Livesay, 20 Dec. 1944, Dorothy Livesay Papers, Queen's University Archives, Kingston.

50 E.B. to Herman Singer, 8 June 1945, Earle Birney Papers, Thomas Fisher Rare Book Library, University of Toronto.

51 E.B. to Carlotta Makins, 5 Sept. 1944, Earle Birney Papers, Thomas Fisher Rare Book Library, University of Toronto.

52 E.B. to Colonel Line, 5 Apr. 1945, Earle Birney Papers, Thomas Fisher Rare Book Library, University of Toronto.

53 E.B. to Martha Birney, 5 June 1945, Earle Birney Papers, Thomas Fisher Rare Book Library, University of Toronto. I have reversed the sentences in this letter.

54 E.B., *Now Is Time* (Toronto: Ryerson Press, 1945), p. 38.

55 E.B. to Alan Crawley, 23 Mar. 1947, Earle Birney Papers, Thomas Fisher Rare Book Library, University of Toronto.

56 Margaret Crosland to E.C., interview, 5 May 1989, Hartfield, England.

57 E.B. *Now Is Time*, pp. 49-50.

58 Corinne Hagon to E.B., 20 May 1945, Earle Birney Papers, Thomas Fisher Rare Book Library, University of Toronto.

59 The book (*Poems,* 1935) is inscribed 10 May 1945, the date of their

first night together. Birney had the book autographed by George Barker in 1959.

60 E.B., "Mappemounde," *Strait of Anian: Selected Poems by Earle Birney* (Toronto: Ryerson Press, 1948), p. 4. The poem was written much earlier.

61 Margaret Crosland to E.C., interview, 5 May 1989.

62 E.B. to Herman Singer, 8 June 1945, Earle Birney Papers, Thomas Fisher Rare Book Library, University of Toronto.

63 Margaret Crosland to E.B., [n.d.] June 1944, Earle Birney Papers, Thomas Fisher Rare Book Library, University of Toronto.

64 Herman Singer to E.B., [n.d.] July 1944, Earle Birney Papers, Thomas Fisher Rare Book Library, University of Toronto.

Chapter 15: Where Is Here?

1 Esther Birney to E.C., interviews, 2 Feb. 1989 and 25 Nov. 1990, Vancouver, B.C.

2 Gabrielle Balwin to E.B., 20 Sept. 1945, Earle Birney Papers, Thomas Fisher Rare Book Library, University of Toronto.

3 *Unit of Five*, ed. Ronald Hambleton (Toronto: Ryerson Press, 1944). The five were: Ronald Hambleton, James Wreford (Watson), Louis Dudek, Raymond Souster and P.K. Page.

4 John Lehmann to E.B., 28 July 1943, Earle Birney Papers, Thomas Fisher Rare Book Library, University of Toronto.

5 Martin, Secker & Warburg to E.B., 20 Apr. 1945; E.B. to Ifor Evans, 16 May 1945; and E.B. to Margaret Crosland, 21 May 1945, Earle Birney Papers, Thomas Fisher Rare Book Library, University of Toronto.

6 Margaret Crosland to E.B., 23 Aug. 1945, Earle Birney Papers, Thomas Fisher Rare Book Library, University of Toronto.

7 E.B. holograph notation, Earle Birney Papers, Thomas Fisher Rare Book Library, University of Toronto.

8 Margaret Crosland to E.C., interview, 5 May 1989, Upper Hartfield, England.

9 Sinclair Ross to E.B., 26 July 1943, Earle Birney Papers, Thomas Fisher Rare Book Library, University of Toronto.

10 E.B. to Margaret Crosland, 25 Sept. 1944, Earle Birney Papers, Thomas Fisher Rare Book Library, University of Toronto.

11 E.B. to E.J. Pratt, 31 May 1945, Earle Birney Papers, Thomas Fisher Rare Book Library, University of Toronto.

12 Charles D. Abbott, Director, Lockwood Memorial Library, University of Buffalo, to E.B., 23 Jan. 1945, Earle Birney Papers, Thomas Fisher Rare Book Library, University of Toronto. The other four poems were: "Man is a Snow," "Winter Saturday," "Climbers" and "World War III."

13 *The War Poets*, ed. Oscar Williams (New York: John Day Co., 1946).

14 Henry W. Wells, "The Awakening in Canadian Poetry," *New England Quarterly* (March 1945), pp. 13-14, and E.B. to Henry W. Wells, 4 June 1945, Earle Birney Papers, Thomas Fisher Rare Book Library, University of Toronto.

15 James Wreford Watson to E.B., 22 June 1944, Earle Birney Papers, Thomas Fisher Rare Book Library, University of Toronto. "Esther said…that we needed you here in Canada as a critic perhaps even more than as a poet."

16 E.J. Pratt to E.B., 8 Aug. 1944, Earle Birney Papers, Thomas Fisher Rare Book Library, University of Toronto.

17 E.B. to Margaret Crosland, 2 Oct. 1944, Earle Birney Papers, Thomas Fisher Rare Book Library, University of Toronto.

18 Dorothy Livesay to E.B., [n.d.] 1944, Dorothy Livesay Papers, Queens University Archives.

19 James Wreford Watson to E.B., 17 July 1943, Earle Birney Papers, Thomas Fisher Rare Book Library, University of Toronto.

20 E.B., "Diary of a Day," unpublished ms., 2 Dec. 1944, Earle Birney Papers, Thomas Fisher Rare Book Library, University of Toronto.

21 "Een Dag," unpublished ms., 26 Jan. 1945, Earle Birney Papers, Thomas Fisher Rare Book Library, University of Toronto.

22 William Robbins to E.B., 12 Jan. 1944, Earle Birney Papers, Thomas Fisher Rare Book Library, University of Toronto.

23 E.B. to Charles Clay, CAA, 8 Dec. 1944, Earle Birney Papers, Thomas Fisher Rare Book Library, University of Toronto.

24 A.J.M. Smith to E.B., 5 Aug. 1944, Earle Birney Papers, Thomas Fisher Rare Book Library, University of Toronto.

25 William McConnell to E.B., 16 Jan. 1944 and [n.d., prob. April] 1944, Earle Birney papers, Thomas Fisher Rare Book Library, University of Toronto.

26 "A Proposal for A Federation of Canadian Writers," 29 July 1944, Copy in William McConnell Papers, Earle Birney Papers, Thomas Fisher Rare Book Library, University of Toronto; also E.B. to Irving Layton, 4 Oct. 1944, and E.B. to Dorothy Livesay, 5 Sept. 1944, Earle Birney Papers, Thomas Fisher Rare Book Library, University of Toronto.

27 E.J. Pratt to E.B., 8 Aug. 1944, Earle Birney Papers, Thomas Fisher Rare Book Library, University of Toronto.

28 E.B. to Dorothy Livesay, 14 Mar. 1945, Dorothy Livesay Papers, Queen's University Archives, Kingston.

29 E.K.Brown, *On Canadian Poetry* (Toronto: Ryerson Press, 1943).

30 Northrop Frye, "On Canadian Poetry," *The Canadian Forum* (Dec. 1943), pp. 207-210.

31 W.W.E. Ross, "On National Poetry," *The Canadian Forum* (July 1944), p. 88.

32 Ralph Gustafson, "Apropos of Canadian Poetry," [name of journal

unknown, clipping in Scrapbook No. 2], pp. 73-74, Earle Birney Papers, Thomas Fisher Rare Book Library, University of Toronto.

33 Dorothy Livesay, "This Canadian Poetry," *The Canadian Forum* (April 1944), pp. 20-21.

34 E.B., "Canadian Poetry," *Calling the West Indies*, Dec. 1944, typescript, Earle Birney Papers, Thomas Fisher Rare Book Library, University of Toronto.

35 E.B. to Dorothy Livesay, Easter Sunday 1944, Dorothy Livesay Papers, Queen's University Archives, Kingston.

36 *Ibid.*

37 E.B. to Dorothy Livesay, 25 June 1944, Dorothy Livesay Papers, Queen's University Archives, Kingston.

38 This is a notion picked up by Frye—or perhaps coincidentally selected by Frye from biblical sources—which he explains in the film *Images of Canada: Journey Without Arrival*, National Film Board of Canada, 1975.

39 Dorothy Livesay to E.B., 12 Mar. 1944, Earle Birney Papers, Thomas Fisher Rare Book Library, University of Toronto.

40 E.B. to A.S.P. Woodhouse, 14 May 1945, Earle Birney Papers, Thomas Fisher Rare Book Library, University of Toronto.

41 Dorothy Livesay to E.B., 25 Jan. 1945, Earle Birney Papers, Thomas Fisher Rare Book Library, University of Toronto.

42 A.S.P. Woodhouse to E.B., 13 Nov. 1945, Earle Birney Papers, Thomas Fisher Rare Book Library, University of Toronto.

43 Miriam Waddington to Esther Birney, [n.d., probably early Aug.] 1945, Earle Birney Papers, Thomas Fisher Rare Book Library, University of Toronto.

44 "Today," "Young Veterans," in E.B., *Now Is Time* (Toronto: Ryerson Press, 1948), p. 55.

45 Ruby Sharp to E.B., 10 Nov. 1945, 13 Jan. 1946 and 8 Mar. 1946, Earle Birney Papers, Thomas Fisher Rare Book Library, University of Toronto.

46 Esther Birney to E.C., interview, 2 Feb. 1989, Vancouver.

Chapter 16: Homeward, Bound

1 Pelham Edgar to E.B., 21 Apr. 1946, Earle Birney Papers, Thomas Fisher Rare Book Library, University of Toronto.

2 G.G. Sedgewick to E.B., 11 Oct. 1945, Earle Birney Papers, Thomas Fisher Rare Book Library, University of Toronto.

3 William Deacon to E.B., 14 Apr. 1946, Earle Birney Papers, Thomas Fisher Rare Book Library, University of Toronto.

4 E.B. to John Sutherland, 21 Aug. 1945, Earle Birney Papers, Thomas Fisher Rare Book Library, University of Toronto.

5 Helmut Blume (head of the German-language section of the CBC International Services under Birney), "Barbed Wire Broadcasts," *Radio Times*, Jan. 1946, Scrapbook No. 2, Earle Birney Papers, Thomas Fisher Rare Book Library, University of Toronto.

6 E.B. to Alan Crawley, 25 Nov. 1945, Earle Birney Papers, Thomas Fisher Rare Book Library, University of Toronto.

7 E.B. to Dorothy Livesay, 13 Jan. 1946, Dorothy Livesay Papers, Queen's University Archives.

8 Alan Crawley to E.B., 7 Feb. 1946, Earle Birney Papers, Thomas Fisher Rare Book Library, University of Toronto.

9 Anne Marriott to E.B., 1 May 1946, Earle Birney Papers, Thomas Fisher Rare Book Library, University of Toronto.

10 "Extract from Minutes of the third meeting," NAC on School Broadcasting, 15-16 March 1946, Royal York Hotel, Toronto, Earle Birney Papers, Thomas Fisher Rare Book Library, University of Toronto.

11 E.B., *Now Is Time* (Toronto: Ryerson Press, 1948).

12 E.B. to Martha Birney, 15 June 1945, Earle Birney Papers, Thomas Fisher Rare Book Library, University of Toronto.

13 S. Morgan-Powell, "Mr. Birney's New Poems," *Montreal Star*, 11 May 1946.

14 Review of *Now Is Time, Canadian Poetry Magazine*, Mar. 1946, pp. 35-36. The review was by Watson Kirkconnell, editor of the journal.

15 E.B. to Elsinore Haultain, Ryerson Press, 5 Feb. 1946, Lorne Pierce Papers, Queen's University Archives.

16 D.S.S. Mackenzie, "Professorial Poets," the *Montreal Gazette*, 2 Mar. 1946.

17 E.K. Brown, "Recent Poetry from Canada," *Poetry* (Chicago), vol. 169 (1946-47), pp. 349-53.

18 Wilhelmina Gordon, rev. of E.B.'s *Now Is Time, Echoes* (Toronto), (Spring 1946), p. 40.

19 Dorothy Livesay to E.B., 1 Jan. 1946, Earle Birney Papers, Thomas Fisher Rare Book Library, University of Toronto.

20 Roy Daniells to E.B., 7 Mar. 1946, Earle Birney Papers, Thomas Fisher Rare Book Library, University of Toronto.

21 E.J. Pratt to E.B., 14 Apr. 1946, Earle Birney Papers, Thomas Fisher Rare Book Library, University of Toronto.

22 Hugh MacLennan, *Two Solitudes* (Toronto: Collins, 1945).

23 Ross Munro, *Gauntlet to Overlord* (Toronto: Macmillan, 1945).

24 Evelyn M. Richardson, *We Keep a Light* (Toronto: Ryerson Press, 1945).

25 Gwethalyn Graham, *Earth and High Heaven* (Philadelphia: Lippincott, 1944).

26 Bill Deacon to E.B., 27 May 1946, Earle Birney Papers, Thomas Fisher Rare Book Library, University of Toronto: "The Governor-General will

speak 5-10 minutes presenting prizes. Winners will reply at 5-10 min-utes, except Birney, who needs 20 because he wants to say something special."

27 E.B., "Has Poetry a Future in Canada?" *The Manitoba Arts Review*, vol. v, no. 1 (Spring 1946), pp. 7-15.

28 E.B.'s speech, as reported in *The Globe and Mail*, 29 June 1946, p. 9. Copies held by the Earle Birney fonds, Special Collections Division, University of Calgary Library.

29 William Deacon to E.B., 22 May 1946, Earle Birney Papers, Thomas Fisher Rare Book Library, University of Toronto.

30 Birney's own account of his editorship of the *Canadian Poetry Magazine* is fully rendered in *Spreading Time*.

31 William Deacon to E.B., 29 May 1946, Earle Birney Papers, Thomas Fisher Rare Book Library, University of Toronto.

32 William Deacon to E.B., 8 July 1946, Earle Birney Papers, Thomas Fisher Rare Book Library, University of Toronto.

33 William Deacon to E.B., 29 Mar. 1946, Earle Birney Papers, Thomas Fisher Rare Book Library, University of Toronto.

34 William Deacon to E.B., 8 July 1946, E.J. Pratt Collection, Box 13, Victoria University Library (Toronto). "...a few members of the Association who are directly interested in poetry felt that your literary creed was too far to the left."

35 E.B. to Elizabeth Campbell, 13 Nov. 1946, Earle Birney Papers, Thomas Fisher Rare Book Library, University of Toronto.

36 E.B. to Charles Bruce, 10 Sept. 1946, Earle Birney Papers, Thomas Fisher Rare Book Library, University of Toronto.

37 E.B. to Anne Marriott, 10 Sept. 1946, Earle Birney Papers, Thomas Fisher Rare Book Library, University of Toronto.

38 E.B. to W.L. MacDonald, 27 Mar.1946, Earle Birney Papers, Thomas Fisher Rare Book Library, University of Toronto.

39 E.B. to Frank Wilcox, 17 Dec. 1946, Earle Birney Papers, Thomas Fisher Rare Book Library, University of Toronto.

40 G.G. Sedgewick to E.B., 18 Mar. 1946, Earle Birney Papers, Thomas Fisher Rare Book Library, University of Toronto.

41 Evelyn Caldwell to E.B., 4 Jan. 1941, Earle Birney Papers, Thomas Fisher Rare Book Library, University of Toronto.

Chapter 17: Day and Night

1 E.B. interviewed by Rex Frost, CFRB Radio, [n.d., probably 30] June 1946, Earle Birney Papers, Thomas Fisher Rare Book Library, University of Toronto.

2 E.B. to Elsinore Haultain, Ryerson Press, 21 Aug. 1946, and Elsinore Haultain to E.B., 10 Sept. 1946, Queen's University Archives, Kingston.

3 E.B. to Gabrielle Baldwin, 22 July 1946, Earle Birney Papers, Thomas Fisher Rare Book Library, University of Toronto.

Chapter 18: Strait Ahead

1 Basil Stuart-Stubbs to E.C., interview, 3 Sept. 1991, Vancouver.

2 E.B. to Carol Coates, 7 May 1947, Earle Birney Papers, Thomas Fisher Rare Book Library, University of Toronto.

3 E.J. Pratt to E.B., 30 Sept. 1947, Earle Birney Papers, Thomas Fisher Rare Book Library, University of Toronto.

4 *Little Anthology of Canadian Poets,* ed. Ralph Gustafson (Norfolk, Conn.: New Directions, 1942); *Anthology of Canadian Poetry,* ed. Ralph Gustafson (Harmondsworth, England: Penguin Books, 1942); *The Book of Canadian Poetry,* ed. A.J.M. Smith (Chicago: Chicago University Press, 1943); *The War Poets,* ed. Oscar Williams (New York: John Day Co., 1945); *Twentieth Century Verse,* ed. Ira Dilworth (Toronto: Clarke, Irwin, 1945); *Poems from New Writing,* ed. John Lehmann (London: J. Lehmann, 1946). And Birney was also included in two other anthologies in the process of being assembled: *A Pocketful of Canada,* ed. John Daniel Robins (Toronto: Collins, 1946) and *A Selection of English Poetry,* ed. W.L. MacDonald (Toronto: Dent, 1946).

5 E.B. to Dorothy Livesay, 13 Jan. 1946, Dorothy Livesay Papers, Queen's University Archives, Kingston.

6 Prof. John Bosher to E.C., interview, 17 May 1990, Toronto.

7 "UBC Offers New Course in Writing," *Vancouver Daily Province,* 19 Mar. 1947, p. 15.

8 Norman Klenman to E.C., 6 January 1992, FAX from Vancouver, property of E.C.

9 Robert Harlow to E.C., 26 Nov. 1990, property of E.C.

10 Ernest Sirluck responded to E.B. with a list of six institutions, 25 Feb. 1948, Earle Birney Papers, Thomas Fisher Rare Book Library, University of Toronto.

11 See his correspondence for 1948-49 with Bob Harlow, Earle Birney Papers, Thomas Fisher Rare Book Library, University of Toronto.

12 E.B. to John Gray, 1 Mar. 1948, Earle Birney Papers, Thomas Fisher Rare Book Library, University of Toronto.

13 E.B. to Lister Sinclair, 9 Nov. 1948, Earle Birney Papers, Thomas Fisher Rare Book Library, University of Toronto.

14 E.B. to Northrop Frye, 10 Mar. 1947, Earle Birney Papers, Thomas Fisher Rare Book Library, University of Toronto.

15 "*Canadian Poetry Magazine* 1946-48," *Spreading Time,* pp. 128-130; reprinted from *Canadian Author & Bookman* (Winter, 1963), pp. 4-5.

16 Louis St. Laurent to E.B., 2 June 1947, Earle Birney Papers, Thomas Fisher Rare Book Library, University of Toronto.

17 E.B. to Northrop Frye, 22 Aug. 1947, Earle Birney Papers, Thomas Fisher Rare Book Library, University of Toronto.

18 "Vincent Massey as Patron," *Canadian Poetry Magazine* (Dec. 1947), p. 9.

19 E.B., as quoted by Sheryl Salloum, *Malcolm Lowry: Vancouver Days* (Madeira Park, B.C.: Harbour Publishing Co., 1987), p. 66. Salloum provides a more lengthy description of their early interaction which was prompted by a letter to Lowry from Sybil Hutchinson, Birney's former U. of T. student and Lowry's acquaintance at McClelland & Stewart.

20 E.B. to Audrey Alexandra Brown, 23 July 1947, Earle Birney Papers, Thomas Fisher Rare Book Library, University of Toronto. I have reversed the phrases from this letter.

21 E.B. to Patrick Waddington, 24 Dec. 1947, Earle Birney Papers, Thomas Fisher Rare Book Library, University of Toronto.

22 E.B. to E.J. Pratt, 14 Jan. 1947, Earle Birney Papers, Thomas Fisher Rare Book Library, University of Toronto.

23 E.B. to Padraig O'Broin, 6 Oct. 1963, Earle Birney Papers, Thomas Fisher Rare Book Library, University of Toronto.

24 E.B. to Dr. Jacob Marcowitz, 19 Apr. 1948, Earle Birney Papers, Thomas Fisher Rare Book Library, University of Toronto.

25 E.B. to Roderick Haig-Brown, who had referred him for this assignment, 12 Apr. 1947, Earle Birney Papers, Thomas Fisher Rare Book Library, University of Toronto.

26 E.B. to James A. O'Connor, 30 Oct. 1947, Earle Birney Papers, Thomas Fisher Rare Book Library, University of Toronto.

27 E.B. to Mary Warr, 4 May 1947, Earle Birney Papers, Thomas Fisher Rare Book Library, University of Toronto.

28 See Birney's correspondence in the Earle Birney Papers, Thomas Fisher Rare Book Library, University of Toronto with: Ryerson Press, E.K. Brown, Roderick Haig-Brown, Margaret E. Ritchie, Malcolm Lowry, W.A. Deacon, A.J.M. Smith, the CAA, and newsclippings in Scrapbook No. 2.

29 E.B. to Sheryl Salloum, interview, [n.d.] 1985, Toronto. I am indebted to Sheryl Salloum for a copy of this interview.

30 Norman Newton to E.C., interview, 22 Nov. 1990, Vancouver.

31 *Ibid.*

32 E.B. to Elizabeth Campbell, 10 Nov. 1948, Earle Birney Papers, Thomas Fisher Rare Book Library, University of Toronto.

33 E.B. to Elizabeth Campbell, 10 Nov. 1948, Earle Birney Papers, Thomas Fisher Rare Book Library, University of Toronto.

34 E.B. to Dave Markson, 7 Mar. 1966, Earle Birney Papers, Thomas Fisher Rare Book Library, University of Toronto.

35 See E.B., "Malcolm Lowry's Search for the Perfect Poem," *Poetry*

Canada Review 7 (autumn 1985), p. 20. Lowry's poems in *Canadian Poetry Magazine* were: "Sestina in a Cantina," vol. 11, no. 1 (Sept. 1947); "Old Freighter in an Old Port," "Port Moody," "Indian Arm," vol. 11, no. 2 (Dec 1947). Other Canadian editors to publish Lowry's poems were: Alan Crawley, *Contemporary Verse*, 21 (summer 1947) and 24 (spring 1948); Ralph Gustafson, *The Penguin Book of Canadian Verse* (Great Britain: Unwin Brothers Ltd., 1958); and A.J.M. Smith, *The Book of Canadian Poetry* (Toronto: University of Chicago Press, 1948).

36 Ben Maartman to E.C., interview, 4 Aug. 1989, Vancouver.

37 Norman Newton to Sheryl Salloum, as published in Salloum, *Malcolm Lowry: Vancouver Days*, pp. 87-88.

38 E.B. to Malcolm Lowry, 1 Jan. 1948, Earle Birney Papers, Thomas Fisher Rare Book Library, University of Toronto.

39 Hilda Thomas to E.C., interview, 23 Nov. 1990, Vancouver.

40 See the front page of *The Vancouver Sun*, 13 April 1948.

41 Hilda Thomas to E.C., interview, 23 Nov. 1990, Vancouver.

42 E.J. Pratt to E.B., 26 Mar. 1948, Earle Birney Papers, Thomas Fisher Rare Book Library, University of Toronto.

43 Dorothy MacDonald, "Book Week Finds B.C. Home of Rising Authors," *The Vancouver Sun*, [late October] 1948, Earle Birney fonds, S.3 MS. Coll. 13, Special Collections Division, University of Calgary Library. The name of the newspaper and the date are inscribed with a query by Birney.

44 Lorne Pierce to E.B., 9 Jan. 1947, Earle Birney Papers, Thomas Fisher Rare Book Library, University of Toronto.

45 E.B. to A.J.M. Smith, 9 Jan. 1948, Earle Birney Papers, Thomas Fisher Rare Book Library, University of Toronto.

46 Lionel Monteith to E.B., 2 July 1947, Earle Birney Papers, Thomas Fisher Rare Book Library, University of Toronto.

47 E.B. to B.K. Sandwell, 19 May 1948, Earle Birney Papers, Thomas Fisher Rare Book Library, University of Toronto.

48 E.B. to Lorne Pierce, 20 Nov. 1947, Earle Birney Papers, Thomas Fisher Rare Book Library, University of Toronto.

49 Lionel Monteith to E.B., 27 Nov. 1948, Earle Birney Papers, Thomas Fisher Rare Book Library, University of Toronto.

50 E.J. Pratt to E.B., 30 Sept. 1947, Earle Birney Papers, Thomas Fisher Rare Book Library, University of Toronto.

51 Brewster Ghiselin to E.B., 6 Oct. 1947, Earle Birney Papers, Thomas Fisher Rare Book Library, University of Toronto.

52 T. Weiss to E.B., 15 Sept. 1947 and 16 Feb. 1948, Earle Birney Papers, Thomas Fisher Rare Book Library, University of Toronto.

53 G.G. Sedgewick to E.B., 30 Mar. 1948, Earle Birney Papers, Thomas Fisher Rare Book Library, University of Toronto.

54 Lionel Monteith to E.B., 24 Jan. 1948, Earle Birney Papers, Thomas Fisher Rare Book Library, University of Toronto. Monteith praised Lister Sinclair, who read on the same program as "the best male reader" he had ever heard.

55 Lionel Monteith, rev. of E.B.'s *Strait of Anian, Outposts* (Autumn 1948), pp. 18-20.

56 Gustav Davidson, rev. of E.B.'s *Strait of Anian, Saturday Review of Literature* (21 Aug. 1948), pp. 22-23.

57 Mary-Etta Macpherson, editor, to E.B., 5 Apr. 1948, Earle Birney Papers, Thomas Fisher Rare Book Library, University of Toronto.

58 "Canada: Case History," *Strait of Anian* (Toronto: Ryerson Press, 1948), p. 6.

59 E.B. to Floris McLaren, 16 Apr. 1948, Earle Birney Papers, Thomas Fisher Rare Book Library, University of Toronto.

60 E.B. to Lionel Monteith, 31 Jan. 1948, Earle Birney Papers, Thomas Fisher Rare Book Library, University of Toronto.

61 C. Day Lewis to E.B., 23 Feb. 1949, Earle Birney Papers, Thomas Fisher Rare Book Library, University of Toronto.

62 E.B. to Marion Saunders, 1 Mar. 1948, and Marion Saunders to E.B., 20 May 1948, Earle Birney Papers, Thomas Fisher Rare Book Library, University of Toronto.

63 E.B. to Philip Child, Bursar, 15 Nov. 1948, Earle Birney Papers, Thomas Fisher Rare Book Library, University of Toronto.

64 "CAA Program, 26th Annual Conference," 7-11 July 1947, Vancouver and Victoria, Earle Birney Papers, Thomas Fisher Rare Book Library, University of Toronto.

65 Lorne Pierce to E.B., 12 Nov. 1948, Earle Birney Papers, Thomas Fisher Rare Book Library, University of Toronto.

66 E.B. to Elizabeth Campbell, 31 Dec. 1948, Earle Birney Papers, Thomas Fisher Rare Book Library, University of Toronto.

67 E.B. to Gustav Davidson, *Saturday Review of Literature*, 22 Nov. 1948, Earle Birney Papers, Thomas Fisher Rare Book Library, University of Toronto.

68 George Woodcock, "Turning New Leaves," rev. of E.B.'s *Selected Poems* (Toronto: McClelland & Stewart, 1966), *The Canadian Forum* (Aug. 1966), p. 115. Woodcock wrote: "When I first visited Birney in his office in the Old Arts Building at the University of British Columbia, more years ago than I care to count, I was surprised to see that he kept his rejection slips and had plastered a wall with them; he seemed to treasure the wounds his poems had suffered as much as their victories."

69 E.B. to Norman Newton, 23 Nov. 1948, Earle Birney Papers, Thomas Fisher Rare Book Library, University of Toronto.

Chapter 19: East of Eden

1 E.B. to Marion Saunders, 29 Mar. 1949, Earle Birney Papers, Thomas Fisher Rare Book Library, University of Toronto.

2 E.B. to Ralph Allen, 19 Jan. 1949, Earle Birney Papers, Thomas Fisher Rare Book Library, University of Toronto.

3 E.B. "Chaucer's Irony," unpublished ms., p. 3, Earle Birney Papers, Thomas Fisher Rare Book Library, University of Toronto.

4 E.B. mentions this novel in a letter to Martha Birney, 11 June 1935, Earle Birney Papers, Thomas Fisher Rare Book Library, University of Toronto.

5 E.B. to Ralph Gustafson, 21 May 1942, Earle Birney Papers, Thomas Fisher Rare Book Library, University of Toronto.

6 E.B. to Elizabeth Campbell, [n.d., probably May] 1949, Earle Birney Papers, Thomas Fisher Rare Book Library, University of Toronto.

7 E.B. reports and letters to Esther, Sept.-Nov. 1944, Earle Birney Papers, Thomas Fisher Rare Book Library, University of Toronto.

8 E.B. reports and letters to Esther, Sept.-Nov. 1944, Earle Birney Papers, Thomas Fisher Rare Book Library, University of Toronto.

9 Gordon Aldridge to E.B., 16 Oct. 1945, Earle Birney Papers, Thomas Fisher Rare Book Library, University of Toronto.

10 Gordon Aldridge to E.B., 4 and 5 June 1945, Earle Birney Papers, Thomas Fisher Rare Book Library, University of Toronto.

11 E.B. to Gordon Aldridge, 26 Mar. 1943, Earle Birney Papers, Thomas Fisher Rare Book Library, University of Toronto.

12 Birney's extensive revisions, which are mainly geared to increasing the accuracy of the several dialects he reproduced and to making other details accurate, can be seen at the University of British Columbia, Special Collections and University Archives Division, Earle Birney Papers.

13 "The Strange Smile of Thomas Turvey," *Here & Now*, vol. II, no. 4 (June 1949), pp. 38-45 and "Turvey Engages a Paratrooper," *Saturday Night* (9 Aug. 1949), p. 21.

14 E.B. to Frank Flemington, assistant editor, 5 Aug. 1949, Earle Birney Papers, Thomas Fisher Rare Book Library, University of Toronto.

15 Jack McClelland to E.C., interview, 19 Dec. 1990, Toronto.

16 E.B. to Morley Callaghan, 4 May 1946, Earle Birney Papers, Thomas Fisher Rare Book Library, University of Toronto.

17 E.B. to Jim Scott, [n.d., probably May] 1949; to James Farrell, 3 May 1949; to Elizabeth Campbell, 7 May 1949; and to John Wardroper and Norman Klenman, 13 July 1949, Earle Birney Papers, Thomas Fisher Rare Book Library, University of Toronto.

18 "Mainly About Books," CBC radio, 9 and 16 March 1949.

19 E.B. to Donald K. Brossard, 3 Feb. 1950, Earle Birney Papers, Thomas Fisher Rare Book Library, University of Toronto.

20 E.B. to Alice Sinclair, 17 Nov. 1949, Earle Birney Papers, Thomas Fisher Rare Book Library, University of Toronto.

21 E. B. to Gordon Aldridge, 10 June 1965, and Gordon Aldridge to E.B., [n.d., probably mid-May] 1967, Earle Birney Papers, Thomas Fisher Rare Book Library, University of Toronto.

22 E.B. to Peggy Todd, 11 Dec. 1949, Earle Birney Papers, Thomas Fisher Rare Book Library, University of Toronto.

23 E.B. to Bill Deacon, 12 Oct. 1949, Earle Birney Papers, Thomas Fisher Rare Book Library, University of Toronto.

24 As reported by E.B. to Eric Nicol, 8 July 1949, Earle Birney Papers, Thomas Fisher Rare Book Library, University of Toronto.

25 E.B. to John Wardroper and Norman Klenman, 13 July 1949, Earle Birney Papers, Thomas Fisher Rare Book Library, University of Toronto.

26 E.B. to Ralph Gustafson, 17 Sept. 1949, Earle Birney Papers, Thomas Fisher Rare Book Library, University of Toronto.

27 E.B. to Mabel Hunter Mackenzie, 7 Apr. 1949, Earle Birney Papers, Thomas Fisher Rare Book Library, University of Toronto.

28 E.B. to E.J. Pratt, [n.d., summer] 1949, Earle Birney Papers, Thomas Fisher Rare Book Library, University of Toronto.

29 The script for this production was written by Birney's friend Rita Allen, and broadcast on "Wednesday Night," 4 Oct. 1950, 8:30–10:00 p.m. EST. Birney was very disappointed in the adaptation (which he believed had been cut from 2 hours to 1 1/2 hours) and complained to the director, exonerating Rita Allen, who in fact had been partly responsible for the flaws Birney noted. (See E.B. to Harry Boyle, 8 May 1950, and E.B. to E.L. Bushnell, 17 Oct. and 21 Nov. 1950, Earle Birney Papers, Thomas Fisher Rare Book Library, University of Toronto.)

30 E.B. to Peggy Todd, 11 Dec. 1949, Earle Birney Papers, Thomas Fisher Rare Book Library, University of Toronto.

31 These two reviews can be consulted at the Earle Birney fonds, 2.2.2.2 MS. Coll. 13, Special Collections Division, University of Calgary Library.

32 E.B. to Malcolm Lowry, [n.d., probably late 1948 or early 1949], University of British Columbia, Special Collections and University Archives Division, Earle Birney Papers.

33 Malcolm Lowry, ms. version in the Earle Birney fonds, 2.2.2.2. MS. Coll. 13, Special Collections Division, University of Calgary Library. The review first appeared in UBC's *Thunderbird*, Vol. 5, No. 1 (Dec. 1949), pp. 24-26. Reprinted in *Earle Birney*, ed. Bruce Nesbitt (Toronto: McGraw-Hill Ryerson Ltd., 1974), pp. 73-75.

34 Ethel Wilson to E.B., 18 Jan. 1958, and E.B. to Ethel Wilson, 20 Jan. 1958, Earle Birney Papers, Thomas Fisher Rare Book Library, University of Toronto. The review was published in Apr. 1950.

35 Hugh MacLennan to E.B., 29 Apr. 1950, Earle Birney Papers, Thomas Fisher Rare Book Library, University of Toronto.

36 Fred Haynes to E.B., [n.d.], Fan Letters file, Earle Birney Papers, Thomas Fisher Rare Book Library, University of Toronto.

37 E.B. to Gaby Baldwin, [n.d.] June 1953, Earle Birney Papers, Thomas Fisher Rare Book Library, University of Toronto.

38 Gordon Black to E.B., 3 Dec. 1949, Earle Birney Papers, Thomas Fisher Rare Book Library, University of Toronto.

39 Gaby Baldwin to E.B., 12 Nov. 1949, Earle Birney Papers, Thomas Fisher Rare Book Library, University of Toronto.

40 See newsclip of Col. Bjorn, Montreal, 5 Dec. 1952, with holograph inscription by E.B. giving this information. See also E.B. to Gabrielle Baldwin, [n.d.] June 1953, "I heard Bjorn was threatening to sue, though he didn't." Earle Birney Papers, Thomas Fisher Rare Book Library, University of Toronto.

41 See correspondence between Bill McConnell and E.B., 1949-50, Earle Birney Papers, Thomas Fisher Rare Book Library, University of Toronto.

42 E.B. to F.E.D. McDowell, 8 May 1950, Earle Birney Papers, Thomas Fisher Rare Book Library, University of Toronto.

43 E.B. to Lister Sinclair, [n.d. probably Sept.] 1949, Earle Birney Papers, Thomas Fisher Rare Book Library, University of Toronto.

44 Elizabeth Campbell, "Who Believes in Fairies?" and "Explanation," *Mail and Empire*, see Elizabeth Campbell's clippings book, property of Elizabeth Campbell, Toronto.

45 Elizabeth Campbell to E.B., 30 Jan. 1949, Earle Birney Papers, Thomas Fisher Rare Book Library, University of Toronto.

46 Elizabeth Campbell to E.B., 7 July 1946, Earle Birney Papers, Thomas Fisher Rare Book Library, University of Toronto.

47 Elizabeth Campbell as quoted by Anne Marriott to E.B., 1 May 1946, Earle Birney Papers, Thomas Fisher Rare Book Library, University of Toronto.

48 Elizabeth Campbell, "Ski Patrol," Part I, is in *The Best Poems of 1941*, selected by Thomas Moult (London: Harcourt Brace, 1941) and Part III, is in *Fact & Fancy* (Toronto: Ginn & Co.).

49 Campbell, "Ski Patrol," excerpts from Parts IV and VII.

50 E.B. to Elizabeth Campbell, 13 Sept. 1946, and Elizabeth Campbell to E.B., 25 Nov. 1946, Earle Birney Papers, Thomas Fisher Rare Book Library, University of Toronto.

51 E.B. to Elizabeth Campbell, 17 Dec. 1946, Earle Birney Papers, Thomas Fisher Rare Book Library, University of Toronto.

52 Elizabeth Campbell to E.B., 12 Feb 1948, Earle Birney Papers, Thomas Fisher Rare Book Library, University of Toronto.

53 E.B. to Elizabeth Campbell, 28 May 1948, Earle Birney Papers,

Thomas Fisher Rare Book Library, University of Toronto.

54 E.B. to Elizabeth Campbell, 3 July and 5 July 1948, Earle Birney Papers, Thomas Fisher Rare Book Library, University of Toronto.

55 Elizabeth Campbell to E.B., 9 July 1948, Earle Birney Papers, Thomas Fisher Rare Book Library, University of Toronto.

56 See first draft of *Turvey*, ms, Special Collections and University Archives Division, Earle Birney Papers, University of British Columbia.

57 Elizabeth Campbell to E.C., interview, 18 Dec. 1993, Toronto.

58 Clyde Gilmour, "Unclownish Humourist," *The Vancouver Sun* magazine supplement, 5 Aug. 1950, Earle Birney fonds, Special Collections Division, University of Calgary Library.

59 E.B. to Elizabeth Campbell, 3 Aug. 1948, Earle Birney Papers, Thomas Fisher Rare Book Library, University of Toronto.

60 E.B. to Elizabeth Campbell, 11 Aug. 1948, Earle Birney Papers, Thomas Fisher Rare Book Library, University of Toronto.

61 Elizabeth Campbell to E.B., 13 Jan. 1949, Earle Birney Papers, Thomas Fisher Rare Book Library, University of Toronto.

62 E.B., holograph inscription in Elizabeth Campbell's copy of *Now Is Time*.

63 E.B. to Elizabeth Campbell, 7 Aug. 1948, Earle Birney Papers, Thomas Fisher Rare Book Library, University of Toronto.

64 See E.B.'s correspondence with Hilda Browne and with Mabel Hunter Mackenzie.

65 E.B. to Margaret Reid Richardson, 8 Aug. 1948, Earle Birney Papers, Thomas Fisher Rare Book Library, University of Toronto.

66 E.B. to Elizabeth Campbell, [n.d., Sept.] 1948, Earle Birney Papers, Thomas Fisher Rare Book Library, University of Toronto.

67 E.B. to Elizabeth Campbell, 16 Sept. 1948, Earle Birney Papers, Thomas Fisher Rare Book Library, University of Toronto.

68 Elizabeth Campbell to E.B., 20 Sept. 1948, Earle Birney Papers, Thomas Fisher Rare Book Library, University of Toronto.

69 Elizabeth Campbell to E.B., 28 Dec. 1948, Earle Birney Papers, Thomas Fisher Rare Book Library, University of Toronto.

70 E.B. to Elizabeth Campbell, 31 Dec. 1948, Earle Birney Papers, Thomas Fisher Rare Book LIbrary, University of Toronto.

71 E.B. to Elizabeth Campbell, 7 Apr. 1949, Earle Birney Papers, Thomas Fisher Rare Book Library, University of Toronto.

72 *Ibid.*

73 E.B. to Lionel Monteith, 31 Jan. 1949, Earle Birney Papers, Thomas Fisher Rare Book Library, University of Toronto.

74 Margaret Crosland to E.B., 4 Apr. 1949, Earle Birney Papers, Thomas Fisher Rare Book Library, University of Toronto.

75 E.B. to Elizabeth Campbell, [n.d. probably May] 1949, Earle Birney Papers, Thomas Fisher Rare Book Library, University of Toronto.

76 See E.B.'s application to Royal Military College, 3 June 1949, Earle Birney Papers, Thomas Fisher Rare Book Library, University of Toronto.

77 Elizabeth Campbell to E.B., 26 May 1949, Earle Birney Papers, Thomas Fisher Rare Book Library, University of Toronto.

78 Elizabeth Campbell to E.B., [n.d. probably May] 1949, Earle Birney Papers, Thomas Fisher Rare Book Library, University of Toronto.

79 E.B. to Wreford Watson, 8 July 1949, Earle Birney Papers, Thomas Fisher Rare Book Library, University of Toronto.

80 See details of the presentation of the brief by Claude Bissell to Vincent Massey and other members of the commission in the *Report*, Earle Birney Papers, Thomas Fisher Rare Book Library, University of Toronto. Birney specifically prepared a report on *Contemporary Verse*, working closely with Bill McConnell, who acted as local secretary of the CWC, after conducting a wide correspondence discussing the matter with literary friends from the time he resigned from *CPM*.

81 Mary McAlpine to E.B., 6 July 1950, Earle Birney Papers, Thomas Fisher Rare Book Library, University of Toronto.

82 E.B. to Jay Macpherson, 18 May 1950, Earle Birney Papers, Thomas Fisher Rare Book Library, University of Toronto.

83 Desmond Pacey to E.B., 11 Apr. 1949, Earle Birney Papers, Thomas Fisher Rare Book Library, University of Toronto.

84 See the correspondence between E.B. and the Woodcocks which began in 1949.

85 Jean Coulthard Adams to E.B., 26 Mar. 1950, Earle Birney Papers, Thomas Fisher Rare Book Library, University of Toronto. This musical version of "Quebec May" won the 1950 CBC song contest.

86 E.B. to Elizabeth Campbell, 15 Aug. 1948, Earle Birney papers, Thomas Fisher Rare Book Library, University of Toronto.

87 Elizabeth Campbell to E.B., 24 Apr. 1949, Earle Birney Papers, Thomas Fisher Rare Book Library, University of Toronto.

88 Elizabeth Campbell to E.B., 16 Nov. 1949, Earle Birney Papers, Thomas Fisher Rare Book Library, University of Toronto.

89 For details, see John Malcolm Brinnin, *Dylan Thomas in America: An Intimate Journal* (Boston: Little, Brown & Co., 1955), pp. 69, 50-51; and Constantine Fitzgibbon, *The Life of Dylan Thomas* (London: J.M. Dent & Sons, Ltd., 1965), pp. 348-359.

90 E.B. to George Woodcock, 28 Apr. 1950, Earle Birney Papers, Thomas Fisher Rare Book Library, University of Toronto; see also Birney's 1985 account in Sheryl Salloum, *Malcolm Lowry: Vancouver Days* (Madeira Park, B.C.: Harbour Publishing Co.), pp. 76-77.

91 E.B. to H. Howard Norman, 17 May 1951, Earle Birney Papers, Thomas Fisher Rare Book Library, University of Toronto.

92 Dylan Thomas to Caitlin Thomas, 6 Apr. 1950, *The Life of Dylan Thomas, op. cit.*, p. 359.

93 Hilda Thomas to E.C., interview 23 Nov. 1990, Vancouver.

94 E.B. to Robert Weaver, 2 May 1949, and Robert Weaver to E.B., 8 June 1949, Earle Birney Papers, Thomas Fisher Rare Book Library, University of Toronto.

95 E.B. to Margaret Parker, 15 May 1950, Earle Birney Papers, Thomas Fisher Rare Book Library, University of Toronto.

96 See E.B.'s correspondence with Bob Allen, 1950, Earle Birney Papers, Thomas Fisher Rare Book Library, University of Toronto. Not all of these adaptations were used. "The Last Griffin" was broadcast on 29 Sept. 1950; "A Party at the Undertaker's" on 14 Nov. 1950; "The Queen of Spades" on 28 Nov. 1950; "The Case of Dr. Trifon" on 21 Nov. 1950; and "The Murder in the Pawnshop" on 7 Nov. 1950.

97 Bob Allen to E.B., 12 Aug. 1950, Earle Birney Papers, Thomas Fisher Rare Book Library, University of Toronto.

98 E.B. to L.A. MacKay, 19 Oct. 1950, Earle Birney Papers, Thomas Fisher Rare Book Library, University of Toronto.

99 E.B. to Helen Hughes, 25 Nov. 1950, Earle Birney Papers, Thomas Fisher Rare Book Library, University of Toronto.

100 E.B. to Howard Moorepark, 11 June 1950, Earle Birney Papers, Thomas Fisher Rare Book Library, University of Toronto. The Canadian issue of *Poetry Commonwealth* (no. 8, spring 1951) was delayed until Jan. 1952, due to the illness of Lionel Monteith, and would be the last issue of the magazine.

101 Michael Joseph Ltd. to E.B., 29 Dec. 1949, Earle Birney Papers, Thomas Fisher Rare Book Library, University of Toronto.

102 E.B. to Louis MacKay, 19 Oct. 1950, Earle Birney Papers, Thomas Fisher Rare Book Library, University of Toronto.

103 E.B. to Howard Moorepark, 5 July, and Howard Moorepark to E.B., [summer] 1950, Earle Birney Papers, Thomas Fisher Rare Book Library, University of Toronto.

104 For a list of these, see E.B. to Ken Johnstone, 12 Dec. 1950, Earle Birney Papers, Thomas Fisher Rare Book Library, University of Toronto.

105 E.B. to Louis MacKay, 19 Oct. 1950, Earle Birney Papers, Thomas Fisher Rare Book Library, University of Toronto.

106 Clyde Gilmour, "Unclownish Humorist," *The Vancouver Sun* magazine supplement, 5 Aug. 1950, p. 3.

Chapter 20: A Trial

1 E.B. to Ralph Gustafson, 7 Sept. 1952, Earle Birney Papers, Thomas Fisher Rare Book Library, University of Toronto.

2 E.B. "On Being a Canadian Author," Canadian Librarians Association, June 1952, Banff, ms., and *CLA Bulletin* vol. 9, no. 3 (Nov. 1952), pp. 77-79, Earle Birney Papers, Thomas Fisher Rare Book Library,

University of Toronto; and "Does Canada Owe Her Authors a Living?" *Mayfair*, 19 Feb. 1953, pp. 36, 73-75.

3 E.B. to Gwladys Downes, [n.d., probably 6] Oct. 1952, Earle Birney Papers, Thomas Fisher Rare Book Library, University of Toronto.

4 See E.B. to E.J. Pratt, 7 Sept. 1952, Earle Birney Papers, Thomas Fisher Rare Book Library, University of Toronto.

5 Dorothy Livesay to E.B., 15 Oct. 1952, Earle Birney Papers, Thomas Fisher Rare Book Library, University of Toronto.

6 E.B. to Dorothy Livesay, 17 Oct. 1952, Dorothy Livesay Papers, Queen's University Archives, Kingston.

7 E.B. to the Dept. of Veteran's Affairs, 3 Oct. 1952, Earle Birney Papers, Thomas Fisher Rare Book Library, University of Toronto.

8 E.B. to George Robertson, 23 Sept. 1951, Earle Birney Papers, Thomas Fisher Rare Book Library, University of Toronto.

9 E.B. to Lorne Pierce, 1 Dec. 1952, Earle Birney Papers, Thomas Fisher Rare Book Library, University of Toronto.

10 E.B. to Gwladys Downes, 18 Dec. 1952, Earle Birney Papers, Thomas Fisher Rare Book Library, University of Toronto.

11 E.B. to George and Inge Woodcock, 14 Jan. 1953, Earle Birney Papers, Thomas Fisher Rare Book Library, University of Toronto.

12 E.B. to Stanley Read, 4 June 1953, Earle Birney Papers, Thomas Fisher Rare Book Library, University of Toronto: "*Maclean's*...tried to get me to delete the homosexual level in the story...because they didn't see it...Others, friends, wanted me to delete the same elements for fear I might be thought to be homosexual myself. Since I'm not, and have never cared much about other people's mistaken ideas of me, I kept the story the way I wrote it."

13 E.B. to George and Inge Woodcock, 14 Jan. 1953, Earle Birney Papers, Thomas Fisher Rare Book Library, University of Toronto.

14 The publishing history of this poem was as follows: "This poem was rejected by several American editors, published obscurely in the Univ. of Kansas City Review, forgotten, reprinted in my *Strait of Anian*, quoted by Adams in the *NYTimes* Book section, picked up by Gustav Davidson for an American number of N.Z. *Arena*, submitted from there back to the U.S. for this Award—and finally announced by the U. of Pennsylvania Press as by 'Earle Birney, the New Zealand poet.' I got the feeling the judges were a little deflated when they discovered I was only a Canadian after all." And later he would comment: "The money was useful but it's always made me feel suspicious about that poem, which otherwise I would think to be one of my best." E.B. to John Sutherland, 7 Nov. 1951 and E.B. to David Bromige, 3 Aug. 1963, Earle Birney Papers, Thomas Fisher Rare Book Library, University of Toronto.

15 E.B. to Peter Stevens, 26 Apr. 1968, Earle Birney Papers, Thomas Fisher Rare Book Library, University of Toronto.

16 Lou Morris to E.B., 12 Nov. 1951, Earle Birney Papers, Thomas Fisher Rare Book Library, University of Toronto.

17 Mary-Etta Macpherson, "A Medal for a Poet," *Canadian Home Journal* (Aug. 1952).

18 "North Star West" was also published in *The Canadian Home Journal* (Nov. 1951), pp. 12-13, and Birney read the poem over the radio in Calgary on 13 June 1952.

19 E.B. to Lorne Pierce, 1 Dec. 1952, Earle Birney Papers, Thomas Fisher Rare Book Library, University of Toronto.

20 E.J. Pratt to E.B., 27 Aug. 1952, Earle Birney Papers, Thomas Fisher Rare Book Library, University of Toronto.

21 E.B. to E.J. Pratt, 7 Sept. 1952, Earle Birney Papers, Thomas Fisher Rare Book Library, University of Toronto.

22 E.B. to Brewster Ghiselin, 13 Feb. 1952, Earle Birney Papers, Thomas Fisher Rare Book Library, University of Toronto.

23 E.B. to Lorne Pierce, 10 Sept. 1951, Earle Birney Papers, Thomas Fisher Rare Book Library, University of Toronto.

24 See Birney's correspondence with Ryerson Press for 1950-51, Earle Birney Papers, Thomas Fisher Rare Book Library, University of Toronto.

25 E.B. to Norman Klenman, 12 Mar. 1952, and E.B. to Marianne de Bade, 19 Mar. 1953, Earle Birney Papers, Thomas Fisher Rare Book Library, University of Toronto.

26 E.B. to George Robertson, 15 Oct. 1952, Earle Birney Papers, Thomas Fisher Rare Book Library, University of Toronto.

27 Ethel Wilson to E.B., 14 May 1952, Earle Birney Papers, Thomas Fisher Rare Book Library, University of Toronto; reprinted in *Ethel Wilson: Stories, Essays, and Letters*, ed. David Stouck (Vancouver: UBC Press, 1987), pp. 68-70.

28 E.B. to Lorne Pierce, 18 Dec. 1951, Earle Birney Papers, Thomas Fisher Rare Book Library, University of Toronto.

29 E.B. to Myra Lazechko-Haas, 15 Oct. 1952, Earle Birney Papers, Thomas Fisher Rare Book Library, University of Toronto.

30 E.B. to Dorothy Livesay, 12 Oct. 1952, Dorothy Livesay Papers, Queen's University Archives, Kingston

31 "Poet Judges Modern Man," *The Globe and Mail*, 11 Oct. 1952, p. 23.

32 Lister Sinclair to E.B., 16 Oct. 1952, Earle Birney Papers, Thomas Fisher Rare Book Library, University of Toronto.

33 *Vancouver News-Herald* as quoted on the dustjacket of *Trial of a City.*

34 E.B. to Lister Sinclair, 20 Oct. 1952, Earle Birney Papers, Thomas Fisher Rare Book Library, University of Toronto.

35 E.B. to Desmond Pacey, 20 Apr. 1957, Earle Birney Papers, Thomas Fisher Rare Book Library, University of Toronto.

36 Hart Crane, "Hurricane," "Key West: An Island Sheaf," *The Complete*

Poems (N.Y.: Livenight Publishing, 1933). This poem in two-line verses is less shaped than "Takkakaw Falls," but it has the same intense rhythm and use of run-on lines and hyperbole for nature description; for example,

> Rescindeth flesh from bone
> To quivering whittlings thinned—
>
> Swept—whistling straw! Battered,
> Lord, e'en boulders now out-leap
>
> Rock sockets, levin-lathered!

37 E.B., description of "Bushed," [n.d.] 1953, Earle Birney Papers, Thomas Fisher Rare Book Library, University of Toronto.

38 See E.B.'s response to Alan Crawley, 17 May 1953, Earle Birney Papers, Thomas Fisher Rare Book Library, University of Toronto.

39 E.B. to Lorne Pierce, 13 Oct. 1952, Earle Birney Papers, Thomas Fisher Rare Book Library, University of Toronto.

40 Roy Daniells to E.B., 29 April 1952, Earle Birney Papers, Thomas Fisher Rare Book Library, University of Toronto.

41 See E.B. correspondence with Ryerson Press for 1951-52 and Doug Glasgow, "Birney Has Trouble," *The Vancouver Sun*, 15 July 1952, Earle Birney Papers, Thomas Fisher Rare Book Library, University of Toronto.

42 E.B. to editors, *The Canadian Forum*, [n.d., after 22 Dec.] 1953, Earle Birney Papers, Thomas Fisher Rare Book Library, University of Toronto.

43 E.B., "Feinting With Praised Damns," ms. [n.d.], Earle Birney Papers, Thomas Fisher Rare Book Library, University of Toronto.

44 E.B. to Lorne Pierce, [n.d., Dec.] 1952, Earle Birney Papers, Thomas Fisher Rare Book Library, University of Toronto.

45 E.B. to Robert Weaver, 27 Nov. 1951, Earle Birney Papers, Thomas Fisher Rare Book Library, University of Toronto.

46 E.B. to John Sutherland, 15 July 1951, Earle Birney Papers, Thomas Fisher Rare Book Library, University of Toronto.

47 E.B. to E.C., interview, 19 July 1982, Toronto.

48 E.B. to John Sutherland, 30 August 1951, Earle Birney Papers, Thomas Fisher Rare Book Library, University of Toronto.

49 See E.B. to Lorne Pierce, 8 Jan. 1953, Earle Birney Papers, Thomas Fisher Rare Book Library, University of Toronto.

50 E.B. to Lorne Pierce, 17 Dec. 1952, Earle Birney Papers, Thomas Fisher Rare Book Library, University of Toronto.

51 E.B. to George and Inge Woodcock, 14 Jan. 1953, Earle Birney Papers, Thomas Fisher Rare Book Library, University of Toronto.

52 E.B. to George Robertson, 14 Jan. 1953, Earle Birney Papers, Thomas Fisher Rare Book Library, University of Toronto.

53 E.B. to E.J. Pratt, 7 Sept. 1952, Earle Birney Papers, Thomas Fisher Rare Book Library, University of Toronto.

54 *Ibid.*

55 E.B. to George Robertson, 6 Oct. 1952, Earle Birney Papers, Thomas Fisher Rare Book Library, University of Toronto.

56 P.H. Newby, Talks Dept. BBC, to E.B., 25 Feb. 1953, Earle Birney Papers, Thomas Fisher Rare Book Library, University of Toronto.

57 E.B. to Archibald Day, 4 March 1953, Earle Birney Papers, Thomas Fisher Rare Book Library, University of Toronto.

58 E.B. to Rosemary Baxter, 6 Mar. 1953, property of Rosemary Baxter, Aberdeen.

59 E.B. to Norman Klenman, 13 May 1953 and E.B. to Archibald Day, 4 Mar. 1953, Earle Birney Papers, Thomas Fisher Rare Book Library, University of Toronto.

60 E.B. to Bill Birney, 10 Mar. 1953, Earle Birney Papers, Thomas Fisher Rare Book Library, University of Toronto.

61 E.B. to Gordon and Jan Baker, 9 Mar. 1953, Earle Birney Papers, Thomas Fisher Rare Book Library, University of Toronto.

62 Bruce Macdonald to E.B., 24 Mar. 1953, Earle Birney Papers, Thomas Fisher Rare Book Library, University of Toronto.

63 See correspondence between the Royal Society and E.B., 19 Feb. and 17 March 1953, Earle Birney Papers, Thomas Fisher Rare Book Library, University of Toronto.

64 E.B. to Pauline Ivey, 14 Nov. 1955, Earle Birney Papers, Thomas Fisher Rare Book Library, University of Toronto.

65 E.B. to Clyde Gilmour, 15 April 1953, Earle Birney Papers, Thomas Fisher Rare Book Library, University of Toronto.

66 E.B. to Brian Elliott, 14 Jan. 1954, Earle Birney Papers, Thomas Fisher Rare Book Library, University of Toronto. I have reversed the sentences.

67 E.B. to Norman Klenman, 13 May 1953, Earle Birney Papers, Thomas Fisher Rare Book Library, University of Toronto.

68 E.B. to George and Inge Woodcock, 17 May 1953, Earle Birney Papers, Thomas Fisher Rare Book Library, University of Toronto.

69 E.B. to Kaye Lamb, 18 Oct. 1952, Earle Birney Papers, Thomas Fisher Rare Book Library, University of Toronto.

70 E.B. to F.R. Scott, 23 Sept. 1952, Earle Birney Papers, Thomas Fisher Rare Book Library, University of Toronto.

71 E.B. to George Robertson, 15 Oct. 1953, Earle Birney Papers, Thomas Fisher Rare Book Library, University of Toronto.

72 E.B. to Brian Elliott, 12 Oct. 1954, Earle Birney Papers, Thomas Fisher Rare Book Library, University of Toronto.

73 E.B. to Herman Singer, 13 May and 15 Nov. 1953, Earle Birney Papers, Thomas Fisher Rare Book Library, University of Toronto.

74 Archibald Ogden to Howard Moorepark, 9 June 1953 and Austen Olney to Howard Moorepark, 9 Nov. 1953, Earle Birney Papers, Thomas Fisher Rare Book Library, University of Toronto.

75 E.B., "Story of Ron & Thelma & Z," Part I, unpublished ms., spring 1937, Earle Birney Papers, Thomas Fisher Rare Book Library, University of Toronto. I am indebted to Tom Reid, library technician, Thomas Fisher Rare Book Library, for drawing this to my attention.

76 E.B. to Ethel Wilson, 28 April 1953, Earle Birney Papers, Thomas Fisher Rare Book Library, University of Toronto.

77 E.B. to Gabrielle Baldwin, 13 May 1953, Earle Birney Papers, Thomas Fisher Rare Book Library, University of Toronto.

78 E.B. to Herman Singer, 13 May 1953, Earle Birney Papers, Thomas Fisher Rare Book Library, University of Toronto.

79 E.B. to Neal Harlow, Bill McConnell, Ernie Perrault, Herman Singer, 13 May 1953, Earle Birney Papers, Thomas Fisher Rare Book Library, University of Toronto.

80 E.B. to Floris McLaren, 17 May 1953, Earle Birney Papers, Thomas Fisher Rare Book Library, University of Toronto.

81 E.B. to Neal Harlow, 13 May 1953, Earle Birney Papers, Thomas Fisher Rare Book Library, University of Toronto.

82 E.B. to Jack and Doris Shadbolt, 17 May 1953, Earle Birney Papers, Thomas Fisher Rare Book Library, University of Toronto.

83 E.B. to Brian Elliott, 14 Jan. 1954, Earle Birney Papers, Thomas Fisher Rare Book Library, University of Toronto.

84 E.B. to George Robertson, 4 June 1953 and E.B. to the Duffs, 5 June 1953 and E.B. to Stan Read, 4 June 1953, Earle Birney Papers, Thomas Fisher Rare Book Library, University of Toronto.

85 E.B. to Dave Marsh, 3 June 1953, Earle Birney Papers, Thomas Fisher Rare Book Library, University of Toronto.

86 E.B. to Brian Elliott, 14 Jan. 1954, Earle Birney Papers, Thomas Fisher Rare Book Library, University of Toronto.

87 E.B. to Gabrielle Baldwin, [n.d.] June 1953, Earle Birney Papers, Thomas Fisher Rare Book Library, University of Toronto.

88 Lois Heiger to E.C., interview, 3 May 1989, London, England.

89 E.B. to Herman Singer, 15 Nov. 1953, Earle Birney Papers, Thomas Fisher Rare Book Library, University of Toronto.

90 E.B. to Robert Weaver, 23 June 1953, Earle Birney Papers, Thomas Fisher Rare Book Library, University of Toronto.

91 See correspondence between E.B. and Gwyn Kinsey, editor, *Saturday Night* for 1953, Earle Birney Papers, Thomas Fisher Rare Book Library, University of Toronto.

92 E.B. to Bruce Macdonald, 14 Jan. 1954, Earle Birney Papers, Thomas Fisher Rare Book Library, University of Toronto.

93 E.B. to Stanley Read, 4 June 1953, Earle Birney Papers, Thomas Fisher

Rare Book Library, University of Toronto.

94 E.B. to George Robertson, 13 Nov. 1953, Earle Birney Papers, Thomas Fisher Rare Book Library, University of Toronto.

95 E.B. to Ralph Gustafson, 31 Jan. 1953, Earle Birney Papers, Thomas Fisher Rare Book Library, University of Toronto.

96 Margaret Stobie, "Critically Speaking," CBC radio, 27 Dec. 1953, Earle Birney fonds, MS Coll. 13, 4.1.9, Special Collections Division, University of Calgary Library.

97 E.B. to Eugenie Perry, 15 Mar. 1955, and E.B. correspondence with Desmond Pacey and Claude Bissell, 1954-56, Earle Birney Papers, Thomas Fisher Rare Book Library, University of Toronto.

98 W.A. Deacon, quotes in review of *Canadian Poetry in English*, chosen by Bliss Carman, Lorne Pierce and V.B. Rhodenizer, *The Globe and Mail*, 18 Sept. 1954, p. 26.

99 E.B. to Son Excellence, M. l'Ambassadeur Dr. Jean Dese, 22 Oct. 1953, Earle Birney Papers, Thomas Fisher Rare Book Library, University of Toronto.

100 Robert Weaver to E.B., 3 Dec. 1952 Earle Birney Papers, Thomas Fisher Rare Book Library, University of Toronto.

101 Ethel Wilson to E.B., 10 April 1953, Earle Birney Papers, Thomas Fisher Rare Book Library, University of Toronto.

102 E.B. to Rosemary Baxter, 29 Sept. 1953, property of Rosemary Baxter, Aberdeen, and Marianne de Bade to E.B., 30 Jan. 1953, Earle Birney Papers, Thomas Fisher Rare Book Library, University of Toronto.

103 E.B. to Herman Singer, 18 Jan. 1954, Earle Birney Papers, Thomas Fisher Rare Book Library, University of Toronto.

104 E.B. to T.S. Eliot, 17 Nov. and T.S. Eliot to E.B., 25 Nov. 1953, Earle Birney Papers, Thomas Fisher Rare Book Library, University of Toronto.

105 As reported by Michael Ames, "Disguised Tea Strainer, No Beard," *The Ubyssey*, 14 Jan. 1954, Earle Birney fonds, Special Collections Division, University of Calgary Library.

106 E.B. to Brian Elliott, 14 Jan. 1954, Earle Birney Papers, Thomas Fisher Rare Book Library, University of Toronto.

107 E.B. to George Robertson, 13 Nov. 1953, Earle Birney Papers, Thomas Fisher Rare Book Library, University of Toronto.

108 E.B. to Jack and Doris Shadbolt, 17 May 1953, Earle Birney Papers, Thomas Fisher Rare Book Library, University of Toronto.

109 E.B. to Brian Elliott, 14 Jan. 1954, Earle Birney Papers, Thomas Fisher Rare Book Library, University of Toronto.

110 E.B. to the Marshes, 3 June 1953, Earle Birney Papers, Thomas Fisher Rare Book Library, University of Toronto.

111 E.B. to Gwyn Kinsey, 29 Oct. 1953, Earle Birney Papers, Thomas Fisher Rare Book Library, University of Toronto.

Chapter 21: In Flight

1 "Mexico in One Jump," *Saturday Night*, 20 Aug. 1955, pp. 27–28; "Canada's Art Colony in Mexico," *Saturday Night*, 15 Oct. 1955, pp. 9–10; "Mexico without Acapulco," *Saturday Night*, 12 Nov. 1955, pp. 43–44.

2 *Time* magazine, 9 Sept. 1957.

3 Reva Brooks to E.C., interviews, 5 and 6 June 1991, San Miguel de Allende, Mexico.

4 Leonard Brooks to E.C., interview, 5 June 1991, San Miguel de Allende, Mexico.

5 E.B. to Bill Hagon, 17 Jan. 1954, Earle Birney Papers, Thomas Fisher Rare Book Library, University of Toronto.

6 Esther Birney to Miriam Waddington, 6 May 1955, National Archives of Canada, Miriam Waddington Papers, MG 31, D 54, vol. 30. The sentences from this letter have been rearranged.

7 E.B. to Pat and John Wardroper, Easter Friday 1954 and to Bruce Macdonald, 14 Jan. 1954, Earle Birney Papers, Thomas Fisher Rare Book Library, University of Toronto.

8 E.B. to Bill Hagon, 17 Jan. 1954, Earle Birney Papers, Thomas Fisher Rare Book Library, University of Toronto.

9 E.B. to Herman Singer, Good Friday and E.B. to Pat and John Wardroper, Easter Friday 1954, Earle Birney Papers, Thomas Fisher Rare Book Library, University of Toronto and to Rosemary Baxter, 20 May 1954, property of Rosemary Baxter.

10 E.B. to Stuart and Ruth Kirby, 23 Apr. 1959, Earle Birney Papers, Thomas Fisher Rare Book Library, University of Toronto.

11 E.B. to Wilfred Eadie, 28 Dec. 1954, Earle Birney Papers, Thomas Fisher Rare Book Library, University of Toronto.

12 E.B. to M.H. Scargill, [n.d., probably late Jan. or early Feb.] 1954, Earle Birney Papers, Thomas Fisher Rare Book Library, University of Toronto.

13 E.B. to David Bromige, 30 Dec. 1962, Earle Birney Papers, Thomas Fisher Rare Book Library, University of Toronto.

14 E.B. to Brian Elliott, 12 Oct. 1954, Earle Birney Papers, Thomas Fisher Rare Book Library, University of Toronto.

15 E.B. to E.J. Pratt, 29 Oct. 1956, Earle Birney Papers, Thomas Fisher Rare Book Library, University of Toronto.

16 See Pauline Ivey to E.B., 10 Nov. 1955 and E.B. to Pauline Ivey, 14 Nov. 1955, Earle Birney Papers, Thomas Fisher Rare Book Library, University of Toronto.

17 E.B. to Herman Singer, 5 Oct. 1954, Earle Birney Papers, Thomas Fisher Rare Book Library, University of Toronto.

18 E.B., notes re: UBC English Dept., [n.d., probably Feb. 1954], 4 pp., Earle Birney Papers, Thomas Fisher Rare Book Library, University of

Toronto.

19 E.B. to Frank Wilcox, [n.d.] Jan. 1955, Earle Birney Papers, Thomas Fisher Rare Book Library, University of Toronto.

20 *Record of Service in the Second World War—The University of British Columbia—Vancouver* (1955).

21 F.R. Scott to E.B., 28 Nov. 1954, Earle Birney Papers, Thomas Fisher Rare Book Library, University of Toronto.

22 E.B. to F.R. Scott, 7 Dec. 1954, Earle Birney Papers, Thomas Fisher Rare Book Library, University of Toronto.

23 "Mammorial Stunzas for Aimee Simple McFarcin," *Prism International,* vol. 1, no. 2 (Winter 1959), pp. 34–35.

24 F.R. Scott to E.B., 18 Dec. 1954, Earle Birney Papers, Thomas Fisher Rare Book Library, University of Toronto.

25 See file of "Fan Letters," Earle Birney Papers, Thomas Fisher Rare Book Library, University of Toronto.

26 E.B. to Campbell Hughes, The Ryerson Press, 9 Jan. 1954 and E.B. to Desmond Pacey, 20 Apr. 1957, Earle Birney Papers, Thomas Fisher Rare Book Library, University of Toronto.

27 Ethel Cox to E.B., 22 Nov. 1954, Earle Birney Papers, Thomas Fisher Rare Book Library, University of Toronto.

28 E.B. to Carlotta Makins, 10 Apr. 1956, Earle Birney Papers, Thomas Fisher Rare Book Library, University of Toronto.

29 E.B. to Bill Hagon, 16 Jan. 1954, Earle Birney Papers, Thomas Fisher Rare Book Library, University of Toronto.

30 E.B. to Pat and John Wardroper, Easter Friday 1954, Earle Birney Papers, Thomas Fisher Rare Book Library, University of Toronto. These short columns on embroidery were published anonymously in 1954–55. E.B. to Elizabeth Cox, 12 Oct. 1954, Earle Birney Papers, Thomas Fisher Rare Book Library, University of Toronto.

31 Esther Birney to Miriam Waddington, 16 Nov. 1954, National Archives of Canada, Miriam Waddington Collection, MG 31, D 54, vol. 30.

32 Esther Birney to Miriam Waddington, 23 Oct. 1953, National Archives of Canada, Miriam Waddington Collection, MG 31, D 54, vol. 30.

33 E.B. to Brian Elliott, 12 Oct. 1954, Earle Birney Papers, Thomas Fisher Rare Book Library, University of Toronto.

34 Earle Birney, 1954 Income Tax Form, Earle Birney fonds, MS. Coll. 13, Special Collections Division, University of Calgary Library.

35 E.B., "Lake O'Hara," Standard Oil Company of British Columbia Limited, Earle Birney fonds, MS Coll. 13, 1.1.9, Special Collections Division, University of Calgary Library.

36 E.B. to Brian Elliott, 12 Oct. and 14 Jan. 1954, Earle Birney Papers, Thomas Fisher Rare Book Library, University of Toronto.

37 Shirley King, "Birney 'Browned Off' Over Writing Novels," *The Ubyssey,* 21 Oct. 1954, Earle Birney Papers, Thomas Fisher Rare Book

Library, University of Toronto.

38 E.B. to Howard Moorepark, 28 Mar. 1955, Earle Birney Papers, Thomas Fisher Rare Book Library, University of Toronto.

39 E.B. to John Wardroper, [n.d., Oct. or Nov.] 1954, Earle Birney Papers, Thomas Fisher Rare Book Library, University of Toronto.

40 Jack McClelland to E.C., interview, 19 Dec. 1990, Toronto.

41 E.B. to Howard Moorepark, 5 Oct. 1954, Earle Birney Papers, Thomas Fisher Rare Book Library, University of Toronto.

42 E.B. to Herman Singer, 5 Oct. and to John Wardroper, 4 Oct. 1954, Earle Birney Papers, Thomas Fisher Rare Book Library, University of Toronto.

43 E.B. to Elizabeth Cox, 13 May 1955, Earle Birney Papers, Thomas Fisher Rare Book Library, University of Toronto.

44 "List of My Correspondents about 1955," Earle Birney fonds, MS.Coll. 13, 7.2.2, Special Collections Division, University of Calgary Library.

45 Esther Birney to E.C., interview, Jan. 1991, Vancouver.

46 E.B. to Norman L. MacKenzie, 18 Mar. 1955, Earle Birney Papers, Thomas Fisher Rare Book Library, University of Toronto.

47 Salary scales for 1954-55, English Department, UBC, Earle Birney Papers, Thomas Fisher Rare Book Library, University of Toronto.

48 E.B. to Herman Singer, Good Friday 1954, Earle Birney Papers, Thomas Fisher Rare Book Library, University of Toronto.

49 E.B. to Rosemary Baxter, 17 May 1955, property of Rosemary Baxter, Aberdeen.

50 E.B. to John Pearson, 12 July 1955, Earle Birney Papers, Thomas Fisher Rare Book Library, University of Toronto.

51 Leonard Brooks to E.C., interview, 5 June 1991, San Miguel de Allende, Mexico, and E.B. to Herman Singer, 18 May 1955, Earle Birney Papers, Thomas Fisher Rare Book Library, University of Toronto.

52 E.B. to Betty Lambert, 25 Feb. 1959, Earle Birney Papers, Thomas Fisher Rare Book Library, University of Toronto.

53 Leonard Brooks to E.C., interview, 5 June 1991, San Miguel de Allende, Mexico.

54 Reva Brooks to E.C., interview, 6 June 1991, San Miguel de Allende, Mexico.

55 E.B. to Margaret Parker, 14 Nov. 1955, Earle Birney Papers, Thomas Fisher Rare Book Library, University of Toronto.

56 Elizabeth Cox to E.B., 31 Jan. 1952 and E.B. to Elizabeth Cox, 11 Feb. 1952, Earle Birney Papers, Thomas Fisher Rare Book Library, University of Toronto.

57 E.B. to Elizabeth Cox, 12 Oct. 1954 and Elizabeth Cox to E.B., 9 Nov. 1954, Earle Birney Papers, Thomas Fisher Rare Book Library, University of Toronto.

58 E.B. to Elizabeth Cox, 13 May and 27 June 1955; Elizabeth Cox to E.B., 24 May 1955, Earle Birney Papers, Thomas Fisher Rare Book Library, University of Toronto.

59 E.B. to Gustav Davidson, 20 Aug. and [n.d.] 1955, Earle Birney Papers, Thomas Fisher Rare Book Library, University of Toronto.

60 E.B. to Herman Singer, 10 Sept. 1955, Earle Birney Papers, Thomas Fisher Rare Book Library, University of Toronto.

61 E.B. to Elizabeth Cox, 27 June and 20 Aug. 1955, Earle Birney Papers, Thomas Fisher Rare Book Library, University of Toronto.

62 E.B. to Elizabeth Cox, 12 Nov. 1955, Earle Birney Papers, Thomas Fisher Rare Book Library, University of Toronto.

63 F.R. Scott, "The Canadian Writers' Conference," *University of Toronto Quarterly*, vol. 25, no. 1 (Oct. 1955), pp. 96–103.

64 E.B. to Herman Singer, 4 Sept. 1955, Earle Birney Papers, Thomas Fisher Rare Book Library, University of Toronto.

65 E.B. to Bill Birney, 13 Aug. and to Pat and John Wardroper, 13 Aug. 1955, Earle Birney Papers, Thomas Fisher Rare Book Library, University of Toronto.

66 E.B. to Phyllis Webb, [n.d., probably Mar.] 1955, Earle Birney Papers, Thomas Fisher Rare Book Library, University of Toronto.

67 Phyllis Webb to E.B., 10 Aug. and 22 Aug. 1955; E.B. to Phyllis Webb, 20 Aug. 1955, Earle Birney Papers, Thomas Fisher Rare Book Library, University of Toronto.

68 Elizabeth Cox to E.B., [n.d.] Aug. and 16 Sept. 1955, Earle Birney Papers, Thomas Fisher Rare Book Library, University of Toronto.

69 E.B. to Rosemary Baxter, 18 Aug. 1955, Earle Birney Papers, Thomas Fisher Rare Book Library, University of Toronto.

70 E.B. to Rosemary Baxter, 25 Oct. 1955, Earle Birney Papers, Thomas Fisher Rare Book Library, University of Toronto.

71 E.B. to Herman Singer, 4 Sept. 1955, Earle Birney Papers, Thomas Fisher Rare Book Library, University of Toronto.

72 E.B. to Herman Singer, 4 Sept. 1955, Earle Birney Papers, Thomas Fisher Rare Book Library, University of Toronto.

73 E.B. to Herman Singer, 5 Dec. 1955, Earle Birney Papers, Thomas Fisher Rare Book Library, University of Toronto.

74 E.B. to Pauline Ivey, 14 Nov. 1955, Earle Birney Papers, Thomas Fisher Rare Book Library, University of Toronto.

75 E.B. to Brian Elliott, [n.d., probably Oct. or Nov.] 1955, Earle Birney Papers, Thomas Fisher Rare Book Library, University of Toronto.

76 E.B. to Elizabeth Cox, 2 Dec. 1955, Earle Birney Papers, Thomas Fisher Rare Book Library, University of Toronto.

77 E.B. to Elizabeth Cox, 2 Dec. 1955, and E.B. to Herman Singer, 5 Dec. 1955, Earle Birney Papers, Thomas Fisher Rare Book Library, University of Toronto.

78 R[oss] D[owson], rev. of *Down the Long Table*, *The Workers' Vanguard*, July 1956, p. 2. I am indebted to Tom Reid, library technician, Thomas Fisher Rare Book Library, for drawing my attention to this review.

79 Norman Klenman to E.B., 7 Feb. 1955, Earle Birney Papers, Thomas Fisher Rare Book Library, University of Toronto.

80 E.B. to Esther Birney, 28 Oct. 1955, Earle Birney Papers, Thomas Fisher Rare Book Library, University of Toronto.

81 Esther Birney to E.C., interview, Jan. 1991, Vancouver.

82 Pauline Ivey to E.B., 22 Dec. 1955, Earle Birney Papers, Thomas Fisher Rare Book Library, University of Toronto.

83 E.B. to Pauline Ivey, 21 Dec. 1956, Earle Birney Papers, Thomas Fisher Rare Book Library, University of Toronto.

84 E.B. to Pauline Ivey, 28 Dec. 1956, Earle Birney Papers, Thomas Fisher Rare Book Library, University of Toronto.

85 E.B. to Elizabeth Cox, 12 Nov. 1955, Earle Birney Papers, Thomas Fisher Rare Book Library, University of Toronto.

86 E.B. to Esther Birney, 30 Dec. 1955, Earle Birney Papers, Thomas Fisher Rare Book Library, University of Toronto.

87 Esther Birney, "About Me & the Jews," [n.d.] 1975, University of British Columbia, Special Collections and University Archives Division, Esther Birney Papers.

88 E.B. to Pauline Ivey, 5 Jan. 1956, Earle Birney Papers, Thomas Fisher Rare Book Library, University of Toronto.

89 Pauline Ivey to E.B., 11 Jan. 1956, Earle Birney Papers, Thomas Fisher Rare Book Library, University of Toronto.

90 E.B. to Elizabeth Cox, 12 Nov. 1955, Earle Birney Papers, Thomas Fisher Rare Book Library, University of Toronto.

91 E.B. to Carlotta Makins, 10 April 1956, Earle Birney Papers, Thomas Fisher Rare Book Library, University of Toronto.

92 E.B. to Phyllis Webb, 12 May 1956, Earle Birney Papers, Thomas Fisher Rare Book Library, University of Toronto.

93 Dorothy Bishop, *The Ottawa Journal*, 19 Nov. and 3 Dec. 1955.

94 E.B. to Art McKenzie of *The Vancouver Province*, 21 Jan. 1956, Earle Birney Papers, Thomas Fisher Rare Book Library, University of Toronto. The Vancouver Sun, Nov. 1955 and *The Vancouver News-Herald*, 12 Nov. 1955. See extracts from book reviews of *Down the Long Table* in Earle Birney fonds, MS. Coll. 13, 2.2.1.4, Special Collections Division, University of Calgary Library.

95 E.B. to H.G. Kimber, *The Globe and Mail*, 7 May 1956, Earle Birney fonds, MS. Coll. 13, 2.2.1.4, Special Collections Division, University of Calgary Library.

96 E.B. to Eugenie Perry, 12 Sept. 1955, Earle Birney Papers, Thomas Fisher Rare Book Library, University of Toronto.

97 Ethel Wilson to E.B., 29 Nov. 1955; Clyde Gilmour to E.B., 3 Dec. 1955; E.J. Pratt to E.B., 8 Nov. 1955; Claude Bissell to E.B., 10 Feb. 1956, Earle Birney Papers, Thomas Fisher Rare Book Library, University of Toronto.

98 E.B. to André Sacriste, 26 Jan. 1956, Earle Birney Papers, Thomas Fisher Rare Book Library, University of Toronto.

99 E.B. to J.B. Priestley, 8 June 1956, Earle Birney Papers, Thomas Fisher Rare Book Library, University of Toronto.

100 E.B. to the Sacristes, 3 Apr. 1955, Earle Birney Papers, Thomas Fisher Rare Book Library, University of Toronto. See other correspondence between the two during 1955-56 for details.

101 E.B. to Brian Elliott, 26 June 1955, Earle Birney Papers, Thomas Fisher Rare Book Library, University of Toronto.

102 E.B. to Elizabeth Cox, 12 Oct. 1954, Earle Birney Papers, Thomas Fisher Rare Book Library, University of Toronto.

103 Heather Spears's works include: *The Danish Portraits* (1967); *From the Inside* (1972); *How to Read Faces* (1986); and *Human Acts* (1988).

104 E.B. to Mrs. Herbert Wilson, 1 May 1955, Earle Birney Papers, Thomas Fisher Rare Book Library, University of Toronto.

105 E.B. to Bill Hagon, 17 Jan. 1954, Earle Birney Papers, Thomas Fisher Rare Book Library, University of Toronto.

106 E.B. to Jay Macpherson, 12 Mar. 1955, Earle Birney Papers, Thomas Fisher Rare Book Library, University of Toronto.

107 E.B. to Phyllis Webb, [n.d., probably Mar.] 1956 and Phyllis Webb to E.B., 8 Mar. 1955, Earle Birney Papers, Thomas Fisher Rare Book Library, University of Toronto.

108 Jay Macpherson sent him *Nineteen Poems*, which he acknowledged on 29 June 1956, Earle Birney Papers, Thomas Fisher Rare Book Library, University of Toronto.

109 E.B. to Miriam Waddington, 15 Mar. 1955, Earle Birney Papers, Thomas Fisher Rare Book Library, University of Toronto.

110 Al Purdy and Curt Lang to E.B., 7 Mar. 1955, Earle Birney Papers, Thomas Fisher Rare Book Library, University of Toronto.

111 E.B. had already been contacted by Al Purdy when Purdy submitted poetry for publication in *CPM* on 20 Oct. 1947. Purdy wrote: "I consciously strive for beauty as well as something that makes a person think a bit. Some people say that the poetry of a nation closely resembles its conversation. I thought that point was particularly true of your long poem 'David.' Yet the trend of most modern poetry seems to be away from this principle…. I would like very much to know whether it's a permanent trend—this swing to the 'ultra-modern.'" To which E.B. replied: "In my regime [as editor of *CPM*], both you and the 'ultra-moderns' as you call them, have a chance, as I believe in giving any craftsman a chance if he is a good enough craftsman." Al Purdy to E.B., 20 Oct. 1947 and E.B. to Al Purdy, 5 Nov. 1947, Earle Birney

Papers, Thomas Fisher Rare Book Library, University of Toronto.

112 E.B. to Lister Sinclair, 1 Dec. 1956, Earle Birney Papers, Thomas Fisher Rare Book Library, University of Toronto.

113 E.B. to Bill Hagon, 17 Sept. 1956, Earle Birney Papers, Thomas Fisher Rare Book Library, University of Toronto.

114 Robert Weaver to E.B., 4 Nov. 1955 and 27 Apr. 1956, Earle Birney Papers, Thomas Fisher Rare Book Library, University of Toronto.

115 E.B. to Charles Allen Smart, 29 July 1956, Earle Birney Papers, Thomas Fisher Rare Book Library, University of Toronto.

116 E.B. to John Pearson, 17 June 1956, Earle Birney Papers, Thomas Fisher Rare Book Library, University of Toronto.

117 See newsclips re: William L. Birney, 28 Nov. 1955, Earle Birney Papers, Thomas Fisher Rare Book Library, University of Toronto.

118 E.B. to André Sacriste, 10 July 1956, Earle Birney Papers, Thomas Fisher Rare Book Library, University of Toronto.

119 E.B. to Eugenie Perry, 12 Sept. 1956, Earle Birney Papers, Thomas Fisher Rare Book Library, University of Toronto.

120 E.B. to André Sacriste, 10 July 1956, Earle Birney Papers, Thomas Fisher Rare Book Library, University of Toronto.

121 E.B. to John Pearson, 12 Aug. 1956, Earle Birney Papers, Thomas Fisher Rare Book Library, University of Toronto.

122 John Pearson to E.B., 16 Aug. 1956, Earle Birney Papers, Thomas Fisher Rare Book Library, University of Toronto.

123 E.B. to Eugenie Perry, 12 Sept. 1956, Earle Birney Papers, Thomas Fisher Rare Book Library, University of Toronto.

124 E.B. to Frank Wilcox, 2 Oct. 1956, Earle Birney Papers, Thomas Fisher Rare Book Library, University of Toronto.

125 E.B. to André and Mimi Sacriste, 2 Oct. and 13 Nov. 1956, Earle Birney Papers, Thomas Fisher Rare Book Library, University of Toronto.

Chapter 22: Circumfluence

1 See E.B. to Harry Scargill, 30 July 1954, Earle Birney Papers, Thomas Fisher Rare Book Library, University of Toronto.

2 See correspondence between E.B. and Brunswick Press, 14 Oct. 1954–1 May 1955, Earle Birney Papers, Thomas Fisher Rare Book Library, University of Toronto.

3 E.B., *Turvey* (Toronto: McClelland & Stewart, 1949), p.41.

4 Published in *Canadian Life* 1949, Earle Birney fonds, MS Coll. 13, 2.1.3, Special Collections Division, University of Calgary Library.

5 "Successful Innocence," *The Times Literary Supplement*, 11 April 1958, Earle Birney fonds, MS Coll. 13, 2.2.2.2, Special Collections Division, University of Calgary Library.

6 E.B. to E.J. Pratt, 28 Nov. 1957, Earle Birney Papers, Thomas Fisher

Rare Book Library, University of Toronto.

7 E.B. to Irving Layton, 20 Feb. 1958, Earle Birney Papers, Thomas Fisher Rare Book Library, University of Toronto.

8 E.B. to Phyllis Webb, 7 Nov. 1957, Earle Birney Papers, Thomas Fisher Rare Book Library, University of Toronto.

9 E.B. to Edmund Blunden, 25 June 1958, Earle Birney Papers, Thomas Fisher Rare Book Library, University of Toronto.

10 E.B. to Prime Minister John Diefenbaker, 27 Feb. 1958, Earle Birney Papers, Thomas Fisher Rare Book Library, University of Toronto.

11 E.B. to Bruce Macdonald, 18 Mar. 1958, Earle Birney Papers, Thomas Fisher Rare Book Library, University of Toronto.

12 E.B. to Beatrice White, 24 Sept. 1958, Earle Birney Papers, Thomas Fisher Rare Book Library, University of Toronto.

13 E.B. to Herman Singer, 24 Nov. 1958, Earle Birney Papers, Thomas Fisher Rare Book Library, University of Toronto.

14 E.B. to Herman Singer, 8 Apr. 1957, Earle Birney Papers, Thomas Fisher Rare Book Library, University of Toronto.

15 E.B. to Lou Crosby, 24 Feb. 1958, Earle Birney Papers, Thomas Fisher Rare Book Library, University of Toronto.

16 E.B. to William Birney, 25 Aug. 1958, Earle Birney Papers, Thomas Fisher Rare Book Library, University of Toronto.

17 E.B. to the Canada Council, 2 Jan. 1958, Earle Birney Papers, Thomas Fisher Rare Book Library, University of Toronto.

18 E.B. to Jim Hall, 21 Apr. 1958, Earle Birney Papers, Thomas Fisher Rare Book Library, University of Toronto.

19 E.B. to Jim Hall, 12 Apr. 1958 and 12 Feb. 1957, Earle Birney Papers, Thomas Fisher Rare Book Library, University of Toronto.

20 E.B. to Stuart Kirby, [n.d., prob. Nov. or Dec.] 1958, Earle Birney Papers, Thomas Fisher Rare Book Library, University of Toronto.

21 E.B. to Merritt Hughes, 25 Feb. 1947, Earle Birney Papers, Thomas Fisher Rare Book Library, University of Toronto.

22 See the long correspondence between Desmond Pacey and E.B. in 1957; Desmond Pacey, *Ten Canadian Poets: A Group of Biographical and Critical Essays* (Toronto: Ryerson Press, 1958).

23 E.B. to Norman Newton, 23 Nov. 1948, Earle Birney Papers, Thomas Fisher Rare Book Library, University of Toronto.

24 E.B. to Jim Hall, 8 Apr. 1959, Earle Birney Papers, Thomas Fisher Rare Book Library, University of Toronto.

25 E.B. to Phyllis Webb and to Sybil Hutchinson, 7 Nov. 1957, Earle Birney Papers, Thomas Fisher Rare Book Library, University of Toronto.

26 E.B. to Alice Frick, 9 April 1957, Earle Birney Papers, Thomas Fisher Rare Book Library, University of Toronto.

27 E.B. to Gwladys Downes, 10 Sept. 1957, Earle Birney Papers, Thomas

Fisher Rare Book Library, University of Toronto.

28 However, a stage production of "Damnation of Vancouver" took place at the University of Washington on 10 Feb. 1957. Birney refused to whitewash his play for the B.C. Centennial officials: "They turfed it back, asking me to throw out the bawdy saloon keeper...and insert a noble pioneering type. I told them where to stick their whole Centennial...and let the play go for its premiere to the University of Washington players in Seattle. After their performance, the play has been discreetly buried." E.B. to Irving Layton, 8 June 1963, Earle Birney Papers, Thomas Fisher Rare Book Library, University of Toronto.

29 "Vancouver Lights–1941," "Pacific Door" and "David," *British Columbia: A Centennial Anthology,* ed. Reginald Eyre Walters (Toronto: McClelland & Stewart, 1958), pp. 97–98, 111, 343–49.

30 Pierre Berton to E.B., 29 Jan. 1958, Earle Birney Papers, Thomas Fisher Rare Book Library, University of Toronto.

31 E.B. to Elizabeth Cox, 13 Feb. 1958, Earle Birney Papers, Thomas Fisher Rare Book Library, University of Toronto.

32 Phyllis Webb, *Even Your Right Eye* (Toronto: McClelland & Stewart, 1956).

33 Irving Layton, *The Bull Calf and Other Poems* (Toronto: Contact Press, 1956).

34 Leonard Cohen, *Let Us Compare Mythologies* (Toronto: Contact Press, 1956).

35 Dorothy Livesay, *Selected Poems, 1926–1956* (Toronto: Ryerson Press, 1957).

36 F.R. Scott, *The Eye of the Needle* (Montreal: Contact Press, 1957). E.B. to Margaret Vatcher, 13 Apr. 1957, Earle Birney Papers, Thomas Fisher Rare Book Library, University of Toronto.

37 See E.B. Income Tax Return and "Statement of Free-Lance Income and Expenses," Earle Birney fonds, MS Coll. 13, Special Collections Division, University of Calgary Library.

38 Esther Birney to Miriam Waddington, [n.d., early March] 1957, Earle Birney Papers, Thomas Fisher Rare Book Library, University of Toronto.

39 E.B. to George Bowering, 23 Nov. 1986, George Bowering Archive, Contemporary Literature Collection, W.A.C. Bennett Library, Simon Fraser University.

40 E.B. to Irving Layton, 11 Sept. 1957, Earle Birney Papers, Thomas Fisher Rare Book Library, University of Toronto.

41 E.B., "Report on UBC Research No. 104," 21 Oct. 1957, Earle Birney Papers, Thomas Fisher Rare Book Library, University of Toronto.

42 E.B. to F.R. Scott, 9 April 1957, Earle Birney Papers, Thomas Fisher Rare Book Library, University of Toronto. F.R. Scott, "The Canadian Authors Meet," *Overture* (Toronto: Ryerson Press, 1945).

43 E.B. to Irving Layton, [n.d., Aug.] 1957 and to A.J.M. Smith, 6 Aug. 1957, Earle Birney Papers, Thomas Fisher Rare Book Library, University of Toronto.

44 E.B. to Frank Wilcox, 20 Jan. 1957, Earle Birney Papers, Thomas Fisher Rare Book Library, University of Toronto.

45 E.B. to John Wardroper, 21 Dec. 1957, Earle Birney Papers, Thomas Fisher Rare Book Library, University of Toronto.

46 Editor of *Modern Language Quarterly* to E.B., 9 Dec. 1957, Earle Birney Papers, Thomas Fisher Rare Book Library, University of Toronto.

47 E.B. to Charles Allen Smart, 16 Oct. 1957, Earle Birney Papers, Thomas Fisher Rare Book Library, University of Toronto.

48 E.B. letter of resignation, 23 Oct. 1957, Earle Birney Papers, Thomas Fisher Rare Book Library, University of Toronto.

49 E.B., "Nuffield Application," 23 Oct. 1957, Earle Birney Papers, Thomas Fisher Rare Book Library, University of Toronto.

50 E.B. to W.H. Howard Norman, 9 May 1958, Earle Birney Papers, Thomas Fisher Rare Book Library, University of Toronto.

51 E.B. to John and Martha Wardroper, 1 July 1958, Earle Birney Papers, Thomas Fisher Rare Book Library, University of Toronto.

52 E.B., "Twenty-third Flight," *Ice Cod Bell or Stone: New Poems*, I (Toronto: McClelland & Stewart, 1962), p. 33.

53 E.B. to Harold Offord, 9 Dec. 1958, Earle Birney Papers, Thomas Fisher Rare Book Library, University of Toronto.

54 E.B. to John and Martha Wardroper, 1 July 1958, and to Betty Lambert, 28 Sept. 1958, Earle Birney Papers, Thomas Fisher Rare Book Library, University of Toronto.

55 E.B. to the Wardropers, 1 July 1958, Earle Birney Papers, Thomas Fisher Rare Book Library, University of Toronto.

56 E.B. to Betty Lambert, 28 Sept. 1958, Earle Birney Papers, Thomas Fisher Rare Book Library, University of Toronto.

57 "UBC Poet Ends Tour of the World," *The Vancouver Province*, 14 Sept. 1959, Earle Birney fonds, MS Coll. 13, 5.5.1, Special Collections Division, University of Calgary Library.

58 E.B. to Betty Lambert, 28 Sept. 1958 and to Robin Howe, 21 Aug. 1958, Earle Birney Papers, Thomas Fisher Rare Book Library, University of Toronto.

59 *Ibid.*

60 E.B. to Bruce Macdonald, [n.d., end Aug.] 1958, Earle Birney Papers, Thomas Fisher Rare Book Library, University of Toronto.

61 E.B. to Betty Lambert, 28 Aug. 1958, Earle Birney Papers, Thomas Fisher Rare Book Library, University of Toronto.

62 E.B. to John Wardroper, [n.d., end Aug.] 1958, Earle Birney Papers, Thomas Fisher Rare Book Library, University of Toronto.

63 E.B. to William McConnell, 26 Oct. 1958, Earle Birney Papers, Thomas Fisher Rare Book Library, University of Toronto.

64 E.B. to Stuart Kirby, 12 Nov. 1958, Earle Birney Papers, Thomas Fisher Rare Book Library, University of Toronto.

65 E.B. to Wilber Stevens, 5 Oct. 1958, Earle Birney Papers, Thomas Fisher Rare Book Library, University of Toronto.

66 Margaret Crosland, *Madame Colette* (London: Peter Owen, 1953); *Jean Cocteau* (London: Peter Nevill, 1955); *The Happy Yes: An Anthology of Marriage Proposals Grave and Gay* (with Patricia Ledward) (London: E. Benn, 1949).

67 E.B. to Rosemary Baxter, 5 Oct. 1958, Earle Birney Papers, Thomas Fisher Rare Book Library, University of Toronto.

68 E.B. to Supervisor, North Library, British Museum, 12 Nov. 1958 and to Dick Fredeman, 28 Nov. 1958, Earle Birney Papers, Thomas Fisher Rare Book Library, University of Toronto.

69 E.B. to Bill McConnell, 26 Oct. 1958, Earle Birney Papers, Thomas Fisher Rare Book Library, University of Toronto.

70 E.B. to Rosemary Baxter, 12 Nov. 1958, Earle Birney Papers, Thomas Fisher Rare Book Library, University of Toronto.

71 E.B. to William Birney, 26 Nov. 1958, Earle Birney Papers, Thomas Fisher Rare Book Library, University of Toronto.

72 E.B. to Robin Howe, 28 Nov. 1958, Earle Birney Papers, Thomas Fisher Rare Book Library, University of Toronto.

73 E.B. to Harry Scargill, 25 Nov. 1958, Earle Birney Papers, Thomas Fisher Rare Book Library, University of Toronto.

74 E.B. to Dick Fredeman, 28 Nov. 1958, Earle Birney Papers, Thomas Fisher Rare Book Library, University of Toronto.

75 E.B. to Bill McConnell, 26 Oct. 1958 and to Claude Bissell, 17 Jan. 1959, Earle Birney Papers, Thomas Fisher Rare Book Library, University of Toronto.

76 Margaret Crosland to E.C., interview, 5 May 1989, Upper Hartfield, England.

77 Jack McClelland to E.B., 3 Dec. 1958; E.B. to Andrew Roberts, 19 July 1959; and E.B. to Ralph Gustafson, 17 Mar. 1959, Earle Birney Papers, Thomas Fisher Rare Book Library, University of Toronto. It appears that Knopf was "blacklisted" by Birney's agent, Howard Moorepark. See E.B. to Andrew Roberts, 20 Oct. 1959, Earle Birney Papers, Thomas Fisher Rare Book Library, University of Toronto.

78 E.B. to John Ciardi, 3 Dec. 1958, Earle Birney Papers, Thomas Fisher Rare Book Library, University of Toronto.

79 E.B. to Frank Flemington, 8 Dec. 1958, Earle Birney Papers, Thomas Fisher Rare Book Library, University of Toronto.

80 E.B. to Norman Newton, 16 Oct. 1950, Earle Birney Papers, Thomas Fisher Rare Book Library, University of Toronto.

81 Elizabeth Cowley to E.B., Dominion Day 1946, Earle Birney Papers, Thomas Fisher Rare Book Library, University of Toronto.

82 E.B. to Stephen Vizinczey, [n.d.] 1969, Earle Birney Papers, Thomas Fisher Rare Book Library, University of Toronto.

83 E.B. to Ken Rexroth, Fri. [n.d., prob. Feb.] 1959 and to Wilfred Watson, 22 Sept. 1958, Earle Birney Papers, Thomas Fisher Rare Book Library, University of Toronto.

84 E.B. to Bruce Macdonald, 14 Jan. 1959, Earle Birney Papers, Thomas Fisher Rare Book Library, University of Toronto.

85 E.B. to Bruce Macdonald, 21 May 1959, Earle Birney Papers, Thomas Fisher Rare Book Library, University of Toronto.

86 E.B., "To Think of It," unpublished poem [n.d., between 13 May-11 Sept. 1959], property of Elizabeth Cowley, London.

87 E.B. to "Tonight," BBC, 8 July 1959, Earle Birney Papers, Thomas Fisher Rare Book Library, University of Toronto.

88 E.B. to Wilber Stevens, 22 May 1959 and to Bruce Macdonald, 21 May 1959, Earle Birney Papers, Thomas Fisher Rare Book Library, University of Toronto.

89 Rosemary Baxter to E.C., explanatory notes on the back of E.B.'s postcard to Rosemary Baxter, 15 Jan. 1959, property of E.C.

90 *Ibid.*

91 E.B. to Elizabeth Cowley, [n.d., prob. 12 June] 1959, property of Elizabeth Cowley, London.

92 E.B. to Merritt Hughes, 9 Jan. 1960, Earle Birney Papers, Thomas Fisher Rare Book Library, University of Toronto.

93 E.B. to Irving Layton, 7 Nov. 1957, Earle Birney Papers, Thomas Fisher Rare Book Library, University of Toronto.

94 E.B., "Consolation for the Stillbirth of a Marriage," [n.d., between 13 May-11 Sept.] 1959, property of Elizabeth Cowley, London.

95 E.B. to Elizabeth Cowley, 11 Sept. 1959, property of Elizabeth Cowley, London.

96 E.B. to Beth and Herman Singer, 12 Nov. 1959, Earle Birney Papers, Thomas Fisher Rare Book Library, University of Toronto.

97 E.B. to Dick Fredeman, 23 Feb. 1959, Earle Birney Papers, Thomas Fisher Rare Book Library, University of Toronto.

98 E.B. to Claude Bissell, 16 Jan. 1959, Earle Birney Papers, Thomas Fisher Rare Book Library, University of Toronto.

99 E.B. to Peggy Stobie, 6 Aug. 1959 and to Beatrice White, 5 Nov. 1959, Earle Birney Papers, Thomas Fisher Rare Book Library, University of Toronto. "'After his Ymage'—Structural Irony in the *Friar's Tale*," *Mediaeval Studies*, vol. 21 (1959), pp. 17-35; "The Squire's Peacock Yeoman," *Review of English Literature*, vol. 1, no. 3 (July 1960), pp. 9-18; "The Franklin's 'Sop in Wyn'," *Notes and Queries*, n.s. 6, no. 9 (Oct. 1959), pp. 345-47; "The Inhibited and Uninhibited: Ironic

Structure in the *Miller's Tale*," *Neophilologus*, vol. 44 (1960), pp. 333-38; "Structural Irony within the 'Summoner's Tale'," *Anglia*, vol. 78 (1960), pp. 204-18; "Chaucer's 'Gentil' Tale," *Neuphilologische Milleilungen*, vol. 61, no. 3 (1960), pp. 257-67.

100 Ernest Sirluck to E.B., Christmas card 1959, Earle Birney Papers, Thomas Fisher Rare Book Library, University of Toronto.

101 E.B. to Al Purdy, 20 Aug. 1959, Earle Birney Papers, Thomas Fisher Rare Book Library, University of Toronto.

102 E.B. to A.J.M. Smith, 2 May 1959, Earle Birney Papers, Thomas Fisher Rare Book Library, University of Toronto.

103 Al Purdy to E.B., 1 Nov. 1959, Earle Birney Papers, Thomas Fisher Rare Book Library, University of Toronto.

104 Ron Everson to E.B., 8 June 1959, Earle Birney Papers, Thomas Fisher Rare Book Library, University of Toronto.

105 E.B. to Alan Crawley, 17 Mar. 1953, Earle Birney Papers, Thomas Fisher Rare Book Library, University of Toronto.

106 E.B. to Howard Moorepark, 2 July 1958, Earle Birney Papers, Thomas Fisher Rare Book Library, University of Toronto.

107 E.B. to Robin Howe, 21 Aug. 1958, Earle Birney Papers, Thomas Fisher Rare Book Library, University of Toronto.

108 E.B. to John Ciardi, 3 Dec. 1959, Earle Birney Papers, Thomas Fisher Rare Book Library, University of Toronto.

109 E.B. to Irving Layton, 6 Oct. 1958, Earle Birney Papers, Thomas Fisher Rare Book Library, University of Toronto. The collection was *A Laughter in the Mind* (Highlands, N.C.: J. Williams, 1958).

110 E.B. to Ethel Wilson, 25 Oct. 1958, Earle Birney Papers, Thomas Fisher Rare Book Library, University of Toronto.

111 E.B. to Betty Lambert, 25 Feb. 1959, Earle Birney Papers, Thomas Fisher Rare Book Library, University of Toronto.

112 E.B. to Heather Spears, 14 Jan. 1959, Earle Birney Papers, Thomas Fisher Rare Book Library, University of Toronto.

113 E.B. to Ralph Gustafson, 17 Mar. 1959, Earle Birney Papers, Thomas Fisher Rare Book Library, University of Toronto.

114 A.J.M. Smith to E.B., 30 Nov. 1959, Earle Birney Papers, Thomas Fisher Rare Book Library, University of Toronto.

115 See Birney's correspondence with the editor of *The New Yorker* in 1959. The poem actually appeared in the 17 Oct. 1960 issue of the magazine.

116 E.B. to Bruce Macdonald, 30 Dec. 1959, Earle Birney Papers, Thomas Fisher Rare Book Library, University of Toronto.

117 E.B., "The Bear on the Delhi Road," *Ice Cod Bell or Stone* (Toronto: McClelland & Stewart, 1962), p. 11.

118 Al Purdy to E.B., 14 Feb. 1960, Earle Birney Papers, Thomas Fisher Rare Book Library, University of Toronto.

119 Ralph Gustafson to E.B., 25 July 1959, Earle Birney Papers, Thomas Fisher Rare Book Library, University of Toronto.

120 E.B. to Al Purdy, 1 Dec. 1959, Earle Birney Papers, Thomas Fisher Rare Book Library, University of Toronto.

121 E.B. to Wilber Stevens, 22 May 1959, Earle Birney Papers, Thomas Fisher Rare Book Library, University of Toronto.

122 E.B. to Joe Langland, 17 Dec. 1959, Earle Birney Papers, Thomas Fisher Rare Book Library, University of Toronto.

123 E.B. to Bruce Macdonald, 20 Sept. 1960, Earle Birney Papers, Thomas Fisher Rare Book Library, University of Toronto.

124 E.B. to John Ciardi, 6 Aug. 1959, Earle Birney Papers, Thomas Fisher Rare Book Library, University of Toronto.

125 E.B. to Robert Weaver, 4 Oct. 1960, Earle Birney Papers, Thomas Fisher Rare Book Library, University of Toronto.

126 E.B., "El Greco: *Espolio*," *Poetry Northwest*, vol. 2, nos. 1–2 (Winter 1960–1), pp. 3–4.

127 E.B., "El Greco: *Espolio*," *Ice Cod Bell or Stone* (Toronto: McClelland & Stewart, 1958), p. 14.

128 E.B. to Elizabeth Cox, 11 Feb. 1952, Earle Birney Papers, Thomas Fisher Rare Book Library, University of Toronto.

129 E.B., "Nobody," *The Plough and the Pen*, ed. Ilona Duczynska and Karl Polanyi (Toronto: McClelland and Stewart, 1963), pp. 170–71; "Midstream" and "Snowscape from a Plane," *Queen's Quarterly*, vol. 65 (Summer 1958), pp. 261–62.

130 E.B., "Address Given at the Third National N.F.C.U.S. Seminar," University of British Columbia, 1960, pp. 2 and 10, Earle Birney fonds, MS.Coll. 13, 1.1.1, Special Collections Division, University of Calgary Library.

131 E.B. to Merritt Hughes, 9 Jan. 1960, Earle Birney Papers, Thomas Fisher Rare Book Library, University of Toronto.

132 E.B. to Carolyn Kitzer, 19 Aug. 1960, Earle Birney Papers, Thomas Fisher Rare Book Library, University of Toronto.

133 Robert Lowell, *Lord Weary's Castle* (New York: Harcourt, Brace, 1947).

134 E.B. to Joe Langland, [n.d., late Dec.] 1959, Earle Birney Papers, Thomas Fisher Rare Book Library, University of Toronto.

Chapter 23: Another Curve of Time

1 E.B. to Claude Bissell, 27 June 1957, and to Irving Layton, 5 Mar. 1958 and 11 Sept. 1957, Earle Birney Papers, Thomas Fisher Rare Book Library, University of Toronto.

2 E.B. to Margaret Vatcher, Canadian Library Association, 13 Apr. 1957, Earle Birney Papers, Thomas Fisher Rare Book Library, University of Toronto.

3 Ruth Witt-Diamant to E.B., 30 Jan. 1960, Earle Birney Papers, Thomas Fisher Rare Book Library, University of Toronto.

4 Bob Dylan, "Ballad of a Thin Man," *Highway '61 Revisited* (Aug. 1965).

5 E.B. to Louis Dudek, [n.d., prob. late Feb.] 1960, Earle Birney Papers, Thomas Fisher Rare Book Library, University of Toronto.

6 E.B. to Louis Dudek, [n.d., prob. late Feb.] 1960, Earle Birney Papers, Thomas Fisher Rare Book Library, University of Toronto.

7 E.B. to Ruth Witt-Diamant, 5 Mar. 1960, and to Carolyn Kitzer, 4 Mar. 1960, Earle Birney Papers, Thomas Fisher Rare Book Library, University of Toronto.

8 Lawrence Ferlinghetti, from "A Coney Island of the Mind," in *The New American Poetry 1945-1960*, ed. Donald M. Allen (New York: Grove Press, 1960), p. 133.

9 E.B. to Wilber Stevens, 31 Mar. 1960, Earle Birney Papers, Thomas Fisher Rare Book Library, University of Toronto.

10 E.B. to Elizabeth Enright, 24 Jan. 1961, Earle Birney Papers, Thomas Fisher Rare Book Library, University of Toronto.

11 E.B. to Judith Bechtold, 28 Oct. 1961, Earle Birney Papers, Thomas Fisher Rare Book Library, University of Toronto.

12 See *TISH: nos. 1-19*, ed. Frank Davey (Vancouver: Talonbooks, 1975).

13 E.B. to Sylvan Karchmer, 5 Oct. 1961, Earle Birney Papers, Thomas Fisher Rare Book Library, University of Toronto.

14 Frank Davey to E.B., 2 May 1961, Earle Birney Papers, Thomas Fisher Rare Book Library, University of Toronto.

15 E.B. to Bruce Macdonald, [n.d., probably 1961], Earle Birney Papers, Thomas Fisher Rare Book Library, University of Toronto.

16 E.B. to Beryl Rowland, 9 Nov. 1961, Earle Birney Papers, Thomas Fisher Rare Book Library, University of Toronto.

17 "The Poet and the University: A Symposium," *Humanities Association of Canada Bulletin*, no. 20, Jan. 1957, pp. 4-15.

18 Robert Bly, *Iron John* (Reading, Mass.: Addison-Wesley, 1990).

19 Robert Bly to E.B., 14 June and 8 Aug. 1960; and E.B. to Robert Bly, 25 June 1960, Earle Birney Papers, Thomas Fisher Rare Book Library, University of Toronto. Birney's friend Ethel Wilson also publically criticized the teaching of creative writing. See E.B.'s rebuttal, 9 Jan. 1961, Earle Birney Papers, Thomas Fisher Rare Book Library, University of Toronto.

20 Esther Birney to Miriam Waddington, 27 Aug. 1960, National Archives of Canada, Miriam Waddington Papers, MG 31, D54, vol. 30.

21 E.B. to Ron Everson, 30 Dec. 1963, Earle Birney Papers, Thomas Fisher Rare Book Library, University of Toronto.

22 Al Purdy to E.B., 30 June 1959, and E.B. to Al Purdy, 20 Aug. 1959, Earle Birney Papers, Thomas Fisher Rare Book Library, University of Toronto.

23 E.B. to Ron Everson, 20 May 1960, Earle Birney Papers, Thomas Fisher Rare Book Library, University of Toronto.

24 E.B. to Phyllis Webb, 24 June 1963, Earle Birney Papers, Thomas Fisher Rare Book Library, University of Toronto.

25 E.B. to Gustav Davidson, 1 Apr. 1961, Earle Birney Papers, Thomas Fisher Rare Book Library, University of Toronto.

26 *Ibid.* According to William McConnell, as quoted by Sheryl Salloum in *Malcolm Lowry: Vancouver Days* (Madeira Park, B.C.: Harbour Publishing Co., 1987), he and his wife Alice also helped Margerie with the Lowry papers (p. 113).

27 For details of E.B.'s work as Malcolm Lowry's unofficial agent, see *Pursued by Furies: A Life of Malcolm Lowry* (Toronto: Random House of Canada, 1993), pp. 415-23, 457-59, 466-67, 484-85, 526-27, 614-15. A number of Birney's letters make it clear that he was assisting Margerie with Lowry's prose as well as his verse. See E.B. to William Jovanovich, 15 Apr. 1961, E.B. to James Dickey, 13 May 1961, E.B. to Mel La Follette, 28 June 1961, and E.B. to Paul Engle, [n.d.] Aug. 1961, Earle Birney Papers, Thomas Fisher Rare Book Library, University of Toronto.

28 Kathleen Sherf, "Unearthing Malcolm Lowry's Two Unknown Volumes of Poetry," *Papers of the Bibliographical Society of Canada*, vol. 29, no. 1 (Spring 1991), pp. 7-22.

29 See correspondence between E.B. and Bruce Macdonald, Nov.-Dec. 1963, Earle Birney Papers, Thomas Fisher Rare Book Library, University of Toronto.

30 E.B., "Turbonave Magnolia," #10, *Near False Creek Mouth* (Toronto: McClelland & Stewart, 1964).

31 E.B. to Nelson Ball, 7 Oct. 1963, Earle Birney Papers, Thomas Fisher Rare Book Library, University of Toronto.

32 E.B. to Elizabeth Cox, 4 Nov. 1963, Earle Birney Papers, Thomas Fisher Rare Book Library, University of Toronto. The meeting was on the evening of 3 Nov. 1963.

33 E.B. to Elizabeth Cox, 13 May 1961, Earle Birney Papers, Thomas Fisher Rare Book Library, University of Toronto.

34 E.B. to Pat Fredeman, 13 May 1961, Earle Birney Papers, Thomas Fisher Rare Book Library, University of Toronto.

35 Fred Cogswell to E.B. 12 Aug. 1964, Earle Birney Papers, Thomas Fisher Rare Book Library, University of Toronto.

36 E.B. to Elizabeth Hicks, 13 Apr. 1960, Earle Birney Papers, Thomas Fisher Rare Book Library, University of Toronto.

37 E.B. to Bill Birney, 29 June 1961, Earle Birney Papers, Thomas Fisher Rare Book Library, University of Toronto.

38 E.B. to Elizabeth Cox, 12 Nov. 1961, Earle Birney Papers, Thomas Fisher Rare Book Library, University of Toronto.

39 E.B. to David Bromige, 3 Aug. 1963, Earle Birney Papers, Thomas

Fisher Rare Book Library, University of Toronto The "old sociologist friend" who lived near the Five Finger Lakes may have been Ed Devereux. Birney also visited Geoffrey Braun and Warren Benson, who had just set "The Hazel Bough" to music.

40 E.B. to Carolyn Kizer, 4 March 1960, Earle Birney Papers, Thomas Fisher Rare Book Library, University of Toronto.

41 E.B., *Ice Cod Bell or Stone* (Toronto: McClelland & Stewart, 1962).

42 Louis Dudek, "'A Tremendous Sense of Delight,'" *Montreal Star*, 26 May 1962; anon. "Tendency to Gimmicks," *Prince George Citizen*, 19 Oct. 1962; John K. Elliott, "Birney's Latest Poems Acquire International Flavour," *London Free Press*, 23 June 1962; Padraig O'Broin, "Birney Brings Cool Pity," *The Globe and Mail*, 2 June 1962; Gwladys Downes, "Critics at Large," CBC radio, June 1962; Robin Skelton, "Birney's Oh, So Clever But a Bit Etaoin Shrdlu," *The Vancouver Sun*, 15 Aug. 1962.

43 Robert Weaver, "The Poetry of Earle Birney," *The Globe and Mail*, 26 May 1962.

44 E.B. to Harnett T. Kane, 4 Aug. 1962, Earle Birney Papers, Thomas Fisher Rare Book Library, University of Toronto.

45 E.B. to Edmund Kerr, 29 Oct. 1961, Earle Birney Papers, Thomas Fisher Rare Book Library, University of Toronto.

46 Irving Layton to E.B., 11 June 1962, Earle Birney Papers, Thomas Fisher Rare Book Library, University of Toronto.

47 Robert Frost, the text reprinted as "Between Prose and Verse," *Atlantic Monthly*, Jan. 1962, p. 53.

48 E.B. to Louis Dudek, [n.d.] 1962, Earle Birney Papers, Thomas Fisher Rare Book Library, University of Toronto.

49 Lionel Kearns, "Lesson," ms. version, attached to E.B. recommendation for Commonwealth Scholarship, 28 Oct. 1961, Earle Birney Papers, Thomas Fisher Rare Book Library, University of Toronto.

50 E.B. to Einar Neilson, 17 Sept. 1961, Earle Birney Papers, Thomas Fisher Rare Book Library, University of Toronto.

51 This was the title of the first show on 25 Jan. 1962. The series was arranged by Alan Campbell, CBC Vancouver.

52 Lawrence Ferlinghetti to E.B., [n.d., prob. mid-July] 1962, Earle Birney Papers, Thomas Fisher Rare Book Library, University of Toronto.

53 Norman Holmes Pearson to E.B., 25 Mar. 1961, Earle Birney Papers, Thomas Fisher Rare Book Library, University of Toronto.

54 George Johnston to E.B. 21 July 1962, National Archives of Canada, George Johnston Papers, MG 31, D 95, vol. 1.

55 Joan Finnegan, "Canadian Poetry Finds its Voice in a Golden Age," *The Globe Magazine*, 20 Jan. 1962, pp. 11-14.

56 E.B. to Irving Layton, 21 April 1962, Earle Birney Papers, Thomas Fisher Rare Book Library, University of Toronto.

57 Tony Friedson to E.B., 8 Oct. 1962, Earle Birney Papers, Thomas Fisher Rare Book Library, University of Toronto.

58 E.B. to Irving Layton, 5 May 1962, Earle Birney Papers, Thomas Fisher Rare Book Library, University of Toronto.

59 *Ibid.*

60 E.B. to Roy Daniells, 7 July 1962, Earle Birney Papers, Thomas Fisher Rare Book Library, University of Toronto. I have rearranged these sentences.

61 Irving Layton to Earle Birney, 2 May 1961, Earle Birney Papers, Thomas Fisher Rare Book Library, University of Toronto. In fact, Layton said it was because he insulted Frye by calling him a castrato.

62 Desmond Pacey to Roy Daniells, 14 May 1962; Northrop Frye to Roy Daniells, 11 May 1962; and Harold G. Files to Roy Daniells, 17 May 1962; University of British Columbia, Special Collections and University Archives Division, Roy Daniells Papers.

63 E.B. to Robert Jordan, 3 Aug. 1962, Earle Birney Papers, Thomas Fisher Rare Book Library, University of Toronto.

64 E.B. to Roy Daniells, 7 July 1962, Earle Birney Papers, Thomas Fisher Rare Book Library, University of Toronto. I have reversed two paragraphs.

65 Norman Mackenzie to Earle Birney, 8 Aug. 1962, Earle Birney Papers, Thomas Fisher Rare Book Library, University of Toronto.

66 Esther Birney to Miriam Waddington, 10 Dec. 1962, National Archives of Canada, Miriam Waddington Papers, MG 31, D54, vol. 30.

67 E.B. to Alan Crawley, 22 Aug. 1962, Alan Crawley Papers, Queen's University Archives, Kingston.

68 E.B. to Harvey Mitchell at UBC, 15 July 1962, Earle Birney Papers, Thomas Fisher Rare Book Library, University of Toronto.

69 The idea itself had been proposed by Birney at a 1960 meeting of the Canada Council with writers and artists. It was popular with artists, but not with the Canada Council. See E.B. to Howard Sergeant, 20 Oct. 1963, Earle Birney Papers, Thomas Fisher Rare Book Library, University of Toronto.

70 E.B. to David Bromige, 30 Dec. 1962, Earle Birney Papers, Thomas Fisher Rare Book Library, University of Toronto.

71 E.B. to Beryl Rowland, 29 July 1962, Earle Birney Papers, Thomas Fisher Rare Book Library, University of Toronto.

72 E.B. to Elizabeth Cox, 13 May 1961, Earle Birney Papers, Thomas Fisher Rare Book Library, University of Toronto.

73 E.B. to Roy Daniells, 30 Jan. 1962, Earle Birney Papers, Thomas Fisher Rare Book Library, University of Toronto.

74 E.B. to Jim Hall, 27 June 1961, Earle Birney Papers, Thomas Fisher Rare Book Library, University of Toronto.

75 E.B. to Kate Simon, 10 Sept. 1962, Earle Birney Papers, Thomas Fisher

Rare Book Library, University of Toronto.

76 E.B. to Warren Benson, 11 Jan. 1963, Earle Birney Papers, Thomas Fisher Rare Book Library, University of Toronto.

77 E.B. to Rosemary Baxter, 11 Dec. 1962, Earle Birney Papers, Thomas Fisher Rare Book Library, University of Toronto.

78 E.B. to David Bromige, 30 Dec. 1962, Earle Birney Papers, Thomas Fisher Rare Book Library, University of Toronto.

79 E.B. to Beth Hosman, 20 May 1963, Earle Birney Papers, Thomas Fisher Rare Book Library, University of Toronto.

80 E.B. to Irving Layton, 7 Jan. 1963, Earle Birney Papers, Thomas Fisher Rare Book Library, University of Toronto.

81 E.B. to Ralph Salisbury, 3 Aug. 1963, Earle Birney Papers, Thomas Fisher Rare Book Library, University of Toronto.

82 E.B. to Bruce Macdonald, [n.d., prob. Feb.] 1963, Earle Birney Papers, Thomas Fisher Rare Book Library, University of Toronto.

83 E.B. to Warren Benson, 8 Oct. 1962, Earle Birney Papers, Thomas Fisher Rare Book Library, University of Toronto.

84 E.B. wrote the letter using "jealous capitals": "THIS IS SERIOUS. Well, I mean, don't be scared away, it's not *too* serious. BUT...consider: I will be free, alone, flush with Can. Council money, free, looking for a quiet spot on the Med. to get some writing done... I can help stake you to the fare, etc. THOUGH I WILL NOT SUPPORT YOU AND SOME SLEEK YOUNG SKI INSTRUCTOR UP MILES BEYOND MY REACH." E.B. to Elizabeth Cowley, 26 Nov. 1962, property of Elizabeth Cowley, London.

85 E.B. to Warren Benson, 10 June 1963, Earle Birney Papers, Thomas Fisher Rare Book Library, University of Toronto.

86 E.B. to Irving Layton, 21 May 1963, Earle Birney Papers, Thomas Fisher Rare Book Library, University of Toronto.

87 E.B. to Judith Bechtold, [n.d., prob. Nov./Dec.] 1962, Earle Birney Papers, Thomas Fisher Rare Book Library, University of Toronto.

88 E.B. to Lew Davidson, 6 June 1963, and E.B. to Irving Layton, 1 Aug. 1963, Earle Birney Papers, Thomas Fisher Rare Book Library, University of Toronto.

89 E.B. to Bernice Singer, 7 Aug. 1961, Earle Birney Papers, Thomas Fisher Rare Book Library, University of Toronto.

90 E.B., "Commemoration Address Service for the Late Chancellor Grauer," 28 Sept. 1961, ms., 4pp., Earle Birney Papers, Thomas Fisher Rare Book Library, University of Toronto.

91 E.B. to Irving Layton, 1 Aug. 1963, Earle Birney Papers, Thomas Fisher Rare Book Library, University of Toronto.

92 E.B. to Irving Layton, 1 Aug. 1963, Earle Birney Papers, Thomas Fisher Rare Book Library, University of Toronto.

93 E.B. to Ralph Salisbury, 3 Aug. 1963, Earle Birney Papers, Thomas

Fisher Rare Book Library, University of Toronto.

94 Ron Everson to E.B., 15 May 1963, Earle Birney Papers, Thomas Fisher Rare Book Library, University of Toronto.

95 Reaney won the 1949 award for poetry for *The Red Heart*; his 1962 drama award was for *The Killdeer and Other Plays*.

96 E.B. to Ron Everson, 15 May 1963, Earle Birney Papers, Thomas Fisher Rare Book Library, University of Toronto.

97 E.B. to Ralph Salisbury, 3 Aug. 1963, and to Ron Everson, 6 June 1963, Earle Birney Papers, Thomas Fisher Rare Book Library, University of Toronto.

98 E.B. to William Birney, 27 July 1963, and to Irving Layton, 7 Nov. 1963, Earle Birney Papers, Thomas Fisher Rare Book Library, University of Toronto.

99 E.B. to William Birney, 27 July 1963, Earle Birney Papers, Thomas Fisher Rare Book Library, University of Toronto.

100 E.B. to Warren Benson, 13 Sept. 1963, Earle Birney Papers, Thomas Fisher Rare Book Library, University of Toronto.

101 E.B. to Paul and Betty Ariola, 31 Dec. 1963, Earle Birney Papers, Thomas Fisher Rare Book Library, University of Toronto.

102 E.B. to David Bromige, [n.d., prob. Apr.] 1963, Earle Birney Papers, Thomas Fisher Rare Book Library, University of Toronto.

103 See E.B.'s correspondence with Dean S.N.F. Chant and Kester Svendson, 1962-63, Earle Birney Papers, Thomas Fisher Rare Book Library, University of Toronto.

104 E.B. to Irving Layton, 21 May 1963, Earle Birney Papers, Thomas Fisher Rare Book Library, University of Toronto.

105 E.B. protested to Dean S.N.F. Chant, 19 Oct. 1963, Earle Birney Papers, Thomas Fisher Rare Book Library, University of Toronto.

106 E.B., "Periodicals Publishing Poetry 1963," typescript list, Earle Birney Papers, Thomas Fisher Rare Book Library, University of Toronto. Birney had poems in 79 of these by 1966.

107 Sybil Hutchinson to E.B., 30 Oct. 1963, Earle Birney Papers, Thomas Fisher Rare Book Library, University of Toronto.

108 Tom Wayman to E.C., 24 Feb. 1992, property of E.C.

109 I am indebted to Tom Wayman for a copy of this collection.

110 Tom Wayman to E.C., interview, 24 Feb. 1992, property of E.C.

111 Peg Robertson to the Creative Writing Dept. of UBC, 9 Nov. 1964, Earle Birney Papers, Thomas Fisher Rare Book Library, University of Toronto.

112 E.B. to Sylvan Karchmer, 15 Mar. 1962, Earle Birney Papers, Thomas Fisher Rare Book Library, University of Toronto.

113 E.B. to David Bromige, 3 Aug. 1963, Earle Birney Papers, Thomas Fisher Rare Book Library, University of Toronto.

114 E.B. to Irving Layton, 21 May 1963, Earle Birney Papers, Thomas

Fisher Rare Book Library, University of Toronto.

115 E.B. to Ron Everson, 30 Dec. 1963, Earle Birney Papers, Thomas
Fisher Rare Book Library, University of Toronto.

116 E.B. to Peter Dale Scott, 1 Sept. 1963, Earle Birney Papers, Thomas
Fisher Rare Book Library, University of Toronto.

117 E.B. to The Editors, *El Corno Emplumado*, 22 Oct. 1963; Margaret
Randall de Mondragan to E.B., 27 Oct. 1963; E.B. to Margaret
Randall de Mondragon, 20 Nov. 1963; and Margaret Randall de
Mondragon to E.B. 2 Dec. 1963, Earle Birney Papers, Thomas Fisher
Rare Book Library, University of Toronto.

118 E.B. to Warren Benson, 30 Dec. 1963, Earle Birney Papers, Thomas
Fisher Rare Book Library, University of Toronto.

119 E.B. to Avo Erisalu, 18 Nov. 1963, Earle Birney Papers, Thomas
Fisher Rare Book Library, University of Toronto.

120 E.B. to A.J.M. Smith, 30 Dec. 1963, Earle Birney Papers, Thomas
Fisher Rare Book Library, University of Toronto.

121 E.B. to Beryl Rowlands, 4 Nov. 1963, and to Elizabeth Cox, 4 Nov.
1963, Earle Birney Papers, Thomas Fisher Rare Book Library,
University of Toronto.

122 E.B. to Warren Benson, 30 Dec. 1963, Earle Birney Papers, Thomas
Fisher Rare Book Library, University of Toronto.

123 E.B. to Einar Neilson, 5 July 1961, Earle Birney Papers, Thomas
Fisher Rare Book Library, University of Toronto.

124 Elizabeth Cox to E.B., 1 Sept. 1962, Earle Birney Papers, Thomas
Fisher Rare Book Library, University of Toronto.

125 Elizabeth Campbell, "Sonnets from a Sequence by Elizabeth K.
Campbell" (1. Dragged Shrieking from the Land; 2. 'We yet do taste
some subtilties of the Isle'; 6. Driftwood, 11. The Mine; 17.
Neighbours; 27. Postscript in January; 36. May: Night of Storm; 39.
When Time Abandoned Us), *The Fiddlehead* (Summer 1961), pp. 36-
39. She had also published a sonnet sequence a year earlier, which were
about her experiences with E.B.: "Five Sonnets" (For Five; Mountain;
The Ship; End of Summer; Boxing Day), *Prism* (Summer 1960), pp.
30-32. These two sonnet sequences illustrate the essential differences
between Campbell's sensibility and Margaret Crosland's: Campbell's
rhythms are gentler, her tone softly and deeply emotional, compared to
the spare, intellectual passion of Crosland's writing.

126 Elizabeth K. Campbell, 'We yet do taste some subtilties of the Isle.'
"Sonnets from a Sequence," p. 36.

127 Elizabeth Cox to E.B., 11 Oct., and E.B. to Elizabeth Cox, 12 Nov.
1961, Earle Birney Papers, Thomas Fisher Rare Book Library,
University of Toronto.

128 Elizabeth Cox to E.B., [n.d., prob. Sept. or Oct.] and 18 Oct. 1963,
Earle Birney Papers, Thomas Fisher Rare Book Library, University of
Toronto.

129 E.B. to Elizabeth Cox, 26 Aug. 1963, Earle Birney Papers, Thomas Fisher Rare Book Library, University of Toronto.

130 E.B. to Ron Everson, 30 Dec. 1963, Earle Birney Papers, Thomas Fisher Rare Book Library, University of Toronto.

131 Gertrude Garbutt, as quoted by Elizabeth Cox to E.B., 8 Jan. 1964, Earle Birney Papers, Thomas Fisher Rare Book Library, University of Toronto.

132 E.B. to Elizabeth Cox, 4 Nov. 1963, Earle Birney Papers, Thomas Fisher Rare Book Library, University of Toronto.

133 E.B. to Elizabeth Cox, 12 Feb. and 7 Jan. 1964, Earle Birney Papers, Thomas Fisher Rare Book Library, University of Toronto.

134 Elizabeth Cox to E.B., [n.d., prob. May] 1964, Earle Birney Papers, Thomas Fisher Rare Book Library, University of Toronto.

135 E.B. to the editor of *Canadian Literature*, 6 Jan. 1964, Earle Birney Papers, Thomas Fisher Rare Book Library, University of Toronto.

136 E.B. to Elizabeth Cox, 12 Feb. 1964, Earle Birney Papers, Thomas Fisher Rare Book Library, University of Toronto.

137 E.B. to Elizabeth Cox, 23 Feb. 1964, Earle Birney Papers, Thomas Fisher Rare Book Library, University of Toronto.

138 E.B. to Ralph Gustafson, 28 May 1964, Ralph Gustafson Papers, Queen's University Archives, Kingston.

139 A $4^{1}/2$ minute animated film of this poem with an introduction by E.B. was made by Elizabeth Lewis, 1988, distributed by McNabb & Connolly, Willowdale, Ont. This film won a Poetry Festival Award (1988), the Certificate of Merit, Chicago International Film Festival (1989) and the Silver Apple Award, National Educational Film & Video Festival, Oakland, Calif. (1989). A villanelle is a mediaeval form of verse with a strict rhyming pattern.

140 Rona Murray, *The Enchanted Adder* (Vancouver: Klanak Press, 1965).

141 Rona Murray to E.C., interview, 9 Feb. 1989, near Sooke, Vancouver Island, B.C.

142 E.B. to Alan Crawley, Easter Sunday 1964, Earle Birney Papers, Thomas Fisher Rare Book Library, University of Toronto.

143 Yvonne Agazarian to E.B., 4 Jan. 1964, Earle Birney Papers, Thomas Fisher Rare Book Library, University of Toronto.

144 George Bowering, 27 Sept. 1964, Earle Birney Papers, Thomas Fisher Rare Book Library, University of Toronto.

145 Daphne Marlatt, [n.d.] Dec. 1964, Earle Birney Papers, Thomas Fisher Rare Book Library, University of Toronto.

146 Lionel Kearns, 15 Oct. 1964, Earle Birney Papers, Thomas Fisher Rare Book Library, University of Toronto.

147 Norman Klenman, 28 Sept. 1964, Earle Birney Papers, Thomas Fisher Rare Book Library, University of Toronto.

148 Betty Lambert, 29 Sept. 1964, Earle Birney Papers, Thomas Fisher

Rare Book Library, University of Toronto.

149 John S. Baxter to Dr. K.N. Naegle at UBC, 15 Oct. 1964, Earle Birney Papers, Thomas Fisher Rare Book Library, University of Toronto.

150 Rosemary Kent-Baxter, Editorial Dept., *Vancouver Times,* to E.B., 21 Oct. 1964, Earle Birney Papers, Thomas Fisher Rare Book Library, University of Toronto.

151 Tom Franck to E.B., 21 Oct. 1964, Earle Birney Papers, Thomas Fisher Rare Book Library, University of Toronto.

152 Peg Robertson to the Creative Writing Dept. at UBC, 9 Nov. 1964, Earle Birney Papers, Thomas Fisher Rare Book Library, University of Toronto.

153 Marya Fiamengo to Dr. K. D. Naegle, Dean of Arts, UBC, 22 Jan. 1965, Earle Birney Papers, Thomas Fisher Rare Book Library, University of Toronto.

154 E.B. to Leonard Cohen, 17 Mar. 1964, Earle Birney Papers, Thomas Fisher Rare Book Library, University of Toronto.

155 E.B. to Geoffrey Pearson, 28 May 1964, Earle Birney Papers, Thomas Fisher Rare Book Library, University of Toronto.

156 E.B. to to Warren Benson, 3 May 1964, Earle Birney Papers, Thomas Fisher Rare Book Library, University of Toronto. The summer school instructor was Errol Hill.

157 E.B. to Alan Crawley, Easter Sunday Mar. 1964, Earle Birney Papers, Thomas Fisher Rare Book Library, University of Toronto.

158 E.B. to Leonard Cohen, 17 Mar. 1964, Earle Birney Papers, Thomas Fisher Rare Book Library, University of Toronto.

159 They read at North York Public Library (Toronto), University of Waterloo, University of Western Ontario (London), University of Toronto, Queen's University (Kingston), Carleton University (Ottawa) and McGill University (Montreal).

160 E.B. to Errol Hill, 28 Sept. 1964, Earle Birney Papers, Thomas Fisher Rare Book Library, University of Toronto.

161 Louis Dudek, "Peripatetic Poets Show their Wares," *The Montreal Star,* 31 Oct. 1964; "Poet's Progress," *Time,* 6 Nov. 1964; *Montreal Gazette,* 27 Oct. 1964; Dubarry Campeau, "Gum Wads Roll as Poets Toll for Elusive Soul," *The Telegram,* 26 Oct. 1964; Ralph Thomas, "Poets Prove Vaudeville Humour still gets Laughs," *Toronto Daily Star,* 28 Oct. 1964; Dusty Vineberg, "Poetic Quartet Ends Campus Tour," *Montreal Star,* 31 Oct. 1964. Sylvan Karchmer, after E.B.'s stint at Oregon, also told him, "You are a thoughtful gentleman, Earle, and we shall not soon see your like again in Eugene." 3 Aug. 1961, Earle Birney Papers, Thomas Fisher Rare Book Library, University of Toronto.

162 E.B. to Irving Layton, Boxing Day 1964, Earle Birney Papers, Thomas Fisher Rare Book Library, University of Toronto. See John Glassco's

description of Cohen's 1962 methods for writing a novel about the Bay of Pigs in the 1963 record of the Foster Poetry Conference, National Archives of Canada, F.R. Scott Papers. To get deeper into the unconscious mind, Cohen proposed noting in a list of disconnected words and phrases the most significant memories that came to mind, then writing a paragraph on each.

163 This was a quality Ron Everson captured in his 1963 poem "The Mail from Mallorca":

> Letter from wandering Birney, right to the edges
> of pages, taking a chance. He goes too far,
> as far out as he can and falls off
> not quite ever...

164 E.B. to Vi and Claire Pratt, [n.d., prob. 21 June 1964], Earle Birney Papers, Thomas Fisher Rare Book Library, University of Toronto.

165 Ralph Gustafson to E.B., 4 June 1964, Earle Birney Papers, Thomas Fisher Rare Book Library, University of Toronto.

166 Ann Robson to E.C., interview, 4 Oct. 1991, Toronto.

Chapter 24: escape artist

1 Esther Birney, "A Beginning," [n.d., probably 1975], ms., 1 p., Special Collections and University Archives Division, Esther Birney Papers, University of British Columbia.

2 Esther Birney, "A Beginning," [n.d., probably 1975], ms., 1 p., Special Collections and University Archives Division, Esther Birney Papers, University of British Columbia.

3 E.B. to Edith Shiffert, 12 Dec. 1964, Earle Birney Papers, Thomas Fisher Rare Book Library, University of Toronto. Birney wrote: "Ikuko is making sukiaki [sic] for Esther and me."

4 Esther Birney to E.C., interview, Jan. 1991, Vancouver.

5 E.B. to Esther Birney, 9 July 1965, Earle Birney Papers, Thomas Fisher Rare Book Library, University of Toronto.

6 Rona Murray to E.C., interview, 9 Feb. 1989, near Sooke, Vancouver Island.

7 E.B. to Irving Layton, [n.d., prob. early Feb.] 1965, Earle Birney Papers, Thomas Fisher Rare Book Library, University of Toronto.

8 Edith Shiffert to E.B., 9 Sept. 1964, Earle Birney Papers, Thomas Fisher Rare Book Library, University of Toronto.

9 Edith Shiffert to E.B., 5 Mar. 1965, Earle Birney Papers, Thomas Fisher Rare Book Library, University of Toronto.

10 E.B. to Alan Crawley, Easter Sunday 1965, Earle Birney Papers, Thomas Fisher Rare Book Library, University of Toronto.

11 He wrote to Sir George Williams University, Carleton University, the University of Toronto and McGill University. To George Johnston at Carleton he turned from helping his "student" find a summer school

to his own interest in teaching with the remark: "another question totally unconnected with the previous part of this letter." 1 Mar. 1965, Earle Birney Papers, Thomas Fisher Rare Book Library, University of Toronto.

12 This information recorded by E.B. in his notes for poetry talks and readings as writer-in-residence at the University of Toronto, [1965 and/or 1966], Earle Birney Papers, Thomas Fisher Rare Book Library, University of Toronto.

13 Ernest Sirluck to E.C., interview, 16 Oct. 1990, Toronto.

14 E.B. to George Bowering, 16 May 1965, Special Collections and University Archives Division, George Bowering Papers, University of British Columbia.

15 E.B. to Esther Birney, 27 Apr. 1965, Earle Birney Papers, Thomas Fisher Rare Book Library, University of Toronto.

16 Esther Birney to E.B., 7 July 1965, Earle Birney Papers, Thomas Fisher Rare Book Library, University of Toronto.

17 E.B. to Fred Cogswell, 9 Mar. 1965, Earle Birney Papers, Thomas Fisher Rare Book Library, University of Toronto.

18 George Johnston to E.B., 4 Mar. 1965, Earle Birney Papers, Thomas Fisher Rare Book Library, University of Toronto.

19 E.B. to Irving Layton, 2 May 1965, Earle Birney Papers, Thomas Fisher Rare Book Library, University of Toronto.

20 E.B. to Irving Layton, [n.d., prob. late May] 1965, Earle Birney Papers, Thomas Fisher Rare Book Library, University of Toronto.

21 Esther Birney to E.B., 7 July 1965, Earle Birney Papers, Thomas Fisher Rare Book Library, University of Toronto.

22 E.B. to Irving Layton, 21 Dec. 1965, Earle Birney Papers, Thomas Fisher Rare Book Library, University of Toronto, and Esther Birney to E.C., interview, 9 June 1994, Vancouver.

23 E.B. to George Bowering, 5 Aug. and 6 Sept. 1965, Earle Birney Papers, Thomas Fisher Rare Book Library, University of Toronto.

24 E.B. to Irving Layton, 9 Oct. 1965, and E.B. to Juditte Sarkanay-Perret, 23 July 1965, Earle Birney Papers, Thomas Fisher Rare Book Library, University of Toronto.

25 Esther Birney to her father, 27 Dec. 1965, Special Collections and University Archives Division, Esther Birney Papers, University of British Columbia.

26 Esther Birney to her father, 27 Dec. 1965, Special Collections and University Archives Division, Esther Birney Papers, University of British Columbia.

27 Esther Birney to her father, 22 Sept. 1965, Special Collections and University Archives Division, Earle Birney Papers, University of British Columbia.

28 E.B. to Esther Birney, 10 July 1965, Earle Birney Papers, Thomas Fisher Rare Book Library, University of Toronto.

29 E.B. to Esther Birney, 10 July 1965, Earle Birney Papers, Thomas Fisher Rare Book Library, University of Toronto.

30 E.B. to Esther Birney, 10 July 1965, Earle Birney Papers, Thomas Fisher Rare Book Library, University of Toronto.

31 bpNichol, *BP Letters* (Toronto: Coach House Press, 1968).

32 bpNichol, Marshall McLuhan and E.B. as quoted by Marilyn Beker in "Concrete Poetry: Sound, not sense," *The Toronto Daily Star*, 12 Aug. 1968, copy in Earle Birney fonds, MS. Coll. 13, Special Collections Division, University of Calgary Library.

33 E.B. to Rosemary Baxter, 6 July 1970, property of Rosemary Baxter, Aberdeen.

34 E.B. unpublished notes, "Poetry of the Deep Image," autumn 1965, Earle Birney Papers, Thomas Fisher Rare Book Library, University of Toronto.

35 Duane Ross, "Pop! Goes the Poet," *Cavalier* (Sept. 1965), p. 60.

36 E.B. to Rosemary Baxter, 12 Dec. 1955, property of Rosemary Baxter, Aberdeen.

37 E.B. made this statement in a radio interview [probably with CBC] on 20 Apr. 1971. See transcript, ms., Earle Birney Papers, Thomas Fisher Rare Book Library, University of Toronto.

38 E.B., different samples of "Like an eddy" for Rosemary Vaughan's use in constructing a mobile. See ms., Sept. 1965, Earle Birney Papers, Thomas Fisher Rare Book Library, University of Toronto.

39 E.B. to Irving Layton, 21 Dec. 1965, Earle Birney Papers, Thomas Fisher Rare Book Library, University of Toronto.

40 E.B. to Alex Trocchi, [n.d., prob. late Oct.] 1965, Earle Birney Papers, Thomas Fisher Rare Book Library, University of Toronto.

41 E.B. to John Gill, 20 May 1967, Earle Birney Papers, Thomas Fisher Rare Book Library, University of Toronto. The programme for the concert, held on 18 May 1967, is in the same collection.

42 E.B. to Tom Wayman, 1 Nov. 1965, to John Gill, 18 Dec. 1967, to Sid Simons, 29 July 1968, to the editors of *The Golden Convulvulus*, 10 Aug. 1965, Earle Birney Papers, Thomas Fisher Rare Book Library, University of Toronto.

43 E.B. to Rona Murray, [n.d., prob. late May] 1967, Earle Birney Papers, Thomas Fisher Rare Book Library, University of Toronto.

44 Gwendolyn MacEwen, *King of Egypt, King of Dreams* (Toronto: Macmillan of Canada, 1971).

45 E.B. to Glen Richards, 1 Apr. 1968, Earle Birney Papers, Thomas Fisher Rare Book Library, University of Toronto.

46 Judy Zacharias to E.B., [n.d., prob. Dec.] 1965; John Robert Colombo to E.B., 20 Dec. 1965; David Cronenberg to E.B., 18 Nov. 1965; E.B. to Kirby Condon, 5 Nov. 1964; and later, to Michael Ondaatje, 28 Nov. 1967; to the Canada Council, 28 Nov. 1967; to bill bissett, 21 July 1966, Earle Birney Papers, Thomas Fisher Rare Book Library,

University of Toronto.

47 E.B. to Paul Potts, 27 Feb. 1939, Earle Birney Papers, Thomas Fisher
   Rare Book Library, University of Toronto.

48 E.B. to Luella Booth, editor *Canadian Poetry Magazine*, 27 Oct 1965,
   Earle Birney Papers, Thomas Fisher Rare Book Library, University of
   Toronto.

49 E.B. to the Secretary of the Royal Society of Canada, 8 April 1968, and
   to Louis Dudek, 3 May 1969, Earle Birney Papers, Thomas Fisher
   Rare Book Library, University of Toronto.

50 Beryl Rowlands published her *Companion to Chaucer Studies* (Toronto
   and New York: Oxford University Press, 1968). Birney wrote her, "I
   was really thrilled…most of all for your dedication and for the wonderful if undeserved things you say about me in your own essay." 21 June
   1968, Earle Birney Papers, Thomas Fisher Rare Book Library,
   University of Toronto.

51 E.B. to Jim Hall, 15 June 1966, Earle Birney Papers, Thomas Fisher
   Rare Book Library, University of Toronto.

52 The lecture was called "Writers and Canadian Universities: Friends or
   Enemies?" and George Bowering, who had invited him and introduced
   him, commented afterwards, "It was like giving a speech to lion-tamers
   and talking about lion-torture."

53 E.B. to E.C., interview, 11 May 1994, Toronto, and E.B. to Irene
   Howard, 12 Dec. 1966, Earle Birney Papers, Thomas Fisher Rare
   Book Library, University of Toronto.

54 Irene Howard to E.B., 15 Dec. 1966, Earle Birney Papers, Thomas
   Fisher Rare Book Library, University of Toronto.

55 E.B. to John Wardroper, 13 Apr. 1966, Earle Birney Papers, Thomas
   Fisher Rare Book Library, University of Toronto.

56 E.B. "Preface," *Selected Poems 1940-1966* (Toronto: McClelland &
   Stewart, 1966), pp. ix-xii.

57 Robert Weaver, "A Big, Strong Book," *The Daily Star*, 4 June 1966, and
   George Woodcock, "Turning New Leaves," *The Canadian Forum*, Aug.
   1966, p. 115.

58 Miriam Waddington, "Poetry of a Frontier World," *The Globe and
   Mail*, 21 May 1966, and E.B. to Miriam Waddington, 8 July 1966,
   National Archives of Canada, Miriam Waddington Papers, MG 31,
   D54, vol. 30.

59 E.B. to Kirby Congdon, 7 Nov. 1966, Earle Birney Papers, Thomas
   Fisher Rare Book Library, University of Toronto.

60 See correspondence between E.B. and Barry Callaghan, 1966, and also
   E.B. to Alan Bevan, 7 Feb. 1967, Earle Birney Papers, Thomas Fisher
   Rare Book Library, University of Toronto.

61 Chester Duncan, "Memorably Canadian," *Winnipeg Free Press*, 6 Aug.
   1966, p. 6.

62 E.B. to Barry Callaghan, 28 Nov. 1967, Earle Birney Papers, Thomas

Fisher Rare Book Library, University of Toronto.

63 E.B. to the Editor, *Toronto Telegram*, 14 Dec. 1966.

64 Hugh McKinley, "Man of Images," *Athens Daily Post*, 23 Mar. 1967, pp. 2, 4.

65 E.B. to George Bowering, 3 Apr. 1966, Special Collections and University Archives Division, George Bowering Papers, University of British Columbia.

66 E.B. to Fred Candelaria, 16 Aug. 1966, and E.B.'s notes to Don Harron, 10 July 1966, Earle Birney Papers, Thomas Fisher Rare Book Library, University of Toronto.

67 E.B. to Irving Layton, 21 Dec. 1965, Earle Birney Papers, Thomas Fisher Rare Book Library, University of Toronto.

68 E.B. to Fred Candelaria, 18 Nov. 1966, Earle Birney Papers, Thomas Fisher Rare Book Library, University of Toronto.

69 E.B. to Joe Rosenblatt, 25 Oct. 1967, Earle Birney Papers, Thomas Fisher Rare Book Library, University of Toronto.

70 Alison Acker to E.C., interview, Dec. 1991, Victoria.

71 Esther Birney to E.C., interviews, 1989 and 1991, Vancouver.

72 E.B. to Jeff Nutall, 22 July 1966, Earle Birney Papers, Thomas Fisher Rare Book Library, University of Toronto.

73 E.B. to Kirby Congdon, 25 Dec. 1966, Earle Birney Papers, Thomas Fisher Rare Book Library, University of Toronto.

74 E.B. to Gina, 19 Feb. 1970, Special Collections and University Archives Division, Earle Birney Papers, University of British Columbia.

75 Although Birney was aware of Alice Munro's work in 1963 and began corresponding with Margaret Laurence when she sought his advice because she was nervous about being writer-in-residence at the University of Toronto in 1969-70 (E.B. to Margaret Laurence, 29 July 1969), he showed no enthusiasm for their writing or Atwood's, compared to his encouragement of many male writers who did not succeed nearly as well as these women.

76 E.B. to Fred Candelaria, 12 Feb. 1965, Earle Birney Papers, Thomas Fisher Rare Book Library, University of Toronto.

77 *The New Romans*, ed. Al Purdy (Edmonton: M.G. Hurtig, 1968).

78 E.B., "Books & Magazines sold to the Toronto Public Library," 1967, Earle Birney fonds, ms. Coll. 13, Special Collections Division, University of Calgary Library.

79 E.B. to Jean Coulthard, 4 Jan. 1967, and E.B. to Bill Stafford, 8 Feb. 1967, Earle Birney Papers, Thomas Fisher Rare Book Library, University of Toronto.

80 E.B. to Margaret Crosland, 10 Apr. 1967, Earle Birney Papers, Thomas Fisher Rare Book Library, University of Toronto.

81 E.B. to Ralph Gustafson, 20 July 1967, Earle Birney Papers, Thomas Fisher Rare Book Library, University of Toronto.

82 E.B. to Phyllis Webb, 9 Aug. 1967, Earle Birney Papers, Thomas Fisher Rare Book Library, University of Toronto.

83 Esther Birney to E.C., interview, 1991, Vancouver.

84 E.B. to Warren Ober, 18 Sept. 1967, Earle Birney Papers, Thomas Fisher Rare Book Library, University of Toronto.

85 Diane Elder, "Birney: A Year in Retrospect," *Chevron*, 22 Mar. 1968.

86 E.B. to Graeme Wilson, 31 Mar. 1968, Earle Birney Papers, Thomas Fisher Rare Book Library, University of Toronto.

87 Peter Stevens, *The McGill Movement: A.J.M. Smith, F.R. Scott and Leo Kennedy* (Toronto: Ryerson Press, 1969). E.B. to Peter Stevens, 26 Apr. 1968, Earle Birney Papers, Thomas Fisher Rare Book Library, University of Toronto.

88 E.B. to Mike Gnarowski, 17 June 1969, Earle Birney Papers, Thomas Fisher Rare Book Library, University of Toronto.

89 E.B. to Peter Stevens, 26 Apr. 1968, Earle Birney Papers, Thomas Fisher Rare Book Library, University of Toronto.

90 Warren Ober to E.B., 14 Mar. 1968, Earle Birney Papers, Thomas Fisher Rare Book Library, University of Toronto.

91 E.B. to Einar and Muriel Neilson, 22 May 1967, Earle Birney Papers, Thomas Fisher Rare Book Library, University of Toronto.

92 The list of lectures was: 1. Concrete poetry: Findlay (Edinburgh), bpNichol, bill bissett; 2. The tradition of shaped poetry, and of audio-visual and "scored" experiments (illustrated with slides); 3. Contemporary poetry in Australia and New Zealand; 4. English language poetry in contemporary Africa; 5. British poets of the '60s; 6. Modern Canadian poetry to 1960 (Scott, Layton, Purdy, Avison, Gustafson, Souster, Reaney, Webb); 7. The new Canadian poets of the '60s (Bowering, Cohen, Kearns, MacEwen, Buckle, Ondaatje, Erisalu); 8. The poetry of French Canada; 9. A reading of E.B.'s poetry. See E.B. to Prof. H. Adams, Chairman, English Dept., University of California, Irvine, 15 May 1967, Earle Birney Papers, Thomas Fisher Rare Book Library, University of Toronto.

93 Tom Wayman to E.C., 28 Nov. 1991, property of E.C., Toronto.

94 E.B. to Maureen Aherrio Maurer, editor of *Haravec: A Literary Magazine from Peru*, 22 June 1968, and E.B. to Sylvan Karchmer, 5 Nov. 1968, Earle Birney Papers, Thomas Fisher Rare Book Library, University of Toronto.

95 E.B. to George Bowering, 31 July 1970, George Bowering Archive, Contemporary Literature Collection, W.A.C. Bennett Library, Simon Fraser University: "[i] threw back the CC medal 3 yrs ago."

96 E.B. to bpNichol, 3 Apr. 1969, Earle Birney Papers, Thomas Fisher Rare Book Library, University of Toronto.

97 E.B. to Grace Perry, 29 July 1969, Earle Birney Papers, Thomas Fisher Rare Book Library, University of Toronto.

98 Earle Birney, *PNOMES, JUKOLLAGES, and OTHER STUNZAS*,

introd. bpNichol (Toronto: Ganglia Press, 1969).

99 The Crawleys reported this intention to the McConnells. Jean & Alan Crawley to Alice & Bill McConnell, [n.d.] Dec. 1967, University of British Columbia, Special Collections and University Archives Division, William McConnell Papers: "[Earle will spend] a short time [in July] in B.C. searching for a piece of land for a garden and with a house for him and Esther and a cat when it is time for him to retire, either in Vancouver or on the island."

100 E.B. to Rosemary Baxter, 13 July 1968, Earle Birney Papers, Thomas Fisher Rare Book Library, University of Toronto.

101 E.B. to Clem Christesen, 17 Apr. 1968, Earle Birney Papers, Thomas Fisher Rare Book Library, University of Toronto.

102 E.B. "i think you are a whole city" (originally titled "for alison"), *Nicely*, vol. 1 (June 1966), p. 4.

103 Alison Acker to E.C., interview, Dec. 1991, Victoria, B.C.

104 "Professor Suggests Literary Export Aid," *The Otage Daily Times*, 7 Oct. 1968, p. 3; "Distinguished Poet on Visit to New Zealand," *New Zealand Herald*, 14 Oct. 1968; "Poet's Apparel" [Christchurch Press], 3 Oct. 1968; E.B. to Richard Tipping, 6 Nov. 1968, Earle Birney Papers, Thomas Fisher Rare Book Library, University of Toronto.

105 E.B. to Mike Gnarowski, 17 June 1969, Earle Birney Papers, Thomas Fisher Rare Book Library, University of Toronto.

106 E.B. to Lysa Tree, 3 Nov. 1968, Earle Birney Papers, Thomas Fisher Rare Book Library, University of Toronto.

107 E.B. to Jack Jensen, 6 Jan. 1969, Earle Birney Papers, Thomas Fisher Rare Book Library, University of Toronto.

108 E.B., handwritten list of guests, probably done from memory, 20 Nov. 1968, Earle Birney Papers, Thomas Fisher Rare Book Library, University of Toronto.

109 E.B. to Stephen Vizinczey, [n.d., 1969], Earle Birney Papers, Thomas Fisher Rare Book Library, University of Toronto.

110 E.B. to Beryl Rowland, 7 Apr. 1969, Earle Birney Papers, Thomas Fisher Rare Book Library, University of Toronto.

111 E.B. to Carol Kerr, 2 July 1969, Earle Birney Papers, Thomas Fisher Rare Book Library, University of Toronto.

112 E.B. to Louis Dudek, 15 Mar. 1969, Earle Birney Papers, Thomas Fisher Rare Book Library, University of Toronto.

113 E.B. to Leonard Brooks, 26 Mar. 1969 and E.B. to Andy Suknaski, 29 July 1969, Earle Birney Papers, Thomas Fisher Rare Book Library, University of Toronto.

114 E.B. to Graeme Wilson, 21 Mar. 1969, Earle Birney Papers, Thomas Fisher Rare Book Library, University of Toronto.

115 James Barber, as quoted by E.B. to Jack Ludwig, 27 Mar. 1969, and E.B. to John Gill, 15 Feb. 1969, Earle Birney Papers, Thomas Fisher Rare Book Library, University of Toronto.

116 Esther Birney to E.C., interview, 10 Feb. 1989, Vancouver.

117 E.B. to Raymond Souster, 19 Mar. 1969, Earle Birney Papers, Thomas Fisher Rare Book Library, University of Toronto.

118 E.B., "Billboards Build Freedom of Choice," *Poetmeat*, 4 (winter 1963-64), p. 15. Reprinted in E.B., *Selected Poems*, p. 32.

119 E.B. to Al Purdy, 30 July 1969, Earle Birney Papers, Thomas Fisher Rare Book Library, University of Toronto.

120 E.B. to Grace Perry, of South Head Press, Five Dock, N.S.W., Australia, 29 July 1969, Earle Birney Papers, Thomas Fisher Rare Book Library, University of Toronto.

121 E.B., "Canada: Case History," *Saturday Night* (July 1969), p. 16.

122 E.B. to Olaf Ruhen, 26 Apr. 1969, Earle Birney Papers, Thomas Fisher Rare Book Library, University of Toronto.

123 E.B. to Esther Birney, 13 June 1969, Earle Birney Papers, Thomas Fisher Rare Book Library, University of Toronto.

124 E.B. to Joe Rosenblatt, 29 July 1969, Earle Birney Papers, Thomas Fisher Rare Book Library, University of Toronto.

125 E.B. to Al Purdy, 30 July 1969, to Tony Kilgallin, 19 Aug. 1969, and E.B. to Albert "Bud" Drake, 29 July 1969, Earle Birney Papers, Thomas Fisher Rare Book Library, University of Toronto.

126 E.B. to Grace Perry, of South Head Press, Five Dock, N.S.W., Australia, 29 July 1969, Earle Birney Papers, Thomas Fisher Rare Book Library, University of Toronto.

127 E.B. to Thomas Jackson, 24 Sept. 1969, Earle Birney Papers, Thomas Fisher Rare Book Library, University of Toronto.

128 E.B. to Doug Fetherling, 31 July 1969, Earle Birney Papers, Thomas Fisher Rare Book Library, University of Toronto.

129 E.B. to Graeme Wilson, 29 July 1969, and to Leonard Brooks, 26 Mar. 1969, Earle Birney Papers, Thomas Fisher Rare Book Library, University of Toronto.

130 E.B. to Elizabeth Cox, 5 Dec. 1969, Earle Birney Papers, Thomas Fisher Rare Book Library, University of Toronto.

131 Alison Acker to E.C., interview, Dec. 1991, Victoria, B.C.

132 Elizabeth Cox to E.B., 17 Dec. 1969, Earle Birney Papers, Thomas Fisher Rare Book Library, University of Toronto.

133 E.B., "Asset Calculations," 1 Apr. 1970, Earle Birney Papers, Thomas Fisher Rare Book Library, University of Toronto.

134 Gabrielle Baldwin to E.B., 16 Dec. 1969, Earle Birney Papers, Thomas Fisher Rare Book Library, University of Toronto.

135 E.B. to Judith Bechtold, 10 Jan. 1970, Special Collections and University Archives Division, Earle Birney Papers, University of British Columbia.

136 E.B. to Rosemary Baxter, 6 July 1970, property of Rosemary Baxter, Aberdeen; E.B. to Frank Davey, 4 Feb. 1970, and E.B. to Gabrielle

Baldwin, 4 Feb. 1970, Earle Birney Papers, Thomas Fisher Rare Book Library, University of Toronto.

137 E.B. to Ralph Gustafson, 27 Jan. 1970, Earle Birney Papers, Thomas Fisher Rare Book Library, University of Toronto.

Chapter 25: A Dry Season

1 Al Purdy to E.B., 18 Nov. 1973, Earle Birney Papers, Thomas Fisher Rare Book Library, University of Toronto. "As I grow old I think of myself as a slightly older Birney (discontent, cantankerous—and certainly the bit about grabbing the first piece of change that comes along is true, which you remarked about both of us the last time I saw you, and damn well other points of similarity too)."

2 Al Purdy to E.B., 20 Mar. 1971, Earle Birney Papers, Thomas Fisher Rare Book Library, University of Toronto.

3 E.B. to Ralph and Betty Gustafson, 18 Nov. 1970, Ralph Gustafson Papers, Queen's University Archives, Kingston.

4 J.H.R. Thomson, interview with E.B., 16 Feb. 1971, transcript and other Birney family documents in M4201, Glenbow Archives, Calgary, Alberta.

5 William and Marsha Birney to E.B. and Esther Birney, Christmas card 1970, Earle Birney Papers, Thomas Fisher Rare Book Library, University of Toronto.

6 E.B. to Rosemary Baxter, 6 July 1970, property of Rosemary Baxter, Aberdeen; and E.B. to Judy Bechtold [Root], 10 Jan. 1970, University of British Columbia, Special Collections and University Archives Division, Earle Birney Papers.

7 E.B. to George Bowering, 31 July 1970, Special Collections and University Archives Division, George Bowering Papers, University of British Columbia.

8 E.B. to William Birney, 24 Oct. 1970, Earle Birney Papers, Thomas Fisher Rare Book Library, University of Toronto.

9 E.B. to Maria des Tombes, [n.d., probably late Oct. or early Nov., 1970], Earle Birney Papers, Thomas Fisher Rare Book Library, University of Toronto.

10 E.B. to Sr. and Sra. Mandrillo, 13 Mar. 1970, Special Collections and University Archives Division, Earle Birney Papers, University of British Columbia.

11 Al Purdy to E.B., 27 July 1971, Al Purdy Papers, Queen's University Archives, Kingston.

12 E.B. to Robert Sward, 1 June 1971, fond Robert Sward, Literary Manuscript Collection, National Library of Canada.

13 E.B. to Ralph Gustafson, 1 Aug. 1972, Ralph Gustafson Papers, Queen's University Archives, Kingston.

14 E.B. to Sr. and Sra. Mandrillo, 13 Mar. 1970, Special Collections and

University Archives Division, Earle Birney Papers, University of British Columbia.

15 E.B. to Al Purdy, 25 May 1970, Al Purdy Papers, Queen's University Archives, Kingston.

16 E.B. to Al Purdy, 16 Dec. 1972, Al Purdy Papers, Queen's University Archives, Kingston.

17 E.B. to Al Purdy, 2 July 1970, Al Purdy Papers, Queen's University Archives, Kingston.

18 E.B., *Rag & Bone Shop* (Toronto: McClelland & Stewart, 1970).

19 E.B. to George Bowering, 31 July 1970, Special Collections and University Archives Division, George Bowering Papers, University of British Columbia.

20 E.B. to Al Purdy, 23 Nov. 1970, Al Purdy Papers, Queen's University Archives, Kingston.

21 E.B. to John Newlove, 16 Nov. 1972, John Newlove Collection, MSS. 70, Department of Archives and Special Collections, University of Manitoba Libraries.

22 E.B. to Dave Markson, 22 May 1970, Special Collections and University Archives Division, David Markson Papers, University of British Columbia.

23 E.B. to Joe Rosenblatt, 25 Jan. and 4 Feb. 1970, Special Collections and University Archives Division, Earle Birney Papers, University of British Columbia.

24 E.B., *Memory No Servant* (Trumansburg, New York: New, 1968).

25 E.B. to Al Purdy, 6 Nov. 1972, Al Purdy Papers, Queen's University Archives, Kingston.

26 E.B. to Al Purdy, 8 Nov. 1972, Al Purdy Papers, Queen's University Archives, Kingston.

27 E.B. to George Bowering, 31 July 1970, Special Collections and University Archives Division, George Bowering Papers, University of British Columbia.

28 E.B. to Al Purdy, 25 May 1970, Al Purdy Papers, Queen's University Archives, Kingston.

29 Viveca Ohm, "Birney Sweeping the Debris from his Poems," *The Vancouver Sun*, 19 Dec. 1970, p. 39.

30 E.B. to Al Purdy, 31 Dec. 1970, Al Purdy Papers, Queen's University Archives, Kingston.

31 E.B. as quoted by Viveca Ohm, "Birney Sweeping the Debris from his Poems," *The Vancouver Sun*, 19 Dec. 1970, p. 39.

32 E.B. to Al Purdy, 3 Aug. 1971, Al Purdy Papers, Queen's University Archives, Kingston.

33 E.B. to Elizabeth Cox, [n.d.] Dec. 1971, property of Elizabeth Cox, Toronto.

34 E.B. to Rosemary Baxter, 29 Nov. 1971, property of Rosemary Baxter,

Aberdeen.

35 E.B. to Ralph Gustafson, 20 June 1972, Ralph Gustafson Papers, Queen's University Archives, Kingston.

36 Rosemary Baxter to E.C., holograph note on the back of E.B. to Rosemary Baxter, 16 Apr. 1971, property of Rosemary Baxter, Aberdeen.

37 E.B. to Elizabeth Cox, [n.d.] Dec. 1971, Earle Birney Papers, Thomas Fisher Rare Book Library, University of Toronto.

38 E.B. to Ralph Gustafson, 1 Aug. 1972, Ralph Gustafson Papers, Queen's University Archives, Kingston.

39 See correspondence between Davey, Downes and E.B., and letters to the editor of the *Victoria Times*, April-May 1966, Earle Birney Papers, Thomas Fisher Rare Book Library, University of Toronto, and Frank Davey Archive, Contemporary Literature Collection, W.A.C. Bennett Library, Simon Fraser University.

40 The two books were published the same year: Frank Davey, *Earle Birney*. Studies in Canadian Literature, No. II (Toronto: Copp Clark, 1971), 127 pp., and Richard Robillard, *Earle Birney*. Canadian Writers, No. 9. New Canadian Library (Toronto: McClelland & Stewart, 1971), 64 pp.

41 E.B. to Frank Davey, 11 July and 23 Aug. 1971, Frank Davey Archive, Contemporary Literature Collection, W.A.C. Bennett Library, Simon Fraser University.

42 E.B. to Frank Davey, 22 Nov. 1971, Frank Davey Archive, Contemporary Literature Collection, W.A.C. Bennett Library, Simon Fraser University.

43 E.B. to Frank Davey, 21 and 22 Dec. 1971, Frank Davey Archive, Contemporary Literature Collection, W.A.C. Bennett Library, Simon Fraser University.

44 Frank Davey to E.B., 5 Jan. and 30 Jan. 1972 and E.B. to Frank Davey, 25 Jan. 1972, Frank Davey Archive, Contemporary Literature Collection, W.A.C. Bennett Library, Simon Fraser University.

45 E.B. to Dorothy Livesay, 28 Dec. 1970 and 4 Aug. 1971, Dorothy Livesay Collection, MSS. 37, Department of Archives and Special Collections, University of Manitoba Libraries.

46 Dorothy Livesay, "The Documentary Poem: A Canadian Genre," *Contexts of Canadian Criticism*, ed. Eli Mandel (Chicago: University of Chicago Press, 1971), p. 279.

47 E.B. to George Bowering, 31 July 1970, Special Collections and University Archives Division, George Bowering Papers, University of British Columbia.

48 E.B., *The Cow Jumped Over the Moon* (Toronto: Holt, Rinehart and W., 1972). See especially pp. 77-79.

49 E.B. to Dorothy Livesay, 19 Mar. 1973, Dorothy Livesay Collection, MSS. 37, Department of Archives and Special Collections, University

of Manitoba Libraries.

50 See all correspondence on this matter in the Dorothy Livesay
Collection, 1973-74, MSS. 37, Department of Archives and Special
Collections, University of Manitoba Libraries.

51 Dorothy Livesay to Eli Mandel, 15 Apr. 1973, Dorothy Livesay
Collection, MSS. 37, Department of Archives and Special Collections,
University of Manitoba Libraries.

52 E.B. to Elizabeth Cox, 25 May 1970, Earle Birney Papers, Thomas
Fisher Rare Book Library, University of Toronto.

53 Elizabeth Cox to E.B., 28 Feb. 1971, property of Elizabeth Cox,
Toronto.

54 E.B. to Elizabeth Cox, 6 Mar. 1971, property of Elizabeth Cox,
Toronto.

55 Birney's reading in Aberdeen ("splendid" according to Rosemary Baxter)
on 26 May 1971. E.B. to Bill and Rosemary Baxter, 16 Apr. and 7
May 1971, property of Rosemary Baxter, Aberdeen.

56 E.B. to Rosemary Baxter, 30 May 1971, property of Rosemary Baxter,
Aberdeen.

57 E.B. to Rosemary Baxter, 18 June 1971, property of Rosemary Baxter,
Aberdeen.

58 Elizabeth Cox to E.B., 20 July 1971, Earle Birney Papers, Thomas
Fisher Rare Book Library, University of Toronto.

59 E.B. to Elizabeth Cox, 3 July 1971, Earle Birney Papers, Thomas Fisher
Rare Book Library, University of Toronto.

60 E.B. to Elizabeth Cox, 4 Aug. 1971, Earle Birney Papers, Thomas
Fisher Rare Book Library, University of Toronto.

61 Elizabeth Cox to E.C., interview, 18 Dec. 1993, Toronto.

62 E.B. to Elizabeth Cox, 21 Aug. 1971, property of Elizabeth Cox,
Toronto.

63 E.B. to Elizabeth Cox, [n.d.] Dec. 1971, property of Elizabeth Cox,
Toronto.

64 Elizabeth Cox to E. B., [n.d., mid-Aug] 1970, Earle Birney Papers,
Thomas Fisher Rare Book Library, University of Toronto.

65 E.B. to Elizabeth Cox, 27 Jan. 1972, Earle Birney Papers, Thomas
Fisher Rare Book Library, University of Toronto.

66 E.B. to Ralph Gustafson, 20 June 1972, Ralph Gustafson Papers,
Queen's University Archives, Kingston.

67 E.B. to Rosemary Baxter, 8 May 1972, property of Rosemary Baxter,
Aberdeen.

68 Elizabeth Cox to E.B., 5 Dec. 1972, Earle Birney Papers, Thomas
Fisher Rare Book Library, University of Toronto.

69 E.B. to Joe Rosenblatt, 18 Dec. 1972, National Archives of Canada, Joe
Rosenblatt Papers, MG 31, D51.

70 E.B. to Patrick Lane, 7 Nov. 1972, Special Collections and University

Archives Division, Patrick Lane Papers, University of British Columbia.

71 E.B. to Rosemary Baxter, 7 Jan. 1972, property of Rosemary Baxter, Aberdeen.

72 E.B. to Ralph Gustafson, 1 Aug. 1972, Ralph Gustafson Papers, Queen's University Archives, Kingston.

73 E.B. to Ralph Gustafson, 13 Feb. 1973, Ralph Gustafson Papers, Queen's University Archives, Kingston.

74 Al Purdy to E.B., 6 Apr. 1973, Al Purdy Papers, Queen's University Archives, Kingston.

Chapter 26: Death To Life

1 E.B. to Elizabeth Brewster, 10 April 1973, National Archives of Canada, Elizabeth Brewster Papers, MG 30, D370, vol. 10.

2 E.B. to Ralph Gustafson, 31 July 1973, Ralph Gustafson Papers, Queen's University Archives, Kingston.

3 Anthony Kilgallin, *Lowry* (Erin, Ont.: Press Porcépic, 1973).

4 Wailan Low to E.C., interview, 9 Jan. 1989, Toronto.

5 Wailan Low to E.C., interview, 9 Jan. 1989, Toronto.

6 Wailan Low to E.C., interview, 28 Jan. 1994, Toronto.

7 Wailan Low to E.C., interview, 9 Jan. 1989, Toronto.

8 E.B. to Esther Birney, 5 July 1973, Earle Birney Papers, Thomas Fisher Rare Book Library, University of Toronto. Wailan Low to Meg Masters, corrections to page proofs, 7 June 1994, property of Penguin Books Canada Limited, Toronto.

9 Esther Birney to E.B., 21 July 1973, Earle Birney Papers, Thomas Fisher Rare Book Library, University of Toronto.

10 Lily Low to Esther Birney, Special Collections and University Archives Division, Esther Birney Papers, University of British Columbia.

11 Esther Birney to E.B., 8 Sept. 1973, Special Collections and University Archives Division, Esther Birney Papers, University of British Columbia.

12 Al Purdy to E.C., interview, 2 Feb. 1994, Sidney, B.C. See also Al Purdy to E.B., 1 May 1976, Al Purdy Papers, Queen's University Archives, Kingston.

13 Elizabeth Cox, envelope dated 20 Dec. 1972, property of Elizabeth Cox, Toronto. Lily Low was actually 23, not 24, at this time.

14 Esther Birney to E.B., 7 Oct. 1973, Earle Birney Papers, Thomas Fisher Rare Book Library, University of Toronto.

15 Lily Low to Robert Sward at Soft Press, Victoria B.C., 20 Aug. 1973, Robert Sward fond, Literary Manuscript Collection, National Library of Canada.

16 E.B. to Dave Markson, 27 Nov. 1973, Special Collections and

University Archives Division, David Markson Papers, University of British Columbia.

17 E.B., *The Bear on the Delhi Road: Selected Poems* (London: Chatto & Windus, 1973).

18 E.B., *what's so big about GREEN?* (Toronto: McClelland & Stewart, 1973).

19 E.B. to Al Purdy, 30 Dec. 1973, Al Purdy Papers, Queen's University Archives, Kingston.

20 E.B. to Wilber Stevens, 22 May 1959, Earle Birney Papers, Thomas Fisher Rare Book Library, University of Toronto.

21 Al Purdy, *Sex and Death* (Toronto: McClelland & Stewart, 1973).

22 E.B. to Al Purdy, 30 Dec. 1973, Al Purdy Papers, Queen's University Archives, Kingston.

23 E.B., "NO BODY," *Ghost in the Wheels: Selected Poems.* Toronto: McClelland & Stewart, 1977, pp. 150-51.

24 E.B., untitled [notes, probably for a lecture on poetry, to which the poem "Najarit" is attached], [n.d., possibly 1965-1968 during various writer-in-residence stints], Earle Birney Papers, Thomas Fisher Rare Book Library, University of Toronto.

25 E.B. to Irving Layton, 8 June 1963, Earle Birney Papers, Thomas Fisher Rare Book Library, University of Toronto.

26 E.B. to Al Purdy, 4 Aug. 1976, Al Purdy Papers, Queen's University Archives. "i wrote a lot of stuff to or about ikuko, but was so disenchanted with her treacheries that almost none of it has been published."

27 E.B., "There Are Delicacies," *Ghost in the Wheels* (Toronto: McClelland & Stewart, 1977), p. 124. E.B. dedicated this poem to Alison Hunt in *Last Makings.*

28 E.B., "SHE IS," *Ghost in the Wheels*, pp. 152-53.

29 Al Purdy to E.B., 30 July 1976, Al Purdy Papers, Queen's University Archives, Kingston.

30 E.B. to Al Purdy, 4 Aug. 1976, Al Purdy Papers, Queen's University Archives, Kingston.

31 Elizabeth Cox to E.C., interview, 18 Dec. 1993, Toronto.

32 Wailan Low to George Johnston, 29 July 1974, National Archives of Canada, George Johnston Papers, MG 31, D 95, vol. 1.

33 E.B. to Ralph Gustafson, 16 May 1974, Ralph Gustafson Papers, Queen's University Archives, Kingston.

34 Ralph Gustafson to E.B., 18 May 1974, Ralph Gustafson Papers, Queen's University Archives, Kingston.

35 Wailan Low to George Johnston, 29 July 1974, National Archives of Canada, George Johnston Papers, MG 31, D 95, vol. 1.

36 E.B. to Ralph Gustafson, 13 June 1974, Ralph Gustafson Papers, Queen's University Archives, Kingston.

37 Wailan Low to George Johnston, 29 July 1974, National Archives of

Canada, George Johnston Papers, MG 31, D 95, vol. 1.

38 Wailan Low to George Johnston, 29 July 1974, National Archives of Canada, George Johnston Papers, MG 31, D 95, vol. 1.

39 E.B., application form for Canada Council travel grant, 5 Sept. 1974, Ralph Gustafson Papers, Queen's University Archives, Kingston.

40 See correspondence between David Stockwood of Goodman & Goodman, Toronto, and Allen N. Fitchen of The University of Chicago Press, Eli Mandel Collection, MSS. 18, Box 4, Fd. 15, Department of Archives and Special Collections, University of Manitoba Libraries.

41 E.B. to Esther Birney, 7 Mar. 1974, Earle Birney Papers, Thomas Fisher Rare Book Library, University of Toronto.

42 E.B. to Dave Markson, 27 Nov. 1973, Special Collections and University Archives Division, David Markson Papers, University of British Columbia.

43 E.B. to Ralph Gustafson, 16 May and 10 Nov. 1974, Ralph Gustafson Papers, Queen's University Archives, Kingston.

44 E.B. to Ralph Gustafson, 16 May 1974, Ralph Gustafson Papers, Queen's University Archives, Kingston.

45 E.B. to Ralph Gustafson, 13 June 1974, Ralph Gustafson Papers, Queen's University Archives, Kingston.

46 Desmond Pacey, *Selections from Major Canadian Writers: Poetry and Creative Prose in English* (Toronto: McGraw-Hill Ryerson, 1974).

47 E.B. to Desmond Pacey, 1 July 1974, National Archives of Canada, Desmond Pacey Papers, MG 30, D 339, vol. 1.

48 E.B. to Esther Birney, 19 May 1974, Earle Birney Papers, Thomas Fisher Rare Book Library, University of Toronto.

49 E.B. to Esther Birney, 7 Mar. 1974, Earle Birney Papers, Thomas Fisher Rare Book Library, University of Toronto.

50 Wailan Low to E.C., interview, 4 Feb. 1994, Toronto.

51 Wailan Low, *Earle Birney: Portrait of a Poet*, NFB film, Donald Winkler director and Tom Daly producer, 1981.

52 E.B. to Ralph Gustafson, 1 Sept. 1974, Ralph Gustafson Papers, Queen's University Archives, Kingston.

53 E.B. to Ralph Gustafson, 18 Oct. 1974, Ralph Gustafson Papers, Queen's University Archives, Kingston.

54 E.B., *The Collected Poems of Earle Birney*, Vols. I & II (Toronto: McClelland & Stewart, 1975).

55 E.B. to Ralph Gustafson, 18 Oct. 1974, Ralph Gustafson Papers, Queen's University Archives, Kingston.

56 Wailan Low to George and Jeanne Johnston, 7 Mar. 1975, National Archives of Canada, George Johnston Papers, MG 31, D 95, vol. 1.

57 E.B. to Ralph Gustafson, 10 Nov. 1974, Ralph Gustafson Papers, Queen's University Archives, Kingston.

58 Wailan Low to George and Jean[ne] Johnston, 16 Oct. 1974, National Archives of Canada, George Johnston Papers, MG 31, D 95, vol. 1.

59 E.B. to Ralph Gustafson, 10 Nov. 1974, Ralph Gustafson Papers, Queen's University Archives, Kingston.

60 E.B. to George Johnston, 25 Dec. 1974, National Archives of Canada, George Johnston Papers, MG 31, D 95, vol. 1.

61 Wailan Low to George and Jeanne Johnston, 7 Mar. 1975, National Archives of Canada, George Johnston Papers, MG 31, D 95, vol. 1.

62 E.B. to Ralph Gustafson, 28 Jan. 1975, Ralph Gustafson Papers, Queen's University Archives, Kingston.

63 E.B. to Ralph Gustafson, 28 Jan. 1975, Ralph Gustafson Papers, Queen's University Archives, Kingston, and Wailan Low to George Johnston, 7 Mar. 1975, National Archives of Canada, George Johnston Papers, MG 31, D95, vol. 1.

64 E.B. to Joe Rosenblatt, 25 Dec. 1974, Earle Birney Papers, Thomas Fisher Rare Book Library, University of Toronto.

65 E.B. to Ralph Gustafson, 11 Mar. 1975, Ralph Gustafson Papers, Queen's University Archives, Kingston.

66 E.B. to Joe Rosenblatt, 21 Feb. 1975, Earle Birney Papers, Thomas Fisher Rare Book Library, University of Toronto.

67 Reva Brooks to E.C., interview, 7 June 1991, San Miguel, Mexico.

68 E.B. to Ralph Gustafson, 18 Oct. 1974, Ralph Gustafson Papers, Queen's University Archives, Kingston.

69 E.B. to George Johnston, 8 May 1975, National Archives of Canada, George Johnston Papers, MG 31, D 95, vol. 1.

70 Wailan Low to Ralph Gustafson, 10 July 1975, Ralph Gustafson Papers, Queen's University Archives, Kingston.

71 Wailan Low to George Johnston, 11 July 1975, National Archives of Canada, George Johnston Papers, MG 31, D 95, vol. 1.

72 E.B. and Wailan Low to George Johnston, 6 Sept. 1975, National Archives of Canada, George Johnston Papers, MG 31, D 95, vol. 1.

73 Wailan Low to George Johnston, 6 Sept. 1975, National Archives of Canada, George Johnston Papers, MG 31, D 95, vol. 1.

74 Numerous friends heard E.B. say this: Bet Cox and the Brooks, among others.

75 E.B. to George Johnston, 17 Sept. 1975, National Archives of Canada, George Johnston Papers, MG 31, D95, vol. 1.

76 E.B. to Al Purdy, 16 Feb. 1976, Al Purdy Papers, Queen's University Archives, Kingston.

77 *Ibid.*

78 *Ibid.*

79 "Fall by Fury," *Fall by Fury & Other Makings* (Toronto: McClelland & Stewart, 1978), pp. 13-14.

80 Tom Wayman, "My Old Master," *Words We Call Home* (Vancouver:

UBC Press, 1990), pp. 357-58.

81 E.B. to Al Purdy, 29 Apr. 1976, Al Purdy Papers, Queen's University Archives, Kingston.

82 Michael Bennett, "Portrait of Artist in his own Land," *The Vancouver Province*, 5 Nov. 1976, p. 23.

83 E.B. to George and Jeanne Johnston, 7 Nov. 1976, National Archives of Canada, George Johnston Papers, MG 31, D95, vol. 1.

Chapter 27: Now Is Time

1 Wailan Low to E.C., interview, 4 Feb. 1994, Toronto; see also the dedication to *Last Leavings*, "For Wailan Low whose devotion made possible the happiest years of my life."

2 Wailan Low to E.C., interview, 17 Feb. 1994, Toronto.

3 E.B. to Al Purdy, 18 Feb. 1980, Al Purdy Papers, Queen's University Archives, Kingston.

4 E.B. to George Bowering, 17 Apr. 1981, fond George Bowering, Literary Manuscript Collection, National Library of Canada.

5 Elizabeth Cox to E.C., interview, 9 May 1994, Toronto.

6 E.B. to George Johnston, 4 June 1983, National Archives of Canada, George Johnston Papers, MG 31, D 95, Interim 16.

7 E.B. to Patrick Lane, 7 Nov. 1972, Patrick Lane Papers, Special Collections and University Archives Division, University of British Columbia.

8 Esther Birney Papers, Special Collections and University Archives Division, University of British Columbia.

9 E.B., "decree absolute," ms. 1975 for 1935, Earle Birney Papers, Thomas Fisher Rare Book Library, University of Toronto; see also E.B., *Last Makings* (Toronto: McClelland & Stewart, 1991), p. 21, where a few changes have been made ("twenty-five and loving and we at last together").

10 E.B., *Alphabeings & Other Seasyours*, ed. Jamie Hamilton (London, Ont.: Pikadilly, 1976) and *The Rugging and the Moving Times: Poems New and Uncollected*, 1976 (Coatsworth, Ont.: Black Moss, 1976).

11 E.B., *Ghost in the Wheels: Selected Poems* (Toronto: McClelland & Stewart, 1977) and *The Damnation of Vancouver*, introd. Wailan Low, NCL No. O11 (Toronto: McClelland & Stewart, 1977).

12 E.B., *Fall by Fury & Other Makings* (Toronto: McClelland & Stewart, 1978).

13 E.B. to Al Purdy, 9 Oct. 1977, Al Purdy Papers, Queen's University Archives, Kingston.

14 Al Purdy to E.B., 18 Nov. 1980, Al Purdy Papers, Queen's University Archives, Kingston.

15 As listed by Michael Ryval, "The Business of Living," *The Canadian* (12 May 1979), pp. 3-6.

16 E.B., "Coming of Age in Erikson, B.C." (Sept. 1980), pp. 29-31, 60-61; "A Chancy Venture" (Oct. 1980), pp. 31-35; "Hot and Cold" (Nov. 1980), pp. 33-36; and "A Camping Week" (Dec. 1980), pp. 31-35; all in *B.C. Outdoors*.

17 E.B., *Words on Waves: Selected Radio Plays of Earle Birney* (Kingston: The Quarry Press & Toronto: CBC Enterprises, 1985).

18 E.B., *Essays on Chaucerian Irony* (Toronto: University of Toronto Press, 1985).

19 E.B., *Copernican Fix* (Toronto: ECW Press, 1985).

20 E.B. to Allan Safarik, 31 Dec. 1978, fond Blackfish Press, Literary Manuscript Collection, National Library of Canada.

21 E.B. to Joe Rosenblatt, 26 Jan. 1981, Joe Rosenblatt Papers, National Archives of Canada, Joe Rosenblatt Papers, Temp. Vol. 35, acc. 82/19.

22 George Bowering to E.B., 26 Sept. 1981, fond George Bowering, Literary Manuscript Collection, National Library of Canada.

23 E.B. to George Johnston, 14 Mar. 1984, George Johnston Papers, MG 31, D95, Interim 16, National Archives of Canada.

24 E.B. to George Johnston, 23 Oct. 1978, George Johnston Papers, MG 31, D95, Interim 16, National Archives of Canada.

25 Michael Walsh, "Birney Movie Shallow," *The Vancouver Province*, 19 Nov. 1981.

26 E.B., "Villanelle," *Poetry & Audience* (Leeds, England), no. 7 (Feb. 1964), p. 4. Reprinted in E.B., *Collected Poems*.

27 Elizabeth Lewis, "Villanelle," 4^{1}/2 minutes, 1988, distributed by McNabb & Connolly, Willowdale, Ont. This film won a Poetry Film Festival Award (1988), the Certificate of Merit, Chicago International Film Festival (1989) and the Silver Apple Award, National Educational Film & Video Festival, Oakland, Calif. (1989). Birney claimed that the poem is an elegy for Betty Lambert's untimely death from cancer at age 50 in 1983, after she had produced five plays and one novel *Crossings* (1979). But it was first published in 1964, almost twenty years before she died. A villanelle is a mediaeval form of verse with a strict rhyming pattern.

28 I am indebted to Norman Klenman for his account of the evening. Norman Klenman to E.C., 6 Jan. 1992, property of E.C., Toronto.

29 E.B. to Seymour Mayne, 18 Feb. year illegible probably 1970, Earle Birney Papers, Thomas Fisher Rare Book Library, University of Toronto.

30 E.B., "Slug in Woods," *The Oxford Book of Canadian Verse* (Toronto: Oxford University Press, 1960), p. 219.

31 Al Purdy, "Preface," *Last Makings* (McClelland & Stewart, 1991), p. xiii.

32 E.B., *pnomes jukollages and other stunzas*, (1969).

33 See Geoffrey Chaucer, *Troilus and Criseide*, Book III, ll. 890-896. I am indebted to Professor Peter Heyworth for assistance with this material.

34 Leonard Cohen, in E.B.'s copy of *The Favourite Game*, Earle Birney Papers, Thomas Fisher Rare Book Library, University of Toronto.

35 John Robert Colombo, *Toronto Daily Star* (4 June 1966).

36 Jack Hodgins to E.C., 3 Feb. 1991, property of E.C.

37 "Vancouver Awards," CKVU Television, VHS video-tape, 13 Mar. 1987, Vancouver. I am indebted to Daryl Duke, then chairman of the board of CKVU-TV, for providing me with a copy of this tape.

38 Barbara Barrett to E.B., 2 Oct. 1930, Earle Birney Papers, Thomas Fisher Rare Book Library, University of Toronto.

39 E.B. to Esther Birney, 7 Sept. 1985, Esther Birney Papers, Special Collections and University Archives Division, University of British Columbia, and E.B. to George Johnston, 30 Aug. 1985, National Archives of Canada, George Johnston Papers, MG 31, D 95, Interim 16.

40 E.B. to George Johnston, 21 June 1986, National Archives of Canada, George Johnston Papers, MG 31, D 95, Interim 16.

41 E.B. to George Johnston, 30 Aug. 1985, National Archives of Canada, George Johnston Papers, MG 31, D 95, Interim 16. From the lines: "Over the hill / & into the bog / I've time just to wave / one muddy hand."

42 E.B. to John Newlove, 26 Sept. 1985, inscribed on a copy of Kelley Jo Burke, "Earle Birney at 80," *Chronicle* (Winter 1984), John Newlove Collection, MSS. 70, Box 18, Folder 12, Department of Archives and Special Collections, University of Manitoba Libraries.

43 E.B. to George Johnston, 26 Feb. 1985, National Archives of Canada, George Johnston Papers, MG 31, D 95, Interim 16.

44 E.B. to George Johnston, 1 Aug. 1986, National Archives of Canada, George Johnston Papers, MG 31, D 95, Interim 16.

45 E.B. to George Johnston, 24 Feb. 1987, National Archives of Canada, George Johnston Papers, MG 31, D 95, Interim 16.

46 Debra Barr to E.C., 24 May-12 June 1992, property of E.C., Toronto.

47 E.B., "Fall by Fury," *Fall By Fury* (Toronto: McClelland & Stewart, 1978), pp. 12-13.

Epilogue

1 E.B., "Vancouver Lights."

2 I visited E.B. in hospital with Wailan Low and saw this myself.

3 Wailan Low to E.C., interview, 4 Feb. 1994, Toronto.

4 Rona Murray to E.C., interview, 9 Feb. 1989, near Sooke, Vancouver Island.

5 E.B. to Corinne and Garrick and Rex Hagon, 6 June 1969, Earle Birney Papers, Thomas Fisher Rare Book Library, University of Toronto.

6 E.B., holograph note, Aug. 1960, Earle Birney Papers, Thomas Fisher Rare Book Library, University of Toronto.

Index

Copyright Acknowledgments